ANNUAL REVIEW OF PSYCHOLOGY

EDITORIAL COMMITTEE (1996)

ANNUAL REVIEW OF PSYCHOLOGY

VOLUME 47, 1996

JANET T. SPENCE, *Editor*
University of Texas, Austin

JOHN M. DARLEY, *Associate Editor*
Princeton University

DONALD J. FOSS, *Associate Editor*
Florida State University

http://annurev.org   science@annurev.org   415-493-4400
ANNUAL REVIEWS INC.   4139 EL CAMINO WAY   P.O. BOX 10139   PALO ALTO, CALIFORNIA 94303-0139

ANNUAL REVIEWS INC.
Palo Alto, California, USA

International Standard Serial Number: 0066-4308
International Standard Book Number: 0-8243-0247-8
Library of Congress Catalog Card Number: 50-13143

Annual Review and publication titles are registered trademarks of Annual Reviews Inc.

The paper used in this publication meets the minimum requirements of American National Standards for Information Sciences—Permanence of Paper for Printed Library
Materials, ANZI Z39.48-1984

Annual Reviews Inc. and the Editors of its publications assume no responsibility for
the statements expressed by the contributors to this *Review.*

Typesetting by Ruth McCue Saavedra and the Annual Reviews Inc. Editorial Staff

PRINTED AND BOUND IN THE UNITED STATES OF AMERICA

ANNUAL REVIEWS INC. is a nonprofit scientific publisher established to promote the advancement of the sciences. Beginning in 1932 with the *Annual Review of Biochemistry,* the Company has pursued as its principal function the publication of high-quality, reasonably priced *Annual Review* volumes. The volumes are organized by Editors and Editorial Committees who invite qualified authors to contribute critical articles reviewing significant developments within each major discipline. The Editor-in-Chief invites those interested in serving as future Editorial Committee members to communicate directly with him. Annual Reviews Inc. is administered by a Board of Directors, whose members serve without compensation.

For the convenience of readers, a detachable order form/envelope is bound into the back of this volume.

Annual Review of Psychology
Volume 47 (1996)

CONTENTS

INDEXES

SOME RELATED ARTICLES IN OTHER *ANNUAL REVIEWS*

From the *Annual Review of Neuroscience,* Volume 18 (1995)

Addictive Drugs and Brain Stimulation Reward, R. A. Wise
Visual Object Recognition, Nikos K. Logothetis, David L. Sheinberg

From the *Annual Review of Anthropology,* Volume 24 (1995)

Science as Culture, Cultures of Science, Sarah Franklin

From the *Annual Review of Sociology,* Volume 21 (1995)

Here and Everywhere: Sociology of Scientific Knowledge, Steven Shapin

From the *Annual Review of Public Health,* Volume 16 (1995)

Factors in the Prevention of Psychopathology and High Risk Behaviors in Children and Adolescents: A Brief Overview, Gloria Johnson-Powell

Mark R Rosenzweig

Annu. Rev. Psychol. 1996. 47:1–32

ASPECTS OF THE SEARCH FOR NEURAL MECHANISMS OF MEMORY

Mark R. Rosenzweig

Department of Psychology, University of California, Berkeley, California 94720-1650

KEY WORDS: brain plasticity, enriched experience, memory formation, neurochemistry of memory, synaptic plasticity

ABSTRACT

The search for neural mechanisms of memory has been under way for more than a century. The pace quickened in the 1960s when investigators found that training or differential experience leads to significant changes in brain neurochemistry, anatomy, and electrophysiology. Many steps have now been identified in the neurochemical cascade that starts with neural stimulation and ends with encoding information in long-term memory. Applications of research in this field are being made to child development, successful aging, recovery from brain damage, and animal welfare. Extensions of current research and exciting new techniques promise novel insights into mechanisms of memory in the decades ahead.

CONTENTS

INTRODUCTION

Plasticity of the nervous system in relation to learning and memory, now a major field of research, has long been an important theme in psychology and related disciplines. William James (1890) was not the first to attribute habit to the plasticity of the nervous system (p. 105) or to write of molecules storing habits in the nerve cells (p. 127). In fact, concepts of brain plasticity in relation to behavior have appeared in various guises over the past two centuries. But only in the 1960s did clear and replicable evidence show that training and experience produce measurable neurochemical and neuroanatomical changes; further evidence soon followed that these neural changes are required for long-term memory. Since then, related research has flourished and branched out in several directions, encouraging a variety of applications. The search has led to some surprising discoveries, to a number of controversies, to the rejection of some hypotheses, and to the opening of new vistas.

This chapter reviews selectively some of this research and some applications that have stemmed from it. These are topics with which I have been concerned for about 50 years. My initial interest was heightened in a graduate seminar Donald O. Hebb gave at Harvard in the summer of 1947, using as the text a mimeographed version of his then unpublished book, *The Organization of Behavior* (Hebb 1949), and I benefitted from further exchanges with him over the years.

PRE-20TH CENTURY SPECULATIONS AND RESEARCH

The Advent of the Science of Memory

From classical antiquity through the Renaissance, practices to improve memory were codified in what became known as the art of memory (Yates 1966). But the *science* of memory began only in 1885, when Hermann Ebbinghaus announced the study-test method and experimental results obtained with it. Clinical observations helped to advance knowledge of memory and its neural bases even before Ebbinghaus's discovery (e.g. Wilks 1864, Ribot 1881), but reciprocal interactions between clinical observations and experimental research stimulated further advances. For example, the recent distinction between declarative and nondeclarative kinds of memory arose from research to find what kind(s) of memory is(are) lost and what is spared after certain kinds of brain damage. This distinction was necessary in order to find the different brain regions used in these two kinds of memory and to understand different kinds of amnesia (Squire et al 1993). The distinction between declarative and nondeclarative kinds of memory is still too recent to be incorporated in standardized tests for assessment of memory, because innovations in such tests usually lag about ten years behind the research literature (Butters et al 1995). I hope that discussion of concepts and findings about mechanisms of memory may foster both further research and applications.

Long before the modern period, speculations about learning and memory and their possible bodily mechanisms led to advice about practices to aid memory or avoid its impairment. Some of this advice now seems ludicrous. Will current formulations seem better grounded to scientists of the future? For example, medieval teachings about memory held that because the brain, which stores memory, is cool and moist (as found in dissections), it needs to be protected against overheating of all sorts; therefore hot foods and strong wine are bad for the memory (Carruthers 1990, p. 50). Although we agree that strong wine impairs retrieval of memory, our explanations are not based on temperature.

Early Speculations about Sites of Learning in the Nervous System

The possibility of testing experimentally whether mental exercise can induce growth of the brain was discussed as early as 1783 in correspondence between the prominent Swiss naturalist Charles Bonnet and a Piedmontese anatomist,

Michele Vincenzo Malacarne (Bonnet 1779–1783). Malacarne agreed to undertake a test of the hypothesis, using an experimental design that anticipated one used 180 years later. He chose as subjects two littermate dogs and also pairs of birds, each pair coming from the same clutch of eggs. In each pair, he gave one animal intensive training while the other received none. After a few years of this treatment, Malacarne sacrificed the animals and compared the brains in each pair. A brief review of the results of this experiment [1793, *Journal de Physique* (Paris) 43:73] claimed positive findings—the trained animals were reported to show more folds in the cerebellum than the untrained.

The prominent German physician Samuel Thomas von Soemmering may have known of Malacarne's work when he wrote the following passage in his major book on human anatomy:

> Does use change the structure of the brain?
> Does use and exertion of mental power gradually change the material structure of the brain, just as we see, for example, that much used muscles become stronger and that hard labor thickens the epidermis considerably? It is not improbable, although the scalpel cannot easily demonstrate this. (1791, Vol. 5, p. 91). [In the edition of 1800, the last phrase was changed to "although anatomy has not yet demonstrated this" (p. 394).]

The idea that exercise or training can enlarge particular brain regions was promoted in the 19th century by two doctrines—phrenology and evolution through inheritance of acquired characteristics. I do not include among the phrenologists the neuroanatomist Franz Joseph Gall, although he is often called the founder or inventor of phrenology (e.g. Wells 1847, Ackerknecht & Vallois 1956). For one thing, Gall called his system "organology" and rejected the term "phrenology," which was invented by his younger colleague Johann Gaspard Spurzheim (Zola-Morgan 1995). More importantly, Gall emphasized the innateness of development of the different "organs" of the cerebral cortex, each of which he hypothesized to correspond to a different mental faculty. Gall rejected the ideas that humankind is indefinitely perfectible and that exercise or education could influence the development of the faculties or the organs of the brain (1819, pp. 252–56). Jean-Baptiste Lamarck, the originator of the doctrine of evolution through inheritance of acquired characteristics, held that the brain and each of its special regions develops through appropriate use of the related faculties, and he criticized Gall's belief that brain development is determined innately [1809 (1914)].

When Spurzheim separated from Gall in 1812 and went to England and later the United States, he created the phrenological movement. This included the idea that development of the faculties and their cerebral organs could be stimulated by exercise (Spurzheim 1815, 1847). Davies (1995) showed how the vogue of phrenology fit with aspects of the American spirit, underscoring the role of heredity and individual differences, but balancing this with the optimistic doctrine of growth and perfectibility through education and exercise. In keeping with their emphasis on differences of individual endowments, the phrenologists urged that programs of education be designed for individuals according to their aptitudes. They also cautioned against overemphasizing intellectual development of children, lest directing too much blood flow to the brain impair development of the body. This point was echoed by other educational theorists, including Herbert Spencer.

Evidence accumulated during the latter part of the 19th century that the brain shows less individual variation in size than other organs and is less affected by changes in body weight. The consensus developed that the gross anatomy of the brain is not affected by experience or training and that the adult brain is essentially fixed anatomically.

Neural Junctions as Sites of Change in Learning

In the 1890s, several scientists speculated that changes at neural junctions might account for memory. This was anticipated, as Finger (1994) points out, by Alexander Bain (1872), an associationist philosopher, who suggested that memory formation involves growth of what we now call synaptic junctions:

> "for every act of memory, every exercise of bodily aptitude, every habit, recollection, train of ideas, there is a specific grouping or coordination of sensations and movements, by virtue of specific growths in the cell junctions" (p. 91).

Such speculations were put on a firmer basis with the enunciation of the neuron doctrine by neuroanatomist Wilhelm von Waldeyer in 1891, largely based on the research of Santiago Ramon y Cajal. Neurologist Eugenio Tanzi (1893) advanced the hypothesis that the plastic changes involved in learning probably take place at the junctions between neurons. He expressed confidence that investigators would soon be able to test by direct inspection the junctional changes he hypothesized to occur with development and training. About 80 years were to elapse, however, before the first results of this sort were announced (e.g. Cragg 1967, Diamond et al 1975, Globus et al 1973, West & Greenough 1972).

Ramon y Cajal, apparently independently of Tanzi, went somewhat further in his Croonian lecture to the Royal Society of London (Cajal 1894). He stated that the higher one looked in the vertebrate scale, the more the neural terminals and collaterals ramified. During development of the individual, neural branching increased, probably up to adulthood. He held it likely that mental exercise also leads to greater growth of neural branches, as he stated with a colorful set of analogies:

The theory of free arborization of cellular branches capable of growing seems not only to be very probable but also most encouraging. A continuous pre-established network—a sort of system of telegraphic wires with no possibility for new stations or new lines—is something rigid and unmodifiable that clashes with our impression that the organ of thought is, within certain limits, malleable and perfectible by well-directed mental exercise, especially during the developmental period. If we are not worried about putting forth analogies, we could say that the cerebral cortex is like a garden planted with innumerable trees—the pyramidal cells—which, thanks to intelligent cultivation, can multiply their branches and sink their roots deeper, producing fruits and flowers of ever greater variety and quality (pp. 467–68).

But he then considered an obvious objection:

You may well ask how the volume of the brain can remain constant if there is a greater branching and even formation of new terminals of the neurons. To meet this objection we may hypothesize either a reciprocal diminution of the cell bodies or a shrinkage of other areas of the brain whose function is not directly related to intelligence (p. 467).

We will return below to this assumption of constancy of brain volume and Ramon y Cajal's hypotheses to permit constancy in the face of increased neuronal ramification.

The neural junctions didn't have a specific name when Tanzi and Ramon y Cajal wrote early in the 1890s, but a few years later neurophysiologist Charles Sherrington (1897) gave them the name "synapse." Sherrington also stated that the synapse was likely to be strategic for learning, putting it in this picturesque way:

Shut off from all opportunities of reproducing itself and adding to its number by mitosis or otherwise, the nerve cell directs its pent-up energy towards amplifying its connections with its fellows, in response to the events which stir it up. Hence, it is capable of an education unknown to other tissues. (p. 1117).

During the first half of the 20th century, psychologists and other scientists proposed memory hypotheses involving either the growth of neural fibrils toward one another to narrow the synaptic gap or more subtle chemical changes at synapses (see review in Finger 1994). But when Karl S. Lashley (1950) reviewed this literature, he concluded that there was no solid evidence to support any of these "growth" theories. Specifically he offered these criticisms: (a) Neural cell growth appears to be too slow to account for the rapidity with which some learning can take place; we will return to this point below. (b) Because he was unable to localize the memory trace, Lashley held there was no warrant to look for localized changes. Lashley's younger colleague Donald O. Hebb (1949) noted some evidence for neural changes and did not let the absence of conclusive evidence deter him from reviving hypotheses about the conditions that could lead to formation of new synaptic junctions and underlie memory. Much current neuroscience research concerns properties of what are now known as Hebbian synapses. Hebb was somewhat amused that his name was connected to this resurrected hypothesis rather than to concepts he considered original (Milner 1993, p. 127).

TRAINING OR EXPERIENCE PRODUCES CHANGES IN THE NEUROCHEMISTRY AND ANATOMY OF CEREBRAL CORTEX

Ten years after Hebb's book was published, his postulate of use-dependent neural plasticity had still not been demonstrated experimentally. It seemed to many that it would not be possible, with available techniques, to find changes in the brain induced by training or experience. At a symposium in 1957 my colleagues and I proposed that an approach to this problem would be to make neurochemical analyses over specific regions of brain. Such an approach might be able to integrate and permit measurement of small changes taking place over many thousands of neural units. If such changes were found, then subsequent analyses might be able to focus down more closely (Rosenzweig et al 1958, p. 338). In the early 1960s two experimental programs announced findings demonstrating that the brain can be altered measureably by training or differential experience. First was the demonstration by our group at Berkeley that both formal training and informal experience in varied environments led to measurable changes in neurochemistry and neuroanatomy of the rodent brain. Soon after came the report of Hubel & Wiesel that occluding one eye of a kitten led to reduction in the number of cortical cells responding to that eye.

The original clues for our discovery came from data on rats given formal training in a variety of problems. We were seeking to examine possible relations between individual differences in brain chemistry and problem-solving ability. We did obtain significant correlations between levels of activity of the enzyme acetylcholinesterase (AChE) in the cerebral cortex and ability to solve spatial problems (e.g. Krech et al 1956, Rosenzweig et al 1958). When we tested the generality of this finding over six different behavioral tests, we found a surprise: As reported at a 1959 symposium, total AChE activity was higher in the cerebral cortex of groups that had been trained and tested on more difficult problems than in those given easier problems, and all the tested groups measured higher in total cortical AChE activity than groups given no training and testing (Rosenzweig et al 1961, p. 102 & Figure 4). It appeared that training could alter the AChE activity of the cortex! To test this hypothesis further, we conducted an experiment in which littermates were either trained on a difficult problem or left untrained. The trained rats developed signifi-

cantly higher cortical AChE activity than their untrained littermates (Rosenzweig et al 1961, p. 103). (As we found later, this experimental design was
similar to Malacarne's in the 18th century.) Control experiments showed that
the results could not be attributed to the fact that the trained rats were underfed
to increase their motivation or were handled.

Instead of continuing to train rats in problem-solving tests, a time-consuming and expensive procedure, we decided to house the animals in different
environments that provided differential opportunities for informal learning.
Measures made at the end of the experiment showed that informal enriched
experience led to increased cortical AChE activity (Krech et al 1960). The
discovery that formal training or differential experience caused changes in
cortical chemistry was soon followed by the even more surprising finding that
enriched experience increased the *weights* of regions of the neocortex (Rosenzweig et al 1962). A recent review notes, "The initial reports by Rosenzweig,
Bennett, Diamond, and their colleagues provided the first evidence that enrichment of the environment could lead to structural changes in the brain" (Bailey
& Kandel 1993, p. 399).

Work by students of Hebb (e.g. Forgays & Forgays 1952) provided the
models for the environments we used in these experiments. Typically, we
assigned littermates of the same sex by a random procedure among various
laboratory environments, the three most common being these: (*a*) a large cage
containing a group of 10 to 12 animals and a variety of stimulus objects, which
were changed daily [this was called the enriched condition (EC) because it
provided greater opportunities for informal learning than did the other conditions; all three conditions provided food and water *ad libitum*]; (*b*) the standard
colony or social condition (SC), with three animals in a standard laboratory
cage; (*c*) SC-size cages housing single animals [this was called the impoverished condition or isolated condition (IC)].

Our first reports of changes in the brain induced by experience were greeted
with skepticism and incredulity. Hebb cautioned me that the more important
the claims, the more careful should be the tests. Over the next several years,
replications and extensions by us (e.g. Bennett et al 1964a) and then by others
(e.g. Altman & Das 1964, Geller et al 1965, Greenough & Volkmar 1973)
gained acceptance for the idea that training or differential experience could
produce measurable changes in the brain. Control experiments demonstrated
that the cerebral differences could not be attributed to differential handling,
locomotor activity, or diet. The brain weight differences caused by differential
experience were extremely reliable, although small in percentage terms. Moreover, these differences were not uniformly distributed throughout the cerebral
cortex: They were almost invariably largest in occipital cortex and smallest in
the adjacent somesthetic cortex; the rest of the brain outside the cerebral cortex
tended to show very little effect (Bennett et al 1964a,b). Thus the learning or

enriched experience caused changes in specific cortical regions and not undifferentiated growth of brain. Later work also showed effects of differential experience in other parts of the brain that have been implicated in learning and formation of memory—the cerebellar cortex (Pysh & Weiss 1979) and the hippocampal dentate gyrus (Juraska et al 1985, 1989).

Further early studies revealed experience-induced changes in other measures, especially in occipital cortex. Increases were reported in cortical thickness (Diamond et al 1964), in sizes of neuronal cell bodies and nuclei (Diamond 1967), in size of synaptic contact areas (West & Greenough 1972), in numbers of dendritic spines per unit of length of basal dendrites (an increase of 10%) (Globus et al 1973), in extent and branching of dendrites (Holloway 1966) [an increase of 25% or more (Greenough & Volkmar 1973)], and in numbers of synapses per neuron (Turner & Greenough 1985); mainly because of the increase in dendritic branching, the neuronal cell bodies are spaced farther apart in cortex of EC rats than in that of IC rats. These effects indicate substantial increases in cortical volume and intracortical connections; they suggest greater processing capacity of the cortical region concerned. They contradict the speculation of Ramon y Cajal (1894) that, with training, neural cell bodies would shrink in order to allow neural arborizations to grow, thus allowing brain volume to remain constant. Instead, larger cell bodies are required to maintain the increased arborization, and the volume of the cortex increases as cell bodies and dendrites grow.

These reports indicated that the number and/or size of synaptic connections increased as a result of training or enriched experience. Some workers declared for one or the other of these possibilities, as when neurophysiologist John C. Eccles (1965) stated his belief that learning and memory storage involve "growth just of bigger and better synapses that are already there, not growth of new connections." But Rosenzweig et al (1972) reviewed findings and theoretical discussions suggesting that negative as well as positive synaptic changes may store memory. Depending upon where in the brain one measures and upon the kind of training or differential experience the organism has undergone, one may find increase in number of synapses, increase in their size, decrease in number, or decrease in size.

Soon after the early publications on neurochemical and anatomical plasticity came another kind of evidence of cortical plasticity—the announcement by Hubel & Wiesel that depriving one eye of light in a young animal, starting at the age at which the eyes first open, reduced the number of cortical cells responding to subsequent stimulation of that eye (Wiesel & Hubel 1963, Hubel & Wiesel 1965, Wiesel & Hubel 1965).

Differential Experience Produces Cerebral Changes
Throughout the Life Span, and Rather Rapidly

Further experiments revealed that relatively short periods of enriched or impoverished experience induced significant cerebral effects at any part of the life span. In contrast, Hubel & Wiesel reported that depriving an eye of light altered cortical responses only if the eye was occluded during a critical period early in life. Later, however, other investigators found that modifying sensory experience in adult animals—especially in the modalities of touch and hearing—could alter both receptive fields of cells and cortical maps, as reviewed by Kaas (1991) and Weinberger (1995).

Initially we supposed that cerebral plasticity might be restricted to the early part of the life span, so we assigned animals to differential environments at weaning (about 25 days of age) and kept them there for 80 days. Later, members of our group obtained similar effects in rats assigned to the differential environments for 30 days as juveniles at 50 days of age (Zolman & Morimoto 1962) and as young adults at 105 days of age (Rosenzweig et al 1963, Bennett et al 1964a). Riege (1971) in our laboratory found that similar effects occurred in rats assigned to the differential environments at 285 days of age and kept there for periods of 30, 60, or 90 days. Two hours a day in the differential environments for a period of 30 or 54 days produced cerebral effects similar to those after 24-hr-a-day exposure for the same periods (Rosenzweig et al 1968). Four days of differential housing produced clear effects on cortical weights (Bennett et al 1970) and on dendritic branching (Kilman et al 1988); Ferchmin & Eterovic (1986) reported that four 10-min daily sessions in EC significantly altered cortical RNA concentrations.

The fact that differential experience can cause cerebral changes throughout the life span, and relatively rapidly, was consistent with our interpretation of these effects as due to learning. Recall also that our original observation of differences in cortical neurochemistry came from experiments on formal training. Later Chang & Greenough (1982) reported that formal visual training confined to one eye of rats caused increased dendritic branching in the visual cortex contralateral to the open eye. Recently single-trial peck-avoidance training in chicks has been found to result in changes in density of dendritic spines (Lowndes & Stewart 1994).

Although the capacity for these plastic changes of the nervous system, and for learning, remain in older subjects, the cerebral effects of differential environmental experience develop somewhat more rapidly in younger than in older animals, and the magnitude of the effects is often greater in the younger animals. Also, continuing plasticity does not hold for all brain systems and types of experience. As noted above, changes in responses of cortical cells to an occluded eye are normally restricted to early development (Wiesel & Hubel 1963), but this restriction may itself be modifiable: Baer & Singer (1986) reported that plasticity of the adult visual cortex could be restored by infusing acetylcholine and noradrenaline. Further work showed that the plastic response of the young kitten brain to occlusion of one eye also depends upon glutamate transmission, because treating the striate cortex with an inhibitor of the glutamate NMDA receptor prevented the changes (Kleinschmidt et al 1987). Thus, whether the brain shows plastic changes in response to a particular kind of experience depends on the brain region, the kind of experience, and also on special circumstances or treatments that enhance or impair plasticity.

ENRICHED EXPERIENCE IMPROVES ABILITY TO LEARN AND TO SOLVE PROBLEMS

Hebb (1949, p. 298–99) reported briefly that when he allowed laboratory rats to explore his home for some weeks as pets of his children and then returned the rats to the laboratory, they showed better problem-solving ability than rats that had remained in the laboratory. Furthermore, they maintained their superiority or even increased it during a series of tests. Hebb concluded that *"the richer experience of the pet group during development made them better able to profit by new experience at maturity*—one of the characteristics of the 'intelligent' human being" (pp. 298–99, italics in the original). The results seemed to show a *permanent* effect of early experience on problem-solving at maturity.

We and others have found that experience in an enriched laboratory environment improves a subject animal's learning and problem-solving ability on a wide variety of tests, although such differences have not been found invariably. One general finding is that the more complex the task, the more likely it is that animals with EC experience will perform better than animals from SC or IC groups (for a review and discussion of various explanations offered for this effect see Renner & Rosenzweig 1987, pp. 46–48).

We were unable, however, to replicate an important aspect of Hebb's report—that over a series of tests, EC rats maintain or increase their superiority over IC rats. On the contrary, we found that IC rats tend to catch up with EC rats over a series of trials; this occurred with each of three different tests, including the Hebb-Williams mazes (Rosenzweig 1971, p. 321). Thus we did not find that early deprivation of experience caused a permanent deficit, at least for rats tested on spatial problems. Also, decreases in cortical weights induced by 300 days in the IC (versus the EC) environment could be overcome by a few weeks of training and testing in the Hebb-Williams mazes (Cummins et al 1973). Below, we note a similar effect in birds.

SIMILAR EFFECTS OF TRAINING AND EXPERIENCE ON BRAIN AND BEHAVIOR OCCUR IN ALL SPECIES TESTED TO DATE

Experiments with several strains of rats showed similar effects of EC vs. IC experience on both brain values and problem-solving behavior, as reviewed by Renner & Rosenzweig (1987, pp. 53–54). Similar effects on brain measures have been found in several species of mammals—mice, gerbils, ground squirrels, cats, and monkeys (reviewed by Renner & Rosenzweig 1987, pp. 54–59), and effects of training on brain values of birds have also been found. Thus the cerebral effects of experience that were surprising when first found in rats have now been generalized to several mammalian and avian species. Anatomical effects of training or differential experience have been measured in specific brain regions of *Drosophila* (Davis 1993, Heisenberg et al 1995). Synaptic changes with training have also been found in the nervous systems of the molluscs *Aplysia* and *Hermissenda*, as reviewed by Krasne & Glanzman (1995). In *Aplysia*, long-term habituation led to decreased numbers of synaptic sites, whereas long-term sensitization led to an increase (Bailey & Chen 1983); this is a case where either a decrease or an increase in synaptic numbers stores memory. Thus, as noted by Greenough et al (1990, p. 164), "experience-dependent synaptic plasticity is more widely reported, in terms of species, than any other putative memory mechanisms."

Experience May Be Necessary for Full Growth of Brain and of Behavioral Potential

Sufficiently rich experience may be necessary for full growth of species-specific brain characteristics and behavioral potential. This is seen in recent research on differential experience conducted with different species of the crow family. Species that cache food in a variety of locations for future use are found to have significantly larger hippocampal formations than related species that do not cache food (Krebs et al 1989, Sherry et al 1989). But the difference in hippocampal size is not found in young birds still in the nest; it appears only after food storing has started, a few weeks after the birds have left the nest (Healy & Krebs 1993). Even more interesting is the finding that this species-typical difference in hippocampal size depends on experience; it does not appear in birds that have not had the opportunity to cache food (Clayton & Krebs 1994). Different groups of hand-raised birds were given experience in storing food at three different ages: either 35–59 days posthatch, 60–83 days, or 115–138 days. Experience at each of these periods led to increased hippocampal size, much as we had found for measures of occipital cortex in the rat.

Thus, both birds and rats appear to retain considerable potential for experience-induced brain growth if it does not occur at the usual early age.

ENRICHED EXPERIENCE AND FORMAL TRAINING EVOKE SIMILAR CASCADES OF NEUROCHEMICAL EVENTS THAT CAUSE PLASTIC CHANGES IN BRAIN

By what processes do enriched experience or formal training lead to plastic changes in cerebral neurochemistry and neuroanatomy? We found early that enriched experience causes increased rates of protein synthesis and increased amounts of protein in the cortex (Bennett et al 1964a). Later, training (imprinting) was reported to increase the rates of incorporation of precursors into RNA and protein in the forebrain of the chick (Haywood et al 1970), and enriched experience in rats was found to lead to increased amounts of RNA (Ferchmin et al 1970, Bennett 1976) and increased expression of RNA in rat brain (Grouse et al 1978). Maze training led to increased ratios of RNA to DNA in rat cortex (Bennett et al 1979). We viewed these findings in the light of the hypothesis, perhaps first enunciated by Katz & Halstead (1950), that protein synthesis is required for memory storage.

Tests of the protein-synthesis hypothesis of memory formation were initiated by Flexner and associates in the early 1960s (e.g. Flexner et al 1962, 1965), and much research followed their design: 1. giving animal subjects brief training that, without further treatment, would yield evidence of retention at a test a few days later; 2. administering to experimental subjects an inhibitor of protein synthesis at various times close to training, while control subjects received an inactive substance; and 3. comparing test performance of experimental and control subjects. By the early 1970s considerable evidence indicated that protein synthesis during or soon after training is necessary for formation of long-term memory (LTM), but the interpretation of the findings was clouded by serious problems: The inhibitors of protein synthesis then available for research (such as puromycin and cycloheximide) were rather toxic, which impeded experiments and complicated interpretation; and it appeared that inhibition of protein synthesis could prevent memory formation after weak training but not after strong training (e.g. Barondes 1970).

A new protein-synthesis inhibitor, anisomycin (ANI), helped to overcome these problems. Schwartz et al (1971) reported that ANI did not prevent an electrophysiological correlate of short-term habituation or sensitization in an isolated ganglion of *Aplysia*, but they did not investigate whether ANI can prevent long-term effects. The discovery by Bennett et al (1972) that ANI is an effective amnestic agent in rodents opened the way to resolving the main challenges to the protein-synthesis hypothesis of LTM formation. ANI is much less toxic than other protein-synthesis inhibitors, and giving doses repeatedly at 2-hr intervals can prolong the duration of cerebral inhibition at amnestic levels. By varying the duration of amnestic levels of inhibition in this way, we found that the stronger the training, the longer protein synthesis had to be inhibited to prevent formation of LTM (Flood et al 1973, 1975). We also found that protein must be synthesized in the cortex soon after training if LTM is to be formed; neither short-term memory (STM) nor intermediate-term memory (ITM) required protein synthesis (e.g. Bennett et al 1972, Mizumori et al 1985, Mizumori et al 1987). Further studies were then designed to find the neurochemical processes that underlie formation of STM and ITM. Lashley's concern, mentioned above, that some kinds of memory appear to be formed too quickly to allow growth of neural connections, ignored the distinction between STM and LTM, even though William James (1890) had already distinguished between these stores (although under different names). Observing this distinction was necessary if one was to look for different mechanisms of the two kinds of memory traces that Hebb distinguished: transient, labile memory traces, on the one hand, and stable, structural traces, on the other.

Much of our work on the neurochemistry of STM and ITM has been done with chicks, which have several advantages for this research, including the following: The chick system is convenient for studying the stages of memory formation because chicks can be trained rapidly in a one-trial peck-avoidance paradigm and can be tested within seconds after training, or hours or days later. Large numbers of chicks can be studied in a single run, so one can compare different agents, doses, and times of administration within the same batch of subjects. Unlike invertebrate preparations, the chick system can be used to study the roles of different vertebrate brain structures and to investigate questions of cerebral asymmetry in learning and memory. The chick system permits study of learning and memory in the intact animal. The successive neurochemical stages occur more slowly in the chick than in the rat, thus allowing them to be separated more clearly. Further advantages have been stated elsewhere (e.g. Rosenzweig 1990, Rosenzweig et al 1992).

Although some amnestic agents, such as ANI, diffuse readily throughout the brain, we found that others affect only a restricted volume of tissue at amnestic concentrations (Patterson et al 1986). Such agents can be used to reveal the roles of different brain structures in different stages of memory formation (e.g. Patterson et al 1986, Serrano et al 1995b).

Using the chick system, several investigators have traced parts of a cascade of neurochemical events from initial stimulation to synthesis of protein and structural changes (e.g. Gibbs & Ng 1977; Ng & Gibbs 1991; Rose 1992a,b; Rosenzweig et al 1992). At some if not all stages, parallel processes occur. Briefly, here are some of the stages: The cascade is initiated when sensory stimulation activates receptor organs, which stimulate afferent neurons by using various synaptic transmitter agents such as acetylcholine (ACh) and glutamate. Inhibitors of ACh synaptic activity, such as scopolamine and pirenzepine, can prevent STM. So can inhibitors of glutamate receptors, including both the NMDA and AMPA receptors. Alteration of regulation of ion channels in the neuronal membrane can inhibit STM formation, as seen in effects of lanthanum chloride on calcium channels and of ouabain on sodium and potassium channels. Inhibition of second messengers is also amnestic—for example inhibition of adenylate cyclase by forskolin or of diacylglycerol by bradykinin. These second messengers can activate protein kinases—enzymes that catalyze addition of phosphate molecules to proteins. We found that two kinds of protein kinases are important in formation, respectively, of ITM or LTM. Agents that inhibit calcium-calmodulin protein kinases (CaM kinases) prevent formation of ITM, whereas agents that do *not* inhibit CaM kinases but *do* inhibit protein kinase A (PKA) or protein kinase C (PKC) prevent formation of LTM (Rosenzweig et al 1992, Serrano et al 1994). From this research, Serrano et al (1995a) were able to predict for a newly available inhibitor of PKC its effective amnestic dose and how long after training it would cause memory to decline. One-trial training leads to increase of immediate early gene messenger RNA in the chick forebrain (Anokhin & Rose 1991) and to increase in the density of dendritic spines (Lowndes & Stewart 1994). Many of these effects occur only in the left hemisphere of the chick, or are more prominent in the left than in the right hemisphere. Thus, learning in the chick system permits study of many steps that lead from sensory stimulation to formation of neuronal structures involved in memory.

The neurochemical cascade involved in formation of memory in the chick is similar to the cascade involved in long-term potentiation in the mammalian brain (e.g. Colley & Routtenberg 1993) and in the nervous systems of invertebrates (e.g. Krasne & Glanzman 1995).

Many of the steps in formation of memory in the chick can also be modulated by opioids and other substances. Opioid agonists tend to impair, and opioid antagonists to enhance, memory formation. Different opioids appear to modulate formation of different stages of memory (e.g. Colombo et al 1992, 1993; Patterson et al 1989; Rosenzweig et al 1992).

Can Parts of the Neurochemical Cascade Be Related to Different Stages of Memory Formation?

Some of the difficulty in attempting to relate parts of the neurochemical cascade to different stages of memory formation comes from problems of defining stages of memory, as discussed more fully elsewhere (Rosenzweig et al 1993). Consider, for example, some very different attempts to state the duration of STM. Early investigators of human STM (Brown 1958, Peterson & Peterson 1959) reported that it lasts only about 30 sec if rehearsal is prevented. Agranoff et al (1966) reported that in goldfish, if formation of LTM is prevented by an inhibitor of protein synthesis, STM can last up to 3 days, although normally LTM forms within an hour after training. Kandel et al (1987) wrote that in *Aplysia*, "A single training trial produces short-term sensitization that lasts from minutes to hours" (p. 17) and that long-term memory is "memory that lasts more than one day" (p. 35). Rose (1995) suggests that, in the chick, memories that persist only a few hours involve a first wave of glycoprotein synthesis, whereas "true long-term memory" requires a second wave of glycoprotein synthesis, occurring about 6 hr after training.

Squire (1987) was not concerned about an apparent discrepancy: Behavioral measures indicated that STM lasts less than a minute whereas neurobiological experiments in both vertebrates and invertebrates have been interpreted as suggesting STM durations of hours or more. In a discussion entitled "Neuropsychology and neurobiology reconciled" (pp. 148–50), Squire suggested that the findings are not incompatible because they refer to different levels of analysis: "[E]xperimental psychology and neuropsychology employ the terms 'short-term' and 'long-term' memory as system-level concepts.... The neurobiological approach analyzes memory at the level of cells and synapses." It is confusing, he suggested, "to assume that stages of synaptic change must reveal themselves literally at the behavioral level." It seems to me that this accepts the discrepancy rather than reconciling the two sets of findings. Moreover, if the behavioral events are based on the neural processes, then it is hard to see how STM events that last less than a minute can depend upon cellular events that require hours to unfold!

Instead of considering that STM can last several hours or even a day or more, it is useful to posit one or more intermediate-term memory (ITM) stages occurring between STM and LTM, as some theorists have done since the 1960s (e.g. McGaugh 1966, 1968). Thus, Gibbs & Ng (1977) referred to a "labile" stage occurring between STM and LTM and later (e.g. 1984) called this the intermediate stage of memory. My coworkers and I have discussed mechanisms of STM, ITM, and LTM in a series of papers (e.g. Rosenzweig et al 1984, 1992, 1993; Mizumori et al 1987; Patterson et al 1988). In investigating effects of protein kinase inhibitors (PKIs) on memory formation in chicks, we reported that those agents that inhibit CaM kinase activity disrupt formation of what some workers with chicks identify as ITM (lasting from about 15 min to about 60 min posttraining); those agents that inhibit PKC, PKA, or PKG, but do not inhibit CaM kinase, disrupt the formation of LTM (Rosenzweig et al 1992, Serrano et al 1994). Other investigators prefer to refer to different phases or stages of LTM rather than use the expression ITM. Thus, studying the LTP analog to memory in slices of rat hippocampus, Huang &

Kandel (1994) reported findings similar to those of Rosenzweig et al (1992) and Serrano et al (1994) with regard to the roles of two classes of protein kinases: Inhibitors of CaM kinase activity disrupted what Huang & Kandel called a transient, early phase of LTP (E-LTP), evoked by moderately strong stimuli and lasting from 1 hr to less than 3 hr after induction of LTP); agents that inhibit PKA, but do not inhibit CaM kinase, disrupt the formation of what they called a later, more enduring phase of LTP (L-LTP), evoked by strong stimulation and lasting at least 6–10 hr. Weak stimuli evoke only short-term potentiation (STP), lasting only 20–30 min. As mentioned above, Rose (1995) suggests that, in the chick, a kind of LTM that lasts a few hours involves a first wave of glycoprotein synthesis, whereas "true long-term memory" requires a second wave of glycoprotein synthesis, occurring about 6 hr after training. But many findings in this area support the hypothesis that at least three sequentially dependent stages of memory formation exist, each dependent on different neurochemical processes. A recent review (DeZazzo & Tully 1995) discusses STM, ITM, and LTM and compares the characteristics of the three stages in fruitflies, chicks, and rats.

The Possibility of Treatments to Improve Cognitive Functioning

The results bearing on stages of memory formation are important not only for investigators of the neurochemistry of memory but also for neuropsychologists and others who work with patients suffering from memory disorders. A review by Kopelman (1992, pp. 136–38) finds mixed results in attempts to distinguish losses of ITM and LTM in Korsakoff's and Alzheimer's patients. If it becomes possible to distinguish patients with disorders of ITM from those with impairment of STM or LTM, then perhaps their deficits can be traced to different disorders of the nervous system. Identification of the neurochemical processes underlying each stage of memory formation could lead to rational pharmacological treatments. If investigators could then understand the genetics involved, they might eventually find genetic treatments for some memory defects.

It should not be overlooked that the advent of effective treatments to ameliorate memory might not be an unmixed blessing; it could lead to social and ethical problems, especially if such treatments could enhance normal cognitive functioning, as René Cassin, one of the authors of the International Declaration of Human Rights, and recipient of the Nobel Peace Prize, warned educators, scientists, and jurists in 1968. Psychologists and neuroscientists whose work may improve the cognitive abilities of individuals share the responsibility to prepare for the social and ethical consequences of their work.

EVIDENCE THAT CERTAIN LEARNING-INDUCED NEUROCHEMICAL PROCESSES AND NEURAL PLASTICITY ARE NECESSARY FOR LONG-TERM MEMORY

What Neurochemical Processes Are Necessary and Sufficient to Store Memories of Various Durations?

As evidence accumulated that learning and experience induce chemical changes in the brain and that inhibiting some chemical processes around the time of learning blocks formation of memory, some investigators tried to devise guidelines and criteria to judge whether such changes and processes are necessary and sufficient for formation of memory. Of course, reports of many studies stated one or more criteria against which to test their findings, but Entingh et al (1975) and Rose (1981) tried to list several guidelines or criteria that would be applicable to a variety of studies.

Research on learning and memory, chiefly with chicks, showed that some neural processes appear to fulfill all the following criteria; those set in italics are paraphrased from Rose (1992a) and given in somewhat different order. Evidence for several of these criteria was shown above: (*a*) *There must be changes in the quantity of the system or substance, or its rate of production or turnover, in some localized region of the brain during memory formation.* (*b*) The amount of change should be related to the strength or amount of training, up to a limit. (*c*) *Stress, motor activity, or other processes that accompany learning must not, in the absence of memory formation, result in the structural or biochemical changes.* (*d*) *If the cellular or biochemical changes are inhibited during the period over which memory formation would normally occur, then memory formation should be prevented and the animal should be amnesic.* However, Flood et al (1973) found cases in which the protein synthesis required for LTM formation was only postponed by inhibition of protein synthesis and occurred later than usual, after the inhibition wore off. (*e*) *Removal of the anatomical site at which the biochemical, cellular, and physiological changes occur should interfere with the process of memory formation, depending upon when, in relation to the training, the region is removed.* But some cases have been found in which, after removal of a primary area for memory formation, memory can be formed in a secondary region. (*f*) *Neurophysiological recording from the sites of cellular change should detect altered electrical responses from the neurons during and/or as a consequence of memory formation.* (*g*) *The time course of the change must be compatible with the time course of memory formation.* (*h*) As Entingh et al (1975, p. 232) pointed out, the brain sites involved in learning and memory storage should be identified by converging evidence from neurochemical changes, localized inhibition of neurochemistry, and electrophysiological recording; lesion studies should be added to this list.

Martinez & Derrick (1996) in this volume discuss whether long-term potentiation (LTP)—which involves neurochemical, electrophysiological, and neuroanatomical changes—is a memory mechanism. While conceding that convincing proof does not exist that LTP is involved in memory, they believe that after 20 years of research on it, "LTP remains the best single candidate for a cellular process of synaptic change that may underlie learning and memory in the vertebrate brain" (p. 198). They review findings of a cascade of neurochemical events underlying LTP that is similar to those found in research on memory formation.

Is Learning-Induced Neuroanatomical Plasticity Necessary for Storage of Long-Term Memory?

Whether learning-induced anatomical changes in the nervous system are necessary for storage of long-term memory has been discussed by several authors, including Morris (1989), Greenough et al (1990), and Martinez & Derrick (1996). Greenough et al (1990, pp. 162–65) note several observations that relate number of synapses and degree of dendritic branching to the amount and sites of learning or experience; evidence for most of these points is given above, and in some cases I here augment the statements of Greenough et al: (*a*) The amount of dendrite per neuron in occipital cortex of the rat reflects the amount of stimulation or complexity in the environment—e.g. the measures are greatest in rats from the enriched condition, least in those from IC, and intermediate in those from SC. (*b*) Similar effects of training or experience occur in young, adult, and old rats. (*c*) Changes in brain measures are induced rapidly by training. (*d*) The changes in dendritic branching are paralleled by changes in numbers of synapses per neuron. (*e*) The synaptic and dendritic changes occur not only in rodents but also in cats and monkeys. (*f*) The synaptic and dendritic changes caused by enriched experience are similar to those induced by traditional learning tasks. Later (pp. 174–76) Greenough et al note (*g*) that learning-based morphological changes are greater than and different from changes induced by mere activity. Also, (*h*) the changes occur in brain regions involved in the learned tasks; if learning is confined to one side of the brain, the synaptic and dendritic changes are also confined to that side. Note that some of the points on this list correspond to some given just above for neurochemical processes.

The fact that training and experience usually lead to increased spacing of cortical neurons should be taken into account in interpreting certain other findings, such as a report by Witelson et al (1994) that received considerable coverage in the news media. They reported, based on a small number of cases, that women have a larger number of neurons in a region of the cortex related to language than do men and speculated that this might be related to women's greater proficiency in language. Actually the measure was not the total number of neurons in the region but *neurons per unit of volume of cortex*. This means closer spacing of neurons, which could as well suggest simpler and less extensive connections of neurons in this region of women's brains, perhaps reflecting less verbal training and experience. At the least, it does not seem compelling to interpret closer packing of neurons as evidence for greater cognitive proficiency.

CHANGES INDUCED BY LEARNING OCCUR IN A VARIETY OF NEURAL NETWORKS

Hebb's main interest was considering how complex neural networks ("phase sequences" and "cell assemblies") could account for phenomena such as perception and memory. He put forth his postulate of synaptic changes only to show that such changes could support the formation of neural networks. But, as Gallistel (1990) notes, most neuroscientists have been more concerned with how synaptic changes can store information than with how neural networks can compute memories. Investigators have proposed a variety of neural circuits and networks in which information could be stored and memorial responses computed; we can classify much current research according to the kinds of networks proposed (Rosenzweig et al 1996), as a few examples will show. The neural circuits range from simple neural chains to parallel distributed circuits.

The simplest neural chain is a monosynaptic reflex arc, and this has been used to describe the mechanism of simple learning (habituation) in the gill withdrawal reflex of *Aplysia* (e.g. Kandel et al 1987, Kupfermann & Kandel 1969). Because the change occurs within the reflex arc, it is sometimes referred to as an intrinsic change (Krasne & Glanzman 1995).

Many simple neural circuits receive input from (or are by-passed by) superordinate circuits, and learning-induced plasticity may occur at the superordinate level. Thus, in eyelid conditioning in mammals, it appears that the site of plasticity necessary for the conditioning is in a higher-order circuit in the cerebellum (Lavond et al 1993), whereas the basic reflex circuit in the brainstem shows no change during training. Considered in relation to the reflex arc, this is sometimes called an extrinsic change.

Even where synaptic changes have been found in a monosynaptic reflex arc, changes sufficient for learning and memory may also take place in other parts of the nervous system. Thus, the gill-withdrawal response of *Aplysia* persists and can be altered by training after surgical removal of the abdominal ganglion (Mpitsos & Lukowiak 1985). The central nervous system of *Aplysia* enters a suppressed state after the animal has eaten or engaged in sexual activity, but even when the CNS is inactivated, the animal still shows the gill-withdrawal response, mediated by the peripheral nervous system. Thus the neural circuitry of the gill-withdrawal response includes cells of the peripheral nervous system, and "the neural circuitry of this behavior is more complex than was hoped, and much of it consists of small diffuse cells that are inaccessible to the neurophysiologist" (Leonard et al 1989, p. 585).

Much current theorizing suggests that the same ensemble of neurons can encode many different memories, each neuron participating to a greater or lesser extent in a particular memory (e.g. McNaughton & Morris 1987). Recent research suggests that modification of the gill-withdrawal response in *Aplysia* may depend on parallel distributed processing (involving synaptic plasticity) in a large ensemble of neurons rather than on a few neurons in a monosynaptic reflex arc. Thus, it appears that approximately 200 of the 1000 neurons in the abdominal ganglion of *Aplysia* respond to a touch to the siphon (Zecevic et al 1989) and that these neurons are involved in respiration as well as gill withdrawal (Wu et al 1994). The different kinds of responses mediated by these neurons appear to be generated by altered activities of a single, large distributed network rather than by separate small networks, each dedicated to a particular response.

Investigation of learning and memory in birds and mammals indicates that they involve neural sites widely distributed in the brain, as Hebb believed likely for cell assemblies. Thompson and his associates (Lavond et al 1993) emphasize that their research on the neural circuit necessary for eyelid conditioning is restricted to "the simplest substrates of aversive conditioning" (p. 318), and they are certain that other structures, including "the hippocampus and cerebral cortex certainly play important roles in more complex learning, as well as being influenced in aversive classical conditioning" (p. 318). Noninvasive imaging techniques now indicate that several brain regions are specifically activated during eyelid conditioning in human subjects. Thus Logan & Grafton (1995) report that brain regions that exhibit significant differences between the unpaired-stimulus control condition and the well-trained state include not only several cerebellar sites but also the pontine tegmentum, ipsilateral inferior thalamus/red nucleus, ipsilateral hippocampal formation, ipsilateral lateral temporal cortex, and bilateral ventral striatum. Similarly, a review of several human neuroimaging studies using various delayed-response tasks to investigate working memory shows that there is typically activation of the dorsal prefrontal cortex, but other regions are also selectively activated depending upon the specific stimuli and task (McCarthy 1995). Tracing the circuits involved is a challenging task that should provide major advances in our understanding of learning and memory.

RESEARCH ON USE-INDUCED BRAIN PLASTICITY IS YIELDING AND SUPPORTING A VARIETY OF APPLICATIONS

Animal research on the effects of experience on brain plasticity and learning is being applied to several areas of human behavior and in other cases has been used as converging or supporting evidence. Thus it is being used to promote child development, successful aging, and recovery from brain damage; it is also being applied to benefit animals in laboratories, zoos, and farms. Let us consider a few of these kinds of application or influence briefly below.

Applications to Child Development

The findings on the effects of differential experience in animals have influenced research on child development or at least have been offered as supporting evidence in favor of giving children adequate experience. An indication of the importance of this approach comes from a major report, "Starting points: Meeting the needs of our youngest children" (1994), issued by the Carnegie Task Force on Meeting the Needs of Young Children. The tenor of the findings is indicated by this quotation:

> Beginning in the 1960s, scientists began to demonstrate that the quality and variety of the environment have direct impact on brain development. Today, researchers around the world are amassing evidence that the role of the environment is even more important than earlier studies had suggested. For example, histological and brain scan studies of animals show changes in brain structure and function as a result of variations in early experience.
>
> These findings are consistent with research in child development that has shown the first eighteen months of life to be an important period of development. Studies of children raised in poor environments—both in this country and elsewhere—show that they have cognitive deficits of substantial magnitude by eighteen months of age and that full reversal of these deficits may not be possible. These studies are based on observational and cognitive assessments; researchers say that neurobiologists using brain scan technologies are on the verge of confirming these findings.
>
> In the meantime, more conventional studies of child development—using cognitive and observational measures—continue to show short- and long-term benefits of an enriched early environment (p. 8).

This is one of the latest contributions to a back-and-forth debate between those who hold that child development proceeds mainly from innate factors with only a small influence of the environment and those who hold that environment can make a major contribution. Gall and Spurzheim differed on this question early in the 19th century.

It is disheartening to note that despite demonstrations over 30 years that lack of adequate intellectual stimulation can cause mental retardation and that appropriate stimulation can foster normal development, few sustained attempts have been made to apply these findings. Hunt (1979), for example, in a chapter in the *Annual Review of Psychology*, presented evidence for the importance of early experience to children's intellectual development. He reviewed several studies showing substantial effects of specific kinds of environmental interventions on particular aspects of child development. One was his own study (Hunt et al 1976) demonstrating the importance of specific caretaking to assure language development of infants in a Teheran orphanage. Hunt also reviewed animal research on effects of differential experience on problem-solving, neuroanatomy, and neurochemistry—research whose inspiration he attributed to Hebb's 1949 book, and which included some of the experiments of the 1960s–1970s described above.

Several factors have complicated attempts to apply research on environmental enrichment to improve the cognitive status of children raised in poor environments. One is that some proponents have overestimated the potential effects of relatively short periods of enrichment and then have been disappointed that the effects were not larger. This has been one of the problems confronting the Head Start program which began in 1963 in the United States (Zigler & Muenchow 1992). Although this and related programs have proved beneficial and cost effective, they were unable to bring participating children up to the scholastic levels of children living in better environments. Another problem is that the human programs involve a variety of interventions, so it is difficult to determine whether the positive effects are attributable to enriched experience and training or to other causes such as improved nutrition and health care. In the words of a recent review of the effects of nutrition on child development, however, "Adequacy of the social and educational environment is as significant as nutrition for mental development (or possibly more significant)" (Sigman 1995, p. 54).

The authors of a new series of studies (Drews et al 1995, Murphy et al 1995, Yeargin-Allsopp et al 1995) conclude that the principal causes of mild retardation (IQ scores between 50 and 70) in an American city appear to be poverty and lack of education of mothers (fewer than 12 years of education). These researchers claim that many cases of mild retardation are preventable and/or treatable by appropriate early training and experience. David Satcher, the Director for the Centers for Disease Control and Prevention, which supported these studies, announced that the Centers will start a demonstration program in 1996 "aimed at promoting the cognitive, communicative, and behavioral development, as well as the health, of children born to women with fewer than 12 years of education" (Satcher 1995, p. 305). Satcher cited the report of the Carnegie Corporation, mentioned above: "[It] goes beyond questions of intellectual function and underscores the importance of early (birth to 3 years) experiential and social factors in brain development. The report emphasizes long-lasting effects of early environmental experience on both brain structure and cognitive function" (Satcher 1995, p. 305).

The problems of finding exactly which factors are most important in enhancing cognitive development should not overshadow the benefits of programs that provide environmental enrichment to children in need of it. I believe that current programs should be expanded to include more children and to retain them for longer periods. Unfortunately, in the United States such programs appear to be in jeopardy in the present political climate.

Enriched Experience Aids "Successful Aging"

Enriched experience, beginning early in life, also helps to ensure maintenance of ability into old age. Thus, infantile handling or later enriched experience helps prevent hippocampal damage caused by stress in rats. Meaney et al (1988, 1991) handled some neonatal rat pups during each of their first 21 days and left other pups unhandled. They examined cognitive function of the rats at different ages from 3 months to 24 months and also measured basal and stress levels of glucocorticoids, numbers of hippocampal neurons, and numbers of glucocorticoid receptors. Chronic excess of glucocorticoids is toxic to neurons, particularly those of the hippocampus, and aged rats are particularly vulnerable (Sapolsky 1992). Handled rats showed improved spatial memory, higher numbers of hippocampal corticoid receptors, and a more rapid return of corticosterone to basal levels after response to a stressful situation. In old age, the handled animals had lower basal levels of corticosterone and lost fewer hippocampal neurons than the unhandled ones.

Young adult rats given 30 days of EC experience beginning at 50 days of age, like rats given infantile handling, showed higher expression of the gene encoding glucocorticoid receptors in the hippocampus, and they also showed induction of genes for nerve growth factors in the hippocampus (Mohammed et al 1993, Olsson et al 1994). The investigators suggest that enriched experience in adulthood, like infantile handling, may protect the aging hippocampus from glucocorticoid neurotoxicity.

Some kinds of learning and performance decline with age after middle adulthood, but other kinds of learning and memory do not. People who continue to learn actively can maintain high levels of performance. For example, professors in their 60s perform as well as professors in their 30s on many tests of learning and memory (Shimamura et al 1995).

Beyond the age of retirement, stimulation and activity continue to contribute to health and mental status. This claim is borne out in a longitudinal study that has assessed the mental abilities of more than 5000 adults, having followed some for as long as 35 years (Schaie 1994). Among the eight variables found to reduce the risk of cognitive decline in old age, three are particularly relevant here: 1. Living in favorable environmental circumstances, as would be the case for persons of high socioeconomic status. Such circumstances include above-average education, histories of occupational pursuits that involve high complexity and low routine, above-average income, and the maintenance of intact families. 2. Substantial involvement in activities typically available in complex and intellectually stimulating environments. Such activities include extensive reading habits, travel, attendance at cultural events, pursuit of continuing education activities, and participation in clubs and professional associations. 3. Being married to a spouse with high cognitive status. Our studies of cognitive similarity in married couples suggest that the spouse who scores less well on tests of cognitive ability at the beginning of marriage tends to maintain or increase his or her scores vis-à-vis the spouse who originally scored higher (Schaie 1994, p. 312).

Terry et al (1995) report that loss of synapses correlates strongly with the severity of symptoms in Alzheimer's disease. Enriched experience produces richer neural networks in the brains of all species so far studied. If similar effects occur in humans, as seems likely, the resulting reserves of connections may protect intellectual function from the effects of Alzheimer's disease.

In adulthood and old age, is use of the nervous system better characterized by the phrase "wear and tear" or by the phrase "use it or lose it" (Swaab 1991)? The research reviewed here, along with many comments on Swaab's paper, mainly support the characterization "use it or lose it." But enriched experience and use of the cognitive faculites are especially effective early in life and set the basis for later use and maintenance of the brain and of mental ability.

Applications to Recovery from or Compensation for Brain Damage

In all parts of the life span, training and enriched experience help in recovery from or compensation for effects of brain damage. We showed this in experiments with rats in the 1970s (Will et al 1977), and research along this line continues. To what degree does experience actually aid in recovery, and to what degree does it only help to compensate for the effects of brain injury? At a minimum, psychological interventions can improve the quality of life of people with injuries of the brain or of the spinal cord. Beyond this, various combinations of physiological and behavioral interventions may combine to bring improvement.

In attempts to promote recovery from brain damage, some neuroscientists are transplanting fetal brain cells into the region of a brain lesion. Psychologists are taking part in this research. Sometimes such neural transplants or implants help to restore function, but often, for reasons that are not yet fully understood, they do not.

A few years ago, investigators started to study the separate and the combined effects of enriched environment and neural transplants (Kelche et al

1988). Under some conditions, neither the enriched experience nor the transplant alone had a beneficial effect but the combination of the two treatments yielded significant improvement in learning. Further work indicates that formal training of rats may be more effective than enriched environment in promoting the effects of brain cell grafts on recovery of learning ability (Kelche et al 1995). The results of such animal research may someday benefit human patients. At present the attempts to help patients with Parkinson's disease by implanting fetal brain cells are garnering mixed results. Perhaps the differences among clinics in success of cell grafts reflect the kinds and amounts of training and stimulation given their patients; such behavioral factors may well interact with the skill of the neurosurgeon. The combination of brain tissue implantation with cognitive training and stimulation may help researchers to elucidate further the neural bases of learning and memory.

Research on Enriched Environments Is Benefiting Animals in Laboratories, Zoos, and Farms

Animals not only contribute to research on mechanisms of memory and effects of environmental enrichment, but they also benefit from such research, as I have described in somewhat more detail elsewhere (Rosenzweig 1984). Newer standards for housing animals in laboratories reflect findings that animals benefit in development of brain and behavior from adequate space and facilities for species-specific activities like running, investigating, and so forth. Zoos are also providing more natural settings and apparatus that permit animals to engage in species-specific activities. Two of my former students who worked with rats in enriched laboratory environments have since worked to improve settings for zoo animals. Some farms have found that animals thrive better in more natural settings.

CONCLUDING COMMENT

The last half century has been a fascinating period in which to observe and take part in the search for mechanisms of memory. The invention of new concepts and the emergence of new experimental techniques have allowed important progress and rejection of inadequate hypotheses. Exciting new techniques promise novel insights. Behavioral research continues to distinguish the various types of learning and memory. Clinical research in interaction with biological research continues to explain problems of learning and memory and to yield methods of alleviating cognitive deficits. The next half century will see many more surprises and advances in this complex and engrossing field.

ACKNOWLEDGMENTS

I thank Dr. Edward L. Bennett for his knowledgable, insightful, and friendly collaboration during more than 40 years. I also thank the colleagues, students, and postdoctoral fellows who collaborated with us and all of the contributors to this field.

The research of our laboratories was supported by grants from the National Science Foundation, the Department of Energy, the National Institute of Mental Health, the Easter Seal Foundation, and the National Institute on Drug Abuse.

Literature Cited

Ackerknecht EH, Vallois HV. 1956. *Franz Joseph Gall, Inventor of Phrenology and His Collection.* Transl. CS Léon, 1956. Madison, WI: Dept. Hist. Med., Univ. Wis. Med. Sch. (From French)

Agranoff BW, Davis RE, Brink JJ. 1966. Chemical studies on memory fixation in goldfish. *Brain Res.* 1:303–9

Altman J, Das GD. 1964. Autoradiographic examination of the effects of enriched environment on the rate of glial multiplication in the adult rat brain. *Nature* 204:1161–63

Anokhin KV, Rose SPR. 1991. Learning-induced increase of early immediate gene messenger RNA in the chick forebrain. *Eur. J. Neurosci.* 3:162–67

Baer MF, Singer W. 1986. Modulation of visual cortical plasticity by acetylcholine and noradrenaline. *Nature* 320:172–76

Bailey CH, Chen M. 1983. Morphological basis of long-term habituation and sensitization in *Aplysia. Science* 220:91–93

Bailey CH, Kandel ER. 1993. Structural changes accompanying memory storage. *Annu. Rev. Physiol.* 55:397–426

Bain A. 1872. *Mind and Body: The Theories of Their Relation.* London: Henry S. King

Barondes SH. 1970. Some critical variables in studies of the effect of inhibitors of protein synthesis on memory. In *Molecular Approaches to Learning and Memory,* ed. WL Byrne, pp. 27–34. New York: Academic

Bennett EL. 1976. Cerebral effects of differential experience and training. In *Neural Mechanisms of Learning and Memory,* ed. MR Rosenzweig, EL Bennett, pp. 279–87. Cambridge, MA: MIT Press

Bennett EL, Diamond MC, Krech D, Rosenzweig MR. 1964a. Chemical and anatomical plasticity of brain. *Science* 164:610–19

Bennett EL, Krech D, Rosenzweig MR. 1964b. Reliability and regional specificity of cerebral effects of environmental complexity and training. *J. Comp. Physiol. Psychol.* 57:440–41

Bennett EL, Orme AE, Hebert M. 1972. Cerebral protein synthesis inhibition and amnesia produced by scopolamine, cycloheximide, streptovitacin A, anisomycin, and emetine in rat. *Fed. Proc.* 31:838

Bennett EL, Rosenzweig MR, Diamond MC. 1970. Time courses of effects of differential experience on brain measures and behavior of rats. In *Molecular Approaches to Learning and Memory,* ed. WL Byrne, pp. 55–89. New York: Academic

Bennett EL, Rosenzweig MR, Morimoto H, Hebert M. 1979. Maze training alters brain weights and cortical RNA/DNA ratios. *Behav. Neural Biol.* 26:1–22

Bonnet C. 1779–1783. *Oeuvres d'Histoire Naturelle et de Philosophie.* Neuchatel: S. Fauche

Brown J. 1958. Some tests of the decay theory of immediate memory. *Q. J. Exp. Psychol.* 10:12–21

Butters N, Delis DC, Lucas JA. 1995. Clinical assessment of memory disorders in amnesia and dementia. *Annu. Rev. Psychol.* 46: 493–523

Cajal RS. 1894. La fine structure des centres nerveux. *Proc. R. Soc. London* 55: 444–68

Carnegie Task Force on Meeting the Needs of Young Children. 1994. *Starting Points: Meeting the Needs of Our Youngest Children.* New York: Carnegie Corp. New York

Carruthers MJ. 1990. *The Book of Memory.* Cambridge, UK: Cambridge Univ. Press

Chang F-LF, Greenough WT. 1982. Lateralized effects of monocular training on dendritic branching in adult split-brain rats. *Brain Res.* 232:283–92

Clayton NS, Krebs JR. 1994. Hippocampal growth and attrition in birds affected by experience. *Proc. Natl. Acad. Sci. USA* 91:7410–14

Colley PA, Routtenberg A. 1993. Long-term potentiation as synaptic dialogue. *Brain Res. Rev.* 18:115–22

Colombo PJ, Martinez JL, Bennett EL, Rosenzweig MR. 1992. Kappa opioid receptor activity modulates memory for peck-avoidance training in the 2-day-old chick. *Psychopharmacology* 108:235–40

Colombo PJ, Thompson KR, Martinez JL, Bennett EL, Rosenzweig MR. 1993. Dynorphin(1–13) impairs memory formation for aversive and appetitive learning in chicks. *Peptides* 14:1165–70

Cragg BG. 1967. Changes in visual cortex on first exposure of rats to light. *Nature* 215:251–53

Cummins RA, Walsh RN, Budtz-Olsen OE, Konstantinos T, Horsfall CR. 1973. Environmentally-induced changes in the brains of elderly rats. *Nature* 243:516–18

Davies JD. 1955. *Phrenology Fad and Science: A 19th Century American Crusade.* New Haven: Yale Univ. Press

Davis R. 1993. Mushroom bodies and *Drosophila* learning. *Neuron* 11:1–14

DeZazzo J, Tully T. 1995. Dissection of memory formulation from behavioral pharmacology to molecular genetics. *Trends Neurosci.* 18:212–18

Diamond MC. 1967. Extensive cortical depth measurements and neuron size increases in the cortex of environmentally enriched rats. *J. Comp. Neurol.* 131:357–64

Diamond MC, Krech D, Rosenzweig MR. 1964. The effects of an enriched environment on the histology of the rat cerebral cortex. *J. Comp. Neurol.* 123:111–19

Diamond MC, Lindner B, Johnson R, Bennett EL, Rosenzweig MR. 1975. Differences in occipital cortical synapses from environmentally enriched, impoverished, and standard colony rats. *J. Neurosci. Res.* 1:109–19

Drews CD, Yeargin-Allsopp M, Decouflé P, Murphy CC. 1995. Variation in the influence of selected sociodemographic risk factors for mental retardation. *Am. J. Public Health* 85:329–34

Eccles JC. 1965. Possible ways in which synaptic mechanisms participate in learning, remembering, and forgetting. In *The Anatomy of Memory*, ed. DP Kimble, p. 97. Palo Alto, CA: Sci. Behav. Books

Entingh D, Dunn A, Wilson JE, Glassman E, Hogan E. 1975. Biochemical approaches to the biological basis of memory. In *Handbook of Psychobiology*, ed. MS Gazzaniga, C Blakemore, pp. 201–38. New York: Academic

Ferchmin P, Eterovic V. 1986. Forty minutes of experience increase the weight and RNA content of cerebral cortex in periadolescent rats. *Dev. Psychobiol.* 19:511–19

Ferchmin P, Eterovic V, Caputto R. 1970. Studies of brain weight and RNA content after short periods of exposure to environmental complexity. *Brain Res.* 20:49–57

Finger S. 1994. *Origins of Neuroscience: A History of Explorations into Brain Function.* New York: Oxford Univ. Press

Flexner JB, Flexner LB, de la Haba G, Roberts RB. 1965. Loss of memory as related to inhibition of cerebral protein synthesis. *J. Neurochem.* 12:535–41

Flexner JB, Flexner LB, Stellar E, de la Haba G, Roberts RB. 1962. Inhibition of protein synthesis in brain and learning and memory following puromycin. *J. Neurochem.* 9:595–605

Flood JF, Bennett EL, Orme AE, Rosenzweig MR. 1975. Relation of memory formation to controlled amounts of brain protein synthesis. *Physiol. Behav.* 15:97–102

Flood JF, Bennett EL, Rosenzweig MR, Orme AE. 1973. The influence of duration of protein synthesis inhibition on memory. *Physiol. Behav.* 10:555–62

Forgays DG, Forgays JW. 1952. The nature of the effect of free-environmental experience on the rat. *J. Comp. Physiol. Psychol.* 45:747–50

Gall JF. 1819. *Anatomie et physiologie du système nerveux en général, et du cerveau en particulier, avec des observations sur la possibilité de recoinnaitre plusieurs dispositions intellectuelles et morales de l'homme et des animaux par la configuation de leurs têtes.* Vol. 4. Paris: N. Maze

Gallistel CR. 1990. *The Organization of Learning.* Cambridge, MA: MIT Press

Geller E, Yuwiler A, Zolman JF. 1965. Effects of environmental complexity on constituents of brain and liver. *J. Neurochem.* 12:949–55

Gibbs ME, Ng KT. 1977. Psychobiology of memory: towards a model of memory formation. *Biobehav. Rev.* 1:113–36

Globus A, Rosenzweig MR, Bennett EL, Diamond MC. 1973. Effects of differential experience on dendritic spine counts in rat cerebral cortex. *J. Comp. Physiol. Psychol.* 82:175–81

Greenough WT, Volkmar FR. 1973. Pattern of dendritic branching in occipital cortex of rats reared in complex environments. *Exp. Neurol.* 40:491–504

Greenough WT, Withers GS, Wallace CS. 1990. Morphological changes in the nervous system arising from behavioral experience: What is the evidence they are involved in learning and memory? In *The Biology of Memory*, ed. LR Squire, E Lindenlaub, pp. 159–85. Stuttgart: Schattauer

Grouse LD, Schrier BK, Bennett EL, Rosenzweig MR, Nelson PG. 1978. Sequence diversity studies of rat brain RNA: effects of environmental complexity on rat brain RNA diversity. *J. Neurochem.* 30:191–203

Haywood J, Rose SPR, Bateson PPG. 1970. Effects of an imprinting procedure on RNA polymerase activity in the chick brain. *Nature* 288:373–74

Healy SD, Krebs JR. 1993. Development of hippocampal specialisation in a food-storing bird. *Behav. Brain Res.* 53:127–30

Hebb DO. 1949. *The Organization of Behavior: A Neuropsychological Theory.* New York: Wiley

Heisenberg M, Heusipp M, Wanke C. 1995. Structural plasticity in the *Drosophila* brain. *J. Neurosci.* 15:1951–60

Holloway RL. 1966. Dendritic branching: some preliminary results of training and complexity in rat visual cortex. *Brain Res.* 2:393–96

Huang YY, Kandel ER. 1994. Recruitment of long-lasting and protein kinase A–dependent long-term potentiation in the CA1 region of hippocampus requires repeated tetanization. *Learn. Mem.* 1:74–82

Hubel DH, Wiesel TN. 1965. Binocular interaction in striate cortex of kittens reared with artificial squint. *J. Neurophysiol.* 28:1041–59

Hunt JM. 1979. Psychological development: early experience. *Annu. Rev. Psychol.* 30:103–43

Hunt JM, Mohandessi K, Ghodssi M, Akiyama M. 1976. The psychological development of orphanage-reared infants: interventions with outcomes (Tehran). *Genet. Psychol. Monogr.* 94:177–226

James W. 1890. *Principles of Psychology,* Vol. 1. New York: Henry Holt

Juraska JM, Fitch JM, Henderson C, Rivers N. 1985. Sex differences in dendritic branching of dentate granule cells following differential experience. *Brain Res.* 333:73–80

Juraska JM, Fitch JM, Washburne DL. 1989. The dendritic morphology of neurons in the rat hippocampus CA3 area. II. Effects of gender and the environment. *Brain Res.* 479:115–19

Kaas JH. 1991. Plasticity of sensory and motor maps in adult mammals. *Annu. Rev. Neurosci.* 14:137–67

Kandel ER, Schacher S, Castellucci VF, Goelet P. 1987. The long and short of memory in *Aplysia*: a molecular perspective. In *Fidia Research Foundation Neuroscience Award Lectures.* Padova: Liviana Press

Katz JJ, Halstead WG. 1950. Protein organization and mental function. *Comp. Psychol. Monogr.* 20:1–38

Kelche C, Dalrymple-Alford JC, Will B. 1988. Housing conditions modulate the effects of intracerebral grafts in rats with brain lesions. *Behav. Brain Res.* 53:287–96

Kelche C, Roeser C, Jeltsch H, Cassel JC, Will B. 1995. The effects of intrahippocampal grafts, training, and postoperative housing on behavioral recovery after septohippocampal damage in the rat. *Neurobiol. Learn. Mem.*28:155–65

Kilman VL, Wallace CS, Withers GS, Greenough WT. 1988. 4 days of differential housing alters dendritic morphology of weanling rats. *Soc. Neurosci. Abstr.* 14:1135

Kleinschmidt A, Baer MF, Singer W. 1987. Blockade of NMDA receptors disrupts experience-dependent plasticity of kitten striate cortex. *Science* 238:355–58

Kopelman MD. 1992. The "new" and the "old": components of the anterograde and retrograde memory loss in Korsakoff and Alzheimer patients. See Squire & Butters 1992, pp. 130–46

Krasne FB, Glanzman DL. 1995. What we can learn from invertebrate learning. *Annu. Rev. Psychol.* 46:585–624

Krebs JR, Sherry DF, Healy SD, Perry VH, Vaccarino AL. 1989. Hippocampal specialisation of food-storing birds. *Proc. Natl. Acad. Sci. USA* 86:1388–92

Krech D, Rosenzweig MR, Bennett EL. 1956. Dimensions of discrimination and level of cholinesterase activity in the cerebral cortex of the rat. *J. Comp. Physiol. Psychol.* 82:261–68

Krech D, Rosenzweig MR, Bennett EL. 1960. Effects of environmental complexity and training on brain chemistry. *J. Comp. Physiol. Psychol.* 53:509–19

Kupfermann I, Kandel ER. 1969. Neuronal controls of a behavioral response mediated by the abdominal ganglion of "Aplysia." *Science* 164:847–50

Lamarck JB. 1809. *Philosophie zoologique.* Transl. H Elliott. 1914. *Zoological Philosophy.* London: Macmillan (From French)

Lashley KS. 1950. In search of the engram. *Symp. Soc. Exp. Biol.* 4:454–82

Lavond D, Kim JJ, Thompson RF. 1993. Mammalian brain substrates of aversive conditioning. *Annu. Rev. Psychol.* 44:317–42

Leonard JL, Edstrom J, Lukowiak K. 1989. Reexamination of the gill withdrawal reflex of *Aplysia californica* Cooper (Gastropoda; Opisthobranchia). *Behav. Neurosci.* 103:585–604

Logan CG, Grafton ST. 1995. Functional anatomy of human eyeblink conditioning determined with regional cerebral glucose metabolism and positron emission tomography. *Proc. Natl. Acad. Sci. USA.* 92:7500–4

Lowndes M, Stewart MG. 1994. Dendritic spine density in the lobus parolfactorius of the domestic chick is increased 24 h after one-trial passive avoidance training. *Brain Res.* 654:129–36

Martinez JL, Derrick BE. 1996. Long-term potentiation and learning. *Annu. Rev. Psychol.* 47:173–203

McCarthy G. 1995. Functional neuroimaging of memory. *Neuroscientist* 1(3):155–63

McGaugh JL. 1966. Time-dependent processes in memory storage. *Science* 153:1351–58

McGaugh JL. 1968. A multi-trace view of memory storage. In *Recent Advances in Learning and Memory*, ed. D Bovet, F Bovet-Nitti, A Oliviero, pp. 13–24. Rome: Roma Accademia Nazionale dei Lincei

McNaughton BL, Morris RGM. 1987. Hippocampal synaptic enhancement and information storage within a distributed memory system. *Trends Neurosci.* 10:408–15

Meaney MJ, Aitkin DH, Bhatnagar S, Van Berkel C, Sapolsky RM. 1988. Effect of neonatal handling on age-related impairments associated with the hippocampus. *Science* 239: 766–68

Meaney MJ, Mitchell JB, Aitkin DH, Bhatnagar S, Bodnoff SR, et al. 1991. The effects of neonatal handling on the development of the adrenocortical response to stress: implications for neuropathology and cognitive deficits in later life. *Psychoneuroendocrinology* 16:85–103

Milner PM. 1993. The mind and Donald O. Hebb. *Sci. Am.* 268(1):124–29

Mizumori SJY, Rosenzweig MR, Bennett EL. 1985. Long-term working memory in the rat: effects of hippocampally applied anisomycin. *Behav. Neurosci.* 99:220–32

Mizumori SJY, Sakai DH, Rosenzweig MR, Bennett EL, Wittreich P. 1987. Investigations into the neuropharmacological basis of temporal stages of memory formation in mice trained in an active avoidance task. *Behav. Brain Res.* 23:239–50

Mohammed AH, Henriksson BG, Soderstrom S, Ebendal T, Olsson T, Seckl JR. 1993. Environmental influences on the central nervous system and their implications for the aging rat. *Behav. Brain Res.* 23:182–91

Morris RGM. 1989. Does synaptic plasticity play a role in learning in the vertebrate brain? In *Parallel Distributed Processing: Implications for Psychology and Neurobiology*, ed. RGM Morris, pp. 248–85. Oxford: Clarendon

Mpitsos GJ, Lukowiak K. 1985. Learning in gastropod molluscs. In *The Mollusca:* Vol. 8. *Neurobiology and Behavior,* ed. AOD Willows, pp. 95–267. Orlando: Academic

Murphy CC, Yeargin-Allsopp M, Decouflé P, Drews CD. 1995. The administrative prevalence of mental retardation in 10-year-old children in metropolitan Atlanta, 1985 through 1987. *Am. J. Public Health* 85:319–23

Ng KT, Gibbs ME. 1991. Stages in memory formation: a review. In *Neural and Behavioural Plasticity: The Use of the Domestic Chick as a Model,* ed. RJ Andrew, pp. 351–69. Oxford: Oxford Univ. Press

Olsson T, Mohammed AH, Donaldson LF, Henriksson BG, Seckl JR. 1994. Glucocorticoid receptor and NGFI-A gene expression are induced in the hippocampus after environmental enrichment in adult rats. *Mol. Brain Res.* 23:349–53

Patterson TA, Alvarado MC, Rosenzweig MR, Bennett EL. 1988. Time courses of amnesia development in two areas of the chick forebrain. *Neurochem. Res.* 13:643–47

Patterson TA, Alvarado MC, Warner IT, Rosenzweig MR, Bennett EL. 1986. Memory stages and brain asymmetry in chick learning. *Behav. Neurosci.* 100:856–65

Patterson TA, Schulteis G, Alvarado MC, Martinez JL, Bennett EL, et al. 1989. Influence of opioid peptides on learning and memory processes in the chick. *Behav. Neurosci.* 103:429–37

Peterson LR, Peterson MJ. 1959. Short-term retention of individual verbal items. *J. Exp. Psychol.* 58:193–98

Pysh JJ, Weiss M. 1979. Exercise during development induces an increase in Purkinje cell dendritic tree size. *Science* 206:230–32

Renner MJ, Rosenzweig MR. 1987. *Enriched and Impoverished Environments: Effects on Brain and Behavior.* New York: Springer-Verlag

Ribot T. 1881. *Les Maladies de la Mémoire.* Paris: J.B. Ballière. Transl. J Fitzgerald. 1883. *The Diseases of Memory.* New York: Humboldt Libr. Pop. Sci. Lit., 46:453–500

Riege WH. 1971. Environmental influences on brain and behavior of old rats. *Dev. Psychobiol.* 4:157–67

Rose SPR. 1981. What should a biochemistry of learning and memory be about? *Neuroscience* 6:811–21

Rose SPR. 1992a. *The Making of Memory.* New York: Doubleday

Rose SPR. 1992b. On chicks and Rosetta stones. See Squire & Butters 1992, pp. 547–56

Rose SPR. 1995. Glycoproteins and memory formation. *Behav. Brain Res.* 66:73–78

Rosenzweig MR. 1971. Effects of environment on development of brain and behavior. In *Biopsychology of Development,* ed. E Tobach, pp. 303–42. New York: Academic

Rosenzweig MR. 1984. Experience, memory, and the brain. *Am. Psychol.* 39:365–76

Rosenzweig MR. 1990. The chick as a model system for studying neural processes in learning and memory. In *Behavior as an*

Indicator of Neuropharmacological Events: Learning and Memory, ed. L Erinoff, pp. 1–20. Washington, DC: NIDA Res. Monogr.

Rosenzweig MR, Bennett EL, Colombo PJ, Lee DW, Serrano PA. 1993. Short-term, intermediate-term, and long-term memories. *Behav. Brain Res.* 57:193–98

Rosenzweig MR, Bennett EL, Martinez JL, Colombo PJ, Lee DW, Serrano PA. 1992. Studying stages of memory formation with chicks. See Squire & Butters 1992, pp. 533–46

Rosenzweig MR, Diamond MC, Bennett EL, Mollgaard K. 1972. Negative as well as positive synaptic changes may store memory. *Psychol. Rev.* 79:93–96

Rosenzweig MR, Krech D, Bennett EL. 1958. Brain chemistry and adaptive behavior. In *Biological and Biochemical Bases of Behavior*, ed. HF Harlow, CN Woolsey, pp. 367–400. Madison, WI: Wis. Univ. Press

Rosenzweig MR, Krech D, Bennett EL. 1961. Heredity, environment, brain biochemistry, and learning. In *Current Trends in Psychological Theory*, pp. 87–110. Pittsburgh: Univ. Pittsburgh Press

Rosenzweig MR, Krech D, Bennett EL. 1963. Effects of differential experience on brain AChE and ChE and brain anatomy in the rat, as a function of stain and age. *Am. Psychol.* 18:430

Rosenzweig MR, Krech D, Bennett EL, Diamond MC. 1962. Effects of environmental complexity and training on brain chemistry and anatomy: a replication and extension. *J. Comp. Physiol. Psychol.* 55:429–37

Rosenzweig MR, Leiman AL, Breedlove SM. 1996. *Biological Psychology*. Sunderland, MA: Sinauer

Rosenzweig MR, Love W, Bennett EL. 1968. Effects of a few hours a day of enriched experience on brain chemistry and brain weights. *Physiol. Behav.* 3:819–25

Sapolsky RM. 1992. *Stress, the Aging Brain and Mechanisms of Neuronal Death.* Cambridge, MA: MIT Press

Satcher D. 1995. Annotation: the sociodemographic correlates of mental retardation. *Am. J. Public Health* 85:304–6

Schaie KW. 1994. The course of adult intellectual development. *Am. Psychol.* 49:304–13

Schwartz JH, Castelluci VF, Kandel ER. 1971. Functioning of identified neurons and synapses in abdominal ganglion of *Aplysia* in absence of protein synthesis. *J. Neurophysiol.* 34:939–63

Serrano PA, Beniston DS, Oxonian MG, Rodriguez WA, Rosenzweig MR, Bennett EL. 1994. Differential effects of protein kinase inhibitors and activators on memory formation in the 2-day-old chick. *Behav. Neural Biol.* 61:60–72

Serrano PA, Rodriguez WA, Bennett EL, Rosenzweig MR 1995a. Protein kinase C inhibitors in two chick brain regions disrupt memory formation. *Pharmacol. Biochem. Behav.* In press

Serrano PA, Rodriguez WA, Pope B, Bennett EL, Rosenzweig MR. 1995b. Protein kinase C inhibitor chelerythrine disrupts memory formation in chicks. *Behav. Neurosci.* 109:278–84

Sherrington CS. 1897. Part III. The central nervous system. In *A Text-Book of Physiology*, ed. M Foster. London: Macmillan

Sherry DF, Vaccarino AL, Buckenham K, Herz RS. 1989. The hippocampal complex of food-storing birds. *Brain Behav. Evol.* 34:308–17

Shimamura A, Berry JM, Mangels JA, Rusting CL, Jurica PJ. 1995. Memory and cognitive abilities in university professors: evidence for successful aging. *Psychol. Sci.* In press

Sigman M. 1995. Nutrition and child development. *Curr. Direct. Psychol. Sci.* 4:52–55

Soemmering ST. 1791. *Von Baue des menschlichen Koerpers*, Vol. 5, Part I. Frankfurt am Main: Barentrapp & Werner

Spurzheim JG. 1815. *Syllabus of a Demonstrative Course of Lectures on Drs. Gall and Spurzheim's Physiognomical System.* Bath, UK: Wood & Co.

Spurzheim JG. 1847. *Education: Its Elementary Principles, Founded on the Nature of Man.* New York: Fowler & Wells. 7th ed.

Squire LR. 1987. *Memory and Brain.* New York: Oxford

Squire LR, Butters N, eds. 1992. *Neuropsychology of Memory.* New York: Guilford

Squire LR, Knowlton B, Musen G. 1993. The structure and organization of memory. *Annu. Rev. Psychol.* 44:453–95

Swaab DF. 1991. Brain aging and Alzheimer's disease, "wear and tear" versus "use it or lose it." *Neurobiol. Aging* 12:317–24

Tanzi E. 1893. I fatti e le induzioni nell'odierna isologia del sistema nervoso. *Rev. Sper. Freniatr.Med. Leg.* 19:419–72

Terry RD, Maslich E, Salmon DP, Butters N, Deteresa R, et al. 1995. Physical basis of cognitive alterations in Alzheimer's disease: synapse loss is the major correlate of cognitive impairment. *Ann. Neurol.* 30:572–80.

Turner AM, Greenough WT. 1985. Differential rearing effects on rat visual cortex synapses. I. Synaptic and neuronal density and synapses per neuron. *Brain Res.* 329:195–203

Weinberger NM. 1995. Dynamic regulation of receptive fields and maps in the adult sensory cortex. *Annu. Rev. Neurosci.* 18:129–58

Wells SR. 1847. Appendix. See Spurzheim 1847, pp. 319–34

West RW, Greenough WT. 1972. Effects of environmental complexity on cortical synapses of rats: preliminary results. *Behav. Biol.* 7:279–84

Wiesel TN, Hubel DH. 1963. Single-cell responses in striate cortex of kittens deprived of vision in one eye. *J. Neurophysiol.* 26:1003–17

Wiesel TN, Hubel DH. 1965. Comparison of the effects of unilateral and bilateral eye closure on cortical unit responses in kittens. *J. Neurophysiol.* 28:1029–40

Wilks S. 1864. Clinical notes on atrophy of the brain. *J. Ment. Sci.* 10:381–92

Will BE, Rosenzweig MR, Bennett EL, Hebert M, Morimoto H. 1977. Relatively brief environmental enrichment aids recovery of learning capacity and alters brain measures after postweaning brain lesions in rats. *J. Comp. Physiol. Psychol.* 91:33–50

Witelson SF, Glezer II, Kigar DL. 1994. Sex differences in numerical density of neurons in human auditory association cortex. *Soc. Neurosci. Abstr.* 20:1425

Wu JY, Cohen LB, Falk CX. 1994. Neuronal activity during different behaviors in *Aplysia*: a distributed organization? *Science* 263:820–23

Yates F. 1966. *The Art of Memory*. London: Routledge & Kegan Paul

Yeargin-Allsopp M, Drews CD, Decouflé P, Murphy CC. 1995. Mild mental retardation in Black and White children in metropolitan Atlanta: a case-control study. *Am. J. Public Health* 85:324–28

Zecevic D, Wu JY, Cohen LB, London JA, Hopp HP, Falk CX. 1989. Hundreds of neurons in the *Aplysia* abdominal ganglion are active during the gill-withdrawal reflex. *J. Neurosci.* 9:3681–89

Zigler E, Muenchow S. 1992. *Head Start: The Inside Story of America's Most Successful Educational Experiment*. New York: Basic Books

Zola-Morgan S. 1995. Localization of brain function: the legacy of Franz Joseph Gall (1758–1828). *Annu. Rev. Neurosci.* 18:359–84

Zolman JF, Morimoto H. 1962. Effects of age of training on cholinesterase activity in the brains of maze-bright rats. *J. Comp. Physiol. Psychol.* 55:794–800

Annu. Rev. Psychol. 1996. 47:33–57

THEORETICAL FOUNDATIONS OF COGNITIVE-BEHAVIOR THERAPY FOR ANXIETY AND DEPRESSION

Chris R. Brewin

Department of Psychology, Royal Holloway, University of London, Egham, Surrey TW20 0EX, United Kingdom

KEY WORDS: appraisal, emotion, schema, conditioning, unconscious

ABSTRACT

Cognitive-behavior therapy (CBT) involves a highly diverse set of terms and procedures. In this review, the origins of CBT are briefly considered, and an integrative theoretical framework is proposed that (*a*) distinguishes therapy interventions targeted at circumscribed disorders from those targeted at generalized disorders and (*b*) distinguishes interventions aimed at modifying conscious beliefs and representations from those aimed at modifying unconscious representations in memory. Interventions aimed at altering consciously accessible beliefs are related to their theoretical bases in appraisal theories of emotion and cognitive theories of emotion and motivation. Interventions aimed at modifying unconscious representations are related to their theoretical bases in learning theory and findings from experimental cognitive psychology. In the review, different formulations of CBT for anxiety disorders and depression are analyzed in terms of this framework, and theoretical issues relating to self-representations in memory and to emotional processing are considered.

CONTENTS

0066-4308/96/0201-0033$08.00

33

INTRODUCTION

Cognitive-behavior therapy (CBT) for anxiety and depressive disorders is well established as a promising and frequently effective treatment (e.g. Chambless & Gillis 1993, Dobson 1989, Hollon et al 1993). CBT is a generic term referring to therapies that incorporate both behavioral interventions (direct attempts to reduce dysfunctional emotions and behavior by altering behavior) and cognitive interventions (attempts to reduce dysfunctional emotions and behavior by altering individual appraisals and thinking patterns). Both types of intervention are based on the assumption that prior learning is currently having maladaptive consequences, and that the purpose of therapy is to reduce distress or unwanted behavior by undoing this learning or by providing new, more adaptive learning experiences.

CBT practitioners believe that symptomatic change follows cognitive change, this cognitive change being brought about by a variety of possible interventions, including the practice of new behaviors, analysis of faulty thinking patterns, and the teaching of more adaptive self-talk. Although incidental cognitive change can be brought about by a variety of interventions, including pharmacological ones (Brewin 1985, Hollon et al 1987), evidence is starting to mount that in behavior therapy (Bandura 1977) and in CBT itself improvement is linked to a corresponding change in cognitions (Blackburn et al 1987, Chambless & Gracely 1988, Clark et al 1994, DeRubeis et al 1990, Firth-Cozens & Brewin 1988, Mattick & Peters 1988; see Chambless & Gillis 1993 for a review). Subsequent maintenance of gains is also often related to cognitive measures (Başoğlu et al 1994, Clark et al 1994, Rush et al 1986, Simons et al 1986). Despite this growing consensus, the actual mechanisms underlying CBT are still poorly understood, and there is considerable disagreement about exactly what has been learned and how change occurs.

HISTORICAL OVERVIEW

One of the most enduring debates about the mechanism of psychological treatment for psychiatric conditions such as anxiety disorders concerns the role in learning of verbal mediation. Traditionally, behaviorists argued that such disorders arose from a learned association between a feared stimulus and an avoidance response and that such conditioned fear was unaffected by a person's conscious beliefs. Numerous observations, particularly of patients with phobias or obsessive-compulsive disorders (OCD), confirmed the irrationality of many fears and the ineffectiveness of treatments relying on simple persuasion. Anxious patients' conscious beliefs and wishes indeed frequently appeared largely irrelevant in the face of overwhelming feelings of fear and the compulsion to avoid them.

These observations led most behaviorists to reject the suggestions put forward by cognitive therapists in the 1970s that conscious thoughts could themselves have an impact on feelings and behavior. But the cognitive therapists were only voicing a generally felt dissatisfaction with the notion that people were entirely at the mercy of their conditioning history and that individual differences in the interpretation of a feared situation, in perceived control, or in the ability to formulate plans and goals had no impact on the outcome of treatment. Despite many empirical demonstrations that conscious beliefs did sometimes influence feelings and behavior, and despite the development of influential cognitive theories of emotion and motivation (e.g. Abramson et al 1978; Bandura 1977, 1986; Lazarus et al 1970; Weiner 1985), the lack of theoretical overlap between the two approaches (i.e. the absence of an explicit role for conditioning in cognitive therapies and the absence of a role for verbal mediation in behavior therapies) led to a prolonged period of mutual denunciation and largely fruitless argument between the two groups of practitioners.

Many of these differences were gradually resolved at a pragmatic level. For example, cognitive therapists were unwilling to abandon highly effective behavioral techniques, and often recommended an integration of both cognitive and behavioral approaches. For instance, Bandura (1977) emphasized that changing behavior was an extremely powerful way to change maladaptive beliefs. Many behavior therapists equally were reassured by the retention of some behavioral interventions and the proposal of highly structured cognitive methods that were subject to empirical test, and they came to appreciate that the broader range of cognitive techniques facilitated the treatment of different kinds of disorder, such as depression, panic disorder, and generalized anxiety disorder (GAD).

At a theoretical level, however, integration between cognitive and behavioral approaches has been less successful. Two main reasons can be identified. First, behavior-therapy techniques have been most effective with disorders involving circumscribed active- or passive-avoidance problems, such as those found in phobias, posttraumatic stress disorder (PTSD), OCD, or pathological grief reactions. Cognitive therapy techniques, on the other hand, have been successfully applied not only to circumscribed problems but also to more generalized problems such as depression, GAD, and, more recently, personality disorder, where the focus is on behavior patterns that occur in a variety of situations. The different clinical foci of the two kinds of therapy have tended to produce different sorts of theory.

The second reason integration is less successful at a theoretical level is that the development of cognitive therapies was not closely tied to a single recognizable strand of basic research and theory in psychology. As is often the case in clinical practice, the development of effective therapies has preceded theoretical understanding. Different therapies use distinctive terms such as "belief," "assumption," "attribution," "expectation," or "schema" and describe what they believe to be the effective ingredient in extremely varied terms (Brewin 1989). For example, Beck et al (1979) described one of the main goals of cognitive therapy for depression as the changing of maladaptive underlying assumptions or schemas. Whereas underlying assumptions were described as conditional beliefs, exemplified in a statement such as "If I am not successful, I can never be happy," schemas were described as stable cognitive structures that contain rules for screening and classifying information. Beck et al, however, often used these terms interchangeably. More recently, the term schema has also been used to refer to so-called core beliefs such as "I am bad" (Beck et al 1990, Young 1990).

In distinguishing between cognitions that are relatively accessible to consciousness, such as automatic thoughts, and so-called deeper cognitions that are less accessible, such as schemas or underlying assumptions, Beck and his colleagues were in agreement with other important theorists such as Ellis (1962) and Meichenbaum (1977). But Beck's usage of the term "schema," although very helpful to therapists, was not clearly specified compared with its usage by cognitive psychologists (e.g. Segal 1988). To cite only one example, Beck implied that the content of schemas consists of propositional knowledge that is potentially accessible to conscious introspection. He did not discuss the possibility that such knowledge might be more implicit or procedural rather than declarative in form, i.e. that it might be neither consciously accessible nor able to be completely captured by a verbal description. Cognitive psychologists, however, argue that people may have no direct access to schematic knowledge, although a person can sometimes infer what it consists of by monitoring the products of schematic processing (Berry & Broadbent 1984, Brewin 1989, Teasdale & Barnard 1993).

Other influential cognitive theories such as the hopelessness theory of depression (Abramson et al 1989) or the self-efficacy theory of behavior change (Bandura 1977) did not distinguish between accessible and underlying cognitions and were concerned only with the modification of conscious attributions or expectations. Similarly, some general cognitive therapies, such as problem-solving therapy (Goldfried & Goldfried 1980), and more specific therapies for panic disorder (Clark & Beck 1988) referred simply to teaching new skills or to identifying and modifying faulty beliefs. Thus, the different cognitive theories and therapies, let alone cognitive and behavior therapy, clearly share no theoretical unity, and some attempt must first be made to address this lack. The natural place to look to fulfill this need is in contemporary theories of cognition and emotion.

A THEORETICAL FRAMEWORK

Progress toward theoretical resolution has been facilitated by three developments: the integration of animal learning theory within more general approaches to information processing (e.g. Dickinson 1987), the general acceptance of the pervasive role of unconscious processing in everyday cognitive operations (e.g. Power & Brewin 1991), and the development of theories that recognize the ability both of conscious appraisal and of unconscious learned associations to generate emotions and behavior (e.g. Ekman 1986, Leventhal 1984).

Cognitive and social psychologists (e.g. Berry & Broadbent 1984, Epstein 1994, Hasher & Zacks 1979, Nisbett & Wilson 1977, Posner & Snyder 1975, Shiffrin & Schneider 1977) have proposed the existence of two cognitive systems with different functions and properties, one that is automatic and outside of awareness and involves large-scale parallel information processing, and one that is more effortful and involves conscious experience. Data from numerous areas of psychology support the idea that most cognitive processing has the potential to include a large amount of information and takes place extremely rapidly and completely outside of awareness. Although we are unaware of this kind of processing, we can become aware of its products, for example, in the forms of thoughts and images. This kind of processing is heavily influenced by previous learning, and new stimuli tend to elicit routinized responses in a relatively inflexible way.

In contrast, conscious processing is slow and deliberate and operates on a tiny fraction of the information available. At the same time, it is extremely adaptable and responsive to new information, which allows for great flexibility in behavior. It is reasonable to suppose that the output of both types of processing is represented in memory. Extensive experimental and neuropsychological evidence suggests the existence of separate nondeclarative (implicit) and declarative (explicit) memory systems, supporting the idea that much of the information stored in memory may not be consciously accessible (see Squire et al 1993 for a review).

Contemporary theories of emotion (Berkowitz 1990, Leventhal 1984) and conditioning (Davey 1992) adopt the view that emotional responses may be influenced both by unconscious learned associations derived from intense or repeated aversive events and by relevant conscious knowledge. Applying a

similar approach to change processes in psychotherapy, Brewin (1989) proposed that persons' knowledge gained through the extensive unconscious parallel processing of their responses to aversive situations, so-called situationally
accessible knowledge, is stored separately from their knowledge gained
through the more limited conscious experience of such situations, so-called
verbally accessible knowledge. Whereas verbally accessible knowledge can in
principle be deliberately interrogated and retrieved, situationally accessible
knowledge can only be retrieved automatically when environmental input
matches features of the stored memories. Thus, in the presence of reminders of
aversive events, a person might become aware of the automatic activation of
emotions, thoughts, images, and behavioral impulses. While the underlying
representation remains inaccessible, its products become available to consciousness and permit a person to make inferences about the material stored in
memory.

In this dual representation theory, both kinds of knowledge—verbally accessible and situationally accessible—can give rise to maladaptive emotions
and behavior. The difference between the two kinds is that when, for example,
emotions are based on verbally accessible knowledge, people know why they
are sad or afraid, whereas when they are based on situationally accessible
knowledge, people must infer indirectly why they feel a particular way. In
either case the recognition of feeling or behaving badly is followed by deliberate, strategic attempts to understand what is happening and to put things right.
This involves a variety of well-described processes such as attribution of the
cause of the problem, generation of coping options and evaluation of their
likely success, and instigation of compensatory behavior (see Brewin 1989 for
a fuller description).

The concept of nondeclarative memory or situationally accessible knowledge can readily include both the learned associations of conditioning theory
and other terms for deeper representations in memory such as emotional
memories (Lang 1979) and schemas (Beck et al 1979). Although in their
original writing Lang and Beck were not explicit about whether these memories were verbally accessible, careful reading suggests that both authors intended them to be more than just records of conscious experience. Rather, their
discussion suggests that the information these memories contain tends to be
quite inclusive (sometimes including a record of physiological responses, for
instance) and is sometimes subject to considerable processing, for example, in
the aggregation of information from similar events. If the information stored
were the product of unconscious parallel processing, it would not be possible
to retrieve it into consciousness. Instead, a person could only know the contents of the memory by inferring them through their awareness, for example,
that certain emotions or images were triggered in certain situations. More
recently Lang (1993) described emotional memories as possessing both a

conscious, language-based meaning component and a more primitive network-based representation of stimuli and responses that is connected to brain centers for afferent and efferent processing.

This framework involving dual representations in memory lends itself readily to the organization of different therapeutic procedures. In the remainder of this review these procedures are divided into those that primarily attempt to alter conscious verbally accessible knowledge and those that attempt to alter deeper or situationally accessible knowledge. Within each group, procedures are divided into those that address circumscribed as opposed to generalized problems. This way of classifying procedures is illustrated in Table 1, which also provides examples of therapies primarily based on these different approaches. In the next section, this framework is related to controversies about the mode of action of CBT for depression and anxiety disorders. Finally, the review concludes with discussion of two current theoretical issues in CBT, the nature of mental representations of the self and the relation of CBT to emotional processing in general.

PROCEDURES TARGETING CONSCIOUS BELIEFS AND REPRESENTATIONS

Circumscribed Disorders

The contention that certain psychological and psychosomatic conditions arise from specific incorrect beliefs has been persuasively argued in recent years. These beliefs are postulated to be consciously held and may be thought of as misconceptions requiring an explicit psychoeducational approach. For example, a person anticipating surgery may have faulty beliefs about the nature or painfulness of the procedures and may be calmed when given the appropriate information (e.g. Johnson et al 1978). Anxiety-related conditions such as stammering, insomnia, and impotence may be exacerbated when a person attributes them wrongly to personal inadequacy or regards them incorrectly as indicative of serious pathology (Storms & McCaul 1976). Teasdale (1985) proposed that depressed mood may be exacerbated by depression about de-

Table 1 Classification of therapies by primary target and scope of problem

	Primary therapy target	
	Conscious representations	Unconscious representations
Circumscribed problems	CT[a] for panic Psychoeducation	Exposure therapy Response prevention
Generalized problems	Problem-solving therapy Self-instruction training	CT for depression and GAD Schema-focused therapy

[a]Cognitive therapy

pression, that is, the belief that normal depressive reactions are pathological and reveal the weakness or inadequacy of the sufferer. Education about the nature of depression, he suggested, can bring about speedy improvement when coupled with simple symptom-management techniques.

Similarly, individuals high in anxiety sensitivity fear that physical symptoms of anxiety have harmful or even catastrophic consequences (Reiss & McNally 1985). Conscious beliefs about the significance of certain bodily sensations are the primary target in cognitive therapy for panic (Clark & Beck 1988). According to the cognitive theory of panic (e.g. Clark 1988), panic arises from specific catastrophic misinterpretations of sensations such as tachycardia or dizziness. Therapy therefore involves a variety of techniques aimed at eliciting and challenging these misinterpretations. For example, panic may be elicited within a therapy session by having the patient read a series of words connected with the feared outcome, graphically demonstrating to the patient the role played by thoughts in producing panic.

These clinical approaches have their roots in appraisal theories of emotion such as those of Lazarus et al (1970) and Weiner (1985). These theorists emphasized the role played by conscious assessments of the meaning and cause of internal and external stimuli and of the coping resources available to deal with any prospective threat.

It should be emphasized, however, that verbally accessible knowledge of this kind may also be subject to automatic processing, outside of awareness, particularly when it is primed by a previous stimulus. It would indeed be strange if conscious knowledge of danger were not processed as rapidly as other kinds of knowledge. Thus, as noted by Clark (1988), catastrophic thoughts may sometimes come to mind so rapidly that patients are barely, if at all, aware of the interpretive process. This phenomenon has been used by Clark to explain panic attacks triggered during sleep. Automatic processing does not differentiate between verbally and situationally accessible knowledge. It is the fact that the thought or belief can on other occasions be directly consciously retrieved that indicates verbally accessible knowledge.

Generalized Disorders

Other disorders such as depression or GAD cannot be so readily traced to specific faulty beliefs. Rather, there are often complex sets of negative beliefs about the self or the external world that are activated in a variety of situations. One approach to treating these generalized disorders is to add to patients' conscious knowledge about their condition by teaching them a set of procedures with which to counter negative mood states. In the section "Conceptualizing CBT for Depression" below, we discuss Barber & DeRubeis's (1989) view that this model can best account for the efficacy of CBT for depression.

Early forms of CBT for anxiety adopted this approach of equipping patients with generally applicable skills. For example, Meichenbaum (1977) emphasized how behavior is controlled at least partly by a person's internal dialogue or inner speech. In his stress-inoculation training, he drew patients' attention to their tendency to make defeatist or anxiety-provoking self-statements when faced with difficult situations. Patients were trained to imagine themselves in feared situations and to practice making positive, adaptive self-statements that emphasized personal control and reduced the anticipated aversiveness of the consequences. These responses were repeated until they became part of the patient's knowledge base of how to cope with anxiety and replaced their previous, less-adaptive repertoire of knowledge and skills.

Another successful approach involving the teaching of generic skills is problem-solving training (D'Zurilla & Goldfried 1971, Goldfried & Goldfried 1980). Patients were first trained to recognize the existence of a problem, assume a solution existed, and inhibit the temptation to act impulsively. They were then taught to reduce the problem to a concrete and manageable form that was susceptible to a solution. Following this, patients generated as many solutions as possible, weighed the advantages and disadvantages of each one, and selected the most promising option. After implementation, the efficacy of the solution was carefully monitored, with a view to trying another solution if the outcome was not satisfactory.

These skills-based approaches in CBT are supported by an enormous body of research into cognitive theories of motivation and self-regulation. The idea of individuals as active planners, problem-solvers, and self-motivators is extremely influential within the area of social cognition (e.g. Bandura 1986, Cantor & Kihlstrom 1987, Carver & Scheier 1981, Karoly & Kanfer 1982, Lazarus 1991, Markus & Wurf 1987, Mischel 1973, Weiner 1985). Among the many processes involved in self-regulation, goal-setting, self-monitoring, the activation and use of standards, self-evaluation, and self-reinforcement are paid considerable attention.

As discussed in more detail elsewhere (Brewin 1988), the awareness of unwanted emotions and behaviors is thought to generate a number of conscious subroutines. These are designed to label or classify the experience, locate the relevant causal agents, assess severity and vulnerability, and generate and assess the likely efficacy and cost/benefit ratio of a number of coping options. Having selected a course of action, such as avoidance, distraction, or confrontation, and having decided how much effort or persistence to put into it, individuals can then monitor the outcome against available standards and can administer appropriate self-reinforcement. Many forms of CBT incorporate various kinds of skills training designed to inform and support patients' coping behavior by reattributing problems to potentially controllable causes, increasing expectations of success, and adding to their conscious knowledge of effective ways to reduce unwanted emotions.

PROCEDURES TARGETING UNCONSCIOUS REPRESENTATIONS

Circumscribed Disorders

Specific phobias are among the most common circumscribed disorders. On the whole, the treatment of phobias has changed little and continues to include an emphasis on helping individuals to undermine habits of cognitive or behavioral avoidance and to achieve habituation to a feared stimulus. On a theoretical level, however, inadequacies in the original behaviorist account of the treatment of phobias led to the adoption of more sophisticated cognitive approaches emphasizing the importance of factors such as attention and memory (Dickinson 1987) and conscious revaluation of the unconditioned stimulus (Davey 1992).

Lang (1979) proposed that the representations underlying phobias, which he termed fear memories, contain three kinds of information: details of the location and physical characteristics of the feared situation (stimulus elements); details of the verbal, physiological, and behavioral responses that occurred in the situation (response elements); and an interpretation of the stimulus and response elements and of their significance for the individual (meaning elements). Drawing on Lang's work, Foa & Kozak (1986) proposed that therapy for phobias works by changing the information in the fear memory: First the memory must be activated, and then new experiences arranged by the therapist (such as within- and between-session habituation to the feared situation) are incorporated into the memory.

The idea that memories, once created, can be altered is a controversial one within cognitive psychology. A popular alternative view is that memory consists of a series of unalterable records with more or less overlapping features. In other words, memory can be added to but not permanently changed (e.g. Morton et al 1985). Consistent with this view, Brewin's (1989) dual representation theory contained the proposal that in therapy new memories are laid down as situationally accessible knowledge. These memories are generally arranged to be as similar as possible to the original fear memory in all respects other than outcome. Patients are encouraged to expose themselves to as good an example as possible of what they fear and to experience the same sensations. In therapy, however, this experience culminates in mastery and the habituation of fear rather than in avoidance. Patients exposed to their feared situations are subsequently more likely to access this new memory—a memory containing fewer fearful response elements and a more benign meaning—than they are to access the original memory containing more fearful response elements and a more threatening meaning.

This formulation, while distinctly similar to that of Foa & Kozak (1986), has some advantages over it. First, it is more parsimonious because it does not postulate that fear memories must be activated for therapy to be effective. A new memory of a therapy experience in which the patient did not become anxious is not such a good match to the original fear memory and thus is less likely to be activated when the originally feared stimulus is encountered in the future. Second, this formulation helps to explain why someone may recover in therapy only to have the fear return. If memories are not changed but are simply overwritten by new memories, relapse may occur when the patient encounters a new situation more similar to the original fear memory than to the new memory created in therapy. After all, the creation within therapy of new situations that match perfectly the original learning experiences is rare. In fact, the incidence of relapse and the return of negative feelings, even after apparently successful therapy, are substantial (Rachman 1980), and thus a successful theory must be able to explain both partial and total therapeutic successes.

Generalized Disorders

In conditions such as depression and GAD, the underlying representations are thought to contain more abstract information than the specific memories underlying phobias. These representations are thought to consist of summaries of numerous aversive experiences produced by complex unconscious computations that abstract common meanings from repeated experiences. One obvious source of repeated aversive events is poor parenting. Anxious and depressed patients, in comparison to controls, are more likely to report having parents who were less warm and affectionate; more punishing, rejecting, and, abusive; less encouraging of autonomy; or more controlling and overprotective (e.g. Brewin et al 1993).

Therapists are obviously going to find it much more difficult to create new therapeutic experiences that share many features with such memories. To begin with, there are many more relevant memories, and these may be very disparate. The patients are much older than they were when the memories were first laid down, and the therapist may be not at all like parental or authority figures from the past. For this reason, treatment of these disorders generally takes longer and is less successful than the treatment of simple phobias.

Brewin (1989) therefore suggested that, rather than create new memories, cognitive therapy for depression attempts instead to limit the ease with which these memories are activated by the current environment. One feature of depression and GAD is that negative mood changes are elicited by a wide range of stimuli. Patients respond to many relatively harmless situations as though these situations contained enormous potential for various psychological and physical threats. The therapist infers the content of these representations by systematically gathering data about the situations that elicit anxiety or depression in a person and about the person's reactions to these situations. Data may be obtained from the patient's own account, from the accounts of family and friends, and by the therapist's own observations of the patient's behavior in the therapy situation.

By drawing attention to the patient's apparent assumptions and challenging these with the use of logic and behavioral experimentation, the therapist can help the patient develop new rules for discriminating situations that are truly threatening from those that merely arouse the feeling of being threatened. This is similar to the process of construct elaboration described by Kelly (1955). Practice in making these discriminations then changes the content of verbally accessible knowledge so that previously threatening situations are reclassified and automatic activation of the unconscious representations is decreased.

This activation-based model of cognitive therapy for depression has several corollaries. First, because the relevant situationally accessible memories are not overwritten and remain available to be reactivated, relapse is more likely here than in the case of specific phobias. Second, the more varied the negative experiences contributing to the formation of the memories (for example, the more the patient experienced rejection at the hands of multiple caregivers), the fewer distinctive stimulus features the memories contain. This is likely to promote overgeneralization and impede the therapist's ability to identify and teach the relevant discriminations. Third, the model clarifies the potential role of cues associated with nontherapeutic events to activate and deactivate unconscious representations. In principle, relevant cues associated with any event may activate or deactivate memories. Consistent with this, negative life events are strongly associated with the onset of depression where there is prior low self-esteem (Brown et al 1986), and positive events are strongly associated with recovery from depression (Brown et al 1992).

A contrasting approach was offered by Teasdale & Barnard (1993). They suggested that depression is frequently maintained by the continued reprocessing of higher-level schematic models related to the experience of depression itself. These representations contain idiosyncratic sensory, proprioceptive, and meaning information synthesized from past experiences of depression and are not able to be fully captured by a verbal description. In their view, models in which the experience of depression is linked with personal inadequacy, helplessness, and hopelessness have to be replaced by alternative models emphasizing the normality of depressive symptoms and the value of positive coping responses. This approach, then, addresses the problem of generalized representations by asserting that, although many experiences and elements may contribute, an essential core concerning the nature of depression is evident for a particular individual. Psychoeducation, coping skills, and other CBT procedures all help to create new models of depression that in time supplant the old maladaptive models.

CONCEPTUALIZING CBT FOR DEPRESSION

The fourfold classification of CBT procedures as targeting conscious and unconscious representations across circumscribed and generalized disorders is something of an oversimplification, although it does appear to capture the differing focus of many cognitive techniques. It also clarifies some of the conceptual debates about the theoretical basis of cognitive treatment. Whereas the debate over CBT for anxiety has mainly concerned the role of behavioral vs cognitive components, the debate over CBT for depression has focused on the exact role played by the cognitive interventions.

As we noted above, Beck et al (1979) identified a number of techniques (e.g. identifying and challenging automatic thoughts, behavioral assignments, and correcting faulty reasoning) that they believed reduced depressed mood in the short run and in the long run altered the content of underlying assumptions and schemas. In contrast, Teasdale (1985) proposed that faulty beliefs about symptoms (depression about depression) lead to the exacerbation of depression and can be corrected with a relatively simple educational intervention plus training in symptom management.

Following a review of proposals put forward by Beck et al (1979), Hollon & Kriss (1984), Teasdale (1985), and Ingram & Hollon (1986), Hollon et al (1988) distinguished three mechanisms that could account for the effectiveness of CBT. These were (a) a change in the content of depressive schemata or in the cognitive processes underlying them, (b) a deactivation of the depressive schemata, and (c) the inculcation of new cognitive or behavioral self-management skills, such as learning to problem-solve, generate a variety of attributions for negative outcomes, and collect evidence germane to these attributions. Following a review of the evidence, Barber & DeRubeis (1989) suggested that the primary mode of action was (c), the development of compensatory skills, but that repeated application of these skills could lead to a change in schemata.

Brewin's (1989) dual representation theory identified two mechanisms in CBT for depression, both aimed at preventing the continued reactivation of situationally accessible memories. He suggested that the therapist's attempts directly to alter the contents of consciousness—for example, by challenging automatic thoughts or instructing patients to distract themselves—disrupt the feedback loop whereby upsetting (automatic) thoughts and images constantly pervade consciousness, reactivate situational memories and maintain depressed mood. Second, as described in more detail in the preceding section, he suggested that the therapist attempts to alter on a more permanent basis the contents of verbally accessible knowledge in order to prevent the reactivation of situational memories through inappropriate stimulus classification.

Finally, Teasdale & Barnard's (1993) interacting cognitive subsystems theory represents a conceptual advance on Teasdale's (1985) ideas. The theory suggests that the function of therapy is to disrupt the repeated synthesis of high-level schematic models containing generic meanings prototypical of previous depressing situations (so-called depressive interlock). Interlock involves numerous cognitive subsystems, which include those responsible for processing sensory and proprioceptive data as well as those that extract meaning at propositional and higher-order (implicational) levels. Disruption of interlock may be achieved in a number of ways. For example, if the models were continually being activated by ongoing stress, problem-solving training aimed at resolving the stress might effectively deactivate them. Physical exercise might alter a person's body state and create a new element capable of disrupting the particular pattern of interlock. As discussed in the previous section, however, Teasdale & Barnard proposed that the main effect of CBT is to disrupt interlock by replacing maladaptive implicational models of depression with more adaptive ones.

In terms of the theoretical framework outlined above, it is clear that Teasdale (1985) and Barber & DeRubeis (1989) emphasized targeting conscious representations, correcting circumscribed faulty beliefs, and teaching generally applicable coping skills and placed less emphasis on the significance of deeper cognitions. Beck et al (1979), on the other hand, primarily targeted the content of underlying assumptions or beliefs that, although not necessarily immediately available to consciousness, are in principle knowable. Both Brewin (1989) and Teasdale & Barnard (1993) explicitly identified the importance of deactivating or changing unconscious (situationally accessible) representations.

In spite of the different emphases contained in these theories, there is a fair measure of agreement that therapists mainly work with consciously available cognitions, even if the aim is to hypothesize about, deactivate, or amend underlying cognitions. There is also agreement about the kind of procedures that are likely to be effective and about the need for repetition and practice.

Greater agreement may not be achievable at present because depression takes many different forms, varying for example in frequency, intensity, chronicity, and symptom pattern. Some depressions are accompanied by negative cognitions whereas others are not (Hamilton & Abramson 1983). Some depressions (chronic or repeated depressions rather than single short episodes) correlate positively with reports of traumatic childhood experiences (Andrews et al 1995). Other depressions are linked specifically to a failure to complete the emotional processing of major life events such as bereavement (Ramsay 1977).

These data support the idea that depression is likely to, but will not necessarily, involve representations of past experience in memory. At present the respective roles of specific event representations and generalized schemas are not well understood. As in the case of anxiety disorders, patients may develop idiosyncratic misinterpretations of their symptoms and adopt coping strategies that exacerbate the problem. Generic psychological treatments for depression such as CBT need to contain provisions for altering misconceptions, equipping patients with more effective skills, and deactivating emotional memories. The particular combination of approaches used depends on the individual presentation.

CONCEPTUALIZING CBT FOR ANXIETY

Until recently only behavioral techniques such as desensitization, flooding, or response prevention were widely accepted as effective in treating anxiety disorders, but now the effectiveness for some disorders of cognitive methods, used alone or in combination with behavioral techniques, is clear. However, purely cognitive techniques tend not to be superior to purely behavioral methods (Rachman 1993). Just as there is disagreement among theorists about how CBT for depression works, there is disagreement about the mechanisms underlying CBT for anxiety. In this section I review evidence suggesting that the disagreement arises because the factors causing and maintaining the disorders are complex and that CBT necessarily reflects this complexity.

Rachman (1990) noted that there are various ways of acquiring fear, either by direct exposure to aversive or traumatic stimuli, by observing others displaying fear, or hearing or reading verbal or written transmission of information about fear and danger. In the latter case, the representations in memory giving rise to subsequent feelings of fear likely are verbally accessible and can presumably be altered by new verbal information, perhaps delivered in the form of an educational intervention. Similarly, some have argued that catastrophic misinterpretations of symptoms based on ignorance or incorrect beliefs can lead to panic disorder (Clark 1988) and prolonged PTSD (Ehlers & Steil 1995). Once again, symptoms based on verbally accessible cognitions should be amenable to treatment by more or less structured cognitive approaches.

In other cases, anxiety reflects the situational activation of unconscious memory structures created through direct exposure to single or repeated aversive experiences. If these memories are circumscribed, as is likely to be the case in many phobias, behavioral interventions can readily be employed. When patients have concluded that these feared situations really are threatening, either from observations of their own behavior or from independent information, these methods are likely to alter the contents not only of situationally accessible knowledge but also of verbally accessible knowledge and result in changes in conscious cognitions as well as in behavior.

As we have seen, the nature of the disorder need have no one-to-one correspondence with a particular type of underlying representation. Thus phobias may be based on unconscious representations, independent conscious representations, or some combination of the two. The particular pattern of response to different treatment approaches depends on the nature of the memories. Although most panic disorder may, in a similar way, be the result of conscious catastrophic misinterpretations, Wolpe & Rowan (1989) suggest that in some patients there are no misinterpretations and that panic is the result of conditioning. In the terms used in this review, the disorder would be said to arise from the activation of situationally accessible knowledge either of previous panic episodes or of related experiences such as fear of similar symptoms in a family member.

Patients also may demonstrate combinations of symptoms that were acquired in different ways. A recent study of patients with panic plus agoraphobia reported that exposure therapy reduced avoidance but not panic, whereas cognitive therapy reduced panic but not avoidance (van den Hout et al 1994).

Social phobia may involve either circumscribed or generalized fears (e.g. Hofmann et al 1995). When discussing treatment of fears that are generalized, as they are in GAD, I distinguish approaches based on compensatory skills training, such as the teaching of relaxation and the modification of negative self-statements, from those based on identifying the content of underlying representations in memory. I suggest that although it may be difficult to alter such representations directly, the content of verbally accessible knowledge can be changed so that they are no longer so easily activated. Effective cognitive therapy for GAD (e.g. Beck & Emery 1985, Butler et al 1991) typically employs both types of procedure.

Recent analyses of OCD (Salkovskis 1985, 1989) and hypochondriasis (Warwick & Salkovskis 1989) underscore the variety and complexity of cases grouped under the same diagnostic category. For example, in OCD Salkovskis identified the frequent tendency of intrusive cognitions to be accompanied by negative automatic thoughts reflecting underlying themes of excessive responsibility for harm to self and others. These thoughts trigger neutralizing behaviors in the form of overt or covert rituals. The neutralizing behaviors presumably originate as conscious strategies for avoiding or terminating the thoughts, but over time their occurrence may become automatic. CBT for these problems involves compensatory skills training in teaching patients not to avoid their negative thoughts, verbal belief modification of the identified automatic thoughts and underlying assumptions, and the overwriting of specific learned associations with behavioral techniques such as response prevention. For example, verbal belief modification can be helpful in reducing anxiety and thus preventing dropouts, facilitating cooperation with response prevention, and maximizing the impact of exposure treatment. The differing combinations and strengths of maladaptive beliefs and neutralizing behaviors and the different relations between them dictate that CBT be comprehensive and flexible if it is to be effective.

THEORETICAL ISSUES

In the final part of this review I touch on two important theoretical issues that follow from my analysis of CBT. I have argued that CBT procedures must be related to the different kinds of representation in memory that underlie the disorder in each patient. In the case of generalized disorders, these usually involve the self, either alone or in relation to significant others. What is known about the representation of the self? Can this information suggest new therapeutic approaches? The other issue is that negative experiences give rise to disorders in some individuals and not in others. It has been suggested that memories of trauma and serious life events have in the normal course of things to be emotionally processed. What is the relation of CBT to this processing?

Mental Representation of Knowledge About the Self

The mental representations thought to underlie depression, social phobia, and GAD are more global and more often concern the self than those thought to underlie more circumscribed disorders such as specific phobias. Such a view is similar to that held by social psychologists such as Markus (1977), who proposed that schemas are structures containing conceptually or empirically related elements that can facilitate the processing of new information about the self.

There is considerable debate about how knowledge concerning the self is represented in memory. For example, Kelly (1955) proposed that the self may be described in relation to a set of idiosyncratic personal constructs, a hierarchically organized system of bipolar dimensions such as good/bad or kind/cruel. A currently popular view is that people have multiple self-representations corresponding to different social roles (e.g. Kihlstrom & Cantor 1984). Higgins et al (1985) suggested that emotions may be generated by discrepancies among self-representations. For example, anxiety is related to discrepancies between the "actual self" and "ought self," and depression to discrepancies between "actual self" and "ideal self."

In contrast, other theorists emphasize the role played by specific memories in self-representation. For example, exemplar-based theories hold that judgments concerning one's character traits are inseparable from specific autobiographical memories: Self-judgments are based on computations carried out on specific examples available in memory. The experiments of Klein & Loftus

(1993) indicate that knowledge about the self in the form of global trait judgments is independent of knowledge in the form of specific autobiographical episodes—both are present and may be accessed and used relatively independently. However, the extent to which judgments and behavior are influenced by specific, concrete past experiences rather than by more abstract, generalized knowledge appears to be much greater than has often been thought. Moreover, the influence of these experiences may occur without a person's conscious awareness (Smith 1990).

Better theoretical understanding of how self-knowledge is represented is essential if we are to comprehend the mechanisms responsible for the success of CBT. To take the example of depression once again, we may ask whether depressed individuals see themselves in wholly negative terms or whether they continue to have access to alternative, more positive self-representations that can be exploited therapeutically. Brewin et al (1992) found that depressed patients were readily able to distinguish among how they would currently describe themselves, how they would usually describe themselves, and how they would have described themselves at some salient prior time, which suggests that alternative self-representations remain accessible even during the depressed episode itself.

Another important issue concerns the role of specific autobiographical memories. Williams (1992) observed that the depressed find it difficult consciously to retrieve specific autobiographical memories, particularly of positive experiences. Williams linked this difficulty to deficits in problem-solving and proposed that memory for specific experiences of success and failure is important if patients are to reassess their past experience in a more adaptive way. He also suggested that the concrete focus of many CBT interventions enhances memory for specific experiences.

Interestingly, given this deficit in conscious retrieval, recent evidence indicates that many depressed patients have high levels of spontaneous intrusive memories of specific autobiographical events—for example, concerning early abuse (Kuyken & Brewin 1994). Moreover, there is a significant association between higher levels of spontaneous memories of abuse and greater difficulty in deliberately retrieving specific autobiographical memories (Kuyken & Brewin 1995).

A related need is to research the connection between generalized self-representations and specific autobiographical memories. Some progress has already been made. Strauman (1990) showed that presenting subjects with words corresponding to their individual self-discrepancies primed the retrieval of specific childhood memories, which suggests a possible origin of global self-beliefs. Andrews & Brewin (1990) interviewed a sample of women with violent partners and found that women with a history of physical or sexual abuse in childhood were more likely to blame the violence in their current relationships on their own characters and not on other factors. Although far from conclusive, these various lines of research suggest that circumscribed memories of trauma may be more relevant to understanding depressive problems than previously suspected, and that CBT for depression may benefit from targeting specific autobiographical memories as well as more generalized self-representations.

Emotional Processing

The notion that specific frightening, distressing, or traumatic experiences create cognitive and emotional disturbances that have to be worked through or processed if they are not to interfere with ordinary life has a long history. More recently this notion has been associated particularly with studies of bereavement (Parkes 1971) and with general models of response to stress and trauma (Horowitz 1976, 1986; Janoff-Bulman 1992).

According to these writers, major stressors or traumas (and attempts to cope with them) can disrupt a person's expectations and goals. Stressors or traumas may contradict important assumptions about a person's own nature (for example, the self is now perceived as capable of thoughts or actions not previously believed possible), the world (for example, the world is now seen as unsafe and unpredictable), and other people (for example, others are now seen as unreliable or untrustworthy). These effects have been viewed as creating a discrepancy between a person's prior assumptions about him- or herself and what that person currently knows to be true. The process of working through is necessary to facilitate the creation of new models consistent with the facts. This process typically involves heightened arousal and an initial response of denial followed by alternating phases of intrusion of traumatic thoughts and memories and attempts to avoid or block them out. It finally ends with the integration of the new information into the person's cognitive models.

Drawing on similar observations and on the work of Lang (1979), Rachman (1980) defined emotional processing as a return to undisrupted behavior after an emotional disturbance has waned. Although many of the phenomena he described were the same as those outlined above, he formulated this process in terms of the absorption and reduction of negative emotions rather than in terms of the creation of new and more adaptive cognitive structures. Applying the concept to the mastery of specific events that evoked fear or sadness, he suggested that psychological treatments such as desensitization and flooding can facilitate this process. He also proposed that obsessions, the return of fear, the incubation of fear, abnormal grief reactions, and nightmares all represented a failure of emotional processing.

These ideas have been very influential, and it is useful to relate them to the distinction between therapies targeting conscious and unconscious representations. The term *emotional processing* is used by such writers as Lang

(1979), Rachman (1980), and Foa & Kozak (1986) to refer primarily to the reduction of negative emotions (particularly fear) by traditional behavioral techniques such as desensitization or exposure therapy [although Rachman (1990) expanded its use to include cognitive changes]. In this review, I have suggested that these techniques help prevent automatic activation of unconscious emotional memories of the aversive event (situationally accessible knowledge).

This process is different from that described by theorists concerned with more general aspects of stress and trauma (e.g. Horowitz 1986, Janoff-Bulman 1992). These theorists appear to focus on persons' conscious preoccupations: Why did this happen to me? What made me behave the way I did? What will happen to me now? These preoccupations lead to a variety of emotional reactions that may include guilt, shame, and anger and to the automatic activation of conscious memories. Recovery is the successful reworking of conscious memories of the event and the creation of new, more inclusive cognitive models in verbally accessible knowledge.

In terms of our analysis, therefore, expressions such as "emotional processing" and "working through" appear to be relevant to modifying both conscious and unconscious representations. In the case of intense but circumscribed fears that have little impact on the rest of a person's life or views of the world, emotional processing entails modifying or overwriting unconscious representations that are producing conditioned fear reactions. In the case of stressors such as bereavement (other than when a person witnesses a traumatic death), emotional processing entails modifying the contents of verbally accessible knowledge to incorporate the new information.

Conditions such as PTSD typically arise from an event that both creates strong conditioned fear reactions and violates many consciously held assumptions. This condition is typically associated with marked cognitive and behavioral avoidance of reminders of the trauma. Discussions of recovery from PTSD tend to focus on either the first (e.g. Foa et al 1989) or the second of these processes (Janoff-Bulman 1992). According to a recent dual representation theory of PTSD (Brewin et al 1994), however, recovery involves both processes.

First, a person undergoing recovery needs to reduce the negative affects generated by the implications of the trauma through a process of consciously reasserting perceived control and achieving an integration of the new information with preexisting concepts and beliefs. This may involve substantial editing of autobiographical memory in order to bring perceptions of the event into line with prior expectations. For example, the behavior of an attacker previously believed to be trustworthy may be reinterpreted, excused, or explained away, or aspects of what was done or said may be forgotten. Alternatively, previous expectations may be adjusted in line with the event; for example, behaviors, neighborhoods, or locations believed to be safe may be reclassified as dangerous, or life goals may be abandoned in favor of less ambitious ones.

The second aspect of emotional processing in PTSD is prevention of the continued automatic reactivation of unconscious representations about the trauma. Following activation and the emergence of their products into consciousness, these unconscious representations may be altered or added to by the pairing of the activated information with changes in concurrent bodily states or contents of consciousness. Changes in bodily states may consist of states of reduced arousal and reduced negative affect. These affective and arousal changes may be brought about by a number of means, including spontaneous or programmed habituation to the traumatic images. Similar changes are expected to follow the conscious restoration of a sense of safety (reduced fear), the abandonment of now unattainable goals (reduced sadness), the absolution of others from responsibility for the trauma (reduced anger), and other attempts to integrate the new information into preexisting expectations. As this process of conscious cognitive restructuring continues, the trauma images can be paired with progressive representations of effective action-outcome sequences and reduced negative affect. In the absence of the negative affect, a reduction in attentional and memory biases, and hence in the accessibility of the memory, may be expected.

This analysis follows Rachman (1980) in suggesting that CBT facilitates emotional processing. I suggest, however, that emotional processing encompasses changes to both verbally and situationally accessible memory.

SUMMARY

The basis of behavior therapy was the assumption that actions and emotions are under the control of learned associations represented in a consciously inaccessible form. Hence its techniques attempt to alter situationally accessible knowledge by changing behavior. In contrast, cognitive therapists accepted that conscious cognitions such as beliefs, plans, and goals also influence behavior and emotions. In addition to trying to change situationally accessible knowledge, they also developed techniques to boost compensatory strategies and to rectify misconceptions in verbally accessible knowledge. Although cognitive and behavior therapies emphasize the importance of different cognitive systems, both therapies are consistent with our understanding of human cognition.

The distinction between verbally accessible knowledge and situationally accessible knowledge also appears central to understanding the different types of cognitive therapy and the theoretical explanations for how they work. Some procedures are clearly designed to change conscious beliefs, others to teach skills, and others to modify less-accessible underlying structures in memory.

Patients with the same diagnosis differ in their past experiences, the way they acquired their disorder, the idiosyncratic meaning they attach to their symptoms, and the strategies they adopt to deal with these symptoms' effects.

The theoretical disunity underlying CBT, although regrettable, is therefore to some extent understandable. CBT has developed pragmatically to deal with often difficult and refractory problems. To achieve its success it has had to deploy a large array of procedures, and to seek to modify beliefs and behavior by whatever means were available. In the process, much has been learned about the factors that impede successful treatment, particularly the strategies of cognitive avoidance and neutralization that may conceal from the therapist and sometimes from patients themselves the true sources of distress. In this process CBT was, arguably, not too badly damaged by the lack of a coherent rationale. I suggest, however, that CBT may in fact have a firm foundation, albeit in such quite disparate areas of psychology as cognition, emotion, and motivation. The next task is to link therapeutic imagination and enthusiasm with a clearer understanding of theory.

ACKNOWLEDGMENTS

I gratefully acknowledge the comments of Michael Eysenck, Andrew MacLeod, and Bernice Andrews on an earlier draft of this article.

Literature Cited

Abramson LY, Metalsky GI, Alloy LB. 1989. Hopelessness depression: a theory-based subtype of depression. *Psychol. Rev.* 96: 358–72

Abramson LY, Seligman MEP, Teasdale JD. 1978. Learned helplessness in humans: critique and reformulation. *J. Abnorm. Psychol.* 87:49–74

Andrews B, Brewin CR. 1990. Attributions of blame for marital violence: a study of antecedents and consequences. *J. Marriage Fam.* 52:757–67

Andrews B, Valentine ER, Valentine JD. 1995. Depression and eating disorders following abuse in childhood in two generations of women. *Br. J. Clin. Psychol.* 34: 37–52

Bandura A. 1977. Self-efficacy: toward a unifying theory of behavioral change. *Psychol. Rev.* 84:191–215

Bandura A. 1986. *Social Foundations of Thought and Action: A Social Cognitive Theory.* Englewood Cliffs, NJ: Prentice-Hall

Barber JP, DeRubeis RJ. 1989. On second

thought: where the action is in cognitive therapy for depression. *Cogn. Ther. Res.* 13:441–57

Başoğlu M, Marks IM, Kiliç C, Brewin CR, Swinson RP. 1994. Alprazolam and exposure for panic disorder with agoraphobia. III. Attribution of improvement to medication predicts relapse. *Br. J. Psychiatr.* 164: 652–59

Beck AT, Emery G. 1985. *Anxiety Disorders and Phobias: A Cognitive Perspective.* New York: Basic Books

Beck AT, Freeman A, Pretzer J, Davis DD, Fleming B, et al. 1990. *Cognitive Therapy of Personality Disorders.* New York: Guilford

Beck AT, Rush AJ, Shaw BF, Emery G. 1979. *Cognitive Therapy of Depression.* New York: Wiley

Berkowitz L. 1990. On the formation and regulation of anger and aggression: a cognitive-neoassociationistic analysis. *Am. Psychol.* 45:494–503

Berry DC, Broadbent DE. 1984. On the relationship between task performance and associated verbalizable knowledge. *Q. J. Exp. Psychol.* 36A:209–31

Blackburn IM, Whalley LJ, Christie JE, Shering A, Goggo M, et al. 1987. Mood, cognition and cortisol: their temporal relationships during recovery from depressive illness. *J. Affect. Disord.* 13:31–43

Brewin CR. 1985. Depression and causal attributions: What is their relation? *Psychol. Bull.* 98:297–309

Brewin CR. 1988. *Cognitive Foundations of Clinical Psychology.* London/Hove, Engl.: Erlbaum

Brewin CR. 1989. Cognitive change processes in psychotherapy. *Psychol. Rev.* 96:379–94

Brewin CR, Andrews B, Gotlib IH. 1993. Psychopathology and early experience: a reappraisal of retrospective reports. *Psychol. Bull.* 113:82–98

Brewin CR, Dalgleish T, Joseph S. 1994. A dual representation theory of post-traumatic stress disorder. Submitted for publication

Brewin CR, Smith AJ, Power M, Furnham A. 1992. State and trait differences in depressive self-perceptions. *Behav. Res. Ther.* 30:555–57

Brown GW, Andrews B, Harris TO, Adler Z, Bridge L. 1986. Social support, self-esteem and depression. *Psychol. Med.* 16:813–31

Brown GW, Lemyre L, Bifulco A. 1992. Social factors and recovery from anxiety and depressive disorders: a test of specificity. *Br. J. Psychiatr.* 161:44–54

Butler G, Fennell M, Robson P, Gelder M. 1991. Comparison of behavior therapy and cognitive behavior therapy in the treatment of generalized anxiety disorder. *J. Consult. Clin. Psychol.* 59:167–75

Cantor N, Kihlstrom JF. 1987. *Personality and Social Intelligence.* Englewood Cliffs, NJ: Prentice-Hall

Carver CS, Scheier MF. 1981. *Attention and Self-Regulation: A Control Theory Approach to Human Behavior.* New York: Springer-Verlag

Chambless DL, Gillis MM. 1993. Cognitive therapy of anxiety disorders. *J. Consult. Clin. Psychol.* 61:248–60

Chambless DL, Gracely EJ. 1988. Prediction of outcome following in vivo exposure treatment of agoraphobia. In *Panic and Phobias,* ed. I Hand, H-U Wittchen, 2:209–20. Berlin: Springer-Verlag

Clark DM. 1988. A cognitive model of panic attacks. In *Panic: Psychological Perspectives,* ed. S Rachman, JD Maser, pp. 71–89. Hillsdale, NJ: Erlbaum

Clark DM, Beck AT. 1988. Cognitive approaches. In *Handbook of Anxiety Disorders,* ed. CG Last, M Hersen, pp. 362–85. Elmsford, NY: Pergamon

Clark DM, Salkovskis PM, Hackmann A, Middleton H, Anastasiades P, Gelder M. 1994. A comparison of cognitive therapy, applied relaxation, and imipramine in the treatment of panic disorder. *Br. J. Psychiatr.* 164:759–69

Davey GCL. 1992. Classical conditioning and the acquisition of human fears and phobias: a review and synthesis of the literature. *Adv. Behav. Res. Ther.* 14:29–66

DeRubeis RJ, Evans MD, Hollon SD, Garvey MJ, Grove WM, Tuason VB. 1990. How does cognitive therapy work? Cognitive change and symptom change in cognitive therapy and pharmacotherapy for depression. *J. Consult. Clin. Psychol.* 58:862–69

Dickinson A. 1987. Animal conditioning and learning theory. In *Theoretical Foundations of Behavior Therapy,* ed. HJ Eysenck, I Martin, pp. 57–79. New York: Plenum

Dobson KS. 1989. A meta-analysis of the efficacy of cognitive therapy for depression. *J. Consult. Clin. Psychol.* 57:414–19

D'Zurilla TJ, Goldfried MR. 1971. Problem solving and behavior modification. *J. Abnorm. Psychol.* 78:197–226

Ehlers A, Steil R. 1995. Maintenance of intrusive memories in posttraumatic stress disorder: a cognitive approach. *Behav. Cogn. Psychother.* In press

Ekman P. 1986. *Telling Lies.* New York: Berkley Books

Ellis A. 1962. *Reason and Emotion in Psychotherapy.* New York: Lyle Stuart

Epstein S. 1994. Integration of the cognitive and the psychodynamic unconscious. *Am. Psychol.* 49:709–24

Firth-Cozens J, Brewin CR. 1988. Attributional change during psychotherapy. *Br. J. Clin. Psychol.* 27:47–54

Foa EB, Kozak MJ. 1986. Emotional processing of fear: exposure to corrective information. *Psychol. Bull.* 99:20–35

Foa EB, Steketee G, Rothbaum BO. 1989. Behavioral/ cognitive conceptualization of post-traumatic stress disorder. *Behav. Ther.* 20:155–76

Goldfried MR, Goldfried AP. 1980. Cognitive change methods. In *Helping People Change,* ed. FH Kanfer, AP Goldstein, pp. 97–130. New York: Pergamon. 2nd ed.

Hamilton EW, Abramson LY. 1983. Cognitive patterns and major depressive disorder: a longitudinal study in a hospital setting. *J. Abnorm. Psychol.* 92:173–84

Hasher L, Zacks RT. 1979. Automatic and effortful processes in memory. *J. Exp. Psychol.: Gen.* 108:356–89

Higgins ET, Klein R, Strauman TJ. 1985. Self-concept discrepancy theory: a psychological model for distinguishing among different aspects of depression and anxiety. *Soc. Cogn.* 3:51–76

Hofmann SG, Newman MG, Ehlers A, Roth WT. 1995. Psychophysiological differences between subgroups of social phobia. *J. Abnorm. Psychol.* 104:224–31

Hollon SD, DeRubeis RJ, Evans MD. 1987. Causal mediation of change in treatment for depression: discriminating between nonspecificity and noncausality. *Psychol. Bull.* 102:139–49

Hollon SD, Evans MD, DeRubeis RJ. 1988. Preventing relapse following treatment for depression: the cognitive pharmacotherapy project. In *Stress and Coping across Development,* ed. TM Field, PM McCabe, N Schneiderman, pp. 227–43. Hillsdale, NJ: Erlbaum

Hollon SD, Kriss MR. 1984. Cognitive factors in clinical research and practice. *Clin. Psychol. Rev.* 4:35–76

Hollon SD, Shelton RC, Davis DD. 1993. Cognitive therapy for depression: conceptual issues and clinical efficacy. *J. Consult. Clin. Psychol.* 61:270–75

Horowitz MJ. 1976. *Stress Response Syndromes.* New York: Jason Aronson

Horowitz MJ. 1986. *Stress Response Syndromes.* New York: Jason Aronson. 2nd ed.

Ingram RE, Hollon SD. 1986. Cognitive therapy of depression from an information processing perspective. In *Information Processing Approaches to Clinical Psychology,* ed. RE Ingram, pp. 259–81. New York: Academic

Janoff-Bulman R. 1992. *Shattered Assumptions: Towards a New Psychology of Trauma.* New York: Free Press

Johnson JE, Rice VH, Fuller SS, Endress MP. 1978. Sensory information, instruction in a coping strategy, and recovery from surgery. *Res. Nurs. Health* 1:4–17

Karoly P, Kanfer FH, eds. 1982. *Self-Management and Behavior Change: From Theory to Practice.* New York: Pergamon

Kelly GA. 1955. *The Psychology of Personal Constructs,* Vols. 1, 2. New York: Norton

Kihlstrom JF, Cantor N. 1984. Mental representation of the self. In *Advances in Experimental Social Psychology,* ed. L Berkowitz, 17:1–47. New York: Academic

Klein SB, Loftus J. 1993. The mental representation of trait and autobiographical knowledge about the self. In *Advances in Social Cognition,* ed. TK Srull, RS Wyer, 5:1–49. Hillsdale, NJ: Erlbaum

Kuyken W, Brewin CR. 1994. Intrusive memories of childhood abuse during depressive episodes. *Behav. Res. Ther.* 32: 525–28

Kuyken W, Brewin CR. 1995. Autobiographical memory functioning in depression and reports of early abuse. *J. Abnorm. Psychol.* In press

Lang PJ. 1979. A bio-informational theory of emotional imagery. *Psychophysiology* 16: 495–512

Lang PJ. 1993. The network model of emotion: motivational connections. In *Advances in Social Cognition,* ed. RS Wyer, TK Srull, 6:109–33. Hillsdale, NJ: Erlbaum

Lazarus RS. 1991. *Emotion and Adaptation.* New York: Oxford Univ. Press

Lazarus RS, Averill JR, Opton EM. 1970. Towards a cognitive theory of emotion. In *Feelings and Emotions,* ed. M Arnold, pp. 207–32. New York: Academic

Leventhal H. 1984. A perceptual-motor theory of emotion. *Adv. Exp. Soc. Psychol.* 17: 117-82

Markus H. 1977. Self-schemata and processing information about the self. *J. Pers. Soc. Psychol.* 35:63–78

Markus H, Wurf E. 1987. The dynamic self-concept: a social psychological perspective. *Annu. Rev. Psychol.* 38:299–337

Mattick RP, Peters L. 1988. Treatment of severe social phobia: effects of guided exposure with and without cognitive restructuring. *J. Consult. Clin. Psychol.* 56: 251–60

Meichenbaum D. 1977. *Cognitive-Behavior Modification.* New York: Plenum

Mischel W. 1973. Toward a cognitive social learning reconceptualization of personality. *Psychol. Rev.* 80:252–83

Morton J, Hammersley RH, Bekerian DA. 1985. Headed records: a model for memory and its failures. *Cognition* 20:1–23

Nisbett RE, Wilson TD. 1977. Telling more than we can know: verbal reports on mental processes. *Psychol. Rev.* 84:231–59

Parkes CM. 1971. Psychosocial transitions: a field for study. *Soc. Sci. Med.* 5:101–15

Posner MI, Snyder CR. 1975. Attention and cognitive control. In *Information Processing and Cognition: The Loyola Symposium,* ed. RL Solso, pp. 55–85. Hillsdale, NJ: Erlbaum

Power MJ, Brewin CR. 1991. From Freud to cognitive science: a contemporary account of the unconscious. *Br. J. Clin. Psychol.* 30:289–310

Rachman S. 1980. Emotional processing. *Behav. Res. Ther.* 18:51–60

Rachman S. 1990. The determinants and treatment of simple phobias. *Adv. Behav. Res. Ther.* 12:1–30

Rachman S. 1993. A critique of cognitive therapy for anxiety disorders. *J. Behav. Ther. Exp. Psychiatr.* 24:279–88

Ramsay RW. 1977. Behavioral approaches to bereavement. *Behav. Res. Ther.* 15: 131–36

Reiss S, McNally RJ. 1985. Expectancy model of fear. In *Theoretical Issues in Behavior Therapy,* ed. S Reiss, RR Bootzin, pp. 107–21. San Diego, CA: Academic

Rush AJ, Weissenburger J, Eaves G. 1986. Do

thinking patterns predict depressive symptoms? *Cogn. Ther. Res.* 10:225–38

Salkovskis PM. 1985. Obsessional-compulsive problems: a cognitive-behavioural analysis. *Behav. Res. Ther.* 23:571–83

Salkovskis PM. 1989. Obsessions and compulsions. See Scott et al 1989, pp. 50–77

Segal ZV. 1988. Appraisal of the self-schema construct in cognitive models of depression. *Psychol. Bull.* 103:147–62

Scott J, Williams JMG, Beck AT, eds. 1989. *Cognitive Therapy in Clinical Practice: An Illustrative Casebook.* London: Routledge

Shiffrin RM, Schneider W. 1977. Controlled and automatic human information processing. II. Perceptual learning, automatic attending, and a general theory. *Psychol. Rev.* 84:127–90

Simons AD, Murphy GE, Levine JE, Wetzel RD. 1986. Cognitive therapy and pharmacotherapy for depression: sustained improvement over one year. *Arch. Gen. Psychiatr.* 43:43–49

Smith ER. 1990. Content and process specificity in the effects of prior experiences. In *Advances in Social Cognition,* ed. TK Srull, RS Wyer, 3:1–59. Hillsdale, NJ: Erlbaum

Squire LR, Knowlton B, Musen G. 1993. The structure and organization of memory. *Annu. Rev. Psychol.* 44:453–95

Storms MD, McCaul KD. 1976. Attribution processes and the emotional exacerbation of dysfunctional behavior. In *New Directions in Attribution Research,* ed. JH Harvey, WJ Ickes, RF Kidd, 1:143–64. Hillsdale, NJ: Erlbaum

Strauman TJ. 1990. Self-guides and emotionally significant childhood memories: a study of retrieval efficiency and incidental negative emotional content. *J. Pers. Soc. Psychol.* 59:869–80

Teasdale JD. 1985. Psychological treatments for depression: How do they work? *Behav. Res. Ther.* 23:157–65

Teasdale JD, Barnard PJ. 1993. *Cognition, Affect, and Change: Re-modelling Depressive Thought.* Hove, Engl.: Erlbaum

van den Hout M, Arntz A, Hoekstra R. 1994. Exposure reduced agoraphobia but not panic, and cognitive therapy reduced panic but not agoraphobia. *Behav. Res. Ther.* 32: 447–51

Warwick HMC, Salkovskis PM. 1989. Hypochondriasis. See Scott et al 1989, pp. 78–102

Weiner B. 1985. An attributional theory of achievement motivation and emotion. *Psychol. Rev.* 92:548–73

Williams JMG. 1992. *The Psychological Treatment of Depression.* London: Routledge. 2nd ed.

Wolpe J, Rowan V. 1989. Panic disorder: a product of classical conditioning. *Behav. Res. Ther.* 27:583–85

Young J. 1990. *Cognitive Therapy for Personality Disorders: A Schema-Focused Approach.* Sarasota, FL: Prof. Resour. Exch.

Annu. Rev. Psychol. 1996. 47:59–86

THE DESIGN AND ANALYSIS OF SOCIAL-INTERACTION RESEARCH

David A. Kenny

Department of Psychology U-20, University of Connecticut, Storrs, Connecticut 06269-1020

KEY WORDS: social interaction, design, observational data, multilevel modeling, Social Relations Model

ABSTRACT

Static models of interacting persons measured at the interval level are reviewed. A discussion of the fundamental sources of variance and key design decisions in social-interaction research is presented. Outlined are the basic designs for social-interaction research and their proper analysis. Multilevel modeling is likely to become the most common data analysis method. Critical issues unique to social-interaction research are examined, particularly the effect of the partner on the interaction actor. Finally, illustrations of analyses from four extended examples are presented.

CONTENTS

INTRODUCTION

A classic definition of psychology is that it is "the "science of behavior." Because behavior, particularly in humans, typically occurs with others present, the design and the analysis of social-interaction data are fundamental issues in psychology. There are several different approaches to the study of social interaction. This review considers one important type of model: static models of interacting human organisms. However, virtually all of the material presented in this review could be applied to interacting animals measured on some variable at the interval level of measurement.

There are two fundamentally different approaches to the analysis of social-interaction data, one dynamic and the other static. The dynamic approach examines sequences of events that unfold over time and searches for cycles or lagged causal effects. For instance, a question considered in the dynamic approach might be: If husbands interrupt their wives, are wives more likely later to interrupt their husbands? The present review is confined to the static approach, which presumes that there is consistency or stability of behavior across interactions. The reader is referred to Bakeman & Gottman (1986) for a discussion of the dynamic approach.

The static approach assumes that relationships and personalities are established and fixed (at least within the time frame of the study); therefore, this model is inappropriate when behaviors are changing. However, it can still be used to study interventions designed to change persons.

Social-interaction research is often described as *naturalistic*. However, the settings in which observations are made are hardly ever totally natural. Often people are aware that they are being observed by others or that their behaviors are being recorded, and this awareness likely changes their behavior (Wickland 1979). Moreover, careful measurement sometimes requires bringing persons into controlled environments, e.g. psychological laboratories. The key feature of social-interaction research is not so much its setting, but rather the fact that the behavior of the interactants is not systematically manipulated by the experimenter. All of the interactants are potentially participants in the research. Therefore, excluded from consideration in this review is research that involves confederates or specially prepared stimuli.

Sometimes the study of social interaction is necessarily unnatural in that persons interact with others with whom they would not otherwise interact. Certain interactions must be created to allow the measurement of specialized sources of variance. Who interacts with whom is a fundamental design issue in social-interaction research.

A final limitation of this review is that it considers only variables that are measured at the interval level of measurement. However, many behavioral measurements are discrete or nominal. For example, in a conversation, a person is at any time either interrupting the partner or not interrupting. To obtain a variable measured at the interval level, the proportion of statements interrupted or rate of interruptions needs to be computed, and therefore the measurements need to be aggregated across time.

The review begins with a discussion of the basic sources of variance in social-interaction data. Next considered is a series of important design decisions that affect the measurement of those sources of variance. Designs that can be used to study social interaction are then explored. Data analysis issues are discussed, as well as the role of time in research of this kind. Finally, analyses from four extended examples are presented.

In the review, I consider a wide range of examples chosen from social, personality, developmental, family, and organizational psychology:

Coie et al (1991): Aggression was measured in 23 five- to six-person groups. Each aggressive act was coded in terms of an initiator and a recipient. The research participants were seven- to nine-year-old African-American males preselected on the basis of sociometric measures.

Cole & Jordan (1991): Members of 121 three-person families—mother, father, and child (a college student)—rated all three family dyads (mother-father, mother-child, and father-child) on cohesion.

Kashy (1991): A total of 77 college students reported on their level of intimacy with 1437 partners. Of interest was the effect of gender on the perception of intimacy.

Landauer et al (1970): Eleven sets of three different mothers attempted to get their preschool child and two other children to comply with a request. Three different tasks were used.

Mael & Alderks (1993): Members of 60 United States Army platoons (average of 16 members) rated team cohesion, which was correlated with performance.

Saavendra & Kwun (1993): Business students in 36 four- to six-person work groups rated one anothers' performance.

Tziner & Eden (1985): The performance of three-person (mover, operator, and loader) Israeli tank crews was related to member ability, a composite based on intelligence, education, language proficiency, and interview. Each person was in only one crew and a single productivity measure was determined for each crew.

Zaccaro et al (1991): In this study, 108 persons interacted in four three-person task-oriented groups with different people. Within each group, each person rated the other two members on leadership.

Each of these studies is much more detailed than can be described in this brief summary, but the summary contains essential information that is referred to in this review. In addition, four of the eight studies are reanalyzed in the final section.

As the title suggests, the review concentrates on the design and analysis of social-interaction research. It does not consider the mechanics and technology of data recording. Nor does it consider in depth issues of reliability and validity of behavioral observation.

SOURCES OF VARIANCE

Consider a cluster of persons. A cluster is a self-contained aggregation of people who interact with one another in smaller subgroups. Examples of clusters are families, fraternities, and organizations. Sometimes the cluster is a synthetic aggregation of people. For instance, in Zaccaro et al (1991) previously unacquainted persons were placed in clusters of size nine, and they interacted in groups of size three.

Persons are observed interacting with other cluster members. Each interaction among cluster members involves a group of persons, and the group size may be as small as two or as large as the cluster. The behavior of one or more of the groups' interactants is observed. Accordingly, a person's response reflects the person, the interaction partners of the group, the group, and the cluster.

In social-interaction research there are fundamental linkages between observations. These linkages refer to the sources of variance or correlation between a pair of scores.

A person may interact in more than one group, and a person's behavior may be consistent from one group to another. This consistency is called the *actor effect*. Many, but not all, individual differences are captured by this term.

The person's partners may also exhibit a degree of consistency when they interact with the person. That consistency is called a *partner effect*. For instance, people may smile more when they are with a particular person. This second type of individual-difference variable is much less frequently studied than the actor effect.

Actor and partner effects may be correlated. For instance, it may be that people smile when they are with someone because that person tends to smile, in which case actor and partner effects are positively correlated.

The people interacting in a group may create a local culture, which may be called a *group effect*. The group effect refers to the collective and not to an individual. It explains the reciprocity or complementarity across the scores of group members.

The same group may be observed more than once. The similarity across these observations is called *uniqueness* and reflects the unique way a person interacts with members of the group, which is different from how the person interacts with others and from how others interact with the person.

Finally, a person is a member of a cluster as well as of a group, a subgroup of the larger cluster. Persons' membership in clusters and subgroups yields *cluster effects,* which may be confounded if the group is the cluster, as it is in the Mael & Alderks (1993) study.

These effects are symbolized by A (actor), P (partner), AP (actor-partner covariance), G (group), U (uniqueness), and C (cluster). A brief description of the effects is presented in Table 1. Of course, a study may contain other variables of interest. The sources of variance included in Table 1 are generic effects that are likely to be present in any study of social interaction.

The model as outlined is essentially identical to the Social Relations Model (SRM) (Kenny 1994) of dyadic behavior. However, some SRM terms have been redefined. "Group" in this review takes on the role of dyadic reciprocity within the SRM, "uniqueness" is relationship less dyadic reciprocity, and "cluster" is replication.

The SRM is a dyadic model, but it is generalized in this review to the study of groups larger than two. However, the model remains fundamentally a dyadic model. In a relationship between a person and others, no differentiation is made among the others. In a truly triadic model, the others would be differentiated. For instance, a person may be asked how much another person

Table 1 Sources of variance in social interaction

Component	Symbol	Definition
Actor	A	Same person, different interaction
Partner	P	Same partner, different interaction
Actor-partner covariance	AP	Actor and partner the same across two interactions
Group	G	Same interaction
Uniqueness	U	Same actor and group at a different time
Cluster	C	Same cluster, different actor and partner
Interaction and error	E	All other variance

in the group likes a third person. This chapter concentrates on dyadic models, but there is some discussion of triadic models in the section on "Triadic Considerations," below. The effect of time is also discussed in a later section of the review.

KEY DESIGN DECISIONS

A series of key design issues is critical in social-interaction research. Even if the interactions are completely unstructured and variables such as who interacts with whom and length of interaction are not controlled at all by the researcher, a design decision about which interactions to sample is still made. For many design issues, I state what I think is the optimal choice. Of course, what is generally optimal is not always possible, and so sometimes the particular application may require a different approach.

First, a decision needs to be made whether to track the identities of an actor's interaction partners. Researchers should generally do so because a person's behavior may depend not only on him- or herself but also on the partner. In the parlance of this chapter, behavior may be determined by the partner as much as by the actor. Ignoring the impact of the partner on an actor's behavior is the most common error in social-interaction research—an error that has been called *pseudounilaterality* by Duncan et al (1984).

The partner may be an important cause of behavior. For instance, in the Coie et al (1991) study of aggressive boys, knowledge of a child's interaction partner when the child is aggressive is important because his aggression may be a function more of his interaction partner than of himself. If a child tends to interact with aggressive partners, he may appear more aggressive than he really is.

Even if the behavior of only one participant in the interaction is observed, recording the identity of the interaction partners is still useful because characteristics of the partners can be controlled in the analysis. For instance, when a person's intimacy in interactions is measured, it is important to know the gender of the partner because interactions with females tend to be more intimate than interactions with males (Reis et al 1985).

The second issue, which is closely related to the first, is the decision whether to observe all of the persons in the interaction. Often in behavioral observation, one person is designated as the focal person and his or her interactions are observed for a fixed time (Ladd 1983). However, only by observing multiple interactants can group effects be measured. Even if the responses of the other participants are not observed, their scores on the independent variables should be recorded.

The third key design issue is the number of participants. Group size can be as small as two[1] or as large as the size of the cluster (in which case cluster and group are confounded). The group size may not be controlled by the researcher, but the researcher may restrict the sample to interactions of only a certain group size. In this review, the focus is on research in which group size is two. Dyads are not only the simplest form of social interaction, but they are also by far the most common in naturalistic social interaction (Bakeman & Beck 1974, James 1953). The review gives limited coverage to design and analysis issues when group sizes are larger than two.

The fourth consideration is whether a person has only one or multiple interactions with the same partner. Single-interaction designs confound uniqueness with error, and so to measure uniqueness there must be multiple interactions.

The fifth issue is the unit of measurement of the outcome variable. Consider first a study of dyads. The outcome can refer to the dyad, the person, or the person's interaction in a particular dyad. In a study of dyadic conversations, gender of person refers to person, interruptions refer to person within dyad, and conversation length refers to the dyad. In groups larger than two, a person may be asked to rate pairs of other persons. For instance, in the Cole & Jordan study (1991), persons were asked to rate the cohesion of pairs of family members. Generally, the researcher should measure at the finest level practical. Some constructs (e.g. productivity) may refer to only the group level and so cannot be measured at the person or dyad level.

A final issue is whether there are fixed[2] roles in groups. In some groups, each person can be distinguished by a fixed characteristic. For instance, in interactions between heterosexual spouses, the role that distinguishes interactants is gender. In traditional nuclear family interactions, persons can be distinguished by the roles of mother, father, and child. Cole & Jordan's (1991) study has this family structure. Also, the individual members of Tziner & Eden's (1985) tank crews had different roles. Analysis of data is quite different when such fixed roles exist.

CATALOG OF DESIGNS

This section pertains to dyadic designs in the analysis of social-interaction data. Three key design decisions imply 12 different designs. Here I discuss the

---

[1]   Solitary behavior could be observed, in which case the "group" size would be one.

[2]   Less frequently, roles may change. For example, in baseball there is a home team and an away team, and teams reverse roles on the basis of their schedule. When interactants can take on more than one role, researchers can create multiple outcome variables. In the baseball team example, for runs scored, there would be two variables: runs scored at home and runs scored on the road.

estimation of sources of variance for these 12 designs and note the special issues that arise in triadic models.

Three factors, discussed in the previous section, determine the type of design. First, the number of groups refers to whether a person interacts in multiple groups or just one.

Second, some groups have a role distinction. For instance, in the study by Landauer et al (1970), all dyads were composed of a mother and a child. In other studies—and this is the case with most laboratory studies of interacting groups—persons are not differentiated by role. When there is a role distinction, e.g. mother-child, the dyad is called *asymmetric;* when there is no role distinction, e.g. between same-gender friends, the dyad is called *symmetric.*

Third, the unit of measurement of the outcome may be at the level of the person or the unit of measurement may be at the level of the dyad or group. Sometimes the data are aggregated to create a group-level measurement when the data are at the individual level. For instance, data on individuals' impressions of marital satisfaction are averaged to create a measure of couple satisfaction. This averaging should only be done when large amounts of group variance have been clearly demonstrated. Finally, only one of the two members of the dyad might be measured. For instance, Landauer et al (1970) measured only children's responses in their study of mother-child dyads.[3] So scores can be measured for each member, for each group as a whole, or for only one member of the group.

When these three factors are combined, there are 12 possible designs. Table 2 presents the 12 combinations, and a roman numeral is used to designate each design.

Design I includes the round-robin design and block designs. In a round-robin design everyone interacts or rates everyone else in the cluster. Such a design was used in Saavendra & Kwun's (1993) peer-rating study and in Coie et al's (1991) study of dyadic aggression. In a block design, the cluster is divided into two subgroups and everyone interacts with or rates everyone else in the other subgroup (DePaulo et al 1987). Kenny (1990) extensively discusses these two designs.

Very often in naturalistic studies, not every person can be observed to interact with every other person. Round-robin designs may be feasible in the laboratory, but on the playground the occurrence of full round-robins may be very rare. Nonetheless, the key design features of Design I are met: Each person interacts with at least two other people, and both persons are measured.

---

[3] Sometimes researchers fail to analyze one dyad member's score, and thus essentially throw away half the data. They engage in this wasteful practice to avoid nonindependence complications, which are discussed in the "Data Analysis" section below.

Table 2 Designs in social interaction research

	Symmetric	Asymmetric
All members measured		
Multiple groups	I	II
Single group	III	IV
Group Score		
Multiple groups	V	VI
Single group	VII	VIII
One member measured		
Multiple groups	IX	X
Single group	XI	XII

Design II is like Design I, but in Design II persons can be distinguished by roles. Cole & Jordan's (1991) family rating study would serve as such a design if each person had been asked to rate the other family members. Instead, they were asked to rate dyads, not individual family members, so the study is triadic, not dyadic. A good example of a dyadic Design II is Cook's (1994) analysis of control in families.

Design III is the prototypical small-group design. Each individual is measured and is a member of only one dyad or group. For instance, Mael & Alderks's (1993) study of cohesiveness in platoons used this design. An important variant of this design is one where the "group members" do not interact, but each "member" is linked to a common person. In the Kashy (1991) study, the group is the set of interaction partners of an informant. Another example would be a study of psychotherapists treating patients on an individual basis in which each therapist sees multiple patients.

Design IV is a group study, but the members can be distinguished from one another by their roles. The Tziner & Eden (1985) study would serve as an example of such a design if Tziner & Eden had measured the individual members in each tank crew. A study of heterosexual married couples that included both members would be an example of this design type.

Designs V through VIII have only a single score for the group. Design V could be either a round-robin or block design in which the scores of the two members of the dyad are be the same. For Design VI, members of an asymmetric dyad provide a single score.

For Design VII, there is again a single score for members of a group. In some sense, Mael & Alderks's (1993) study of platoons has this structure, if the rating the platoon leader gives the platoon is considered the variable. An example of Design VIII is the Tziner & Eden study of the productivity of tank crews. The groups are asymmetric because each member of the crew has a different role.

Design IX for dyads has been called the half-block design (Kenny 1990). It is like a block design, but only one of the two members of the dyad is measured. If there is an asymmetry between members in such a design, the design type is X. The Landauer et al (1970) study of children's obedience is an example of this type.

Examples of Designs XI and XII are studies with data obtained from a classroom survey. In these designs, only one member of the dyad or group is surveyed. An example of Design XI would be a classroom survey in which each person rated his or her roommate, and an example of Design XII would be a survey in which a person reported on his or her dating partner. Sometimes researchers have complicated designs, but they throw away data to create Designs XI and XII.

Identification of Variance Components

For each design, information about different sources of variance may be able to be estimated. The effects of design decisions on variance-component estimation are summarized in Table 3.

If actor and partner variances are to be estimated, the design must have multiple groups. The definition of both actor and partner effects requires that the person interact in more than one group. If both members are measured and there are multiple groups, then actor and partner variance can be estimated. If the dyads are asymmetric (Design II), then actor and partner variances can be estimated for each role.

If there is only a group score and there are multiple partners (Designs V and VI), then one single individual-difference variance term can be estimated. That term would equal the sum of actor and partner effects, and so its variance would be the actor variance plus the partner variance plus twice the actor-partner covariance.[4]

If only one of the group members is measured and the design is multiple groups, whether actor and partner variances can be estimated is not straightforward. The clearest case is Design X in which there are asymmetric dyads. If only one person in one role always is measured and the person in the other role is always the partner, then actor variance for one role can be measured, and partner variance for the other role can be measured. However, the actor-partner covariance cannot be estimated.

To measure group variance, there are two different possibilities. If the design is multiple group, then estimates are straightforward. If the design is

---

[4] Less commonly, the single score might represent actor minus partner; e.g. in a study of worker productivity, the score represents how much more or less the actor produces than the partner.

Table 3 The Effect of design decisions on the estimation of variance components

Actor and partner effects
   Complete information: multiple groups, both members measured
   Confounded with each other: multiple groups, group score
   No actor-partner covariance: multiple groups, asymmetric dyad, one member (always the same role) measured
Group effects
   Complete information: multiple groups, both members measured
   Assume no actor and partner effects: single group, both members measured

single group, then group effects are estimable only if actor and partner variances are set to zero.

Triadic Considerations

When the group has three or more members, there are several important complications to consider beyond the scope of dyadic research. These complications are only sketched here. The first concerns whether the measurement is triadic. When persons i, j, and k are in a group, does person i separately interact with or rate both j and k, and is i's behavior measured for all of those interactions?

A second issue in triadic research is the meaning of the group effect. In dyadic research, the group effect is defined as the effect over and above individual-level effects of actor and partner. In triadic research, a group effect can be defined as an effect beyond both individual and dyadic effects. In triadic research, there are then three levels of effects: the person, the dyad, and the triad.

A third issue concerns design. Does person i interact with person j only when k is a member of the group, or does person i interact with j, k, m, and so on? The issue is whether all possible triads or just a subset is formed.

Table 4 presents three multiple-group designs for research using three-person groups. In each design, the person rotates into different groups and interacts with different persons. In the first design, each person is in a group with everyone once, but only once. Kenny et al (1993) call this the *classic rotation design*. Zaccaro et al (1991) used this design to study the stability of leadership behavior. This design's analysis is discussed in Kenny & Hallmark (1992) and Kenny et al (1993). Later in this review, the Zaccaro et al (1991) data are reanalyzed.

In the second design in Table 4, all possible groups are formed. For this and the next design, dyadic actor and partner effects can be estimated given individual-level measurements. A dyadic actor effect means that a person's score can increase or decrease if a particular other person is in the group. A dyadic

Table 4 Examples of triadic multiple group designs

Interact with everyone only once: classic rotation design			
ABC	ADG	AEI	AFH
DEF	BEH	BFG	BDI
GHI	CFI	CDH	CEG

All possible groups: factorial rotation				
ABC	ACD	ADF	BCF	CDE
ABD	ACE	AEF	BDE	CDF
ABE	ACF	BCD	BDF	CEF
ABF	ADE	BCE	BEF	DEF

All possible groups with roles	
$A_1B_1C_1$	$A_2B_1C_1$
$A_1B_1C_2$	$A_2B_1C_2$
$A_1B_2C_1$	$A_2B_2C_1$
$A_1B_2C_2$	$A_2B_2C_2$

partner effect refers to the presence of a dyad in the group, which results in an increase in the performance of anyone who is in the group.

In the last design, persons are assigned or have different roles. The roles are designated as A, B, and C, and for each role there are two persons, 1 and 2. This design is analogous to a repeated-measures design, and its analysis is somewhat similar. Kenny et al (1993) present a reanalysis of Rosenberg et al's (1955) study, which used a variant of this design.

CF Bond, B Horn, and DA Kenny (unpublished manuscript) considered in more detail the complications of triadic design in the analysis of social-interaction data. In essence, they developed a triadic generalization of the SRM. The basic model is complex and contains 7 variances and 16 covariances, whereas the SRM contains just 3 variances and 2 covariances.

DATA ANALYSIS

Generalizability theory (Cronbach et al 1972, Shavelson & Webb 1991) provides a broad framework for the estimation of models from social-interaction data. This theory was developed for the analysis of educational and personality tests but can serve as a platform for understanding the fundamental sources of variance in social-interaction data.

The statistical methods available for estimating these models are of two general types: analysis of variance (ANOVA) and multilevel models. Before discussing these models, I elaborate in some detail a key distinction within generalizability theory.

Fixed vs Random Variables

Researchers are often interested in the effect of one variable on another. For instance, Landauer et al (1970) were interested in whether children complied more or less when their mother asked them to perform a task as opposed to when a stranger asked them to perform a task. Tziner & Eden (1985) tested whether the abilities of the individuals, dyads, or triads determined the performance of the tank crew. Kashy (1991) wanted to know whether people view same- or opposite-gender interactions as more intimate.

Causal variables in social-interaction research are typically fixed variables. A fixed variable usually has a finite number of levels, all of which are sampled. Of interest to researchers is the difference in the outcome variable between levels of that variable. Gender is a prototypical fixed variable.

In contrast, a random variable has many levels, only some of which are sampled in a particular study. In the discussion of "sources of variance" above, four major random variables in social-interaction studies were presented: person (both actor and partner), group, interaction or uniqueness, and cluster. The researcher is interested in the variance of the random variable, not mean differences. For example, researchers are usually not interested in whether Dave interrupts others more than does Charles, but rather in whether people in general differ from one another in interruption rate.

Even if the researcher is not primarily interested in random sources of variance, for the following reasons random effects must still be considered. First, when the focus is on individual-level fixed effects (e.g. effects due to gender or age), it is important to demonstrate individual-level variance (either actor or partner) in the data. If there were not variance at that level, it is unlikely that the fixed effect at that level would be important. Second, random effects serve as the error terms in testing fixed effects. For example, in conventional between-subjects ANOVA, the person (a random effect) serves as the error in the test of fixed effects (e.g. gender). If the fixed variable is a repeated measure, its interaction with the random variable of person serves as error term. Social-interaction data usually contain multiple random effects, and often these sources of variance are used as error terms to test fixed effects.

The analysis of the sources of random variation in a social-interaction study can be complicated. Fortunately, some effects that are assumed to vary randomly may not, in fact, do so when observed empirically. If an effect does not vary, it need not be included in the model. For instance, if the mean did not vary significantly across clusters, cluster could be dropped from the model. In the Landauer et al (1970) study, mother, the person attempting to influence the child, does not affect compliance much, and so mother could be dropped from the model. Models with fewer random effects result in more efficient estimation and testing of fixed effects. Both an analysis for and a test of the random sources of variance are necessary before testing the fixed effects.

The relationship between a fixed and a random variable may be termed either *nested* or *crossed*. With nesting, multiple levels of a variable are grouped within another variable. For instance, persons are nested within their genders. Two variables are said to be crossed when all possible combinations are formed. Gender and cluster are crossed when all clusters contain both males and females.

It is helpful to understand at what level a fixed variable varies. As stated in the section above on sources of variance, there are four fundamental levels of generalization in social-interaction data: cluster, person, group, and interaction. A fixed variable usually varies primarily at one of these levels. Examples of cluster-level variables are organizational type and school size, examples of person-level variables are gender and age, examples of group-level variables are similarity of the couple and family income, and examples of interaction-level variables are attraction and time of interaction.

A key determination is whether a fixed variable interacts with a random variable with which it is crossed. Consider a study of the effect of sociometric classification (rejected vs nonrejected) on aggression. Sociometric classification varies within clusters in the Coie et al (1991) study. It might be assumed that the difference in aggressiveness among sociometric types is the same in each cluster, or it might be assumed that the difference varies across clusters. As a second example, in the Kashy (1991) study, it is important to know whether the partner gender effect interacts with actor. That is, do some persons report more intimate interactions with female partners than do other persons?

The analysis of social-interaction research should examine the effects of fixed and random variables simultaneously. However, as discussed in the section above on key design decisions, for some designs, sources of random variation are confounded. In principle, research in a given area begins with an analysis of random effects. After random effects are identified, fixed effects at that level can be investigated to elucidate the causes of that random variation.

Analysis of Variance and Multiple Regression

Researchers often analyze social-interaction data by averaging the behaviors of each actor across each group in which the actor is a member and by then performing an ANOVA or a multiple regression (MR), in which actor is used as the unit of analysis. Typically, partner, group, and cluster effects are ignored.[5] The researcher implicitly assumes that partner, group, and cluster have no effects, an assumption that is rarely tested.

---

[5] Laudably, Coie et al (1991) explicitly considered cluster effects.

The major problem with using person as the unit of analysis is that the error term used in statistical tests is improper, and so p values are biased. Using actor as the unit ignores important sources of variance, and so scores are nonindependent. Two actors from the same cluster are likely to have correlated scores for the following reasons: (*a*) They interact with the same partners, (*b*) they interact with each other, and (*c*) they are members of the same cluster. Violation of the independence assumption can seriously distort significance test results (Kenny 1995, Kenny & Judd 1986). Although the violation of the independence assumption often leads to too liberal tests of significance, it can sometimes lead to much too conservative a test.

Researchers less frequently use observation as the unit. Often when this is done, variation due to actor, partner, group, and cluster is ignored, and so the significance testing is also likely to be misleading.

Some designs lend themselves naturally to the appropriate use of standard techniques. Single-group designs in which either a group or one member is measured (Designs VII, VIII, XI, and XII in Table 2) often use ANOVA or MR and treat actor or group as the unit of analysis. Because only a single score is measured, there is no aggregation of data, and therefore nonindependence is not introduced by aggregation. Also, because there is only a single score for each group, nonindependence due to group is not a problem. The only source of nonindependence in this analysis is cluster. Tziner & Eden (1985) appropriately used MR to analyze Design VIII.

Note that the designs most appropriate for the use of standard methods are the weakest in terms of estimating multiple sources of variance. One wonders whether investigators choose very weak designs so they can use the analysis tools with which they are more familiar.

ANOVA or MR can also be used to analyze Design IV. Group serves as the unit of analysis and role becomes a repeated measure. So for instance, if Tziner & Eden (1985) had analyzed their individual-level variable of ability as a dependent variable, role (mover, operator, and loader) would have been the repeated measure, and tank group the unit of analysis. Given that there are more than two roles, MANOVA would likely have been more appropriate than ANOVA.

Finally, Design IX requires a variant of repeated-measures ANOVA. Actor becomes the subject in the analysis, and partner the repeated measure. The Landauer et al (1970) study has essentially this structure. Child takes on the role of subject, and mother takes on the role of repeated measure.

Generalizability theory (Cronbach et al 1972, Shavelson & Webb 1991) can be used as a framework to estimate effects within ANOVA for more complicated designs. However, the application of that theory within an ANOVA framework is limited in that generally the designs must be perfectly balanced (equal group sizes), with no missing data, and the fixed variables must be categorical. Determining expected mean squares with unbalanced designs can be difficult and time consuming. Moreover, the solution may refer only to the study at hand and may be of little use for future work. Because of these difficulties, multilevel models, which I discuss below, are gaining favor.

When there are multiple clusters, one can sometimes use conventional analysis strategies by using cluster as unit. One first estimates all of the fixed effects within each cluster. However, no significance tests are performed within-cluster. With cluster as unit of analysis, one uses a *t*-test to determine whether the mean of a given fixed effect (or variance component) is significantly different from zero. In the reanalysis of the Landauer et al (1970) study, below, this strategy is used. Although this chapter is generally critical of aggregation of data, the use of cluster as unit is defensible because ordinarily clusters are independent of one another. Thus, aggregating across independent units is defensible whereas aggregating across nonindependent units is not (e.g. actors).

Estimation of Fixed Actor and Partner Effects in Group Research

Person-level fixed variables are usually assumed to affect only actor effects, but they may also affect partner effects. Considered in this section is the simultaneous estimation of actor and partner effects of a fixed variable for Designs III or IV (see Table 2). To estimate partner effects, the mean or the sum of the scores on the fixed variable of those in the group besides the actor is used to predict a person's response. For instance, in the study of platoon cohesiveness by Mael & Alderks (1993), if the researcher were interested in the effect of race on platoon cohesiveness, race could be shown to have two effects. The first is the actor effect: Do African-Americans or whites report greater levels of cohesiveness? The partner-effect variable concerns the effect of the race of others: Is there more cohesiveness when there are more African-Americans in the platoon? The partner effect would be operationalized as the mean proportion of those in the platoon, besides the respondent, who are white.

Fixed partner effects can be estimated using designs for which random partner effects cannot be estimated. In order to estimate both actor and partner effects, all group members should be measured, and the fixed effect must vary both within and between groups. That is, within a group, members must vary on the fixed variable, and the sum of the fixed variable cannot be the same in all groups. If Design IV is used, actor and partner effects cannot be estimated for the variable that distinguishes members because that variable does not vary between groups.

There are two predictors in a model. The person's own score on the independent variable and the score of the partner (or for groups larger than two, the average or sum of all the partners' scores). Within sociology, there is a long-established tradition of contextual analysis (Boyd & Iverson 1979) in which the group mean for the fixed variable as well as the score of the person is used to predict the outcome variable. In contextual analysis, the mean includes the actor's own score, whereas the partner effect is the mean (or sum) of the scores *excluding the actor.* The two formulations are mathematically equivalent in that one can be derived from the other. However, the partner-effect formulation seems more appropriate because it avoids the part-whole problem. That is, in contextual analysis, a person's score contributes both to the actor and to the group mean.

When groups are larger than two, theory dictates whether the partner effect is captured either by the mean or by the sum of the scores of the others in the group, but the choice matters only when group size varies. There may be another weighting scheme besides a linear one. For instance, according to social impact theory (Latane 1981), the partner has less impact as the group size increases. Thus, this theory predicts weaker partner effects as group size increases. It is also possible to weight individuals differentially, as opposed to equally, in forming the partner effect.

No matter how the partner effect is measured, an ordinary regression equation containing actor and partner effects should not usually be estimated because there may be nonindependence in the scores of members of the same group. The estimation and testing of both actor and partner effects of a fixed variable are surprisingly difficult. Kraemer & Jacklin (1979) pioneered an approach that has been generalized by Kenny (1996). In this approach, the analysis is performed twice, once on the group means and once on the variation within groups. These two sets of regression analyses are then pooled to provide estimates and tests of partner effects. If the groups are asymmetric, structural equation modeling can estimate fixed actor and partner effects (Kenny 1996).

The possibility may exist of an interaction between a fixed actor effect and its partner effect. For dyads, the interaction is a group-level variable and can represent similarity between the two members. Very often, measures of similarity, heterogeneity, and discrepancy can be viewed as the interaction between actor and partner effects. As in any interaction, the main effects of actor and partner should be controlled.

SRM Analyses

Since participating in Warner et al's (1979) study, I have been keenly interested in the analysis of social-interaction data, particularly dyadic data with multiple partners (especially Design I). The reader is referred to the most recent summary of the approach that my colleagues and I have developed (Kenny 1994). In essence, the approach is ANOVA. Expected means squares and cross-products are determined for different designs. Bond & Lashley (1995) present estimates of the variance of the SRM components for the round-robin design.

The estimation approach resembles random-effects ANOVA. Linear combinations of mean squares are used to estimate unknown variance and covariance components. Unlike traditional ANOVA, the designs are rarely balanced, and there are numerous sources of nonindependence. As a result, determining the expected mean squares can be complicated.

The approach is not flexible when data are missing or the design is not (as is often the case with studies in natural settings) a perfect round-robin or block. Other analytic techniques (e.g. average squared difference or multilevel models) must be used in these cases. Another major weakness of SRM analyses is their inability to handle some fixed variables, most notably fixed variables at the level of the dyad. The approach also uses specialized software that is not generally accessible (Kenny 1994).

Related work that also employs expected mean squares can be used to analyze Design III (Kenny & La Voie 1985) (see Table 2) and the classic rotation design presented in Table 4 (Kenny & Hallmark 1992).

Average Squared Differences

Kenny & Judd (1996) describe a very general estimation approach for nonindependent data structures. The approach relies on the statistical fact that the average of all possible squared differences among scores equals twice the variance. The squared difference between every pair of scores is expressed in terms of unknown variances and covariances. Squared differences that have the same expectation are averaged, and these averages are used to solve for unknown variance and covariance components. What makes this method especially useful is that expectations can be obtained in a relatively straightforward fashion, whereas in ANOVA, expectations of mean squares can often be complicated. However, the method is both computationally and statistically inefficient and does not have a straightforward test of significance. It is, however, very general and is more similar to ANOVA methods than the procedure discussed in the next section. The Kenny & Judd approach is applied to the Zaccaro et al (1991) study in the "Illustrations" section of the review.

Confirmatory Factor Analysis

For some models, confirmatory factor analysis can be used to estimate the variance of random effects. When roles are fixed, as they are in the Cole & Jordan (1991) data set, the data can often be separated into discrete variables and then analyzed by confirmatory factor analysis. Computer programs such as EQS and LISREL can be used.

A detailed discussion of confirmatory factor analysis models for Design II may be found in Kashy & Kenny (1990), and an excellent example may be found in Cook (1994). A reanalysis of the Cole & Jordan (1991) data set, presented in the "Illustrations" section below, uses confirmatory factor analysis.

Multilevel Analysis

Multilevel modeling (Bryk & Raudenbush 1992) is a new approach within generalizability theory that provides a very general approach to the estimation of models of social interaction. It can easily handle models with both fixed and random variables as well as models with multiple random variables. However, unlike ANOVA methods, tests of variance of random effects are large-sample tests and so are tested using a chi-square, not an F-test. Generally maximum likelihood estimation is used with iterative solutions. Thus, there are no simple formulas for variances and estimates of fixed effects. Rather, complicated algorithms are used to converge on a solution. For large models, the estimation can be intensive and time-consuming. Given the rapid improvement in the speed of computers, however, these computational difficulties should not prove to be an obstacle.

In traditional ANOVA methods, missing data are a problem, but missing data (at least in moderate amounts) present no serious estimation difficulty for multilevel modeling. Also, amalgams of designs (e.g. both symmetric and asymmetric dyads) and constraints on parameters can be easily estimated in multilevel modeling. A further advantage of multilevel modeling is the ease it allows in specifying whether a term is needed in the model. If, for example, there is no evidence of gender-by-cluster interaction, then it would not need to be included in the model.[6]

Specialized computer software is often used to estimate multilevel models. The most notable programs are HLM (Bryk et al 1994), ML3 (Prosser et al 1991), and MIXREG (Hedeker 1993). Programs are currently available within SAS and BMDP to estimate these models. Major improvements in speed, user friendliness, and range of analyzable designs will likely be made in the next decade.

Multilevel modeling was developed for nested designs; it can more naturally handle single-partner designs where persons are nested in groups (Designs III and IV). However, it can handle all of the designs mentioned in this review even though in some designs effects are crossed (TAB Snijders & DA

---

[6] If group size varies, it can be determined whether actor and partner effects vary as the group size changes. An effect would be correlated across different group sizes. For instance, whether a person's sociability is the same in dyadic and group interaction could be tested (Sullivan 1995). One could also test whether group variance changes as a function of group size.

Kenny, unpublished manuscript). For instance, actor and partner effects are crossed factors in Designs I and II.

Multilevel models have been infrequently used in social-interaction studies. Most applications have been either in educational settings or in over-time developmental or evaluation studies.

TIME AND TASK EFFECTS

If a person interacts with others at multiple times, a structuring of interactions across time may be observed. The time effect can be measured when there are multiple interactions. For instance, time may interact with actor or partner effects. Some actors' scores may improve over time, and others may decline. Various models of growth (e.g. linear or exponential) may be considered.

In some social interaction studies, particularly laboratory ones, participants are given more than one task. For instance, Zaccaro et al (1991) investigated leadership using four different tasks. Also, Landauer et al (1970) used three different compliance tasks. Task and time may need to be counterbalanced by a latin square, which was done in both these studies. Like time, task may interact with random variables.

Change may be studied within the static approach by splitting the data into early and late observations. In this way, the causal effects between actor and partner effects can be estimated. For example, if a child initiates prosocial behavior, is he or she later the recipient of prosocial acts?

ILLUSTRATIONS

Four original data sets are reanalyzed. Different designs and estimation techniques are illustrated. The analyses reveal the wealth of information that can be obtained from social-interaction data.

Cole & Jordan (1991) Study of Family Cohesiveness

In this study, members of three-person families—mother, father, and child—rated the three family dyads (mother-father, mother-child, and father-child) on cohesiveness. There is a total of nine variables, each of which is designated by three letters. For instance, MFC means the mother's rating of father-child cohesiveness. Because the rating is of a dyad, MFC is the same as MCF.

Because there are fixed roles, the data can be analyzed by confirmatory factor analysis. Table 5 presents the basic structure of the model, which is different from the multitrait-multimethod model proposed by Cole & Jordan (1991).

Table 5 Cole & Jordan (1991) factor loading matrix and factor variances (M = mother; F = father; C = child)

	Actor			Partner			Dyad		
	M	F	C	M	F	C	MF	MC	FC
MMF	1	0	0	1	1	0	1	0	0
MMC	1	0	0	1	0	1	0	1	0
MFC	1	0	0	0	1	1	0	0	1
FMF	0	1	0	1	1	0	1	0	0
FMC	0	1	0	1	0	1	0	1	0
FFC	0	1	0	0	1	1	0	0	1
CMF	0	0	1	1	1	0	1	0	0
CMC	0	0	1	1	0	1	0	1	0
CFC	0	0	1	0	1	2	0	0	1
Variance	$.23^a$	$.08^a$	$.27^a$	$.36^a$	$.15^a$	$.44^a$	-.16	.10	.08

[a] $p < .05$.

There are nine factors and all the loadings are fixed to 1. Because the solution is not standardized, loadings can be 1 or larger. There are three actor effects (mother, father, and child), three partner effects, and three dyadic effects. Each of these effects becomes a factor in the confirmatory factor analysis.

As shown in the last row of Table 5, there are actor effects (differences in perceived cohesiveness) and partner effects (agreement about who promotes cohesiveness). However, there is no evidence for any dyadic effects in the data set.[7] The model can be reestimated with these dyadic factors dropped.

Note that in Table 5 the variance for the MF dyad is negative. Estimated negative variances are possible for random effects and are interpreted as if they were zero.

Zaccaro et al (1991) Study of Leadership Stability

Zaccaro et al (1991) were interested in the stability of leadership across interactions. Their design is the classic rotation design (see the first design in Table 4). In this instance, each cluster contained nine persons, and each person interacted in a group with two different persons four times. Within each group, the person rated both partners on leadership. The net result was that each person interacted once and only once with every one else in the cluster. The study also included four different tasks, one for each of the person's groups.

[7] The covariance matrix should be analyzed, but only the correlation matrix is presented in Cole & Jordan (1991).

Task and time were counterbalanced, but only task is considered in the analysis that follows.

Kenny et al (1993) consider two alternative specifications of the group effect. The first is that group is an emergent phenomenon. The second is that the group effect is an individual effect added to every score. Here a third procedure is adopted. When person i rates j and k is a third member, the rating is assumed to be affected by the fact that k is a member of the group. This effect is called the *bystander effect* because it refers to neither the actor nor the partner but to the third person in the group. There are three covariances in the model: actor-partner, actor-bystander, and partner-bystander. Nine sources of random variance result:

Actor stable: Does a person see others as leaders across the four groups?

Actor unstable: Does a person see others as leaders in some groups but not in others?

Partner stable: Is a person seen as a leader across the four groups?

Partner unstable: Is a person seen as a leader in one group and not in another?

Bystander stable: If k is in the group, do i and j see each other as leaders?

Bystander unstable: Does the bystander effect vary across time?

Cluster: Is there more leadership in some clusters than in others?

Cluster by task: Does the task effect vary by cluster?

Error: How much is the rating of leadership affected by other factors?

The only fixed factor in this study is task.

The Kenny & Judd (1996) average squared difference method was used to determine expected mean squares for this model. Table 6 presents the estimates of variance for each of the components. Except for the terms involving cluster, cluster is the unit of analysis, and a t-test is used to evaluate whether the mean of the component is different from zero. Tests of variances are one tailed, and tests of covariances are two tailed. The task effect was evaluated with an MANOVA of the four tasks with cluster as the unit of analysis. The test of the task effect is statistically significant, $F(3,9) = 7.115$, $p<.01$.

Perhaps the most important result of the test is the presence of stable-partner variance. A large portion of the partner variance is stable, 38% [$= .049/(.049 + .079)$]. Therefore, when a person was seen as a leader in one group, that person was also seen as a leader in the next group that he or she was in. This value is a little smaller than that reported in Zaccaro et al (1991) because they did not estimate a bystander effect.

The bystander variance is marginally significant. The presence of a person in the group may change the ratings of others' leadership in the group. The partner-bystander correlation can help in interpreting the bystander effect. It indicates that if one person is seen as a leader, others in the group are not seen as leaders. In essence, leadership creates followership.

Table 6 Estimates of variance for the Zaccaro et al (1991) leadership study

Variance	Absolute	Relative
Actor stable	.066[a]	.153
Actor unstable	-.000	.000
Partner stable	.049[a]	.114
Partner unstable	.079[a]	.183
Bystander stable	.011[b]	.026
Bystander unstable	-.018	.000
Cluster	.021[c]	.049
Cluster by time	.008[c]	.019
Error	.197[c]	.457
Covariance	Raw	r
Actor-partner	-.014	-.238
Actor-bystander	.017	.627
Partner-bystander	-.014	-.628

[a]$p < .05$
[b]$p < .10$
[c]Not tested.

Landauer et al (1970) Study of Mother-Child Compliance

Landauer et al (1970) is by far the oldest study considered in this review, but it is one of the best. The investigators' original analysis is sophisticated, especially for its time.[8] Clusters consisted of three mothers and their preschool children. Each mother attempted to get her own child and the other two children to comply with a request to perform a task (e.g. to pick up toys). There were three different tasks, and each mother made a different request to each child.

The outcome measure is compliance, and its measurement is fairly complex. Landauer et al (1970) rank-ordered the children on the basis of compliance within the three tasks. In the reanalysis, the ranks were converted to normalized ranks, which gives the ranks a quasi-normal distribution. To make the results more interpretable, the scores were divided by the square root of the error variance, which results in a solution with an error variance of one. There are five sources of random variance:

Cluster: Is there more compliance in some sets of three mothers and children than in others?

---

[8] There appears to be a minor typographical error in the reporting of the data from this study. The seventh observation from the sixth group should be −.9, not 2.8. It is a testimony to the carefulness of the authors that this error could even be detected.

Mother: Can some mothers get children to obey them more than other mothers?

Child: Do some children comply more than other children?

Cluster by relationship: Are mothers more effective at getting their own children to obey in some clusters than in others?

Error: Are there random sources of variance?

One fixed effect is relationship: parent vs nonparent. Finally, there is one covariance: mother-child (Do compliant children have persuasive mothers?). ANOVA expected mean squares were determined, and cluster was the unit of analysis.

Table 7 presents the basic results. Most of the conclusions here are identical to those of Landauer et al (1970). Of the systematic random effects, cluster explains the most variance. Child explains almost the same amount as cluster, but that effect is only marginally significant. Mother explains even less variance, and its effect is not significant. Relationship does not appear to interact with cluster.

By far the largest effect (standardized effect of −1.09) is the fixed effect of relationship. Mothers were singularly unsuccessful at getting their own child to obey them. Children complied with the requests of strangers much more often than with their own mothers' requests.

The correlation between mother effects and child effects is positive and large. Mothers who had compliant children were more successful persuaders. Although the effect is plausible, given the relatively small amounts of mother variance, the correlation should be treated with caution.

Table 7 Estimates of variance for the Landauer et al (1970) mother-child compliance study using normalized ranks

Variance		
Cluster	.331[a]	
Mother	.158	
Child	.316[b]	
Cluster by relationship	.014[a]	
Error	1.000[a]	
Fixed effect		
Relationship[c]	-1.089[d]	
Covariance	Raw	r
Mother-child	.180[a]	.808

[a]Not tested.

[b]$p < .10$.

[c]Parent-child minus non-parent-child.

[d]$p < .05$.

Kashy (1991) Study of Gender Differences in Intimacy

In this study, 77 respondents reported their level of intimacy with 1437 partners. The outcome variable was the average intimacy across all interactions with a partner. The central question was the role of gender in perceived intimacy. The multilevel computer program HLM (Bryk et al 1994) was used to analyze the data.

There are three fixed effects in the model:

Actor gender: Which gender reports the more intimate interactions?
Partner gender: Are interactions with males or females reported to be more intimate?
Same- vs opposite-gender: Are interactions with same- or opposite-gender partners reported to be more intimate?

There are also three random effects in the study:

Actor: Do some people report their interactions as more intimate than do others?
Actor by partner gender: Are some people more intimate with female partners than with male partners?
Error: Is there random variation in the scores?

The results for all these effects are presented in Table 8 as Model I.

For the fixed effects, both actor gender and same- vs opposite-gender are significant. More intimacy was reported when the actor was female than when the actor was male, and there was more reported intimacy in opposite-gender interactions.

Table 8 Estimates and tests of coefficients and variance components for the Kashy (1991) study

	Model	
	I	II
Fixed effects		
Actor gender[a]	.540[b]	.540[b]
Partner gender[a]	.108	.112
Same versus opposite gender	-.376[b]	-.372[b]
Random effects (variances)		
Actor	.853[b]	.854[b]
Actor by partner gender	.025	—[c]
Error	1.888[d]	1.909[d]

[a]Female minus male.

[b]$p < .05$

[c]Set to zero.

[d]Not tested.

For the random effects, actor variance was significant: Some people report more intimacy in their interactions than do others. However, the interaction of actor with partner gender was not significant. The effect of partner gender is basically the same for all dyads. Because this interaction was not significant, the model was reestimated and the effects were again tested and presented in Table 8 as Model II.

SUMMARY

Social-interaction data possess a rich potential that is rarely utilized. Social-interaction researchers invest considerable time and effort gathering the necessary data, yet they rarely recover much information from it. The major purpose of this chapter has been to encourage a greater willingness to explore the data in more depth.

However, it is important to understand the limitations of the approach presented in this review. The focus has been almost exclusively univariate in the sense that there is only a single outcome measure. Multiple outcomes were designated as replications in order to separate uniqueness from error. The variables could, as an alternative, be ordered in a causal sequence.

Moreover, dynamic models have not been presented. They are treated elsewhere (e.g. Bakeman & Gottman 1986). Additionally, the outcomes considered here are assumed to be measured at the interval level of measurement. Typically, behavioral variables are measured at the nominal level. Multilevel models have been developed for the analysis of nominal outcomes.

One clear recommendation stemming from this review is that researchers need to gather more data than they usually do. Researchers need to determine with whom a person is interacting, the characteristics of that person, and that person's behavior. Sometimes researchers must make arrangements to ensure that certain persons interact with others.

Another recommendation is to measure and estimate partner effects. All too often the partner is ignored in social interaction (Duncan et al 1984). Either the partner's behavior is not measured, or his or her effects on the other are ignored. The partner presents some serious complications in the analysis, but these complications can be understood and analyzed. In fact, sometimes the partner effect is the central research focus. For instance, learning in the classroom often takes place in groups. It has been hypothesized that high-ability children can facilitate others' learning—i.e. that there are partner effects.

Aggregation of data should generally be avoided, because it may result in a loss of information about random variables and because it may create nonindependent units. If possible, the analysis should do the aggregation. Sometimes, however, the outcome measure requires aggregation. For instance, Saavendra & Kwun (1993) were interested in how variable the responses were.

The analysis of social-interaction data must be done in much more depth. Researchers have often attempted to use the standard data-analytic techniques of analysis of variance and multiple regression to analyze social-interaction data. Often these tools are inappropriate; sometimes they provide only limited information about the fundamental sources of variance. What is even worse is that sometimes their use constrains researchers in their determination of how the data are gathered and what questions are asked.

A proper analysis of social-interaction data is often difficult using conventional methods. However, we are soon going to see analytic tools that are much easier for the researcher to use. The researcher need only specify the sources of variance and they will be estimated by complicated algorithms. The estimation procedure is likely to be a form of multilevel modeling.

Finally, I hope this chapter is read not so much as a discussion about what is wrong with the analysis of social-interaction data but rather as a consideration of what can be done. Researchers, reviewers, editors, and granting agencies need to accept the complexities in social interaction. Never can the complete complexity be captured in a single study, but I hope that we will allow for more complexity of social interaction than we have in the past.

ACKNOWLEDGMENTS

I wish to acknowledge the support of grants from the National Science Foundation DBS 9307949 and the National Institute of Mental Health R01 MH-51964. Deborah A. Kashy provided extensive comments on a previous version of this review.

Literature Cited

Bakeman R, Beck S. 1974. The size of informal groups in public. *Environ. Behav.* 6: 378–90

Bakeman R, Gottman JM. 1986. *Observing Interaction.* New York: Cambridge

Bond CF Jr, Lashley BR. 1995. Social relations analysis of dyadic interaction: exact and estimated standard errors. *Psychometrika.* In press

Boyd L, Iverson G. 1979. *Contextual Analysis: Concepts and Statistical Techniques.* Belmont, CA: Wadsworth

Bryk AS, Raudenbush SW. 1992. *Hierarchical Linear Models: Applications and Data Analysis Methods.* Newbury Park, CA: Sage

Bryk AS, Raudenbush SW, Congdon RT.

1994. *HLM 2–3: Hierarchical Linear Modeling with the HLM/2L and HLM/3L Programs.* Chicago: Scientific Software

Coie JD, Dodge KA, Terry R, Wright V. 1991. The role of aggression in peer relations: an analysis of aggression episodes in boys' play groups. *Child Dev.* 62:812–26

Cole DA, Jordan AE. 1991. Assessment of cohesion and adaptability in component family dyads: a question of convergent and discriminant validity. *J. Couns. Psychol.* 36: 456–63

Cook WL. 1994. A structural equation model of dyadic relationships within the family system. *J. Consult. Clin. Psychol.* 62:500–9

Cronbach LJ, Gleser GC, Nanda H, Rajaratnam N. 1972. *The Dependability of Behav-*

ioral Measurements: Theory of Generalizability of Scores and Profiles. New York: Wiley

DePaulo B, Kenny DA, Hoover C, Webb W, Oliver PV. 1987. Accuracy of person perception: Do people know what kinds of impressions they convey? J. Pers. Soc. Psychol. 52:303–15

Duncan S, Kanki BG, Mokros H, Fiske DW. 1984. Pseudounilaterality, simple-rate variables, and other ills to which interaction research is heir. J. Pers. Soc. Pscyhol. 6: 1335–48

Hedeker D. 1993. MIXREG: A FORTRAN Program for Mixed-Effects Linear Regression Models. Chicago: Univ. Illinois Press

James J. 1953. The distribution of free-forming small group size. Am. Soc. Rev. 18:569–70

Kashy DA. 1991. Levels of analysis of social interaction diaries: separating the effects of person, partner, day, and interaction. PhD thesis. Univ. Conn.

Kashy DA, Kenny DA. 1990. Analysis of family research designs: a model of interdependence. Commun. Res. 17:462–82

Kenny DA. 1990. Design issues in dyadic research. In Review of Personality and Social Psychology: Research Methods in Personality and Social Psychology, ed. C Hendrick, MS Clark, 11:164–84. Newbury Park, CA: Sage

Kenny DA. 1994. Interpersonal Perception: A Social Relations Analysis. New York: Guilford

Kenny DA. 1995. The effect of nonindependence on significance testing in dyadic research. Pers. Relat. 2:67–75

Kenny DA. 1996. Models of nonindependence in dyadic research. J. Soc. Pers. Rel. In press

Kenny DA, Hallmark BW. 1992. Rotation designs in leadership research. Leadersh. Q. 3:25–41

Kenny DA, Hallmark BW, Sullivan PS, Kashy DA. 1993. The analysis of designs in which individuals are in more than one group. Br. J. Soc. Pscyhol. 32:173–90

Kenny DA, Judd CM. 1986. Consequences of violating the independence assumption in analysis of variance. Pscyhol. Bull. 99: 422–31

Kenny DA, Judd CM. 1996. A general procedure for the estimation of interdependence. Psychol. Bull. In Press

Kenny DA, La Voie L. 1985. Separating individual and group effects. J. Pers. Soc. Pscyhol. 48:339–48

Kraemer HC, Jacklin CN. 1979. Statistical analysis of dyadic social behavior. Pscyhol. Bull. 86:217–24

Ladd GW. 1983. Social networks of popular, average, and rejected children in school settings. Merrill-Palmer Q. 29:283–307

Landauer TK, Carlsmith JM, Leeper M. 1970. Experimental analysis of the factors determining obedience of four-year-old children to adult females. Child Dev. 41:601–11

Latane B. 1981. The psychology of social impact. Am. Psychol. 36:343–56

Mael FA, Alderks CE. 1993. Leadership team cohesion and subordinate work unit morale and performance. Mil. Psychol. 5:141–58

Prosser R, Rasbash J, Goldstein H. 1991. ML3: Software for Three-Level Analysis. London: Univ. London

Reis HT, Senchak M, Solomon B. 1985. Sex differences in the intimacy of social interaction: further examination of potential explanations. J. Pers. Soc. Pscyhol. 48: 1204–17

Rosenberg S, Erlick DE, Berkowitz L. 1955. Some effects of varying combinations of group members on group performance measures and leadership behaviors. J. Abnorm. Soc. Pscyhol. 51:195–203

Saavendra R, Kwun SK. 1993. Peer evaluation in self-managing work groups. J. Appl. Pscyhol. 78:450–62

Shavelson RJ, Webb NM. 1991. Generalizability Theory: A Primer. Newbury Park, CA: Sage

Sullivan PS. 1995. Interpersonal perception in dyadic and group settings: a social relations analysis. PhD thesis. Univ. Conn.

Tziner A, Eden D. 1985. Effects of crew composition on crew performance: Does the whole equal the sum of its parts? J. Appl. Pscyhol. 70:85–93

Warner R, Kenny DA, Stoto M. 1979. A new round robin analysis of variance for social interaction data. J. Pers. Soc. Pscyhol. 37: 1742–57

Wickland RA. 1979. The influence of self-awareness on human behavior. Am. Sci. 67: 187–93

Zaccaro SJ, Foti RJ, Kenny DA. 1991. Self-monitoring and trait-based variance in leadership: an investigation of leader flexibility across multiple group situations. J. Appl. Pscyhol. 76:308–15

Annu. Rev. Psychol. 1996. 47:87–111

PERSONALITY: Individual Differences and Clinical Assessment

James N. Butcher and Steven V. Rouse

University of Minnesota, Department of Psychology, Minneapolis, Minnesota, 55455

KEY WORDS: clinical assessment, validity, Five-Factor Model, managed care, computerized assessment

ABSTRACT

Research in clinical personality assessment continues to be produced at a high rate. The MMPI/MMPI-2 remains the most popular instrument for both clinical application and psychopathology research. Two other clinical personality instruments, the Rorschach and TAT, continue to find a place in research and clinical assessment. Some new instruments have surfaced recently to deal with areas, such as personality disorders, that have been considered inadequately addressed. There is a growing recognition that the Five-Factor Model is too superficial for clinical assessment that requires more refined and broadened patient information. Clinical personality assessment has successfully survived a number of past challenges. The newest challenge stems from the health-care revolution, in which managed-care providers are reluctant to pay for assessment because of shrinking funds. Psychologists need to develop models for incorporating assessment information into the treatment process. The future is likely to see more extensive research and theoretical development in this endeavor.

CONTENTS

0066-4308/96/0201-0087$08.00

INTRODUCTION

The annual yield of personality assessment research continues to grow, and the number of new journals and books devoted to personality test applications has increased over the past decade. Much of this research centers on the use of clinical assessment techniques, and we focus this review on clinical personality assessment, in part because past *Annual Review of Psychology* assessment topics have tended to focus on nonclinical personality assessment instruments.

In order to give the appropriate amount of weight to the measures extensively used in clinical research, we conducted a review of the research literature on clinical personality assessment published over the past 20 years. Our review (see Table 1) highlights measures considered to be standard instruments, as well as some newer tests. A recent survey of clinical practitioners by Watkins et al (1995) indicates that these tests, identified in Table 1 as most often studied by researchers, are also the ones most frequently used by clinicians. Watkins et al surveyed 1000 clinical psychologists to ascertain the assessment measures that were used and concluded that the Minnesota Multiphasic Personality Inventory (MMPI-2), Rorschach, and Thematic Apperception Test (TAT) were the most popular personality tests. Sentence Completion Tasks, not included in this review, were also among the top four procedures used.

Several other considerations influenced our choice of which assessment instruments to include in this review. We opted to limit our review to instruments and studies that focus on assessment of adult psychopathology; we do not address adolescent or child assessment measures. We limit our review to formal assessment procedures—psychological tests—and do not include interview, behavioral observations, psychophysiological measures of personality, or nonstandard construction tasks such as figure drawings. Finally, we focus on research published between 1994 (give or take a few months in 1993) and March of 1995.

Table 1   Frequency of published research on clinical assessment methods over a 20-year period[a]

Year	BPI	DPI	MCMI	MMPI	MMPI2	NEO	PAI	16PF	Rors	TAT
1974				185				12	99	55
1975				176				15	76	67
1976				200				27	85	57
1977				217				21	67	52
1978				208				15	73	38
1979				171				11	81	41
1980			1	189				16	69	42
1981				151				10	94	48
1982			1	216				32	94	65
1983			2	261		1		79	114	53
1984			7	273		1		72	100	57
1985			22	242		1		75	101	59
1986	3		17	249		1		79	112	49
1987	2		22	233		2		56	96	59
1988	4		31	262		4		64	100	42
1989	3	1	43	235	5	8		70	119	37
1990	5		68	222	11	9		62	134	55
1991	4		41	219	33	20		45	81	32
1992	4		42	210	55	19	1	41	124	48
1993	2		60	132	49	32	3	28	96	29
1994[b]	4		27	88	50	28	3	17	54	13
Total	31	1	384	4339	203	126	7	847	1969	998

[a]BPI (Basic Personality Inventory); DPI (Differential Personality Inventory); MCMI (Millon Clinical Multiaxial Inventory, MCMI-II, MCMI-III); MMPI (Minnesota Multiphasic Personality Inventory), MMPI-2 (MMPI-2, MMPI-A); NEO (NEO Personality Inventory, NEO-FFI, NEO-PI-R); PAI (Personality Assessment Inventory); Rors (Rorschach Inkblot Method); TAT (Thematic Apperception Test)

[b]"1994" includes those 1994 references that had been indexed by PsychLit as of March 1995, as well as several references published during 1995.

OVERVIEW OF CLINICAL ASSESSMENT MEASURES FOR 1994

Minnesota Multiphasic Personality Inventory (MMPI/MMPI-2)

The MMPI-2 appears to be continuing in the tradition of its predecessor, the MMPI, as the most frequently researched clinical instrument. There were 321 articles/books published on the MMPI/MMPI-2/MMPI-A in the current review period, with an increased number of articles (101) published on MMPI-2 and MMPI-A. Articles centered around several themes: exploring the relationship between the MMPI-2 and the original version (Brophy 1993; Chojnacki

& Walsh 1994; Colligan et al 1994; Edwards et al 1993a,b; Han et al 1995), evaluating the MMPI-2 scales against external criteria (Ben-Porath et al 1993, Berger 1994, Boone 1994a, Clark ME 1994, Elwood 1993, Lovitt 1993, Meyer 1993, Morrison et al 1994); further exploring internal relationships (Endler et al 1993, Keiller & Graham 1993, Timbrook et al 1993, Ward 1994), examining the test's generalizability with diverse populations (Bagby et al 1994a, Ben-Porath et al 1995, Butcher 1994b, Butcher 1995a, Canul & Cross 1994, Deardorff et al 1993, Derksen & de Mey 1994, Hargrave et al 1994, Khan et al 1993, Lamb et al 1994, Long et al 1994, Lucio et al 1994, Megargee 1994, Poreh & Whitman 1993, Priest & Meunier 1993, Rogers et al 1993a, Stevens et al 1993, Svanum & Ehrmann 1993, Talbert et al 1994, Timbrook & Graham 1994, Whitworth & McBlaine 1993), and assessing test validity, which is discussed below.

Two controversial interchanges appeared during this period that may be of interest to researchers and clinicians. The first debate is contained in four articles discussing the continuity of code types between the MMPI and MMPI-2. The debate was initiated in two articles by Dahlstrom (1992) and Humphrey & Dahlstrom (1995), who questioned whether code types derived by the two versions of the inventory produce the same classifications. Dahlstrom's conclusions were based largely on samples of normal-range profiles that tended to have attenuated elevations and minimal differences among scale scores. Tellegen & Ben-Porath (1993) and Ben-Porath & Tellegen (1995), in a rebuttal and critique of Dahlstrom's conclusions, provided a rationale and explanation for refining code-type interpretation to produce better defined and more stable codes. In general, they found that most of the shifting from one set of norms to the other resulted from profiles that were not clearly defined; that is, the scores in the profile were close to one another, within the standard error of measurement. Tellegen & Ben-Porath (1993) concluded that if well-defined codes were used, then the codes were stable and tended not to vary substantially between the two versions of the inventory.

A second debate involved a critique of the MMPI and MMPI-2 by Helmes & Reddon (1993), who questioned the entire basis of the original MMPI, such as the way the scales were derived, the psychometric properties of the scales, and the scales' vulnerability to response sets. Helmes & Reddon (1993) also criticized some of the decisions made in revising the MMPI-2. A reply by YS Ben-Porath, A Tellegen, RL Graham, and JN Butcher (unpublished manuscript) questioned the accuracy of many of Helmes & Reddon's criticisms. Ben-Porath et al specifically noted that Helmes & Reddon (1993) critiqued the MMPI clinical scales on the basis of uses that no longer apply to these scales. Ben-Porath et al also noted that Helmes & Reddon failed to provide any empirical justification for their suggestions that so-called modern personality inventories may offer advantages over the MMPI-2. Readers interested in issues central to the psychometric structure of objective personality question-naires would probably find these discussions informative.

Rorschach

Criticisms of the Rorschach abound, and many academic psychologists have expressed the belief that knowledge of projective testing is not as important as it used to be and that use of projective tests will likely decline in the future (Durand et al 1988, Piotrowski & Zalewski 1993, Watkins 1991). However, the continued broad interest in the Rorschach is clearly noted in the data shown in Table 1. For each year reviewed and for the summation of the 20 years, the Rorschach Inkblot technique was the second most fre-quently researched personality assessment method. Moreover, most PhD and PsyD clinical psychology training programs include formal instruction in the use of the Rorschach (Frohnauer et al 1988, Piotrowski & Zalewski 1993), and the majority of the internship sites approved by the American Psychological Association place a high value on knowledge of the method (Durand et al 1988). The Rorschach continues to be listed among the most frequently used methods for assessing personality in a variety of clinical settings and is often surpassed only by the MMPI or MMPI-2 (Archer et al 1991, Ball et al 1994, Lees-Haley 1992, Ornberg & Zalewski 1994, Piotrowski et al 1993, Wat-kins 1991, Watkins et al 1995). Recent trends have focused on the use of the Rorschach as a companion to the MMPI-2, rather than as an alternative, which allows for the integration of the strengths of these two diverse ap-proaches (Acklin 1993; Archer & Krishnamurthy 1993a,b; Lovitt 1993; Meyer 1993; Weiner 1993). Much of the strength of the Rorschach method in con-temporary assessment comes from the broad use of the Exner Comprehensive System (Exner 1991, 1993, 1995; Exner & Weiner 1994), which provides a more reliable and objective basis for interpretation than was available prior to its introduction.

A number of recent Rorschach studies have addressed clinical problems or populations such as adolescents in residential treatment (Abraham et al 1994), dependent patients (Bornstein et al 1993), alexithymia (Bornstein & O'Neill 1993), thought-disordered patients (Harris 1993, Perry & Braff 1994), criminal offenders (Heraute 1993), borderline and narcissistic patients (Hilsenroth et al 1993), paranoid schizophrenics (Johnson & Quinlan 1993), women who com-mit murder (Kaser-Boyd 1993), and sex-crime murderers (Meloy et al 1994).

Whether viewed from the perspective of research attention or practical usage, the Rorschach Inkblot technique remains among the most popular per-sonality assessment methods, and predictions about the technique's demise appear both unwarranted and unrealistic.

Thematic Apperception Test (TAT)

The TAT continues to be used as a clinical assessment tool and research instrument to study motivation and fantasy. Although much of the research on the TAT centers around nonclinical studies of, for example, studies in industry (Jacobs & McClelland 1994), with normal populations such as the aging (Shanan 1993), or in problem solving in normals (Alvarado 1994; Peterson & Ulrey 1994; Ronan et al 1993, 1995; Zeldow & McAdams 1993), clinical samples are still emphasized. Studies have reported on Alzheimer's disease (Johnson 1994), schizophrenic parents (Karon & Widener 1994), juvenile delinquents (Pinkerman et al 1993, Zeiller & Barnoud 1993), and sexually abused girls (Ornduff et al 1994, Pistole & Ornduff 1994). Research continues to be conducted on norms (Zhang et al 1993) and on the development of scoring methods for protocols (Hibbard et al 1994, Ronan et al 1993).

Sixteen Personality Factors (16PF)

Because of its nonpathology-oriented item content, the 16PF inventory is used and researched primarily with nonclinical samples; however, there were a number of clinically related assessment studies during the period of review. Research centered on such factors as alcoholism (Rodriguez 1994); heritability of hostility (Cates et al 1993); juvenile delinquency (Gerstein & Briggs 1993); personality factors in medical disease such as renal disease (Hernandez-Moreno et al 1993), cancer (Nair et al 1993), and myocardial infarction (Pruneti et al 1993); somatic disorders (Rotenberg & Michailov 1993); and war-related stress (Poikolainen 1993).

Millon Clinical Multiaxial Inventory (MCMI/MCMI-II/MCMI-III)

The MCMI/MCMI-II/MCMI-III personality scales were developed by Millon (1977, 1987, 1994) to aid in the classification of personality disorders according to the *Diagnostic and Statistical Manual (DSM)* in defined clinical populations. The MCMI instruments are firmly based on a categorical model of psychopathology, in contrast with the trend described by Ben-Porath (1994) toward dimensional models. We were able to locate 384 publications on the MCMI published since 1980. During the current review period, 87 articles were published covering such topics as differential diagnosis (Guthrie & Mobley 1994), limitations on use of the test (Wakefield & Underwager 1993), and its susceptibility to response bias (Dyer 1994). Clinical research on the MCMI has been increasing, as noted in Table 1. As described in Millon's manual (Millon 1994), the MCMI-III was developed for use with psychiatric patients. The test developer did not employ normative scores based on a normal population but used base rate scores to place a patient's score into a disordered category. Consequently, anyone taking the test is assumed to be a patient, and the scales simply address the type of personality disorder they might have. This makes the instrument likely to produce false positives when it is used with nonclinical populations. However, efforts have been made to extend the MCMI instruments to nonclinical populations (Grillo et al 1994, King 1994, McKee & Klohn 1994). The success of this broadening of the MCMI's scope to nonclinical samples has not yet been assessed (Berry et al 1995).

Basic Personality Inventory (BPI) and Personality Assessment Inventory (PAI)

The BPI (Jackson 1989) and the PAI (Morey 1991) are general psychopathology scales that were devised as alternatives to the MMPI. The constructs measured by these instruments bear a close resemblance to those measured by the MMPI and MMPI-2. The developers of the BPI and PAI describe efforts to assess similar pathologic domains with very similar scales developed by a rational scale-construction approach. Both instruments contain fewer items, however, than the MMPI-2. The BPI has been available for about nine years and the PAI for about four. As yet, few studies exist from which to obtain a clear picture of their effectiveness as clinical measures. For the 9-year period, we found only 31 articles on the BPI, and for the 4-year period only 7 articles for the PAI. It will take more research with a broad range of patients to determine how well these measures perform in clinical assessment. One recent study by Grigoriadis et al (1994) provided a direct comparison of the effectiveness between the BPI and the MMPI-2 at predicting symptoms and reported that both instruments significantly discriminated symptoms, with comparable hit rates for the MMPI-2 (84%) and the BPI (81%).

Revised NEO Personality Inventory (NEO-PI-R)

The NEO-PI-R, along with a shorter companion test, the NEO Five-Factor Inventory (NEO-FFI), has been developed to assess the five broad domains of the so-called Five-Factor Model of Personality (Costa & McCrae 1992a). Recent research has examined the use of the NEO scales in the context of vocational interest (Gottfredson et al 1993, Holland et al 1993), alcoholism (Martin & Sher 1994), suicide (Duberstein et al 1994), PTSD (Talbert et al 1993), and Alzheimer's disease (Strauss et al 1993).

As clinical assessment tools, the NEO scales have been criticized for their narrowness. Ben-Porath & Waller (1992) noted that five broad factors are unlikely to provide information specific enough for the needs of clinical applications. As a response to such criticism, a hierarchical framework has been proposed for the NEO-PI-R. For each of the five broad domains, six so-called facet scores, subfactors, have been developed in an effort to provide the specific level of information necessary for clinicians (Costa & McCrae 1995). Contradictory findings have been obtained, however, regarding the validity of the hierarchical organization of the 30 facets within the five domains. Confirmatory factor analysis of the 30 facets does not consistently reproduce the five domains of the NEO-PI-R (Parker et al 1993, Piedmont & Weinstein 1993). Costa & McCrae (1995) acknowledge that the examination of a NEO-PI-R profile may reveal discrepancies between a domain score and its subordinate facets. For example, a client may obtain an average-level score on one domain, but facet scores within that domain may range from very low to very high. They argue, however, that this is not a source of concern; if it is true that the domains provide only the superficial information that one would need to know to interact with a stranger, one should recall that "the new patient is always a stranger to the clinician, and individuals—especially individuals in psychotherapy—are often strangers to themselves. Analysis of personality at the domain level is only a starting place, but it is a very good starting place" (p. 44). One would hope, however, that a clinical assessment technique would allow a clinician to learn more about a person's psychological functioning than one knows about a stranger. If the domain scores provide clinicians with no more than superficial hypotheses, they may have limited clinical utility. Ben-Porath & Waller (1992) also criticized the absence of validity scales on the NEO-PI-R as a major hindrance to the use of this test in clinical assessment.

ASSESSMENT OF PROTOCOL VALIDITY

Central to personality assessment is the credibility of a patient's self-report. Has the individual taking the test produced a valid, interpretable protocol? Personality assessment instruments, in order to be effective, must have validity scales that can appraise the subject's level of cooperation, willingness to share personal information, and degree of response exaggeration. For example, Harkness & Hogan (1995) have argued that if assessments are viewed as communications from patients, it is important to evaluate the intent or pragmatic purpose of such communications. More comprehensive assessment measures are needed to appraise the client's motivation in responding to the test items. In a recent informative review of research on the use of validity scales to assess malingering, Berry et al (1995) compared several personality scales and pointed out the extent to which these instruments addressed invalidating response sets.

Among personality scales the MMPI-2 contains the most extensive validity indicators (Bagby et al 1995; Berry et al 1991a, 1992, 1995; Schretlen et al 1992). In addition to the traditional MMPI validity scales (Cannot Say, L, F, and K) several new validity scales have been introduced. Two new response inconsistency scales, the Variable Response Inconsistency Scale (VRIN) and the True Response Inconsistency Scale (TRIN), have become standard validity indicators for random responding and acquiescence and have been the subject of a number of recent investigations (Berry et al 1991b, 1992). Additional scales intended to assess infrequent responding have been incorporated in the standard invalidity measures, the F(B) or Back F Scale (Berry et al 1991b) and the F(p) or Inpatient Psychopathology Scale (Arbisi & Ben-Porath 1995). These measures were developed to assess infrequent or exaggerated responding under special conditions. The F(B) scale assesses infrequent responding to items in the back of the MMPI-2 booklet (Iverson et al 1995). The F(p) scale assesses infrequent or exaggerated responding in populations with high base rates of psychopathology (Arabisi & Ben-Porath 1995). A new scale meant to assess virtuous self-presentation has been published (Butcher & Han 1995), and several studies examining its effectiveness at detecting symptom underreporting have been completed (Baer et al 1995, Lim 1994, Rhodes 1995). Empirical research on MMPI-2 validity scales covers a broad range of designs, questions, and populations (Bagby et al 1994a,b; Berry et al 1994; Boone 1994b; Borum & Stock 1993; Butcher 1994b; Coons 1993; Costello et al 1993; Dannenbaum & Lanyon 1993; DuAlba & Scott 1993; Dush et al 1994; Ganellin 1994; Gallucci 1993; Graham 1993; Lamb et al 1994; Leckart 1994; Munley et al 1993; Owens & Harms 1993; Rogers et al 1993a; Rothke et al 1994; Timbrook et al 1993; Weed 1993; Wetter et al 1992, 1993).

The MCMI addresses invalidating response conditions by including measures such as the Validity Index for symptom overreporting, random responding, and faking; the Disclosure Scale to assess whether the individual was responding openly to items; the Debasement Scale to assess whether the individual was answering openly; and the Desirability Scale to determine whether the individual minimizes problems (Choca et al 1992, Millon 1994). Some support can be found in the literature for the validity measures in the MCMI-II; however, Berry et al (1995) pointed out that the validity indices for the MCMI scales were developed on a "small and highly selected derivation sample and rational determination of BR scores suggests the need for careful cross-validation in clinically relevant samples." Several studies in the period under review have addressed the utility of the Millon validity indicators (Bishop 1993; Craig et al 1994; Dyer 1994; Grillo et al 1994; Wierzbicki 1993a,b).

The PAI contains four validity scales: Inconsistency, Infrequency, Impression Management Negative (NIM), and Positive Impression Management (PIM). There is little information, outside of the test manual, available on the effectiveness of these scales at detecting invalidating conditions. One article (Rogers et al 1993b) in the period of our review examined the effectiveness of Negative Impression Management at detecting simulated psychopathology. The NIM scale was effective at detecting feigned schizophrenia, marginally effective in detecting feigned depression, and ineffective at detecting feigned generalized anxiety disorder.

The BPI does not address protocol validity directly, in part because the test developer considers that "deliberate efforts to distort responses are rare in clinical applications of psychological tests" (Jackson 1989, p. 22). However, two measures that can be considered validity indicators are the Denial and Deviation scales. These measures have recently been studied with prison inmates by Kroner & Reddon (1994).

Berry et al (1995) noted that the NEO-PI-R does not address response validity and recommended against using the instrument in situations in which "malingering is an important consideration," because no normal validity scales are included in the test. The NEO-PI-R contains only one validity item that simply asks respondents whether they have answered honestly. In addition, the test manual for the NEO-PI-R recommends examining the answer sheet for unusual response patterns, such as use of contiguous "Strongly Agree" responses. Berry et al (1995) considered the NEO-PI-R's approach to assessment of malingering to be ineffective.

Finally, some recent research has assessed malingering or defensive responding on the Rorschach. Ganellen (1994) evaluated whether a defensive response set would distort responses to the Rorschach in such a way that patients might conceal psychological problems. Frueh & Kinder (1994) conducted a study to determine whether individuals who malingered PTSD symptoms could be detected. Both studies reported indices that provide clues to assessing deviating response conditions on the Rorschach.

ASSESSMENT OF AXIS II DISORDERS

Assessment of personality disorder can be reliably obtained by structured interview, such as the SCID-II or the SIDP-R; however, these approaches require extensive time to administer. Widiger & Sanderson (1995) recommended that clinicians first administer and score one of the personality disorder questionnaires to guide the structured interview. Several personality assessment techniques are available for this purpose.

Assessment of personality disorder was an active area of research in the period under review. New measures have been introduced; for example, the Schedule for Normal or Abnormal Personality (SNAP) (Clark 1994), the Wisconsin Personality Disorders Inventory (Klein et al 1993), and the Hare Psychopathy Checklist—Revised (Hare 1992). However, most of the studies reported involve existing measures such as the MCMI (Alexander 1993, Antoni 1993, Chick et al 1993, Divac-Jovanovic et al 1993, Inch & Crossley 1993, Norman et al 1993, Patrick 1993, Reich 1993, Soldz et al 1993, Swirsky Sacchetti et al 1993, Tisdale & Pendleton 1993, Wetzler & Marlow 1993,

Widiger & Corbitt 1993), the MMPI (Chatham et al 1993, Schotte et al 1993, Schubert 1993, Serper et al 1993, Swirsky Sacchetti et al 1993, Trull 1993, Wetzler & Marlowe 1993), and the Rorschach (Berg et al 1993, Gacono 1993, Harris 1993, Hilsenroth et al 1993, Murray 1993, Rossel et al 1993). Personality disorder scales have been developed for the original MMPI (Bagby 1990, Morey et al 1985) and for the MMPI-2 (Somwaru & Ben-Porath 1995).

The extensive research effort in this area is a result of the desire to provide more objective differentiation in personality disorder, on Axis II conditions. With the recent publication of *DSM-IV* (APA 1994) and some restructuring of disorders on Axis II, further research in this area is likely. As in the past, much of the research in the assessment of personality disorder centers on antisocial personality—perhaps because it can be reliably diagnosed (Widiger & Sanderson 1995).

CAN THE FIVE-FACTOR MODEL BE USEFUL IN CLINICAL ASSESSMENT?

Recent literature in the field of personality assessment continues to focus on the so-called Five-Factor Model (FFM), or Big Five, a set of factor-analytically derived constructs proposed to map the basic underlying structure of personality organization. Because we do not share its adherents' view that this approach provides such a comprehensive model, we refer to it here as the Five-Factor Approach (FFA). Readers who are unfamiliar with the FFA are referred to McCrae & John (1992) and McAdams (1992) for an introduction to its strengths and weaknesses. Proponents of the FFA have made dramatic claims about its usefulness for the study and assessment of personality structure. Some believe the existence of five, and only five, factors to be an empirical fact as undeniable as the existence of seven continents on earth (McCrae & John 1992) and as valuable as the cartographic convention of using four directional poles (i.e. north, south, east, and west) in geography and navigation (Goldberg 1993). Despite this enthusiasm, numerous critics have resisted the invitation to "jump on the Big Five bandwagon" (Ben-Porath & Waller 1992, Butcher 1994c, Davis & Millon 1993, Epstein 1994, Eysenck 1992, Kline & Barrett 1994, McAdams 1992, Montag & Levin 1994, Pervin 1994, Van Heck et al 1994). Recent criticism has focused on the FFA's inability to incorporate stage theories, such as ego development and moral development (Loevinger 1994), its reliance on the lexical hypothesis i.e. that important individual differences in personality are encoded in common languages (Pervin 1994)], and its dependence upon the potentially arbitrary method of factor analysis (Block 1995). On this last point, Loevinger (1994, p. 6) wrote, "There is no reason to believe that the bedrock of personality is a set of orthogonal...factors, unless you think that nature is constrained to present us a world in rows and columns. That would be convenient for many purposes, particularly given the statistical programs already installed on our computers. But is it realistic?"

Proponents of the model have suggested that Axis II diagnoses contained in the *DSM-III-R* (APA 1987) and *DSM-IV* (APA 1994) can be conceptualized in the terminology of the FFA (Costa & McCrae 1990, 1992b; Costa & Widiger 1994; Widiger & Costa 1994). Widiger (1993) argued that the use of a categorical diagnostic system can no longer be justified by empirical research; dimensional models may be more effective. On the basis of theoretical and empirical relationships, an attempt was made to demonstrate how each of the Axis II disorders could be meaningfully related to constructs from the FFA. Five broad factors, however, appeared to be insufficient to describe the differences among the disorders, and Widiger was required to invoke 30 so-called facets of the Big Five. For example, in Widiger's conceptualization, Schizoid Personality Disorder could be understood as low levels of Hostility, Self-Consciousness, Warmth, Gregariousness, Excitement Seeking, Positive Emotions, Feelings, and Achievement Striving, along with a high level of Compliance. Unfortunately, within the factors, Widiger occasionally had to invoke contradictory facets. For example, Dependent Personality Disorder was hypothesized to relate to a high level of Warmth and a low level of Assertiveness; both of these characteristics, however, are listed as facets of a single factor, Extraversion. In attempting to show that these disorders could be conceptualized as different configurations of the Big Five, Widiger demonstrated that these disorders can only be conceptualized as different configurations of the "Little Thirty." Used alone, the five factors are too broad to lend themselves to specific behaviors of clinical concern (Benjamin 1993). For example, to conceptualize Borderline Personality Disorder merely as high levels of Extraversion, Openness, and Neuroticism and low levels of Agreeableness and Conscientiousness does not allow for a comprehensive understanding of the problematic behavior patterns.

A variety of criticism has been raised against such procrustean attempts to force Axis II disorders into the artificial structure of the FFA. First, empirical research has not supported the hypothesized relationship between the FFA and Axis II disorders. Using a measure of personality disorders and the five factors, Clark (1993) found that each personality disorder scale was only modestly related to one of the five factors. As a result, differentiation among the personality disorder scales was not possible. For example, Neuroticism was significantly related to both Avoidant Personality Disorder ($r^2 = .16$) and Dependent Personality Disorder ($r^2 = .18$). Because no other factor was related to either of these two personality disorder scales, and because each had similar r^2 values, it would not be possible to discriminate between these very different disorders using only the five factors.

Second, the FFA is insufficient because many of the concepts that are important in the assessment of personality pathology were systematically underrepresented in the development of the FFA (Tellegen 1993, Waller & Zavala 1993). Allport and Odbert believed that affect-laden and evaluative terms were inappropriate for the scientific study of personality; as a result, such terms were excluded from their original list of trait terms. However, affective trait terms are important aspects of many Axis II disorders, and evaluative terms are necessary to represent personality pathology (Tellegen 1993). Ironically, the term "agreeable," which is now used to define one of the five factors, was originally considered to be an evaluative term and therefore not appropriate for the study of personality traits (Waller & Zavala 1993). When highly inclusive criteria, allowing both affective terms and evaluative terms, are used to construct a lexicon of trait terms, seven factors are required to account for the variance. Of these seven factors, five bear some resemblance to the FFA, although the meanings are slightly different owing to the inclusion of terms that would have been eliminated by Allport and Odbert. The two factors that cannot be absorbed into the FFA are Positive Valence, which is conceptualized as a continuum from Excellent to Ordinary, and Negative Valence, which is conceptualized as a continuum from Decent to Cruel (Tellegen 1993, Waller & Zavala 1993). Although Shopshire & Craik (1994) argued that they obtained an FFA-like solution by factor-analyzing diagnostic criteria for *DSM-III-R* Axis II disorders, the evaluative nature of the criteria makes it difficult to reconcile their solution with the nonevaluative FFA. In addition, in the case of some major structural differences (e.g. two factors were needed to account for Introversion and Extraversion; no Openness component emerged), some components bear only superficial resemblance to their FFA counterparts. For example, the component labeled "Conscientiousness-Perfectionism" was most highly related to aspects of paralyzing perfectionism and ethical rigidity. It would be difficult to argue that ineffectuality and inflexibility are merely extreme variants of conscientiousness, efficiency, and dependability. Although they bear similar titles, they appear to be two different psychological constructs.

Third, the method by which the FFA was developed could represent an analysis of common linguistic structure, not one of personality or behavior. To argue that the lexical approach is more than just a semantic exercise, one would need to demonstrate that casual observers are capable of perceiving and discriminating among the important aspects of personality pathology (Schacht 1993). If these concepts are accessible to the casual observer, it would be more meaningful to refer to these as general folk concepts, not psychological concepts. In this case, the FFA is not appropriate for the scientific study of personality because the maturation of a scientific discipline usually involves the development of concepts that explain common phenomena in ways that are not possible for folk concepts (Tellegen 1993). It is not desirable to reduce the study of personality pathology to the common denominator of folk concepts that appear in common language (Schacht 1993).

Critics are not arguing that the FFA's constructs are unrelated to psychopathology; they are, however, unwilling to accept the assertion that the important aspects of personality pathology can be comfortably nested within the Big Five. Recent research demonstrates that various symptoms of psychopathology are statistically related to the factors of the FFA (Hart & Hare 1994, Trull & Sher 1994, Zuroff 1994). However, the relationships observed indicate that the FFA cannot sufficiently account for the variance in measures of pathology.

An alternative dimensional representation of Axis II disorders is the Personality Psychopathology Five, or the PSY-5 (Harkness & McNulty 1994). Unlike the FFA, which emerged from lists of nonevaluative trait terms in the common language, the PSY-5 were developed through the factor analysis of a set of terms that included both nonadaptive descriptors (i.e. representative diagnostic criteria for the Axis II disorders in the *DSM-III-R*) and adaptive descriptors (i.e. markers of several normal personality traits). Five factors emerged from the heterogeneous set of descriptors: Aggressiveness, Psychoticism, Constraint, Negative Emotionality/Neuroticism, and Positive Emotionality/Extraversion. The measurement of the PSY-5 constructs in the MMPI-2 is described by Harkness et al (1995). Although there are some surface-level similarities between the PSY-5 dimensions and the FFA, the PSY-5 are likely to be mapping a different universe of psychological concepts because it originated from diagnostic criteria of nonadaptive personality. For example, Harkness & McNulty (1994) argued that while the PSY-5 factor Constraint and the FFA factor Conscientiousness may appear similar at a superficial level, they are tapping two distinctly different constructs; the characteristics of a person with a low level of Constraint (e.g. impulsivity, rule breaking, abandonment of traditional morality) are dissimilar to traditional markers of low Conscientiousness (e.g. disorganization, inefficiency). Although substantial research would be necessary before one could argue that the PSY-5 adequately represents the structure of personality pathology, the PSY-5 is intuitively more appealing than the FFA because it originated not from nonevaluative common terms but from *DSM* diagnostic criteria. Those who are dissatisfied with categorical models in assessment of abnormal behavior and are seeking dimensional replacements (Widiger 1993) may find the PSY-5 more appropriate than the less pathologically oriented items in the Big Five.

COMPUTER-BASED PERSONALITY ASSESSMENT

During the period considered in this review several general guidelines or reviews of computer-based assessment applications appeared. The American

Psychological Association (APA 1993) published the *Guidelines for Computer-Based Assessment*. The impact of computers in several areas has been addressed: personality (Eyde et al 1993), behavioral assessment (Farrell 1993), psychological intervention (Bloom 1992), memory assessment (Crook et al 1992), and offender classification (Jemelka et al 1992). Several articles were published on the role of computer-based testing in contemporary psychological assessment (Butcher 1994a, First 1994, Flowers et al 1993, Spinhoven et al 1993). The most extensive psychometric utilization of computer capability in computer-based personality assessment has involved efforts to apply IRT-based models and other adaptive testing techniques for item administration in order to abbreviate the task (Holden et al 1991; Roper et al 1991, 1995).

CLINICAL ASSESSMENT IN MANAGED CARE

One of the most formidable challenges facing mental-health practitioners today is determining what role clinical assessment will have in the evolving system of managed mental health care. In one respect clinical assessment, because of its relatively low cost and objective methods, appears to fit well in managed-care service delivery. On the other hand, in an era of shrinking funds available for mental-health services psychological assessment may be eliminated from the health-care loop unless assessment psychologists can document that psychological testing provides treatment-relevant and cost-effective information and is relevant and valid for treatment planning. With the ever-increasing focus on the need for effective, abbreviated treatment, psychological assessment has come to be viewed by many as an essential component of efficient mental-health treatments. Objective psychological testing has also been considered one means of assuring accountability in service provision because tests can be used to evaluate progress in treatment as well as to guide practitioners toward appropriate services. By developing methods and strategies for client evaluation, assessment psychologists help patients to benefit from the use of mental-health services. The most highly developed and widely used assessment-treatment feedback model being incorporated in health maintenance organizations today for treatment planning is an MMPI/MMPI-2–based feedback used to facilitate the treatment process (Butcher 1990, Erdberg 1979, Finn & Tonsager 1992, Quirk et al 1995). The incorporation of psychological-test feedback in therapy can help to focus treatment. A high-quality problem-focused assessment can help build the therapeutic alliance and can in and of itself have therapeutic potency (Finn & Tonsager 1992). Assessment will likely be combined with therapy more frequently in the future as managed mental health care programs evolve.

ETHICS AND TESTING

The recent revision of the APA's (1992) Ethical Principles of Psychologists and Code of Conduct is the most significant in a decade (Keith-Speigel 1994). Assessment psychologists should examine those aspects of the code that relate to psychological testing. Prominent themes in the new ethical code are competence and qualified use of assessment procedures (see standards 2.02 and 2.06). Because of the harm that can result from their misapplication, the code recognizes that clinical psychologists must be formally trained in the use of assessment instruments (Canter et al 1994). Moreland et al (1995) argued that much of the criticism that has been aimed at psychological assessment in the past resulted from misuse of tests by unqualified individuals; test publishers, they suggested, should more carefully qualify those permitted to purchase their instruments. Today most publishers qualify purchasers based only on educational degree and licensure status, despite the fact that passing the national licensing examination guarantees no competence in psychological testing. Moreland et al proposed a qualification system based on competencies. An example of an empirically based qualification form was presented that acknowledges seven factors of testing competency: comprehensive assessment, proper test use, psychometric knowledge, maintenance of the integrity of test results, accuracy of scoring, appropriate use of norms, and the provision of interpretive feedback. Although the practicality of this proposal should be examined, it appears to match the spirit of the new ethics code.

A substantial change in the new code of ethics is the mandate to use assessment techniques that are appropriate to an "individual's gender, age, race, ethnicity, national origin, religion, sexual orientation, disability, language, or socioeconomic status" (APA 1992, p. 1603). Whereas the code has been criticized for not providing practical guidelines for solving problems in this controversial area (Dana 1994), it highlights the need to consider a client's age (Morin & Colecchi 1995), gender (Worell & Robinson 1995), neurological functioning (Gass & Ansley 1995), ethnic background, and language (Gray-Little 1995, Okazaki & Sue 1995, Velásquez 1995) in the selection of personality assessment techniques.

One arena in which assessment psychologists may face ethical dilemmas is forensic assessment (Butcher & Pope 1993, Pope et al 1993), particularly in cases that affect the welfare of a child (Brodinsky 1993, McAnulty 1993, Otto & Butcher 1995, Small & Melton 1994) or when the psychologist receives a subpoena or court order requesting that "raw" psychological data (such as test scores or item responses) be released to individuals who are not qualified to interpret them (Tranel 1994). Butcher & Pope (1993) discussed several ethical issues that should be considered by forensic psychologists while conducting psychological assessment, such as using tests that fit the task at hand, using tests that fit the individual, and considering the accuracy and validity of computerized interpretive reports.

CONCLUSIONS

Research in clinical personality assessment continues to be carried out at a high rate. Although new instruments are being published to address clinical problems, traditional assessment approaches continue to elicit broad usage and further research. The MMPI (now MMPI-2) remains the most popular instrument for both clinical application and psychopathology research. Two other clinical personality instruments with a long tradition, the Rorschach and TAT, continue to find a place in research and clinical assessment despite perennial predictions of their forthcoming demise.

A number of new assessment instruments have surfaced recently and promise to more fully address areas, such as personality disorders, that traditional instruments may inadequately have addressed. Many recognize the Five-Factor Model as too superficial to help much in clinical assessment, which requires more refined and broadened personality and symptom foci than are provided through the narrow lens of only five factors.

Researchers remain concerned over the veracity of the assessment results they obtain from their clients, and a number of new approaches have been evolving to assess response bias that could invalidate test performance. New personality instruments that do not provide a comprehensive enough means of accounting for invalidating conditions are not likely to gain many followers in assessment settings in which response motivations require careful consideration.

Clinical personality assessment has faced and successfully survived a number of challenges in the past, ranging from behavioristic reductionism to the invasion-of-privacy controversy. The newest challenge stems from the health-care revolution, in which managed-care providers are reluctant to pay for assessment out of the shrinking health-care dollar. Assessment psychologists need to gear up for this challenge and are currently doing so by developing models for the incorporation of assessment information into treatment itself in order to bring psychometric sophistication to the art of behavior change. The future is likely to see more extensive research and theoretical development in this endeavor.

Literature Cited

Abraham PP, Lepisto BL, Lewis MG, Schultz L. 1994. An outcome study: changes in Rorschach variables of adolescents in residential treatment. *J. Pers. Assess.* 62: 505–14

Acklin MW. 1993. Integrating the Rorschach and the MMPI in clinical assessment: conceptual and methodological issues. *J. Pers. Assess.* 60:125–31

Alexander PC. 1993. The differential effects of abuse characteristics and attachment in the prediction of long-term effects of sexual abuse. *J. Interpers. Violence* 8: 346–62

Alvarado N. 1994. Empirical validity of the Thematic Apperception Test. *J. Pers. Assess.* 63:59–79

American Psychiatric Association. 1987. *Diagnostic and Statistical Manual of Mental Disorders, Revised.* Washington DC: Am. Psychiatr. Assoc. 3rd ed.

American Psychiatric Association. 1994. *Diagnostic and Statistical Manual of Mental Disorders.* Washington, DC: Am. Psychiatr. Assoc. 4th ed.

American Psychological Association. 1992. Ethical principles of psychologists and code of conduct. *Am. Psychol.* 47: 1597–1611

American Psychological Association. 1993. *Guidelines for Computer-Based Tests and Interpretation.* Washington, DC: Am. Psychol. Assoc.

Antoni M. 1993. The combined use of the MCMI and MMPI. See Craig 1993, pp. 279–302

Arbisi PA, Ben-Porath YS. 1995. An MMPI-2 infrequent response scale for use with psychopathological populations: the F(p) Scale. *Psychol. Assess.* In press

Archer RP, Krishnamurthy R. 1993a. A review of MMPI and Rorschach interrelationships in adult samples. *J. Pers. Assess.* 62: 277–93

Archer RP, Krishnamurthy R. 1993b. Combining the Rorschach and the MMPI in the assessment of adolescents. *J. Pers. Assess.* 60:132–40

Archer RP, Maruish M, Imhof EA, Piotrowski C. 1991. Psychological test usage with adolescent clients: 1990 survey findings. *Prof. Psychol. Res. Pract.* 22:247–52

Baer RA, Wetter MW, Nichols DS, Greene R, Berry DTR. 1995. Sensitivity of MMPI-2 validity scales to underreporting of symptoms. *Psychol. Assess.* In press

Bagby RM. 1990. Status of the MMPI personality disorder scales on the MMPI-2. *MMPI-2 News Profiles* 1:8

Bagby RM, Buis T, Nicholson RA. 1995. Relative effectiveness of the standard validity scales in detecting fake-bad and fake-good responding: replication and extension. *Psychol. Assess.* 7:84–92

Bagby RM, Rogers R, Buis T. 1994a. Detecting malingering and defensive responding on the MMPI-2 in a forensic inpatient sample. *J. Pers. Assess.* 62:191–203

Bagby RM, Rogers R, Buis T, Kalemba V. 1994b. Malingered and defensive response styles on the MMPI-2: an examination of validity scales. *Assessment* 1:31–38

Ball JD, Archer RP, Imhof EA. 1994. Time requirements of psychological testing: a survey of practitioners. *J. Pers. Assess.* 63: 239–49

Benjamin LS. 1993. Dimensional, categorical, or hybrid analyses of personality: a response to Widiger's proposal. *Psychol. Inq.* 4:91–95

Ben-Porath YS. 1994. The MMPI and MMPI-2: fifty years of differentiating normal and abnormal personality. See Strack & Lorr 1994, pp. 361–401

Ben-Porath YS, McCully E, Almagor M. 1993. Incremental validity of the MMPI-2 content scales in the assessment of personality and psychopathology by self-report. *J. Pers. Assess.* 61:557–75

Ben-Porath YS, Shondrick DD, Stafford KP. 1995. MMPI-2 and race in a forensic diagnostic sample. *Crim. Just. Beh.* 22:19–32

Ben-Porath YS, Tellegen A. 1992. Continuity and changes in MMPI-2 validity indicators: points of clarification. *MMPI-2 News Profiles* 3:6–8

Ben-Porath YS, Tellegen A. 1995. How (not) to evaluate the comparability of MMPI and MMPI-2 profile configurations: a reply to Humphrey and Dahlstrom. *J. Pers. Assess.* In press

Ben-Porath YS, Waller NG. 1992. Five big issues in clinical personality assessment: a rejoinder to Costa and McCrae. *Psychol. Assess.* 4:23–25

Berg JL, Packer A, Nunno VJ. 1993. A Rorschach analysis: parallel disturbance in thought and in self/object representation. *J. Pers. Assess.* 61:311–23

Berger P. 1994. *Psychopathologic correlates of female incarcerated infanticides, filicides, and homicides on the MMPI-2.* PhD thesis. Forest Inst. Prof. Psychol.

Berry DTR, Baer RA, Harris MJ. 1991a. Detection of malingering on the MMPI: a meta-analysis. *Clin. Psychol. Rev.* 11: 585–91

Berry DTR, Lamb DG, Wetter MW, Baer RA. 1994. Ethical considerations in research on coached malingering. *Psychol. Assess.* 6:16–17

Berry DTR, Wetter M, Baer R. 1995. Assessment of malingering. See Butcher 1995b, pp. 236–48

Berry DTR, Wetter MW, Baer RA, Larsen L, Clark C, Monroe K. 1992. MMPI-2 random responding indices: validation using a self-report methodology. *Psychol. Assess.* 4:340–45

Berry DTR, Wetter MW, Baer RA, Widiger TA, Sumpter JC, et al. 1991b. Detection of random responding on the MMPI-2: utility of F, Back F, and VRIN scales. *Psychol. Assess.* 3:418–23

Bishop DR. 1993. Validity issues in using the Millon-II with substance users. *Psychol. Rep.* 73:27–33

Block J. 1995. A contrarian view of the five-factor approach to personality description. *Psychol. Bull.* In press

Bloom BL. 1992. Computer-assisted psychological intervention: a review and commentary. *Clin. Psychol. Rev.* 12:169–97

Boone DE. 1994a. Validity of the MMPI-2 Depression content scale with psychiatric inpatients. *Psychol. Rep.* 74:159–62

Boone DE. 1994b. Reliability of the MMPI-2 subtle and obvious scales with psychiatric inpatients. *J. Pers. Assess.* 62:346–51

Bornstein RF, Manning KA, Krukonis AB, Rossner SC. 1993. Sex differences in dependency: a comparison of objective and projective measures. *J. Pers. Assess.* 61: 169–81

Bornstein RF, O'Neill RM. 1993. Construct validity of a self-report measure of alexithymia in a psychiatric inpatient sample. *J. Clin. Psychol.* 49:841–46

Borum R, Stock HV. 1993. Detection of deception in law enforcement applicants: a preliminary investigation. *Law Hum. Behav.* 17:157–66

Brodinsky DM. 1993. On the use and misuse of psychological testing in child custody evaluations. *Prof. Psychol. Res. Pract.* 24: 213–19

Brophy AL. 1993. Cooke's disturbance index on the MMPI-2. *Psychol. Rep.* 72:345–46

Butcher JN. 1990. *The MMPI-2 in Psychological Treatment.* New York: Oxford Univ. Press

Butcher JN. 1994a. Psychological assessment by computer: potential gains and problems to avoid. *Psychol. Ann.* 24:20–24

Butcher JN. 1994b. Psychological assessment of airline pilot applicants with the MMPI-2. *J. Pers. Assess.* 62:31–44

Butcher JN. 1994c. *Trends in personality assessment: What will the new century be like?* Presented at Annu. Meet. Am. Psychol. Assoc., 102nd, Los Angeles

Butcher JN. 1995a. *International Adaptations of the MMPI-2: A Handbook of Research and Clinical Applications.* Minneapolis: Univ. Minn. Press

Butcher JN, ed. 1995b. *Clinical Personality Assessment: Practical Approaches.* New York: Oxford Univ. Press. 10th ed.

Butcher JN, Han K. 1995. Development of an MMPI-2 scale to assess the presentation of self in a superlative manner: the S Scale. In *Advances in Personality Assessment,* ed. JN Butcher, CD Spielberger, pp. 25–50. Hillsdale, NJ: Erlbaum

Butcher JN, Pope KS. 1993. Seven issues in conducting forensic assessment: ethical responsibilities in light of new standards and new tests. *Ethics Behav.* 3:267–88

Canter MB, Bennett BE, Jones SE, Nagy TF. 1994. *Ethics for Psychologists: A Commentary on the APA Ethics Code.* Washington, DC: Am. Psychol. Assoc.

Canul GD, Cross HJ. 1994. The influence of acculturation and racial identity attitudes on Mexican-Americans' MMPI-2 performance. *J. Clin Psychol.* 50:736–45

Cates DS, Houston BK, Vavak CR, Crawford MH. 1993. Heritability of hostility-related emotions, attitudes, and behaviors. *J. Behav. Med.* 16:237–56

Chatham PM, Tibbals CJ, Harrington ME. 1993. The MMPI and the MCMI in the evaluation of narcissism in a clinical sample. *J. Pers. Assess.* 60:239–51

Chick D, Sheaffer CI, Goggin WC, Sison GF. 1993. The relationship between MCMI personality scales and clinician-generated DSM-III-R personality disorder diagnoses. *J. Pers. Assess.* 61:264–76

Choca J, Shanley L, Van Denburg E. 1992. *Interpretive Guide to the Millon Multiaxial Personality Inventory.* Washington, DC: Am. Psychol. Assoc.

Chojnacki JT, Walsh WB. 1994. The consistency between scores of the Harris-Lingoes subscales of the MMPI and MMPI-2. *J. Pers. Assess.* 62:157–65

Clark LA. 1993. Personality disorder diagnosis: limitations of the Five-Factor model. *Psychol. Inq.* 4:100–4

Clark LA. 1994. *Schedule for Nonadaptive and Adaptive Personality: Manual for Administration, Scoring, and Interpretation.* Minneapolis: Univ. Minn. Press

Clark ME. 1994. Interpretive limitations of the MMPI-2 Anger and Cynicism content scales. *J. Pers. Assess.* 63:89–96

Colligan RC, Morey LC, Offord KP. 1994. The MMPI/MMPI-2 Personality Disorder scales: contemporary norms for adults and adolescents. *J. Clin. Psychol.* 50:168–200

Coons PM. 1993. Use of the MMPI to distinguish genuine from factitious multiple personality disorder. *Psychol. Rep.* 73:401–2

Costa PT Jr, McCrae RR. 1990. Personality disorders and the five-factor model of personality. *J. Pers. Disord.* 4:362–71

Costa PT Jr, McCrae RR. 1992a. *Manual for the Revised NEO Personality Inventory (NEO-PI-R) and NEO Five-Factor Inven-*

tory (NEO-FFI). Odessa, FL: Psychol. Assess. Resour.

Costa PT Jr, McCrae RR. 1992b. The five-factor model of personality and its relevance to personality disorders. *J. Pers. Disord.* 6:343–59

Costa PT Jr, McCrae RR. 1995. Domains and facets: hierarchical personality assessment using the Revised NEO Personality Inventory. *J. Pers. Assess.* 64:21–50

Costa PT Jr, Widiger TA. 1994. *Personality Disorders and the Five-Factor Model of Personality.* Washington, DC: Am. Psychol. Assoc.

Costello RM, Schneider SL, Schoenfeld LS. 1993. Applicants fraud in law enforcement. *Psychol. Rep.* 73:179–83

Craig RJ, ed. 1993. *The Millon Clinical Multiaxial Inventory: A Clinical Research Information Synthesis.* Hillsdale, NJ: Erlbaum

Craig RJ, Kuncel R, Olson RE. 1994. Ability of drug abusers to avoid detection of substance use on the MCMI-II. *J. Soc. Behav. Pers.* 9:95–106

Crook TH, Youngjohn JR, Larrabee GJ. 1992. Multiple equivalent test forms in computerized everyday memory battery. *Arch. Clin. Neuropsychol.* 7:221–32

Dahlstrom WG. 1992. Comparability of two-point high-point code patterns from original MMPI norms to MMPI-2 norms for the restandardization sample. *J. Pers. Assess.* 59:153–64

Dana RH. 1994. Testing and assessment ethics for all persons: beginning and agenda. *Prof. Psychol. Res. Pract.* 24:349–54

Dannenbaum SE, Lanyon RI. 1993. The use of subtle items in detecting deception. *J. Pers. Assess.* 61:501–10

Davis RD, Millon T. 1993. The Five-Factor model for personality disorders: apt or misguided? *Psychol. Inq.* 4:104–9

Deardorff WW, Chino AF, Scott DW. 1993. Characteristics of chronic pain patients: factor analysis of the MMPI-2. *Pain* 54: 153–58

Derksen J, de Mey H. 1994. De MMPI-2. Een "oudgediende" opnieuw in stelling gebracht. (The MMPI-2: an "old reliable" revised.) *Psycholoog* 29:138–42

Divac-Jovanovic M, Svrakic D, Lecic Tosevski D. 1993. Personality disorders: model for conceptual approach and classification. I. General model. *Am. J. Psychother.* 47:558–71

DuAlba L, Scott RL. 1993. Somatization and malingering for workers' compensation applicants: a cross-cultural MMPI study. *J. Clin. Psychol.* 49:913–17

Duberstein PR, Conwell Y, Caine ED. 1994. Age differences in the personality characteristics of suicide completers: preliminary findings from a psychological autopsy

study. *Psychiatr.: Interpers. Biol. Process.* 57:213–24

Durand VM, Blanchard EB, Mindell JA. 1988. Training in projective testing: survey of clinical training directors and internship directors. *Prof. Psychol. Res. Pract.* 19: 236–38

Dush DM, Simons LE, Platt M, Nation PC. 1994. Psychological profiles distinguishing litigating and nonlitigating pain patients: subtle, and not so subtle. *J. Pers. Assess.* 62:299–313

Dyer FJ. 1994. Factorial trait variance and response bias in MCMI-II personality disorder scales. *J. Pers. Disord.* 8:121–30

Edwards DW, Morrison TL, Weissman HN. 1993a. The MMPI and MMPI-2 in an outpatient sample: comparisons of code types, validity scales, and clinical scales. *J. Pers. Assess.* 61:1–18

Edwards DW, Morrison TL, Weissman HN. 1993b. Uniform versus linear T scores on the MMPI-2/MMPI in an outpatient psychiatric sample: differential contributions. *Psychol. Assess.* 5:499–500

Elwood RW. 1993. The clinical utility of the MMPI-2 in diagnosing unipolar depression among male alcoholics. *J. Pers. Assess.* 60: 511–21

Endler NS, Parker JDA, Butcher JN. 1993. A factor analytic study of coping styles and the MMPI-2 content scales. *J. Clin. Psychol.* 49:523–27

Epstein S. 1994. Trait theory as personality theory: Can a part be as great as the whole? *Psychol. Inq.* 5:120–22

Erdberg P. 1979. A systematic approach to providing feedback from the MMPI. In *MMPI Clinical and Research Trends,* ed. CS Newmark, pp. 328–42. New York: Praeger

Exner JE. 1991. *The Rorschach: A Comprehensive System,* Vol. 2, *Interpretation.* New York: Wiley

Exner JE. 1993. *The Rorschach: A Comprehensive System,* Vol. 1, *Basic Foundations.* New York: Wiley. 2nd ed.

Exner JE. 1995. Why use personality tests? A brief historical view. See Butcher 1995b, pp. 10–18

Exner JE, Weiner IB. 1994. *The Rorschach: A Comprehensive System,* Vol. 3, *Assessment of Children and Adolescents.* New York: Wiley

Eyde L, Kowal D, Fishburne FJ. 1993. *The Computer and the Decision Making Process.* Hillsdale, NJ: Erlbaum

Eysenck HJ. 1992. Four ways five factors are not basic. *Pers. Individ. Differ.* 6:667–73

Farrell AD. 1993. Computers and behavioral assessment: current applications, future possibilities, and obstacles to routine use. *Behav. Assess.* 13:159–79

Finn SE, Tonsager ME. 1992. Therapeutic effects of providing MMPI-2 test feedback to college students awaiting therapy. *Psychol. Assess.* 4:278–87

First MB. 1994. Computer-assisted assessment of DSM-III-R diagnoses. *Psychol. Ann.* 24: 25–29

Flowers JV, Booraem CD, Schwartz B. 1993. Impact of client computerized rapid assessment instruments on counselors and client outcome. *Comput. Hum. Serv.* 10:9–18

Frohnauer LA, Vavak C, Hardin KN. 1988. Rorschach use in APA-approved clinical training programs: an update. *J. Train. Pract. Prof. Psychol.* 2:45–48

Frueh BC, Kinder BN. 1994. The susceptibility of the Rorschach Inkblot Test to malingering of combat-related PTSD. *J. Pers. Assess.* 62:280–98

Gacono CB. 1993. Some thoughts on Rorschach findings and psychophysiology in the psychopath. *Br. J. Proj. Psychol.* 38: 42–52

Gallucci NT. 1993. Influence of elevated K-scale scores on the validity of adolescent Minnesota Multiphasic Personality Inventories. *J. Clin. Child Psychol.* 22:375–81

Ganellin RJ. 1994. Attempting to conceal psychological disturbance: MMPI defensive response sets and the Rorschach. *J. Pers. Assess.* 63:423–37

Gass CS, Ansley J. 1995. Personality assessment of neurologically impaired patients. See Butcher 1995b, pp. 192–209

Gerstein LH, Briggs JR. 1993. Psychological and sociological discriminants of violent and nonviolent serious juvenile offenders. *J. Addict. Offend. Couns.* 14:2–13

Goldberg LR. 1993. The structure of phenotypic personality traits. *Am. Psychol.* 48: 26–34

Gottfredson GD, Jones EM, Holland JL. 1993. Personality and vocational interest: the relation of Holland's six interest dimensions to five robust dimensions of personality. *J. Couns. Psychol.* 40:518–24

Graham RL. 1993. MMPI-2 obvious and subtle items: predictive and discriminant validity. *Diss. Abstr. Intl.* 53:3773

Gray-Little B. 1995. The assessment of psychopathology in racial and ethnic minorities. See Butcher 1995b, pp. 141–57

Grigoriadis S, Fekken GC, Nussbaum D. 1994. *MMPI-2 or BPI, which to use?* Presented at Annu. Meet. Am. Psychol. Assoc., 102nd, Los Angeles

Grillo J, Brown RS, Hilsabeck R, Price JR. 1994. Raising doubts about claims of malingering: implications of the relationship between MCMI-II and MMPI-2 performances. *J. Clin. Psychol.* 50:651–55

Guthrie PC, Mobley BD. 1994. A comparison of the differential diagnostic efficiency of three personality disorder inventories. *J. Clin. Psychol.* 50:656–65

Han K, Weed N, Calhoun R, Butcher JN. 1995. Psychometric characteristics of the MMPI-2 Cook-Medley Hostility Scale. *J. Pers. Assess.* In press

Hare RD. 1992. *The Hare Psychopathology Checklist—Revised.* Odessa, FL: Psychol. Assess. Resour.

Hargrave GE, Hiatt D, Ogard EM, Karr C. 1994. Comparison of the MMPI and the MMPI-2 for a sample of peace officers. *Psychol. Assess.* 6:27–32

Harkness AR, Hogan R. 1995. The theory and measurement of traits: two views. See Butcher 1995b, pp. 28–41

Harkness AR, McNulty JL. 1994. The Personality Psychopathology Five (Psy-5): issue from the pages of a diagnostic manual instead of a dictionary. See Strack & Lorr 1994, pp. 291–315

Harkness AR, McNulty JL, Ben-Porath YS. 1995. The Personality Psychopathology Five (PSY-5): constructs and MMPI-2 scales. *Psychol. Assess.* 7:104–14

Harris D. 1993. The prevalence of thought disorder in personality-disordered outpatients. *J. Per. Assess.* 61:112–20

Hart SD, Hare RD. 1994. Psychopathy and the big five: correlations between observers' ratings of normal and pathological personality. *J. Pers. Disord.* 8:32–40

Helmes E, Reddon JR. 1993. A perspective on developments in assessing psychopathology: a critical review of the MMPI and MMPI-2. *Psychol. Bull.* 113:453–71

Heraute JC. 1993. Une nouvelle approche diagnostique et prognostique du fonctionnement psychologique de la personne deliquante ou criminelle a partir du Rorschach: l'etude des rapports entre violence, inhibition et socialisation banale. (A Rorschach-based approach to the diagnostic and prognostic assessment of psychological functioning in criminal offenders: a study on the relationship between violence, inhibition, and banal socialization). *Anal. Psicol.* 11:115–28

Hernandez-Moreno L, Carbonell Masia C, Ramos Brieva J. 1993. Dessarrollo de un indice de probabilidad de adaptacion psicosocial de los enfermos renales cronicos (IPAPERC). [Development of an index of probability of psychosocial adaptation for chronic renal patients (IPAPERC).] *Actas Luso Esp. Neurol. Psiquiatr. Cienc. Afines* 21:51–55

Hibbard SR, Farmer L, Wells C, Difillipo E, Barry W, et al. 1994. Validation of Cramer's defense mechanism manual for the TAT. *J. Pers. Assess.* 63:197–210

Hilsenroth MJ, Hibbard SR, Nash MR, Handler L. 1993. A Rorschach study of narcissism, defense, and aggression in borderline, narcissistic, and Cluster C personality disorders. *J. Pers. Assess.* 60:346–61

Holden RR, Fekken GC, Cotton DH. 1991. Assessing psychopathology using structured test-item response latencies. *Psychol. Assess.* 3:111–18

Holland JL, Johnston JA, Asama NF, Polys SM. 1993. Validating and using the Career Beliefs Inventory. *J. Career Dev.* 19: 233–44

Humphrey DH, Dahlstrom WG. 1995. The impact of changing from the MMPI to the MMPI-2 on profile configurations. *J. Pers. Assess.* In press

Inch R, Crossley M. 1993. Diagnostic utility of the MCMI-I and MCMI-II with psychiatric outpatients. *J. Clin. Psychol.* 49:358–66

Iverson GL, Franzen MD, Hammond JA. 1995. Examination of inmates' ability to malinger on the MMPI-2. *Psychol. Assess.* 7:118–21

Jackson D. 1989. *Basic Personality Inventory Manual.* Port Huron, MI: Sigma Assess. Syst.

Jacobs RL, McClelland DC. 1994. Moving up the corporate ladder: a longitudinal study of the leadership motive pattern and managerial success in women and men. *Cons. Psychol. J. Pract. Res.* 46:32–41

Jemelka RP, Wiegand GA, Walker EA, Trupin EW. 1992. Computerized offender assessment: validation study. *Psychol. Assess.* 4: 138–44

Johnson DR, Quinlan DM. 1993. Can the mental representations of paranoid schizophrenics be differentiated from those of normals? *J. Pers. Assess.* 60:588–601

Johnson JL. 1994. The Thematic Apperception Test and Alzheimer's disease. *J. Pers. Assess.* 62:314–19

Karon BP, Widener AJ. 1994. Is there really a schizophrenogenic parent? *Psychoanal. Psychol.* 11:47–61

Kaser-Boyd N. 1993. Rorschachs of women who commit homicide. *J. Pers. Assess.* 60:458–70

Keiller SW, Graham JR. 1993. The meaning of low scores on MMPI-2 clinical scales of normal subjects. *J. Pers. Assess.* 61: 211–23

Keith-Speigel P. 1994. The 1992 Ethics Code: boon or bane. *Prof. Psychol. Res. Pract.* 25:315–16

Khan FI, Welch TL, Zillmer EA. 1993. MMPI-2 profiles of battered women in transition. *J. Pers. Assess.* 60:100–11

King RE. 1994. Assessing aviators for personality pathology with the Millon Clinical Multiaxial Inventory (MCMI). *Aviat. Space Environ. Med.* 65:227–31

Klein MH, Benjamin LS, Rosenfeld R, Treece C, Greist JH. 1993. The Wisconsin Personality Disorder Inventory. I. Development, reliability, and validity. *J. Pers. Disord.* 7: 285–303

Kline P, Barrett P. 1994. Studies with the PPQ

and the 5-factor model of personality. *Eur. Rev. Appl. Psychol.* 44:35–42

Kroner DG, Reddon JR. 1994. Relationship among clinical and validity scales of the Basic Personality Inventory. *J. Clin. Psychol.* 50:522–28

Lamb DG, Berry DTR, Wetter MW, Baer RA. 1994. Effects of two types of information on malingering of closed head injury on the MMPI-2: an analog investigation. *Psychol. Assess.* 6:8–13

Leckart B. 1994. A revised dissimulation scale applicable to the MMPI-2. *Am. J. Forensic Psychol.* 12:5–15

Lees-Haley PR. 1992. Psychodiagnostic test usage by forensic psychologists. *Am. J. Forensic Psychol.* 10:25–30

Lim J. 1994. *Detecting faking on the MMPI-2 profiles: differentiating between faking-bad, denial, and claiming extreme virtue.* PhD thesis. Univ. Minn.

Loevinger J. 1994. Has psychology lost its conscience? *J. Pers. Assess.* 62:2–8

Long KA, Graham JR, Timbrook R. 1994. Socioeconomic status and MMPI-2 interpretation. *Meas. Eval. Couns. Dev.* 27:158–77

Lovitt R. 1993. A strategy for integrating a normal MMPI-2 and dysfunctional Rorschach in a severely compromised patient. *J. Pers. Assess.* 60:141–47

Lucio E, Reyes-Lagunes I, Scott RL. 1994. MMPI-2 for Mexico: translation and adaptation. *J. Pers. Assess.* 63:105–16

Martin ED, Sher KJ. 1994. Family history of alcoholism, alcohol use disorder, and the five-factor model of personality. *J. Studies Alcohol.* 55:81–90

McAdams DP. 1992. The five-factor model in personality: a critical appraisal. *J. Pers.* 60: 329–61

McAnulty RD. 1993. Expert psychological testimony in cases of alleged child sexual abuse. *Arch. Sexual Behav.* 22:311–24

McCrae RR, John OP. 1992. An introduction to the Five Factor Model and its applications. *J. Pers.* 60:175–215

McKee GR, Klohn LS. 1994. MCMI profiles of pretrial defendants. *Psychol. Rep.* 74: 1346

Megargee EI. 1994. Using the Megargee MMPI-based classification system with MMPI-2s of male prison inmates. *Psychol. Assess.* 6:337–44

Meloy JR, Gacono CB, Kenney L. 1994. A Rorschach investigation of sexual homicide. *J. Pers. Assess.* 62:58–67

Meyer GJ. 1993. The impact of response frequency on the Rorschach constellation indices and on their validity with diagnostic and MMPI-2 criteria. *J. Pers. Assess.* 60: 153–80

Millon T. 1977. *Manual for the Millon Clinical Multiaxial Inventory.* Minneapolis: Natl. Comp. Syst.

Millon T. 1987. *Manual for the Millon Clinical Multiaxial Inventory—II.* Minneapolis: Natl. Comp. Syst.

Millon T. 1994. *Manual for the Millon Clinical Multiaxial Inventory-III.* Minneapolis: Natl. Comp. Syst.

Montag I, Levin J. 1994. The five factor model and psychopathology in nonclinical samples. *Pers. Individ. Differ.* 17:1–7

Moreland KL, Eyde LD, Robertson GJ, Primoff ES, Most RB. 1995. Assessment of test user qualifications: a research-based measurement procedure. *Am. Psychol.* 50: 14–23

Morey LC. 1991. *Personality Assessment Inventory: Professional Manual.* Odessa, FL: Psychol. Assess. Resour.

Morey LC, Waugh MH, Blashfield RK. 1985. MMPI scales for DSM-III personality disorders. *J. Pers. Assess.* 49:245–51

Morin CM, Colecchi CA. 1995. Psychological assessment of older adults. See Butcher 1995b, pp. 172–91

Morrison TL, Edwards DW, Weissman HN. 1994. The MMPI and MMPI-2 as predictors of psychiatric diagnosis in an outpatient sample. *J. Pers. Assess.* 62:17–30

Munley PH, Bains DS, Bloem WD. 1993. F scale elevation and PTSD MMPI profiles. *Psychol. Rep.* 73:363–70

Murray JF. 1993. The Rorschach search for the borderline holy grail: an examination of personality structure, personality style, and situation. *J. Pers. Assess.* 61:342–57

Nair L, Deb S, Mandal J. 1993. A study on repression-sensitization, personality characteristics and early childhood experiences of male cancer patients. *J. Pers. Clin. Stud.* 9:87–94

Norman DK, Blais MA, Herzog D. 1993. Personality characteristics of eating-disordered patients as identified by the Millon Clinical Multiaxial Inventory. *J. Pers. Disord.* 7:1–9

Okazaki S, Sue S. 1995. Cultural considerations in psychological assessment of Asian-Americans. See Butcher 1995b, pp. 107–19

Ornberg B, Zalewski C. 1994. Assessment of adolescents with the Rorschach: a critical review. *Assessment* 1:209–17

Ornduff SR, Feedenfeld RN, Kelsey RM, Critelli JW. 1994. Object relations of sexually abused female subjects: a TAT analysis. *J. Pers. Assess.* 63:223–38

Otto R, Butcher JN. 1995. Computer assisted psychological assessment in child custody evaluations. *Fam. Law Q.* 29(1):79–96

Owens RG, Harms LO. 1993. Differential responses of female forgers to MMPI items. *J. Offend. Rehabil.* 19:165–71

Parker JD, Bagby RM, Summerfeldt LJ. 1993. Confirmatory factor analysis of the Revised NEO Personality Inventory. *Pers. Individ. Differ.* 15:463–66

Patrick J. 1993. Validation of the MCMI-1 Borderline Personality Disorder scale with a well-defined criterion sample. *J. Clin. Psychol.* 49:28–32

Perry W, Braff DL. 1994. Information-processing deficits and thought disorder in schizophrenia. *Am. J. Psychol.* 151:363–67

Pervin LA. 1994. A critical analysis of current trait theory. *Psychol. Inq.* 5:103–13

Peterson C, Ulrey LM. 1994. Can explanatory style be scored from TAT protocols? *Pers. Soc. Psychol. Bull.* 20:102–6

Piedmont RL, Weinstein HP. 1993. A psychometric evaluation of the new NEO-PI-R facet scales for agreeableness and conscientiousness. *J. Pers. Assess.* 60:302–18

Pinkerman JE, Haynes JP, Keiser T. 1993. Characteristics of psychological practice in juvenile court clinics. *Am. J. Forensic Psychol.* 11:3–12

Piotrowski C, Keller JW, Ogawa T. 1993. Projective techniques: an international perspective. *Psychol. Rep.* 72:179–82

Piotrowski C, Zalewski C. 1993. Training in psychodiagnostic testing in APA-approved PsyD and PhD clinical psychology programs. *J. Pers. Assess.* 61:394–405

Pistole DR, Ornduff SR. 1994. TAT assessment of sexually abused girls: an analysis of manifest content. *J. Pers. Assess.* 63: 211–22

Poikolainen K. 1993. Does fear of war impair mental health among psychiatric patients? *Nord. J. Psychol.* 47:455–57

Pope KS, Butcher JN, Seelen J. 1993. *The MMPI, MMPI-2, & MMPI-A in Court: A Practical Guide for Expert Witnesses and Attorneys.* Washington, DC: Am. Psychol. Assoc.

Poreh A, Whitman D. 1993. MMPI-2 schizophrenia spectrum profiles among schizotypal college students and college students who seek psychological treatment. *Psychol. Rep.* 73:987–94

Priest W, Meunier GF. 1993. MMPI-2 performance of elderly women. *Clin. Gerontol.* 14:3–11

Pruneti CA, L'Abbate A, Steptoe A. 1993. Personality and behavioral changes in patients after myocardial infarction. *Res. Comm. Psychol. Psychiatr. Behav.* 18:37–51

Quirk MP, Strosahl K, Kreilkamp T, Erdberg P. 1995. Personality feedback consultation in a managed mental health care practice. *Prof. Psychol. Res. Pract.* 26:27–32

Reich J. 1993. The MCMI and DSM-III anxiety disorders. See Craig, pp. 173–78

Rhodes BC. 1995. *The Superlative Scale: Does anonymity dilute the overly virtuous response set on the MMPI-2 profiles of aviators?* PhD diss. Am. School Prof. Psychol.

Rodriguez M. 1994. Influence of sex and family history of alcoholism on cognitive functioning in heroin users. *Eur. J. Psychol.* 8: 29–36

Rogers R, Bagby RM, Chakraborty D. 1993a. Feigning schizophrenic disorders on the MMPI-2: detection of coached simulators. *J. Pers. Assess.* 60:215–26

Rogers R, Ornduff SR, Sewell KW. 1993b. Feigning specific disorders: a study of the Personality Assessment Inventory (PAI). *J. Pers. Assess.* 60:554–60

Ronan GF, Colavito VA, Hammontree SR. 1993. Personal problem-solving system for scoring TAT responses: preliminary validity and reliability data. *J. Pers. Assess.* 61: 28–40

Ronan GF, Date AL, Weisbrod M. 1995. Personal problem-solving scoring of the TAT: sensitivity to training. *J. Pers. Assess.* 64: 119–31

Roper BL, Ben-Porath YS, Butcher JN. 1991. Comparability of computerized adaptive and conventional testing with the MMPI-2. *J. Pers. Assess.* 57:278–90

Roper BL, Ben-Porath YS, Butcher JN. 1995. Comparability and validity of computerized adaptive testing with the MMPI-2. *J. Pers. Assess.*

Rossel F, Cedraschi C, Merceron C. 1993. Erotization of morbid in false-self personalities. Special Issue: Intl. Rorschach Congr. 1993. *Br. J. Proj. Psychol.* 38: 71–78

Rotenberg VS, Michailov AN. 1993. Characteristics of psychological defense mechanisms in healthy testees and in patients with somatic disorders. *Homeostasis Heal. Dis.* 34:54–58

Rothke SE, Friedman AF, Dahlstrom WG, Greene RL. 1994. MMPI-2 normative data for the F-K index: implications for clinical, neuropsychological, and forensic practice. *Assessment* 1:1–15

Schacht TE. 1993. How do I diagnose thee? Let me count the dimensions. *Psychol. Inq.* 4:115–18

Schretlen D, Wilkins SS, Van Gorp WG, Bobholz JH. 1992. Cross-validation of a psychological test battery to detect faked insanity. *Psychol. Assess.* 4:77–83

Schotte C, de Doncker D, Maes M, Cluydts R. 1993. MMPI assessment of the DSM-III-R histrionic personality disorder. *J. Pers. Assess.* 60:500–10

Schubert E. 1993. Personality disorders and overseas missions: guidelines for the mental health professional. *J. Psychol. Theol.* 21:18–25

Serper MR, Bernstein DP, Maurer G, Harvey PD. 1993. Psychological test profiles of patients with borderline and schizotypal personality disorders: implications for DSM-IV. *J. Pers. Disord.* 7:144–54

Shanan J. 1993. Die Jerusalemer Langsschnittuntersuchungen der mittleren Lebensjahre und des Alterns—JESMA (The Jerusalem longitudinal study on mid-adulthood and aging—JESMA.) *Z. Gerontol.* 26:151–55

Shopshire MS, Craik KH. 1994. The five-factor model of personality and the DSM-III-R personality disorders: correspondence and differentiation. *J. Pers. Disord.* 8: 41–52

Small MA, Melton GB. 1994. Evaluation of child witnesses for confrontation by criminal defendants. *Prof. Psychol. Res. Pract.* 25:228–33

Soldz S, Budman S, Demby A, Merry J. 1993. Representation of personality disorders in circumplex and five-factor space: explorations with a clinical sample. *Psychol. Assess.* 5:41–52

Somwaru DP, Ben-Porath YS. 1995. *Development and reliability of MMPI-2 based* personality disorder scales. Presented at Annu. Symp. Recent Dev. MMPI-2 MMPI-A, 30th, St. Petersburg Beach, FL

Spinhoven P, Labbe MR, Rombouts R. 1993. Feasibility of computerized psychological testing with psychiatric outpatients. *J. Clin. Psychol.* 49:440–47

Stevens MJ, Kwan K, Graybill DF. 1993. Comparison of MMPI-2 scores of foreign Chinese and Caucasian-American students. *J. Clin. Psychol.* 49:23–27

Strack S, Lorr M, eds. 1994. *Differentiating Normal and Abnormal Personality.* New York: Springer

Strauss ME, Pasupathi M, Chatterjee A, 1993. Concordance between observers in description of personality change in Alzheimer's disease. *Psychol. Aging* 8:475–80

Svanum S, Ehrmann LC. 1993. Screening for maladjustment in college students: an application of receiver operating characteristic curve to MMPI scales. *J. Pers. Assess.* 60:397–410

Swirsky-Sacchetti T, Gorton G, Samuel S, Sobel R. 1993. Neuropsychological function in borderline personality disorder. *J. Clin. Psychol.* 49:385–96

Talbert FS, Albrecht JW, Boudewyns PA, Hyer LA, Touze J, Lemmon CR. 1994. A comparison of MMPI and MMPI-2 in PTSD assessment. *J. Clin. Psychol.* 50:578–85

Talbert FS, Braswell LC, Albrecht JW, Hyer LA. 1993. NEO-PI profiles in PTSD as a function of trauma level. *J. Clin. Psychol.* 49:663–69

Tellegen A. 1993. Folk concepts and psychological concepts of personality and personality disorder. *Psychol. Inq.* 4:122–30

Tellegen A, Ben-Porath YS. 1993. Code type comparability of the MMPI and MMPI-2: analysis of recent findings and criticisms. *J. Pers. Assess.* 61:489–500

Timbrook RE, Graham JR. 1994. Ethnic differences on the MMPI-2? *Psychol. Assess.* 6: 212–17

Timbrook RE, Graham JR, Keiller SW, Watts D. 1993. Comparison of the Weiner-Harmon Subtle-Obvious scales and the standard validity scales in detecting valid and invalid MMPI-2 profiles. *Psychol. Assess.* 5:53–61

Tisdale M, Pendleton L. 1993. The use of the MCMI with eating disorders. See Craig 1993, pp. 147–57

Tranel D. 1994. The release of psychological data to nonexperts: ethical and legal considerations. *Prof. Psychol. Res. Pract.* 25: 33–38

Trull TJ. 1993. Temporal stability and validity of two personality disorder inventories. *Psychol. Assess.* 5:11–18

Trull TJ, Sher KJ. 1994. Relationship between the five-factor model of personality and Axis I disorders in a nonclinical sample. *J. Abnorm. Psychol.* 103:350–60

Velásquez RJ. 1995. Personality assessment of Hispanic clients. See Butcher 1995b, pp. 120–39

Van Heck GL, Perugini M, Caprara G, Froger J. 1994. The Big Five as tendencies in situations. *Pers. Individ. Differ.* 16:715–31

Wakefield H, Underwager R. 1993. Misuse of psychological tests in forensic settings: some horrible examples. *Am. J. Forensic Psychol.* 11:55–75

Waller NG, Zavala JD. 1993. Evaluating the Big Five. *Psychol. Inq.* 40:131–34

Ward LC. 1994. MMPI-2 assessment of positive attributes: a methodological note. *J. Pers. Assess.* 62:559–61

Watkins CE. 1991. What have surveys taught us about the teaching and practice of psychological assessment? *J. Pers. Assess.* 56: 426–37

Watkins CE, Campbell VL, Nieberding R, Hallmark R. 1995. Contemporary practice of psychological assessment by clinical psychologists. *Prof. Psychol. Res. Pract.* 26:54–60

Weed NC. 1993. An evaluation of the efficacy of MMPI-2 indicators of validity. *Diss. Abstr. Intl.*53:3800

Weiner IB. 1993. Clinical considerations in the conjoint use of the Rorschach and the MMPI. *J. Pers. Assess.* 60:148–152

Wetter MW, Baer RA, Berry DT, Robison LH, Sumpter J. 1993. MMPI-2 profiles of moti-vated fakers given specific symptom information. *Psychol. Assess.* 5:317–23

Wetter MW, Baer RA, Berry DT, Smith GT, Larsen L. 1992. Sensitivity of the MMPI-2 validity scales to random responding and malingering. *Psychol. Assess.* 4:369–74

Wetzler S, Marlowe DB. 1993. The diagnosis and assessment of depression, mania, and psychosis by self-report. *J. Pers. Assess.* 60:1–31

Whitworth RH, McBlaine DD. 1993. Comparison of the MMPI and MMPI-2 administered to Anglo- and Hispanic-American university students. *J. Pers. Assess.* 61: 19–27

Widiger TA. 1993. The DSM-III-R categorical Personality Disorder diagnoses: a critique and an alternative. *Psychol. Inq.* 4:75–90

Widiger TA, Corbitt EM. 1993. The MCMI-II personality disorder scales and their relationship to DSM-III-R diagnosis. See Craig 1993, pp. 181–201

Widiger TA, Costa PT Jr. 1994. Personality and personality disorders. *J. Abnorm. Psychol.* 103:78–91

Widiger TA, Sanderson CJ. 1995. Assessing personality disorders. See Butcher 1995b, pp. 380–94

Wierzbicki M. 1993a. Use of MCMI subtle and obvious subscales to detect faking. *J. Clin. Psychol.* 49:809–14

Wierzbicki M. 1993b. The relationship between MCMI subtlety and severity. *J. Pers. Assess.* 61:259–63

Worell J, Robinson D. 1995. Issues in clinical assessment with women. See Butcher 1995b, pp. 158–71

Zeiller B, Barnoud S. 1993. Enfants et adolescents criminels: aspects psychopathologiques. (Delinquent children and adolescents: Psychopathological aspects). *Anal. Psicol.* 11:87–98

Zeldow PB, McAdams DP. 1993. On the comparison of TAT and free speech techniques in personality assessment. *J. Pers. Assess.* 60:181–85

Zhang T, Xu S, Cai Z, Chen Z. 1993. Research on the Thematic Apperception Test: Chinese revision and norms. *Acta Psychol. Sin.* 25:314–23

Zuroff DC. 1994. Depressive personality styles and the five-factor model of personality. *J. Pers. Assess.* 63:453–72

Annu. Rev. Psychol. 1996. 47:113–42

HEALTH PSYCHOLOGY:
Psychological Factors and Physical Disease from the Perspective of Human Psychoneuroimmunology

Sheldon Cohen and Tracy B. Herbert

Department of Psychology, Carnegie Mellon University, Pittsburgh, Pennsylvania 15213

KEY WORDS: stress, social support, personality, upper respiratory infection, immune function

ABSTRACT

This review addresses the importance of studies of human psychoneuroimmu-nology in understanding the role of psychological factors in physical illness. First, it provides psychologically and biologically plausible explanations for how psychological factors might influence immunity and immune system–mediated disease. Second, it covers substantial evidence that factors such as stress, negative affect, clinical depression, social support, and repression/denial can influence both cellular and humoral indicators of immune status and function. Third, at least in the case of the less serious infectious diseases (colds, influenza, herpes), it considers consistent and convincing evidence of links between stress and negative affect and disease onset and progression. Although still early in its development, research also suggests a role of psychological factors in autoim-mune diseases. Evidence for effects of stress, depression, and repression/denial on onset and progression of AIDS and cancer is less consistent and inconclusive, possibly owing to methodological limitations inherent in studying these complex illnesses, or because psychological influences on immunity are not of the magnitude or type necessary to alter the body's response in these cases. What is missing in this literature, however, is strong evidence that the associations between psychological factors and disease that do exist are attributable to immune changes.

0066-4308/96/0201-0113$08.00

CONTENTS

INTRODUCTION

Much of psychoneuroimmunology's popularity with both the public and the psychological community derives from its promise to explore and explain the common belief that our personalities and emotions influence our health. Can depression, anxiety, psychological distress, social support, or an optimistic view alter our ability to resist infection, autoimmune diseases, or cancer? What are the biological pathways through which psychological characteristics and states yield physical changes? Can we alter immunity and hence disease susceptibility through psychological intervention? Several hundred studies published in the past decade address the relation of psychological characteristics and states to immune function and to health outcomes thought to be determined by immune alterations. In this chapter we highlight what we have learned about the importance of immunity as a link between the mind and the body.

WHAT IS PSYCHONEUROIMMUNOLOGY?

Psychoneuroimmunology (PNI) is the study of the interrelations between the central nervous system and the immune system. The term interrelations is used because the assumption is that the relations are bidirectional. Work with animals has advanced our understanding of this bidirectionality and has provided evidence for nerves connecting the central nervous system (CNS) and the immune system (e.g. Felten et al 1985), for neuroendocrine-induced alterations of specific immune functions (e.g. Shavit et al 1984), and for the existence of chemicals called cytokines that are produced by the immune system, cross the blood-brain barrier, and alter the function of the CNS (review in Rabin et al 1989). An important step in establishing that the CNS and immune system interact was accomplished by psychologists working with animal models who demonstrated that immune system change could be induced by classically conditioned stimuli (review in Ader & Cohen 1993).

The interests of psychoneuroimmunologists working with humans overlap with those of animal researchers, but human psychoneuroimmunologists' emphases are different. Examples of overlap in focus include studies of classical conditioning of human immune response (e.g. Bovbjerg et al 1990, Buske-Kirschbaum et al 1992) and demonstrations of immune-system effects on the CNS as reflected in human performance (Smith et al 1988). The most obvious difference, however, is that the human literature is primarily concerned with behavior and psychological traits and states as drivers of CNS and immune response. The major foci of human studies include establishing whether there is an association between psychological traits and states and immunity, what the biological and behavioral pathways are that are responsible for such relations, and whether psychologically induced changes in immunity are responsible for changes in susceptibility to immune system–mediated disease.

WHAT IS IMMUNE FUNCTION?

The Immune System

The immune system protects the body from damage by invading microorganisms—bacteria, viruses, fungi, and parasites. These foreign materials are called antigens. Most immune system cells are located in the bone marrow, thymus, lymph nodes, spleen, tonsils, appendix, and Peyer's patches (clumps of immune tissue in the small intestines). Because there is no easy way to access the cells of these organs, PNI work with humans is primarily limited to the study of immune processes occurring in circulating peripheral blood. Circulating blood transports immune components between organs of the immune system and sites of inflammation. Components of the immune system that circulate in blood (e.g. some types of white blood cells and antibody) survey for and combat against invading antigens. Therefore, peripheral blood plays a key role in inflammatory and immune processes.

Tests of Immune Function

In this section, we describe the immune system tests most commonly used in human PNI research. Most of the tests evaluate the role of immune cells in peripheral blood.

ENUMERATIVE TESTS   The enumerative assay most often used involves simply counting the numbers or percentages of different kinds of white blood cells in the peripheral blood. The white blood cells relevant to this chapter are neutrophils, monocytes, and lymphocytes, including natural killer (NK), T, and B lymphocytes. Quantifying the number of circulating cells is important both because the body cannot respond adequately to antigenic response without a minimum number of each type of immune cell and because an optimal response requires a balance of the various cell types. Both increases and decreases in numbers of circulating cells suggest alterations in the immune system. However, the changes found in the PNI literature are usually quite small, and whether these changes indicate compromised immune function is theoretically unclear.

FUNCTIONAL TESTS   Immune response can be divided into *cellular* immunity, in which immune cells directly combat antigens, and *humoral* immunity, in which products of immune cells (e.g. antibody) combat antigens. Although the cellular and humoral subsystems work together in many instances, the functional tests we describe primarily explore the integrity of one or the other.

Lymphocytes are the key cells controlling the immune response. The ability of these cells to proliferate rapidly in the face of an antigenic challenge is essential to an adequate response. Lymphocyte proliferation is a test of cellular immunity that examines how effectively stimulated lymphocytes divide. Lymphocytes are stimulated through incubation with substances (mitogens) capable of nonspecifically inducing T or B lymphocytes to divide. It is assumed that greater proliferation indicates more effective cell function. Commonly used mitogens include phytohemagglutinin (PHA), concanavalin A (Con A), and pokeweed mitogen (PWM).

NK cells may be thought of as serving a surveillance function; they can detect and kill damaged or altered (e.g. infected or cancerous) cells. The NK cell cytotoxic activity assay, another test of cellular immunity, is used to determine how effectively NK cells kill transformed cells. In this assay, immune cells are incubated with tumor cells and tumor-cell killing is measured.

The functional tests described up to this point are in vitro tests; cells are removed from the body and their function is studied in the laboratory. Three in vivo tests that assess the function of cells in the living organism are also used in this literature. One, the quantification of antibodies (Ab) to herpesviruses, is used to *indirectly* assess cellular immune competence (e.g. Glaser & Gottlieb Stematsky 1982). Almost everyone has been exposed to the common herpesviruses. These viruses differ from most other known viruses in that after exposure, they are present in the body all of the time, although often in latent states. When the immune system is suppressed, latent virus replicates. Antibodies are protein molecules produced by the immune system that have the ability to attach to a specific antigen, mark it for destruction, and prevent it from causing infection. Ab is produced in response to the herpes viral replication, and the amount of Ab produced fluctuates in relation to the amount of virus produced. Hence higher levels of herpesvirus Ab are interpreted as indirect evidence of compromised cellular immune function.

A more direct test of cellular immunity is the delayed-type hypersensitivity response. In this test, small amounts of antigen are introduced by injection into the skin. A hypersensitivity response is one in which swelling and redness occur at the site of injection. The inflammation is generated by the reaction of the antigen with antigen-specific T lymphocytes. Inflammation is expected in response to the antigens, and the larger the inflammation, the more "competent" the cellular immune system is assumed to be.

Finally, in an in vivo test assessing the competence of the humoral arm of the immune system, individuals are inoculated with an antigen, and the amount of Ab produced in response to that specific antigen is quantified. Depending on the specific type of Ab, it can be quantified from either blood or mucosal secretions (e.g. saliva, nasal discharge). The more Ab produced in response to an antigen, the more "competent" the humoral system is assumed to be.

Immunity and Disease

The immune system's defense against invading microorganisms is composed of a complex cascade of events. Moreover, the exact nature of any given immune response varies with the invaded organism's history of exposure, the type of antigen, and the route of entry into the body. Practically, human PNI researchers are limited to assessing a small number of rough markers of immune function rather than anything that resembles a true estimate of the body's ability to resist disease. For these and other reasons addressed later (see the section entitled "Do Psychological Factors Influence Immune System–Mediated Disease?"), PNI studies with immune (but not disease) outcomes are informative about the interrelation among behavior, the CNS, and the immune system, but do not necessarily indicate changes in resistance to disease. In the sections that follow, we first discuss studies on the relations between psychological factors and immunity, and then studies of the relations between psychological factors and the onset and progression of immune system–mediated disease. The review is limited to studies of the psychological factors that have received the most attention, including stressful life events, clinical depression, negative affect, social support, and repression/denial.

HOW COULD PSYCHOLOGICAL FACTORS INFLUENCE IMMUNITY AND DISEASE?

Figure 1 presents a simplified view of how psychological factors might alter immunity and disease susceptibility. As discussed above, psychological variables may influence immunity through direct innervation of the CNS and immune systems or through hormonal pathways. Behavioral changes that are associated with personality characteristics or that occur as adaptations or coping responses in the face of stressful events or negative emotional states may

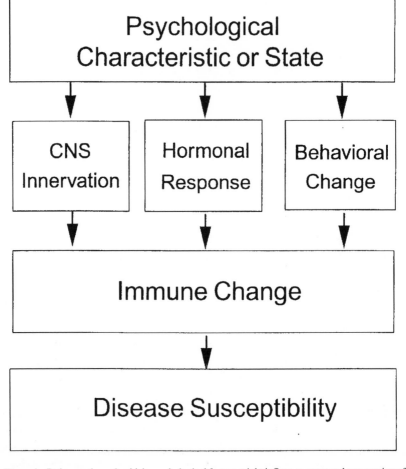

Figure 1   Pathways through which psychological factors might influence onset and progression of immune system–mediated disease. For simplicity, arrows are drawn in only one direction, from psychological characteristics to disease. No lack of alternative paths is implied.

also influence immunity. For example, persons experiencing negative affect often engage in poor health practices, such as smoking, poor dietary practices, and poor sleeping habits (Cohen & Williamson 1988), which may have immunosuppressive effects (Kiecolt-Glaser & Glaser 1988).

DO PSYCHOLOGICAL FACTORS INFLUENCE IMMUNITY AND DISEASE?

Stress

Stressful life events are commonly believed to alter immunity and hence susceptibility to immune system–mediated disease. When demands imposed by events exceed individuals' abilities to cope, a psychological stress response composed of negative cognitive and emotional states is elicited. It is these responses that are thought to influence immune function through their effects on behavioral coping and neuroendocrine response.

NATURALISTIC STRESSORS   In a series of studies, Glaser, Kiecolt-Glaser, and colleagues investigated the impact of medical school examinations on medical students' cellular immune function. In the typical study, students' psychological stress levels and immune responses were assessed during a low-stress baseline period (e.g. just following vacation) and again during a series of important exams. Students reported more stress during exams and showed a decrease in the function of a range of indicators of cellular immune response, including decreased NK activity (Kiecolt-Glaser et al 1984, Glaser et al 1986), lymphocyte proliferation (Glaser et al 1985b, 1987, 1993), lymphocyte production of the chemical messenger gamma interferon (Glaser et al 1986, 1987), as well as an increase in production of antibody to herpesviruses (Glaser et al 1985a, 1987, 1991).

In a study of the role of positive (e.g. accomplishing a goal, experiencing a good interaction with their bosses) and negative (e.g. losing keys, having arguments) daily events in humoral immunity, Stone et al (1994) had community volunteers ingest a capsule containing an innocuous novel protein daily for 12 weeks. The protein acted as an antigen to which the immune system responded by producing antibody. To evaluate the role of daily events in antibody production, volunteers also completed daily diaries and gave daily saliva samples that were used to assess amounts of secretory Immunoglobulin A (sIgA) antibody produced in response to the novel antigen. The reporting of more desirable events was concurrently related to greater sIgA antibody production, and the reporting of more undesirable events was related to less. Desirable events were also associated with increases in sIgA production over two subsequent days. These data provide evidence for the role of day-to-day events in immune regulation as well as suggest the benefit of positive events in health outcomes.

Two studies explored the impact of perceived stress on the body's ability to produce antibodies (develop immunity) in response to the standard series of three hepatitis B vaccinations. Glaser et al (1992) did not find a prospective relation between negative affect and seroconversion (initial production of hepatitis B antibodies) in response to the first injection. They did, however, find that those who did not seroconvert were more stress reactive (reported more stress in response to a subsequent exam period) than those who seroconverted. In contrast, Jabaaij et al (1993) found that greater perceived stress assessed after the second hepatitis B vaccination was associated with less antibody production (among those who seroconverted) in response to the third injection. It is unclear, however, whether these differences in antibody level are great enough to influence the degree of protection against infection provided by the vaccination.

Stressful events that last for a longer term, e.g. months or even years, have similar potential to influence the immune system. One example is the set of studies assessing stress effects on residents of the area surrounding the Three Mile Island (TMI) nuclear power plant. TMI was the site of a serious accident in 1979, and the distress among area residents has remained high (Baum et al 1985). Recently, almost 10 years after the accident, McKinnon et al (1989) found more antibody to herpesviruses in TMI residents than in demographically matched control-group residents, suggesting lower cellular immune competence in the former.

Studies on the impact of the chronic stress associated with caregiving for relatives with Alzheimer's disease (AD) report mixed results. Kiecolt-Glaser et al (1987b) found that caregiving was associated with distress and elevated levels of herpesvirus antibody. The caregivers did not differ from the low-stress control group, however, in a variety of health behaviors thought to affect cellular immunity. In contrast, in a similar study, Irwin et al (1991) found no difference in NK activity between caregivers and controls. Finally, Esterling et al (1994b) compared AD caregivers, former AD caregivers (i.e. those whose AD relative had died at least two years previously), and controls. Former and current caregivers did not differ from each other and had poorer NK-cell response to stimulatory chemicals than the control group. These data suggest that psychological and immunological consequences of chronic stressors may persist beyond the cessation of the actual stressor.

If stress is reliably associated with immune change, can stress-reduction interventions prevent that change? The few existing studies are less than convincing in that regard. However, only one actually addressed the effectiveness of an intervention in the face of a common stressful event. In this study, medical students were trained in relaxation techniques just prior to first-year exams. The intervention did not influence stress-induced changes in cellular immune function (Kiecolt-Glaser et al 1986). In a second study of relaxation training in medical students, neither the training nor immune measurement coincided with a common stressful event (McGrady et al 1992), but researchers did find increased lymphocyte proliferation in response to PHA and Con A in the relaxation group following the four-week intervention. Finally, elderly adults residing in a geriatric care facility who were trained in relaxation techniques showed improved cellular immune response, including increased NK activity and decreased levels of herpes antibody (Kiecolt-Glaser et al 1985). Work on relaxation training as a stress-reducing intervention is inconclusive. However, the literature suggests that relaxation training may be sufficient to temporarily alter the relation between usual background levels of stress and immune response, but not sufficient to influence stress-induced perturbations in immunity caused by external stressors.

ACUTE STRESSORS IN THE LABORATORY   Several studies have assessed the effects of acute (i.e. lasting 5–20 minutes) psychological stressors (e.g. speech task, Stroop color word interference task, mental arithmetic) on immune response. The most consistent immune changes following stressor exposure include increased NK and suppressor/cytotoxic T cell numbers and decreased proliferative responses to mitogens, particularly PHA (e.g. Herbert et al 1994, Manuck et al 1991, Naliboff et al 1991, Zakowski et al 1992). One study has shown that immune changes in both cell numbers and function can be found as soon as five minutes after the onset of the stressor (Herbert et al 1994). Most immune parameters return to a resting level by one hour following the cessation of the stressor (Kiecolt-Glaser et al 1992), although some evidence indicates that NK activity remains depressed for as long as 48 hours (Sieber et al 1992). Moreover, stress-elicited immune responses found in the laboratory are at least partly attributable to a dispositional style of responding to stress. This is suggested by data indicating that stress-induced immune responses are reliable across time and tasks (Marsland et al 1995). The existence of dispositional immune reactive styles allows the possibility that greater immune reactivity may place people at risk for stress-elicited immune related disease (Boyce et al 1995, Cohen & Manuck 1995).

Laboratory studies are ideal for exploring biologic mechanisms linking psychological stress to immune change. For example, Manuck et al (1991) concluded that individuals characterized by high sympathetic nervous system (SNS) activation (i.e. large increases in blood pressure, heart rate, and SNS hormones epinephrine and norepinephrine) in the face of acute stressors also showed the largest immune changes. Those demonstrating little or no sympathetic reactivity showed little or no change. This result has been replicated several times (Bachen et al 1995, Herbert et al 1994, Zakowski et al 1992).

The correlations between sympathetic and immune response suggest that stress-elicited SNS response may drive the immune changes. However, this evidence is merely correlational and does not establish a causal chain.

Two recent experimental studies have attempted to provide evidence that would allow a causal inference regarding the mediating role of the SNS in the relation between acute stress and immune change. These studies are similar to earlier work in that persons exposed to stressors are compared to those not so exposed. However, these studies also include a second factor. Subjects are administered either placebos or pharmacological agents that prevent hormones produced by the SNS from binding to and therefore interacting with immune cells (adrenergic blockers). If the effects of stress on cellular immune function are mediated by the SNS, the pharmacological agents should effectively eliminate stress-induced change in the immune system. In one study, Bachen et al (1995) demonstrated that administering the adrenergic blocker labetalol prevented stress-induced increases in NK-cell number and NK activity and decreases in lymphocyte proliferation in response to mitogen. Benschop et al (1994) have also shown that the adrenergic blocker propranolol prevents the stress-induced increase in NK-cell number and NK activity. Both studies therefore suggest that these immune changes are caused by sympathetic activation following stressor exposure. The interpretation that the SNS is the primary mediator of these effects is also supported by studies that investigate stress-induced immune changes in the context of other key hormonal systems involved in immune regulation. For example, studies have failed to implicate either cortisol (Manuck et al 1991; Zakowski et al 1992, 1994) or opioids (Naliboff et al 1995) in acute stress-induced suppression of either lymphocyte proliferation or NK-cell activity.

Although laboratory stress studies provide valuable information, important questions remain unanswered. For example, to what extent do acute stressor effects found in the laboratory simulate more chronic real-life stressful events, and is laboratory immune reactivity a dispositional marker of susceptibility to stress-elicited disease (Boyce et al 1995, Cohen & Manuck 1995)?

Affect

Research on the role of negative affect in immune response has focused on clinical depression. However, recent work examines relations between different affective states, both negative and positive, and immune response in healthy populations.

DEPRESSIVE DISORDERS   Investigation of the immunologic correlates of clinical depression has received considerable attention. A recent meta-analysis of over 40 studies shows that when compared to healthy controls, clinically depressed individuals have lowered proliferative response to PHA, Con A, and

PWM; lowered NK activity; higher numbers of circulating white blood cells (primarily neutrophils and monocytes); and lowered numbers of NK, B, T, helper T, and suppressor/cytotoxic T cells (Herbert & Cohen 1993a). Longitudinal data also suggest that when people recover from depression, decreased NK activity is no longer evident (Irwin et al 1992). The relations between depression and immune outcomes are strongest in both older and hospitalized samples. However, it remains unclear whether this is because these groups suffer from more severe depression or whether age or hospitalization otherwise moderate the relation between depression and immunity.

Although these findings are reliable across studies included in the meta-analysis, there is variability in results. One reason for the variability is methodological: Few research groups have achieved high-quality designs. To limit variability, patients must be assessed when they are drug free, they must be carefully age- and sex-matched with comparison subjects, and appropriate controls must be used to deal with the day-to-day variability of immune assays (Schleifer et al 1993). One study, now a classic, that achieved these goals is also one of the largest and most carefully controlled studies of clinical populations to date. Schleifer et al (1989) found that, consistent with the meta-analysis, depression was associated with immunosuppression primarily among older patients and hospitalized patients.

As discussed earlier, relations between depression and immunity may sometimes be attributable to behavioral factors. Depressed persons sleep less, exercise less, have poorer diets, smoke more, and use alcohol and other drugs more often than do nondepressed persons (Gregory & Smeltzer 1983, Grunberg & Baum 1985). Although many studies now focus on physically healthy, drug-free subjects, relations between health behaviors and depression or immunity are generally not assessed. The few studies that included statistical controls for health practices such as weight and recent weight loss (Schleifer et al 1989), cigarette use, and alcohol consumption (Irwin et al 1987, 1990) suggest that these health practices do not account for alterations in immune function among depressed persons.

MOOD   What do we know about the relation between normal fluctuations in mood and immune response? Relatively little. Moreover, most studies address relations between negative mood states and immunity, with only scattered work addressing the role of positive moods. A recent meta-analysis of this literature suggests that depressed mood in nonclinical samples is associated with decreased proliferative responses to mitogens and decreased NK activity (Herbert & Cohen 1993a). However, the effect sizes are considerably smaller (in fact, about half the size) than those found for clinical depression. Only a handful of studies investigate relations between anxiety and immunity. These studies found that anxious mood is associated with decreased NK activity (Locke et al 1984) and decreased proliferative response to both PHA and Con A (Linn et al 1981).

Several studies examine the associations of positive and negative mood states with immune outcomes. For example, a daily diary study examined the relations between positive and negative mood states and antibody response to an orally ingested novel antigen over eight weeks (Stone et al 1987). Antibody levels were higher on days when respondents reported high positive mood states and lower on days when they reported high negative mood states. These results were replicated in a subsequent study that monitored mood and anti-body levels over a 12-week period (Stone et al 1994).

In a handful of experimental studies, specific affective states were induced in healthy subjects and the subsequent acute immune changes were docu-mented. For example, Knapp et al (1992) had subjects recall positive and negative experiences to induce "positive" and "negative" mood states. Both positive and negative moods were associated with decreased proliferative re-sponses to PHA and increased numbers of neutrophils. Similar immune effects of positive and negative mood were attributed to the fact that all subjects reported increased levels of excitement (arousal) during the mood inductions, regardless of the valence of the mood.

Futterman et al (1994) used actors in a within-subjects design and induced mood using written scenarios that depicted four different emotional states: high-arousal positive, high-arousal negative, low-arousal positive, and low-arousal negative. Although NK activity was not associated with mood condi-tion, the proliferative response of lymphocytes to PHA was differentially sensitive to mood valence. That is, proliferation increased following positive moods and decreased following negative moods.

Thus different moods may be associated with different immune responses. Clear interpretation of this work is impeded by a lack of consensus on the dimensions in which mood should be classified. However, existing work sug-gests that the dimensions of valence and arousal may be important ones in relating moods to immune function.

Interpersonal Relationships

Substantial evidence implicates interpersonal relationships in the maintenance of health (Cohen 1988, House et al 1988). A series of prospective studies shows that belonging to a strong social network is associated with longevity (reviewed by House et al 1988) and that perceptions of available support protect persons from the pathogenic effects of stressful events (reviewed by Cohen & Wills 1985). What is not clear, however, is the extent to which these effects are mediated by support-induced changes in immune function. Recent studies of loneliness, separation and divorce, perceptions of support, and disclosure of traumatic events have begun to elucidate the impact of interpersonal relationships on immunity and immune system–mediated illness.

In their studies of first-year medical students, Kiecolt-Glaser and Glaser (Glaser et al 1985a, Kiecolt-Glaser et al 1984) found that persons higher in self-reported loneliness had lower NK activity and higher levels of herpesvirus antibody than those who described themselves as less lonely. In a related study, lonelier psychiatric inpatients had poorer NK cell function and lower proliferative responses to PHA than did patients who reported less loneliness (Kiecolt-Glaser et al 1984). Because loneliness is generally associated with psychological distress and negative affect (Peplau & Perlman 1982), these relations might be explicable in the same terms as the effects of negative emotions described above.

There is substantial evidence that poorer marital relations and marital disruption (separation and divorce) are associated with poorer health (Verbrugge 1979). Recent work has searched for potential effects of marital discord on immune function. Kiecolt-Glaser et al (1987a) found that 16 separated and divorced (S/D) women had higher levels of herpes antibody, a lower percentage of NK cells, and lower lymphocyte proliferative response to PHA and Con A than a comparison group of 16 married women. In a similar study, Kiecolt-Glaser et al (1988) found that 32 S/D men reported having more infectious illnesses and had higher levels of herpes antibody than their 32 married counterparts. Finally, a study that categorized newlywed couples on the basis of observed interactions (Kiecolt-Glaser et al 1993) found that those who exhibited more negative or hostile behaviors showed greater decreases over 24 hours in NK activity and proliferative response to PHA and Con A.

Perceived availability of social support has also been associated with immune function. A study of 256 elderly adults (Thomas et al 1985) found that blood samples from persons reporting they had confiding relationships proliferated more in response to PHA than samples from those without confiding relationships. Moreover, this relation was unchanged by controlling for psychological distress and health practices. Similar results were found in a study of 23 spouses of patients with cancer (Baron et al 1990). Six different provisions of social support (including emotional and instrumental forms of support) were associated with higher NK activity and better proliferative response to PHA (but not to Con A). Better immune response among supported persons could not be explained by greater depression or more numerous stressful life events among those with less social support. Glaser et al (1992) found that medical students reporting more available social support produced more antibody in response to a hepatitis B vaccination than those reporting less support, but two studies of HIV-positive men were less successful in establishing relations between social support and immunity (Goodkin et al 1992, Perry et al 1992). However, HIV infection compromises the immune system to a degree so severe that the relatively small effects of social support on immune function might be undetectable.

Many of the beneficial health effects of interpersonal relationships are attributed to receipt or availability of emotional support—someone to talk to about problems (Cohen & Wills 1985). A related literature has examined the potential health benefits associated with persons' disclosure of traumatic events. Pennebaker and his colleagues (Pennebaker & Beall 1986) reported that college students instructed to write about both the emotions and facts associated with a traumatic event had fewer subsequent visits to the health center than those instructed to write about emotions or facts alone. In a follow-up study of the role the immune system might play in the beneficial process of trauma disclosure (Pennebaker et al 1988), 50 healthy undergraduates were assigned to write about either personal and traumatic events or trivial topics. They wrote for 20 minutes a day on four consecutive days. Immunologic data were collected before the study began (baseline), at the end of the intervention, and at six-week and four-month follow-ups. Blood drawn from subjects who wrote about traumatic events was more responsive to PHA (but not Con A). There were no relations between disclosure and alcohol intake, caffeine intake, or exercise over the course of the study. In addition, subjects revealing traumatic events made fewer visits to the health center in the six weeks following the intervention than did members of the control group. Unfortunately, the data do not support an immune pathway because the lymphocyte proliferation data were *not* correlated with health-center visits. This absence of correlation also suggests that increases in health center visits may be driven by psychological influences on decision processes rather than by influences on actual illness (Cohen & Williamson 1991).

Research on how social-support interventions affect immune system function in stressed samples is in its infancy. Existing studies provide only suggestive evidence. Three visits a week for a month by college students to geriatric-home residents resulted in no detectable effects on residents' cellular immune response (Kiecolt-Glaser et al 1985); nor did an intervention (of unspecified length) that provided emotional support and information about finding new jobs modify the decrease in lymphocyte proliferation to PHA suffered by a group of Swedish women who were unemployed for over nine months (Arnetz et al 1987). However, a six-session group intervention with melanoma patients was associated with decreased psychological distress and increased NK activity six months after the intervention (Fawzy et al 1993). This intervention was run by professional facilitators and included such elements as stress management training and education about cancer. How to design appropriate and effective social support interventions is a controversial and as yet unresolved question. Appropriate design depends on definitions of social resources to be provided, the nature of the population, the source of the support, strategies for structuring group interaction, and the duration of the intervention.

Personality

The study of the role of personality in health has a long history (Friedman 1990). However, relations between personality characteristics and immunity have received little attention. Personality characteristics correlated with measures of immune status include power motivation (e.g. Jemmott et al 1983, 1990), pessimistic style (Kamen-Siegel et al 1991), and repression (Esterling et al 1993). We limit our discussion to repression/denial because it has been studied in relation both to immune function and to immune system–mediated disease [acquired immunodeficiency syndrome (AIDS) and cancer].

Repression/denial represents a coping strategy against threatening information and is characterized by denial or minimization of distress and negative emotions. Repressors react to stressful stimuli with higher autonomic arousal than persons reporting high anxiety or distress (Weinberger et al 1979).

Esterling et al (1993) found no association of repression with herpesvirus antibodies when repression was operationalized in terms of a low score in trait anxiety and a high score in defensiveness. However, higher scores on a personality inventory assessing repression were associated with the suppression of cellular immune function as indicated by higher levels of herpesvirus antibody in two independent samples (Esterling et al 1990, 1994a). These relations held even after controlling for medication use and a range of health practices. In contrast, Antoni et al (1990) found that gay males who were about to be tested for HIV status who scored higher on a denial coping scale had a *greater* proliferative response to PHA. This work suggests the possibility of a link between repression/denial and cellular immune response but also suggests that the scale used to measure repression/denial is important.

DO PSYCHOLOGICAL FACTORS INFLUENCE IMMUNE SYSTEM–MEDIATED DISEASE?

Invasion of the body by a disease-causing agent is not sufficient cause for disease. Disease occurs when host defenses are compromised or unable to recognize the foreign material. This is why psychological variables that influence immunity have the potential to influence the onset and progression of immune system–mediated diseases. What is less clear is whether psychologically induced changes in immunity are of the magnitude or type that would alter the ability of the body to fight disease (Cohen & Williamson 1991, Laudenslager 1987, O'Leary 1990). Below, we review a selection of studies that addresses the role of psychological factors in the onset and progression of infectious diseases, autoimmune diseases, and cancer. We limit ourselves primarily to prospective or intervention studies and to studies in which disease outcomes are biologically verified or physician documented.

Infectious Disease

UPPER RESPIRATORY INFECTIONS (URI)   Early prospective work by Meyer & Haggerty (1962) indicated that both disruptive daily events and chronic family stress were associated with greater risk for upper respiratory infections. Similar results were reported by Graham et al (1986). Measures of life stress were collected from members of 94 families before and during a six-month period in which diary data on subjects' respiratory symptoms were collected daily. Illness episodes were validated by nose and throat cultures. Although high- and low-stress groups were almost identical with respect to demographics and health practices, the high-stress groups experienced more verified episodes of illness and more days with symptoms of respiratory illness.

In a study of susceptibility to influenza (Clover et al 1989), 246 individuals in 58 families completed instruments assessing family relationships and individual stressful life events prior to the start of flu season. Stressed ("rigid and chaotic") families showed greater incidence of disease than nonstressed ("balanced") families. However, illness was not related to individual stressful life events.

Increased incidence of URI under stress in these studies may be attributable to stress-induced increases in exposure to infectious agents rather than to stress-induced immunosuppression. For example, persons under stress often seek out others, which increases the probability of exposure. A series of studies using a procedure through which volunteers are intentionally exposed to a virus (viral-challenge trials) provides control for exposure. In these prospective designs, psychological factors are assessed before volunteers are intentionally exposed to an upper respiratory virus. Whether or not persons develop biologically verified clinical illness over the course of 7 to 10 days of quarantine is then assessed as the dependent variable.

Three recent viral-challenge trials suggest interesting relations between psychological stress and URI susceptibility. In a study of 394 volunteers (Cohen et al 1991, 1993), measures of stressful life events, perceived stress, and negative affect all predicted the probability of developing a cold, with greater stress linearly related to greater probability. The relations that Cohen et al reported were found consistently across five different URI viruses. Moreover, these results could not be explained by stress-elicited differences in health practices such as smoking and alcohol consumption or in the numbers of various white blood cell populations or total (nonspecific) antibody levels. It is interesting to note that stressful life events predicted susceptibility independently of (and through a different biological mechanism than) perceived stress and negative affect. In another study, Stone et al (1992) replicated the relation between stressful life events and susceptibility to URI and identified the same biological pathway as in the work of Cohen et al (1993). Finally, in a viral-challenge study examining predictors of disease severity (rather than episode onset), Cohen et al (1995a) found that state (but not trait) negative affect measured just prior to viral exposure was associated with more severe colds and influenza as measured by the amount of mucus produced over the course of the illness.

In sum, both stressful life events and psychological stress (perceptions and negative affect) are associated with increased susceptibility to upper respiratory infections. These effects are not generally explicable in terms of stress-elicited changes in health behaviors. However, neither is there any direct evidence yet that increased susceptibility is attributable to stress-induced immunosuppression.

HERPESVIRUS INFECTIONS   Herpesviruses are thought to be responsible for cold sores, genital lesions, infectious mononucleosis, and mononucleosis syndrome and deafness in neonates (Kiecolt-Glaser & Glaser 1987). Herpesviruses differ from most other known viruses in that after exposure, they are present in individuals all the time, although often in latent states. The cellular immune response plays a key role both in protection from initial herpesvirus infection and in keeping latent herpesviruses from becoming active (Glaser & Gotlieb-Stematsky 1982). As discussed earlier, one explanation for the increase in herpesvirus antibodies often associated with stressful conditions is that stress suppresses cellular immune function, which allows the latent virus to become active. Is stress associated with a recurrence of clinical disease (lesions) after a period of herpesvirus latency?

In a series of studies of student nurses conducted in the 1970s, negative moods at the beginning of the school year were generally associated with greater numbers of subsequent episodes of verified oral herpes (Friedmann et al 1977, Katcher et al 1973, Luborsky et al 1976). Similar evidence for stress-induced recurrence is provided by both retrospective (e.g. Kemeny et al 1989) and prospective studies of genital herpes (Goldmeier & Johnson 1982, McLarnon & Kaloupek 1988; see critiques in Cohen & Williamson 1991). A recent study of 125 college students provides an elegant test of the role of stress in herpes recurrence through an examination of several specific causal models (Hoon et al 1991). This work indicates that stress increases vulnerability to illness in general (nonherpes) and that it is this increase in nonspecific vulnerability that results in herpes recurrence. Hoon et al did not address the physiological basis for this vulnerability, but because the illness vulnerability measure was heavily influenced by highly prevalent infectious diseases (colds and influenza), an immune basis is plausible.

In sum, herpes studies generally support a relation between negative emotional states and disease recurrence. However, the evidence is not entirely consistent, and methodological limitations warrant cautious interpretation of these results. Moreover, existing work does not establish the extent to which such effects are mediated through immune or behavioral pathways.

AIDS   Not all persons exposed to the HIV virus become infected. After exposure, both the number of years to manifestation of clinical symptoms and the severity of illness at all stages of AIDS vary tremendously. Poor nutrition, drug use, repeated HIV exposure, and other concurrent viral infections can all accelerate HIV disease progression. However, even after these factors are accounted for, a good deal of variability in response to the virus is unexplained. Psychological variables are thought to contribute to host resistance to the HIV virus by altering relevant behavioral practices and hormonal and immune environments (Baum & Nesselhof 1988, Kemeny 1994, Schneiderman et al 1994).

Studies of the roles of stress and negative affect in the progression of HIV infection are inconsistent in their conclusions. Burack et al (1993) found that HIV-positive gay men who were depressed at baseline showed greater declines than a nondpressed control group in numbers of T-helper cells (an important prognostic indicator of HIV) over a subsequent period of five years. However, depression was not associated with either the onset of AIDS or mortality. In contrast, in another study of HIV-positive gay men, Lyketsos et al (1993) found no association between depression and changes in T-helper cell counts, AIDS onset, or mortality over a subsequent period of eight years. In a recent study (Kemeny et al 1995), HIV-positive men who recently lost an intimate partner to AIDS showed an increase in levels of an immune marker of disease progression (serum neopterin) as well as a decrease in lymphocyte proliferation in response to PHA. Neither immune change was explicable in terms of use of recreational drugs, alcohol, or smoking. Finally, Kessler et al (1991) did not find correlations between recent losses or stressful life events during the six months prior to baseline and two disease outcomes—T-helper cell count and onset of symptoms associated with AIDS over the subsequent two to three years. All of these studies can be faulted for focusing on baseline stress and depression as predictors of the long-term course of disease. These variables are not stable over time and there is a need to examine triggers closer to the time of disease onset (Cohen et al 1995b).

Investigations of the role of denial in AIDS are inconsistent. Ironson et al (1994) studied disease progression in initially asymptomatic HIV-positive men involved in a behavioral intervention program. Persons who denied their diagnosis did poorly on markers of disease progression one year later (poorer PHA-stimulated proliferation and greater decline in T-helper cells) and reported more symptoms two years later. Immune function at one year was associated with symptoms at a two-year follow-up, but no direct test of immune mediation of the association between denial and symptoms was conducted. In contrast, Reed et al (1994) reported that HIV-positive gay men who refuse to accept their disease and its implications live nine months longer than those who realistically accept them.

Finally, in a single study of social support (Theorell et al 1995), 48 hemophiliac patients who were infected with the HIV virus were followed for five years. Those who reported less access to emotional support at baseline showed a greater decline in T-helper cells over the course of the study than those with stronger support systems. There were no differences between groups in number of symptoms of AIDS or in rates of mortality.

INTERVENTIONS   Two studies investigated the potential impact of stress management interventions on immune markers of AIDS progression. A study of men diagnosed with HIV infection (Coates et al 1989) found no differences in T-helper cell numbers or lymphocyte proliferation between treated and untreated patients. In a study of individuals' responses to being diagnosed HIV positive (Antoni et al 1991), those who received stress management prior to notification responded with a better immune status (greater T-helper and NK cell numbers and greater PHA-stimulated lymphocyte proliferation) than no-treatment controls. Both of these studies had small sample sizes and short follow-ups, and neither preselected participants for particular vulnerabilities (e.g. depression). Intervention work is of great theoretical and practical importance and further studies using various proven approaches as well as improved methodologies should be the highest priority.

Evidence reported above is at best mixed in its support for a role of psychological variables in the progression of HIV infections. Investigations of the role of psychological factors in AIDS, however, pose difficult methodological challenges. Time since infection is usually indeterminable; there is difficulty in controlling for effects of medication; and the work published to date has lacked sufficient time-lines for assessing mortality. Further work attending to the stability of the psychological predictors, recognizing that psychological factors may have different influences on different stages of disease, and assessing alternative explanations for relations would be welcome.

Autoimmune Diseases

In autoimmune disease, the body begins to attack its own cells and organs. The immune system produces antibodies that attack its own tissues (autoantibodies), and T lymphocytes fail to discriminate self from nonself and attack normal body tissue (Rabin et al 1989). Autoimmune disorders include rheumatoid arthritis (RA), insulin-dependent diabetes, lupus, Graves disease, inflammatory bowel disease, and multiple sclerosis. Each is associated with different organs and with somewhat differing immune processes. Most of the work on the role of psychological factors in autoimmune disease has involved patients with RA. The primary symptom of RA is inflammation of the joints, and progression of the disease leads to erosion of cartilage and finally to joint-cavity destruction.

Numerous clinical observations and several retrospective studies suggest that psychological factors, including stressful life events (Homo-Delarche et al 1991, Rimón et al 1977) and less-supportive atmospheres (DeVellis et al 1986, Moos & Solomon 1964), play a role in the onset and exacerbation of autoimmune diseases. More impressive are studies evaluating the effectiveness of cognitive-behavioral interventions on RA progression (review in Young 1992). Although not all interventions are successful in affecting disease outcomes (e.g. Parker et al 1988, Strauss et al 1986), many have been. For example, Bradley et al (1987) assigned RA patients to one of three groups. The first was a cognitive-behavioral program consisting of biofeedback training, RA education, relaxation training, behavioral goal setting, and use of self-rewards. The second included a social support condition consisting of small group meetings with family members or friends to discuss RA education, current coping strategies, and the development of improved coping methods. The third group was a no-treatment control. Compared with the other two groups, the patients assigned to the cognitive-behavioral program showed greater reductions in pain intensity, inflammation, and serum levels of rheumatoid factor (a marker of disease progression) immediately posttreatment. However, these benefits were no longer evident six months later. O'Leary et al (1988) also used a cognitive-behavioral intervention and compared disease outcomes of patients undergoing the intervention with patients assigned to a control group that received only printed information (i.e. a bibliotherapy control). The treatment group met once each week for two hours over a five-week period, and assessments of disease outcome were made immediately before and after the five weeks of intervention. When compared with the control group, patients receiving the cognitive-behavioral intervention reported reduced pain, and rheumatologists who were blind to patient group assignment found improved joint conditions among these patients.

Finally, Radojevic et al (1992) conducted a six-week-long intervention and assigned RA patients to one of four groups: cognitive-behavioral intervention with family support, cognitive-behavioral intervention alone, education with family support, or a no-treatment control group. The family support component of the intervention differed depending on the condition, although in both groups family members attended the meetings. In the cognitive-behavioral intervention, family support consisted of learning how RA affects the family environment and how the family can assist the patient in coping with pain and in helping the patient to increase his/her functioning. In the education group, patients received emotional support from family during sessions and were encouraged to discuss illness-related problems between sessions with their family members. Regardless of whether family support was available, RA patients in the cognitive-behavioral interventions showed improvement in joint exam, reduced swelling severity, and fewer swollen joints two months after the intervention, compared with the other two groups.

At this point it is unclear why some interventions with RA patients resulted in improved health and others did not, although possible reasons include differences in patient adherence to the interventions' requirements; differing amounts of practice to maintain gains; or differences in such patient characteristics as severity of disease, amount of disability, and sex (Young 1992). Moreover, none of the existing work directly addresses how (i.e whether by means of immune changes, behavioral changes, etc) psychological factors alter disease progression.

Cancer

Cancer comprises a large and heterogeneous group of diseases characterized by the uncontrolled proliferation of cells. Because the immune system is thought to play important roles in tumor surveillance and in preventing the progression and metastatic spread of tumors, psychological factors associated with immunity are considered potential contributors to cancer onset and progression (Anderson et al 1994). The immune function emphasized as a link between psychological factors and cancer is NK activity. The presumed importance of NK activity is based on the combination of reliable findings associating psychologic variables with NK activity (Herbert & Cohen 1993a,b) and on the association of depressed NK activity and increased metastases in animal models (Gorelik & Herberman 1986). However, different cancers are very different diseases, and immune and psychological factors may play a role in some but not in others (Holland 1990, Rabin et al 1989). Similarly, psychological and immune processes may vary at different phases of tumor growth—tumor induction, growth, and metastases (Sklar & Anisman 1981).

We reviewed work suggesting that both depressed affect and clinical depression have been associated with changes in immune function (including lower NK activity). Depression has also received considerable attention as a contributor to cancer; however, the results are not entirely consistent. This work includes prospective epidemiological studies of initially healthy persons that predict subsequent cancer incidence and mortality as well as studies that predict survival among diagnosed cancer patients.

Evidence from prospective incidence and mortality studies is mixed. In a 20-year follow-up of 2020 men who completed the Minnesota Multiphasic Personality Inventory in 1957–1958, those with higher depression scores had twice the risk of dying of cancer 17 (Shekelle et al 1981) and 20 years (Persky et al 1987) later than did their less depressed counterparts. These effects were nonspecific to site or type of cancer and could not be explained by differences in health practices. It is interesting to note that when a formula was used to calculate whether patients were "clinically depressed" from the self-reported scale, no relation to cancer was found (Bieliauskas & Garron 1982). Gross-sarth-Maticek et al (1983, 1985) found that persons with long-lasting hope-lessness and depression were more likely than those neither hopeless nor depressed to develop cancer over a 10-year follow-up. This relation was inde-pendent of a series of biological predictors of disease onset. Several 10- to 20-year prospective studies have failed to find that clinical depression as assessed by self-report depression scales placed people at risk for either cancer incidence or cancer mortality (Hahn & Petitti 1988, Kaplan & Reynolds 1988, Zonderman et al 1989). Depression has, however, been associated with mark-ers of disease progression (Levy et al 1985) and shorter survival among patients diagnosed with cancer (e.g. Derogatis et al 1979, Weisman & Worden 1975).

Why are existing data inconsistent? Work on the role of depression in cancer incidence and mortality has focused on undifferentiated cancer out-comes, and greater emphasis on specific disease types and sites may be neces-sary to clarify this literature. The temporal instability of both depressive affect and clinical depression and the possible role of more acute depressive episodes in cancer onset and progression also need to be recognized (Cohen et al 1995b). This requires repeated measures of depression over the course of longitudinal studies as well as testing at shorter intervals between depression and disease onset.

Evidence discussed above addressed the role of interpersonal relationships and support in immunity. Among cancer patients, greater access to social support has been associated with better prognostic indicators (Levy et al 1985) and longer survival (Funch & Marshall 1983, Weisman & Worden 1975). However, the effects of social support on survival may occur for younger but not for older women (Funch & Marshall 1983), and both disease onset and mortality may be associated with social isolation among women but not men (Reynolds & Kaplan 1990). This work is consistent with other research on the role of social support and suggests that different social structures and re-sources may have different implications for different populations, particularly as defined by gender and age.

Finally, a 15-year study suggests that patients who respond to nonmetas-tatic breast cancer with a fighting spirit or with denial have less recurrence and longer lives than patients with stoic acceptance (fatalism) or helpless responses (Greer 1991). Partial replications of this work have been reported (Dean & Surtees 1989, DiClemente & Temoshok 1985). Greer (1991) cautions that these results have been found in the context of breast and cervical cancer and that generalizations to other cancers are not warranted.

Although there are many consistencies in these correlational literatures, as a whole they must be viewed in light of several concerns and qualifications. The problems associated with cancer (e.g. undetected premorbid states, difficulty in quantifying severity at any stage, differences in biology of different tumors, difficulty in assessing and controlling for medication and compliance with medical regimens) make it difficult (and often impossible) to design studies that eliminate important alternative explanations. Correlations may be spurious—i.e. derived from other variables such as toxic workplaces, viruses, or chronic infections that influence both psychological characteristics and cancer (Sklar & Anisman 1981). Moreover, although psychological variables may affect survival, the contribution is relatively small and is overshadowed by biological factors. Hence psychological variables are least likely to play a role in later and more serious stages of disease (e.g. Cassileth et al 1985, Jamison et al 1987).

INTERVENTIONS   Two recent intervention studies provide the most provocative and convincing evidence for a role of psychological factors in cancer progression. In one (Fawzy et al 1993), 66 malignant-melanoma patients were randomly assigned to either an intervention or a no-treatment control group. The intervention combined education, stress management, coping skills, and discussion with patients and facilitators and consisted of six 90-minute sessions. Six months after the intervention ended, participants in the intervention group showed reduced psychologic distress, enhanced immune function (increased NK activity), and changes in immune cell counts (decreased T cells, increased lymphocytes) when compared with patients in the control group. The intervention also decreased recurrence and increased survival as assessed six years later. Alterations in immune outcomes, however, did not explain the intervention's effect on mortality. In the other intervention study (Spiegel et al 1989), 58 patients with metastatic breast cancer were randomly assigned to either an intervention or a no-treatment control group. The intervention consisted of weekly 90-minute meetings for one year. The highly structured meeting focused on various problems associated with terminal illness and on ways to improve relationships. Ten years later, there was an 18-month survival advantage associated with the intervention. No immune measures were assessed. These studies are conceptually important because they are experimental demonstrations of the significance of psychological factors, and they are practically important because they suggest a significant role for psychological interventions in cancer survival. Ongoing attempts to replicate and extend this work will help us evaluate their validity as well as identify behavioral and immune mechanisms responsible for reported outcomes.

CONCLUSIONS

The literature discussed in this chapter is in many ways impressive. First, it provides psychologically and biologically plausible explanations for how psychological factors might influence immunity and immune system–mediated disease. Second, it provides substantial evidence that psychological factors can influence both cellular and humoral indicators of immune status and function. Third, at least in the case of the less serious infectious diseases (colds, influenza, herpes), it includes consistent and convincing evidence of links between stress and disease onset and progression. Although still early in its development, research on autoimmune diseases (at least on RA) also suggests the potential role of psychological factors. Evidence for effects of psychological factors on AIDS and cancer is less consistent and inconclusive. This may be because of methodological limitations inherent in studying these complex illnesses, or it may be because psychological influences on immunity are just not of the magnitude or type necessary to alter the body's response in these cases. Further development and evaluation of psychosocial interventions may be the best approach for providing evidence that allows clear causal inference and at the same time has clinical implications. What is missing in this literature, however, is strong evidence that the associations between psychological factors and disease that do exist are attributable to immune changes. Many of the relations reported in this chapter may be attributable to psychologically induced changes in health behaviors (e.g. health practices such as smoking and alcohol consumption, or degree of adherence to medical regimens); better measurement and control of these variables are essential. Moreover, the inclusion in future studies of immune measures based on the role of the immune system in the specific disease under study may help provide evidence for a direct link among psychological factors, immunity, and disease.

ACKNOWLEDGMENTS

Drs. Cohen and Herbert's contributions were supported by a Research Scientist Development Award (K02MH00721) and a grant (MH50430) from the National Institute of Mental Health, respectively. We are indebted to Drs. Andrew Baum, Bruce Rabin, and Mario Rodriguez for their comments on an earlier draft and to Janet Schlarb and Susan Kravitz for their aid in preparing the chapter.

Literature Cited

Ader R, Cohen N. 1993. Psychoneuroimmunology: conditioning and stress. *Annu. Rev. Psychol.* 44:53–85

Anderson BL, Kiecolt-Glaser JK, Glaser R. 1994. A biobehavioral model of cancer stress and disease course. *Am. Psychol.* 49:389–404

Antoni MH, August S, LaPerriere A, Baggett HL, Klimas N, et al. 1990. Psychological and neuroendocrine measures related to functional immune changes in anticipation of HIV-1 serostatus notification. *Psychosom. Med.* 52:496–510

Antoni MH, Baggett HL, Ironson G, LaPerriere A, August S, et al. 1991. Cognitive-behavioral stress management intervention buffers distress responses and immunologic changes following notification of HIV-1 seropositivity. *J. Consult. Clin. Psychol.* 59:906–15

Arnetz BB, Wasserman J, Petrini B, Brenner S-O, Levi L, et al. 1987. Immune function in unemployed women. *Psychosom. Med.* 49:3–12

Bachen EA, Manuck SB, Cohen S, Muldoon MF, Raible R, et al. 1995. Adrenergic blockage ameliorates cellular immune responses to mental stress in humans. *Psychosom. Med.* In press

Baron RS, Cutrona CE, Hicklin D, Russell DW, Lubaroff DM. 1990. Social support and immune function among spouses of cancer patients. *J. Pers. Soc. Psychol.* 59:344–52

Baum A, Nesselhof EA. 1988. Psychological research and the prevention, etiology, and treatment of AIDS. *Am. Psychol.* 43:900–6

Baum A, Schaeffer MA, Lake CR, Fleming R, Collins DL. 1985. Psychological and endocrinological correlates of chronic stress at Three Mile Island. In *Perspectives on Behavioral Medicine*, ed. R Williams, 2:201–17. San Diego: Academic

Benschop RJ, Nieuwenhuis EES, Tromp EAM, Godaert GLR, Bailieux RE, van Doornen LJP. 1994. Effects of ß-adrenergic blockade on immunologic and cardiovascular changes induced by mental stress. *Circulation* 89:762–69

Bieliauskas LA, Garron DC. 1982. Psychological depression and cancer. *Gen. Hosp. Psychiatr.* 4:187–95

Bovbjerg DH, Redd WH, Maier LA, Holland JC, Lesko LM, et al. 1990. Anticipatory immune suppression and nausea in women receiving cyclic chemotherapy for ovarian cancer. *J. Consult. Clin. Psychol.* 58:153–57

Boyce WT, Chesney M, Alkon A, Tschann JM, Adams S, et al. 1995. Psychobiologic reactivity to stress and childhood respiratory illnesses. *Psychosom. Med.* In press

Bradley LA, Young LD, Anderson KO, Turner RA, Agudelo CA, et al. 1987. Effects of psychological therapy on pain behavior of rheumatoid arthritis patients: treatment outcome and six-month followup. *Arthritis Rheum.* 30:1105–14

Burack JH, Barrett DC, Stall RD, Chesney MA, Ekstrand ML, Coates TJ. 1993. Depressive symptoms and CD4 lymphocyte decline among HIV-infected men. *J. Am. Med. Assoc.* 270:2568–73

Buske-Kirschbaum A, Kirschbaum C, Stierle H, Lehnert H, Hellhammer D. 1992. Conditioned increase of natural killer cell activity (NKCA) in humans. *Psychosom. Med.* 54:123–32

Cassileth BR, Lusk EJ, Miller DS, Brown LL, Miller C. 1985. Psychosocial correlates of survival in advanced malignant disease. *N. Engl. J. Med.* 312:1551–55

Clover RD, Abell T, Becker LA, Crawford S, Ramsey JCN. 1989. Family functioning and stress as predictors of influenza B infection. *J. Fam. Pract.* 28:535–39

Coates TJ, McKusick L, Kuno R, Stites DP. 1989. Stress reduction training changed number of sexual partners but not immune function in men with HIV. *Am. J. Public Health* 79:885–87

Cohen S. 1988. Psychosocial models of the role of social support in the etiology of physical disease. *Health Psychol.* 7:269–97

Cohen S, Doyle WJ, Skoner DP, Fireman P, Gwaltney JM Jr, Newsom JT. 1995a. State and trait negative affect as predictors of objective and subjective symptoms of respiratory viral infections. *J. Pers. Soc. Psychol.* 68:159–69

Cohen S, Kessler RC, Underwood Gordon LG. 1995b. Strategies for measuring stress in studies of psychiatric and physical disorders. In *Measuring Stress: A Guide for Health and Social Scientists*, ed. S Cohen, RC Kessler, L Underwood Gordon, pp. 3–26. New York: Oxford

Cohen S, Manuck SB. 1995. Stress, reactivity and disease. *Psychosom. Med.* In press

Cohen S, Tyrrell DAJ, Smith AP. 1991. Psychological stress and susceptibility to the common cold. *N. Engl. J. Med.* 325: 606–12

Cohen S, Tyrrell DAJ, Smith AP. 1993. Negative life events, perceived stress, negative affect, and susceptibility to the common cold. *J. Pers. Soc. Psychol.* 64:131–40

Cohen S, Williamson GM. 1988. Perceived stress in a probability sample of the United States. In *The Social Psychology of Health*, ed. S Spacapan, S Oskamp, pp. 31–67. Newbury, CA: Sage

Cohen S, Williamson GM. 1991. Stress and infectious disease in humans. *Psychol. Bull.* 109:5–24

Cohen S, Wills TA. 1985. Stress, social support, and the buffering hypothesis. *Psychol. Bull.* 2:310–57

Dean C, Surtees PG. 1989. Do psychological factors predict survival in breast cancer? *J. Psychosom. Res.* 33:561–69

Derogatis LR, Abeloff MD, Melisaratos N. 1979. Psychological coping mechanisms and survival time in metastatic breast cancer. *J. Am. Med. Assoc.* 242:1504–8

DeVellis RF, DeVellis B, McEvoy H, Sauter SV, Harring K, Cohen JL. 1986. Predictors of pain and functioning in arthritis. *Health Educ. Res.: Theory Pract.* 1:61–67

DiClemente RJ, Temoshok L. 1985. Psychological adjustment to having cutaneous malignant melanoma as a predictor of follow-up clinical status. *Psychosom. Med.* 47:81 (Abstr.)

Esterling BA, Antoni MH, Fletcher MA, Margulies S, Schneiderman N. 1994a. Emotional disclosure through writing or speaking modulates latent Epstein-Barr virus antibody titers. *J. Consult. Clin. Psychol.* 62: 130–40

Esterling BA, Antoni MH, Kumar M, Schneiderman N. 1990. Emotional repression, stress disclosure responses, and Epstein-Barr viral capsid antigen titers. *Psychosom. Med.* 52:397–410

Esterling BA, Antoni MH, Kumar M, Schneiderman N. 1993. Defensiveness, trait anxiety, and Epstein-Barr virus capsid antigen antibody titers in healthy college students. *Health Psychol.* 12:132–39

Esterling BA, Kiecolt-Glaser JK, Bodnar JC, Glaser R. 1994b. Chronic stress, social support, and persistent alterations in the natural killer cell response to cytokines in older adults. *Health Psychol.* 13:291–98

Fawzy FI, Fawzy NW, Hyun CS, Elashoff R, Guthrie D, et al. 1993. Malignant melanoma: effects of an early structured psychiatric intervention, coping, and affective state on recurrence and survival six years later. *Arch. Gen. Psychiatr.* 50:681–89

Felten DL, Felten SY, Carlson SL, Olschowka JA, Livnat S. 1985. Noradrenergic sympathetic innervation of lymphoid tissue. *J. Immunol.* 135:755S–65S

Friedmann E, Katcher AH, Brightman VJ. 1977. Incidence of recurrent herpes labialis and upper respiratory infection: a prospective study of the influence of biologic, social and psychologic predictors. *Oral Surg. Oral Med. Oral Pathol.* 43:873–78

Friedman HS. 1990. *Personality and Disease.* New York: Wiley

Funch DP, Marshall J. 1983. The role of stress, social support and age in survival from breast cancer. *J. Psychosom. Res.* 27:77–83

Futterman AD, Kemeny ME, Shapiro D, Fahey JL. 1994. Immunological and physiological changes associated with induced positive and negative mood. *Psychosom. Med.* 56: 499–511

Glaser R, Gottlieb-Stematsky TE. 1982. *Human Herpesvirus Infections: Clinical Aspects.* New York: Marcel Dekker

Glaser R, Kiecolt-Glaser JK, Bonneau RH, Malarkey W, Kennedy S, Hughes J. 1992. Stress-induced modulation of immune response to recombinant hepatitis B vaccine. *Psychosom. Med.* 54:22–29

Glaser R, Kiecolt-Glaser JK, Speicher CE, Holliday JE. 1985a. Stress, loneliness, and changes in herpesvirus latency. *J. Behav. Med.* 8:249–60

Glaser R, Kiecolt-Glaser JK, Stout JC, Tarr KL, Speicher CE, Holliday JE. 1985b. Stress-related impairments in cellular immunity. *Psychiatr. Res.* 16:233–39

Glaser R, Pearson GR, Bonneau RH, Esterling BA, Atkinson C, Kiecolt-Glaser JK. 1993. Stress and the memory T-cell response to the Epstein-Barr virus in healthy medical students. *Health Psychol.* 12:435–42

Glaser R, Pearson GR, Jones JF, Hillhouse J, Kennedy S, et al. 1991. Stress-related activation of Epstein-Barr virus. *Brain Behav. Immun.* 5:219–32

Glaser R, Rice J, Sheridan J, Fertel R, Stout JC, et al. 1987. Stress-related immune suppression: health implications. *Brain Behav. Immun.* 1:7–20

Glaser R, Rice J, Speicher CE, Stout JC, Kiecolt-Glaser JK. 1986. Stress depresses interferon production by leukocytes concomitant with a decrease in natural killer cell activity. *Behav. Neurosci.* 100:675–78

Goldmeier D, Johnson A. 1982. Does psychiatric illness affect the recurrence rate of genital herpes? *Br. J. Vener. Dis.* 54:40–43

Goodkin K, Blaney NT, Feaster D, Fletcher MA, Baum A, et al. 1992. Active coping style is associated with natural killer cell cytotoxicity in asymptomatic HIV-1 seropositive homosexual men. *J. Psychosom. Res.* 36:635–50

Gorelik E, Herberman R. 1986. The role of natural killer "NK" cells in the control of tumor growth and metastatic spread. In

Cancer Immunology: Innovative Approaches to Therapy, ed. R Herberman, pp. 151–76. Boston: Martinez Nijhoff

Graham NMH, Douglas RB, Ryan P. 1986. Stress and acute respiratory infection. *Am. J. Epidemiol.* 124:389–401

Greer S. 1991. Psychological response to cancer and survival. *Psychol. Med.* 21:43–49

Gregory MD, Smeltzer MA. 1983. *Psychiatry: Essentials of Clinical Practice.* Boston: Little, Brown

Grossarth-Maticek R, Kanazir DT, Schmidt P, Vetter H. 1985. Psychosocial and organic variables as predictors of lung cancer, cardiac infarct and apoplexy: some differential predictors. *Pers. Individ. Differ.* 6:313–21

Grossarth-Maticek R, Kanazir DT, Vetter H, Schmidt P. 1983. Psychosomatic factors involved in the process of cancerogenesis. *Psychother. Psychosom.* 40:191–210

Grunberg NE, Baum A. 1985. Biological commonalities of stress and substance abuse. In *Coping and Substance Use,* ed. S Shiffman, TA Wills, pp. 25–62. San Diego: Academic

Hahn RC, Petitti DB. 1988. Minnesota Multiphasic Personality Inventory–rated depression and the incidence of breast cancer. *Cancer* 61:845–48

Herbert TB, Cohen S. 1993a. Depression and immunity: a meta-analytic review. *Psychol. Bull.* 113:472–86

Herbert TB, Cohen S. 1993b. Stress and immunity in humans: a meta-analytic review. *Psychosom. Med.* 55:364–79

Herbert TB, Cohen S, Marsland AL, Bachen EA, Rabin BS, et al. 1994. Cardiovascular reactivity and the course of immune response to an acute psychological stressor. *Psychosom. Med.* 56:337–44

Holland JC. 1990. Behavioral and psychosocial risk factors in cancer: human studies. In *Handbook of Psychooncology—Psychological Care of the Patient with Cancer,* ed. JC Holland, JH Rowland, pp. 705–26. NY: Oxford Univ. Press

Homo-Delarche F, Fitzpatrick F, Christeff N, Nunez EA, Bach JF, Dardenne M. 1991. Sex steroids, glucocorticoids, stress and autoimmunity. *J. Steroid Biochem. Molec. Biol.* 40:619–37

Hoon EF, Hoon PW, Rand KH, Johnson J, Hall NR, Edwards NB. 1991. A psycho-behavioral model of genital herpes recurrence. *J. Psychosom. Res.* 35:25–36

House JS, Landis KR, Umberson D. 1988. Social relationships and health. *Science* 241: 540–45

Ironson G, Friedman A, Klimas N, Antoni M, Fletcher MA, et al. 1994. Distress, denial and low adherence to behavioral interventions predict faster disease progression in gay men infected with human immunodeficiency virus. *Int. J. Behav. Med.* 1:90–105

Irwin M, Brown M, Patterson T, Hauger R, Mascovich A, Grant I. 1991. Neuropeptide Y and natural killer cell activity: findings in depression and Alzheimer caregiver stress. *FASEB J.* 5:3100–7

Irwin M, Lacher U, Caldwell C. 1992. Depression and reduced natural killer cytotoxicity: a longitudinal study of depressed patients and control subjects. *Psychol. Med.* 22: 1045–50

Irwin M, Patterson T, Smith TL, Caldwell C, Brown SA, et al. 1990. Reduction of immune function in life stress and depression. *Biol. Psychiatr.* 27:22–30

Irwin M, Smith TL, Gillin JC. 1987. Low natural killer cytotoxicity in major depression. *Life Sci.* 41:2127–33

Jabaaij L, Grosheide PM, Heijtink RA, Duivenvoorden HJ, Ballieux RE, Vingerhoets AJJM. 1993. Influence of perceived psychological stress and distress on antibody response to low dose rDNA hepatitis B vaccine. *J. Psychosom. Res.* 37:361–69

Jamison RN, Burish TG, Wallston KA. 1987. Psychogenic factors in predicting survival of breast cancer patients. *J. Clin. Oncol.* 5:768–72

Jemmott JB III, Borysenko JZ, Borysenko M, McClelland DC, Chapman R, et al. 1983. Academic stress, power motivation, and decrease in secretion rate of salivary secretory immunoglobulin A. *Lancet* I:1400–2

Jemmott JB III, Hellman C, Locke SE, Kraus L, Williams RM, Valeri CR. 1990. Motivational syndromes associated with natural killer cell activity. *J. Behav. Med.* 13: 53–73

Kamen-Siegel L, Rodin J, Seligman MEP, Dwyer J. 1991. Explanatory style and cell-mediated immunity in elderly men and women. *Health Psychol.* 10:229–35

Kaplan GA, Reynolds P. 1988. Depression and cancer mortality and morbidity: prospective evidence from the Alameda County study. *J. Behav. Med.* 11:1–13

Katcher AH, Brightman VJ, Luborsky L, Ship I. 1973. Prediction of the incidence of recurrent herpes labialis and systemic illness from psychological measures. *J. Dent. Res.* 52:49–58

Kemeny ME. 1994. Stressful events, psychological responses, and progression of HIV infection. In *Handbook of Human Stress and Immunity,* ed. R Glaser, J Kiecolt-Glaser, pp. 245–66. New York: Academic

Kemeny ME, Cohen F, Zegens L. 1989. Psychological and immunological predictors of genital herpes recurrence. *Psychosom. Med.* 51:195–208

Kemeny ME, Weiner H, Duran R, Taylor SE, Visscher B, Fahey JL. 1995. Immune system changes following the death of a partner in HIV positive gay men. *Psychosom. Med.* In press

Kessler RC, Foster C, Joseph J, Ostrow D, Wortman C, et al. 1991. Stressful life events and symptom onset in HIV infection. *Am. J. Psychiatr.* 148:733–38

Kiecolt-Glaser JK, Cacioppo JT, Malarkey WB, Glaser R. 1992. Acute psychological stressors and short-term immune changes: what, why, for whom, and to what extent? *Psychosom. Med.* 54:680–85

Kiecolt-Glaser JK, Fisher LD, Ogrocki P, Stout JC, Speicher CE, Glaser R. 1987a. Marital quality, marital disruption, and immune function. *Psychosom. Med.* 49:13–34

Kiecolt-Glaser JK, Garner W, Speicher CE, Penn GM, Holliday J, Glaser R. 1984. Psychosocial modifiers of immunocompetence in medical students. *Psychosom. Med.* 46: 7–14

Kiecolt-Glaser JK, Glaser R. 1987. Psychosocial influences on herpes virus latency. In *Viruses, Immunity and Mental Disorders,* ed. E Kurstak, ZJ Lipowski, PV Morozov, pp. 403–11. New York: Plenum

Kiecolt-Glaser JK, Glaser R. 1988. Methodological issues in behavioral immunology research with humans. *Brain Behav. Immun.* 2:67–68

Kiecolt-Glaser JK, Glaser R, Shuttleworth EC, Dyer CS, Ogrocki P, Speicher CE. 1987b. Chronic stress and immunity in family caregivers of Alzheimer's disease victims. *Psychosom. Med.* 49:523–35

Kiecolt-Glaser JK, Glaser R, Strain E, Stout J, Tarr K, et al. 1986. Modulation of cellular immunity in medical students. *J. Behav. Med.* 9:5–21

Kiecolt-Glaser JK, Glaser R, Williger D, Stout J, Messick G, et al. 1985. Psychosocial enhancement of immunocompetence in a geriatric population. *Health Psychol.* 4: 25–41

Kiecolt-Glaser JK, Kennedy S, Malkoff S, Fisher L, Speicher CE, Glaser R. 1988. Marital discord and immunity in males. *Psychosom. Med.* 50:213–29

Kiecolt-Glaser JK, Malarkey WB, Chee M, Newton T, Cacioppo JT, et al. 1993. Negative behavior during marital conflict is associated with immunological down-regulation. *Psychosom. Med.* 55:395–409

Knapp PH, Levy EM, Giorgi RG, Black PH, Fox BH, Heeren TC. 1992. Short-term immunological effects of induced emotion. *Psychosom. Med.* 54:133–48

Laudenslager ML. 1987. Psychosocial stress and susceptibility to infectious disease. In *Viruses, Immunity and Mental Disorders,* ed. E Kurstak, ZJ Lipowski, PV Morozov, pp. 391–402. New York: Plenum

Levy S, Herberman R, Maluish A, Schliew B, Lippman M. 1985. Prognostic risk assessment in primary breast cancer by behavioral and immunological parameters. *Health Psychol.* 4:99–113

Linn BS, Linn MW, Jensen J. 1981. Anxiety and immune responsiveness. *Psychol. Rep.* 49:969–70

Locke SE, Kraus L, Leserman J, Hurst MW, Heisel JS, Williams RM. 1984. Life change stress, psychiatric symptoms, and natural killer cell activity. *Psychosom. Med.* 46: 441–53

Luborsky L, Mintz J, Brightman VJ, Katcher AH. 1976. Herpes simplex virus and moods: a longitudinal study. *J. Psychosom. Res.* 20:543–48

Lyketsos CG, Hoover DR, Guccione M, Senterfitt W, Dew MA, et al. 1993. Depressive symptoms as predictors of medical outcomes in HIV infection. *J. Am. Med. Assoc.* 270:2563–67

Manuck SB, Cohen S, Rabin BS, Muldoon MF, Bachen EA. 1991. Individual differences in cellular immune response to stress. *Psychol. Sci.* 2:111–15

Marsland AL, Manuck SB, Fazzari TV, Steward CJ, Rabin BS. 1995. Stability of individual differences in cellular immune responses to acute psychological stress. *Psychosom. Med.* 57:295–98

McGrady A, Conran P, Dickey D, Garman D, Farris E, Schumann-Brzezinski C. 1992. The effects of biofeedback-assisted relaxation on cell mediated immunity, cortisol, and white blood cell count in healthy adult subjects. *J. Behav. Med.* 15:343–54

McKinnon W, Weisse CS, Reynolds CP, Bowles CA, Baum A. 1989. Chronic stress, leukocyte subpopulations, and humoral response to latent viruses. *Health Psychol.* 8:389–402

McLarnon LD, Kaloupek DG. 1988. Psychological investigation of genital herpes recurrence: prospective assessment and cognitive-behavioral intervention for a chronic physical disorder. *Health Psychol.* 7: 231–49

Meyer RJ, Haggerty RJ. 1962. Streptococcal infections in families. *Pediatrics* 29: 539–49

Moos RH, Solomon GF. 1964. Personality correlates of the rapidity of progression of rheumatoid arthritis. *Ann. Rheum. Dis.* 23: 145–51

Naliboff BD, Benton D, Solomon GF, Morley JE, Fahey JL, et al. 1991. Immunological changes in young and old adults during brief laboratory stress. *Psychosom. Med.* 53:121–32

Naliboff BD, Solomon GF, Gilmore SL, Benton D, Morley JE, Fahey JL. 1995. The effects of the opiate antagonist naloxone on measures of cellular immunity during rest and brief psychological stress. *J. Psychosom. Res.* In press

O'Leary A. 1990. Stress, emotion, and human immune function. *Psychol. Bull.* 108: 363–82

O'Leary A, Shoor S, Lorig K, Holman HR. 1988. A cognitive-behavioral treatment for rheumatoid arthritis. *Health Psychol.* 7:527–44

Parker JC, Frank RG, Beck NC, Smarr KL, Buescher KL, et al. 1988. Pain management in rheumatoid arthritis patients: a cognitive-behavioral approach. *Arthritis Rheum.* 31:593–601

Pennebaker JW, Beall SK. 1986. Confronting a traumatic event: toward an understanding of inhibition and disease. *J. Abnorm. Psychol.* 95:274–81

Pennebaker JW, Kiecolt-Glaser JK, Glaser R. 1988. Disclosures of traumas and immune function: health implications for psychotherapy. *J. Consult. Clin. Psychol.* 56:239–45

Peplau LA, Perlman D, eds. 1982. *Loneliness: A Source Book of Current Theory, Research, and Therapy.* New York: Wiley

Perry S, Fishman B, Jacobsberg L, Frances A. 1992. Relationships over 1 year between lymphocyte subsets and psychosocial variables among adults with infection by human immunodeficiency virus. *Arch. Gen. Psychiatr.* 49:396–401

Persky VW, Kempthorne-Rawson J, Shekelle RB. 1987. Personality and risk of cancer: 20-year follow-up of the Western Electric Study. *Psychosom. Med.* 49:435–49

Rabin BS, Cohen S, Ganguli R, Lysle DT, Cunnick JE. 1989. Bidirectional interaction between the central nervous system and immune system. *Crit. Rev. Immunol.* 9:279–312

Radojevic V, Nicassio PM, Weisman MH. 1992. Behavioral intervention with and without family support for rheumatoid arthritis. *Behav. Ther.* 23:13–30

Reed GM, Kemeny ME, Taylor SE, Wang HJ, Visscher BR. 1994. Realistic acceptance as a predictor of decreased survival time in gay men with AIDS. *Health Psychol.* 13:299–307

Reynolds P, Kaplan GA. 1990. Social connections and risk for cancer: prospective evidence from the Alameda County study. *Behav. Med.* 16:101–10

Rimón R, Belmaker RH, Ebstein R. 1977. Psychosomatic aspects of juvenile rheumatoid arthritis. *Scand. J. Rheum.* 6:1–10

Schleifer SJ, Eckholdt HM, Cohen J, Keller SE. 1993. Analysis of partial variance (APV) as a statistical approach to control day to day variation in immune assays. *Brain Behav. Immun.* 7:243–52

Schleifer SJ, Keller SE, Bond RN, Cohen J, Stein M. 1989. Major depressive disorder and immunity: role of age, sex, severity, and hospitalization. *Arch. Gen. Psychiatry* 46:81–87

Schneiderman N, Antoni M, Ironson G, Klimas N, LaPerriere A, et al. 1994. HIV-1, immunity, and behavior. In *Handbook of Human Stress and Immunity,* ed. R Glaser, J Kiecolt-Glaser, pp. 267–300. New York: Academic

Shavit Y, Lewis JW, Terman GW, Gale RP, Liebesking JC. 1984. Opioid peptides mediate the suppressive effect of stress on natural killer cell cytotoxicity. *Science* 223:188

Shekelle RB, Raynor WJ Jr, Ostfeld AM, Garron DC, Bieliauskas LA, et al. 1981. Psychological depression and seventeen-year risk of death from cancer. *Psychosom. Med.* 43:117–25

Sieber WJ, Rodin J, Larson L, Ortega S, Cummings N, et al. 1992. Modulation of human natural killer cell activity by exposure to uncontrollable stress. *Brain Behav. Immun.* 6:141–56

Sklar LS, Anisman H. 1981. Stress and cancer. *Psychol. Bull.* 89:369–406

Smith AP, Tyrrell DAJ, Al-Nakib W, Coyle KB, Donovan CB, et al. 1988. The effects of experimentally induced respiratory virus infections on performance. *Psychol. Med.* 18:65–71

Spiegel D, Bloom J, Kraemer H, Gotthel E. 1989. Effect of psychosocial treatment on survival of patients with metastatic breast cancer. *Lancet* 2:901

Stone AA, Bovbjerg DH, Neale JM, Napoli A, Valdimarsdottir H, et al. 1992. Development of common cold symptoms following experimental rhinovirus infection is related to prior stressful life events. *Behav. Med.* 8:115–20

Stone AA, Cox DS, Valdimarsdottir H, Jandorf L, Neale JM. 1987. Evidence that secretory IgA antibody is associated with daily mood. *J. Pers. Soc. Psychol.* 52:988–93

Stone AA, Neale JM, Cox DS, Napoli A, Valdimarsdottir H, Kennedy-Moore E. 1994. Daily events are associated with a secretory immune response to an oral antigen in men. *Health Psychol.* 13:440–46

Strauss GD, Spiegel JS, Daniels M, Spiegel T, Landsverk J, et al. 1986. Group therapies for rheumatoid arthritis. *Arthritis Rheum.* 29:1203–9

Theorell T, Blomkvist V, Jonsson H, Schulman S, Berntorp E, Stigendal L. 1995. Social support and the development of immune function in human immunodeficiency virus infection. *Psychosom. Med.* 57:32–36

Thomas PD, Goodwin JM, Goodwin JS. 1985. Effect of social support on stress-related changes in cholesterol level, uric acid level, and immune function in an elderly sample. *Am. J. Psychiatr.* 142:735–37

Verbrugge LM. 1979. Marital status and health. *J. Marriage Fam.* 41:267–85

Weinberger DA, Schwartz GE, Davidson RJ.

1979. Low-anxious, high-anxious, and repressive coping styles: psychometric patterns and behavioral and physiological responses to stress. *J. Abnorm. Psychol.* 88: 369–80

Weisman A, Worden J. 1975. Psychological analysis of cancer deaths. *Omega: J. Death Dying* 6:61–75

Young LD. 1992. Psychological factors in rheumatoid arthritis. *J. Consult. Clin. Psychol.* 60:619–27

Zakowski SG, Cohen L, Hall MH, Wollman K, Baum A. 1994. Differential effects of active and passive laboratory stressors on immune function in healthy men. *Int. J. Behav. Med.* 1:163–84

Zakowski SG, McAllister CG, Deal M, Baum A. 1992. Stress, reactivity, and immune function in healthy men. *Health Psychol.* 11:223–32

Zonderman AB, Costa PT, McCrae RR. 1989. Depression as a risk for cancer morbidity and mortality in a nationally representative sample. *J. Am. Med. Assoc.* 262:1191–95

Annu. Rev. Psychol. 1996. 47:143–72

VERBAL LEARNING AND MEMORY:
Does the Modal Model Still Work?

Alice F. Healy and Danielle S. McNamara

Department of Psychology, Muenzinger Building, University of Colorado, Campus Box 345, Boulder, Colorado 80309-0345

KEY WORDS: memory models, primary memory, sensory memory, secondary memory, working memory

ABSTRACT

This chapter focuses on recent research concerning verbal learning and memory. A prominent guiding framework for research on this topic over the past three decades has been the modal model of memory, which postulates distinct sensory, primary, and secondary memory stores. Although this model continues to be popular, it has fostered much debate concerning its validity and specifically the need for its three separate memory stores. The chapter reviews research supporting and research contradicting the modal model, as well as alternative modern frameworks. Extensions of the modal model are discussed, including the search of associative memory model, the perturbation model, precategorical acoustic store, and permastore. Alternative approaches are discussed including working memory, conceptual short-term memory, long-term working memory, short-term activation and attention, processing streams, the feature model, distinctiveness, and procedural reinstatement.

CONTENTS

0066-4308/96/0201-0143$08.00

INTRODUCTION

This chapter focuses on recent research concerning verbal learning and memory. A prominent guiding framework for research on this topic over the past three decades has been the modal model of memory (Atkinson & Shiffrin 1968, Glanzer & Cunitz 1966, Waugh & Norman 1965), which postulates distinct sensory, primary, and secondary memory stores. Although this model continues to be popular, it has fostered much debate concerning its validity and, specifically, the need for its three separate memory stores. In this chapter, we review research supporting and research contradicting the modal model as well as alternative modern frameworks. We begin by summarizing the empirical support for the original model. The remainder of the chapter addresses in turn issues concerning each of the three memory stores.[1]

BACKGROUND

An initial statement of what has since been termed the modal model can be traced to James (1890), who distinguished between primary and secondary memory. James described primary memory as that which is held momentarily in consciousness and secondary memory as unconscious but permanent. An important impetus to modern versions of the modal model was the discovery that a short sequence of items is forgotten within seconds when rehearsal is prevented by a distractor task interpolated between item presentation and recall (Brown 1958, Peterson & Peterson 1959; but see Melton 1963). Other findings that also invited the distinction between primary and secondary memory included neuropsychological studies of amnesic patients unable to form new long-term memories (Milner 1966, but see Graf et al 1984) and studies showing that short-term memory (STM) tended to rely on phonetic coding and long-term memory (LTM) on semantic coding (Baddeley 1966, but see Shulman 1971).

---

[1] It should be noted that this chapter is not intended to cover the entire spectrum of recent research on verbal learning and memory. For example, space limitations do not allow us to review indirect measures (Richardson-Klavehn & Bjork 1988), mathematical models (Raaijmakers & Shiffrin 1992), or neuropsychological studies (Squire et al 1993) of memory.

Modern descriptions of the modal model were presented by Waugh & Norman (1965) and Glanzer & Cunitz (1966), and the fullest description was provided by Atkinson & Shiffrin (1968), who added sensory memory to the primary and secondary memory dichotomy. Specifically, Atkinson & Shiffrin postulated three distinct memory stores: sensory registers (with separate registers for different senses, including visual, auditory, and haptic), short-term store (STS or primary memory), and long-term store (LTS or secondary memory).[2] In terms of a computer metaphor, these stores constitute the essential permanent structural features, or hardware, of the system. In addition, Atkinson & Shiffrin postulated various control processes, or subject strategies, constituting the software of the system. One control process was given most extensive consideration: rote rehearsal. The concept of a rehearsal buffer in STS was used to describe this process.

Although much of their empirical work involved the continuous paired-associate paradigm, Atkinson & Shiffrin (1968) also devoted considerable attention to performance in the standard free-recall task. According to the simple version of their model applied to free recall, each stimulus item enters a fixed-capacity rehearsal buffer and displaces a randomly selected item already there when the capacity (about four items) is exceeded. As long as an item is in the buffer, information about it is transferred to a permanent LTS. The amount of information transferred is a linear function of the time in the buffer. At the time of test, subjects initially output the items still remaining in the buffer and then make a fixed number of searches of LTS. Crucial to this version of the modal model, as well as to earlier versions, are the assumptions that an item may be retained in the STS buffer as well as in LTS at the same time and that recall of any particular item, including those presented most recently, can derive from information in both STS and LTS.

The Atkinson & Shiffrin (1968) model accounts for the bowed serial position function and the effects of such variables as the presence of a distractor task, the rate of item presentation, and the list length. Specifically, the advantage for the most recently presented items (the recency effect) is explained by the fact that those items remain in the buffer at the time of test. The advantage for the items presented initially (the primacy effect) is explained by the fact that those items stay in the buffer longer than subsequent items. Because the buffer starts out empty, the initial items are not displaced by subsequent items until the buffer is full. Most crucial are the model's explanations of why some variables have different effects on the prerecency (primacy and middle) and recency portions of the serial position function. It is assumed that when a

---

[2] Note that STM and LTM refer to retention over brief and long time intervals, respectively, whereas STS and LTS refer to hypothetical temporary and permanent memory systems, respectively.

distractor task, such as mental arithmetic, is interpolated between list presentation and recall, the most recent items are no longer in the buffer at the time of recall. Indeed under standard conditions, the prerecency items are unaffected but the recency effect is eliminated by a distractor task. In contrast, presentation rate and list length affect the prerecency, but not the recency, portions of the serial position function. A fast presentation rate leads to lower levels of recall for prerecency positions because rapidly presented items remain in the buffer for a shorter time and, thus, less information is transferred about them to LTS. The level of recall for prerecency positions is lower for a given item in a long than in a short list because subjects are assumed to make a fixed number of searches of LTS, so that the probability of retrieving a particular item is lower when there are more items. The recency items are not affected by either rate of presentation or list length because they are recalled largely from the buffer rather than from LTS.

Early problems for the Atkinson & Shiffrin (1968) model were raised by Craik & Lockhart (1972), who proposed instead a levels-of-processing framework. The central postulate of that framework is that information is encoded to different levels and that the level of processing determines the subsequent rate of forgetting. A distinction is drawn between Type I processing, which maintains an item at a shallow level, and Type II processing, which promotes a deeper level of encoding. Demonstrations that maintaining information at a shallow level of processing do not necessarily lead to enhanced long-term retention were taken as evidence against the Atkinson & Shiffrin model's assumption that transfer to LTS is a function of time in the rehearsal buffer. However, as Raaijmakers (1993) recently pointed out, the Atkinson & Shiffrin model made a distinction between the control processes of rehearsal and coding that is analogous to the distinction between Type I and Type II processing.

PRIMARY MEMORY

The controversy about the distinction between primary and secondary memory still exists today, as was most evident in a series of recent articles addressing the question "Short-Term Memory: Where Do We Stand?" This current debate is best exemplified by two sets of opposing quotations from articles in this series. Crowder (1993) stated: "The popularity of short-term stores grew during a time when we were busy inventing such storage receptacles. Nowadays that attitude seems archaic and, to some of us, even downright quaint" (p. 143). In contrast, Shiffrin (1993) summarized the current situation as follows: "Over the years, a metatheoretical view of short-term memory has developed. This view, closely related to the 'modal' model from the 1960s, is supported by an increasing base of neurophysiological data, and a wide variety of empirical findings....The main problem with this view is the fact that it encompasses virtually everything that we are concerned with in human cognition—a *successful* model would almost be a general model of cognition" (p. 193).

Crowder's (1993) empirical challenges to the concept of STM concerned both the Brown-Peterson distractor task and the recency effect in free recall. He pointed to two observations that are inconsistent with the idea that primary memory is responsible for the rapid forgetting observed across the retention interval in the distractor task. First, Keppel & Underwood (1962) found that there is no forgetting across the retention interval on the first trial of a series of trials. Second, Turvey et al (1970) showed that there is no effect of delay on forgetting when the retention interval is varied between, rather than within, subjects.

Crowder (1993) also pointed to three observations that are inconsistent with the idea that primary memory is responsible for the recency effect in free recall because of recency effects found in LTM. First, Roediger & Crowder (1976) demonstrated a recency effect in students' recall of the names of the United States presidents. Second, Baddeley & Hitch (1977) found a recency effect for rugby team members' recall of the teams they played against that season. Third, Bjork & Whitten (1974) discovered a recency effect in the continuous-distractor paradigm, in which a distractor task follows the presentation of each item in the list including the final item, so that primary memory could not affect recall performance. Later, Koppenaal & Glanzer (1990) changed the distractor task in the continuous-distractor paradigm after the last list item and found depressed performance, suggesting that recency does reflect a temporary rehearsal buffer. However, Neath (1993a) showed that changing the distractor task depressed performance even for prerecency items (see also Thapar & Greene 1993).

Some of these empirical challenges to the modal model can be dismissed by two general considerations. First, information can be encoded in secondary memory even with rapid stimulus presentation, so that retention can derive from secondary memory as well as primary memory in the distractor task. For example, Keppel & Underwood's (1962) finding of no forgetting on the first trial in the distractor paradigm is easily understood in terms of the lack of proactive interference on secondary memory in the first trial. Thus, secondary memory can support first-trial retention. Second, not all bowed serial position functions have the same specific shape or the same underlying causes. For example, the shape of the serial position functions for the recall of presidents' names has a much larger recency effect than is typically found in free-recall tasks of episodic memory, and frequency of exposure to the different presidents' names readily accounts for this serial position function. Likewise, Raaijmakers (1993) recently pointed out that the modal model does not assume that STS is the cause of all recency effects. An advantage for recency items can also be predicted by the modal model from the fact that retrieval from LTS is often based on cues from the current context, and the recency items are more closely linked to the current context than are earlier items.

Modern Extensions of the Modal Model

Although the original modal model continues to have its proponents, it has been revised and extended in recent theoretical developments. We focus here on two of these modern extensions of the modal model that maintain as fundamental the distinction between primary and secondary memory. The first, the Search of Associative Memory (SAM) model (Raaijmakers & Shiffrin 1981, Shiffrin & Raaijmakers 1992), is a direct descendent of the Atkinson & Shiffrin (1968) model and has most extensively addressed free recall. The second, the perturbation model (Estes 1972, Lee 1992), is primarily aimed at performance in the Brown-Peterson distractor task using the specific paradigm introduced by Conrad (1967).

SEARCH OF ASSOCIATIVE MEMORY MODEL   The SAM model elaborates the Atkinson & Shiffrin (1968) model primarily in its description of the search and retrieval processes from LTS that occur at the time of the memory test. At the heart of the SAM model is the idea that events are stored in memory as images (i.e. as separate, unitized representations) and that LTS is accessed via retrieval cues. The strength of a given cue in terms of its link to a given memory image is determined both by preexisting relationships and by rehearsal and coding processes conducted in STS. For example, the link strength between an item cue and the image of another item in the same list depends in part on the time that the two items were rehearsed together in the STS buffer. The three most important types of retrieval strength include self-strength (from an item as a cue to itself as a target), associative strength (between different items), and context strength (for linking the context cue to a target item).

SAM has been successfully fit to many aspects of free recall, paired associate recall, and interference paradigms, as well as to recognition. For recall, the subject is assumed to generate cues at each stage of the search, starting with the context cue and then employing other types of cues, with weights assigned to the different cues on the basis of their salience. Because the sum of the weights is assumed to be limited, the weights can be viewed as reflecting the limited capacity of STS at the time of retrieval. The cues combine multiplicatively for recall, which allows the search process to be focused on those memory images that are most strongly linked to all of the cues. Each retrieval attempt involves sampling one memory image based on its strength relative to that of all other images stored in LTS. A search termination occurs on the basis of unsuccessful search cycles, although a rechecking process sometimes follows initial termination. After sampling an image of an item, recall of that item depends on its recovery, which is an exponential function of the sum of the weighted strengths of the cues to the image. Most impressive is the fact that SAM can account for the part-list cuing effect in free recall, which is the finding that the likelihood of recalling a given list item decreases when other list items are given as test cues (Raaijmakers & Shiffrin 1981). SAM's explanation of the part-list cuing effect, unlike some others, can also account for its reversal in a delayed testing situation (Raaijmakers 1993).

Recognition in the version of SAM used by Gillund & Shiffrin (1984) does not occur as a search but rather as a function of global activation (but see Mensink & Raaijmakers 1988 for a different approach). Although for recall the overall strength of a set of cues to a particular target depends on the product of the individual cue strengths, recognition is largely a direct-access process dependent on the sum of activation strengths. This difference between recall and recognition retrieval processes is central to the explanation of the list-strength effect (Ratcliff et al 1990, Shiffrin et al 1990). Strengthening some items in a list decreases the free recall of other items but has either no effect or a positive effect on the recognition of other items. The interfering list-strength effects are, therefore, attributed by SAM to retrieval processes occurring in free recall but not in recognition. Murnane & Shiffrin (1991a) take the list-strength findings as crucial evidence against memory models that postulate that structural interference occurs when storing multiple inputs in memory, such as composite storage models (e.g. Murdock 1982). Unlike SAM, these models do not assume a distinct localized memory trace or image but assume instead that a memory trace is part of a combination or superimposition of multiple traces. Ironically, however, the crucial assumption SAM makes to account for the list strength effect involves a type of composite storage; it is assumed that repetitions of the same item in the same context are stored in a single memory image (Murnane & Shiffrin 1991b). SAM must also make an additional assumption, referred to as the "differentiation hypothesis," according to which the activation produced by an unrelated item cue is less on a stronger image than on a weaker image, presumably because the stronger image is easier to differentiate from the cue (Shiffrin et al 1990).

Although SAM is a descendent of the modal model, some of its more recent assumptions resemble those of the alternative levels-of-processing framework. For example, Shiffrin et al (1989) made the point that the units of storage used by SAM depend on coding operations, and longer and deeper operations result in higher-order units. Also, in accord with the notion of encoding specificity, Clark & Shiffrin (1987) postulated context sensitive encoding, which reflects the fact that the coding of a particular item is influenced by the other items in the same group, and test performance is best when the group of test items matches the group of study items.

Although SAM is able to account for the full range of accuracy findings in explicit, episodic memory paradigms, it has not yet been applied to fit reaction time data in recognition, or to many implicit memory and semantic memory tasks (but see Raaijmakers 1993 for some insights into how SAM could be applied in those situations). Other challenges for SAM include complete explanations of the mirror effect in recognition memory (whereby the recognition of new items as unfamiliar, mirrors the recognition of old items as familiar; see Glanzer & Adams 1990) and the learning of crossed-list associates (e.g. hot-slow, fast-cold; see Humphreys et al 1989).

PERTURBATION MODEL   The perturbation model (Estes 1972, Lee & Estes 1981) was designed to account for four principal findings from the Brown-Peterson distractor paradigm. First, there is a steep retention function reflecting rapid forgetting. Second, there are symmetrical bowed serial position functions at each retention interval in the recall of order, but not item, information. Third, there are gradually declining positional uncertainty curves, reflecting the fact that a letter substituted for another at recall usually comes from a neighboring serial position. Fourth, when to-be-remembered items are divided into separate segments, there is a recall advantage for the most recently presented segment.

According to the perturbation model, codes for immediate recall of order information are arranged in a hierarchical structure containing multiple levels. These levels include the position of the item within a segment, the segment containing the item, and the specific trial on which the segment occurred. The hierarchy of codes is repeatedly reactivated, and at each reactivation there is some probability that the relative position of neighboring items, segments, or trials will be transposed (perturbed). In the original version of the perturbation model, there was a single free parameter, theta, the probability of a perturbation at a given level of the hierarchy in primary memory. In a later version (Healy et al 1987), a second parameter, alpha, was added to the perturbation model. This parameter is the probability that a memory code will be subject to the perturbation process; hence, 1-alpha is the probability of storing position information in secondary memory. In other words, the perturbation model now has two free parameters, the first reflecting primary-memory rehearsal processes and the second reflecting secondary-memory encoding processes.

The necessity for including the secondary-memory parameter was demonstrated in a series of experiments by Cunningham et al (1984) and Healy et al (1987) who compared two conditions, both involving the presentation of two segments of items on a given trial but the recall of only one segment. Subjects were either told in advance (precue), or at the end of the distractor task (postcue), which one of the two segments was to be recalled. Performance was consistently above the chance level and better in the precue condition than in the postcue condition, even at retention intervals up to 30 sec. It was found that the perturbation model was able to fit the data only when the secondary-memory parameter was included. Of particular note is the fact that only the secondary-memory parameter varied in the data fits; the primary-memory parameter was constant throughout these data fits (and equal to the value used by Lee & Estes 1981).

The constant value of the primary memory parameter across experiments implies that there is a fixed rate of forgetting from primary memory that can be measured using the Brown-Peterson distractor paradigm. However, Muter (1980) argued that the rate of forgetting from primary memory is underestimated by the Brown-Peterson paradigm because, in a typical experiment using the distractor task, subjects are repeatedly tested, so that they develop a high expectancy to recall after the distractor period. Muter offered an alternative paradigm in which subjects were led to expect either to recall immediately or to perform a distractor task without subsequent recall. Subjects were tested following a distractor-filled retention interval on only a few critical trials. Muter, and subsequently Sebrechts et al (1989), found a dramatic increase in forgetting rate on the critical trials such that the probability of correct recall approached floor-level performance after only 2–4 sec. However, more recently, Cunningham et al (1993) used two new versions of the distractor task to reduce the involvement of secondary memory processing. This reduction was achieved either by manipulating subject expectancy to recall or by manipulating the importance of the to-be-recalled material. With both methods, recall performance was substantially depressed at all retention intervals (including immediate recall); there was no evidence of a more rapid forgetting rate, only a change in the asymptotic performance level. Cunningham et al found that the perturbation model provided a close fit to the obtained data when they kept the primary-memory parameter at the level used in previous experiments and varied only the secondary-memory parameter such that the involvement of secondary memory processes was minimized. These results indicate that the distractor task remains a valid paradigm to study primary memory and the perturbation model provides a valuable tool for describing forgetting from primary memory.

Although the perturbation model was developed to account for STM processes, Nairne (1991) argued that the model can also be applied to situations involving LTM. In particular, Nairne showed that the model with just the single parameter, theta, for the perturbation rate could explain the results of experiments involving the reconstruction of order information from LTM. The model accounted for the symmetrical bowed serial position functions and the gradually declining positional uncertainty curves for both list selection and placement of an item in a list.

Subsequently, Nairne (1992) reported an experiment that examined the retention of position information over intervals ranging from 30 sec to 24 h and compared the data to predictions based on the perturbation model. In applying the perturbation model to this situation, which spanned both STM and LTM, Nairne again used the version of the model with only the single parameter theta reflecting perturbation rate. However, he inadvertently added another parameter, because he assumed that there was an opportunity for perturbation once every 6 sec in the first 30-sec interval but once every 24 min thereafter. In other words, the forgetting rate was very rapid over the period corresponding to immediate retention but was considerably slower over longer retention intervals. This observation suggests that a two-parameter model (one for primary memory and another for secondary memory) is necessary. In fact, even with the two separate forgetting rates in Nairne's application of the perturbation model, the observed proportion of correct responses was significantly greater than the predicted proportion for the 24-h retention interval.

Although the two-parameter version of the perturbation model can be viewed as an extension of the modal model because it maintains as fundamental the distinction between primary and secondary memory, Estes (1991) challenged another underlying assumption of the modal model, which he terms the "trial-unit" assumption, by which each trial is considered as a discrete episode. Estes observed that item intrusions on a given trial are derived largely from the recall responses of the previous trial. These item intrusions were given in the same position as they occurred in the previous recall output, whether or not that position matched the previous stimulus input. Items from previous trials that were not recalled on those trials usually did not intrude into the recall responses of the given trial. These findings were taken as evidence against the trial-unit model and in favor of an alternative continuum model, in which there are no strict boundaries separating representations of items from successive trials. More recently, Estes (1994) provided a formal account of this phenomenon in terms of his array model of classification, with the assumption that each to-be-remembered item on a trial includes a context feature which it shares with the other items from the same trial, but which differs from those of items from previous trials, with the difference increasing with greater distance between the trials.

To examine intrusions of responses from rehearsal on a previous trial, Estes (1991) included a condition in which to-be-remembered letters were followed by distractor digits and then recalled after a delay during which subjects rehearsed the letters aloud. He found that items rehearsed out of the correct input position were less likely to be recalled than were those rehearsed in the input position. Also, when the recall and rehearsal positions were not the same, the majority of the items were recalled in their correct input position. This finding suggested that recall order was not a simple repetition of rehearsal.

Unrehearsed items were likely to be recalled in their input position or in a neighboring position, although the recall occurred with a lower probability and with less precise positional information than that for rehearsed items. To explain these observations, Estes contrasted the direct recall track, from input to recall, with an indirect track, from rehearsal to recall. The indirect track is stronger because the rehearsal context, relative to the input context, is more similar to the recall context. By postulating two different recall tracks, Estes seems to be moving towards memory models with multiple STM systems. We turn next to a discussion of models of this type.

Additional Memory Systems

Although the modal model has traditionally been described as containing a single primary memory store, the Atkinson & Shiffrin (1968) version did distinguish between the rehearsal process and other control processes in STS. This distinction foreshadowed subsequent theorizing that has broken down primary memory into separate systems.

WORKING MEMORY Undoubtedly the most influential model that analyzes primary memory into separate systems is Baddeley's working memory model (Baddeley 1992), which emphasizes the active processing rather than the passive storage of information that occurs in primary memory. Because of experiments using a dual-task technique in which a concurrent memory load of three or six digits had no influence on the recency part of a free-recall test for words but had small effects on performance of reasoning and prose comprehension, Baddeley & Hitch (1974) argued against a unitary limited-capacity STS. They proposed instead a multicomponent working memory model, including a limited-capacity attentional system, the central executive, supported by two slave systems, the phonological (or articulatory) loop and the visuo-spatial sketchpad (or scratchpad).

The phonological loop has received the most empirical support. It contains a phonological (i.e. speech-based) store along with an articulatory control process. The store maintains information by means of subvocal rehearsal, and without such rehearsal, information rapidly decays from the store over a period of seconds. There are at least six robust effects that are explained in terms of the phonological loop (Baddeley 1992). First is the phonological similarity effect, whereby immediate recall is lower for items that are phonologically similar than for those that are dissimilar, presumably because the similar material contains fewer phonologically distinctive features. Second is the irrelevant speech effect, whereby spoken material irrelevant to the memory task and from a different speaker disrupts immediate memory performance, presumably because all spoken material automatically enters the phonological store irrespective of its meaning (Salame & Baddeley 1989). Third is the phonological sandwich effect, in which irrelevant spoken material is interpolated between to-be-remembered items. This effect is like that of irrelevant speech and has been explained in a similar manner, but both the list and interpolated items are by the same speaker in this case (Baddeley et al 1991). Fourth is the word-length effect, whereby immediate serial recall of words depends on their spoken duration, presumably because shorter words are rehearsed more rapidly than longer words. In fact, it has been shown that subjects recall roughly as many words as they can say in 2 sec (Baddeley et al 1975). Fifth is articulatory suppression, whereby immediate memory for visually presented material is depressed by requiring subjects to articulate irrelevant material during stimulus presentation, presumably because the irrelevant material blocks the articulatory control process and prevents other material from entering the phonological store. Supporting this description is the finding that articulatory suppression eliminates the phonological similarity, irrelevant speech, and word length effects (Baddeley et al 1984). Sixth are observations involving patients with deficiencies in immediate memory who do not show phonological similarity or word-length effects (Vallar & Shallice 1990), and patients with deficiencies in speech articulation but unimpaired language processing who do show such effects (Baddeley & Wilson 1985), presumably because the former patients, but not the latter, have a defective phonological store.

Questions have been raised concerning the usefulness of the phonological loop (Baddeley 1992) because patients with phonological deficiencies appear to have normal functioning outside the laboratory and show only minor problems with sentence comprehension (Butterworth et al 1986). However, such a patient was shown to have a marked problem learning Russian vocabulary (Baddeley et al 1988); hence, the phonological loop does seem to play an important role in long-term phonological learning. Also, Gathercole & Baddeley (1990) found that subjects with delayed development of language had a reduced-capacity phonological loop. With normal subjects, a deficit in the phonological loop can be simulated by the use of articulatory suppression, which, similarly, has been shown to disrupt new phonological learning but not paired-associate learning (Papagno et al 1991).

There has been less progress in understanding either the visuo-spatial sketchpad or the central executive. Secondary tasks, ranging from nonvisual spatial tracking tasks (Baddeley & Lieberman 1980) to nonspatial visual observation tasks (Logie 1986), have been used to pinpoint the nature of the processing of the sketchpad. These tasks have shown that the sketchpad involves both spatial and visual processing and is distinct from the verbal processing associated with the phonological loop. The central executive is an attentional control system that is in charge of both strategy selection and integration of information from various sources, including the two slave systems. Baddeley (1992) pointed to randomly generating letters as a useful secondary task to load the central executive, neuropsychological studies of frontal lobe damage as providing valuable insights into the operation of the central executive, and a model of attentional control as the most promising candidate for the core of the central executive.

Baddeley (1992) showed how his tripartite system can illuminate the cognitive functions affected by various diseases and those used in various tasks. For example, various secondary tasks were used to disrupt the central executive and the two slave systems in normal and Alzheimer's disease patients (Baddeley et al 1986, Spinnler et al 1988). The results suggested that the Alzheimer impairment lay with the central executive rather than the slave systems. Likewise, studies using a similar methodology to analyze chess performance provided evidence that both the visuo-spatial sketchpad and the central executive play important roles in coding and memory during chess but that verbal coding is not used.

Baddeley & Hitch (1993), while retaining their working memory model, have proposed a new explanation for the recency effect in free recall in terms of a simple temporal or ordinal discrimination hypothesis, so that recency reflects registration in implicit memory by a priming process. They proposed that recall involves reactivating nodes for items in a network and that more recent items are primed and thus reactivated more easily. In support of their hypothesis of recency as priming, they assessed recency in terms of Tulving & Schacter's (1990) five criteria for priming: They pointed to (a) intact performance in amnesia for recency items, (b) developmental dissociation between recency items and the rest of the list, with no developmental effect on recency items, (c) drug dissociation between recency items and the rest of the list, with no effect of drugs on recency items, (d) functional independence, whereby recall of earlier list items is influenced by different factors than is recall of recency items, and (e) at least some hint of stochastic independence (but see Hintzman & Hartry 1990 for issues concerning stochastic independence), whereby initial recall of recency items is independent of their subsequent recall from LTM. Baddeley & Hitch argued further that although recency reflects implicit learning, it depends on the use of an explicit retrieval strategy in which the last items in the list are output first.

CONCEPTUAL SHORT-TERM MEMORY   Although Baddeley's (1992) phonological loop seems to play little role in sentence understanding, Potter (1993) has proposed a distinct conceptual STM (CSTM) that is not evident in the standard paradigms for studying STM but plays an important role in everyday reading, scene perception, and sentence processing. This conceptual memory is laid down and decays very rapidly (within 1 sec). When a visual stimulus is presented, such as a sentence, the conceptual output goes to CSTM and the phonological output to conventional STM (i.e. the phonological loop). CSTM holds considerable information, most of which is rapidly lost unless it is relevant to a conceptual structure that is consolidated into LTM.

Potter has used the technique of rapid serial visual presentation (RSVP) of pictures or words to a fixed location on a computer screen to study CSTM. In one set of her studies (Potter 1976), RSVP pictures were presented either with immediate rapid semantic detection (e.g. respond to a picture of a picnic) or a recognition test following the sequence. Subjects performed well on the detection task, but performance was near chance levels on recognition. This finding is consistent with rapidly decaying CSTM. Likewise, Potter (1993) reviewed a study involving RSVP with words, in which words could be identified in two-word lists at very rapid rates (faster than 3 words/sec), but those same rates yielded memory span performance for longer lists well below that in the standard STM task with slower presentation rates (e.g. 1 word/sec). When the RSVP lists consisted of sentences (Potter et al 1986), even longer lists of words were recalled nearly perfectly even at high rates, suggesting that they were parsed and understood immediately. Thus, words at fast rates enter Potter's CSTM but not conventional STM.

Lombardi & Potter (1992) and Potter & Lombardi (1990) proposed that immediate recall of RSVP sentences involves regeneration from a conceptual representation formed from the activated part of LTM. The verbatim nature of RSVP sentence recall reflects the fact that the lexical items in the sentence were activated more than other lexical items. In support of this hypothesis, subjects' sentence recall included intrusions of closely synonymous words from an interpolated secondary word-matching distractor task, even when the sentences were presented extremely rapidly. In another study involving RSVP sentence recall (Potter et al 1993), ambiguous misspelled words (e.g. *dack* which could be a misspelling of *duck* or *deck*) were replaced by subjects in their recall protocols with the correctly spelled words appropriate to the sentence context. This finding suggests that the sentence context was processed conceptually despite the rapid rate of sentence presentation.

Potter (1993) related CSTM to conceptual priming but noted that concept reactivation cannot account for the formation of episodic-specific links among word representations, as occurs with the RSVP presentation of a sentence. CSTM provides the basis for encoding information in LTM according to Potter's account and can be viewed either as a separate episodic representation or as an activated part of LTM. In the light of this latter view, Potter's approach can be seen as similar to an approach taken recently by Ericsson & Kintsch (1995).

LONG-TERM WORKING MEMORY   Ericsson & Kintsch (1995) raised the question as to whether the standard definition of working memory as limited, temporary storage can be applied to tasks such as reading text and skilled performance by experts, especially because these activities can be interrupted and later resumed without major detriments in performance. To resolve this question, Ericsson & Kintsch proposed a mechanism based on skilled use of storage in long-term working memory (LT-WM) in addition to the temporary storage of information in short-term working memory (ST-WM). This work is an extension of Chase & Ericsson's (1982) skilled memory theory, which accounts for a tenfold increase in digit span by individuals given extensive training. This training overcame the proactive interference caused by previous storage of similar information in memory. Chase & Ericsson proposed that such individuals draw on their acquired knowledge and on systems of retrieval cues, or retrieval structures.

Ericsson & Kintsch (1995) took issue with the assumption that it is slow both to retrieve information from LTM and to store new information in LTM. Although they acknowledged that it does indeed take up to 1 sec to re-trieve—and 10 sec to store—unfamiliar information in LTM, it takes much less time for an expert to retrieve or store relatively familiar information in LTM. Likewise, although the estimate of STM capacity as about four chunks of information (Broadbent 1975) applies well to a wide range of simple cogni-tive activities, for more complex tasks such a small working-memory capacity is insufficient (Anderson 1983, Newell 1990).

To accommodate the increased memory performance by chess experts, Chase & Simon (1973) argued that the experts relied on larger chunks in STM. However, Ericsson & Kintsch (1995) pointed to findings that chess experts can recall up to nine different patterns of chess pieces (Cooke et al 1993), and that interpolated tasks do not depress performance by such experts, as suggest-ing storage in LTM rather than STM. Similarly, the performance of memory-span experts seems to reflect storage in LTM because of small decrements in performance with STM interference before list recall, accurate recall of all lists at the end of a session, and improvement specific to the type of material practiced.

Ericsson & Kintsch's (1995) account is that subjects use LT-WM for a skilled activity when they have a large body of relevant knowledge and can anticipate future memory demands. The use of LT-WM relies on a stable retrieval structure, which is all that needs to be available in ST-WM, along with a cue indicating the relevant type of information required. In contrast, Schneider & Detweiler (1988) argued that LTM cannot be used as working memory because of the build-up of retroactive interference, and Baddeley (1990) used the finding that expert mental abacus calculators can recall no more than one sequence of digits (Hatano & Osawa 1983) as evidence against the use of storage in LTM for this task. Ericsson & Kintsch addressed these issues by pointing out that temporal distinctiveness and elaborative encoding can overcome the build-up of retroactive interference and that temporal distinctiveness is poor in the task of mental abacus calculation.

Ericsson & Kintsch (1995) used Kintsch's (1988) construction-integration model to explain how the constructed representation of a previously read text is kept accessible in LT-WM so that new information can be encoded and integrated with previous information. Glanzer et al (1984) interrupted text reading with an unrelated task and then allowed reading to resume. The effect was to increase reading time for the first sentence after reading resumed but not to influence speed or accuracy of answers to comprehension questions. Ericsson & Kintsch took these findings as evidence that the disruptions led to a loss of retrieval cues in ST-WM; comprehension was not disrupted because the information was stored in LT-WM. They further proposed that superior text comprehension is due to superior skill encoding information in LT-WM and making it accessible via cues in ST-WM. Contrary to the assumption by Just & Carpenter (1992) that good readers have more room in active memory than poor readers (see Engle et al 1992 for a similar view), Ericsson & Kintsch proposed that good readers produce a more extensive retrieval structure for LT-WM so that their effective working memory is larger without an increase in the size of active memory.

SHORT-TERM ACTIVATION AND ATTENTION   The relationship between STM and LTM has also been explored by Cowan (1993, 1994), who pointed out that there have been two definitions for STM, one (deriving from James 1890) that is the current focus of attention, and the other that is currently activated in LTM. These two definitions have sometimes been used interchangeably, but they cannot be equivalent given evidence for activation outside of awareness, including priming (i.e. activation) from a previously attended item. Cowan represents STM as a nested subset of LTM; the currently activated features are a subset of LTM, and the focus of attention is a subset of the activated memory.

Cowan et al (1990) supported the hypothesis that STM includes both attended and unattended information by examining immediate retention for attended and unattended stimuli. Subjects silently (or by whispering) read a novel and simultaneously heard speech syllables presented through headphones. They were given comprehension tests and asked to write a sentence summarizing recently read material. On crucial test trials they were asked to recognize the speech syllables heard, after a variable delay filled with the reading. A rapid memory decay was found for the speech syllables. Performance was improved on shorter delays if subjects shifted their attention away from reading, as evidenced by their not whispering during a short interval on either side of the target syllable. If subjects consistently divided their attention between the two channels by responding to particular syllables, then little forgetting of the target syllables was evident even at the longest (10 sec) delay.

Thus, there was memory for unattended syllables, and subtle attentional shifts improved memory.

Cowan et al (1992) examined STM loss by studying memory decay during subjects' overt verbal recall of a list. They used words identical in number of phonemes and syllables but different in pronunciation length. They found that longer words at the beginning of the list depressed forward recall, whereas longer words at the end of the list depressed backward recall. This finding suggests that while subjects recall words from the list the other words decay from activation. Cowan (1993) proposed that when a list is recalled, memory decays during word output but is reactivated during the pauses between words [see Schweickert (1993) for a candidate model of this process]. Individual differences in immediate memory span are then attributed not to the speed of pronouncing words but to the efficiency of covert processing between words. This hypothesis is supported by Cowan's (1992) finding of (a) a correlation for four-year old children between span and duration of recall but not between span and speech rate and (b) faster spoken recall of lists less than span length, with the reduction in speed located entirely within the pauses between words.

Central to Cowan's (1993) framework is the distinction between STM and LTM. Two findings taken as support of a separate STM are the recency effect and the word length effect in immediate recall. The recency effect in the continuous-distractor paradigm, which relies on LTM, has been taken as weakening the support for a separate STM (Greene 1986). However, Cowan et al (1994) provided evidence that the word length effect was not the same in immediate recall and in the continuous-distractor paradigm. They manipulated the syllable length of the words on a list and asked subjects for backward recall. For the immediate recall procedure, increased word length of the items in the second half of the list depressed recall, but the reverse was found (i.e. better performance with longer words) for the continuous-distractor procedure. Further, in support of Cowan's (1993) proposal that STM is the activated portion of LTM, Hulme et al (1991) found a linear relation between immediate memory span and speech rate, with a higher intercept for words than for nonwords, so that lexical familiarity in LTM made a difference in STM.

Unitary Memory System

Although the evidence presented for additional memory systems is quite compelling, Roediger (1993) persuasively discussed the interpretive problems created by a proliferation of memory stores. In contrast, some theories postulate a unitary memory system. We will concentrate on one such theory proposed by Crowder & Neath (1991) because it was specifically formulated as an alternative to the modal model. Crowder & Neath argued that the Brown-Peterson distractor paradigm, rather than isolating STM, serves to temporally magnify the retention of a particular item, as if it were under a microscope. They used this microscope analogy to suggest that the same principles apply to STM as to LTM. Following Murdock (1960), they focused on the principle of distinctiveness, which they used to explain serial position functions in both STM and LTM. Murdock measured distinctiveness of a serial position by computing the difference between its ordinal number and that of all the other positions in the list. In addition, he accounted for the asymmetry of the serial position function by transforming the ordinal numbers into log values (see Johnson 1991 for a recent discussion and elaboration of these ideas). This theory necessarily assumes a constant shape of serial position functions across learning conditions (e.g. variations in presentation rate and item familiarity), and indeed the serial position function for serial learning is constant when normalized (i.e. plotted as the proportion of the total number of correct responses made at each position in the list). Neath (1993b) extended Murdock's formulation by using the actual durations of the interstimulus and retention intervals when calculating the temporal distinctiveness of an item.

Following Glenberg (1987), Neath & Crowder (1990) employed the continuous-distractor paradigm to study temporal distinctiveness. They compared a control condition with equal temporal spacing (interpolated arithmetic) between successive list items to an increasing condition, in which the spacing increased as the list progressed, and to a decreasing condition, in which the spacing decreased. They showed that for items presented visually the recency effect was largest in the increasing condition (in which the distinctiveness of the recency items was greatest) and smallest in the decreasing condition (in which the distinctiveness of the primacy items was greatest). They also conducted a parallel experiment using the Brown-Peterson distractor paradigm in which they interpolated digits between the to-be-remembered letters with a constant, increasing, or decreasing number of digits. The increasing condition showed the most recency and the decreasing condition the least. Thus, the results in the two situations were parallel despite the fact that the first relied on LTM and the second on STM.

Also consistent with this view is a study by Wright et al (1985) with data from monkeys, pigeons, and humans viewing four slides followed by a retention interval and then a recognition probe. At immediate testing, there was a pure recency effect with no primacy effect, whereas with delayed testing there was greater primacy with increasing delay until there was pure primacy and no recency. Crowder & Neath (1991) explained these findings by proposing that the retrieval orientation was initially from the recency end of the list but after a delay shifted to the primacy end. Neath (1993b) replicated these findings in studies with human subjects recognizing pictures of snowflakes that could not be easily verbalized. Whereas the duration of the retention interval was varied in this study, in a subsequent study, Neath & Knoedler (1994) varied the duration of the interstimulus interval and also found results consistent with the distinctiveness model. Further, Neath & Knoedler applied the same model to experiments by Gernsbacher & Hargreaves (1988) and their own follow-up experiment on sentence processing. These experiments showed a response-time advantage for verifying the second-mentioned of two participants after a short retention interval (analogous to a recency effect), but an advantage for verifying the first-mentioned participant after a longer interval (analogous to a primacy effect). Thus, the distinctiveness model can account for a wide range of memory phenomena, including STM and LTM paradigms, experiments with animals and humans, and tasks ranging from picture recognition to sentence processing. Nevertheless, it is not clear to us how this model would account for the full range of empirical phenomena we have reviewed in support of multistore models.

Summary

The modal model has been successfully elaborated both in terms of secondary memory search and retrieval processes and in terms of primary memory forgetting processes. Nevertheless, there is strong empirical evidence that distinctions are necessary beyond the modal model's dichotomy between primary and secondary memory. In particular, there is evidence for separate phonological and visuo-spatial processing and for a distinction between indirect and direct recall tracks or, similarly, between short-term activation and attention. Evidence also points to an additional very short-term conceptual memory and a more active involvement of LTM in skilled performance. The concept of distinctiveness accommodates a wide range of findings previously attributed to primary memory, but it seems doubtful that it can provide a comprehensive account.

SENSORY MEMORY

We now consider the front end of the modal model: sensory memory. The modal model includes separate memories for each sense, including visual, auditory, and haptic. Because visual sensory (iconic) memory has been shown to be useful for only a fraction of a second [and perhaps not useful at all outside artificial laboratory tasks (see Haber 1983)], and because haptic and other senses play little role in verbal memory tasks, we concentrate here only on auditory sensory (echoic) memory.

Precategorical Acoustic Store

The strongest evidence for a distinct auditory sensory memory came from three interrelated observations in immediate serial recall of auditorily presented words (usually digits): (a) the recency effect (the advantage for the last item of the list), (b) the stimulus suffix effect (the elimination of the recency effect with the presentation of a redundant word presented after the list as a recall cue), and (c) the modality effect (the elimination of the recency effect with visual presentation of the list). These findings prompted Crowder & Morton (1969) to postulate an auditory sensory memory, which they termed precategorical acoustic store (PAS); their description of PAS was subsequently extended by Crowder (1978) to include effects of auditory masking. The store was labeled precategorical because it was found to be sensitive to physical (e.g. the voice of the speaker) but not semantic (e.g. the meaning of the words) characteristics of the items. The store was labeled acoustic because it seemed to depend on auditory presentation of the items. However, both of these characteristics of PAS have been disputed in recent years.

The precategorical nature of PAS was disputed by findings indicating that the suffix effect depended on the subjects' interpretation of the suffix as either speech or nonspeech. For example, Neath et al (1993) used as a suffix the word "baa." Half of the subjects were told that it was an actual sheep sound while the other half of the subjects were told that it was produced by a person. The suffix effect was observed only for the subjects who thought that the suffixes were spoken by a human. The acoustic nature of PAS was disputed because of studies showing that silently mouthed or lipread stimuli produced suffix effects even when the lists of to-be-remembered items were heard (Greene & Crowder 1984).

Both of these problems for PAS can be resolved by viewing it as a speech memory rather than an acoustic memory because it is well known that visual articulatory information, such as lip movements, affects speech perception (McGurk & MacDonald 1976) and that the interpretation by listeners of a specific sound as speech or nonspeech affects the way it is perceived (Liberman 1982). Work in speech perception has also revealed important differences in the perception of vowels and stop consonants (Healy & Repp 1982). This revised PAS account (Crowder 1983) can, thus, easily accommodate the fact that vowels but not stop consonants show suffix and modality effects for auditory (Crowder 1971) and lipread (de Gelder & Vroomen 1994) stimuli (but see Turner et al 1987 for different findings with mouthed stimuli).

An important challenge to this revised account of PAS is that modality effects have also been reported in paradigms involving LTM, such as the continuous-distractor paradigm (Gardiner & Gregg 1979). However, Greene (1992) pointed out that these long-term modality effects (unlike the parallel short-term effects) are not found for serial recall of digits. Hence, it may not be necessary to use the same explanation for both short-term and long-term modality effects. Nevertheless, alternative theoretical frameworks have been proposed to account for the full range of modality effects. One such account is Glenberg's (1987) temporal distinctiveness theory, which is based on the assumption that temporal discrimination is more accurate for auditory than for visual presentation of items. In support of this distinction between auditory and visual information, Glenberg et al (1989) found an advantage for auditory, relative to visual, presentation in the reproduction of temporal rhythms. On the other hand, Schab & Crowder (1989) disputed this distinction because they found little auditory advantage in the estimation of temporal durations.

Processing Streams

Penney (1989) also rejected the PAS account of the short-term modality effect and proposed an alternative account in terms of separate processing streams for auditory and visual items. According to her account, auditorily presented items automatically elicit both A (acoustic) and P (phonological) codes. The A code is sensory-based and produced only for stimuli that are heard. The P code is internally generated and is analogous to Baddeley's (1992) phonological loop, including information about words, phonemes, and articulation. Visually presented items are normally represented in the P code, but not automatically so. In addition, they elicit a visually-based code analogous to Baddeley's (1992) visuo-spatial sketchpad. Penney's support for the separate streams involves five different lines of evidence: (a) less interference with two concurrent verbal tasks when two modalities, rather than a single modality, are employed, as in attentional studies; (b) improved memory when list items are presented in two different modalities; (c) modality selective interference effects, including suffix effects and effects of different distractor tasks; (d) the advantage for recall organized by modality, as opposed to time of presentation; and (e) STM deficits that are modality specific.

Penney (1989) raised two primary criticisms against the PAS model. The first concerns its underestimation of both the capacity and duration of auditory sensory memory. Penney argued that the A code represents at least five items and lasts as long as a minute. Second, and most importantly, she pointed to demonstrations of long-term modality effects, such as that found by Gathercole & Conway (1988) extending throughout a list of 30 items. Because long-term and short-term modality effects react differently to some variables, she proposed that these two effects reflect different mechanisms but that both reflect properties of the A code. Three properties of the A code emphasized by Penney are (a) its large capacity and the fact that it does not decay but is subject to interference, (b) its specialization for coding sequential associations between items, and (c) the automatic nature of its generation and maintenance. However, with Penney's proposed large capacity for the A code, it appears difficult to provide an explanation for the typical modality and suffix effects, which are limited to the final position in immediate serial recall.

Feature Model

Nairne's (1988, 1990) feature model is an alternative framework in which to interpret recency effects in serial recall. Nairne postulated two types of memory trace features—modality independent, which coincide with the inner voice, and modality dependent, which reflect perceptual aspects of the stimuli. The modality-dependent features are analogous to Penney's (1989) A code and visuo-spatial sketchpad code, whereas the modality-independent features are analogous to her P code. Nairne postulated similar modality-dependent features from speech, lipread, and mouthed stimuli, which are all output of a language-analysis system. Thus, the modality-dependent features are perceptual, not sensory. In contrast, the modality-independent features correspond to STM or articulatory coding.

According to Nairne (1988), particular trace features are used at recall if they are discriminable (distinctive) and salient (useful or relevant). Recall is based on a reconstructive process in which the features of the memory trace are compared with features of candidate items. There is no decay as a source of forgetting in this account (as there is in the PAS account). Rather, forgetting results purely from overwriting, which occurs feature by feature, such that a subsequent feature can overwrite an earlier feature only if it is the same type (modality-dependent or modality-independent). Overwriting also occurs only for items in the same perceptual group (Frankish 1989). Recency results because the final list item does not suffer from overwriting of modality-dependent features unless there is a suffix. The modality-independent features of the final list item are overwritten by rehearsal and other inner voice activities that occur at the end of the list even when there is no suffix.

An important aspect of Nairne's (1988) model is the fact that he is able to account for the presence of visual recency effects, which occur for deaf subjects with American Sign Language (Shand & Klima 1981) and for hearing subjects with abstract (Broadbent & Broadbent 1981) and unusual (Campbell et al 1983) visual stimuli. According to Nairne, auditory features are not stronger, more distinctive, or more durable than visual features. Visual stimuli usually fail to exhibit recency because of overwriting by visual events after the end of the list and because subjects generally use auditory, rather than visual, features as discriminative cues in recall. Nairne's account is, thus, similar to Shand & Klima's (1981) primary linguistic code account, according to which recency effects occur when the stimuli are presented in the modality consistent with the dominant format used for STM coding. However, by Nairne's account, subjects may be led by some task demands to attend to linguistically irrelevant visual features. If the salience of visual features is enhanced in a particular task, then visual recency effects should occur according to Nairne's model, but not according to the PAS model.

Nairne (1988) accounts for long-term modality effects in a manner similar to that of Glenberg's (1987) temporal distinctiveness theory. Time of occurrence is associated with a broader temporal region for visual traces because they are largely composed of modality-independent features, as are the neighboring traces for inner-voice activity.

Summary

Just as attempts were made to use distinctiveness as an explanation for previous findings attributable to primary memory, it has been used as an explanation for previous findings attributable to auditory sensory memory, especially because of parallel effects found in LTM. Nevertheless, there remains powerful evidence for a separate type of processing associated with speech perception; that is, there is support for a distinction between acoustic and phonological codes or, similarly, between modality-dependent and independent features.

SECONDARY MEMORY

According to some versions of the modal model, including the simple version of the Atkinson & Shiffrin (1968) model that was applied to free recall, storage in secondary memory is permanent, with forgetting attributable solely to retrieval, rather than storage, failures. This proposed durability of storage in secondary memory is in sharp contrast to the rapid loss of information from primary memory. Hence, we concentrate our discussion of secondary memory on the issue of its permanency and durability. (For more inclusive summaries of the literature on long-term retention, see Healy & Sinclair 1995, Schmidt & Bjork 1992.)

Permastore

Although it is difficult to study retention over long delay intervals in the laboratory, an ingenious naturalistic cross-sectional method was developed by Bahrick (1984) to study retention over periods up to 50 years. This method employs a large number of subjects who acquired the same knowledge at different times in the past. These subjects must estimate the degree of their original acquisition of the material and the extent to which they rehearsed the material after acquisition. Retention tests are performed and a retention function is calculated on the basis of the subjects' date of original acquisition and then corrected, through multiple regression, for such factors as degree of original acquisition and extent of rehearsal. Bahrick used this method to study the retention of Spanish learned in the classroom by more than 700 subjects whose last exposure to a Spanish course was from 0 to approximately 50 years prior to the retention test. Rehearsal was very low and not a good predictor of performance on the retention test, which was instead predicted to a large extent by original acquisition level and training in other Romance languages. The retention function indicated an exponential decline in performance across the first 6 years, after which there was a stable asymptote for about 30 years, followed by a final decline probably attributable to aging. Because so much knowledge was maintained across the long delays with little intervening rehearsal, Bahrick introduced the concept of permanent memory, or "permastore."

Although Bahrick's (1984) findings have been disputed (Hintzman 1993), more recent work has provided converging evidence for the notion of permastore. Using the same techniques, Conway et al (1991) assessed retention over a 12-year period of material learned in a cognitive psychology course. After a rapid decline in performance across the first four years, there was a stable asymptote for the remaining eight years. Further, in a cross-sectional study of bilingual Hispanic immigrants, Bahrick et al (1994) found essentially no loss of Spanish knowledge over a 50-year period of residence in the United States. It is important to note that the subjects in this study were at least 10 years old when they entered the United States and, thus, had a solid foundation in Spanish before immigrating and that most of them continued to speak about as much Spanish as English after entering the United States. Using a different method, in which subjects were given recognition tests for former single-season television programs, Squire (1989) supported the finding that considerable knowledge may be maintained in memory for a lifetime even in the absence of rehearsal. However, he also found a gradual and continuous loss in performance, and no evidence of a stable asymptote. This finding is consistent with demonstrations that forgetting functions follow a power law (Anderson & Schooler 1991, Wixted & Ebbesen 1991). Squire attributed the discrepancy between his findings and those of Bahrick to the higher degree of learning and the greater degree of internal organization for the learned material in Bahrick's studies.

Procedural Reinstatement

Remarkable durability of memory has also been found in laboratory studies of skill acquisition and retention (Healy & Bourne 1995). For example, in an experiment in which subjects were given extensive training in single-digit multiplication, Fendrich et al (1993) found considerable improvements in the speed with which subjects provided the answers to the problems across 12 sessions of training and no deterioration in performance speed across delay intervals up to 14 months after training. This high degree of skill retention was coupled, however, with a striking specificity in the skill acquired. Rickard et al (1994) found that extensive training on specific multiplication and division problems (e.g. _ = 4 × 7) did not transfer to parallel problems with the complementary operation (e.g. 28 = _ × 7). To account for the observed skill durability and specificity, Healy et al (1992a) proposed a procedural reinstatement principle, according to which superior long-term retention results when the procedures (the motoric, perceptual, and cognitive operations) used at the time of acquisition are reinstated (duplicated) at the time of the retention test. This procedural reinstatement principle draws on the distinction between procedural and declarative knowledge proposed by Anderson (1983) as well as the notion proposed by Kolers & Roediger (1984) that memory representations cannot be divorced from the procedures used to acquire them.

The procedural reinstatement principle can be divided into two hypotheses, one concerning the use of procedures during study of material and the second concerning the use of the same procedures during the retention test. Support for each of these hypotheses was provided in studies of the generation effect (better memory for material that is generated than for material that is simply read by subjects) in episodic memory for the list of answers to simple arithmetic problems shown during an experimental session. The relevant procedures in this memory task are the arithmetic operations linking the problems to the answers. Crutcher & Healy (1989) showed that subjects' memory for the list of answers to multiplication problems was enhanced when subjects were required during study to perform the multiplication operations themselves as opposed to reading the answer with the problem. Generating or reading the answer per se was not crucial, because reading and verifying an answer did enhance performance, whereas using a calculator to generate the answer did not. McNamara & Healy (1995b) showed that enhanced memory for the list of answers to arithmetic problems only occurred when subjects were able at the retention test to recall the problem operands encountered during study and use them as retrieval cues for the list of answers. That is, a retention advantage was only found when subjects were able to reinstate at test the arithmetic procedures performed at study. The procedural reinstatement account of the generation effect is similar to other accounts (e.g. McDaniel et al 1990). However, the procedural reinstatement account has the advantage of explaining a broader range of findings concerning the generation effect (e.g. McNamara & Healy 1995a, Roediger & McDermott 1993) as well as findings in other domains, including long-term retention of nonverbal as well as verbal material.

Summary

The modal model generally assumes that secondary memory is permanent. Evidence for durability comes from naturalistic cross-sectional studies of knowledge acquisition and from laboratory studies of skill acquisition. Procedural reinstatement has been used to explain both durability and specificity of training.

CONCLUSION

Does the modal model still work? Some of the alternative frameworks, including distinctiveness and procedural reinstatement, can explain a wider scope of memory findings, including those spanning both short and long retention intervals and both verbal and nonverbal material. However, it seems clear from the studies reviewed here that these alternative frameworks cannot account for the full set of findings used to support the modal model. It is also clear, though, that the modal model needs to be elaborated along the lines reviewed here. In any event, this review has convinced us that the modal model is still useful as a means to frame the current literature on verbal learning and memory.

ACKNOWLEDGMENTS

Preparation of this chapter was supported in part by Army Research Institute Contract MDA903-93-K-0010 to the University of Colorado (Alice Healy, Principal Investigator) and a James S McDonnell Foundation Postdoctoral Fellowship Award to Danielle McNamara. We are indebted to James Parker for his invaluable help preparing this chapter and Lyle Bourne, Bob Crowder, Bill Estes, Don Foss, Bill Marmie, Bill Oliver, and Larry Pinneo for their helpful comments on earlier versions of this chapter.

Literature Cited

Anderson JR. 1983. *The Architecture of Cognition.* Cambridge, MA: Harvard Univ. Press

Anderson JR, Schooler LJ. 1991. Reflections of the environment in memory. *Psychol. Sci.* 2:396–408

Atkinson RC, Shiffrin RM. 1968. Human memory: a proposed system and its control processes. In *The Psychology of Learning and Motivation: Advances in Research and Theory,* ed. KW Spence, JT Spence, 2:89–195. New York: Academic

Baddeley AD. 1966. Short-term memory for word sequences as a function of acoustic, semantic and formal similarity. *Q. J. Exp. Psychol.* 18:362–65

Baddeley AD. 1990. *Human Memory: Theory and Practice.* Boston: Allyn & Bacon

Baddeley AD. 1992. Is working memory working? The fifteenth Bartlett lecture. *Q. J. Exp. Psychol.* 44A:1–31

Baddeley AD, Hitch GJ. 1974. Working memory. In *The Psychology of Learning and Motivation: Advances in Research and Theory,* ed. GH Bower, 8:47–89. New York: Academic

Baddeley AD, Hitch GJ. 1977. Recency reexamined. In *Attention and Performance,* ed. S Dornic, 6:647–67. Hillsdale, NJ: Erlbaum

Baddeley AD, Hitch GJ. 1993. The recency effect: implicit learning with explicit retrieval? *Mem. Cogn.* 21:146–55

Baddeley AD, Lewis VJ, Vallar G. 1984. Exploring the articulatory loop. *Q. J. Exp. Psychol.* 36:233–52

Baddeley AD, Lieberman K. 1980. Spatial working memory. In *Attention and Performance,* ed. RS Nickerson, 8:521–39. Hillsdale, NJ: Erlbaum

Baddeley AD, Logie R, Bressi S, Della Sala S, Spinnler H. 1986. Dementia and working memory. *Q. J. Exp. Psychol.* 38A:603–18

Baddeley AD, Papagno C, Norris D. 1991. Phonological memory and serial order: a sandwich for TODAM. See Hockley & Lewandowsky 1991, pp. 175–94

Baddeley AD, Papagno C, Vallar G. 1988.

When long-term learning depends on short-term storage. *J. Mem. Lang.* 27:586–95

Baddeley AD, Thomson N, Buchanan M. 1975. Word length and the structure of short-term memory. *J. Verbal Learn. Verbal Behav.* 14:575–89

Baddeley AD, Wilson B. 1985. Phonological coding and short-term memory in patients without speech. *J. Mem. Lang.* 24: 490–502

Bahrick HP. 1984. Semantic memory content in permastore: fifty years of memory for Spanish learned in school. *J. Exp. Psychol.: Gen.* 113:1–29

Bahrick HP, Hall LK, Goggin JP, Bahrick LE, Berger SA. 1994. Fifty years of language maintenance and language dominance in bilingual Hispanic immigrants. *J. Exp. Psychol.: Gen.* 123:264–83

Bjork RA, Whitten WB. 1974. Recency-sensitive retrieval processes in long-term free recall. *Cogn. Psychol.* 6:173–89

Broadbent DE. 1975. The magic number seven after fifteen years. In *Studies in Long-Term Memory,* ed. A Kennedy, A Wikes, pp. 3–18. London: Wiley

Broadbent DE, Broadbent MHP. 1981. Recency effects in visual memory. *Q. J. Exp. Psychol.* 33A:1–15

Brown J. 1958. Some tests of the decay theory of immediate memory. *Q. J. Exp. Psychol.* 10:12–21

Butterworth B, Campbell R, Howard D. 1986. The uses of short-term memory: a case study. *Q. J. Exp. Psychol.* 38A:705–37

Campbell R, Dodd B, Brasher J. 1983. The sources of visual recency: movement and language in serial recall. *Q. J. Exp. Psychol.* 35A:571–87

Chase WG, Ericsson KA. 1982. Skill and working memory. In *The Psychology of Learning and Motivation: Advances in Research and Theory,* ed. GH Bower, 16: 1–58. New York: Academic

Chase WG, Simon HA. 1973. The mind's eye in chess. In *Visual Information Processing,* ed. WG Chase, pp. 215–81. New York: Academic

Clark SE, Shiffrin RM. 1987. Recognition of multiple-item probes. *Mem. Cogn.* 15: 367–78

Conrad R. 1967. Interference or decay over short retention intervals. *J. Verbal Learn. Verbal. Behav.* 6:49–54

Conway MA, Cohen G, Stanhope N. 1991. On the very long-term retention of knowledge acquired through formal education: twelve years of cognitive psychology. *J. Exp. Psychol.: Gen.* 120:395–409

Cooke NJ, Atlas RS, Lane DM, Berger RC. 1993. Role of high-level knowledge in memory for chess positions. *Am. J. Psychol.* 106:321–51

Cowan N. 1992. Verbal memory span and the timing of spoken recall. *J. Mem. Lang.* 31: 668–84

Cowan N. 1993. Activation, attention, and short-term memory. *Mem. Cogn.* 21: 162–67

Cowan N. 1994. Mechanisms of verbal short-term memory. *Curr. Dir. Psychol. Sci.* 3: 185–89

Cowan N, Day L, Saults JS, Keller TA, Johnson T, Flores L. 1992. The role of verbal output time in the effects of word length on immediate memory. *J. Mem. Lang.* 31:1–17

Cowan N, Lichty W, Grove TR. 1990. Properties of memory for unattended spoken syllables. *J. Exp. Psychol.: Learn. Mem. Cogn.* 16:258–69

Cowan N, Wood NL, Borne DN. 1994. Reconfirmation of the short-term storage concept. *Psychol. Sci.* 5:103–6

Craik FIM, Lockhart RS. 1972. Levels of processing: a framework for memory research. *J. Verbal Learn. Verbal Behav.* 11: 671–84

Crowder RG. 1971. The sound of vowels and consonants in immediate memory. *J. Verbal Learn. Verbal Behav.* 10:587–96

Crowder RG. 1978. Mechanisms of auditory backward masking in the stimulus suffix effect. *Psychol. Rev.* 85:502–24

Crowder RG. 1983. The purity of auditory memory. *Philos. Trans. R. Soc. London* B302:251–65

Crowder RG. 1993. Short-term memory: Where do we stand? *Mem. Cogn.* 21: 142–45

Crowder RG, Morton J. 1969. Precategorical acoustic storage (PAS). *Percept. Psychophys.* 5:365–73

Crowder RG, Neath I. 1991. The microscope metaphor in human memory. See Hockley & Lewandowsky 1991, pp. 111–25

Crutcher RJ, Healy AF. 1989. Cognitive operations and the generation effect. *J. Exp. Psychol.: Learn. Mem. Cogn.* 15:669–75

Cunningham TF, Healy AF, Till RE, Fendrich DW, Dimitry CZ. 1993. Is there really very rapid forgetting from primary memory? The role of expectancy and item importance in short-term recall. *Mem. Cogn.* 21: 671–88

Cunningham TF, Healy AF, Williams DM. 1984. Effects of repetition on short-term retention of order information. *J. Exp. Psychol.: Learn. Mem. Cogn.* 10:575–97

de Gelder B, Vroomen J. 1994. Memory for consonants versus vowels in heard and lipread speech. *J. Mem. Lang.* 33:737–56

Engle RW, Cantor J, Carullo JJ. 1992. Individual differences in working memory and comprehension: a test of four hypotheses. *J. Exp. Psychol.: Learn. Mem. Cogn.* 18: 972–92

Ericsson KA, Kintsch W. 1995. Long-term

working memory. *Psychol. Rev.* 102: 211–45

Estes WK. 1972. An associative basis for coding and organization in memory. In *Coding Processes in Human Memory,* ed. AW Melton, E Martin, pp. 161–90. Washington, DC: Winston

Estes WK. 1991. On types of item coding and sources of recall in short-term memory. See Hockley & Lewandowsky 1991, pp. 155–73

Estes WK. 1994. *Classification and Cognition. Oxford Psychology Series, No. 22.* New York: Oxford Univ. Press

Fendrich DW, Healy AF, Bourne LE Jr. 1993. Mental arithmetic: training and retention of multiplication skill. In *Cognitive Psychology Applied,* ed. C Izawa, pp. 111–33. Hillsdale, NJ: Erlbaum

Frankish C. 1989. Perceptual organization and precategorical acoustic storage. *J. Exp. Psychol.: Learn. Mem. Cogn.* 15:469–79

Gardiner JM, Gregg VH. 1979. When auditory memory is not overwritten. *J. Verbal Learn. Verbal Behav.* 18:705–19

Gathercole SE, Baddeley AD. 1990. Phonological memory deficits in language disordered children: Is there a causal connection? *J. Mem. Lang.* 29:336–60

Gathercole SE, Conway MA. 1988. Exploring long-term modality effects: Vocalization leads to best retention. *Mem. Cogn.* 16: 110–19

Gernsbacher MA, Hargreaves DJ. 1988. Accessing sentence participants: the advantage of first mention. *J. Mem. Lang.* 27: 699–717

Gillund G, Shiffrin RM. 1984. A retrieval model for both recognition and recall. *Psychol. Rev.* 91:1–67

Glanzer M, Adams JK. 1990. The mirror effect in recognition memory: data and theory. *J. Exp. Psychol.: Learn. Mem. Cogn.* 16:5–16

Glanzer M, Cunitz AR. 1966. Two storage mechanisms in free recall. *J. Verbal Learn. Verbal Behav.* 5:351–60

Glanzer M, Fischer B, Dorfman D. 1984. Short-term storage in reading. *J. Verbal Learn. Verbal Behav.* 23:467–86

Glenberg AM. 1987. Temporal context and recency. In *Memory and Learning: The Ebbinghaus Centennial Conference,* ed. DS Gorfein, RR Hoffman, pp. 173–90. Hillsdale, NJ: Erlbaum

Glenberg AM, Mann S, Altman L, Forman T, Procise S. 1989. Modality effects in the coding and reproduction of rhythms. *Mem. Cogn.* 17:373–83

Graf P, Squire LR, Mandler G. 1984. The information that amnesic patients do not forget. *J. Exp. Psychol.: Learn. Mem. Cogn.* 10:164–78

Greene RL. 1986. Sources of recency effects in free recall. *Psychol. Bull.* 99:221–28

Greene RL. 1992. *Human Memory: Paradigms and Paradoxes.* Hillsdale, NJ: Erlbaum

Greene RL, Crowder RG. 1984. Modality and suffix effects in the absence of auditory stimulation. *J. Verbal Learn. Verbal Behav.* 23:371–82

Haber RN. 1983. The impending demise of the icon: a critique of the concept of iconic storage in visual information processing. *Behav. Brain Sci.* 6:1–54

Hatano G, Osawa K. 1983. Digit memory of grand experts in abacus-derived mental calculation. *Cognition* 15:95–110

Healy AF, Bourne LE Jr, eds. 1995. *Learning and Memory of Knowledge and Skills: Durability and Specificity.* Thousands Oaks, CA: Sage

Healy AF, Fendrich DW, Crutcher RJ, Wittman WT, Gesi AT, et al. 1992a. The long-term retention of skills. See Healy et al 1992b, pp. 87–118

Healy AF, Fendrich DW, Cunningham TF, Till RE. 1987. Effects of cuing on short-term retention of order information. *J. Exp. Psychol.: Learn. Mem. Cogn.* 13:413–25

Healy AF, Kosslyn SM, Shiffrin RM, eds. 1992b. *From Learning Processes to Cognitive Processes: Essays in Honor of William K. Estes,* Vol. 2. Hillsdale, NJ: Erlbaum

Healy AF, Repp BH. 1982. Context independence and phonetic mediation in categorical perception. *J. Exp. Psychol.: Hum. Percept. Perform.* 8:68–80

Healy AF, Sinclair GP. 1995. The long-term retention of training and instruction. In *Handbook of Perception and Cognition,* ed. EL Bjork, RA Bjork, Vol. 10. New York: Academic. In press

Hintzman DL. 1993. Twenty-five years of learning and memory: Was the cognitive revolution a mistake? See Meyer & Kornblum 1993, pp. 359–91

Hintzman DL, Hartry AL. 1990. Item effects in recognition and fragment completion: Contingency relations vary for different subsets of words. *J. Exp. Psychol.: Learn. Mem. Cogn.* 16:955–69

Hockley WE, Lewandowsky S, eds. 1991. *Relating Theory and Data: Essays on Human Memory in Honor of Bennet B. Murdock.* Hillsdale, NJ: Erlbaum

Hulme C, Maughan S, Brown GDA. 1991. Memory for familiar and unfamiliar words: evidence for a long-term memory contribution to short-term memory span. *J. Mem. Lang.* 30:685–701

Humphreys MS, Bain JD, Pike R. 1989. Different ways to cue a coherent memory system: a theory for episodic, semantic, and procedural tasks. *Psychol. Rev.* 96:208–33

James W. 1890. *The Principles of Psychology.* New York: Henry Holt

Johnson GJ. 1991. A distinctiveness model of

serial learning. *Psychol. Rev.* 98:204–17

Just MA, Carpenter PA. 1992. A capacity theory of comprehension: individual differences in working memory. *Psychol. Rev.* 99:122–49

Keppel G, Underwood BJ. 1962. Proactive inhibition in short-term retention of single items. *J. Verbal Learn. Verbal Behav.* 1: 153–61

Kintsch W. 1988. The role of knowledge in discourse comprehension: a construction-integration model. *Psychol. Rev.* 95: 163–82

Kolers PA, Roediger HL III. 1984. Procedures of mind. *J. Verbal Learn. Verbal Behav.* 23:425–49

Koppenaal L, Glanzer M. 1990. An examination of the continuous distractor task and the "long-term recency effect". *Mem. Cogn.* 18:183–95

Lee CL. 1992. The perturbation model of short-term memory: a review and some further developments. See Healy et al 1992b, pp. 119–41

Lee CL, Estes WK. 1981. Item and order information in short-term memory: evidence for multilevel perturbation processes. *J. Exp. Psychol.: Hum. Learn. Mem.* 7:149–69

Liberman AM. 1982. On finding that speech is special. *Am. Psychol.* 37:148–67

Logie RH. 1986. Visuo-spatial processing in working memory. *Q. J. Exp. Psychol.* 38A: 229–47

Lombardi L, Potter MC. 1992. The regeneration of syntax in short term memory. *J. Mem. Lang.* 31:713–33

McDaniel MA, Riegler GL, Waddill PJ. 1990. Generation effects in free recall: further support for a three-factor theory. *J. Exp. Psychol.: Learn. Mem. Cogn.* 16:789–98

McGurk H, MacDonald J. 1976. Hearing lips and seeing voices. *Nature* 264:746–48

McNamara DS, Healy AF. 1995a. A generation advantage for multiplication skill training and nonword vocabulary acquisition. See Healy & Bourne 1995, pp. 132–67

McNamara DS, Healy AF. 1995b. A procedural explanation of the generation effect: the use of an operand retrieval strategy for multiplication and addition problems. *J. Mem. Lang.* 34:399–416

Melton AW. 1963. Implications of short-term memory for a general theory of memory. *J. Verbal Learn. Verbal Behav.* 2:1–21

Mensink GJ, Raaijmakers JGW. 1988. A model for interference and forgetting. *Psychol. Rev.* 95:434–55

Meyer DE, Kornblum S, eds. 1993. *Attention and Performance,* Vol. 14. Cambridge, MA: MIT Press

Milner B. 1966. Amnesia following operation on the temporal lobes. In *Amnesia,* ed. C Whitty, O Zangwill, pp. 109–33. London: Butterworths

Murdock BB Jr. 1960. The distinctiveness of stimuli. *Psychol. Rev.* 67:16–31

Murdock BB Jr. 1982. A theory for the storage and retrieval of item and associative information. *Psychol. Rev.* 89:609–26

Murnane K, Shiffrin RM. 1991a. Interference and the representation of events in memory. *J. Exp. Psychol.: Learn. Mem. Cogn.* 17:855–74

Murnane K, Shiffrin RM. 1991b. Word repetitions in sentence recognition. *Mem. Cogn.* 19:119–30

Muter P. 1980. Very rapid forgetting. *Mem. Cogn.* 8:174–79

Nairne JS. 1988. A framework for interpreting recency effects in immediate serial recall. *Mem. Cogn.* 16:343–52

Nairne JS. 1990. A feature model of immediate memory. *Mem. Cogn.* 18:251–69

Nairne JS. 1991. Positional uncertainty in long-term memory. *Mem. Cogn.* 19: 332–40

Nairne JS. 1992. The loss of positional certainty in long-term memory. *Psychol. Sci.* 3:199–202

Neath I. 1993a. Contextual and distinctive processes and the serial position function. *J. Mem. Lang.* 32:820–40

Neath I. 1993b. Distinctiveness and serial position effects in recognition. *Mem. Cogn.* 21:689–98

Neath I, Crowder RG. 1990. Schedules of presentation and temporal distinctiveness in human memory. *J. Exp. Psychol.: Learn. Mem. Cogn.* 16:316–27

Neath I, Knoedler AJ. 1994. Distinctiveness and serial position effects in recognition and sentence processing. *J. Mem. Lang.* 33: 776–95

Neath I, Surprenant AM, Crowder RG. 1993. The context-dependent stimulus suffix effect. *J. Exp. Psychol.: Learn. Mem. Cogn.* 19:698–703

Newell A. 1990. *Unified Theories of Cognition.* Cambridge, MA: Harvard Univ. Press

Papagno C, Valentine T, Baddeley AD. 1991. Phonological short-term memory and foreign-language vocabulary learning. *J. Mem. Lang.* 30:331–47

Penney CG. 1989. Modality effects and the structure of short-term verbal memory. *Mem. Cogn.* 17:398–422

Peterson LR, Peterson MJ. 1959. Short-term retention of individual verbal items. *J. Exp. Psychol.* 58:193–98

Potter MC. 1976. Short-term conceptual memory for pictures. *J. Exp. Psychol.: Hum. Learn. Mem.* 2:509–22

Potter MC. 1993. Very short-term conceptual memory. *Mem. Cogn.* 21:156–61

Potter MC, Kroll JF, Yachzel B, Carpenter E, Sherman J. 1986. Pictures in sentences: understanding without words. *J. Exp. Psychol.: Gen.* 115:281–94

Potter MC, Lombardi L. 1990. Regeneration in the short-term recall of sentences. *J. Mem. Lang.* 29:633–54

Potter MC, Moryadas A, Abrams I, Noel A. 1993. Word perception and misperception in context. *J. Exp. Psychol.: Learn. Mem. Cogn.* 19:3–22

Raaijmakers JGW. 1993. The story of the two-store model of memory: past criticisms, current status, and future directions. See Meyer & Kornblum 1993, pp. 467–88

Raaijmakers JGW, Shiffrin RM. 1981. Search of associative memory. *Psychol. Rev.* 88: 93–134

Raaijmakers JGW, Shiffrin RM. 1992. Models for recall and recognition. *Annu. Rev. Psychol.* 43:205–34

Ratcliff R, Clark SE, Shiffrin RM. 1990. List-strength effect. I. Data and discussion. *J. Exp. Psychol.: Learn. Mem. Cogn.* 16: 163–78

Richardson-Klavehn A, Bjork RA. 1988. Measures of memory. *Annu. Rev. Psychol.* 39:475–543

Rickard TC, Healy AF, Bourne LE Jr. 1994. On the cognitive structure of basic arithmetic skills: operation, order, and symbol transfer effects. *J. Exp. Psychol.: Learn. Mem. Cogn.* 20:1139–53

Roediger HL III. 1993. Learning and memory: progress and challenge. See Meyer & Kornblum 1993, pp. 509–28

Roediger HL III, Crowder RG. 1976. A serial position effect in recall of United States presidents. *Bull. Psychon. Soc.* 8:275–78

Roediger HL III, McDermott KB. 1993. Implicit memory in normal human subjects. In *Handbook of Neuropsychology,* ed. F Boller, J Grafman, 8:63–131. Amsterdam: Elsevier

Salame P, Baddeley AD. 1989. Effects of background music on phonological short-term memory. *Q. J. Exp. Psychol.* 41A: 107–22

Schab FR, Crowder RG. 1989. Accuracy of temporal coding: auditory-visual comparisons. *Mem. Cogn.* 17:384–97

Schmidt RA, Bjork RA. 1992. New conceptualizations of practice: common principles in three paradigms suggest new concepts for training. *Psychol. Sci.* 3:207–17

Schneider W, Detweiler M. 1988. A connectionist/control architecture for working memory. In *The Psychology of Learning and Motivation: Advances in Research and Theory,* ed. GH Bower, 21:53–119. New York: Academic

Schweickert R. 1993. A multinomial processing tree model for degradation and reintegration in immediate recall. *Mem. Cogn.* 21:168–75

Sebrechts MM, Marsh RL, Seamon JG. 1989. Secondary memory and very rapid forgetting. *Mem. Cogn.* 17:693–700

Shand MA, Klima ES. 1981. Nonauditory suffix effects in congenitally deaf signers of American Sign Language. *J. Exp. Psychol.: Hum. Learn. Mem.* 7:464–74

Shiffrin RM. 1993. Short-term memory: a brief commentary. *Mem. Cogn.* 21:193–97

Shiffrin RM, Murnane K, Gronlund S, Roth M. 1989. On units of storage and retrieval. In *Current Issues in Cognitive Processes: The Tulane Floweree Symposium on Cognition,* ed. C Izawa, pp. 25–68. Hillsdale, NJ: Erlbaum

Shiffrin RM, Raaijmakers J. 1992. The SAM retrieval model: a retrospective and prospective. See Healy et al 1992b, pp. 69–86

Shiffrin RM, Ratcliff R, Clark SE. 1990. List-strength effect. II. Theoretical mechanisms. *J. Exp. Psychol.: Learn. Mem. Cogn.* 16: 179–95

Shulman HG. 1971. Similarity effects in short-term memory. *Psychol. Bull.* 75:399–415

Spinnler H, della Sala S, Bandera R, Baddeley AD. 1988. Dementia, ageing and the structure of human memory. *Cogn. Neuropsychol.* 5:193–211

Squire LR. 1989. On the course of forgetting in very long-term memory. *J. Exp. Psychol.: Learn. Mem. Cogn.* 15:241–45

Squire LR, Knowlton B, Musen G. 1993. The structure and organization of memory. *Annu. Rev. Psychol.* 44:453–95

Thapar A, Greene RL. 1993. Evidence against a short-term-store account of long-term recency effects. *Mem. Cogn.* 21:329–37

Tulving E, Schacter DL. 1990. Priming and human memory systems. *Science* 247: 301–6

Turner ML, La Pointe LB, Cantor J, Reeves CH, Griffeth RH, Engle RW. 1987. Recency and suffix effects found with auditory presentation and with mouthed visual presentation: They're not the same thing. *J. Mem. Lang.* 26:138–64

Turvey MT, Brick P, Osborn J. 1970. Proactive interference in short-term memory as a function of prior-item retention interval. *Q. J. Exp. Psychol.* 22:142–47

Vallar G, Shallice T, eds. 1990. *Neuropsychological Impairments of Short-Term Memory.* Cambridge: Cambridge Univ. Press

Waugh NC, Norman DA. 1965. Primary memory. *Psychol. Rev.* 72:89–104

Wixted JT, Ebbesen EB. 1991. On the form of forgetting. *Psychol. Sci.* 2:409–415

Wright AA, Santiago HC, Sands SF, Kendrick DF, Cook RG. 1985. Memory processing of serial lists by pigeons, monkeys, and people. *Science* 229:287–89

Annu. Rev. Psychol. 1996. 47:173–203

LONG-TERM POTENTIATION AND LEARNING

Joe L. Martinez, Jr. and Brian E. Derrick

The University of Texas, San Antonio, Texas 78249-0662

KEY WORDS: memory, hippocampus, synaptic plasticity, Hebb, neural networks

ABSTRACT

Long-term potentiation (LTP), a relatively long-lived increase in synaptic strength, remains the most popular model for the cellular process that may underlie information storage within neural systems. The strongest arguments for a role of LTP in memory are theoretical and involve Hebb's Postulate, Marr's theory of hippocampal function, and neural network theory. Considering LTP research as a whole, few studies have addressed the essential question: Is LTP a process involved in learning and memory? The present manuscript reviews research that attempts to link LTP with learning and memory, focusing on studies utilizing electrophysiological, pharmacological, and molecular biological methodologies. Most evidence firmly supports a role for LTP in learning memory. However, an unequivocal experimental demonstration of a contribution of LTP to memory is hampered by our lack of knowledge of the biological basis of memory and of the ways in which memories are represented in ensembles of neurons, the existence of a variety of cellular forms of LTP, and the likely resistance of distributed memory stores to degradation by treatments that incompletely disrupt LTP.

CONTENTS

INTRODUCTION

All neurobiologists would agree that information is acquired, stored, and re-trieved by the brain; memory is a thing in a place in a brain. Unfortunately, we do not understand completely how any brain encodes memory as a biological entity. However, the brain's cellular architecture provides clues. All brains consist of individual cellular units or neurons. Most neurons have the same parts: a dendritic tree, cell-body, axon, and synaptic buttons. The majority of neurons communicate with each other across a synaptic space via neurotrans-mitters and neuromodulators. In mammalian brains, billions of neurons inter-connect in vast networks via even more billions of synapses. This fact leads to our first assertion about memory.

Assertion 1: Memory Is Stored in Networks of Neurons

The brain accomplishes all of its remarkable activity through networks of neurons. A single neuron is unlikely to encode a specific memory; rather, ensembles of neurons participate in maintaining a representation that serves as a memory. Such ensembles require dynamic interactions among neurons and an ability to modify these interactions. This implies a need for use-dependent changes in synaptic function and leads to the second assertion about memory.

Assertion 2: Memory Is Stored through Changes in Synaptic Function

Hebb (1949) increased our understanding of how networks of neurons might store information with the provocative theory that memories are represented by reverberating assemblies of neurons. Hebb recognized that a memory so represented cannot reverberate forever and that some alteration in the network must occur to provide integrity both to make the assembly a permanent trace and to make it more likely that the trace could be reconstructed as a remem-brance. Thus, our second assertion is that, because neurons communicate with each other only at synapses, the activity of the assembly or network is most easily (perhaps only) altered by changes in synaptic function. Hebb (1949) formalized this idea in what is known as Hebb's Postulate: "When an axon of cell A is near enough to excite cell B and repeatedly or persistently takes part in firing it, some growth process or metabolic change takes place in one or both cells such that A's efficiency, as one of the cells firing B, is increased." Hebb's Postulate is very close to a modern-day definition of long-term potentiation (LTP) and leads to two more assertions about why LTP could be a mechanism of memory storage.

Assertion 3: LTP Could Operate in Networks of Neurons to Store Memory in a Manner Similar to That in Hebb's Postulate

Bliss & Lomo (1973) first reported that tetanic stimulation of the perforant path in anesthetized rabbits increased the slope of the population excitatory post-synaptic potential (EPSP) recorded extracellularly in the dentate gyrus and reduced the threshold for eliciting a population action potential (population spike). They defined LTP as potentiation that lasted longer than 30 min, although they observed LTP for several hours. Later studies showed that LTP recorded in animals with permanent indwelling electrodes lasted from weeks to months (Barnes 1979). Moreover, LTP is found in many areas of neocortex (Bear & Kirkwood 1993).

A line of reasoning that led to the conclusion that LTP is a mechanism of memory is derived from theoretical studies on neural networks. Marr (1971) described an associative network in area CA3 of the hippocampus in which distributed patterns of activity were imposed on principal cells; the trace became established as a result of strengthening synaptic connections. Since the work of Hebb (1949) and the discovery of LTP (Bliss & Lomo 1973), these theoretical connections among neurons that strengthen as a result of activity are referred to as Hebb Synapses.

Synaptic strengthening as described by the Hebb Rule could increase without bound. Because such a Hebbian mechanism would lead to saturation, anti-Hebb processes were suggested (Stent 1973, Sejnowski 1977). Recently there has been a surge of interest in long-term depression (LTD) both as a memory mechanism (homosynaptic or associative LTD) and as a process that normalizes synaptic weights in networks (homosynaptic and heterosynaptic LTD; cf Morris 1989b, Linden & Conner 1995, Rolls 1989, Derrick & Martinez 1995).

The use of the Hebb Rule in a distributed memory system can lead to efficient storage of a number of representations within the same network (also called correlation matrix memories; see McNaughton & Morris 1987), which can be regenerated with partial input (pattern completion). The notion of correlation matrix memories resolves the seeming paradox of how specific memories or representations are stored in nonspecific (distributed) stores. Further, any particular part of the network is not essential for pattern completion; the performance of the entire network deteriorates gradually as more and more units are damaged or eliminated. This feature, referred to as graceful degradation, is a natural by-product of distributed memory stores (Rolls 1989, Rumelhart & McClelland 1986) and is characteristic of neural systems (see Rumelhart & McClelland 1986). Moreover, storage of memory within distributed systems rests on the ability of neurons to form synapse-specific alterations in synaptic strength. Thus we come to our third assertion about memory. If memory is stored in networks of neurons and if network efficiency is mediated by persistent activity (Hebb's Postulate), then LTP induced by persistent stimulation of an afferent pathway is at least one likely mechanism by which the brain stores information.

Together these three assertions provide a powerful rationale for the claim that LTP is a substrate of memory. However, because no one has isolated a memory trace, LTP cannot be studied in a known memory network. Thus the evidence reviewed in this paper is correlational and inferential. Before we consider the evidence, we discuss three other similarities between LTP and learning that some consider support the notion that LTP is a memory mechanism: LTP is specific to tetanized inputs, it is associative, and it lasts a long time. In our view, these arguments unfortunately focused discussion on similarities between classical conditioning and LTP that, to date, remain merely similarities.

LTP Is Specific to Tetanized Inputs

Since the time of Pavlov (1927), conditioned reflexes have been thought to involve specific neural pathways. In fact, simple neural reflexes may be incorporated into conditioned reflexes. LTP is specific in this way in that only tetanized afferents show potentiation, so-called homosynaptic LTP. Unfortunately, the idea of specificity of tetanized afferents has become clouded with reports that LTP induction might involve gases, such as nitrous oxide (NO), that readily diffuse into adjacent neurons (O'Dell et al 1991, Schuman & Madison 1991). Also, evidence suggests that maintenance of LTP involves retrograde messengers that also may affect neighboring neurons (Bonhoeffer et al 1989). This lack of specificity has advantages over a strict Hebb Rule in that diffuse alterations in presynaptic elements (referred to as volume learning) may permit the storage of the temporal order of inputs (Montague & Sejnowski 1994).

LTP Is Associative

Another interesting property of LTP, which led some researchers to suggest that it is a memory mechanism, is associativity. If weak non-LTP-inducing stimulation in one afferent is paired with strong LTP-inducing stimulation in another afferent to the same cell population, then the weakly stimulated afferent exhibits LTP (Levy & Steward 1979, McNaughton et al 1978). The property of associativity is reminiscent of classical conditioning, in which a neutral CS is associated with a strong UCS to induce conditioning (Makintosh 1974). As the argument goes, because neural afferents in associative LTP act in a way similar to neural activity in classical conditioning, and because the mechanism of associative LTP is the same as in LTP, at least in N-methyl-D-aspartate (NMDA) receptor–dependent systems LTP is a memory mechanism. This proposition has been roundly criticized. The critics' view (Gallistel 1995) is that the temporal constraints of associative LTP are dissimilar to those of classical conditioning. In addition, the necessary ordering of CS and UCS are absent in associative LTP, and a mechanism as simple as associative LTP cannot account for the behavioral complexity observed in classical conditioning.

Today most researchers would agree that associative LTP is not classical conditioning (Diamond & Rose 1994). LTP does, however, bear comparison to a psychological example of learning. Associative LTP, described by Hebb (1949) as the simultaneous activity of sensory afferents, is more similar to sensory preconditioning than classical conditioning (Mackintosh 1974). Sensory preconditioning is the association of two sensory stimuli—for example, a tone and a light—by repeated pairing. The comparison of associative LTP and sensory preconditioning is straightforward: The stimuli need not be presented in a particular order, nor does a UCS need be present, as in classical conditioning. However, temporal contiguity for the presentation of the two stimuli is required (Kelso & Brown 1986, Mackintosh 1974). In our view, it is more proper to compare associative LTP to sensory preconditioning than to classical conditioning. An interesting observation in this regard is that hippocampal lesions appear to abolish sensory preconditioning (Port et al 1987).

From a behavioral point of view, LTP is more analogous to sensitization, and LTD is more analogous to habituation—both forms of nonassociative learning—than either is to classical conditioning. Habituation may be defined authoritatively as a "response decrement as a result of repeated stimulation" (Harris cited in Thompson & Spencer 1966). Sensitization may be defined as a response increment as a result of repeated (usually strong) stimulation (Thompson & Spencer 1966). LTP and LTD are response increments and decrements that result from repeated stimulation (Bliss & Lomo 1973, Dudek & Bear 1993). Most researchers would not agree that LTP is analogous to sensitization because induction of LTP requires that a threshold number of fibers have to be simultaneously active (McNaughton et al 1978). Cooperativity could involve associative interactions within the postsynaptic target or among presynaptic fibers (whereas Hebbian associativity implies a postsynaptic associative effect of multiple fibers).

The comparison of LTD and habituation has not been made, but a parametric analysis of habituation is available (Thompson & Spencer 1966). Habituation and sensitization were recognized quite early to be separate processes, and dishabituation was viewed as sensitization induced simultaneously with habituation (Thompson & Spencer 1966). An analogous contemporary conundrum is whether depotentiation represents the addition of separate and oppositely signed processes, or the cellular reversal of LTP (Bear & Malenka 1994). While the comparisons of LTP and LTD to psychological phenomena will undoubtedly continue, it seems that simple isomorphisms do not exist.

LTP Lasts a Long Time as Does Long-Term Memory

The lasting nature of LTP has been used as an argument both for (Barnes 1979) and against (Gallistel 1995) LTP as a memory mechanism; the latter is supported by the fact that LTP does not last a lifetime, as do some memories (Squire 1987). However, any number of properties of networks—for example, reactivation (Hebb 1949)—may extend the biological integrity of a memory. Further, most studies characterizing LTP longevity observed LTP at hippocampal sites. Because the hippocampus is viewed as having a temporally restricted role in memory in both animals and humans (Barnes 1988, Zola-Morgan & Squire 1993), there is no a priori reason to expect permanent changes within the hippocampus. Thus, longevity comparisons between hippocampal LTP and long-term memories are not meaningful. Memory is not a unitary phenomenon, and memory systems likely include anatomically distinct structures and even perhaps distinct neural mechanisms (Schacter & Tulving 1994). Perhaps synaptic plasticity within other parts of the brain—in neocortical regions, for example—lasts longer than hippocampal LTP.

In our view the findings discussed to this point offer compelling reasons to consider LTP (and LTD) likely biological mechanisms of memory. This extensive prologue was required because the evidence supporting such an interpretation is not convincing to some (Keith & Rudy 1990, Gallistel 1995) and because each set of studies supporting this view carries interpretational difficulties. We now turn to a discussion of the evidence. First, we briefly list the known cellular mechanisms for LTP; for more extensive reviews of cellular mechanisms, see Bliss & Collingridge (1993), Bramham (1992), and Johnston et al (1992). Then we discuss electrophysiological correlations between LTP and learning, induction of LTP and its effect on learning, the pharmacological properties of learning and LTP, and new studies that attempt to determine simultaneously the genetic basis of LTP and learning.

CELLULAR MECHANISMS OF LTP INDUCTION

Several different forms of LTP have been described (Bliss & Collingridge 1993). In the hippocampus, two major forms of LTP are NMDA receptor-dependent (Collingridge et al 1983) or opioid receptor-dependent (Bramham 1992). Each is discussed.

NMDA-Receptor-Dependent LTP and Associative LTP

NMDA is a voltage-dependent glutamate receptor subtype. For LTP induction, the NMDA receptor must be activated by the neurotransmitter glutamate and simultaneously there must be sufficient depolarization of the postsynaptic membrane to relieve a Mg^{2+} block in the NMDA-associated ion channel, which allows the entry of Ca^{2+} into the postsynaptic terminal. Ca^{2+} activates any number of Ca^{2+}-sensitive second messenger processes. Because NMDA receptors are sensitive to both presynaptic transmitter release and postsynaptic depolarization, they act as Hebbian coincidence detectors. This property can explain cooperativity and associativity through temporal and spatial summation. Thus, activated NMDA receptors at synapses that are proximal to active sites of depolarization may be depolarized sufficiently to relieve the Mg^{2+} block and initiate the cascade of events that leads to LTP induction. This cascade may occur even though the activity of that particular synapse alone was not sufficient to induce LTP. Thus, NMDA receptors can account for the association of two separate afferent projections to the same cell, one strongly and the other weakly active (Kelso & Brown 1986, Levy & Steward 1979), and for the cooperative requirement that a threshold number of fibers be active. Recently Bashir et al (1993) suggested that other glutamate receptors, particularly the metabotropic subtype, may contribute to the induction of LTP.

The maintenance of NMDA-receptor-dependent LTP is less well understood. In a contemporary review a distinction was suggested between short-term potentiation (STP), which decays in about one hour, followed by three stages of LTP (LTP_{1-3}) requiring, respectively (*a*) protein kinase activation and protein phosphorylation, (*b*) protein synthesis from existing mRNAs, and (*c*) gene expression (Bliss & Collingridge 1993). Behavioral approaches to learning suggested that these same cellular processes are involved in the establishment of long-term memory (Brinton 1991).

Opioid-Receptor-Dependent LTP and Associative LTP

Although less well known and less completely studied (Bramham 1991a,b; Breindl et al 1994; Derrick et al 1991; Ishihara 1990; Martin 1983), this form of LTP is the predominant form of plasticity within extrinsic afferents to the hippocampal formation (mossy-fiber CA3, lateral-perforant-path dentate gyrus, lateral-perforant-path CA3) and is present in more afferent projections to the hippocampal formation than is NMDA-receptor-dependent LTP (medial-perforant-path dentate gyrus, medial-perforant-path CA3). Thus if the hippocampus is important in memory formation, as much data suggests, then opioid-receptor-dependent LTP and its relationship to NMDA-receptor-dependent LTP need to be understood.

LTP induction in the mossy-fiber CA3 and lateral-perforant-path CA3 pathways depends on the activation of μ-opioid receptors (Derrick et al 1992, but see Weisskopf et al 1993) and induction in the perforant-path dentate pathway depends on δ-opioid receptors (Bramham et al 1991a, 1992). Therefore, more than one form of opioid-receptor-dependent LTP exists in the hippocampus. We refer to the different forms as LTP_μ (mossy-fiber CA3 and lateral-perforant-path CA3) and LTP_δ (lateral-perforant-path dentate).

The time courses of NMDA-receptor-dependent and LTP_μ differ in that the former reaches its maximum almost immediately and can begin to decay, whereas the latter takes approximately an hour to reach its maximum and shows no decay (Derrick & Martinez 1989). These different time courses of augmentation and decay are relevant to our understanding of the operation of these forms of LTP in neural networks.

Associative opioid-receptor-dependent LTP in the mossy-fiber CA3 system appears to have constraints regulating induction that are different from those regulating associative NMDA-receptor-dependent LTP. The mossy fibers also show cooperativity in that a sufficient number of fibers have to be activated in order to observe LTP (Derrick & Martinez 1994b, McNaughton et al 1978, but see Chattarji et al 1989). Induction of LTP in the mossy fibers also is dependent on a sufficient number of tetanizing pulses, presumably to insure the release of opioid peptides (Derrick & Martinez 1994a); peptides in general are only released after trains of impulses (Peng & Horn 1991). Associative LTP of mossy-fiber responses can be observed with stimulation of the convergent commissural pathway only when trains of mossy-fiber pulses are used (Derrick & Martinez 1994b). The commissural-CA3 system expresses NMDA-receptor-dependent LTP (Derrick & Martinez 1994b), and the induction of associative mossy-fiber LTP is blocked by both opioid- and NMDA-receptor antagonists (Derrick & Martinez 1994b).

Research findings in the area of mossy-fiber LTP are controversial. Although it is generally agreed that LTP in this pathway depends on trains of pulses and the presence of extracellular Ca^{2+}, the site of Ca^{2+} entry, either pre- or postsynaptically, is in dispute (Williams & Johnston 1989, Zalutsky & Nicoll 1990), as is the necessity of postsynaptic depolarization (Jaffe & Johnston 1990). One group of researchers even refuses to ascribe the lofty title of LTP to the phenomenon of synaptic enhancement in mossy fibers and refers to LTP in this pathway as mossy-fiber potentiation because it is nonassociative and, according to them, rapidly decremental (Staubli 1992, Staubli et al 1990).

The controversy may arise because the preparation of the hippocampal in vitro slice may compromise the integrity of the mossy-fiber system (Dailey et al 1994), and different species, particularly rat and guinea pig, which are favorite subjects, have different distributions of opioids and opioid receptors (McLean et al 1987). Future research, particularly in vivo, should resolve some of the controversy.

ELECTROPHYSIOLOGICAL APPROACHES TO RELATING LTP TO LEARNING

Studies addressing the contribution of LTP to learning have been approached at an electrophysiological level to answer two major questions: Does learning induce changes in synaptic responses that are similar to LTP? Does the induction of LTP alter learning?

Does Learning Produce LTP-like Changes?

We limit our review to those studies that measured changes in the population EPSP rather than the population spike, owing to general agreement that excitatory postsynaptic potentials (EPSPs) changes reflect changes in synaptic function, whereas changes in the population spike amplitude may reflect other mechanisms (Bliss & Lynch 1988).

Changes in population EPSPs can be observed in perforant-path dentate gyrus responses during exploratory behaviors. The phenomenon was initially named short-term exploratory modulation, or STEM (Sharp et al 1985). This initial study demonstrated that exploration produced increases in perforant-path synaptic responses over the course of exploration and that the increases persisted for short periods of time after exploration. The initial and subsequent studies (Green et al 1990) revealed that STEM was not dependent on handling, novelty, repeated stimulation, or increased locomotion. Like LTP, STEM results in an apparent increase in the field EPSP and can be blocked by the NMDA-receptor antagonist MK 801 (Erickson et al 1990). However, unlike LTP, STEM is relatively short lived: It lasts only 20–40 min (Sharp et al 1985).

Evidence suggesting that STEM was not an LTP-like process emerged in 1993 with the report of additive effects of STEM and LTP (Erickson et al 1993) and changes in STEM that are distinct from those observed with LTP (Erickson et al 1993). A strong correlation between the magnitude of STEM and simultaneously recorded 2–3°C fluctuations in brain temperature (Moser et al 1993a), presumably resulting from physical activity that occurred during exploratory behavior, also was reported. STEM-like changes could also be induced with intense activity or with passive heating. More recent studies (Moser et al 1993b) suggest that, when temperature-induced alterations in conduction velocity are controlled, small changes in perforant-path dentate field potentials may actually reflect changes due to exploration. However, this effect is short lived. STEM may represent endogenously occurring short-term potentiation (STP), the rapidly decaying process that precedes the generation of stimulation-induced LTP.

Ex vivo study is a different approach to the problem of detecting electro-physiological changes in evoked responsiveness following learning. The responsiveness of in vitro hippocampal slices removed from animals exposed to an enriched environment were compared with responsiveness of slices from animals exposed to a standard laboratory environment (Green & Greenough 1986). Rearing animals in complex environments produces anatomical changes in cortex that are thought to be a result of learning (Bennett et al 1964, Greenough et al 1973, Rosenzweig et al 1962). In this study, the slope of perforant-path dentate responses was assessed. The magnitude of field EPSP slopes was larger in rats raised in a complex environment than in rats housed in standard laboratory conditions, effects that are similar to those observed after LTP induction in this pathway (Bliss & Lomo 1973). Electrophysiological measures of antidromic (nonsynaptic) volleys and of the presynaptic-fiber volley (number of fibers activated) revealed no differences between the rearing conditions. Thus the field EPSP slopes elicited by equivalent volleys were significantly larger, which suggests that the differences arise from an enhancement of perforant-path synaptic transmission. The increased dentate responsiveness was not observed in animals that were removed from complex housing three to four weeks prior to testing, which suggests the effects were transient, as is LTP (Barnes 1979).

More recently, one group of researchers recorded responses in another hippocampal system, the mossy-fiber projections, as animals learned a radial arm maze (Mitsuno et al 1994). Incremental increases were observed in mossy-fiber field EPSPs over the course of learning. Changes in evoked responsiveness were evident three days after learning. Taken together, these studies show that learning induces changes in hippocampal responsiveness that resemble those observed following LTP induction.

Why should changes in evoked-response amplitude following a single learning episode be detectable? According to the view of distributed memory systems, changes underlying learning should occur in a very small fraction of the available synapses, and there is no reason to expect that such sparse changes would be evident in synaptic activation evoked by the stimulation of thousands of afferent fibers activated by a stimulating electrode. However, the hippocampal memory system could have a small capacity and utilize most synapses when storing information. In such a system an evoked response might reveal the existence of a stored memory. However, in order for new information to be stored, the information in this low-capacity system would either have to be erased or have to decay rapidly. Some researchers suggest that the mossy-fiber projections to CA3 represent a low-capacity store (Lynch & Granger 1986) because LTP in mossy fibers can decay quite rapidly (within hours) in vitro (Mitsuno et al 1994). However, learning-induced LTP-like changes in evoked mossy-fiber responses are observed three days after the cessation of training, arguing against the neural changes representing a transient, low-capacity store.

One clever strategy eliminates this problem of "looking for a needle in a haystack." Synapse-specific changes in responses mediated by a large number of afferents need not be observed. Rather, the evoked response is employed as an integral part of the learning task. Detection of salient learning-induced change in a large number of randomly stimulated fibers is not necessary; instead, the activity of the fibers is incorporated into the learning task. This strategy was employed by several laboratories and provides consistent and convincing electrophysiological evidence for a role of LTP in learning.

In one set of studies, a shuttle avoidance task with a footshock as an unconditioned stimulus was employed (Matthies et al 1986, Ott et al 1982, Reymann et al 1982). High-frequency perforant-path stimulation was the conditioned stimulus. Low-frequency evoked responses were recorded in the dentate gyrus before, during, and after 10 daily training sessions. Overall daily changes of the field EPSP slope roughly corresponded to changes in learned behavior. However, the relationships among the measures each day were more complex; improved performance was not correlated with response magnitude within the daily trials. The LTP-like increase in responses was apparent only at the start of the second day of training, which suggests that a consolidation process occurs after the training and prior to the session the following day. Nevertheless, the increases in the field EPSP paralleled learning across days, with asymptotic performance occurring on the days of asymptotic LTP. An important observation was that animals that were poor learners and did not acquire the task also failed to show an increase in dentate responses. The stimulation may have induced LTP that was independent of any learning-induced changes in neural function. However, the stimulation trains used as a CS did not produce any changes in the EPSP during the initial 40 trials on the first day of training. Thus, it is not likely that the CS stimulation induced LTP.

An interpretational difficulty of the above study is that the hippocampus is not necessary for learning of the active-avoidance task; in fact, hippocampal lesions or NMDA-receptor antagonists can facilitate active- or passive-avoidance learning, respectively (Mondadori et al 1989, Nadel 1968, Ohki 1982, Shimai & Ohki 1980). Thus increases observed in perforant-path responses that parallel learning may reflect ancillary learning of other aspects of the CS, such as context (Kim & Fanselow 1992). However, in a subsequent study, colchicine lesions of the dentate gyrus eliminated both the evoked response and the ability of perforant-path stimulation to serve as a CS (Ruthrich et al 1987). These lesions did not alter conditioning to other CSs nor did they alter conditioned emotional response to the footshock. Together, these data suggest that the increases in responses of activated perforant-path dentate synapses contributed to the learning of the CS aspects of an active-avoidance response.

In a similar study (Laroche et al 1989), high-frequency stimulation served as a CS for a footshock that elicited behavioral suppression. Learning of the perforant-path stimulation-shock association occurred only when the trains were of an intensity sufficient to elicit LTP. Further, inhibition of LTP induction by prior tetanization of commissural afferents, which inhibits LTP induction by engaging inhibitory mechanisms, produced substantial deficits in learning. Furthermore, chronic infusion of AP5, a selective NMDA antagonist, blocked both LTP induction and the ability of the stimulation to serve as a CS. A significant correlation existed between the magnitude of LTP produced by these various treatments and the acquisition of the conditioned response. The decay of LTP induced in this behavioral paradigm was observed in the following 31-day period and correlated with retention of the conditioned response (Laroche et al 1991).

In the experiments mentioned above, it was assumed that stimulation of the perforant path can serve as a sensory-like conditioning stimulus. However, the degree to which the perforant path is normally involved in representing a sensory CS is unknown. Further, because the stimulation produced a potentiated synaptic response, the correlation between LTP and learning may reflect merely an increase in the salience of the perforant-path stimulation. For this reason such an approach may be of limited utility. An alternative strategy is to stimulate structures or pathways that actually mediate sensory input. Studies by Roman and colleagues (Roman et al 1987, 1993) used such an approach by recording monosynaptic responses in the olfactory (piriform) cortex elicited by stimulation of sensory projections from the olfactory bulb (the lateral olfactory tract, or LOT). These studies are notable in that they depart from the study of LTP restricted to the hippocampus and address the contribution of LTP to learning at other cortical sites. In these studies, patterned LOT stimulation was used as a discriminative cue for the presence of water. Stimulation of this olfactory pathway apparently produced something like a sensory event, because rats responded to burst stimulation with sniffing and exploring, as though they detected an odor, and such stimulation served as a CS in an olfactory discrimination learning task. Performance in this task using stimulation as a CS was remarkably similar to that observed with actual odors as CSs. Comparison of monosynaptic responses during the acquisition of discrimination learning revealed increases in the monosynaptic LOT piriform cortex responses, an effect that persisted at least 24 hours after training. Thus patterned stimulation did not produce synaptic potentiation unless the association of the cue and the water reward was learned. A significant correlation was found between the increase in the field EPSP slope and the number of correct responses. Although the magnitude of LTP and behavioral responses among animals was quite variable, better responding was associated with larger changes in the field EPSP slopes within individual animals (Roman et al 1993). Of particular interest is the observation that the burst stimulation, which is thought to be optimal for LTP induction at other sites (Staubli & Lynch 1987), was ineffective by itself in inducing LTP. Rather, a long-term depression of responses was observed following stimulation of naive rats in a non-learning situation. Because the LOT pathway is known to be resistant to LTP induction in vivo (Racine et al 1983, Stripling et al 1991) but not in vitro (Jung et al 1990, Kanter & Haberly 1993) or during learning (Roman et al 1987, 1993), these data suggest that LTP induction is actively inhibited in vivo. It is tempting to speculate that attentional or other mechanisms are engaged during conditioning that enable LTP induction in this cortical structure.

Together these studies provide positive support for the idea that LTP may be involved in conditioning because LTP-like increases in evoked potentials exist following learning in CS pathways that are chosen for experimental convenience. A more direct experimental approach to the question of whether LTP is a mechanism of learning is to induce LTP and then determine whether it influences later learning.

Does the Induction of LTP Influence Learning?

LTP induced prior to learning might impair learning by saturating LTP processes that normally participate in the learning; LTP induced after learning might obscure prior learning by occluding any distributed pattern of synaptic changes that were formed as a result of learning. Alternatively, LTP may enhance or impair learning by activating modulatory mechanisms (Martinez et al 1991).

In one study the effects of LTP induction on the acquisition of classically conditioned nictitating membrane response (NMR) were assessed (Berger 1984). The rationale for this study arose from the observation that changes in hippocampal pyramidal-cell activity parallel changes in the acquisition of the conditioned behavioral response (Berger et al 1983, Berger 1984) as well as from the possibility that the increase in hippocampal unit firing resulted from plastic events within the hippocampus. LTP induced unilaterally in the perforant path facilitated the subsequent acquisition of a classically conditioned NMR in rabbits (Berger 1984). Given that the hippocampus is not essential for learning of simultaneous classical conditioning of the NMR (although it appears important in the acquisition of more complex aspects of classical conditioning; see Berger & Orr 1983), this effect may be of a modulatory nature, rather than a direct effect on an essential learning mechanism.

An opposite effect was observed using spatial learning in a circular maze (McNaughton et al 1986). Bilateral, supposedly saturating LTP stimulation of the angular bundle, which carries both the lateral and medial aspects of the perforant-path projections, disrupted performance either prior to or immediately after learning. In an important control procedure, LTP that was induced after the task was well learned did not disrupt performance. Subsequent studies (Castro et al 1989) expanded this initial observation. The strategy was to saturate LTP by stimulating rats every day for a 19-day period. On the final day, the ability of the rats to find a hidden platform in the Morris water maze was assessed. A single probe trial was used to measure performance of rats when the hidden platform was removed, and the time a rat spent in each quadrant was determined. Rats that received LTP-inducing stimulation displayed deficits in learning, whereas rats that received only low-frequency non-LTP-inducing stimulation acquired the task and spent more time in the quadrant where the hidden platform was during acquisition. As a control, the ability to locate a visible platform was assessed, and in this case no difference was observed between the stimulation groups, which indicates that the stimulation did not affect any sensory capacity. Rats in which LTP was induced and then allowed to decay did not show any learning deficits. Taken together, these data suggest that LTP itself, rather than nonspecific effects of stimulation, is essential for learning because saturation-impaired acquisition of the spatial learning task and the ability to learn returned with the decay of the LTP.

Several laboratories, including the laboratory of origin, reported difficulties in replicating the LTP saturation effect (Jeffery & Morris 1993, Robinson 1992, Sutherland et al 1993). A number of reasons may explain the failure to replicate. First, although the stimulation parameters used may have resulted in the saturation of LTP in those afferents stimulated, stimulation of the angular bundle with a single stimulation electrode may not sufficiently tetanize all fibers that course through this structure. Second, LTP saturation does not prevent the induction of LTD (Linden & Conner 1995), which also is a potential memory mechanism (Sejnowski 1977, Stent 1973). Other reasons for lack of replication of the LTP saturation effect were delineated in a recent study (Barnes et al 1994) in which LTP saturation induced deficits in reversal training to a circular maze, but not in a water maze, which suggests different task susceptibility to LTP saturation. The extent of saturation was addressed by measuring the induction of the immediate early gene *zif*, whose induction was correlated with the quantity of LTP induction in the dentate. LTP saturation procedures induced *zif* mostly in the dorsal hippocampus. Thus, if *zif* marks those cells that potentiated, then perhaps LTP was neither saturated nor induced in the more ventral regions of the hippocampus in those experiments that did not replicate the saturation effect. Barnes et al (1994) believe this interpretation is supported by findings from the same study in which maximal electroconvulsive shock (ECS) treatments, which produce a synaptic potentiation (Stewart et al 1994) that is NMDA-receptor-dependent (Stewart & Reid 1994), also led to significant deficits in acquisition and reversal of the water maze task. The potentiation produced by either ECS or LTP-inducing stimulation was not additive, and ECS induced *zif* throughout the hippocampus. Seizures were observed in some animals, which apparently did not influence learning: When ECS treatment induced seizures without inducing LTP, no deficits were observed. The deficits were highly correlated with the amount of LTP induced. Although an interpretational problem is that multiple ECS treatments may produce effects that alter learning as a result of actions that are unrelated to the induction of LTP, the results of Barnes et al (1994) are consistent with the view that a large degree of hippocampal inactivation is needed to reliably induce learning deficits (Jarrard 1986, McNaughton et al 1989). In this view, information stored in a distributed memory system is quite resistant to degradation, and the partial saturation of LTP or preservation of a process such as LTD may be sufficient to permit substantial learning.

Although the enhancement of classical conditioning (Berger 1984) and the impairment of spatial maze learning (Barnes et al 1994, Castro et al 1989, McNaughton et al 1986) apparently are contradictory effects, the differences in the findings of these studies reflect, in our view, a differential contribution of the hippocampus, and therefore hippocampal LTP, to classical conditioning of the NMR and spatial learning, which are distinctly different memory tasks that appear to require distinct memory systems (Thompson 1992). Because the hippocampus is not required for acquisition of the NMR response but is required for acquisition of spatial mazes, the roles of LTP in these two kinds of learning are likely different, and thus the studies cannot be compared directly.

PHARMACOLOGICAL APPROACHES RELATING LTP TO LEARNING

Subsequent to the demonstration of the important role for the NMDA-type glutamate receptors in LTP induction, a number of behavioral researchers rushed to characterize the effects of NMDA-receptor antagonists on learning. As in all pharmacological studies attempting to study learning, the inference of causality from a specific action of a drug is problematic (Martinez et al 1991). Drug-related side effects and determination of the drug's specific site of action are always issues. Further, in the studies reviewed below, the drug has to be administered before the initiation of conditioning if it is to block the induction of any LTP that might contribute to the learning. Being thus present early, the drug might induce an effect on learning through a sensory, motor, motivational, attentional, or other variable (Martinez et al 1991). As noted below, these concerns complicate the interpretation of studies using this strategy.

Many studies examined the effect of selective NMDA-receptor antagonists on a variety of learning tasks (Kim et al 1991, Walker & Gold 1991), including tasks thought to depend on hippocampal function (Robinson et al 1990, Staubli et al 1986). Here we limit our discussion to pharmacological studies that address both hippocampus-based learning and LTP induction and that use relatively localized, or at least intra-CNS, administration of drugs, so that as far as possible the effects described are the result of an action of the drug in a circumscribed area of the brain. The most comprehensive and elegant studies (Morris et al 1986) examined intracerebroventricular (ICV) administration of AP5, the selective NMDA antagonist, on learning in a Morris water maze task. Prior research indicated that the hippocampus is important in the acquisition of this task, that is, when the rats are required to learn the location of the platform with respect to distal cues in the environment (Morris et al 1982). In the initial studies (Morris et al 1986), the nature of the memory impairment induced by the NMDA antagonist was assessed with (*a*) measures of latency on acquisition trials, (*b*) measures of performance on a probe trial with the platform removed, and (*c*) a reversal procedure, by which animals were additionally trained with the platform in a different location. For each of these measures a significant impairment was observed in the animals infused with AP5. Potential sensorimotor impairments induced by the drug were assessed with a visual discrimination task using the same water maze apparatus. In this circumstance, the NMDA antagonist had no apparent effect. The effect of AP5 on LTP induction also was assessed in these studies to compare the behavior-impairing and LTP-induction-impairing action of AP5. LTP was induced by stimulation of the perforant-path dentate synapse. The drug had no effect on the low-frequency evoked responses; however, AP5 impaired acquisition of the maze and AP5 completely blocked LTP induction.

A striking impairment of task acquisition was not observed; although the animals receiving AP5 showed longer latencies to escape than control animals, learning in the drug-treated group paralleled that in the control animals. Thus a learning curve was observed. However, because animals with hippocampal lesions show a similar early acquisition deficit (Morris et al 1982), the authors suggested that learning in the Morris water maze can involve nonspatial elements and that other, hippocampus-independent strategies are employed in the initial stages of learning. In this view, spatial deficits should be most apparent at the point of asymptotic learning, and performance in the probe trials should be sensitive to spatial-learning deficits. Thus, for many researchers, the most convincing indication of memory deficits is observed in the probe trials. As noted earlier, in this test the platform is removed, and the amount of time an animal spends in the quadrant where the platform was located is measured.

Animals treated with the NMDA antagonist showed no preference for the original location of the platform. By contrast, animals that received either saline or the inactive stereoisomer of AP5 showed a significant preference for the quadrant where the platform had been located, which indicates that the animals treated with AP5 had no spatial memory of the platform. The acquisition curve, as measured by decreased latencies, therefore indicates that the animals had learned to escape from the maze using a nonspatial strategy.

The results of reversal tests are more ambiguous (Morris et al 1986). In a reversal test the platform is moved to a location different from that of the original training. The degree of animals' learning is reflected by the persistence of the animals in returning to the place of original learning and by the acquisition of the new platform location. The animals that received AP5 showed no acquisition of the new location of the escape platform, whereas the control groups showed substantial preference for the quadrant of original training and readily learned the new location of the platform. The interpretational problem with this study is that the AP5-treated animals' performance at the beginning of reversal training was as poor as the control animals', which suggests a negative transfer effect of some original learning.

Other critics noted that some rats fell off the platform during training and suggested that the impairment produced by AP5 was because of motor deficits (Keith & Rudy 1990). Further control experiments suggest that falling off the platform did not have an aversive effect on performance in water maze learning (Morris 1990). As an added measure, pretraining within the water maze using the visual discrimination task prior to ICV infusion demonstrated that the apparent sensorimotor deficit revealed by platform instability could be overcome by pretraining. Spatial learning impairments resulting from AP5 administration were still observed in these pretrained rats. It has been noted (Keith & Rudy 1990) that the rats receiving AP5 showed performance deficits on the first trials before learning had occurred, and that this deficit may reflect a side effect of the drug on sensorimotor function. However, later studies that more closely examined learning in the early trials showed no effect of moderate doses of AP5 on performance in the first trial (Davis et al 1992). Goddard (1986) objected that the discrimination learning experiment is not a good test of sensorimotor impairment because ICV administration of AP5 probably results in lower concentrations of AP5 at sites important for visual discrimination. However, actual measurement of the dispersion of AP5 following ICV administration showed that it was evenly distributed within the brain (Butcher et al 1990). Subsequent studies indicated that localized infusion of AP5 within the visual cortex did not produce impairments in the visual discrimination task (Butcher et al 1991). Together these results suggest that the impairment of performance in the water maze produced by AP5 is the result of the effects mediated by the actions of this drug at hippocampal sites.

As noted by the embattled originators of these NMDA-antagonist studies, it would be erroneous to conclude that AP5 causes the learning deficit because AP5 blocked LTP (Morris 1989a). AP5 may affect learning, for example, because AP5 has an effect on hippocampal theta rhythm, and treatments that disrupt theta rhythm can block acquisition of learning tasks (Winson 1978). Thus, as discussed above, many factors impede the interpretation of a drug effect, including the selectivity of the drug's actions, side effects, drug dispersion, and the site of drug action.

Another way to demonstrate that two separate drug effects, such as impaired spatial learning and impaired induction of LTP, are related is to compare the dose response curves of the drug's separate effects. Different dose response functions may show that the drug was acting on different processes, and identical dose response functions may show that the drug was acting on a common process. In subsequent studies (Davis et al 1992) identical dose response curves were observed for both impairment of spatial learning and blocking of LTP induction. Furthermore, concentrations of AP5, measured in the brain using high-performance liquid chromatography (HPLC) microdialysis, that impaired learning and that blocked LTP were the same; no concentration of AP5 was observed to block LTP without affecting learning (Butcher et al 1991). Lastly, the extracellular concentrations that were measured during the block of LTP induction in vivo matched the concentrations that were effective in blocking LTP induction in vitro.

Further studies (Morris 1989a) addressed the question of the effect of AP5 on both the acquisition and retrieval of a spatial-learning task. The reasoning in these studies was as follows: NMDA-receptor activation, although essential for LTP induction in many hippocampal pathways, is not essential for either the expression or the maintenance of LTP. If AP5 alters memory by blocking LTP induction, then any deleterious effects of AP5 should be limited to the acquisition period, and AP5 should not impair performance on a spatial-learning task when administered following training. This strategy also addresses, to some degree, the possible sensorimotor and LTP-independent effects of NMDA-receptor antagonists, because any performance deficit seen in these conditions could not be because of any effect on acquisition. AP5, when infused into rats by ICV administration following asymptotic acquisition of the water maze task, has no effect on the retrieval of learned spatial information, as assessed using probe trials. Moreover, in these same rats, the doses of AP5 that had no effect on performance following training effectively blocked new learning in a subsequent reversal test. The lack of effects on performance of an already learned task suggests that the AP5 is not producing sensorimotor impairment that interferes with performance of the task. Taken together, these studies provide striking evidence that AP5 may impair learning through blocking the induction of LTP.

The recent data implicating metabotropic glutamate receptors in the induction of LTP prompted assessment of the role of these glutamate receptors in spatial learning. Richter-Levin et al (1994) reported that perfusion of the metabotropic antagonist [RS]-α-methyl-4-carboxyphenylglycine (MCPG) did not produce deficits in animals during acquisition of a Morris water maze, although a significant deficit was observed in probe trials given 24 h after the last training trial. In these same animals, equivalent quantities of MCPG attenuated the magnitude but did not block the induction of perforant-path dentate LTP. Thus antagonism of metabotropic glutamate receptors produces some deficits in LTP and spatial learning.

The studies employing NMDA-receptor antagonists to assess the contribution of hippocampal LTP to learning have been the subject of particularly intense scrutiny (see Keith & Rudy 1990). However, in our view, the fact that spatial learning is not blocked completely by NMDA-receptor antagonists is not surprising. Several pathways in the hippocampus, including the mossy-fiber pathway (Derrick et al 1992), the lateral perforant path to area CA3 (Breindl et al 1994), and the lateral perforant path to dentate (Bramham et al 1991a,b; but see Zhang & Levy 1992) display LTP_μ and LTP_δ, which are both opioid receptor-dependent and NMDA receptor-independent. In addition, both NMDA-receptor-dependent and NMDA-receptor-independent mechanisms of LTP induction are observed within the CA1 region (Teyler & Grover 1993). As mentioned above with respect to the saturation experiments of McNaughton and colleagues, when viewed from the perspective of distributed memories, partial sparing of function may be sufficient to permit learning. Such reasoning leads to the conclusion that the alteration of any one of the LTP systems within the hippocampus may not be sufficient to produce a total or even a profound deficit in spatial learning. That localized NMDA-receptor blockade does produce observable deficits, and that these deficits are similar to, although less severe than, those observed with extensive hippocampal lesions, suggest not only that NMDA-receptor-dependent mechanisms, and perhaps LTP, contribute to spatial learning, but also that they may be a fundamental mechanism of information storage.

Does Learning of a Spatial Task Involve Hippocampal Opioid Systems?

Given that opioid receptor antagonists impair the induction of LTP in opioidergic afferents, opioid receptor antagonists would be expected to impair spatial learning. However, systemic administration of naloxone is reported to facilitate acquisition of a spatial water maze as measured by latency to find the platform (Decker et al 1989). These studies employed intraperitoneal administration of naloxone 5 min prior to training, which may be insufficient time for intraperitoneally administered naloxone to block sufficiently opioid receptors at central sites. For example, intraperitoneal naloxone effects on evolved hippocampal responses are observed only 10–15 min following intraperitoneal naloxone administration (Martinez & Derrick 1994). Thus training may not have been given at an optimum time following drug administration. In addition, opioid antagonists exert effects on opioid systems that influence learning that may be independent of hippocampal opioid systems (Martinez et al 1991), and alterations in these opioid systems by systemic administration of opioid receptor antagonists may also alter learning. In support of this interpretation, other studies employing local application of opioids into the hippocampus produce an impairment of spatial learning. For example, local administration of dynorphins impairs spatial learning (McDaniel et al 1990), and dynorphins impair LTP induction in both the mossy-fiber CA3 and perforant-path dentate synapses via actions on kappa receptors (Wagner et al 1993, Weisskopf et al 1993). To date, no studies have addressed the effect of selective blockade of hippocampal μ or δ receptors in spatial learning, but local blockade of opioid receptors is likely to produce spatial learning deficits because, like opioid receptor blockade (Derrick et al 1992), elimination of specific metabotropic glutamate receptors selectively impairs mossy fiber LTP, and elimination of these metabotropic receptors also impairs spatial learning (Conquet et al 1994).

KNOCKOUT MUTANTS, LTP, AND HIPPOCAMPALLY DEPENDENT LEARNING

The molecular biological revolution has arrived in force in the area of LTP and learning. A paradox of learning is that it is expressed as activity among neurons, though the biological changes that underlie memories are stored within neurons. The molecular biological revolution taught us that enduring alterations of cell function, as must occur in long-term memory storage, are controlled by gene expression and resultant protein production. Thus, for every sustained memory there is likely a chain of events leading from the initiation of activity at a synaptic receptor, to the activity of second messenger systems, to intermediate early gene induction, and to secondary gene induction in every cell that participates in the memory network. The same is likely true for LTP (but see Lisman 1989).

A number of research groups are endeavoring to trace the chain of cellular events that underlie induction and maintenance of LTP (Grant et al 1992, Silva et al 1992a,b). In these studies single genes, controlling what are hoped to be specific events within cells, can be eliminated and the resultant effect can be studied simultaneously in whole animals minus one gene, so-called knockouts, for LTP and learning. In this method the gene of interest, usually a well-characterized gene, is cloned and in most cases altered so that important regulatory regions of the gene are nonfunctional. This altered DNA is introduced into embryonic stem cells derived from blastocysts. The gene combines with the DNA of the stem cells, and those cells in which the gene is inserted at appropriate regions of the DNA (via homologous recombination) can be isolated and inserted into developing blastocysts. Subsequent cells arising from these altered cells all lack the knockout gene. The resulting animal is a heterozygous chimera (combination of normal and mutant cells) that, with cross breeding, can generate progeny that are homozygous for the knocked-out targeted gene.

One reason to target genes is that these genetic procedures have the potential to overcome the current limitations of pharmacology. In studies of genes related to LTP, an area of focus in the study of transgenes has been kinases. Although data strongly suggest LTP induction involves a variety of kinases, including protein kinase C (Malinow et al 1989), calmodulin kinase (Malenka et al 1989), and tyrosine kinases (O'Dell et al 1991), these studies are limited by the fact that currently available kinase inhibitors lack a high degree of selectivity. Further, for a given kinase, the kinase family to which it belongs is composed of a number of subtypes, which appear to have varied functions. It would be of great utility to selectively impair the function of specific kinase isoforms, a feat that is achieved by the use of knockout mutants.

The first study that attempted to trace the events underlying induction and maintenance of LTP (Grant et al 1992) compared various knockouts of genes coding for particular tyrosine kinases. Deletion of one specific tyrosine kinase found in the *fyn* gene altered the amount of current necessary to induce LTP in area CA1. Traditional measures of synaptic function appeared normal, such as the maximal EPSP amplitudes and measures of paired-pulse facilitation, a short-term augmentation of synaptic response that appears to depend on residual presynaptic Ca^{2+}. The *fyn*-knockout rats appeared incapable of learning the location of a hidden platform in a Morris water maze.

Unfortunately, this study is difficult to interpret. First, the hippocampus displayed obvious anatomical abnormalities, including an increase in granule and pyramidal cells. The dendrites of pyramidal cells in stratum radiatum showed disorganization and were less tightly packed, as were the cell bodies. Given the altered neural architecture, the synaptic volume might have been reduced, which may explain the reduced ability of high-intensity stimulation to produce LTP, although this is perhaps unlikely because low-frequency evoked EPSP amplitudes in the *fyn* knockouts are not different from those of wild-type controls. There were impairments in visual function because *fyn* knockouts were initially poor at performing a visual discrimination where the platform was visible, although they eventually reached latencies comparable to wild-type controls. The authors also noted that "overtraining in spatial tasks masked the *fyn* learning deficit." Apparently then, the animals could learn, and the deletion of the *fyn* gene only altered the sensitivity of the knockout animals to such parametric aspects of training as the number of training trials needed to evidence learning. Because the *fyn* knockouts could express LTP, these data do not support a conclusion that LTP is a substrate of memory, because LTP and learning clearly do not depend on the presence of the *fyn* gene (Deutsch 1993).

In a second wave of studies other researchers (Silva et al 1992b) engineered knockout mice that were deficient in α-calcium-calmodulin-dependent kinase II (α-CaMKII). The kinase α-CaMKII, in contrast with tyrosine kinase FYN, is localized to the brain and is neuron specific. The α-CaMKII mutants showed no overt physical or neuroanatomical abnormalities. Measures of post-synaptic function, such as the maximal EPSP amplitudes, in Schaffer-CA1 responses appeared normal, but paired-pulse potentiation was reduced in mu-tant mice. Activation of NMDA receptors appeared to elicit normal responses. Although the probability of induction of LTP was greatly reduced in the mutants, LTP in some animals was virtually indistinguishable from LTP ob-served in wild-type controls.

A subsequent study (Silva 1992a) assessed the ability of α-CaMKII mu-tants to learn the Morris water maze. These mutants apparently had a defect in their visual function, because they showed an initial deficit in the visual discrimination task. However, these mutant mice eventually matched the wild-type animals in performance. The α-CaMKII mutants were also impaired in their ability to find the hidden platform on the first session of training in the Morris water maze and were always slower than the wild-type control mice; that the mutants did learn is shown by the fact that their latencies to find the platform decreased over sessions. For the probe trial, the mutant mice took roughly twice as long to find the platform. An additional test employed a randomly located platform. Some trials were conducted with the hidden plat-form randomly located at other sites. Mutant mice took as long to find refuge at the random sites as to find refuge at the original location, whereas wild-type mice took less time to find the original location and longer times to find the random platforms, which indicates negative transfer. The results of the random probe test therefore suggest that the mutant mice did not know the spatial location of the hidden platform, although they apparently were able to use some strategy to escape the maze. Mutant animals were the equal of their wild-type cousins in learning a + maze, which does not exact any spatial ability from its students. The α-CaMKII mutants showed greater activity in open field and did not evidence habituation of activity. Thus the evidence suggests that the α-CaMKII mutants did have a deficit in the ability to learn the spatial maze. What is not so clear is whether this spatial deficit is related to LTP. In the mutant mice only the probability of LTP induction was altered; LTP induction was not abolished. If a mutant did show LTP, then the LTP was indistinguishable from that observed in wild-type controls. The deficit in paired-pulse potentiation in the mutant mice is also problematic. Such an alteration could be important for hippocampal function that is unrelated to LTP but that is manifested as a spatial deficit.

Another group targeted protein kinase C (Abeliovich et al 1993) and selected the PKC$_\gamma$ isoform, both because inhibitors of PKC prevent induction of NMDA-receptor-dependent LTP in CA1 (Malinow et al 1989) and because PKC$_\gamma$ is specific to neurons in the CNS and is expressed postnatally. The probability of LTP induction was reduced in the mutants much as it had been in previous studies employing knockouts; but if the mutant mice were first treated with low-frequency stimulation, then the LTP was indistinguishable from that observed in wild-type controls. An interesting finding, however, was that expression of LTD was not impaired. In spite of coordination deficits, the mutant mice learned the Morris water maze at the same rate as did the wild-type controls and performed similarly in the probe and random probe tests. The authors believe the mutant mice did exhibit a mild spatial deficit because during the probe test the mutants crossed the hidden platform site less often than the controls, even though they were searching the correct quadrant. In contrast with their behavior in the spatial maze, the PKC$_\gamma$ mutants did show deficits in contextual-fear conditioning in that they froze significantly less after return to a chamber where they experienced footshock. There is evidence that acquisition of a contextual-fear task depends on both the hippocampus and NMDA receptors (Kim et al 1991, 1992; Kim & Fanselow 1992). Conditioned fear (measured by observing freezing in response to a tone in a novel environment), which is thought to be independent of hippocampal function, was not impaired. The results do not support a role for PKC$_\gamma$ in either LTP or spatial learning because the mutant mice could learn the Morris water maze and, if stimulated appropriately, displayed LTP.

Departing from the study of the kinases, other groups targeted genes specific for subtypes of the glutamate receptor. One group (Sakimura et al 1995) created mice with a mutation of the GluRε subunit of the NMDA-receptor channel. No obvious morphological brain abnormalities were observed, probably because this gene is expressed after development. However, the mutants appeared jumpy and had an apparently enhanced startle response. LTP could be induced in the mutants but at a reduced magnitude (smaller percentage increase from baseline). As in the case of the PKC$_\gamma$ mutants, low-frequency stimulation prior to LTP restored some function but not to the level of the wild-type control. During training in the Morris water maze the mutants showed an initial latency deficit that disappeared by the end of training. During the transfer test the mutants searched the previously correct quadrant, crossed the trained site—though not at the same level of efficiency as the wild-type mice—and were less precise in their crossings. The authors consider their findings positive evidence for the participation of the GluRε subunit of the NMDA receptor in both LTP and the acquisition of spatial learning. Yet, as in the other studies reviewed, the gene mutation did not abolish either LTP or spatial learning, in which case this gene cannot be necessary for either.

The metabotropic glutamate receptor (mGlu) is implicated in LTP induction, though this conclusion remains controversial (Bashir et al 1993, Manzoni et al 1994). Activation of the metabotropic glutamate receptor 1 (mGluR1) may activate G-protein-coupled second messenger processes, and these processes may play an important role in LTP induction, acting like a metabolic switch that enables the induction of LTP. Recently one research group created an mGluR1 mutant to test involvement of mGluR1 in LTP and contextual-fear conditioning (Aiba et al 1993). This receptor subtype is plentiful in the dentate gyrus and CA3 areas and is apparently restricted to the presynaptic side of the Schaffer collateral projection to area CA1. These mGluR1 mutants had ataxia and were poor breeders but had brains that appeared normal. Synaptic transmission, STP, and paired-pulse potentiation were normal. LTP was observed in the mGluR1 mutants, but as in the GluRε mutants its magnitude was reduced. Low-frequency priming had no effect. The mGluR1 mutants were impaired in the hippocampus-dependent contextual-fear conditioning task and exhibited less freezing than did the wild-type controls in the cage where they were shocked. By contrast, the mutants learned as well as the wild-type animals to freeze in response to the tone and thus showed normal learning in response to this hippocampus-independent form of fear conditioning. The authors concluded that the mGluR1 receptor is not necessary for induction of LTP but that it modulates neural plasticity, apparently expressed as the magnitude of LTP. Because the mutant animals were moderately impaired in their learning, Aiba et al posited that the mGluR1 receptor is not necessary for learning of the contextual-fear response but perhaps participates in some way.

A quite different set of results was found by another group who created an mGluR1 mutant (Conquet et al 1994). These mutants exhibited ataxia as well. A neurological exam of the mutants revealed a complete loss of the righting reflex and reduced locomotor activity. LTD in cerebellar slices was severely reduced. Synaptic transmission appeared normal in the Schaffer collateral-commissural pathway to CA1, medial and lateral perforant pathways to dentate, and mossy-fiber and associational pathways in CA3. LTP was normal in all pathways except the mossy-fiber CA3 pathway, where it was greatly reduced. In the visible platform version of the Morris water maze the mutant mice were initially slower than the wild-type mice, but after three sessions they were indistinguishable from controls. However, in the hidden-platform version of the maze, the mGluR1 mutants could not find the platform and evidenced no learning. Because the mutant mice did learn the visually guided maze, the authors concluded that the deficit observed with respect to the hidden platform was due to an impairment of spatial ability mediated by mGluR1 receptors and probably in the mossy-fiber CA3 system, because LTP was reduced only in the mossy fiber-CA3 system. If the authors' interpretation of the data is correct, then deficits in the mossy-fiber system cannot be compensated by correctly functioning NMDA-receptor-dependent systems in other hippocampal pathways. This suggests an important role for both the dentate gyrus and LTP_μ in its mossy-fiber projections to area CA3 in learning (Marr 1971, McNaughton et al 1989).

The knockout strategy has provided some evidence that LTP and LTD are substrates of learning. What the knockout gains in specificity of elimination is lessened by the complexity of the mutant creature that develops without a particular gene. For example, is synaptic transmission in the mutant normal? In both the knockout studies and studies using selective drugs, it is assumed that if low-frequency synaptic transmission is not altered, then synaptic transmission is normal. However, there is no reason to believe that normal hippocampal function involves exclusively low-frequency activity; rather, high-frequency information is important for aspects of hippocampal function independent of its potential involvement in LTP induction. Such activity may be greatly influenced by the absence of a gene, as evidenced by the alterations in facilitation in one study (Silva et al 1992b). Other basic questions concern whether an animal's motor system is competent to perform what is required and whether the animal can see the elevated platform. We find it curious in these mutant studies that learning is measured in vivo and induction of LTP is measured in vitro in the hippocampal slice. This strategy is based on the as-yet-uncertain assumption that LTP observed in the slice is identical to that observed in vivo.

The most striking study, the last in this review, is undoubtedly that by Conquet et al (1994), in which five pathways in the hippocampus were characterized for normal synaptic transmission and induction of LTP. The learning deficit, which was impressive, may be related in an unexpected manner to malfunctioning in the mossy-fiber system, a pathway known to exhibit NMDA-receptor-independent, opioid-receptor-dependent LTP_μ (Derrick et al 1991, Harris & Cotman 1986). Prior to this study, most researchers assumed NMDA-receptor-independent LTP had a relatively unimportant role and attached primary importance to NMDA-receptor-dependent LTP in spatial learning.

To be fair, however, the knockout studies do demonstrate deficits in hippocampal LTP that mirror deficits in hippocampus-dependent learning, and if we apply the same explanation of graceful degradation as we have previously, then it is not surprising that some memory is evident in a distributed neural system.

However, it remains disquieting that, even within a discrete afferent system, no single specific kinase appears essential for the induction of NMDA-receptor-dependent LTP. Such findings, suggesting as they do the existence of parallel intracellular cascades, are problematic for reductionists trying to delineate the essential components of a successful molecular cascade. From a larger view, these results emphasize that no single approach will be sufficient to elucidate the role of LTP in memory, even though the knockout approach is powerful and increases our understanding of the relationship between LTP and learning.

CONCLUSION

The rationale for considering LTP a memory mechanism is strong. The absence of proof that LTP is involved in memory results from our current uncertainties about what memory is and how we should observe it. The occurrence of multiple forms of LTP, together with the distributed nature of hippocampal information storage, makes it difficult to identify the processes necessary to hippocampal memory and to implicate specific LTP processes in memory. Thus we should proceed cautiously in interpreting negative findings. Might LTP emerge as an epiphenomenon unrelated to learning or memory? If it does, then the focus of research would shift to such other potential neural mechanisms of memory storage as LTD, population spike potentiation, and presynaptic facilitation. After 20 years under scrutiny, however, LTP remains the best single candidate for the primary cellular process of synaptic change that underlies learning and memory in the vertebrate brain.

ACKNOWLEDGMENTS

The writing of this review was supported by DA 04195, NSF 3389, and the Ewing Halsell Endowment of The University of Texas at San Antonio. We thank Professors David Jaffe, Ray Kesner, Mark Rosenzweig, Tracy Shors, and Richard Thompson for their helpful comments.

Literature Cited

Abeliovich A, Paylor R, Chen C, Kim JJ, Wehner JM, Tonegawa S. 1993. PKC gamma mutant mice exhibit mild deficits in spatial and contextual learning. *Cell* 75(7):1263–71

Aiba A, Chen C, Herrup K, Rosenmund C, Stevens CF, Tonegawa S. 1993. Reduced hippocampal long-term potentiation and context-specific deficit in associative learning in mGluR1 mutant mice. *Cell* 79(2): 365–75

Barnes CA. 1979. Memory deficits associated with senescence: a neurophysiological and behavioral study in the rat. *J. Comp. Physiol. Psychol.* 93:74–104

Barnes CA. 1988. Spatial learning and memory processes: the search for their neurobiological mechanisms in the rat. *Trends Neurosci.* 11:163–69

Barnes CA, Jung MW, McNaughton BL, Korol DL, Andreasson K, Worley PF. 1994. LTP saturation and spatial learning disruption: effects of task variables and saturation levels. *J. Neurosci.* 14(10): 5793–5806

Bashir ZI, Bortolotto ZA, Davies CH, Berretta N, Irving AJ, et al. 1993. Induction of LTP in the hippocampus needs synaptic activation of glutamate metabotropic receptors. *Nature* 363(6427):347–50

Bear MF, Kirkwood A. 1993. Neocortical long-term potentiation. *Curr. Opin. Neurobiol.* 3:197–202

Bear MF, Malenka RC. 1994. Synaptic plasticity: LTP and LTD. *Curr. Opin. Neurobiol.* 4(3):389–99

Bennett EL, Diamond MC, Krech D, Rosenzweig MR. 1964. Chemical and anatomical plasticity of brain. *Science* 146:610–19

Berger TW. 1984. Long-term potentiation of hippocampal synaptic transmission affects rate of behavioral learning. *Science* 224(4649):627–30

Berger TW, Orr WB. 1983. Hippocampectomy selectively disrupts discrimination reversal conditioning of the rabbit nictitating membrane response. *Behav. Brain Res.* 8(1): 49–68

Berger TW, Rinaldi PC, Weisz DJ, Thompson RF. 1983. Single-unit analysis of different hippocampal cell types during classical conditioning of rabbit nictitating membrane response. *J. Neurophysiol.* 50(5): 1197–1219

Blazis DE, Fischer TM, Carew TJ. 1993. A neural network model of inhibitory information processing in Aplysia. *Neural Comput.* 5(2):213–27

Bliss TVP, Collingridge GL. 1993. A synaptic model of memory: long-term potentiation in the hippocampus. *Nature* 361 :31–39

Bliss TVP, Lomo T. 1973. Long-lasting potentiation of synaptic transmission in the dentate area of the anesthetized rabbit following stimulation of the perforant path. *J. Physiol.* 232:331–56

Bliss TVP, Lynch MA. 1988. Long-term potentiation of synaptic transmission in the hippocampus: properties and mechanisms. In *LTP: From Biophysics to Behavior*, ed. P Landfield, SA Deadwyler, pp. 3–72. New York: Liss

Bonhoeffer T, Staiger V, Aertsen A. 1989. Synaptic plasticity in rat hippocampal slice cultures: local "Hebbian" conjunction of pre- and postsynaptic stimulation leads to distributed synaptic enhancement. *Proc. Natl. Acad. Sci. USA* 86(20):8113–17

Bramham CR. 1992. Opioid receptor–dependent long-term potentiation: peptidergic regulation of synaptic plasticity in the hippocampus. *Neurochem. Int.* 20:441–55

Bramham CR, Milgram NW, Srebro B. 1991a. Delta opioid receptor activation is required to induce LTP of synaptic transmission in the lateral perforant path in vivo. *Brain Res.* 567(1):42–50

Bramham CR, Milgram NW, Srebro B. 1991b. Activation of AP5-sensitive NMDA receptors is not required to induce LTP of synaptic transmission in the lateral perforant path. *Eur. J. Neurosci.* 3:1300–8

Breindl AB, Derrick BE, Rodriguez SB, Martinez JL Jr. 1994. Opioid receptor–dependent long-term potentiation at the lateral perforant path–CA3 synapse in rat hippocampus. *Brain Res. Bull.* 33(1): 17–24

Brinton RE. 1991. Biochemical correlates of learning and memory. See Martinez & Kesner 1991, pp. 199–257

Butcher SP, Davis S, Morris RGM. 1990. A dose-related impairment of spatial learning by the NMDA receptor antagonist, 2-amino-5-phosphonovalerate (AP5). *Eur. Neuropsychopharmacol.* 1(1):15–20

Butcher SP, Hamberger A, Morris RGM. 1991. Intracerebral distribution of DL-2-amino-phosphonopentanoic acid (AP5) and the dissociation of different types of learning. *Exp. Brain Res.* 83(3):521–26

Castro CA, Silbert LH, McNaughton BL, Barnes CA. 1989. Recovery of learning following decay of experimental saturation of LTE at perforant path synapses. *Nature* 342:545–48

Chattarji S, Stanton PK, Sejnowski TJ. 1989. Commissural synapses, but not mossy fiber synapses, in hippocampal field CA3 exhibit associative long-term potentiation and depression. *Brain Res.* 495(1):145–50

Collingridge GL, Kehl SJ, McLennan H. 1983. Excitatory amino acids in synaptic transmission in the Schaffer collateral-commissural pathway of the rat hippocampus. *J. Physiol.* 334:33–46

Conquet F, Bashir ZI, Davies CH, Daniel H, Ferraguti F, et al. 1994. Motor deficit and impairment of synaptic plasticity in mice lacking mGluR1. *Nature* 372(6503): 237–43

Dailey ME, Buchanan J, Bergles DE, Smith SJ. 1994. Mossy fiber growth and synaptogenesis in rat hippocampal slices in vitro. *J. Neurosci.* 14(3):1060–78

Davis S, Butcher SP, Morris RGM. 1992. The NMDA receptor antagonist D-2-amino-5-phosphonopentanoate (D-AP5) impairs spatial learning and LTP in vivo at intracerebral concentrations comparable to those that block LTP in vitro. *J. Neurosci.* 12(1): 21–34

Decker MW, Introini-Collison IB, McGaugh JL. 1989. Effects of naloxone on Morris water maze learning in the rat: enhanced acquisition with pretraining but not post-training administration. *Psychobiology* 17:270–75

Derrick BE, Martinez JL Jr. 1989. A unique,

opioid peptide–dependent form of long-term potentiation is found in the CA3 region of the rat hippocampus. *Adv. Biosci.* 75:213–16

Derrick BE, Martinez JL Jr. 1994a. Opioid receptors underlie the frequency-dependence of mossy fiber LTP induction. *J. Neurosci.* 14(7):4359–67

Derrick BE, Martinez JL Jr. 1994b. Frequency-dependent associative LTP at the mossy fiber-CA3 synapse. *Proc. Natl. Acad. Sci. USA* 91(22):10290–94

Derrick BE, Martinez JL Jr. 1995. Associative LTD at the Hippocampal Mossy Fiber–CA3 Synapse. *Soc. Neurosci. Abstr.* 21:603

Derrick BE, Rodriguez SB, Lieberman DN, Martinez JL Jr. 1992. Mu opioid receptors are associated with the induction of LTP at hippocampal mossy fiber synapses. *J. Pharmacol. Exp. Ther.* 263: 725–33

Derrick BE, Weinberger SB, Martinez JL Jr. 1991. Opioid receptors are involved in an NMDA receptor–independent mechanism of LTP induction at hippocampal mossy fiber–CA3 synapses. *Brain Res. Bull.* 27: 219–23

Deutsch JA. 1993. Spatial learning in mutant mice. *Science* 262(5134):760–63

Diamond DM, Rose GM. 1994. Does associative LTP underlie classical conditioning? *Psychobiology* 22(4):263–69

Dudek SM, Bear MF. 1993. Bidirectional long-term modification of synaptic effectiveness in the adult and immature hippocampus. *J. Neurosci.* 13:2910–18

Erickson CA, McNaughton BL, Barnes CA. 1993. Comparison of long-term enhancement and short-term exploratory modulation of perforant path synaptic transmission. *Brain Res.* 615(2):275–80

Erickson CA, McNaughton BL, Barnes CA. 1990. Exploration-dependent enhancement of synaptic responses in rat fascia dentata is blocked by MK801. *Soc. Neurosci. Abstr.* 16:442

Gallistel R. 1994. Interview with Randy Gallistel. *J. Cogn. Neurosci.* 6(2): 174–79

Gallistel R. 1995. Is long-term potentiation a plausible basis for memory? In *Brain and Memory: Modulation and Mediation of Plasticity*, ed. JL McGaugh, NMWeinberger, G Lynch, pp. 328–37. New York: Oxford Univ. Press

Goddard GV. 1986. A step nearer a neural substrate. *Nature* 319:721–22

Grant SG, O'Dell TJ, Karl KA, Stein PL, Soriano P, Kandel ER. 1992. Impaired long-term potentiation, spatial learning, and hippocampal development in *fyn* mutant mice. *Science* 258(5090):1903–10

Green EJ, Greenough WT. 1986. Altered synaptic transmission in dentate gyrus of rats reared in complex environments: evidence from hippocampal slices maintained in vitro. *J. Neurophysiol.* 55(4):739–50

Greenough EJ, McNaughton BL, Barnes CA. 1990. Exploration-dependent modulation of evoked responses in fascia dentata: dissociation of motor, EEG, and sensory factors, and evidence for a synaptic efficacy change. *J. Neurosci.* 10(5):1455–71

Greenough WT, Volkmar FR, Juraska JM. 1973. Effects of rearing complexity on dendritic branching in frontolateral and temporal cortex of rat. *Exp. Neurol.* 41: 371–78

Harris EW, Cotman CW. 1986. Long-term potentiation of guinea pig mossy fiber responses is not blocked by *N*-methyl D-aspartate antagonists. *Neurosci. Lett.* 70: 132–37

Hebb DO. 1949. *The Organization of Behavior.* New York: Wiley

Ishihara K, Katsuki H, Sugimura M, Kaneko S, Satoh M. 1990. Different drug-susceptibilities of long-term potentiation in three input systems to the CA3 region of the guinea pig hippocampus in vitro. *Neuropharmacology* 29(5):487–92

Jaffe D, Johnston D. 1990. Induction of long-term potentiation at hippocampal mossy fibers follows a Hebbian rule. *J. Neurophysiol.* 64:948–60

Jarrard JE. 1986. Selective hippocampal lesions and behavior. In *The Hippocampus*, ed. RL Isaacson, KH Pribram, 4:93–122. New York: Plenum

Jeffery KJ, Morris RGM. 1993. Cumulative long-term potentiation in the rat dentate gyrus correlates with, but does not modify, performance in the water maze. *Hippocampus* 3(2):133–40

Johnston D, Williams S, Jaffe D, Gray R. 1992. NMDA-receptor-independent long-term potentiation. *Annu. Rev. Physiol.* 54: 489–505

Jung MW, Larson J, Lynch G. 1990. Long-term potentiation of monosynaptic EPSPs in rat piriform cortex in vitro. *Synapse* 6(3):279–83

Kanter ED, Haberly LB. 1993. Associative long-term potentiation in piriform cortex slices requires GABAA blockade. *J. Neurosci.* 13(6):2477–82

Keith JR, Rudy JW. 1990. Why NMDA receptor–dependent long-term potentiation may not be a mechanism of learning and memory: a reappraisal of the NMDA receptor blockade strategy. *Psychobiology* 18(3): 251–57

Kelso SR, Brown TH. 1986. Differential conditioning of associative synaptic enhancement in hippocampal brain slices. *Science* 232(4746):85–87

Kim JJ, DeCola JP, Landeira-Fernandez J, Fanselow MS. 1991. N-methyl-D-aspartate receptor antagonist APV blocks acquisition but not expression of fear conditioning. *Behav. Neurosci.* 105(1):126–33

Kim JJ, Fanselow MS. 1992. Modality-specific retrograde amnesia of fear. *Science* 256: 675–77

Kim JJ, Fanselow MS, DeCola JP, Landeira-Fernandez J. 1992. Selective impairment of long-term but not short-term conditional fear by the *N*-methyl-D-aspartate antagonist APV. *Behav. Neurosci.* 106(4):591–96

Laroche S, Doyere V, Bloch V. 1989. Linear relation between the magnitude of long-term potentiation in the dentate gyrus and associative learning in the rat: a demonstration using commissural inhibition and local infusion of an N-methyl-D-aspartate receptor antagonist. *Neuroscience* 28(2): 375–86

Laroche S, Doyere V, Redini Del Negro C. 1991. What role for LTP in learning and the maintenance of memories? In *LTP: A Debate of the Current Issues*, ed. M Baudry, JL Davis, pp. 301–16. London: MIT Press

Levy WB, Steward O. 1979. Synapses as associative memory elements in the hippocampal formation. *Brain Res.* 175(2):233–45

Linden DJ, Connor JA. 1995. Long-term synaptic depression. *Annu. Rev. Neurosci.* 8: 319–57

Lisman J. 1989. A mechanism for the Hebb and the anti-Hebb processes underlying learning and memory. *Proc. Natl. Acad. Sci. USA* 86(23):9574–78

Lynch G, Granger R. 1986. Variations in synaptic plasticity and types of memory in corticohippocampal networks *J. Cogn. Neurosci.* 4(3):189–99

Makintosh NJ. 1974. *The Psychology of Animal Learning*. London: Academic

Malenka RC, Kauer JA, Perkel DJ, Mauk MD, Kelly PT, et al. 1989. An essential role for postsynaptic calmodulin and protein kinase activity in long-term potentiation. *Nature* 340(6234):554–57

Malinow R, Schulman H, Tsien RW. 1989. Inhibition of postsynaptic PKC or CaMKII blocks induction but not expression of LTP. *Science* 245(4920):862–66

Manzoni OJ, Weisskopf MG, Nicoll RA. 1994. MCPG antagonizes metabotropic glutamate receptors but not long-term potentiation in the hippocampus. *Eur. J. Neurosci.* 6(6):1050–54

Marr D. 1971. Simple memory: a theory of archicortex. *Philos. Trans. R. Soc. London Ser. B* 262:23–81

Martin MR. 1983. Naloxone and long-term potentiation of hippocampal CA3 field potentials in vitro. *Neuropeptides* 4:45–50

Martinez JL Jr, Derrick BE. 1994. Opioid receptors contribute to lateral perforant path–CA3 responses days, but not hours,

following LTP induction. *Soc. Neurosci. Abstr.* 20:897

Martinez JL Jr, Kesner RP. 1991. *Learning and Memory: A Biological View.* San Diego: Academic

Martinez JL Jr, Schulteis G, Weinberger SB. 1991. How to increase and decrease the strength of memory traces: the effects of drugs and hormones. See Martinez & Kesner 1991, pp. 149–287

Matthies H, Ruethrich H, Ott T, Matthies HK, Matthies R. 1986. Low-frequency perforant path stimulation as a conditioned stimulus demonstrates correlations between long-term synaptic potentiation and learning. *Physiol. Behav.* 36(5):811–21

McDaniel KL, Mundy WR, Tilson HA. 1990. Microinjection of dynorphin into the hippocampus impairs spatial learning in rats. *Pharmacol. Biochem. Behav.* 35(2): 429–35

McLean S, Rothman RB, Jacobson AE, Rice KC, Herkenham M. 1987. Distribution of opiate receptor subtypes and enkephalin and dynorphin immunoreactivity in the hippocampus of the squirrel, guinea pig, rat and hamster. *J. Comp. Neurol.* 255: 497–510

McNaughton BL, Barnes CA, Meltzer J, Sutherland RJ. 1989. Hippocampal granule cells are necessary for normal spatial learning but not for spatially-selective pyramidal cell discharge. *Exp. Brain Res.* 76(3): 485–96

McNaughton BL, Barnes CA, Rao G, Baldwin J, Rasmussen M. 1986. Long-term enhancement of hippocampal synaptic transmission and the acquisition of spatial information. *J. Neurosci.* 6(2):563–71

McNaughton BL, Douglas RM, Goddard GV. 1978. Synaptic enhancement in fascia dentata: cooperativity among coactive afferents. *Brain Res.* 157:277–93

McNaughton BL, Morris RGM. 1987. Hippocampal synaptic enhancement and information storage within a distributed memory system. *Trends Neurosci.* 10:408–15

Mitsuno K, Sasa M, Ishihara K, Ishikawa M, Kikuchi H. 1994. LTP of mossy fiber-stimulated potentials in CA3 during learning in rats. *Physiol. Behav.* 55(4):633–38

Mondadori C, Weiskrantz L, Buerki H, Petschke F, Fagg GE. 1989. NMDA receptor antagonists can enhance or impair learning performance in animals. *Exp. Brain Res.* 75(3):449–56

Montague PR, Sejnowski TJ. 1994. The predictive brain: temporal coincidence and temporal order in synaptic learning mechanisms. *Learn. Mem.* 1:1–33

Morris RGM. 1989a. Synaptic plasticity and learning: selective impairment of learning rats and blockade of long-term potentiation in vivo by the *N*-methyl-D-aspartate receptor antagonist AP5. *J. Neurosci.* 9(9): 3040–57

Morris RGM. 1989b. Does synaptic plasticity play a role in information storage in the vertebrate brain? In *Parallel Distributed Processing: Implications for Psychology and Neurobiology*, ed. RGM Morris, pp. 248–85. Oxford: Clarendon

Morris RGM. 1990. It's heads they win, tails I lose! *Psychobiology* 18:261–66

Morris RGM, Anderson E, Lynch GS, Baudry M. 1986. Selective impairment of learning and blockade of long-term potentiation by an *N*-methyl-D-aspartate receptor antagonist AP5. *Nature* 319(6056):774–76

Morris RGM, Garrud P, Rawlins JN, O'Keefe J. 1982. Place navigation impaired in rats with hippocampal lesions. *Nature* 297(5868):681–83

Moser E, Mathiesen I, Andersen P. 1993a. Association between brain temperature and dentate field potentials in exploring and swimming rats. *Science* 259(5099): 1324–26

Moser E, Moser MB, Andersen P. 1993b. Synaptic potentiation in the rat dentate gyrus during exploratory learning. *NeuroReport* 5(3):317–20

Nadel L. 1968. Dorsal and ventral hippocampal lesions and behavior. *Physiol. Behav.* 3(6):891–900

O'Dell TJ, Kandel ER, Grant SG. 1991. Long-term potentiation in the hippocampus is blocked by tyrosine kinase inhibitors. *Nature* 353(6344):558–60

Ohki Y. 1982. The effects of hippocampal lesions on two types of avoidance learning in rats: effects on learning to be active or to be inactive. *Jpn. J. Psychol.* 53(2): 65–71

Ott T, Ruthrich K, Reymann L, Lindenau L, Matthies H. 1982. Direct evidence for the participation of changes in synaptic efficacy in the development of behavioral plasticity. In *Neuronal Plasticity and Memory Formation,* ed. CA Marsan, H Matthies, pp. 441–52. New York: Raven

Pavlov IP. 1927. *Conditioned Reflexes.* London: Oxford Univ. Press

Peng Y, Horn JP. 1991. Continuous repetitive stimuli are more effective than bursts for evoking LHRH release in bullfrog sympathetic ganglia. *J. Neurosci.* 11:85–95

Port RL, Beggs AL, Patterson MM. 1987. Hippocampal substrate of sensory associations. *Physiol. Behav.* 39(5):643–47

Racine RJ, Milgram NW, Hafner S. 1983. Long-term potentiation phenomena in the rat limbic forebrain. *Brain Res.* 260(2): 217–31

Reymann KG, Ruthrich H, Lindenau L, Ott T, Matthies H. 1982. Monosynaptic activation of the hippocampus as a conditioned stimu-

lus: behavioral effects. *Physiol. Behav.* 29(6):1007–12

Richter-Levin G, Errington ML, Maegawa H, Bliss TV. 1994. Activation of metabotropic glutamate receptors is necessary for long-term potentiation in the dentate gyrus and for spatial learning. *Neuropharmacology* 33(7):853–57

Robinson GS, Crooks GB, Shinkman PG, Gallagher M. 1990. Behavioral effects of MK-801 mimic deficits associated with hippocampal damage. *Psychobiology* 17(2): 156–64

Robinson GB. 1992. Maintained saturation of hippocampal long-term potentiation does not disrupt acquisition of the eight-arm radial maze. *Hippocampus* 2(4):389–95

Rolls ET. 1989. Parallel distributed processing in the brain: implications of the functional architecture of neuronal networks in the hippocampus. In *Parallel Distributed Processing: Implications for Psychology and Neurobiology*, ed. RGM Morris, pp. 286–307. Oxford: Clarendon

Roman FS, Chaillan FA, Soumireu-Mourat B. 1993. Long-term potentiation in rat piriform cortex following discrimination learning. *Brain Res.* 601(1–2):265–72

Roman FS, Staubli U, Lynch G. 1987. Evidence for synaptic potentiation in a cortical network during learning. *Brain Res.* 418(2):221–26

Rosenzweig MR, Krech D, Bennett EL, Diamond MC. 1962. Effects of environmental complexity and training on brain chemistry and anatomy: a replication and extension. *J. Comp. Physiol. Psychol.* 55:429–37

Rumelhart D, McClelland J. 1986. *Parallel Distributed Processing,* Vol. 1. Cambridge: MIT Press

Ruthrich H, Dorochow W, Pohle W, Ruthrich HL, Matthies H. 1987. Colchicine-induced lesion of rat hippocampal granular cells prevents conditioned active avoidance with perforant path stimulation as conditioned stimulus, but not conditioned emotion. *Physiol. Behav.* 40(2):147–54

Sakimura K, Kutsuwada T, Ito I, Manabe T, Takayama C, et al. 1995. Reduced hippocampal LTP and spatial learning in mice lacking NMDA receptor epsilon 1 subunit. *Nature* 373(6510):151–55

Schacter DL, Tulving E. 1994. What are the memory systems of 1994? In *Memory Systems 1994,* ed. DL Schacter, E Tulving, pp. 1–38. Cambridge: MIT Press

Schuman EM, Madison DV. 1991. A requirement for the intercellular messenger nitric oxide in long-term potentiation. *Science* 254(5037):1503–6

Sejnowski TJ. 1977. Storing covariance with nonlinearly interacting neurons. *J. Math. Biol.* 4(4):303–21

Sharp PE, McNaughton BL, Barnes CA. 1985. Enhancement of hippocampal field potentials in rats exposed to a novel, complex environment. *Brain Res.* 339(2):361–65

Shimai S, Ohki Y. 1980. Facilitation of discriminated rearing-avoidance in rats with hippocampal lesions. *Percept. Mot. Skills* 50(1):56–8

Silva AJ, Paylor R, Wehner JM, Tonegawa S. 1992a. Impaired spatial learning in alpha-calcium-calmodulin kinase II mutant mice. *Science* 257(5067):206–11

Silva AJ, Stevens CF, Tonegawa S, Wang Y. 1992b. Deficient hippocampal long-term potentiation in alpha-calcium-calmodulin kinase II mutant mice. *Science* 257(5067): 201–6

Squire LR. 1987. *Memory and Brain.* New York: Oxford Univ. Press

Staubli U. 1992. A peculiar form of potentiation in mossy fiber synapses. *Epilepsy Res. Suppl.* 7:151–57

Staubli U, Larson J, Lynch G. 1990. Mossy fiber potentiation and long-term potentiation involve different expression mechanisms. *Synapse* 5(4):333–35

Staubli U, Lynch G. 1987. Stable hippocampal long-term potentiation elicited by 'theta' pattern stimulation. *Brain Res.* 435:227–34

Staubli U, Thibault O, Lynch G. 1986. Antagonism of NMDA receptors impairs acquisition, but not retention, of olfactory memory. *Behav. Neurosci.* 103:54–60

Stent G. 1973. A physiological mechanism for Hebb's postulate of learning. *Proc. Natl. Acad. Sci. USA* 70:997–1001

Stewart CA, Jeffery K, Reid I. 1994. LTP-like synaptic efficacy changes following electroconvulsive stimulation. *NeuroReport* 5(9):1041–44

Stewart CA, Reid IC. 1994. Ketamine prevents ECS-induced synaptic enhancement in rat hippocampus. *Neurosci. Lett.* 178(1):11–14

Stripling JS, Patneau DK, Gramlich CA. 1991. Characterization and anatomical distribution of selective long-term potentiation in the olfactory forebrain. *Brain Res.* 542(1): 107–22

Sutherland RJ, Dringenberg HC, Hoesing JM. 1993. Induction of long-term potentiation at perforant path dentate synapses does not affect place learning or memory. *Hippocampus* 3(2):141–47

Teyler TJ, Grover L. 1993. In *Synaptic Plasticity: Molecular, Cellular and Functional Aspects,* ed. M Baudry, RF Thompson, JL Davis, pp. 73–86. Cambridge: MIT Press

Thompson RF. 1992. Memory. *Curr. Opin. Neurobiol.* 2(2):203–8

Thompson RF, Spencer WA. 1966. Habituation: a model phenomenon for the study of the neuronal substrates of behavior. *Psych. Rev.* 173:16–43

Wagner JJ, Terman GW, Chaukin C. 1993. Endogenous dynorphins inhibit excitatory neurotransmission and block LTP induction in hippocampus. *Nature* 36:(6428): 451–54

Walker DL, Gold PE. 1991. Effects of the novel NMDA antagonist NPC 12626, on long-term potentiation, learning and memory. *Brain Res.* 549(2):213–21

Weisskopf MG, Zalutsky RA, Nicoll RA. 1993. The opioid peptide dynorphin mediates heterosynaptic depression of hippocampal mossy fibre synapses and modulates long-term potentiation. *Nature* 362: 423–27

Williams S, Johnston D. 1989. Long-term potentiation of hippocampal mossy fibers is blocked by postsynaptic injection of calcium chelators. *Neuron* 3:583–88

Winson J. 1978. Loss of hippocampal theta rhythm results in spatial memory deficit in the rat. *Science* 201(4351):160–63

Zalutsky RA, Nicoll RA. 1990. Comparison of two forms of long-term potentiation in single hippocampal neurons. *Science* 248: 1619–24

Zalutsky RA, Nicoll RA. 1992. Mossy fiber long-term potentiation shows specificity but no apparent cooperativity. *Neurosci. Lett.* 138:193–97

Zhang DX, Levy WB. 1992. Ketamine blocks the induction of LTP at the lateral entorhinal cortex-dentate gyrus synapses. *Brain Res.* 593(1):124–27

Zola-Morgan S, Squire LR. 1993. Neuroanatomy of memory. *Annu. Rev. Neurosci.* 16:547–63

Annu. Rev. Psychol. 1996. 47:205–35

CROSS-CULTURAL SOCIAL AND ORGANIZATIONAL PSYCHOLOGY

Michael Harris Bond

Department of Psychology, Chinese University of Hong Kong, Shatin NT, Hong Kong

Peter B. Smith

School of Social Sciences, University of Sussex, Falmer, Brighton BN1 9QN, England

KEY WORDS: individualism-collectivism, independence-interdependence, self-concept, social influence, work behavior

ABSTRACT

This review considers recent theoretical and empirical developments in cross-cultural studies within social and organizational psychology. It begins with a description of the importance and the difficulties of universalizing psychological science. It then continues with an examination of theoretical work on both the internal-proximal and the external-distal constraints that mediate culture's influence on behavior. Influences on social cognition are documented by describing research on self-concept, self-esteem, emotions, attribution processes, person perception, interpersonal attraction, and justice. Group processes are addressed in the areas of leadership, decision-making, and negotiation, and research in organizational psychology is examined with respect to work motivation and work behavior. The review concludes that considerable improvement is evident in recent cross-cultural research. However, future research must include a broader range of cultures and attend more closely to the levels at which cultural effects should be analyzed, and cultural samples must be unpacked in more psychologically useful ways.

CONTENTS

0066-4308/96/0201-0205$08.00

[A] human race speaking many tongues, regarding many values, and holding different convictions about the meaning of life sooner or later will have to consult all that is human.

G Murphy (1969, p. 528)

INTRODUCTION

An American social psychologist, new to the cross-cultural area, attended the 1994 Congress of the International Association for Cross-Cultural Psychology. He later wrote:

> I have a sense that the field is suffering not just from an identity crisis, but from the overwhelming magnitude of that task we are undertaking and the enormous difficulty of doing valuable research in this area. I heard some fine talks, but it is clear that the field is really in its infancy, and to my way of thinking, it confronts the most difficult domain of knowledge in the social sciences. I found it stimulating and exciting, but also a bit daunting. I think we just have to plunge ahead and make the mistakes that will ultimately lead to progress (W Stephan, personal communication).

These astute observations capture the essence of our current challenge in cross-cultural psychology. Where have we cross-cultural psychologists come from? What have we found? Whither are we going? These are the issues we shall address in deciding if cross-cultural social and organizational psychology has indeed come of age.

The Promise of the Cross-Cultural Approach

Psychology is the scientific study of human behavior. Its presumptive goal is to achieve universal status by generalizing results found in particular ecological, social, legal, institutional, and political settings. Such generalization requires testing in maximally different cultures. "In no other way can we be certain that what we believe to be...regularities are not merely peculiarities, the product of some limited set of historical or cultural or political circumstances" (Kohn 1987, p. 713).

Tests for generalizability often produce extensive discrepancies (Amir & Sharon 1987). Of course, these discrepancies can arise because of differences in testing methods. "To obviate the possibility that differences in findings are merely artifacts of differences in method, one tries to design studies to be comparable with one another in their methods, to establish both linguistic and conceptual equivalence in the wording of questions and in the coding of answers, and to establish truly equivalent indices of the underlying concepts" (Kohn 1987, p. 720).

This requirement is no mean challenge, and early, obvious failures have left cross-cultural psychology with a dubious legacy. Today, however, psychologists show greater vigilance and sophistication about the equivalence issue (van de Vijver & Leung 1996). Consequently, we may feel more confident about the validity of differences found across cultural settings.

With methodological concerns minimized, one can use discrepancies to comprehend the anomalous. As Kohn (1987) has noted, "what appear to be cross-national differences may really be instances of lawful regularities, if thought of in terms of some larger, more encompassing interpretation" (p. 716). This is mind-stretching work, but it is, however, essential if psychology is to claim universality. Carefully wrought cross-cultural psychology can serve as a midwife to this heady enterprise.

The Current Scene

The growth is illustrated by the recent appearance of textbooks in cross-cultural psychology as a whole (Berry et al 1992, Brislin 1993, Lonner & Malpass 1994, Segall et al 1990), cross-cultural social psychology (Matsumoto 1994, Moghaddam et al 1993, Smith & Bond 1994, Triandis 1994), and cross-cultural organizational psychology (Adler 1991, Erez & Earley 1993, Triandis et al 1993a), as well as by the appearance of volumes arising from the congresses of the International Association for Cross-Cultural Psychology (Bouvy et al 1994, Keats et al 1989, Iwawaki et al 1992, Pandey et al 1995) and of a completely new edition of the *Handbook of Cross-Cultural Psychology* (Berry et al 1996). The growth of cross-cultural research and the attention given to this area of study is encouraging. But how well positioned are we? How much progress are we able to report since the publication, in this series, of reviews of cross-cultural psychology by Kagitcibasi & Berry (1989) and Shweder & Sullivan (1993)?

Research in psychology is dominated by Americans. Prestigious psychology journals are largely monopolized by North Americans, who rarely cite the work of outsiders and who work on questions that are often themselves culturally distinctive (Hogan & Emler 1978). The state of affairs extends to cross-cultural psychology itself. Content analysis of the *Journal of Cross-Cultural Psychology* since its inception in 1970 reveals that, even there, North American theories and authors predominate (Ongel & Smith 1994). This ethnocentrism, as noted by Moghaddam et al (1993), is fueled by the general use of the English language in journals and at international conferences.

One small inroad into this North American domination of the field is the emergence of psychology both from and about Asian cultures (Bond 1986, 1995; Gudykunst 1993; Komin 1990; Misumi 1985). Sustained by the economic development of the Five Dragons, this work has stimulated and been responsive to the construct of cultural collectivism. Given researchers' predilection for two-culture comparisons, however, an East Asian variant of collectivism may be gaining a disproportionate scientific ascendancy (Singelis 1994). We need to decenter collectivism by undertaking studies in South America, Africa, and the former Communist Bloc (A Realo et al, submitted).

We note in fairness that many North American psychologists and journal editors are promoting the visibility of psychologists and psychology within other cultural groups (Rosenzweig 1992). There is some indication of growing reliance upon theories held by scholars indigenous to India (Adair et al 1993) and other countries (Kim & Berry 1993). Some textbooks are introducing more cross-cultural material, and the journal *Psychology and Developing Societies* has been established.

Greater attention is also being given to the development of procedures for ensuring the equivalence of measurements made at different locations. For instance, item response theory can be used to assess the equivalence of questionnaire responses (Bontempo 1993, Ellis et al 1993); careful thought can be given to item appropriateness (Lonner 1980); and cultural differences in response bias can be mapped (Hui & Triandis 1989, Marin & Marin 1991, Marin et al 1993) and controlled for by within-subject standardization of responses (Leung & Bond 1989). Methodological prerequisites are enumerated for valid cross-cultural experiments (Earley & Mosakowski 1995) and for studies of organizations (Lytle et al 1995, Shenkar & von Glinow 1994). All these developments contribute to a gradual cultural decentering of psychology, but the remaining obstacles are real and considerable (Ongel & Smith 1994, p. 50):

High on the list of further impediments…must lie the difficulty of assembling diverse and truly collaborative research teams where members contribute equally toward research designs that will have validity in a number of different cultural settings. The development of such teams takes time, tact, and resources, and publication pressures militate against setting them up. Where some of the collaborating researchers are from high power distance cultures, [and hence are more likely to defer to project leaders from cultures low in power distance,] or are former graduate students of their present research partners, the encouragement to rely on established Western measures and theories is further intensified.

We hope this review will empower voices of science from other cultures to contribute to the universalizing of psychology.

THEORETICAL DEVELOPMENTS

Definitions of culture abound, and the sheer number displays the complexity of their referent (Krewer & Jahoda 1993, Misra & Gergen 1993, Soudjin et al 1990). We adopt Poortinga's (1992) broad position on culture as a set of "shared constraints that limit the behavior repertoire available to members of a certain…group" (p. 10). These "boundary conditions for behavior" (p. 12) include the internal constraints of genetic and cultural transmission and the external constraints of ecological, socioeconomical, historical, and situational contexts, with a range of distal to proximal effects within each type of constraint.

This definition of culture may be married to a position of universalism, in which "it is assumed that the same psychological processes are operating in all humans independent of culture" (Poortinga 1992, p. 13). Cultural constraints then limit and shape the behavioral expression of the universal process. Universals, as these psychological processes are called, are grist for the cross-cultural psychology mill. They may be identified conceptually by careful attention to the anthropological literature (Lonner 1980), by historical exegesis (Adamopoulos 1988), or through evolutionary analyses (Chasiotis & Keller 1994). Alternatively, they may also be identified empirically through careful cross-cultural replications, as seen in Kohn et al's (1990) work on class structure, job specialization, and the transmission of values in three cultures, or in Costa & McCrae's (1992) work on the Big Five factors of personality.

What typology of cultures and their behavioral constraints shall be used in the search for universals? We address this question on the basis of Poortinga's differentiation between internal and external constraints, each of which involves culturally transmitted values and beliefs in eco-socio-historical contexts.

Theories of Internal-Proximal Constraints

VALUES   The dominant development of the past decade in theories of internal-proximal constraints has been Schwartz's (1992, 1994) work on values. A wide reading by Schwartz of previous theory, methodology, and cultural anthropology preceded the creation of a comprehensive values instrument that has been carefully administered to equivalent samples of teachers and students in almost 50 countries. The results of this work form the basis of a circumplex model of 10 universal value domains at the individual level (1992) and 7 at the cultural level with scores for 38 culture regions (1994). These culture-level scores have been related to Hofstede's (1980) four dimensions of cultural variation and to both Hofstede's and the Chinese Culture Connection's (1987) nation scores (Bond 1995). Schwartz's country-level scores have also been related to country-level indices of physical, economic, and social health (Chan & Bond 1995). In terms of both convergent and external validity, the Schwartz domains appear most promising.

Schwartz's initial work, however, was at the individual level, and his culture-level work was predicated on this foundation. Future cross-cultural work can proceed at the individual level through use of the Schwartz Value Survey (Feather 1994, Leung et al 1994). Such a "translation" of the Survey to the individual was not possible with Hofstede's (1980) classic results, eager as many psychologists were to leap from the study of culture to the study of the individual. We hope that Schwartz will soon publish the average scores of people from his culture samples on the 10 individual-level domains [as Bond (1988) did for the Chinese Culture Connection's nation scores (1987)], so researchers can work at their preferred level of study.

An additional development is Smith et al's (1995a) analysis of the Trompenaars (1993) data base. Data from 43 countries were derived from a questionnaire designed to show seven patterns of cultural variation. Smith et al identified two separate dimensions, i.e. conservatism–egalitarian commitment and loyal involvement–utilitarian involvement, which had been conflated in Hofstede's (1980) discussion of collectivism. This empirical refinement of the collectivism construct is important, given its current ascendancy in cross-cultural studies (Kim et al 1994, Triandis 1995) and its further refinement at the individual level into horizontal as well as vertical components (Singelis et al 1995).

BELIEFS   Values tap what is important, beliefs what is true. Scales measuring cultural constructs sometimes mix values and beliefs together. It is important, however, for theoretical (Feather 1988) and empirical (Leung et al 1994) reasons to keep these constructs separate. For example, Smith et al (1995b) have analyzed responses from 43 countries to Rotter's (1966) locus of control scale.

This scale is used to tap beliefs, not values, about internal vs external control of reinforcement. Smith et al found three dimensions of belief about causality, only one of which paralleled Rotter's original formulation. These dimensions of beliefs along which countries may be arrayed overlap only moderately with country measures of value.

Locus-of-control beliefs are important in predicting individual behavior and are closely related to discussions of key cultural differences in individuals' experiences of control, harmony, and submission with respect to the environment. The experience of personal agency and people's needs to believe in their personal agency are probably universal; therefore, we would hope that locally valid measures of this belief will be developed and its role in explaining cross-cultural differences examined.

Other beliefs that vary cross-culturally, e.g. beliefs about a just world (Furnham 1993), global interdependencies (Der-Kerabetian 1992), and work behaviors (Furnham et al 1993), are promising areas for explaining cultural differences in behavior. A taxonomy of such beliefs would help to move the field beyond its excessive reliance on values (K Leung & MH Bond, unpublished observations).

Theories of External-Distal Constraints

Factor-analytic studies of ecological, social, economic, and political indicators may be exploited to provide a taxonomy of external-distal constraints on individual behavior. Studies in the 1970s yielded many factors, but economic development or so-called modernization was invariably the first obtained. The fact that this dimension is only one among many has been used to dismiss simplistic assertions about convergence (Smith & Bond 1994). We expect that variations along the remaining dimensions give considerable scope for nations and their constituent cultures to exert varying influences, once economic development has been partialled out (Bond 1991).

With the notable exceptions of Berry (1979) and Triandis (1984), recent researchers have been loath to grasp the nettle of external-distal constraints. The variables involved are perceived by many to lie outside the discipline. Their translation into the psychological realm is considered tenuous and uncharted or else probably isomorphic with cultural value dimensions. Although understandable, such avoidance is lamentable, especially in light of ubiquitous calls for cross-disciplinary integration (Easton & Shelling 1991, Gabrenya 1988). Much may be achieved in this area, however, as a recent study by Linssen & Hagendoorn (1994) on European nationality stereotypes can attest.

Almost all current models of cultural difference are thus proximal rather than distal. Fiske (1992), however, proposes a model of four domains of social relationship present in all cultures: communal sharing, authority ranking, equality matching, and market pricing. According to Fiske, cultural difference is defined in terms of the relative reliance on these four bases of relationship. Fiske (1993) replicated results of an earlier US study showing that when Koreans, Chinese, Bengalis, and Liberians made errors in naming a person, their errors referred to others within the same relationship type.

SOCIAL COGNITION

The Self-Concept

Triandis (1990), who has focused on the close relation of the self to the in-group and on the greater distance of the self from the out-group, hypothesizes that cultural collectivism leads its members to make more social responses on the "Who Are You?" test (Bochner 1994). Triandis (1993) defines culture-level collectivism as a cultural syndrome encompassing a broad range of behaviors. Triandis has also developed measures of the corresponding individual-level construct, allocentrism-idiocentrism, both within and across cultures (Triandis et al 1993b).

Markus & Kitayama (1991) have focused instead on the sense of interdependence that characterizes the experience of self in collective cultural systems. Such a socially shared, normative construction of the self has challenging implications for developmental (Kagitcibasi 1995), personality (Miller 1994), and social (Singelis et al 1995) areas of psychology. Surprisingly, attempts to measure the interdependent and independent components of the self-concept have shown them to be orthogonal, not bipolar constructs (Gudykunst et al 1994, Singelis 1994). Persons from collectivist cultures feel more interdependence, and interdependent peoples in all cultures endorse values such as restrictive conformity, prosociality, and security. Individuals from individualistic cultures feel more independence, and independent people in all cultures endorse self-direction (Gudykunst et al 1994). Scores on interdependence are positively related to emotional contagion (TM Singelis 1994, unpublished data) and embarrassability (Singelis & Sharkey 1995), both within and across cultures.

Self-concept clarity (SCC) is "the extent to which an individual's specific self-beliefs are clearly and confidently defined, internally consistent, and temporarily stable" (JD Campbell, PD Trapnell, SJ Heine, IM Katz, L Lavallee, DR Lehman, submitted). These authors argue that people with an interdependent self-concept should have less clarity. As a test of this prediction, they compared samples of Japanese and Canadians, who represent persons from a collectivist and individualist culture, respectively, and showed that Japanese are indeed lower on SCC than Canadians.

GENDER SELF-CONCEPT   Williams & Best (1990) examined sex stereotypes in 30 countries and concluded that there is substantial agreement among cultures concerning the psychological characteristics differentially associated with men and women. The ratings were scored for activity, strength of affective meaning, and favorability. The content of the male stereotype turned out to be more active and stronger in affective meaning, but not any more favorable. Across cultures, stronger male stereotypes, i.e. greater attribution of affectively active, strong characteristics to males than to females, are associated with lower levels of literacy and socioeconomic development and with a lower proportion of women enrolled in college.

Best & Williams (1994) also showed that in all cultures, men and women differ in their self-reports of masculine and feminine characteristics, although the gender difference is typically less than that reflected in gender stereotypes. Best & Williams also reported that the gender difference in total affective meaning of self-reports was greater in countries in which power distance was high (i.e. more authoritarian social structure) and social-economic level, percentage of Christians, and proportion of female college graduates were low.

ETHNIC IDENTITY   Weinreich (1986) defines ethnic identity as "that part of the totality of one's self-construal made up of those dimensions that express the continuity between one's construal of past ancestry and future aspirations in relation to ethnicity" (p. 308). This is a complex construct, and measures of one's ethnic identification can include assessments of one's ethnicity-related practices, the importance one attaches to those practices, one's subjective self-labeling, and the evaluation given to this self-labeling and to one's ascribed ethnicity (Rosenthal & Feldman 1992). Weinreich has developed an idiographic technique called Identity Structure Analysis (ISA) that has been applied to cases of ethnic identification and conflicts arising from bicultural parenting, intergroup conflict, and superordinate group demands (Weinreich 1995).

Weinreich's thinking concerns how the individual negotiates the often treacherous cross-currents of ethnic identities ascribed to that individual by others. University students in Hong Kong, for example, perceive themselves as similar to but distinct from typical Hong Kong Chinese. They ascribe to themselves elements of a valued Western identity in equal measure to their Hong Kong identity (Weinreich et al 1994). This creative synthesizing of local identities provides an escape from the intergroup conflict that must arise when there is no alternative to ascribed ethnic identity. The identifications achieved by individuals rather than ascribed to them by others then become the basis for various forms of intergroup behavior, such as linguistic differentiation (Giles & Viladot 1994) and styles of conflict management (Ting-Toomey et al 1994).

Self-Esteem

Because self-esteem is central to Western theories of psychopathology and social functioning (Taylor & Brown 1988), self-esteem measures have been much used in non-Western research (Leung & Leung 1992) and in cross-cultural comparisons (Bond & Cheung 1983).

Are self-esteem measures derived from cross-culturally equivalent ways of construing self-concept, from which self-esteem derives? The work of Watkins & Dong (1994) with Chinese, Nepalese, Nigerian, Filipino, and Australian children, using the Shavelson model (Shavelson & Bolus 1982) of the self-concept, confirms construct validity across cultures. Such models of the self-concept are, however, individualistic in conceptualization. When collective or group-based elements of the self-concept are included, construct similarity may break down.

Measures of self-esteem used in cross-cultural comparisons are often based on evaluations of one's individual attributes rather than on one's group attributes (Feather & McKee 1993). Cross-cultural comparisons may therefore miss differences in self-evaluation derived from one's collective identity (Luhtanen & Crocker 1992). Reported cultural differences in self-esteem may be misleading if the construct has not been fully assessed. Debates about whether people from certain cultural groups are more socially modest or internally depressed (DeGooyer & Williams 1992) may thus be premature.

The assessment question may also affect construct validity. Individually based levels of self-esteem seem to be derived from similar components of personality across cultural groups (Ho 1994) and to be meaningfully related to social responses in different cultures (Feather & McKee 1993). Collectively derived measures of self-esteem, however, predict important outcomes like psychological well-being for some ethnic groups but not for others (Crocker et al 1994). How one measures self-esteem across cultures will obviously affect what one discovers about the concept.

Emotion

The cross-cultural study of emotion (Mesquita & Frijda 1992) has been stimulated by Markus & Kitayama's (1991) seminal paper and a subsequent conference (Kitayama & Markus 1994). However, as Frijda & Mesquita (1994) have observed, cross-cultural researchers on emotion have been preoccupied with labels. Given the interpersonal focus of this chapter, we endorse Frijda & Mesquita's definition of emotions as "first and foremost, modes of relating to the environment: states of readiness for engaging, or not engaging, in interaction with that environment" (p. 51). Aspects of that engagement include "modifying inter-individual interactions...at the moment;...regulating the balance of power;...determining general patterns of social interaction;...and...motivating social cohesion" (pp. 82–83).

This centrality of emotion in social life underscores its importance for understanding cross-cultural differences in behavior. Recent work has been concentrated on appraisal of the events that generate emotions (Ellsworth 1994). The dimensions of appraisal appear to be universal (Mauro et al 1992), as are appraisal patterns activated by many emotionally relevant situations (Mesquita 1993). The weight accorded to certain of these dimensions (e.g. controllability, causal agency) varies across cultures, as does the importance of certain emotions. These differences are explained by variations in cultural independence-interdependence, a construct that accounts for differences in the social embeddedness of the emotions (Frijda & Mesquita 1994).

In recent years fewer cross-cultural studies have examined how emotions are communicated to others (Russell 1994) and how emotional displays affect the responses of others to the actor, to the ongoing interaction, and to their social group (Frijda & Mesquita 1994). Such additional work would be most welcome to the field.

Attribution Processes

Although a great deal of research on diverse aspects of attribution theory has been carried out, it has been criticized for committing the "fundamental attribution researcher's error" (Russell 1982), the assumption on the part of researchers that their conceptualization of what is under investigation corresponds to their subjects' ideas. The criticism particularly has force in cross-cultural research. Because researchers' conceptualizations and measures are almost always Western-based and subjects' attributional models are not, the dangers of "imposed-etic" research (Berry 1989) are present.

Watkins & Cheng (1995), for instance, showed that the perceived dimensions underlying the Revised Causal Dimension Scale, which was developed using American subjects, do not reflect the dimensions of causality used by Hong Kong students. The investigators argue that this difference arises because of the relative Chinese emphasis on the role of effort as an explanation for achievement (Leung 1995a). This difference in factor structure renders suspect cross-cultural comparisons on relative frequency of causal attribution categories. Part of a cross-culturalist's answer to this inconsistency is to work with more open-ended causal accounts (Kashima & Triandis 1986), which permit indigenous constructs such as the Chinese *yuan* (fatedness) (Yang & Ho 1988) to be included. Local instruments can then be developed that assess the dimensionality of causal categories in various cultures (Luk & Bond 1992). Equivalent categories may then be compared across cultures on issues such as salience, self-esteem maintenance, interpersonal modesty, and responsibility attribution. Crittenden (1995) explores these concerns within Chinese attribution research.

Nevertheless, a promising research theme has emerged in the study of attribution processes. Shweder & Bourne (1982) argued that many non-Western cultures inculcate a "holistic world view" that promotes "context-dependent, occasion-bound thinking." Accordingly, attributions made by members of non-Western cultures are more external/situational (Morris & Peng 1994). In research consistent with this assessment of non-Western attribution processes, Newman (1993) found US allocentrics less willing to make trait attributions, while Kashima et al (1992) found non-Westerners less likely to believe that others' behaviors are consistent with internal loci such as attitudes. This less-personal attributional logic can also aid our understanding of cultural variations in social processes such as morality judgments (Miller & Bersoff 1992).

INTERPERSONAL BEHAVIOR

Person Perception

Dixon (1977) asserts that trait terms are used in every known language to distinguish persons. Studies of implicit personality theory in any language studied to date indicate that a five-factor model can describe the organization of perceived personality (Bond 1994; see Butcher & Rouse, this volume). The apparent universality of the broad categories of extroversion, agreeableness, conscientiousness, emotional stability, and openness to experience may arise from their importance in directing universal types of social behaviors such as association, subordination, and formality (Bond & Forgas 1984).

Within the general framework of this model, culture exercises its influence by accentuating certain of the Big Five dimensions over others. In free-response trait descriptions of themselves (Ip & Bond 1995) or of others (Chang et al 1994), Chinese, for example, use the category of conscientiousness more often and use the category of agreeableness less often than do Americans. Moreover, the rated importance of each of the five categories varies among cultural groups (Williams et al 1995), and these categories are differentially weighted in guiding social behavior (Bond & Forgas 1984).

Such differences may be explained by an ecological model emphasizing the adaptive significance of certain types of responding in different cultural environments (Zebrowitz-McArthur 1988). The universally adaptive significance of caring for immature members of the species is obvious. As a result, physical cues of immaturity, such as babyfacedness (McArthur & Berry 1987) and vocal softness (Peng et al 1993), have been related pan-culturally to personality perceptions of dependence and weakness. Similarly, mating with youthful members of the species is biologically adaptive, so people with youthful gaits are regarded as sexier across cultures (Montepare & Zebrowitz 1993). Likewise, the cues for physical attractiveness enjoy considerable universality (Perrett et al 1994) and connote reproductive fitness (Cunningham 1986). It may be for this latter, biological reason that the personalities of attractive persons are judged as more sociable across cultures (L Albright, Q Dong, TE Malloy, DA Kenney, D Yu, submitted). Through these examples, we can see how our common biological agenda accounts for universals of personality perceptions. The variable cultural impact of cues such as vocal speed (Peng et al 1993) or smiling (Matsumoto & Kudoh 1993) is harder to explain persuasively, because the linkage of these cues to dimensions of culture is less apparent.

Interpersonal Attraction

People in individualistic cultures believe that internal dispositions drive behavior (Kashima et al 1992); therefore topics like interpersonal attraction and love engage Western psychologists almost exclusively (Hogan & Emler 1978). However, owing to modernization and the attendant increase in personal choice it offers people, scientific interest in interpersonal attraction is growing outside the West (Hatfield & Rapson 1993). This is a welcome development because only scattered evidence about the processes of interpersonal attraction exists from other cultures (Cheng et al 1995, Rai & Rathore 1988, Rodrigues & Iwawaki 1986). This evidence generally confirms Western models of similarity or balance.

Future work in other cultures must focus on the nature of attraction itself. For example, Shaver et al (1991) found that the mainland Chinese conceptualization of passionate love is dramatically different from Italian and American conceptualizations. Similarly, Ellis et al (1995) found that Mexicans assign a different subjective meaning to love than do Americans or Spaniards. Clearly, conceptual equivalence of key terms is an issue that must be carefully assessed in this area.

Cross-cultural work on behavioral benchmarks such as mate preferences (Liston & Salts 1988), friendship selection (Goodwin & Tang 1991), sexual activity (Hatfield & Rapson 1993), or attachment style (Wu & Shaver 1992) sidesteps this equivalence problem. The marriage relationship, for example, entails similar social requirements in all cultures, so it is perhaps not surprising that a high degree of cross-cultural agreement was found in Buss et al's (1990) multicultural study of desired spousal attributes. One complex of qualities, including chastity in women, domestic skills, and interest in home and children did, however, vary negatively as a function of cultural modernity. This latter variable and its associate, individualism, have been related to the importance of love itself in establishing and maintaining the marriage bond (KK Dion & KL Dion 1991, 1993; Levine et al 1995) and to the style of loving likely to be found in heterosexual relationships (KL Dion & KK Dion 1993).

Research into how individualism and other cultural dimensions affect interpersonal attraction is still needed as modernization proceeds.

Justice

The topic of justice was first explored cross-culturally in the context of resource allocation. Bond et al (1982) argued and found that the concern of people in collectivist cultures for maintaining harmony should result in egalitarian resource divisions, and that the concern of people in individualistic cultures for performance should result in equitable resource divisions. Need-based allocations are also more likely in collectivist cultures because of concerns for group solidarity (Berman et al 1985).

Subsequent studies have revealed inconsistencies in research results based on the above reasoning (e.g. Chen 1995). Leung (1995b) has advanced a contextual model to integrate conflicting results. He argues that the nature of the social relationship between the allocator of the reward and the recipient (in-group or out-group member) and of the role relationship (supervisor allocating rewards to other performers, or coworkers allocating them to self and coworker) mediates the impact of culture on reward allocation. According to Leung, collectivists should only show an egalitarian division when allocating to an in-group member who is also a coworker. Otherwise, equity is observed. Leung (1995b) encourages cross-cultural researchers to test his model explicitly. He also challenges them to measure directly putative mediating variables such as performance enhancement that underlie reward distribution (Bond et al 1992). Only then can we build persuasive, pan-cultural theories of social behavior (Messick 1988).

Justice researchers have also focused on resource allocation procedures. Procedural concerns involve both the formal steps and the interpersonal style followed by allocators to reach their decisions (Tyler & Bies 1990). Judgments based on procedural justice are typically more convincing in cultures where authority and the decisions of people in power are widely accepted than are judgments based on outcome fairness. Tyler et al (submitted) extended this research across cultures. They argued that the preference for low power distance, which is evident in the United States, is associated with a relative emphasis on procedural rather than instrumental judgments in evaluating authorities. This conclusion was supported by Tyler et al both cross-culturally using Japanese respondents and within culture using an individual measure of preferred power distance.

Psychologists have recently examined human rights observance (Clemence et al 1995, Doise et al 1991, Humana 1992). Doise et al (1994) have linked individuals' positions on human rights to value structures. Future research might additionally consider the distinction between procedural and instrumental concerns.

GROUP PROCESSES

Many social scientists interested in group behavior assume that the phenomena identified in North America are universals. Whether these phenomena vary in strength by culture and whether indigenous approaches may identify wholly different additional phenomena is unclear. Studies of several known behavioral phenomena have found substantially different effects. Social loafing (Latané et al 1979) is not only absent but is significantly reversed in China (Earley 1989), Israel (Earley 1993), and Japan (Matsui et al 1987). In the China and Israel studies, subjects' endorsement of collectivist values predicted enhancement rather than curtailment of performance in group settings. Earley (1994) compared business employees in China and the United States and found Chinese performance was enhanced by a collectively focused training input, whereas US employees responded better to an individually focused input. Employees' collectivism scores predicted both culture-level and individual-level effects.

Bond & Smith (1995) report a meta-analysis of 133 replications of the Asch conformity study. After design variations are accounted for, Hofstede's collectivism scores predict higher levels of conformity. Replications of this type, however, can only detect the type of social influence processes captured by the Asch paradigm. Fernandez Dols (1992) proposes that in some cultures conformity processes may operate in a rather different manner. He finds a higher incidence of "perverse" norms in Spain than in Anglo countries. These are norms that are agreed to exist but that are only rarely enforced. Triandis (1995) identified cultures in which this type of norm is widespread as "loose" rather than "tight." Whereas the Asch paradigm shows conformity to depend upon majority size, Fernandez Dols argued that within a system of perverse norms, authority figures can maintain control by determining when norms will be enforced and when they will not.

Basic aspects of group performance, such as productivity and conformity, thus differ substantially by culture. These differences may well prove problematic in multicultural teams. Merritt & Helmreich (1995) found that US airline pilots and flight attendants endorsed lower power distance and collectivism than did pilots and attendants within the same airlines from seven East Asian countries. Anglo student groups were found to be less cooperative toward others than were non-Anglo groups (Cox et al 1991) and more in favor of risk-taking (Watson & Kumar 1992). However, although culturally diverse student teams experienced more difficulties in working together initially, Watson et al (1993) found their related performance three months later superior to that of culturally homogeneous teams.

Leadership

In his summary of an extensive program of leadership research in Japan, Misumi (1985) proposed that researchers distinguish between *general* or universal functions that effective leaders must carry out and the *specific* ways in which these functions are expressed. The P (Task Performance) and M (Group Maintenance) general leadership functions that, according to Misumi, predict leadership effectiveness resemble dimensions postulated by North American researchers. The more significant aspect of Misumi's Japanese results is that they consistently indicate that different *specific* behaviors contribute to each function in differing situations. Smith et al (1989) obtained similar results in their comparison of assembly-line workers' perceptions of supervisors in Japan, Hong Kong, the United States, and Great Britain. For instance, a *specific* behavior such as eating lunch with one's work team was associated with a high M score in some locations but not in others.

Misumi's work suggests a way in which one can better understand apparent contradictions between the results of different leadership studies. We may expect that studies that used relatively *general* characterizations of leader style will yield evidence of cross-cultural consistency in effectiveness, whereas studies of more *specific* leader attributes will detect cultural or organizational contingencies. In the remainder of this paragraph we consider studies that have used *general* style measures. Smith et al (1992) found that work teams within Japan, Hong Kong, the United States, and Great Britain led by leaders rated high for P and M all achieved higher work quality. Bass & Avolio's (1993) review of cross-cultural tests of their theory of transformational leadership indicates greater efficacy of the transformational style from 14 countries. Furthermore, Campbell et al (1993) found no difference in preference for participation in decision-making between US and Singaporean business students. Finally, Furnham & Stringfield (1994) found no difference in ratings on attributes such as innovation and commitment among Chinese and non-Chinese managers working for a Hong Kong airline. The results of these studies are as one may expect for studies using generalized measures of leader style.

Other cross-cultural studies of leadership (reviewed by Dorfman 1995) have been influenced by Western contingency theories and have consequently focused more upon *specific* attributes of effective leadership than the *general* functions that may underlie variations in leadership style. Okechuku (1994) found differences in the perceived traits associated with managers' ratings of effective subordinates in Canada, Hong Kong, and China, as did Black & Porter (1991), who compared managers' ratings in the United States and Hong Kong. Gerstner & Day (1994) asked students originally from eight different nations residing in the United States to rate how well 59 traits typified a business leader. The three country-level dimensions that were identified correlated highly with Hofstede dimensions of individualism, power distance, and uncertainty avoidance. Ayman & Chemers (1991) found some support for Fiedler & Chemers' (1984) contingency-based leader match theory among Mexican workers. Schmidt & Yeh (1992) compared leader influence in Japan, Taiwan, Australia, and Great Britain. Although a broadly similar range of influence strategies was found, they factored together distinctively within each national sample. Howell et al (1995), who contrasted business-leader effectiveness in Japan, Korea, Taiwan, Mexico, and the United States, found general effects for leader supportiveness and contingent reward, but cultural specificity for participation in decision-making and contingent punishment. Jago et al (1993) compared preferences to participate of managers in the United States and six European countries and found differences were correlated positively with power-distance scores for the seven countries. The Industrial Democracy in Europe International Research Group (IDE) (1993) carried out a longitudinal replication study of participation in 10 European countries and found differences reported in an earlier study were still apparent, though somewhat attenuated. These studies confirm that when more specific measures of leader style are employed, cultural differences are more apparent.

Decision-Making

If the generality of some measures of leader style leaves unclear the relation of leader behavior to cultural constraints, then studies on the making of specific managerial decisions may provide greater clarity. Smith & Peterson (1988) proposed an analysis of leadership based around the concept of "event management," i.e. the exercise of choice in how events are managed. They suggest that managers handle events on the basis of their own experience, consultation with others, reliance upon rules, and so forth. Smith et al (1994a) surveyed managers in 16 countries and found that in individualist, low power distance nations, managers rely more heavily on their own experience and training than do those from collectivist, high power distance countries. Hofstede's country-level value measures thus predict reported managerial behaviors, despite a 25-year gap in data collection. Further studies of event management show differences in how Japanese, British, and American electronic assembly work teams handle events (Peterson et al 1990). Work teams judged most effective by their supervisors show, in Japan, more reliance on peers; in the United States, more reference to superiors; and, in Great Britain, greater self-reliance (Smith et al 1994b). Tse et al (1988) found Chinese managers more inclined than Hong Kong Chinese or Canadians to refer to their superiors. Wang & Heller (1993) compared decision-making of British and Chinese managers and found both nation and type of decision affected the degree of subordinate participation and supervisor consultation.

Yates & Lee (1995) found Chinese and several other East Asian groups (but not Japanese) more confident than Americans that their decisions were correct. They attribute this to a greater propensity to select the first adequate problem solution that is identified rather than to survey a range of alternatives before deciding. Radford et al (1991, 1993) found differences in decision-making style between Australian and Japanese students. Consistent with US counterparts from earlier research, Australians favored the "choice" style, which emphasizes careful individual thought. The Japanese, however, reported greater use of three other styles, which all involved greater reference to others. As Yates & Lee also found, the Japanese were less confident of their decisions. These differences may be explicable in terms of variations in individualism-collectivism among East Asian countries, Australia, and the United States.

Negotiation

Group processes within cross-cultural negotiation should provide particularly clear illustrations of the effects of divergence in values across cultures. Studies of intracultural simulated buyer-seller negotiations indicate that while cooperative problem-solving strategies are most effective in the United States, competitive behavior works better in Russia (Graham et al 1992), Taiwan (Graham et al 1988), Germany, Great Britain (Campbell et al 1988), Mexico, and Francophone Canada (Adler et al 1987). Similarly, Gabrenya (1990) found that US students cooperated on a task better with strangers than did Taiwanese students. These results support the view that members of collectivist cultures are more competitive with out-groups than are members of individualist cultures. This proposition is tested more directly by DKS Chan, HC Triandis, PJ Carnevale, A Tam, MH Bond (submitted), who compared intracultural negotiation behavior of Hong Kong Chinese and US students and obtained measures of their individualist or collectivist values. Hong Kong students responded more to cooperation and yielded to an in-group negotiator more than to an out-group negotiator. Similar differences were obtained by Trubisky et al (1991), who compared intracultural conflict resolution preferences of US and Taiwanese students. The authors of both studies attributed their results to differences in individualism-collectivism. In a more detailed review of culture and negotiation, Leung (1995b) concludes that behavior is influenced both by variations in individualism-collectivism and by specific situational demands.

How closely the processes of intracultural and intercultural negotiation parallel one another remains unclear. Tse et al (1994) compared intracultural and intercultural negotiating behaviors of Chinese and Canadian executives. Neither party modified its approach when negotiating cross-culturally. Chinese negotiators sought to avoid conflict more than the Canadians, and when conflict did arise Chinese favored withdrawal or consultation with superiors more strongly. However, Adler & Graham (1989) did find some changes in negotiators' behavior when they engaged in intercultural negotiations. Japanese negotiators achieved lower payoffs negotiating with Americans than with other Japanese. Anglophone Canadians achieved lower payoffs in negotiations with Francophone Canadians, despite the fact that the Francophones became more cooperative when negotiating interculturally. Some caution is needed in equating payoff with success in this type of study because collectivists may regard maintenance of long-term links as a more important success criterion than short-term payoff.

Three studies show how social context and understanding of the other party's preferred communication styles are crucial to successful outcome. Qualitative analyses are provided by Goldman (1994) for US-Japanese negotiations and by Kimmel (1994) for US-Iraqi negotiations prior to the Gulf War. Marriott (1993) reports how seating arrangements affected Japanese-Australian business negotiations.

ORGANIZATIONAL BEHAVIOR

Work Motivation

The role of work may be expected to reflect salient dimensions of a society's values. The Meaning of Working International Team (MOW) (1987) performed surveys in the United States, Japan, and six West European countries and found so-called "work centrality" highest in Japan. The MOW study has been replicated and extended to China and six East European countries (SA Ruiz Quintanilla & GW England, submitted). The MOW team conclude that work meanings can be represented along a single axis on which, at one end, are situated the costs to the individual and, at the other end, the collective benefits of work. The Work Socialization of Youth project (WOSY) (Touzard 1992) is a longitudinal study that compares work role socialization in seven West European countries and Israel and uses the same concepts developed by the MOW team. The WOSY researchers found that changes in patterns of work meaning over the first three years at work were predicted by both individual- and country-level variables, but the researchers did not analyze their results in terms of cross-cultural theory (Claes & Ruiz Quintanilla 1993).

Misra et al (1990) found greater linkage between work and family concerns in India than in Canada. Schwalb et al (1992) found that Japanese employees reported being motivated by the task itself, self-improvement, and financial reward, in contrast with a greater US emphasis upon affiliation, social concern, and recognition. Holt & Keats (1992) compared Anglo, Chinese, Lebanese, and Aboriginal Australians. While all valued achievement highly, the degree to which achievement related to work varied greatly. These results indicate the need for revision of the earlier view that achievement motivation is particularly strong in individualist cultures, and that individualistic entrepreneurialism is a prerequisite for economic development (McClelland 1961). Achievement motivation, at least in East Asian collectivist cultures, is more socially oriented (Yu 1995, Yu & Yang 1994), which may also foster entrepreneurial activity (Redding 1990). Whether achievement motivation centers upon work is dependent upon the values of a culture, and this variation can lead to unexpected findings. Xie & Jamal's (1993) study of Chinese managers, for example, illustrates that Type A managers reported more job stress than Type B managers, as in Western studies. However, the two groups showed no difference in psychosomatic problems, and Type A managers spent more time with their families. Thus the Western pattern of compulsive working with attendant health risks appears here to be attenuated by the centrality of family within Chinese culture.

Agarwal (1993) found positive effects of reliance on rules and normalization in handling role conflict and ambiguity among salespersons in India, but negative effects in the United States. Dubinsky et al (1992) compared role ambiguity and role conflict among salespersons in the United States, Japan, and Korea. Few effects due to culture were detected. Several researchers have examined the relation of work stress to Hofstede scores for particular countries. Shenkar & Zeira (1992) studied role ambiguity of chief executives within international joint ventures in Israel. Role ambiguity was greatest where the scores for power distance and masculinity among partners' countries were most divergent. Peterson et al (1995) surveyed managers in 21 countries and reported role overload was greatest in high power distance, collectivist nations whereas reported role ambiguity was greatest in low power distance, individualist nations.

Work Behavior

Several studies discussed earlier that were designed to identify dimensions of cultural variation were based upon employees' reported values or behavior. This section considers more specific aspects of work behavior. Luthans et al (1993) made an observational study of Russian managers and compared the results to earlier studies of US managers. Although the pattern of their activities showed considerable similarities, the Russians spent less time on networking and more on planning, controlling, and coordinating. Boisot & Liang (1992) observed a small sample of Chinese managers. The managers spent more time with their superiors and received much more written material from them than was the case in earlier US studies.

Comparisons between Hong Kong and US managers have proved popular. Schermerhorn & Bond (1991) compared managers' preferred influence tactics and found Hong Kong respondents preferred assertiveness and the Americans preferred rationality, exchange, and ingratiation. Ralston et al (1992, 1993) found Hong Kong managers rated higher for Machiavellianism, external locus of control, dogmatism, and Confucian Work Dynamism. Most of these effects were found also among mainland Chinese managers. Black & Porter (1991) compared performance appraisals received by managers in the United States and Hong Kong with managers' self-rated traits derived from US leadership theory. High correlations between traits and performance appraisals were found in the United States but were not found for either Chinese or US managers working in Hong Kong. Similar conclusions were reached by Furnham & Stringfield (1993), who found that quite different traits were significantly linked to performance measures among Chinese and European managers working for the same Hong Kong airline.

Bochner & Hesketh (1994) studied Australian bank employees whose ethnic identity was with either high (e.g. Hong Kong) or low (e.g. Great Britain) power distance cultures. The high power distance group reported significantly more behaviors likely to be expected from high power distance, collectivist cultures and reported experiencing more discrimination than did respondents from the majority, low power distance group. Wong & Birnbaum-More (1994) found that among banks in Hong Kong the degree of centralization and hierarchy could be predicted by the Hofstede power distance score of the country owning the bank.

Organizational researchers have also sought to delineate the relationship between organizational culture and national culture. Morris et al (1994) compared the incidence of entrepreneurial corporate climate in US, South African, and Portuguese organizations. Within-country analyses revealed that within the United States and South Africa, respondents' endorsement of moderate levels of individualism-collectivism was associated with the highest endorsement of entrepreneurial values. Van Muijen & Koopman (1994) report results from the FOCUS 92 group, which surveyed perceptions of organizational climate in 10 European nations. Differences in mean country scores on preference for innovation paralleled Hofstede's individualism scores, but rules-orientation did not accord with any of the Hofstede scores. Janssens et al (1995) compared perceptions of safety policy within US, French, and Argentinian plants of the same US multinational corporation. Although a company-wide policy was in force, its implementation varied in ways that were interpreted in terms of individualism-collectivism. Hofstede et al (1990) identified six dimensions of organizational culture within organizations in Denmark and the Netherlands. Hofstede et al (1993) further illustrated the importance of employing the appropriate level of data analysis in characterizing individual values, organizational culture, or national culture.

CONCLUSIONS

Kagitcibasi & Berry (1989) concluded that three trends were apparent within the field of cross-cultural psychology in the late 1980s: a focus upon individualism-collectivism, increasing concern to develop indigenous psychologies, and the search for cultural universals. Our coverage indicates that since then the first of these issues has attracted the attention of more and more researchers. While this increased attention has served to focus cross-cultural psychology more clearly, it has led to the comparative neglect of other approaches deriving from Kagitcibasi & Berry's second and third areas. The search for universals and an emphasis upon indigenous culture-specifics are often cast as contradictory enterprises that exemplify contrasting etic and emic approaches. Yet these concepts are no more separable than nature and nurture. If the recently emerging dimensions of culture identified by Hofstede, Schwartz, Smith and others are to guide future research in fruitful directions, the methodological problems stemming from the etic-emic dilemma must be more clearly addressed.

Berry (1989) proposes a sequence in research whereby parallel indigenous studies within two or more societies may lead to a validly generalized universal or derived etic, in contrast to the currently much more widespread reliance on imposed-etic measures drawn from a small number of Western countries. Although many believe Berry's procedure is preferable, imposed-etic measures will likely continue to be much more widely used. In these circumstances, we need estimates of what types of cultural variance are missed by imposed-etic measures. Studies designed from a non-Western starting point such as the one by the Chinese Culture Connection (1987) are crucial. The increasing number of recent studies whose results compare well with already identified dimensions of cultural variation also enhance the argument for convergent validity (Bond 1995). The testing of hypotheses linking emergent dimensions of cultural values or beliefs to external-distal country-level data is another welcome trend (Best & Williams 1994; DKS Chan, submitted; Smith et al 1995a,b; Williams 1993)

However, numerous pitfalls along the path toward a well-validated framework for cross-cultural studies remain. First, this review demonstrates how the sampling of national cultures within recent studies is woefully biased. Current studies heavily overrepresent North America, East Asia, and Western Europe, with consequent neglect of Latin American, African, East European, Arab, South Asian, and other societies. Second, the strongly individualistic values of the cultures from which most researchers are drawn result in confusion regarding the appropriate levels of analysis of cross-cultural data. Most current culture-level analyses are based upon aggregation of individual-level data, and reviewers used by major North American journals rather often require that researchers engage in individual-level data analyses, which is inappropriate to a culture-level analysis. Appropriate-level variables must be used if we are to understand variation at a given level (Hofstede et al 1993). Equally invalid extrapolations are also widespread in the reverse direction: Researchers infer that because culture X has certain values, individuals within that culture will share those values. Separate individual-level variables are needed. Schwartz's (1994) recent large-scale surveys show how individual-level analyses yield results different from culture-level analyses and provide relatively comprehensive guidelines with respect to intracultural continuities in the structure of values.

Third, how do we define the boundaries of one's cultural samples? Most studies use national affiliation, but the existing and increasing cultural diversity of many nations makes this strategy unsatisfactory. However, if future researchers routinely include measures of the salient values and ethnic identities of the samples they study, comparisons with other studies with somewhat more established theoretical roots may be made. Furthermore, the growing cultural heterogeneity both of nations and of smaller social systems within them will require that researchers progress from documenting contrasts between different cultures toward examining the ways in which individuals and groups from different cultures relate to one another. In doing so, they may broaden the cultural range encompassed by existing literatures concerning intergroup relations, stereotyping, conflict, communication, and so forth.

Although the methodological problems facing cross-cultural researchers should not be minimized, we do not wish to conclude this review on a pessimistic note. Cross-cultural social and organizational psychology has for the first time a theoretical framework upon which studies may be designed and relevant samples may be selected. That framework must be scrutinized, of course, but a set of dimensions of cultural variation proven to predict social phenomena is now available to researchers. While the definition of individualism and collectivism as polar opposites will certainly prove unable to integrate the full range of global variations in social behavior, further progress can be expected in defining just how many dimensions are required for optimal parsimony.

Literature Cited

Adair JG, Puhan BN, Vohra H. 1993. The indigenisation of psychology: empirical assessment of progress in Indian research. *Int. J. Psychol.* 28:761–73

Adamopoulos J. 1988. Interpersonal behavior: cross-cultural and historical perspectives. See Bond 1988, pp. 196–207

Adler NJ. 1991. *International Dimensions of Organizational Behavior.* Boston: PWS-Kent. 2nd ed

Adler NJ, Graham JL. 1989. Cross-cultural comparison: the international comparison fallacy. *J. Int. Bus. Stud.* 20:515–38

Adler NJ, Graham JL, Schwarz T. 1987. Business negotiations in Canada, Mexico and the United States. *J. Bus. Res.* 15: 411–29

Agarwal S. 1993. Influence of formalisation on role stress, organizational commitment and work alienation of salespersons: a cross-national comparative study. *J. Int. Bus. Stud.* 24:715–39

Amir Y, Sharon I. 1987. Are social psychological laws cross-culturally valid? *J. Cross-Cult. Psychol.* 18:383–470

Ayman R, Chemers MM. 1991. The effect of leadership match on subordinate satisfaction in Mexican organisations: some moderating influences of self-monitoring. *Appl. Psychol.: Int. Rev.* 40:299–314

Bass BM, Avolio B. 1993. Transformational leadership: a response to critiques. In *Leadership Theory and Research,* ed. MM Chemers, R Ayman, pp. 49–80. San Diego: Academic

Berman JJ, Murphy-Berman V, Singh P. 1985. Cross-cultural similarities and differences in perceptions of fairness. *J. Cross-Cult. Psychol.* 16:55–67

Berry JW. 1979. A cultural ecology of social behavior. In *Advances in Experimental Social Psychology,* ed. L Berkowitz, 12: 177–206. New York: Academic

Berry JW. 1989. Imposed etics-emics-derived etics: the operationalisation of a compelling idea. *Int. J. Psychol.* 24:721–35

Berry JW, Poortinga YH, Segall MH, Dasen PR. 1992. *Cross-Cultural Psychology: Research and Applications.* Cambridge: Cambridge Univ. Press

Berry JW, Segall MH, Kagitcibasi C, eds. 1996. *Handbook of Cross-Cultural Psychology,* Vol. 3, *Social Psychology, Personality and Psychopathology.* Needham, MA: Allyn & Bacon. In press

Best DL, Williams JE. 1994. Masculinity/femininity in the self and ideal self-descriptions of university students in fourteen countries. See Bouvy et al 1994, pp. 297–306

Black JS, Porter LW. 1991. Managerial behaviors and job performance: a successful

manager in Los Angeles may not succeed in Hong Kong. *J. Int. Bus. Stud.* 22:99–113

Bochner S. 1994. Cross-cultural differences in the self concept: a test of Hofstede's individualism/collectivism distinction. *J. Cross-Cult. Psychol.* 25:273–83

Bochner S, Hesketh B. 1994. Power distance, individualism/collectivism and job-related attitudes in a culturally-diverse work group. *J. Cross-Cult. Psychol.* 25:233–57

Boisot M, Liang XG. 1992. The nature of managerial work in the Chinese enterprise reforms: a study of six directors. *Organ. Stud.* 13:161–84

Bond MH, ed. 1986. *The Psychology of the Chinese People.* Hong Kong: Oxford Univ. Press

Bond MH. 1988. *The Cross-Cultural Challenge to Social Psychology.* Newbury Park, CA: Sage

Bond MH. 1991. Chinese values and health: a cross-cultural examination. *Psychol. Health* 5:137–52

Bond MH. 1994. Trait theory and cross-cultural studies of person perception. *Psychol. Inq.* 5:114–17

Bond MH, ed. 1995. *Handbook of Chinese Psychology.* Hong Kong: Oxford Univ. Press. In press

Bond MH, Cheung TS. 1983. The spontaneous self-concept of college students in Hong Kong, Japan, and the United States. *J. Cross-Cult. Psychol.* 14:153–71

Bond MH, Forgas JP. 1984. Linking person perception to behavioral intention across cultures: the role of cultural collectivism. *J. Cross-Cult. Psychol.* 15:337–52

Bond MH, Leung K, Schwartz S. 1992. Explaining choices in procedural and distributive justice across cultures. *Int. J. Psychol.* 27:211–25

Bond MH, Leung K, Wan KC. 1982. How does cultural collectivism operate? The impact of task and maintenance contributions on reward allocation. *J. Cross-Cult. Psychol.* 13:186–200

Bond R, Smith PB. 1995. Culture and conformity: a meta-analysis of the Asch line judgment task. *Psychol. Bull.* In press

Bontempo R. 1993. Translation fidelity of psychological scales: an item response theory analysis of an individualism-collectivism scale. *J. Cross-Cult. Psychol.* 24:149–66

Bouvy AM, van de Vijver FJR, Boski P, Schmitz P, eds. 1994. *Journeys into Cross-Cultural Psychology.* Amsterdam: Swets & Zeitlinger

Brislin R. 1993. *Understanding Culture's Influence on Behavior.* Fort Worth, TX: Harcourt, Brace, Jovanovich

Buss DM, Abbott M, Angelitner A, Asherian

A, Biaggio A, et al. 1990. International preferences in selecting mates: a study of 37 cultures. *J. Cross-Cult. Psychol.* 21: 5–47

Campbell D, Bommer W, Yeo E. 1993. Perceptions of appropriate leadership style: participation versus consultation across two cultures. *Asia Pac. J. Manage.* 10:1–19

Campbell N, Graham JL, Jolibert A, Meissner HG. 1988. Marketing negotiations in France, Germany, the United Kingdom and the United States. *J. Mark.* 52:49–62

Chan SCN, Bond MH. 1995. *Cultural values and social health.* Presented at Eur. Congr. Psychol., Athens

Chang YC, Lin W, Lohnstamm GA. 1994. *Parents' free descriptions of children's characteristics—a verified study of the Big Five in Chinese children.* Presented at Int. Soc. Stud. Behav. Dev., Beijing

Chasiotis A, Keller H. 1994. Evolutionary psychology and developmental cross-cultural psychology. See Bouvy et al 1994, pp. 6–82

Chen CC. 1995. New trends in rewards allocation preferences: a Sino-US comparison. *Acad. Manage. J.* 38:408–28

Cheng C, Bond MH, Chan SC. 1995. The perception of ideal best friends by Chinese adolescents. *Int. J. Psychol.* 30:91–108

Chinese Culture Connection. 1987. Chinese values and the search for culture-free dimensions of culture. *J. Cross-Cult. Psychol.* 18:143–64

Claes R, Ruiz Quintanilla SA. 1993. Work meaning patterns in early career. *Eur. Work Organ. Psychol.* 3:311–23

Clemence A, Doise W, Rosa AS, Gonzalez L. 1995. La representation sociale des droits de l'homme: une recherche internationale sur l'etendue et les limites de l'universalite. *Int. J. Psychol.* In press

Costa PT Jr, McCrae RR. 1992. Four ways five factors are basic. *Pers. Indiv. Diff.* 13: 653–65

Cox T, Lobel S, McLeod PL. 1991. Effects of ethnic group cultural differences on cooperative and competitive behavior on a group task. *Acad. Manage. J.* 34:827–47

Crittenden KS. 1995. Causal attribution processes among the Chinese. See Bond 1995

Crocker J, Luhtanen R, Blaine B, Broadnax S. 1994. Collective self-esteem and psychological well-being among White, Black, and Asian college students. *Pers. Soc. Psychol. Bull.* 20:503–13

Cunningham MR. 1986. Measuring the physical in physical attractiveness: quasi-experiments on the sociology of female facial beauty. *J. Pers. Soc. Psychol.* 50:925–35

DeGooyer MJ, Williams JE. 1992. A comparison of self-concepts in Japan and the United States. See Iwawaki et al 1992, pp. 279–88

Der-Kerabetian A. 1992. World-mindedness and the nuclear threat: a multinational study. *J. Soc. Behav. Pers.* 7:293–303

Dion KK, Dion KL. 1991. Psychological individualism and romantic love. *J. Soc. Behav. Pers.* 6:17–33

Dion KK, Dion KL. 1993. Individualistic and collectivistic perspectives on gender and the cultural context of love and intimacy. *J. Soc. Issues* 49:53–69

Dion KL, Dion KK. 1993. Gender and ethnocultural comparisons in styles of love. *Psychol. Women Q.* 17:463–73

Dixon RMW. 1977. Where have all the adjectives gone? *Stud. Lang.* 1:19–80

Doise W, Dell' Ambrogio P, Spini D. 1991. Psychologie sociale et Droits del' Homme. *Rev. Int. Psychol. Soc.* 4:257–77

Doise W, Spini D, Jesuino JC, Ng SH, Emler N. 1994. Values and perceived conflicts in the social representations of human rights: feasibility of a cross-national study. *Swiss J. Psychol.* 53:240–51

Dorfman PW. 1995. International and cross-cultural leadership research. See Punnett & Shenkar 1995

Dubinsky A, Michaels RE, Kotabe M, Lim CU, Moon HC. 1992. Influence of role stress on industrial salespeople's work outcomes in the United States, Japan and Korea. *J. Int. Bus. Stud.* 23:77–99

Earley PC. 1989. Social loafing and collectivism: a comparison of the United States and the People's Republic of China. *Adm. Sci. Q.* 34:565–81

Earley PC. 1993. East meets West meets Mideast: further explorations of collectivistic and individualistic work groups. *Acad. Manage. J.* 36:319–48

Earley PC. 1994. Self or group: cultural effects of training on self-efficacy and performance. *Adm. Sci. Q.* 39:89–117

Earley PC, Erez M, eds. 1996. *New Perspectives on International Industrial/Organizational Psychology.* San Francisco: Jossey Bass. In press

Earley PC, Mosakowski E. 1995. A framework for understanding experimental research in an international and intercultural context. See Punnett & Shenkar 1995

Easton D, Shelling CS, eds. 1991. *Divided Knowledge: Across Disciplines, Across Cultures.* Newbury Park, CA: Sage

Ellis BB, Becker P, Kimmel HD. 1993. An item response theory evaluation of an English version of the Trier Personality Inventory (TPI). *J. Cross-Cult. Psychol.* 24: 133–48

Ellis BB, Kimmel HD, Diaz Guerrero R, Canas J, Bajo MT. 1995. Love and power in Mexico, Spain and the United States. *J. Cross-Cult. Psychol.* 25:525–40

Ellsworth PC. 1994. Sense, culture, sensibility. See Kitayama & Markus 1994, pp. 23–50

Erez M, Earley PC. 1993. *Culture, Self-Identity and Work.* New York: Oxford Univ. Press

Feather NT. 1988. From values to actions: recent applications of the expectancy-value model. *Aust. J. Psychol.* 40:105–24

Feather NT. 1994. Values, national identification and in-group favouritism. *Br. J. Soc. Psychol.* 33:467–76

Feather NT, McKee IR. 1993. Global self-esteem and attitudes toward the high achiever for Australian and Japanese students. *Soc. Psychol. Q.* 56:65–76

Fernandez Dols JP. 1992. Procesos escabrosos en psicologia social: el concepto de norma perversa. *Rev. Psicol. Soc.* 7:243–55

Fiedler FE, Chemers MM. 1984. *Improving Leadership Effectiveness: The Leader Match Concept.* New York: Wiley

Fiske AP. 1992. The four elementary forms of sociality: framework for a unified theory of social relations. *Psychol. Rev.* 99:689–723

Fiske AP. 1993. Social errors in four cultures: evidence about universal forms of social relations. *J. Cross-Cult. Psychol.* 24:463–94

Frijda NH, Mesquita B. 1994. The social roles and functions of emotions. See Kitayama & Markus 1994, pp. 51–87

Furnham A. 1993. Just world beliefs in twelve societies. *J. Soc. Psychol.* 133:317–29

Furnham A, Bond MH, Heaven P, Hilton D, Lobel T, et al. 1993. A comparison of Protestant work ethic beliefs in thirteen nations. *J. Soc. Psychol.* 133:185–97

Furnham A, Stringfield P. 1993. Personality and occupational behavior: Myers-Briggs Type indicator correlates of managerial practices in two cultures. *Hum. Relat.* 46:827–48

Furnham A, Stringfield P. 1994. Congruence of self and subordinate ratings of managerial practices as a correlate of supervisor evaluation. *J. Occup. Organ. Psychol.* 67:57–68

Gabrenya WK. 1988. Social science and social psychology: the cross-cultural link. See Bond 1988, pp. 48–66

Gabrenya WK. 1990. *Dyadic social interaction during task behavior in collectivist and individualist societies.* Presented at Workshop on Individualism-Collectivism, Seoul, Korea

Gerstner CR, Day DV. 1994. Cross-cultural comparison of leadership prototypes. *Leadersh. Q.* 5:121–34

Gielen UP. 1994. American mainstream psychology and its relationship to international and cross-cultural psychology. In *Advancing Psychology and Its Applications: International Perspectives,* ed. AL Comunian, UP Gielen, pp. 26–40. Milan: Angel

Giles HA, Viladot A. 1994. Ethnolinguistic differentiation in Catalonia. *Multilingua: J.*

Cross-Cult. Interlang. Commun. 13:301–12

Goldman A. 1994. The centrality of 'ningensei' to Japanese negotiating and interpersonal relationships: implications for US-Japanese communication. *Int. J. Intercult. Relat.* 18:29–54

Goodwin R, Tang D. 1991. Preferences for friends and close relationship partners. *J. Soc. Psychol.* 131:579–81

Graham JL, Evenko LI, Rajan MN. 1992. An empirical comparison of Soviet and American business negotiations. *J. Int. Bus. Stud.* 23:387–418

Graham JL, Kim DK, Lin CY, Robinson R. 1988. Buyer-seller negotiations around the Pacific Rim: differences in fundamental exchange processes. *J. Consum. Res.* 15:48–54

Gudykunst WB, ed. 1993. *Communication in Japan and the United States.* Albany: S. Univ. NY

Gudykunst WB, Matsumoto Y, Ting-Toomey S, Nishida T, Karimi H. 1994. *Measuring self-construals across cultures: a derived-etic analysis.* Int. Commun. Assoc., Sydney

Hatfield E, Rapson RL. 1993. Historical and cross-cultural perspectives on passionate love and sexual desire. *Annu. Rev. Sex Res.* 4:67–97

Ho EKF. 1994. *Validating the five-factor model of personality.* BA thesis. Chinese Univ. Hong Kong

Hofstede G. 1980. *Culture's Consequences: International Differences in Work-Related Values.* Beverly Hills, CA: Sage

Hofstede G, Bond MH, Luk CL. 1993. Individual perceptions of organisational cultures: a methodological treatise on levels of analysis. *Organ. Stud.* 14:483–503

Hofstede G, Neuyen B, Ohayv DD, Sanders G. 1990. Measuring organizational cultures: a qualitative and quantitative study across twenty cases. *Adm. Sci. Q.* 35:286–316

Hogan RT, Emler NP. 1978. The biases in contemporary social psychology. *Soc. Res.* 45:478–534

Holt J, Keats DM. 1992. Work cognitions in multicultural interaction. *J. Cross-Cult. Psychol.* 23:421–43

Howell JP, Dorfman PW, Hibino S, Lee JK, Tate U. 1995. Leadership in Western and Asian countries: commonalities and differences in effective leadership processes and substitutes across cultures. Las Cruces: New Mex. State Univ.

Hui CH, Triandis HC. 1989. Effects of culture and response format on extreme response style. *J. Cross-Cult. Psychol.* 20:296–309

Humana C. 1992. *World Human Rights Guide.* New York: Oxford

Industrial Democracy in Europe International Research Group. 1993. *Industrial Democ-*

racy in Europe Revisited. Oxford: Oxford Univ. Press

Ip GWM, Bond MH. 1995. Culture, values, and the spontaneous self-concept. *Asian J. Psychol.* 1:30–36

Iwawaki S, Kashima Y, Leung K, eds. 1992. *Innovations in Cross-Cultural Psychology.* Amsterdam: Swets & Zeitlinger

Jago AG, Reber G, Bohnisch W, Maczynski J, Zavrel J, et al. 1993. *Culture's consequence? A seven nation study of participation.* Presented at Decis. Sci. Inst., Washington, DC

Janssens M, Brett J, Smith FJ. 1995. Confirmatory cross-cultural research: testing the viability of a corporate-wide safety policy. *Acad. Manage. J.* 38:364–82

Kagitcibasi C, Berry JW. 1989. Cross-cultural psychology: current research and trends. *Annu. Rev. Psychol.* 40:493–531

Kagitcibasi C. 1995. *Family and Human Development Across Cultures: A View from the Other Side.* Hillsdale, NJ: Erlbaum

Kashima Y, Siegel M, Tanaka K, Kashima ES. 1992. Do people believe behaviors are consistent with attitudes? Towards a cultural psychology of attribution processes. *Br. J. Soc. Psychol.* 31:111–24

Kashima Y, Triandis HC. 1986. The self-serving bias in attributions as a coping strategy: a cross-cultural study. *J. Cross-Cult. Psychol.* 17:83–97

Keats DM, Munro D, Mann L. 1989. *Heterogeneity in Cross-Cultural Psychology.* Amsterdam: Swets & Zeitlinger

Kim U, Berry JW, eds. 1993. *Indigenous Psychologies: Research and Experience in Context.* Newbury Park, CA: Sage

Kim U, Triandis HC, Kagitcibasi C, Choi SC, Yoon G, eds. 1994. *Individualism and Collectivism: Theory, Method and Applications.* Newbury Park, CA: Sage

Kimmel PR. 1994. Cultural perspectives on international negotiations. *J. Soc. Issues* 50: 179–96

Kitayama S, Markus HR, eds. 1994. *Emotion and Culture: Empirical Studies of Mutual Influence.* Washington, DC: Am. Psychol. Assoc.

Komin S. 1990. Culture and work-related values in Thai organisations. *Int. J. Psychol.* 25:681–704

Kohn ML. 1987. Cross-national research as an analytic strategy. *Am. Soc. Rev.* 52: 713–31

Kohn ML, Schoonbach C, Schooler C, Slomczynski KM. 1990. Position in the class structure and psychological functioning in the United States, Japan and Poland. *Am. J. Soc.* 95:964–1008

Krewer B, Jahoda G. 1993. Psychologie et culture: vers une solution de Babel? *Int. J. Psychol.* 28:367–76

Latané B, Williams K, Harkins S. 1979. Many hands make light the work: causes and consequences of social loafing. *J. Pers. Soc. Psychol.* 37:822–32

Leung JP, Leung K. 1992. Life satisfaction, self-concept and relationship with parents in adolescence. *J. Youth Adolesc.* 21: 653–65

Leung K. 1995a. Beliefs in Chinese culture. See Bond 1995

Leung K. 1995b. Negotiation and reward allocations across cultures. See Earley & Erez 1996

Leung K, Bond MH. 1989. On the empirical identification of dimensions for cross-cultural comparison. *J. Cross-Cult. Psychol.* 20:133–51

Leung K, Bond MH, Schwartz S. 1994. *How To Explain Cross-Cultural Differences: Values, Valences and Expectancies?* Hong Kong: Chinese Univ.

Levine R, Sato S, Hashimoto T, Verma J. 1995. Love and marriage in eleven cultures. *J. Cross-Cult. Psychol.* In press

Linssen H, Hagendoorn L. 1994. Social and geographic factors in the explanation of the content of European nationality stereotypes. *Br. J. Soc. Psychol.* 33:165–82

Liston A, Salts CJ. 1988. Mate selection values: a comparison of Malaysian and United States students. *J. Comp. Fam. Stud.* 19: 361–70

Lonner WJ. 1980. The search for psychological universals. See Triandis & Lambert 1980, pp. 143–204

Lonner WJ, Malpass R, eds. 1994. *Psychology and Culture.* Boston: Allyn & Bacon

Luhtanen R, Crocker J. 1992. A collective self-esteem scale: self-evaluation of one's social identity. *Pers. Soc. Psychol. Bull.* 18: 302–18

Luk CL, Bond MH. 1992. Chinese lay beliefs about the causes and cures of psychological problems. *J. Clin. Soc. Psychol.* 11: 140–57

Luthans F, Welsh DHB, Rosenkrantz SA. 1993. What do Russian managers really do? An observational study with comparisons to US managers. *J. Int. Bus. Stud.* 24: 741–61

Lytle A, Brett JM, Barsness ZI, Tinsley CH, Janssens M. 1995. A paradigm for confirmatory cross-cultural research in organizational behavior. *Res. Organ. Behav.* 17: 167–214

Marin G, Gamba RJ, Marin BV. 1993. Extreme response style and acquiescence among Hispanics: the role of acculturation and education. *J. Cross-Cult. Psychol.* 23:498–509

Marin G, Marin BV. 1991. *Research with Hispanic Populations.* Newbury Park, CA: Sage

Markus HR, Kitayama S. 1991. Culture and the self: implications for cognition, emotion and motivation. *Psychol. Rev.* 98:224–53

Marriott H. 1993. Spatial arrangements in Australian-Japanese business communication. *J. Asian Pac. Commun.* 4:107–26

Matsui T, Kakuyama T, Onglatco ML. 1987. Effects of goals and feedback on performance in groups. *J. Appl. Psychol.* 72:407–15

Matsumoto D. 1994. *People: Psychology from a Cultural Perspective.* Pacific Grove, CA: Brooks/Cole

Matsumoto D, Kudoh T. 1993. American-Japanese cultural differences in attributions of personality based on smiles. *J. Nonverbal Behav.* 17:231–43

Mauro R, Sato K, Tucker J. 1992. The role of appraisal in human emotions: a cross-cultural study. *J. Pers. Soc. Psychol.* 62:301–17

McArthur LZ, Berry DS. 1987. Cross-cultural agreement in perceptions of babyfaced adults. *J. Cross-Cult. Psychol.* 18:165–92

McClelland DC. 1961. *The Achieving Society.* Princeton, NJ: Van Nostrand

Merritt AC, Helmreich RL. 1995. Human factors on the flightdeck: the influence of national culture. *J. Cross-Cult. Psychol.* In press

Mesquita B. 1993. *Cultural variations in emotions: a comparative study of Dutch, Surinamese and Turkish people in the Netherlands.* PhD thesis. Univ. Amsterdam

Mesquita B, Frijda NH. 1992. Cultural variations in emotions: a review. *Psychol. Bull.* 412:179–204

Messick DM. 1988. On the limitations of cross-cultural research in social psychology. See Bond 1988, pp. 41–47

Miller JG. 1994. Cultural diversity in the morality of caring: individually oriented versus duty-based interpersonal moral codes. *Cross-Cult. Res.* 28:3–39

Miller JG, Bersoff DM. 1992. Culture and moral judgment. How are conflicts between justice and interpersonal responsibilities resolved? *J. Pers. Soc. Psychol.* 62:541–54

Misra S, Gergen K. 1993. On the place of culture in psychological science. *Int. J. Psychol.* 28:225–44

Misra S, Ghosh R, Kanungo RN. 1990. Measurement of family involvement: a cross-national study of managers. *J. Cross-Cult. Psychol.* 21:232–48

Misumi J. 1985. *The Behavioral Science of Leadership.* Ann Arbor: Univ. Mich. Press

Moghaddam FM, Taylor DM, Wright SC. 1993. *Social Psychology in Cross-Cultural Perspective.* New York: Freeman

Montepare JM, Zebrowitz LA. 1993. A cross-cultural comparison of impressions created by age-related variations in gait. *J. Nonverbal Behav.* 17:55–68

Morris MH, Davis DL, Allen JW. 1994. Fostering corporate entrepreneurship: cross-cultural comparisons of the importance of individualism versus collectivism. *J. Int. Bus. Stud.* 25:65–89

Morris MW, Peng KP. 1994. Culture and cause: American and Chinese attributions for social and physical events. *J. Pers. Soc. Psychol.* 67:949–71

Murphy G. 1969. Psychology in the year 2000. *Am. Psychol.* 24:523–30

Newman LS. 1993. How individualists interpret behavior: idiocentrism and spontaneous trait inference. *Soc. Cogn.* 11:243–69

Okechuku C. 1994. The relationship of six managerial characteristics to the assessment of managerial effectiveness in Canada, Hong Kong and the People's Republic of China. *J. Occup. Organ. Psychol.* 67:79–86

Ongel U, Smith PB. 1994. Who are we and where are we going? JCCP approaches its 100th issue. *J. Cross-Cult. Psychol.* 25:25–53

Pandey J, Sinha D, Bhawuk DPS, eds. 1995. *Asian Contributions to Cross-Cultural Psychology.* New Delhi: Sage

Paranjpe AC, Ho DYF, Rieber RW, eds. 1988. *Asian Contributions to Psychology.* New York: Praeger

Peng Y, Zebrowitz LA, Lee HK. 1993. The impact of cultural background and cross-cultural experience on impressions of American and Korean speakers. *J. Cross-Cult. Psychol.* 24:203–20

Perrett DI, May KA, Yoshikawa S. 1994. Facial shape and judgments of female attractiveness. *Nature* 368:239–42

Peterson MF, Smith PB, Bond MH, Misumi J. 1990. Personal reliance on alternative event management processes in four countries. *Group Organ. Stud.* 15:75–91

Peterson MF, Smith PB, Akande D, Ayestaran S, Bochner S, et al. 1995. Role stress by national culture and organizational function: a 21 nation study. *Acad. Manage. J.* 38:429–52

Poortinga Y. 1992. Towards a conceptualization of culture for psychology. See Iwawaki et al 1992, pp. 3–17

Punnett BJ, Shenkar O, eds. 1995. *Handbook of International Management Research.* Oxford: Blackwell. In press

Radford MH, Mann L, Ohta Y, Nakane Y. 1991. Differences between Australia and Japan in reported use of decision processes. *Int. J. Psychol.* 26:35–52

Radford MH, Mann L, Ohta Y, Nakane Y. 1993. Differences between Australian and Japanese students in decisional self-esteem, decisional stress and coping styles. *J. Cross-Cult. Psychol.* 24:284–97

Rai SN, Rathore J. 1988. Attraction as a function of cultural similarity and proportion of similar attitudes related to different areas of life. *Psychol. Ling.* 18:47–57

Ralston DA, Gustafson DJ, Elsacs PM, Cheung FM, Terpstra RH. 1992. Eastern values: a comparison of managers in the United States, Hong Kong and the People's Republic of China. *J. Appl. Psychol.* 77: 664–71

Ralston DA, Gustafson DJ, Terpstra RH, Holt DH, Cheung FM, et al. 1993. The impact of managerial values on decision-making behavior: a comparison of the United States and Hong Kong. *Asia. Pac. J. Manage.* 10:21–37

Redding SG. 1990. *The Spirit of Chinese Capitalism.* Berlin: de Gruyter

Rodrigues A, Iwawaki S. 1986. Testing the validity of different models of interpersonal balance in the Japanese culture. *Psychologia* 29:123–31

Rosenthal DA, Feldman SS. 1992. The nature and stability of ethnic identity in Chinese youth: effects of length of residence in two cultural contexts. *J. Cross-Cult. Psychol.* 23:214–27

Rosenzweig MR. 1992. *International Psychological Science: Progress, Problems and Prospects.* Washington, DC: Am. Psychol. Assoc.

Rotter JB. 1966. Generalised expectancies for internal versus external control of reinforcement. *Psychol. Monogr.* 80:(Whole No. 609)

Russell DW. 1982. The Causal Dimension Scale: a measure of how individuals perceive causes. *J. Pers. Soc. Psychol.* 42: 1137–45

Russell JA. 1994. Is there universal recognition of emotion from facial expression? A review of the cross-cultural studies. *Psychol. Bull.* 115:102–41

Schermerhorn JR, Bond MH. 1991. Upward and downward influence tactics in managerial networks: a comparative study of Hong Kong Chinese and Americans. *Asia Pac. J. Manage.* 8:147–58

Schmidt SM, Yeh RS. 1992. The structure of leader influence: a cross-national comparison. *J. Cross-Cult. Psychol.* 23:251–64

Schwalb DW, Schwalb BJ, Harnisch DL, Maehr ML, Akabane K. 1992. Personal investment in Japan and the USA: a study of worker motivation. *Int. J. Intercult. Relat.* 16:107–24

Schwartz SH. 1992. The universal content and structure of values: theoretical advances and empirical tests in 20 countries. In *Advanced Experimental Social Psychology,* ed. MP Zanna, 25:1–65. New York: Academic

Schwartz SH. 1994. Beyond individualism/collectivism: new cultural dimensions of values. See Kim et al 1994, pp. 85–119

Segall MH, Dasen PR, Berry JW, Poortinga YH. 1990. *Human Behavior in Global Perspective: An Introduction to Cross-Cultural Psychology.* New York: Pergamon

Shavelson RJ, Bolus R. 1982. Self-concept: the interplay of theory and methods. *J. Educ. Psychol.* 74:3–17

Shaver PR, Wu S, Schwartz JC. 1991. Cross-cultural similarities and differences in emotion and its representation: a prototype approach. In *Review of Personality and Social Psychology,* ed. MS Clark, 13: 175–212. Beverley Hills, CA: Sage

Shenkar O, von Glinow MA. 1994. Paradoxes in organizational theory and research: using the case of China to illustrate national contingency. *Manage. Sci.* 40:56–71

Shenkar O, Zeira Y. 1992. Role conflict and role ambiguity of chief executive officers in international joint ventures. *J. Int. Bus. Stud.* 23:55–75

Shweder RA, Bourne EJ. 1982. Does the concept of the person vary cross-culturally? In *Cultural Conceptions of Mental Health and Therapy,* ed. AJ Marsella, GM White, pp. 97–137. Dordrecht: Reidel

Shweder RA, Sullivan MA. 1993. Cultural psychology: Who needs it? *Annu. Rev. Psychol.* 44:497–523

Singelis TM. 1994. The measurement of independent and interdependent self-construals. *Pers. Soc. Psychol. Bull.* 20:580–91

Singelis TM, Sharkey WF. 1995. Culture, self-construal and embarassability. *J. Cross-Cult. Psychol.* In press

Singelis TM, Triandis HC, Bhawuk DW, Gelfand M. 1995. Horizontal and vertical dimensions of individualism and collectivism: a theoretical and measurement refinement. *Cross-Cult. Res.* 29:240–75

Smith PB, Bond MH. 1994. *Social Psychology Across Cultures: Analysis and Perspectives.* Boston: Allyn & Bacon

Smith PB, Dugan S, Trompenaars F. 1995a. National culture and managerial values: a dimensional analysis across 43 nations. *J. Cross-Cult. Psychol.* In press

Smith PB, Misumi J, Tayeb MH, Peterson MF, Bond MH. 1989. On the generality of leadership styles across cultures. *J. Occup. Psychol.* 62:97–110

Smith PB, Peterson MF. 1988. *Leadership, Organizations and Culture: An Event Management Model.* London: Sage

Smith PB, Peterson MF, Akande D, Callan V, Cho NG, et al. 1994a. Organizational event management in 14 countries: a comparison with Hofstede's dimensions. See Bouvy et al 1994, pp. 364–73

Smith PB, Peterson MF, Misumi J. 1994b. Event management and work team effectiveness in Japan, Britain and the USA. *J. Occup. Organ. Psychol.* 67:33–44

Smith PB, Peterson MF, Misumi J, Bond MH. 1992. A cross-cultural test of Japanese PM leadership theory. *Appl. Psychol.: Int. Rev.* 41:5–19

Smith PB, Trompenaars F, Dugan S. 1995b. The Rotter locus of control scale in 43 countries: a test of cultural relativity. *Int. J. Psychol.* 30:377–400

Soudjin KA, Hutschmaekers GTM, Van de Vijver FJR. 1990. Culture conceptualizations. In *The Investigation of Culture: Current Issues in Cultural Psychology,* ed. FJR van de Vijver, GTM Hutschmaekers, pp. 19–39. Tilburg, Holland: Tilburg Univ. Press

Taylor SE, Brown JD. 1988. Illusion and well-being: a social psychological perspective on mental health. *Psychol. Bull.* 103:193–210

Ting-Toomey S, Yee-Jung KK, Shapiro RB, Garcia W. 1994. *Ethnic identity salience and conflict styles in four ethnic groups: African Americans, Asian Americans, European Americans, and Latino Americans.* Presented at Annu. Meet. Speech Commun. Assoc., New Orleans

Touzard H, ed. 1992. *Int. Rev. Soc. Psychol.* 5(1):whole issue

Triandis HC. 1984. Toward a psychological theory of economic growth. *Int. J. Psychol.* 19:79–95

Triandis HC. 1990. Cross-cultural studies of individualism and collectivism. In *Nebraska Symposium Motivation, 1989,* ed. JJ Berman, 37:41–134. Lincoln: Univ. Nebr. Press

Triandis HC. 1993. Collectivism and individualism as cultural syndromes. *Cross-Cult. Res.* 27:155–80

Triandis HC. 1994. *Culture and Social Behavior.* New York: McGraw-Hill

Triandis HC. 1995. *Individualism and Collectivism.* Boulder, CO: Westview

Triandis HC, Dunnette M, Hough LM, eds. 1993a. *Handbook of Industrial and Organizational Psychology,* Vol. 4, *Cross-Cultural Studies.* Palo Alto, CA: Consulting Psychologists. 2nd ed.

Triandis HC, McCusker C, Betancourt H, Iwao S, Leung K, et al. 1993b. An emic-etic analysis of individualism-collectivism. *J. Cross-Cult. Psychol.* 24:366–83

Triandis HC, Lambert WW, eds. 1980. *Handbook of Cross-Cultural Psychology,* Vol. 1, *Perspectives.* Boston: Allyn & Bacon

Trompenaars F. 1993. *Riding the Waves of Culture.* London: Brealey

Trubisky P, Ting-Toomey S, Lin SL. 1991. The influence of individualism-collectivism and self-monitoring on conflict styles. *Int. J. Intercult. Relat.* 15:65–84

Tse DK, Francis J, Walls J. 1994. Cultural differences in conducting intra- and inter-cultural negotiations: a Sino-Canadian comparison. *J. Int. Bus. Stud.* 25:537–55

Tse DK, Lee KH, Vertinsky I, Wehrung DA.

1988. Does culture matter? A cross-cultural study of executives' choice, decisiveness and risk adjustment in international marketing. *J. Mark.* 52:81–95

Tyler TR, Bies RJ. 1990. Beyond formal procedures: the interpersonal context of procedural justice. In *Applied Social Psychology and Organizational Settings,* ed. JS Carroll, pp. 77–98. Hillsdale, NJ: Erlbaum

Tyler TR, Lind EA, Huo YJ. 1995. Culture and reactions to authority: influence of situational and dispositional factors. *J. Pers. Soc. Psychol.* In press

van de Vijver FJR, Leung K. 1996. Methods and data analytic procedures in cross-cultural research. See Berry et al 1996

van Muijen J, Koopman P. 1994. The influence of national culture on organizational culture: a comparative study between ten countries. *Eur. Work Organ. Psychol.* In press

Wang ZM, Heller FA. 1993. Patterns of power distribution and managerial decision-making in Chinese and British industrial organizations. *Int. J. Hum. Res. Manage.* 4:113–28

Watkins D, Cheng C. 1995. The Revised Causal Attribution Scale: a confirmatory factor analysis with Hong Kong subjects. *Br. J. Educ. Psychol.* 65:249–52

Watkins D, Dong Q. 1994. Assessing the self-esteem of Chinese school children. *Educ. Psychol.* 14:129–37

Watson WE, Kumar K. 1992. Differences in decision-making regarding risk-taking: a comparison of culturally diverse and culturally homogeneous task groups. *Int. J. Intercult. Relat.* 16:53–65

Watson WE, Kumar K, Michaelsen LK. 1993. Cultural diversity's impact on interaction process and performance: comparing homogeneous and diverse task groups. *Acad. Manage. J.* 36:590–602

Weinreich P. 1986. The operationalization of identity theory in racial and ethnic relations. In *Theories of Race and Ethnic Relations,* ed. J Rex, D Mason, pp. 299–324. Cambridge: Cambridge Univ. Press

Weinreich P. 1995. Operationalization of ethnic identity: illustrative case studies of orientations to the European Community. In *National Identities in Europe: Problems and Controversies,* ed. E Sonsa. Lisbon: Portuguese Comm. to EC/ISPA. In press

Weinreich P, Luk C, Bond MH. 1994. *Ethnic identity: identification with other cultures, self-esteem and identity confusion.* Int. Conf. Immigr., Lang. Acquis., Patterns Soc. Integr., Jerusalem

Williams JE. 1993. *Young adults' views of aging: a 19 nation study.* Presented at Inter-Am. Soc. Psychol. Congr., Santiago, Chile

Williams JE, Best D. 1990. *Sex and Psyche:*

Gender and Self Viewed Cross-Culturally. Newbury Park, CA: Sage

Williams JE, Saiz JL, FormyDuval DL, Munick ML, Fogle EE, et al. 1995. Cross-cultural variation in the importance of psychological characteristics: a seven country study. *Int. J. Psychol.* In press

Wong GYY, Birnbaum-More M. 1994. Culture, context and structure: a test on Hong Kong banks. *Organ. Stud.* 15:99–123

Wu S, Shaver PR. 1992. *Conceptions of love in the United States and the People's Republic of China.* Presented at Int. Soc. Study Pers. Relat., 6th, Orono, ME

Xie JL, Jamal M. 1993. The Type A experiences: stress, job-related attitudes and nonwork behavior: a study of managers in China. *Int. J. Manage.* 10:351–60

Yang KS, Ho DYF. 1988. The role of *yuan* in Chinese social life: a conceptual and empirical analysis. See Paranjpe et al 1988, pp. 163–81

Yates JF, Lee JW. 1995. Chinese decision-making. See Bond 1995

Yu AB. 1995. Ultimate Chinese concern, self, and achievement motivation. See Bond 1995

Yu AB, Yang KS. 1994. The nature of achievement motivation in collectivist societies. See Kim et al 1994, pp. 239–50

Zebrowitz-McArthur L. 1988. Person perception in cross-cultural perspective. See Bond 1988, pp. 245–65

Annu. Rev. Psychol. 1996. 47:237–71

STEREOTYPES

James L. Hilton

Department of Psychology, University of Michigan, Ann Arbor, Michigan 48106

William von Hippel

Department of Psychology, Ohio State University, Columbus, Ohio 43210

KEY WORDS: prejudice, group relations, discrimination, expectancies

ABSTRACT

The stereotyping literature within psychology has grown considerably over the past decade. In large part, this growth can be attributed to progress in understanding the individual mechanisms that give rise to stereotypic thinking. In the current review, the recent psychological literature on stereotypes is reviewed, with particular emphasis given to the cognitive and motivational factors that contribute to stereotype formation, maintenance, application, and change. In addition, the context-dependent function of stereotypes is highlighted, as are the representational issues that various models of stereotypes imply.

CONTENTS

0066-4308/96/0201-0237$08.00

237

INTRODUCTION

On the Question of "Why?": The Context-Dependent Function of Stereotypic Thinking

Why do people engage in stereotypic thinking? Should stereotypes be seen as the inevitable by-products of a miserly cognitive style, for example, or do they result from deep-seeded personality and motivational variables? Do stereotypes emerge in response to frustration, or do they stem from a need to go beyond the information given? Are stereotypes a consequence of our evolutionary heritage, or a product of our particular culture?

We devote relatively little attention to this interesting question of why stereotypes exist. (For excellent reviews, see Smith 1993, Snyder & Miene 1994, Stroebe & Insko 1989.) We believe stereotypic thinking typically serves multiple purposes that reflect a variety of cognitive and motivational processes. Sometimes, for example, stereotyping emerges as a way of simplifying the demands on the perceiver (Bodenhausen et al 1994a,b; Macrae et al 1994c). Stereotypes make information processing easier by allowing the perceiver to rely on previously stored knowledge in place of incoming information. Stereotypes also emerge in response to environmental factors, such as different social roles (cf Eagly 1995), group conflicts (Robinson et al 1995), and differences in power (Fiske 1993). Other times stereotypes emerge as a way of justifying the status quo (Jost & Banaji 1994, Sidanius 1993), or in response to a need for social identity (Hogg & Abrams 1988). Thus, when it comes to the question of "why," we think the answer can most often be found in the notion of context-dependent functionality. Put simply, stereotyping emerges in various contexts to serve particular functions necessitated by those contexts.

The "How" and "When" of Stereotypic Thinking

In this review, we address the more limited questions of "how" and "when" stereotypic thinking emerges, organizing it into sections devoted to the representation, formation, maintenance, application, and change of stereotypes. It is important to note how motivational factors, traditionally considered key ingredients in answering the "why" of stereotyping, are treated in this review. We consider motivation in a more limited way, assuming that stereotypes are not only formed and maintained *for* a variety of motivational reasons but *through* a variety of motivational factors as well. That is, considerable research shows that motivation and emotion play just as important a role in the "when" and "how" of stereotyping as they do in the "why" of stereotyping (Dovidio & Gaertner 1993, Erber 1991, Haddock et al 1993, Hass et al 1992, Islam & Hewstone 1993b, Jussim et al 1995, Mullen 1991, Murray et al 1990, Wilder & Shapiro 1991, Yzerbyt et al 1994).

We highlight a variety of affective and motivational factors that influence when and how stereotypes manifest themselves. As will be evident, motivation frequently determines when stereotyping emerges, but more often than not cognitive processes serve as the mechanism for these motivational effects, determining how motivational processes influence perception, judgment, and behavior. For example, people typically require more evidence to convince them that a disliked person is intelligent rather than unintelligent (Ditto & Lopez 1993). In terms of stereotyping, this finding suggests that motivational factors can lead to rapid confirmation yet slow or begrudging disconfirmation of a negative expectancy, even when the stereotype concerns a dimension that is irrelevant to the root of the disfavor (see also Hilton et al 1991). In contrast, motivation to like a particular person can have the opposite effect, bringing about a generalized reduction in negative stereotypes concerning the particular person's group (Klein & Kunda 1992; see also Pendry & Macrae 1994).

In a related vein, Spencer & Fein (1994) demonstrated that motivation can have an impact on stereotyping by increasing the likelihood that certain cognitive processes will take place. They hypothesized that subjects who had experienced a threat to their self-esteem would be motivated to activate their stereotypes as a means of making themselves feel better through downward social comparison (Crocker & Luhtanen 1990, Fein & Spencer 1993). Consistent with this logic, subjects who had experienced a threat to their self-esteem showed evidence of stereotype activation even when they were cognitively busy, a circumstance under which nonthreatened subjects did not show evidence of activation (see section on Automaticity).

Affect can also have opposite effects on stereotyping, as a function of the type of information processing with which it is associated. For example, affect can inhibit stereotype formation by interfering with the development of illusory correlations (Hamilton et al 1993, Stroessner et al 1992), or it can facilitate stereotype formation, maintenance, and application by increasing perceptions of group homogeneity (Stroessner & Mackie 1992, 1993), the likelihood that deviant group members will be assimilated to the group stereotype (Wilder 1993), and reliance on stereotypes as a cognitive shortcut (Bodenhausen et al 1994a,b). Thus the outcome of affective processes differs dramatically as a function of the mental operations in which the perceiver is engaged.

Taken together, these studies suggest that motivation and affect play significant roles in stereotyping through their impact on cognition. Although preferences influenced judgments in Ditto & Lopez's experiment, for example, they did so through a cognitive mechanism. Subjects did not simply decide that the more likeable person was also more intelligent. Rather, they selectively set high or low standards of evidence that had to be obtained before they could be convinced of who was the more intelligent person (see also Macrae et al 1992). Similarly, subjects in Klein & Kunda's experiment allowed their desires to influence their beliefs about a person by changing the cognitions underlying these beliefs (see also Klein & Kunda 1993, Kunda 1990, Sanitioso et al 1990). Thus a cognitive process mediated, and thereby justified, the influence of subjects' preferences in these experiments (see also Schaller 1992). Finally, in Spencer & Fein (1994), although a threat to subjects' self-esteem caused them to stereotype an out-group member, again the mechanism was a cognitive one: Motivation facilitated stereotype activation, which in turn served to bolster subjects' self-esteem (Fein & Spencer 1993).

Definitions and Directions

Stereotypes have been defined in a variety of ways (see Gardner 1994, Hamilton & Sherman 1994). In this review we adopt the standard viewpoint that stereotypes are beliefs about the characteristics, attributes, and behaviors of members of certain groups. More than just beliefs about groups, they are also theories about how and why certain attributes go together. The nature and purpose of these theories are likely to play an important role in determining when stereotypes are applied and when they are likely to change (cf Leyens et al 1992, Oakes & Turner 1990, Snyder & Miene 1994, Rothbart & Taylor 1992, Wittenbrink 1994). Furthermore, although stereotypes are not necessarily negative in nature, stereotypes about out-group members are more likely to have negative connotations than those about in-group members, even when the attributes they include may seem objectively positive (cf Esses et al 1993, 1994). As Allport (1954) observed, "[T]he personality qualities admired in Abraham Lincoln are deplored in the Jews" (p. 189). Consistent with this viewpoint, negative stereotypes have been shown to be predictive of intergroup attitudes even when positive stereotypes are not (Stangor et al 1991).

Stereotypes can be defined as beliefs about certain groups, but from whence do these beliefs come? There are two sources. The first are mental representations of real differences between groups. That is, stereotypes are sometimes accurate representations of reality (see Judd & Park 1993, Jussim 1991, Swim 1994), or at least of the local reality to which the perceiver is exposed (Rothbart et al 1984). Under this circumstance, stereotypes operate much like object schemas, allowing easier and more efficient processing of information about others. Like schemas in general, these stereotypes may cause perceivers to gloss over or fail to notice individual differences (von Hippel et al 1993), but otherwise there is little reason to believe that they cause people to deviate from accurate perceptions. These stereotypes are selective, however, in that they are localized around group features that are the most distinctive (Nelson & Miller 1995), that provide the greatest differentiation between groups, and that show the least within-group variation (Ford & Stangor 1992).

Whereas a variety of stereotypes are based on real group differences (e.g. cultural stereotypes about food preferences), we believe that stereotypes based on relatively enduring characteristics of the person (such as race, religion, and gender) have enormous potential for error. Thus, the second route to stereotyping occurs when stereotypes are formed about various groups independent of real group differences. This issue is the central focus of this review. That is, what are the psychological mechanisms that allow stereotypes to be formed, maintained, and applied even if there are no corresponding group differences? To address this issue, we first discuss how stereotypes are represented in the head of the individual, as assumptions about representation underlie current understandings of stereotyping and stereotype change.

REPRESENTATION

The question of how stereotypes are represented is interesting from at least two perspectives. First, different representational models lead to different predictions concerning the ways stereotypes are formed, maintained, applied, and changed. Second, although assumptions about representation underlie a great deal of the recent research on formation, maintenance, application, and change, the representational models themselves have received relatively little direct attention. We now briefly outline the gist of five distinct representational models. [For a more thorough treatment of representational issues, see Fiske & Taylor (1991), Hamilton & Sherman (1994), and Smith & Zárate (1992).]

In the *prototype* model, which is perhaps the most widely cited, people carry around neither a set of defining features that constitute the stereotype nor much information about individual group members. Instead, perceivers store abstracted representations of a group's typical features and judge individual group members on the basis of similarity comparisons between the individual and the prototype (Cantor & Mischel 1978). In other words, the prototype representation is an "averaged" representation of the category across many attributes, with no set of group attributes seen as defining. Moreover, the prototype model assumes that knowledge about the stereotype is organized hierarchically (Devine & Baker 1991, Johnston & Hewstone 1992). Thus it is possible to talk about "base level" categories and "subtypes." Indeed, one implication of the prototype model is that stereotype change is accomplished through the creation of subtypes (see section on stereotype change).

A second implication of the prototype model is that it predicts that perceivers will often fail to apply stereotypes to individual group members. Because reactions to individual group members are based on a comparison between the prototype and the individual, *any features,* even nondiagnostic ones, that reduce the similarity between the individual and the prototype should decrease reliance on the stereotype. Consistent with this aspect of prototype theory, numerous studies have documented the diluting power that nondiagnostic information has, although explanations for this effect differ (Fein & Hilton 1992, Krueger & Rothbart 1988).

Recently, a number of investigators have proposed an exemplar-based alternative to prototype and other abstraction-based models (Anderson & Cole 1990, Linville et al 1989, Smith 1990, Smith & Zárate 1992). According to the *exemplar* model, perceivers do not store abstract representations of groups. Instead, groups are represented through particular, concrete exemplars. The stereotype of African-Americans as athletic, for example, is thought to be stored in the form of specific individuals (e.g. Michael Jordan, Carl Lewis). Which exemplars are called to mind upon encountering an individual depends on how attention is directed. Because of this feature, exemplar models place considerable emphasis on the role that goals and context play in determining which stereotypes are activated and applied (Smith & Zárate 1992). Thus, one implication of this model is that a particular stereotype will not always be activated and applied when members of the stereotyped group are encountered, or even when the same member is encountered on different occasions. A second implication is that it should be possible to observe dramatic (if not necessarily permanent) changes in the stereotype as a result of experience with a single counter-stereotypic exemplar.

A number of researchers have proposed "blended" models in which stereotypes are represented as both prototypes and exemplars (Hamilton & Mackie 1990, Klein et al 1992). Although this broadening of the concepts captures more of the data, it also blurs the distinction between abstraction-based and instance-based models (Hamilton & Sherman 1994).

A third representation model is *associative networks,* in which stereotypes are thought of as networks of linked attributes (Carlston 1992, Manis et al 1988, Stephan & Stephan 1993). Different theorists define "attributes" differently (e.g. some see the attributes as traits, others as beliefs, and still others as behaviors) as well as the links between them (e.g. some see the links as simple associations, others see them as causal connections, and still others see them as associations with affective tags; for a thorough review, see Wyer & Carlston 1994). Despite the differences, however, these models share the assumption that the associations can be activated automatically, and thus that stereotypes can operate outside the perceivers' awareness and/or control. Similarly, these models suggest that stereotypes change only slowly and incrementally, as the attributes that make up the stereotype are extensively interconnected.

A fourth model proposes that stereotypes are represented as *schemas*. Although "schema" has become a catch-all term, here we use it simply to refer to Kant's notion of a knowledge representation at its most abstract level. Rather than assuming that information is represented in the form of averaged traits, exemplars, or networked attributes, the schematic view considers stereotypes as generalized, highly abstract beliefs about groups and their members (cf Fiske & Taylor 1991). The stereotype of men, for example, may contain the general belief that they are aggressive, without tying that belief to particular instantiations of aggression, specific contexts or exemplars, or particular organizational structures (e.g. prototypes or associative networks). Moreover, because schema-based models assume that information is represented more abstractly than in other models, one implication of schema-based representation is that the potential for assimilation should be high. That is, because the representation of the group is devoid of specifics, the possibility for assimilating even inconsistent individuals should be substantial (Hilton & von Hippel 1990).

Finally, some have argued that stereotypes can be viewed as *base rates* (Beckett & Park 1995, Judd & Park 1993, Nelson et al 1990), though base rates are not representations per se but rather are a way of thinking about how stereotypes operate. Given people's ability to use base rates, two things should follow from this perspective. First, stereotypes should often be ignored when individuating information is available. Second, greater experience with the stereotype (i.e. the base rate) should lead to more appropriate (i.e. Bayesian) integration of the individuating information and the base rate (Gigerenzer et al 1988). With regard to the first point, although a number of studies have found that stereotypes are often diluted by individuating information (e.g. Hilton & Fein 1989, Krueger & Rothbart 1988), there is controversy about whether it is possible to make a meaningful distinction between base rate and individuating information in the context of a stereotype (cf McCauley 1994). There has been less research on the second point, although studies by Nelson et al (1990) on gender and height estimation suggest that people do integrate individuating and base-rate information in some situations.

Although it is possible to identify competing representational models, investigators have devoted relatively little attention to testing them against one another. They have tended to adopt a model (often implicitly) and then conduct research under the notion that if that model is correct, certain phenomena should manifest themselves. (For example, if stereotypes are represented as prototypes, there should be evidence of dilution in the presence of nondiagnostic information.) Researchers have not often proposed that "X should happen *if, and only if,* the model of representation it implies is correct." Indeed, most of the representational models have yet to be spelled out in sufficient detail to allow testable competing predictions, and, ironically, when such refinement occurs, it often renders the models *less* rather than more distinguishable (Barsalou 1990).

All of which leaves us with a bit of a paradox. On the one hand, assumptions about representation are implicit in virtually all the recent research on stereotype formation, maintenance, application, and change. On the other hand, there has been little effort directed at specifying the details of various representational models. Although there are obvious exceptions to this generalization (e.g. Bodenhausen et al 1995, Linville & Fischer 1993, Mullen & Johnson 1995, Park & Hastie 1987, Park et al 1991, Sherman 1994, Smith & Zárate 1992), the different representational models have served more as heuristic tools for examining stereotyping than as topics of investigation in their own right.

FORMATION

Having briefly examined issues of representation, we now turn to the questions of how and when stereotypes are formed. We attempt to identify those processes that cause stereotypes to emerge, independent of preexisting differences among groups.

Self-Fulfilling Prophecies

Perhaps the best-known route to stereotype formation is the creation of group differences through self-fulfilling prophecies. Self-fulfilling prophecies emerge when people hold expectancies that lead them to alter their behavior, which in turn causes the expected behaviors to be exhibited by people who are targets of the expectancies. For example, teachers who expect some of their students to excel elicit superior performance from those students (Rosenthal & Jacobson 1968). Similarly, college students who believe that their conversational partners are physically attractive elicit more sociable behavior from those partners (Snyder et al 1977). Whereas early research focused on demonstrating that self-fulfilling prophecies occur, recent research has focused on specifying the conditions under which self-fulfilling prophecies emerge (for reviews see Hilton & Darley 1991, Jussim 1991, Snyder 1992).

Nonconscious Detection of Covariation

One possible route to stereotype formation is through the generalization from the behaviors of one group member to the evaluation of others. Research on covariation detection suggests that this process need not be a conscious one.

For although conscious ability to detect correlations is rather poor (Nisbett & Ross 1980), the ability to detect correlations nonconsciously is quite remarkable (Lewicki 1986). Furthermore, once an initial contingency between two events has been detected nonconsciously, people behave as if the relationship continues to exists long after the contingency has been removed (Hill et al 1989). For example, Hill et al (1990) presented subjects with a series of faces in which the location of the nostrils, which varied vertically by 1/8 inch, covaried with bogus personality profiles. As in previous research, subjects soon nonconsciously abstracted the relationship. When subjects were later presented with faces for which there was no longer any feedback concerning the accuracy of the earlier association, their nonconscious belief in the rule not only remained intact but actually strengthened with additional presentations of new faces. Thus, the encoding rule that subjects had earlier learned nonconsciously *gained in strength in the absence of supporting evidence.*

Such self-perpetuation of bias may play an important role in the formation of social stereotypes. In the absence of self-perpetuation effects, the role of nonconscious detection of covariation in stereotyping is limited to stereotypes that are based on a kernel of truth. Because of self-perpetuation effects, however, all that is necessary to initiate a stereotype is an encounter with a few stereotypic individuals (e.g. a few passive women or a few hostile African-Americans), and perceivers will continue to strengthen their belief in the stereotype in the absence of supportive evidence. Given the existence of self-fulfilling prophecies and the prevalence of subtle stereotyping in the arts, media, etc (Zuckerman & Kieffer 1994), it seems highly likely that there will always be at least a few (actual or portrayed) stereotype-congruent individuals available to initiate such self-perpetuating stereotypes. In addition, because contingencies are easier to learn when they are associated with individuals with whom one has little experience rather than with individuals with whom one has a great deal of experience (Cacioppo et al 1992), nonconscious detection of covariation is likely to play a larger role in the development of stereotypes about out-groups rather than in-groups. Furthermore, because the detection of covariation and consequent changes in evaluation take place outside conscious awareness, self-perpetuating biases could exert an influence even as perceivers attempt to behave in an egalitarian fashion (see Devine & Monteith 1993, Monteith 1993).

Illusory Correlation

Erroneous or "illusory" detection of correlation has the potential to play a major role in the formation and maintenance of social stereotypes about minority groups. A great deal of research has demonstrated that people can come to perceive minority groups in a more negative light than majority groups, even when the groups behave identically. One explanation of this effect is that negative behaviors become associated with minority group members at encoding by virtue of their shared distinctiveness (for reviews of the distinctiveness perspective, see Hamilton & Sherman 1989, Mullen & Johnson 1990). Consistent with this analysis, people spend more time encoding distinctive (minority) information than other information, and disruption of this increased processing can inhibit the formation of illusory correlations (Stroessner et al 1992; see also Johnson & Mullen 1994). Similarly, illusory correlations are attenuated when a minority group is made less distinctive by the presence of an even smaller minority group or another minority group with an increased preponderance of negative behavior (Sherman et al 1989). These findings suggest that the minority group is distinctive only by virtue of its relation to the majority group.

Despite findings like these in support of the distinctiveness explanation, recent research has led to another explanation of the processes by which illusory correlations are formed (Fiedler 1991, Fiedler & Armbruster 1994, Smith 1991; see also McGarty et al 1993). Specifically, information loss, or forgetting, has been proposed as a route that can lead perceivers to form illusory correlations. Essentially, this account proposes that as a function of probabilities, people are probabilistically more likely to forget the ratio of positive to negative behaviors when the ratio is based on a smaller (i.e. minority) rather than a larger (i.e. majority) sample. Because of this differential forgetting, people's impressions of minority groups are less extreme than their impressions of majority groups. When groups exhibit primarily positive behaviors, people have more moderate and thereby more negative impressions of the minority group, and when groups exhibit primarily negative behaviors, people have more moderate and thereby more positive impressions of the minority group. The key to this explanation is that the locus of illusory correlations is proposed to be at retrieval, suggesting that loss of information in storage and failure at retrieval may be at least partially responsible for the effect.

The problem with the information-loss account of illusory correlation effects is that it cannot accommodate evidence (e.g. Johnson & Mullen 1994, Stroessner et al 1992) that distinctive information does indeed receive greater processing than nondistinctive information. For this reason, an alternative distinctiveness explanation has been offered, according to which it is not only distinctiveness at encoding that facilitates illusory correlations but also postencoding distinctiveness as well (McConnell et al 1994b; see also McConnell et al 1994a). According to this account, it does not matter whether a behavior originally seemed distinctive as it was processed but only whether a behavior comes to be distinctive in the context of all other behaviors that were processed from the same sources. So long as a behavior becomes distinctive prior to the judgment task (e.g. by virtue of the eventual preponderance of other behaviors that are inconsistent with it), it will have the tendency to facilitate the formation of illusory correlations.

Although illusory correlations have proven to be fairly robust, a number of conditions prevent their formation. Most importantly, because illusory correlations rely on item memorability, they only emerge when people are making judgments of a group in a memory-based fashion. Whenever judgments of a group are made on-line, such as when information is self-relevant (Schaller 1991) or when people are processing information about a source from whom they expect a great degree of internal consistency (McConnell et al 1994a, 1995), no correlation is perceived between distinctive events. In addition, factors that disrupt the processing of information, such as the presence of cognitive load or a positive or negative mood state, also inhibit the formation of illusory correlations (Hamilton et al 1993, Stroessner et al 1992). Thus, the role of illusory correlations in stereotype formation appears to be limited to conditions in which people are evaluating groups without inordinate demands on their attention and in a memory-based fashion.

Out-Group Homogeneity

Out-group members are not only perceived as possessing less desirable traits than in-group members, they are seen as more homogeneous as well. A consequence of the so-called out-group homogeneity effect is that people believe that most out-group members share the attributes of the specific out-group members whom they encounter (Park & Hastie 1987) and that group-level stereotypes are likely to describe individual group members (Park et al 1991).

Although the out-group homogeneity effect is well documented, there is considerable disagreement about the cause of the effect and about its measurement (see Judd et al 1991, Ostrom & Sedikides 1992). On the one hand, Linville and her colleagues (Linville et al 1989, Linville & Fischer 1993) have proposed an exemplar model, according to which perceptions of out-group homogeneity are caused by the fact that people know more in-group members than out-group members and thereby retrieve more instances when making in-group rather than out-group variability judgments. This greater retrieval of in-group instances leads, on average, to greater perceptions of in-group heterogeneity. A related model has been proposed by Kashima & Kashima (1993) in which it is not the number of exemplars but rather the dissimilarity of the exemplars that leads to judgments of heterogeneity. On the other hand, Park, Judd, and their colleagues (Park & Judd 1990, Park et al 1991) have proposed an abstraction/exemplar model, wherein group variability information is stored as part of an abstract group stereotype. According to this model, group variability judgments do not necessitate exemplar retrieval, but exemplars (particularly the self as an exemplar) are nevertheless often retrieved in the case of judgments concerning in-groups but not out-groups. Thus, it is the selective retrieval of exemplars that causes increased perceptions of variability among in-groups as compared with out-groups.

A variety of situations exacerbate or attenuate the tendency to perceive out-groups as more homogeneous than in-groups. For example, minority groups are seen as more homogeneous than majority groups, an effect that holds even in impressions of a minority member's own group (Bartsch & Judd 1993). Similarly, thinking about group members in terms of subgroups attenuates perceptions of in-group and out-group homogeneity (Park et al 1992),[1] whereas thinking about groups in terms of their self-defining traits exacerbates perceptions of in-group and out-group homogeneity (Kelly 1989). Finally, group competition exacerbates the out-group homogeneity effect (Judd & Park 1988), as indeed it exacerbates a variety of in-group biases (Weber 1994).

These relationships between perceived homogeneity and factors such as group competition and knowledge of group stereotypes suggest that perceptions of out-group homogeneity may be critically associated with stereotyping, prejudice, and discrimination (cf Diehl & Jonas 1991, Quattrone 1986). In support of such a possibility, people have been shown to discriminate in a minimal group situation against homogeneous out-groups when they do not discriminate against heterogeneous out-groups (Vanbeselaere 1991; see also Simon et al 1990).

MAINTENANCE

Regardless of how they are formed, stereotypes are maintained through a variety of processes. In this section, we review the major routes to stereotype maintenance.

Priming

The way that we process information, even unambiguous information, is heavily influenced by information that we have previously encountered. Bruner (1957) argued that prior experience operates on current perception by making certain categories more "accessible" during the interpretation of incoming information. Variously known as "category accessibility," "implicit memory," and "priming," the impact of prior experience on ongoing perception and cognition is pervasive. If a single conclusion can be made from hundreds of experiments in cognitive and social psychology, it is this: Prior experience determines what we see and hear, how we interpret that information, and how we store it for later use (Sedikides & Skowronski 1991).

---

[1]   Park et al also demonstrated that in-groups are perceived to have more subgroups than outgroups, suggesting that perceptions of subgroups may be a critical factor contributing to the out-group homogeneity effect (see also Kraus et al 1993).

In the realm of stereotyping, priming plays a dramatic role in the perception and evaluation of out-group members. For example, after exposure to television commercials in which women are portrayed as sexual objects, males are more likely to encode the next female they encounter in a sexual fashion, paying more attention to her appearance and style of dress than to what she says (Rudman & Borgida, in press). Interestingly, males also *behave* in a more sexual way toward the woman after viewing these commercials, asking sexist questions, scooting their chair closer to the woman's, and spending more time gazing at her body (see also Bargh & Gollwitzer 1994, Bargh et al 1995, McKenzie-Mohr & Zanna 1990). It seems that priming a particular domain makes people more likely to use that domain in later evaluations, even when the earlier priming experience should be completely irrelevant to the current task (Sherman et al 1990).

The influence of priming is not limited to conscious information processing; rather, assimilative priming effects emerge even when the initial priming episode takes place outside conscious awareness (Perdue et al 1990). Such priming effects also manifest themselves at the level of the social category, with conscious or nonconscious activation of a social category causing an individual's behavior to be interpreted along category-relevant dimensions (Ford et al 1994, Macrae et al 1994a). Indeed, priming a social category can inhibit activation of other categories (Macrae et al 1994a). Moreover, because race, gender, and age information all seem capable of automatically activating associated stereotypes (see section on Automaticity), the mere presence of a female, African-American, or older person may increase the likelihood that this individual's behavior is interpreted in a stereotype-congruent fashion, even if the perceiver has not consciously encoded the target's social category. Thus, despite the fact that social behaviors can often be interpreted in a variety of ways, and all individuals are members of many social categories, priming may nevertheless lock perceivers into a stereotypic frame of reference (Skowronski et al 1993).

Once a behavior has been interpreted in a particular way, this interpretation has long-term consequences for its evaluation (Smith et al 1992). In Smith et al's experiments, subjects were presented with behaviors that could be interpreted along two different dimensions, with opposite evaluative connotations. Smith et al found that when subjects initially rated behaviors along a dimension on which the behaviors seemed positive, they later evaluated the behaviors more positively than when they had rated them along a dimension on which they seemed negative. This priming effect was as apparent one week later as it was one hour later and was actually strongest for behaviors that subjects could no longer recollect having encountered. These findings suggest that a single prior experience with a behavior, even if long forgotten, can later exert a strong assimilative influence on how that behavior is interpreted.

If the events that lead to assimilative priming effects were randomly deter-mined, the Smith et al findings would simply suggest that we should hope that, for whatever reason, people are primed to interpret our behaviors along their most favorable dimensions. Recent evidence suggests, however, that events only prime evaluations when the events are stereotype-congruent (Banaji et al 1993; see also Banaji & Greenwald 1995). For example, in Banaji et al's experiments, priming the construct of dependency had an impact on sub-sequent evaluations of female targets but did not influence evaluations of male targets. Similarly, priming aggression influenced evaluations of males but not females. These findings suggest that even *random* priming events (e.g. daily experiences, stories in the news) facilitate stereotype maintenance by selec-tively influencing interpretations only when they are stereotype congruent. These findings also suggest that multiply interpretable behaviors tend to be interpreted to the detriment of the stereotyped group. Because the cultural stereotype holds that African-American males are hostile and unintelligent (Devine 1989), for example, a stereotyping perceiver is primed by the mere presence of an African-American to interpret his behaviors as consistent with these traits. For this reason, if he were to do something friendly but stupid, it would likely be regarded as stupid, whereas his unfriendly but intelligent behavior would likely be regarded as unfriendly.

Assimilation Effects

An important and long-studied route to stereotype maintenance is through assimilation. Put simply, individuals often are perceived as more similar to their stereotype than they really are. For example, a student athlete is more likely to be judged guilty of cheating than a nonathlete (Bodenhausen 1990), an angry housewife is seen as less aggressive than an angry construction worker (Kunda & Sherman-Williams 1993), and an African-American pan-handler is seen as more threatening than a Caucasian pan-handler (von Hippel et al 1995). These are examples of individuals being assimilated to their group stereotype.

How divergent can such behaviors be from the stereotype and still be assimilated to it? Most evidence suggests that the behaviors must fit at least within the tails of the distributions from which they are thought to emanate, or they will be contrasted away from their group of origin (Manis et al 1988, Wilder & Thompson 1988; see also Krueger & Clement 1994). Thus, an African-American who behaves in a highly intelligent manner will actually seem more intelligent—rather than less intelligent—than a comparable Cauca-sian (Jussim et al 1987). This tendency is qualified, however, by people's processing capabilities. When the ability to process information is disrupted, such as in situations that are anxiety provoking, individuals who would other-wise be perceived as deviant are assimilated to their stereotype (Wilder 1993).

Furthermore, people who have a high need to perceive consistency or structure in their environment are more likely to assimilate behaviors to their stereotypes than people who have a low need to perceive consistency (Neuberg & Newsom 1993).

The tendency to assimilate is also moderated by a perceiver's expectations of consistency from members of the stereotyped group. When perceivers hold high expectations of consistency, behaviors are assimilated to stereotypes that would otherwise be perceived as outside the distribution of expected behaviors and thus contrasted away (Hilton & von Hippel 1990). Because natural groups vary a great deal in the extent to which consistency is expected from group members (cf Ostrom & Sedikides 1992), different groups show different proclivities for assimilation. Very large and heterogeneous groups (such as females or African-Americans) are likely to be associated with lower expectations of internal consistency than smaller and more homogeneous groups (such as tax accountants or football players). Importantly, by virtue of their seeming homogeneity (see section on Out-Group Homogeneity), out-groups will be associated with higher levels of perceived internal consistency than in-groups. Thus, there is a greater tendency to assimilate incongruent behaviors to the group stereotype when the behaviors are associated with smaller rather than larger groups and when they are associated with out-groups rather than in-groups. Moreover, because factors such as intergroup competition (Judd & Park 1988) and lack of intergroup contact (Islam & Hewstone 1993a) increase perceptions of out-group homogeneity, such variables are likely to increase the tendency toward assimilation of individuals to the group stereotype as well.

Somewhat related to the notion that people assimilate divergent individuals to their group stereotype is the idea of category accentuation, or the tendency to perceive categories as more distinct from one another than they really are. In a demonstration of this phenomenon, Krueger et al (1989) found that when the distance between categories is exacerbated by the addition of new category members, people are adept at adjusting their perceptions of the category. When the distance between categories is attenuated by the addition of new members, however, people do not sufficiently adjust their perception of the categories to accommodate the new members (see also Ford & Stangor 1992, Krueger & Rothbart 1990).

Attributional Processes

Although attributional processes tend to be a ubiquitous component of social perception (Carlston & Skowronski 1994), they are particularly likely to be initiated by behaviors that are incongruent with perceivers' prior expectancies (Kanazawa 1992). The attribution processes that are aroused by incongruency tend to be highly sophisticated in nature, with a variety of factors converging to bias the attributional outcome in ways that maintain the stereotype. Indeed, one striking finding from the social perception literature is the remarkable flexibility with which people use attributional logic (Hewstone 1990, Major & Crocker 1993).

At the most basic level, perceivers sometimes simply refuse to make any inferences at all when confronted with stereotype incongruency (Maass et al 1989, 1995; Rubini & Semin 1994; see also Hamilton et al 1992), a finding that is important for two reasons. First, when making memory-based judgments people tend to remember and rely on their abstractions in place of the original behaviors that led to the abstractions (Srull & Wyer 1989). Second, and somewhat relatedly, abstractly encoded information tends to be more resistant to disconfirmation and more stable over time than information that is encoded at a concrete level (Semin & Fiedler 1988). Taken together, these tendencies suggest that perceivers are more likely to remember, believe, rely on, and communicate stereotype-congruent information than stereotype-incongruent information.

Attributional processing can also be inhibited by stereotype-congruent information. People typically engage in attributional processing only until they have found a sufficient cause for the behaviors they are witnessing. Once such sufficiency has been achieved, attributional processing usually ceases. Because the stereotype itself provides a sufficient explanation for many stereotype-congruent events, stereotypes can block people's ability to notice and interpret covariation between stereotype-irrelevant factors and the stereotype-congruent event (Sanbonmatsu et al 1994).

Finally, when behaviors are open to alternative explanations, people make very different types of inferences from stereotype-congruent vs stereotype-incongruent information (for a review, see Hewstone 1990). For example, people are more likely to infer dispositional or internal causes for stereotype-congruent rather than incongruent behaviors (Jackson et al 1993, Yee & Eccles 1988). People are also more likely to infer dispositional causes for negative out-group and positive in-group behaviors than for positive out-group and negative in-group behaviors (Hewstone & Jaspars 1984). Pettigrew (1979) has labeled this tendency the "ultimate attribution error" and has proposed that it underlies a variety of in-group biases. It is worth noting, however, that although the tendency to protect group esteem by attributing negative in-group and positive out-group information to situational causes is a common finding, the tendency to enhance group esteem by attributing positive in-group and negative out-group information to dispositional causes is relatively rare (Weber 1994; see also Islam & Hewstone 1993b).

Memory Processes

It is clear from the research cited in this review that a number of information-processing strategies are biased toward stereotype formation and maintenance.

The question remains, however, as to what role memory plays in this process. The evidence that currently exists suggests that people often have better memory for information that is incongruent, rather than congruent, with their stereotypes and expectancies (for reviews see Rojahn & Pettigrew 1992, Stangor & McMillan 1992). This general finding suggests that memory processes actually serve to undermine stereotyping. There are, however, three important reasons to believe that this is not so.

First, incongruent information is better remembered than congruent information because it instigates attributional processing, as people attempt to make sense of the incongruency (Sherman & Hamilton 1994). This attributional processing might conceivably result in a change of meaning, or perhaps discounting, of the incongruent behavior. Either way, this attributional processing leads to better recall of incongruent rather than congruent information and also causes the incongruent information to no longer seem incongruent with the original expectancy. Thus, to the extent that a perceiver engages in cognitive effort to explain away a seeming inconsistency, the perceiver is both more likely to be successful in discounting or reinterpreting the information and more likely to remember the (no longer) incongruent information as a consequence of the extensive cognitive processing (von Hippel et al 1995). Because so many social behaviors are inherently ambiguous, this reinterpretation process and the resultant dissociation between memory and judgment are likely to be quite common. Consequently, despite the seeming inconsistency between memory and judgment, memory incongruency effects should not be taken as evidence that memory serves to undermine stereotyping.

Second, although the memory incongruency effect emerges when people are allowed to process information at their leisure, when task demands are heavy (as they commonly are in social interaction) people tend to show better memory for stereotype-congruent information (Macrae et al 1993, Stangor & Duan 1991). Presumably this increased memory for congruent information arises because people do not have the opportunity to engage in the inconsistency-resolution processes that lead to the memory incongruency effect (Sherman & Hamilton 1994; see also Vonk & van Knippenberg 1995).

Third, in their meta-analytic review, Stangor & McMillan (1992) found that incongruent information is better remembered than congruent information only when the perceiver believes that the target is relatively homogeneous. For groups from which little internal consistency is expected (such as large groups like African-Americans and women), perceivers should remember more congruent rather than incongruent information. Stangor & McMillan also found that the tendency to remember incongruent information is moderated by the strength of the perceiver's expectancy. When the perceiver holds an expectancy that is of weak to moderate strength, incongruency effects emerge. When the perceiver holds a strong stereotype or expectancy, congruent information is actually more likely to be remembered than incongruent information. This finding suggests that people who are highly prejudiced, and thereby likely to hold strong stereotypes, have memories that primarily support their stereotypes (von Hippel et al 1995).

APPLICATION

Probably the most important consequence of stereotypes is that they can lead to unfair, negative outcomes when they are applied to members of stereotyped groups. In this section, we review evidence for when and how stereotypes are likely to be applied.

Automaticity

Under the right circumstances, and with extensive practice, information processing becomes automatic (Bargh 1994). Devine (1989) has proposed that automaticity develops in the activation of social stereotypes just as it does with a variety of other cognitive tasks. She has argued that because our culture is suffused with information pertaining to the stereotype of African-Americans, the activation of the African-American stereotype becomes automatized at a young age for most Americans. Importantly, however, as people grow older and begin to evaluate and reflect on their beliefs, those who are not prejudiced learn to suppress or replace the automatically activated stereotypic thoughts in favor of more egalitarian ones. This suppression or replacement of stereotypic cognitions is proposed to be an effortful process that requires conscious cognitive resources from the perceiver. Devine's theory is important both as a process model of stereotype activation and application and for its implications for stereotype use under a variety of circumstances. If group membership and the accompanying stereotypic information are automatically encoded whenever a member of a social category is encountered, the potential for that stereotype to be applied is manifestly increased.

Although there continues to be relatively little published research concerning the automatic activation and subsequent suppression of stereotypes, the evidence that does exist supports several aspects of Devine's theory. For example, nonconscious presentation of age (Perdue & Gurtman 1990), gender (Klinger & Beall 1992), and race (Macrae et al 1994b, Wolfe et al 1995) information has been found to activate associated evaluations and stereotypes (see also Perdue et al 1990). Furthermore, whereas nonconscious priming of gender information leads to equivalent activation of gender stereotypes among people who consciously endorse them and people who do not, conscious priming leads to differential activation among people who express different attitudes toward women (Klinger & Beall 1992).

Despite such evidence that stereotypes are activated automatically, a recent paper has challenged this notion. In a clever pair of experiments, Gilbert & Hixon (1991) demonstrated that cognitive busyness inhibits activation of the Asian-American stereotype but facilitates application of it. These findings suggest that stereotypes require conscious attention and effort to be activated and thus are not automatic. An important caveat, however, that must be considered is that in Gilbert & Hixon's (1991) experiments subjects had no particular reason to engage in stereotypic processing.

In an effort to determine whether cognitively busy subjects in Gilbert & Hixon's experiments could have activated their stereotypes had they been more motivated to do so, Spencer & Fein (1994) replicated the experiments but added a manipulation of threat to self-esteem. Because motivation to stereotype is enhanced when people experience a threat to their self-esteem (see sections On the Question of "Why?" and The "How" and "When" of Stereotypic Thinking), Spencer & Fein (1994) hypothesized that even cognitively busy subjects would activate their stereotypes when they had been threatened. Consistent with this prediction, they found that although cognitively busy subjects who had not been threatened did not show any evidence of stereotype activation, cognitively busy subjects who had experienced a threat to their self-esteem did show evidence of activation of the Asian-American stereotype. In follow-up research, Wolfe et al (1995) demonstrated that stereotypes concerning African-Americans were also not activated when subjects were cognitively busy, unless subjects had experienced a threat to their self-esteem. This effect emerged despite the fact that the stereotypes were primed subliminally and were never available to conscious awareness. These data suggest that activation of stereotypes can be accomplished with minimal cognitive resources by persons who are motivated to stereotype others.

How is it that stereotypes can be activated automatically, but only when the perceiver is motivated to do so? The solution to this seeming inconsistency lies in the conditional nature of automaticity. As Bargh (1989) has noted, automaticity is not a unitary construct. Rather, different types of automaticity require different levels of processing on the part of the perceiver. It seems likely that stereotype activation is at the level of *goal-dependent automaticity* in that the perceiver must have a specific goal (e.g. denigration or impression formation) for the stereotype to be activated automatically (Spencer & Fein 1994).

Attributional Ambiguity: Self-Deception and Self-Presentation

Above, we noted that attributional processes contribute to the maintenance of stereotypes. Recent research suggests that they also play an important role in stereotype application, on both the perceiver's and the target's side of the interaction. On the perceiver's side, people typically will not exhibit behaviors that could be seen as prejudiced when the conditions surrounding those behaviors make the meaning of the behavior attributionally clear. When choosing to sit far away from a disabled person would unambiguously be attributed to avoidance, for example, subjects choose to sit close to the disabled person. In contrast, when the meaning of the seating choice is ambiguous, subjects disproportionately choose to sit away from the person (Snyder et al 1979). In a related way, simply creating the illusion that evaluations are based on individuating information can free people to apply their stereotypes when they otherwise would not (Yzerbyt et al 1994). This finding is somewhat reminiscent of the research of Darley & Gross (1983), who found that subjects were unwilling to make stereotypic judgments in the absence of individuating information.

On the target's side of the interaction, the importance of attributional ambiguity has become evident in the work of Crocker & Major (1989, Crocker et al 1991, Major & Crocker 1993). They argued that members of stigmatized groups are often confronted with attributionally ambiguous feedback concerning their performance. Negative feedback can be attributed to poor performance, but it can also be attributed to the prejudices of the evaluator. Similarly, positive feedback can be attributed either to good performance or to a desire on the part of the evaluator to avoid appearing prejudiced. Crocker & Major argued that this ambiguity leads to a variety of cognitive, affective, and motivational outcomes. Ambiguity can, for example, buffer members of a stigmatized group against negative feedback but it can also undermine self-esteem following positive feedback (Crocker et al 1991).

Prejudice

Prejudice has traditionally been viewed as the application of social stereotypes. According to Allport's (1954) classic definition, prejudice is "an antipathy based on a faulty and inflexible generalization" (p. 9). Thus, prejudice is seen both as an outgrowth of stereotyping and as negative evaluations of group members. In support of Allport's theorizing, the evaluative nature of people's attitudes toward members of different groups (prejudice) has been shown to be linked to the overall evaluative connotation of their beliefs (stereotypes) about group members (Eagly & Mladinic 1989; Haddock et al 1993, 1994; Stephan et al 1994; see also Kleinpenning & Hagendoorn 1991, 1993).[2] Prejudice is clearly more than just antipathy, however, as it is comprised of different emotions in different contexts among different people (Altemeyer 1994; Batson & Burris 1994; Gaines & Reed 1995; Haslam et al 1992; Kleinpenning & Hagendoorn 1991, 1993; Smith 1993; Swim et al 1995).

---

[2] However, this relationship may be mediated by emotional responses or symbolic beliefs (Esses et al 1993, Haddock et al 1993).

A variety of theories of prejudice have emerged in the past decade or so that are linked only loosely, if at all, to the stereotypes that people hold about members of the targeted groups. Although these theories differ in whether people are thought to be consciously aware of their prejudices and in the importance placed on this awareness, they hold in common the view that negative evaluative or emotional responses to group members are the primary components of prejudice. For example, according to aversive racism (Dovidio & Gaertner 1991), most people embrace egalitarian values yet have negative affect toward African-Americans. As a consequence, this negative affect is excluded from consciousness but has an important impact on behavior whenever the person can be unaware of the influence of her or his prejudices (e.g. when the behavior is attributionally ambiguous). Thus, for aversive racism, prejudice is nonconscious and it must remain so in order for it to have an impact on judgment and behavior.

Modern racism (McConahay 1986) and symbolic racism (Sears 1988) are similar to aversive racism in that the negative affect at the root of prejudice must be rationalized by linking it to nonracial issues such as politics in order for it to avoid conflict with egalitarian values. Because modern racism and symbolic racism link prejudice to politics, however, they are open to the criticism that they are simply tapping political conservatism and are not inherently measures of prejudice (Sniderman et al 1991).

Ambivalent racism (Hass et al 1991) is similar to these other theories of prejudice in that it holds that people are deeply conflicted about their prejudiced feelings. In ambivalent racism, people's egalitarian ideals lead them to embrace equality and feel a sense of sympathy for the underdog, but their Protestant work ethic suggests that individuals are responsible for their own fate. These conflicting values lead ambivalent racists to heap great praise on successful African-Americans but simultaneously to denigrate African-Americans who are not perceived as embracing the Protestant work ethic. This ambivalence is also thought to lead to a fundamental instability in the reactions of such people to African-Americans, depending upon which sentiments are most available at the time a judgment or behavior is required.

Devine and her colleagues (Devine et al 1991, Devine & Monteith 1993, Monteith 1993, Monteith et al 1993) have recently proposed a somewhat orthogonal conception of prejudice that revitalizes Allport's (1954) early notions of prejudice with and without compunction. According to this model, the critical difference between high- and low-prejudice individuals is that low-prejudice individuals have internalized standards for how they should respond to group members, and they experience feelings of guilt and self-criticism whenever they violate these standards. These feelings, in turn, motivate vigilance and an increased consistency among personal standards, thoughts, and behaviors. High-prejudice persons, on the other hand, follow external societal standards for how they should respond to group members, and as a consequence they feel only generalized negative affect, as well as other-directed affect such as anger and irritation, when they violate these standards. These feelings should, if anything, only increase the prejudice of such individuals, as they blame the group members for their own negative reactions to them.

Finally, it should be noted that prejudice has historically been defined not only as negative attitudes or affect directed toward particular groups but also as a tendency to prejudge members of a group on the basis of their group membership (cf Brewer 1994). The idea that prejudice contains a processing component (such as prejudgment) has been recaptured in a recent proposal that prejudice should be conceived and operationalized as the tendency to engage in stereotypical processing of group members (von Hippel et al 1995). Such a notion of prejudice differs from the theories discussed above by suggesting that not only negative evaluations define prejudice but also the way people process information about others. This notion of prejudice also differs from the theories discussed above in that it explicitly links prejudice with stereotyping. Prejudiced people are defined as those who show stereotypic biases in their encoding of members of a particular group, and nonprejudiced people are defined as those who do not show such biases. Consistent with these ideas, von Hippel et al (1995) demonstrated that a process measure of prejudice (derived from Maass et al 1989, 1995) can predict evaluations of group members when an evaluation-based measure, derived from modern racism theory, cannot (see also Dovidio et al 1995, Fazio et al 1995).

CHANGE

Determining the conditions under which stereotypes change has been a central concern of recent research (for reviews see Hewstone 1989, Stroebe & Insko 1989). Within this research, two related questions have been asked. First, what are the cognitive and motivational resources necessary for the processing of stereotype-inconsistent information (cf Brewer 1988, Fiske & Neuberg 1990, Hewstone 1989)? In general, the assumption has been that it is easier to maintain a stereotype than to change it, as numerous processes contribute to the maintenance of even unimportant stereotypes (see section on Maintenance). Second, assuming that the perceiver has sufficient motivation and resources to engage in stereotype revision, what form will the revision take?

Models of Change

To date, four models of change have been proposed. The *bookkeeping* model (Rothbart 1981) posits that stereotypes are updated incrementally. Each inconsistency that is processed leads to a small change in the stereotype. The *conversion* model (Rothbart 1981) posits that stereotype change occurs in a dramatic fashion, but only after some critical level of inconsistency has been encountered. The *subtyping* model (Brewer et al 1981) posits that inconsistent information is simply recategorized under a new subsidiary classification. Finally, *exemplar-based* models assume that stereotypes consist of representations of specific individuals (Smith & Zárate 1992). From this perspective, stereotypes change when new exemplars are added or when different exemplars are retrieved. Thus, like the bookkeeping model, an exemplar-based model suggests that stereotypes change in response to each processed inconsistency. Because the stereotype of the group is dependent upon the exemplars called to mind rather than on an abstracted representation, however, an exemplar-based model allows for much greater change than the bookkeeping model does in response to perceived inconsistency or a new perspective on the part of the perceiver.

The subtyping model of stereotype change has received the lion's share of attention (Hewstone et al 1992a, Johnston & Hewstone 1992, Kunda & Oleson 1995). In large part, this is because there are two theories concerning the impact of subtyping. One view of subtyping holds that it serves primarily to maintain stereotypic beliefs. If, for example, we expect Germans to be efficient but we meet an inefficient German professor, we may form a subtype of German professors that includes the expectation that German professors are inefficient (Weber & Crocker 1983). Notice that this process renders inefficiency among German professors less surprising, while preserving the belief that Germans, in general, are efficient. Allport (1954) anticipated this line of reasoning when he discussed the functions of refencing.

Work by Brewer (Brewer 1988, Brewer et al 1981), however, challenges the notion that subtypes serve primarily to maintain stereotypes. According to Brewer's analysis, as our perceptions of groups become sufficiently differentiated, subtypes replace superordinate categorizations and become base level categories themselves. Like furniture dealers who find the concept of "chair" too general to have any utility, our experience with some groups (e.g. men and women, young and old) is sufficiently rich to render the superordinate categorizations (e.g. men, old people) relatively uninformative. As a consequence, people are likely to rely on subtypes of such groups rather than on the group in general when making stereotype-relevant judgments. In support of such a possibility, activation of certain female subtypes has been shown to inhibit activation of competing subtypes (Rudman & Borgida, in press). To the extent that subtyping leads to changes in base level categorization in such a fashion, it contributes to meaningful stereotype change in the sense that greater variability is likely to be reflected in perceiver's responses to members of the same superordinate category (Park et al 1992).

To date, investigators have obtained at least some evidence to support all four models (Hewstone et al 1992b). What has remained difficult has been to specify the conditions under which each model is likely to apply, with evidence for different models sometimes emerging from the same set of data (e.g. Weber & Crocker 1983). Two important factors contribute to this confusion. First, investigators have yet to agree on what constitutes appropriate measures of change. Consider, for example, research on subtyping. At one extreme, representational change accompanied by little change in the perception of the "typical" group member has been taken as evidence of subtyping (e.g. Devine & Baker 1991, Johnston & Hewstone 1992). At the other extreme, subtyping has been inferred when specific conditions promote stability in the perception of the group despite the atypicality of specific group members (e.g. Kunda & Oleson 1995). Second, evidence for the various models of stereotype change seems to be differentially likely to emerge depending upon the particular function served by the stereotype for a particular individual in a particular context (Snyder & Miene 1994). Thus, the context-dependent functionality of stereotyping probably plays just as important a role in stereotype change as it does in the formation, maintenance, and application of stereotypes.

Inhibition

A question that is tightly tied to issues of stereotype change, particularly in the wake of recent analyses concerning the lack of intentionality associated with many stereotypes (Devine 1989, Devine et al 1991, Perdue & Gurtman 1990), is whether stereotypes can be inhibited by conscious action on the part of the perceiver. Macrae, Bodenhausen, and their colleagues (Bodenhausen & Macrae 1996; Macrae et al 1994b,c) have conducted a number of studies investigating the effect that conscious suppression of stereotypic thinking has on stereotype activation. Building on Wegner's (1994) model of thought suppression, they proposed that the ironic monitoring process caused by suppression leads to repeated activation of the content of the stereotype. This repeated activation, in turn, serves to prime the contents of the stereotype. When suppressors subsequently encounter members of stereotyped groups, the primed content of the stereotype leads them to interpret the target's behavior in stereotype-consistent ways. Consistent with this analysis, Macrae et al (1994b) found that subjects who had been instructed to suppress stereotypic thoughts were more likely to avoid interacting with the target of the stereotype than were subjects given no such instructions.

The Macrae et al results suggest that suppression does not provide a very effective route to stereotype inhibition. Extending this line of reasoning, recent work by Hilton et al (1993) provides an alternative way of thinking about stereotype inhibition. Specifically, Hilton et al argued that stereotypes should be viewed as naive theories about groups. These theories are linked to perceivers' general knowledge, and they provide explanatory frameworks for information about the group. In other words, stereotypes consist of knowledge about the attributes associated with a particular group and the causal connections between attributes (see also Sedikides & Anderson 1994).

It follows from this line of reasoning that one way to change stereotypes is to examine the causal links between stereotyped attributes. When confronted with the category "African-American male," for example, both high- and low-prejudiced individuals may anticipate meeting a man who is likely to be poor (Devine 1989). But whereas the prejudiced individual is willing to attribute this characteristic to the dispositional nature of African-American males, the nonprejudiced person has an explanation based on limited opportunity and structural barriers. As a consequence, the affective response to the target may depend importantly upon the explanation given (Weiner 1990; see also Whitley 1990). This view of stereotyping suggests that one way to inhibit stereotypic reactions to a target is to think more about the explanations, not to suppress thinking.

Finally, it should be noted that not all strategies of thought control are equally likely to be doomed to failure. People can be quite successful at monitoring their own responses when they feel they have violated their personal standards (Monteith 1993). Indeed, this issue of personal standards may be a critical factor in determining when suppression will fail or succeed. Consider the work of Macrae et al (1994b) and Monteith and her colleagues. In the Macrae et al (1994b) experiments, subjects were asked to suppress their stereotypes about skinheads. Given the typical beliefs about skinheads, it seems likely that the subjects had no strong desire not to stereotype skinheads and thus did not inhibit the priming effects that emerged as a consequence of their earlier stereotype suppression. In the Monteith (1993, Monteith et al 1993) experiments, nonprejudiced subjects did have a strong desire not to stereotype homosexuals and thus were more successful in their efforts to inhibit stereotypic responding. This notion of personal commitment or involvement in the goal to *not* stereotype seems to play a critical role and can also be seen in research on outcome dependency and accountability. Specifically, this research has shown that causing people to become personally involved with the targets of their stereotypes or accountable for the consequences of their stereotyping leads them to individuate the targets and rely less on stereotypes in their judgments (Schaller et al 1995, Tetlock 1992).

GENERAL CONCLUSIONS

We began this review by suggesting that it is difficult to settle on a single account of why stereotypes emerge, because stereotypes serve different functions in different contexts. In some situations, stereotypes simplify the processing demands on the perceiver. In other situations, they enrich perception by enabling the perceiver to go beyond the information given. In still other situations, they help the perceiver justify a particular conclusion or behavior. Consistent with these observations, the literature reviewed here suggests that stereotypes are formed and maintained through a variety of cognitive and motivational processes. Sometimes stereotypes are born from self-fulfilling prophecies, while other times they have their genesis in illusory correlations and perceptions of out-group homogeneity. Similarly, sometimes stereotypes are nurtured by our tendency to assimilate events to primed categories, while other times they are maintained by our tendency to remember information selectively. Thus, to the extent that there is a single message to be gleaned from the current review, it is that there is indeed no single message: Stereotypic thinking is clearly multiply mediated.

Nevertheless, although the field has made significant progress toward understanding individual mechanisms that are implicated in stereotypic thinking, we are struck by four areas of research in which the questions continue to outweigh the answers. First, it is evident from this review that we know much more about where stereotypes come from than about how to make them go away. On the positive side, the multiply mediated nature of stereotypes implies that a variety of factors should attenuate stereotypic thinking. Consistent with this logic, several factors have been found to influence the processes that contribute to stereotypic thinking. As noted above, for example, illusory correlations are less likely to emerge when evaluations are made on-line or when information processing is disrupted. Similarly, perceptions of out-group homogeneity can be reduced by encouraging cooperation and fostering individuation. Thus, it is possible to imagine a variety of interventions that could be deployed to combat the processes that lead to stereotypic thinking (see also Leippe & Eisenstadt 1994, Mackie et al 1992).

On the negative side, however, the multiply mediated nature of stereotypic thinking also implies that stereotypes are unlikely to respond to a single cure. To the extent that stereotypes are formed and maintained through a variety of processes that work individually and in concert, it becomes difficult to imagine interventions that successfully block all of the routes to stereotypic thinking. Indeed, the literature reviewed here suggests that the intervention side of the stereotyping problem is even more complicated than we might have originally imagined.

Second, this review suggests that we are only just beginning to get a handle on the nonconscious components of stereotyping. Beginning with Brewer's (1988) suggestion that category-relevant features are likely to be activated automatically upon an encounter with a category member, a substantial number of important papers have changed the way we think about stereotype activation and application. Following in this tradition, research by Greenwald & Banaji (1995) and Banaji & Greenwald (1995) and many others is beginning to challenge traditional ideas of what it means to hold a stereotype and how it is that stereotypes manifest themselves. Although there is naturally some controversy about the meaning and importance of the nonconscious components of stereotypes, the research on nonconscious stereotyping strongly suggests that simply asking people to describe members of various groups will, at best, provide an incomplete understanding of their stereotypes.

Third, we still know little about the consequences of stereotyping for the stereotyped individual. While a number of researchers have decried the paucity of research on the "victims" of stereotyping (e.g. Gaines & Reed 1995), the issue continues to be explored by relatively few individuals. It is worth noting, however, that the research that does exist suggests that the paradigms and problems that are proving fruitful in the study of the so-called perpetrators of stereotyping may also prove fruitful in the study of the victims of stereotyping (e.g. Crocker & Major 1989, Crocker et al 1991, Frable 1993, Frable et al 1990, Major & Crocker 1993).

Finally, the extensive research on the cognitive roots of stereotyping suggests that a fertile but relatively unexplored approach is to examine the impact of individual differences in cognitive functioning on the stereotyping process (see Ford & Kruglanski 1996, Neuberg & Newsom 1993, Schaller et al 1995). The literature reviewed herein highlights the important role that cognitive factors (and often the motivations behind them) play in stereotype formation, maintenance, application, and change. Nowhere should this be more apparent than in individual differences in cognitive styles and capabilities. And yet, while there has been a substantial amount of research on individual differences in proclivities toward stereotyping and prejudice (Altemeyer 1994; Devine 1989; Dovidio & Gaertner 1991; Haddock et al 1993, 1994; Monteith 1993), almost no research has taken advantage of the central findings of the stereotyping literature and searched for individual differences in the tendency to form illusory correlations, for example, or to perceive out-group homogeneity. Undoubtedly, much of what we currently regard as error variance in the tendency to show such biases has important causes and significant practical and theoretical implications for our understanding of stereotypes and stereotyping.

ACKNOWLEDGMENTS

We gratefully thank Marilynn Brewer, Steve Fein, Deborah Frable, Tony Greenwald, Geoff Haddock, Neal Macrae, Allen McConnell, Margo Monteith, Alex Rothman, Norbert Schwartz, John Skowronski, Jeff Sherman, Jim Sherman, Eliot Smith, Phil Tetlock, and Michael Zárate for their helpful comments on earlier drafts of the manuscript. Order of authorship was determined alphabetically; both authors contributed equally.

Literature Cited

Allport G. 1954. *The Nature of Prejudice.* Cambridge, MA: Addison-Wesley

Altemeyer B. 1994. Reducing prejudice in right-wing authoritarians. See Zanna & Olson 1994, pp. 131–48

Anderson SM, Cole SW. 1990. Do I know you? The role of significant others in general social perception. *J. Pers. Soc. Psychol.* 59:235–46

Banaji MR, Greenwald AG. 1995. Implicit gender stereotyping in judgments of fame. *J. Pers. Soc. Psychol.* 68:181–98

Banaji MR, Hardin C, Rothman AJ. 1993. Implicit stereotyping in person judgment. *J. Pers. Soc. Psychol.* 65:272–81

Bargh JA. 1989. Conditional automaticity: varieties of automatic influence in social perception and cognition. In *Unintended Thought,* ed. JS Uleman, JA Bargh, pp. 3–51. New York: Guilford

Bargh JA. 1994. The four horsemen of automaticity: awareness, intention, efficiency, and control in social cognition. See Wyer & Srull 1994, pp. 1–40

Bargh JA, Gollwitzer PM. 1994. Environmental control of goal-directed action: automatic and strategic contingencies between situations and behavior. In *Nebraska Symposium on Motivation,* ed. R Dienstbier, 41:73–124. Lincoln: Univ. Nebr. Press

Bargh JA, Raymond P, Pryor JB, Strack F. 1995. Attractiveness of the underling: an automatic power→sex association and its consequences for sexual harrassment and aggression. *J. Pers. Soc. Psychol.* 68:768–81

Barsalou LW. 1990. On the indistinguishability of exemplar memory and abstraction in category representation. See Srull & Wyer 1990, pp. 61–88

Bar-Tal D, Graumann CF, Kruglanski AW, Stroebe W, eds. 1989. *Stereotyping and Prejudice: Changing Conceptions.* New York: Springer-Verlag

Bartsch RA, Judd CM. 1993. Majority-minority status and perceived ingroup variability revisited. *Eur. J. Soc. Psychol.* 23:471–83

Batson CD, Burris CT. 1994. Personal religion: depressant or stimulant of prejudice and discrimination? See Zanna & Olson 1994, pp. 149–69

Beckett NE, Park B. 1995. Use of category versus individuating information: making base rates salient. *Pers. Soc. Psychol. Bull.* 21:21–31

Bodenhausen GV. 1990. Stereotypes as judgmental heuristics: evidence of circadian variations in discrimination. *Psychol. Sci.* 1:319–22

Bodenhausen GV, Kramer GP, Süsser K. 1994a. Happiness and stereotypic thinking in social judgment. *J. Pers. Soc. Psychol.* 66:621–32

Bodenhausen GV, Macrae CN. 1996. The self-regulation of intergroup perception: mechanisms and consequences of stereotype suppression. In *Foundations of Stereotypes and Stereotyping,* ed. CN Macrae, M Hewstone, C Stangor. Guilford Press. In press

Bodenhausen GV, Schwartz N, Bless H, Wänke M. 1995. Effects of atypical exemplars on racial beliefs: enlightened racism or generalized appraisals? *J. Exp. Soc. Psychol.* 31:48–63

Bodenhausen GV, Sheppard LA, Kramer GP. 1994b. Negative affect and social judgment: the differential impact of anger and sadness. *Eur. J. Soc. Psychol.* 24:45–62

Brewer MB. 1988. A dual process model of impression formation. In *Advances in Social Cognition,* ed. TK Srull, RS Wyer Jr, 1:1–36. Hillsdale, NJ: Erlbaum

Brewer MB. 1994. The social psychology of prejudice: getting it all together. See Zanna & Olson 1994, pp. 315–29

Brewer MB, Dull V, Lui L. 1981. Perceptions of the elderly: stereotypes as prototypes. *J. Pers. Soc. Psychol.* 41:656–70

Bruner JS. 1957. On perceptual readiness. *Psychol. Rev.* 64:123–52

Cacioppo JT, Marshall-Goodell BS, Tassinary LG, Petty RE. 1992. Rudimentary determinants of attitudes: classical conditioning is more effective when prior knowledge about the attitude stimulus is low than high. *J. Exp. Soc. Psychol.* 28:207–33

Cantor N, Mischel W. 1978. Prototypes in person perception. In *Advances in Experimental Social Psychology,* ed. L Berkowitz, 12:3–52. New York: Academic

Carlston DE. 1992. Impression formation and the modular mind: the Associated Systems Theory. In *The Construction of Social Judgments,* ed. L Martin, A Tesser, pp. 301–41. Hillsdale, NJ: Erlbaum

Carlston DE, Skowronski JJ. 1994. Savings in relearning of trait information as evidence for spontaneous trait inference generation. *J. Pers. Soc. Psychol.* 66:840–56

Crocker J, Luhtanen R. 1990. Collective self-esteem and ingroup bias. *J. Pers. Soc. Psychol.* 58:60–67

Crocker J, Major B. 1989. Social stigma and self-esteem: the self-protective properties of stigma. *Psychol. Rev.* 96:608–30

Crocker J, Voelkl K, Testa M, Major B. 1991. Social stigma: the affective consequences of attributional ambiguity. *J. Pers. Soc. Psychol.* 54:840–46

Darley JM, Gross PH. 1983. A hypothesis-confirming bias in labeling effects. *J. Pers. Soc. Psychol.* 44:20–33

Devine PG. 1989. Stereotypes and prejudice: their automatic and controlled components. *J. Pers. Soc. Psychol.* 56:5–18

Devine PG, Baker SM. 1991. Measurement of racial stereotype subtyping. *Pers. Soc. Psychol. Bull.* 17:44–50

Devine PG, Monteith MJ. 1993. The role of discrepancy-associated affect in prejudice reduction. See Mackie & Hamilton 1993, pp. 317–44

Devine PG, Monteith MJ, Zuwerink JR, Elliot AJ. 1991. Prejudice with and without compunction. *J. Pers. Soc. Psychol.* 60: 817–30

Diehl M, Jonas K. 1991. Measure of national stereotypes as predictors of latencies of inductive versus deductive stereotypic judgments. *Eur. J. Soc. Psychol.* 21:317–30

Ditto PH, Lopez DA. 1993. Motivated skepticism: use of differential decision criteria for preferred and nonpreferred conclusions. *J. Pers. Soc. Psychol.* 63:568–84

Dovidio JF, Brigham JC, Johnson BT, Gaertner SL. 1995. Stereotyping, prejudice, and discrimination: another look. *Foundations of Stereotypes and Stereotyping,* ed. N Macrae, M Hewstone, C Stangor. New York: Guilford. In press

Dovidio JF, Gaertner SL. 1991. Changes in the nature and assessment of racial prejudice. In *Opening Doors: An Appraisal of Race Relations in Contemporary America,* ed. H Knopke, J Norrell, R Rogers, pp. 201–41. Tuscaloosa: Univ. Ala. Press

Dovidio JF, Gaertner SL. 1993. Stereotypes and evaluative intergroup bias. See Mackie & Hamilton 1993, pp. 167–193

Eagly AH. 1995. The science and politics of comparing women and men. *Am. Psychol.* 50:145–58

Eagly AH, Mladinic A. 1989. Gender stereotypes and attitudes toward women and men. *Pers. Soc. Psychol. Bull.* 15:543–58

Erber R. 1991. Affective and semantic priming: effects of mood on category accessibility and inference. *J. Exp. Soc. Psychol.* 27: 480–98

Esses VM, Haddock G, Zanna MP. 1993. Values, stereotypes, and emotions as determinants of intergroup attitudes. See Mackie & Hamilton 1993, pp. 137–66

Esses VM, Haddock G, Zanna MP. 1994. The role of mood in the expression of intergroup stereotypes. See Zanna & Olson 1994, pp. 77–102

Fazio RH, Jackson SR, Dunton BC, Williams CJ. 1995. Variability in automatic activation as an unobtrusive measure of racial attitudes: a bona fide pipeline? *J. Pers. Soc. Psychol.* In press

Fein S, Hilton JL. 1992. Attitudes toward groups and behavioral intentions toward individual group members: the impact of nondiagnostic information. *J. Exp. Soc. Psychol.* 28:101–24

Fein S, Spencer SJ. 1993. *Self-esteem and stereotype-based downward social comparison.* Presented at Annu. Meet. Am. Psychol. Assoc., 101st, Toronto

Fein S, Spencer SJ. 1994. *Self-affirmation processes in stereotyping and prejudice.* Presented at Annu. Meet. Pers. Mem. Interest Group, Lake Tahoe, CA

Fiedler K. 1991. The tricky nature of skewed frequency tables: an information loss account of distinctiveness-based illusory correlations. *J. Pers. Soc. Psychol.* 60:24–36

Fiedler K, Armbruster T. 1994. Two halves may be more than one whole: category-split effects on frequency illusions. *J. Pers. Soc. Psychol.* 66:633–45

Fiske ST. 1993. Controlling other people: the impact of power on stereotyping. *Am. Psychol.* 48:621–28

Fiske ST, Neuberg SL. 1990. A continuum of impression formation, from category-based to individuating processes: influences of information and motivation on attention and interpretation. In *Advances in Experimental Social Psychology,* ed. MP Zanna, 23: 1–74. New York: Academic

Fiske ST, Taylor SE. 1991. *Social Cognition.* New York: McGraw-Hill

Ford TE, Kruglanski AW. 1996. Effects of epistemic motivations on the use of accessible construct in social judgments. *Pers. Soc. Psychol. Bull.* In press

Ford TE, Stangor C. 1992. The role of diagnosticity in stereotype formation: perceiving group means and variances. *J. Pers. Soc. Psychol.* 63:356–67

Ford TE, Stangor C, Duan C. 1994. Influence of social category and category-associated trait accessibility on judgments of individuals. *Soc. Cogn.* 12:149–68

Frable DES. 1993. Dimensions of marginality: distinctions among those who are different. *Pers. Soc. Psychol. Bull.* 19:370–80

Frable DES, Blackstone T, Scherbaum C. 1990. Marginal and mindful: deviants in social interactions. *J. Pers. Soc. Psychol.* 59:140–49

Gaines SO, Reed ES. 1995. Prejudice: from Allport to DuBois. *Am. Psychol.* 50: 96–103

Gardner RC. 1994. Stereotypes as consensual beliefs. See Zanna & Olson 1994, pp. 1–32

Gigerenzer G, Hell W, Blank H. 1988. Presentation and content: the use of base rates as a continuous variable. *J. Exp. Psychol.: Hum. Percept. Perform.* 14:513–25

Gilbert DT, Hixon JG. 1991. The trouble of thinking: activation and application of stereotypic beliefs. *J. Pers. Soc. Psychol.* 60:509–17

Greenwald AG, Banaji MR. 1995. Implicit social cognition: attitudes, self-esteem, and stereotypes. *Psychol. Rev.*102:4–27

Haddock G, Zanna MP, Esses VM. 1993. Assessing the structure of prejudicial attitudes: the case of attitudes toward homosexuals. *J. Pers. Soc. Psychol.* 65: 1105–18

Haddock G, Zanna MP, Esses VM. 1994. Mood and the expression of intergroup attitudes: the moderating role of affect intensity. *Eur. J. Soc. Psychol.* 24:189–205

Hamilton DL, Gibbons P, Stroessner SJ, Sherman JW. 1992. Stereotypes and language use. In *Language and Social Cognition*, ed. K Fiedler, GR Semin, pp. 102–28. Newbury Park, CA: Sage

Hamilton DL, Mackie DM. 1990. Specificity and generality in the nature and use of stereotypes. See Srull & Wyer 1990, pp. 99–110

Hamilton DL, Sherman JW. 1994. Stereotypes. In *Handbook of Social Cognition*, Vol. 2, *Applications*, ed. RS Wyer Jr, TK Srull, pp. 1–68. Hillsdale, NJ: Erlbaum

Hamilton DL, Sherman SJ. 1989. Illusory correlations: implications for stereotype theory and research. See Bar-Tal et al 1989, pp. 59–82

Hamilton DL, Stroessner SJ, Mackie DM. 1993. The influence of affect on stereotyping: the case of illusory correlations. See Mackie & Hamilton 1993, pp. 39–61

Haslam SA, Turner JC, Oakes PJ, McGarty C, Hayes BK. 1992. Context-dependent variation in social stereotyping. I. The effects of intergroup relations as mediated by social change and frame of reference. *Eur. J. Soc. Psychol.* 22:3–20

Hass RG, Katz I, Rizzo N, Bailey J, Eisenstadt D. 1991. Cross-racial appraisal as related to attitude ambivalence and cognitive complexity. *Pers. Soc. Psychol. Bull.* 17: 83–92

Hass RG, Katz I, Rizzo N, Bailey J, Moore L. 1992. When racial ambivalence evokes negative affect, using a disguised measure of mood. *Pers. Soc. Psychol. Bull.* 18: 786–97

Hewstone M. 1989. Changing stereotypes with disconfirming information. See Bar-Tal et al 1989, pp. 207–23

Hewstone M. 1990. The "ultimate attribution error"?: a review of the literature on intergroup causal attribution. *Eur. J. Soc. Psychol.* 20:311–35

Hewstone M, Hopkins N, Routh DA. 1992a. Cognitive models of stereotype change. I. Generalization and subtyping in young people of the police. *Eur. J. Soc. Psychol.* 22:219–34

Hewstone M, Jaspars JMF. 1984. Social dimensions of attribution. In *The Social Dimension: European Developments in Social Psychology*, ed. H Tajfel, 2:379–404. Cambridge: Cambridge Univ. Press

Hewstone M, Johnston L, Aird P. 1992b. Cognitive models of stereotype change. II. Perceptions of homogeneous and heterogeneous groups. *Eur. J. Soc. Psychol.* 22: 235–49

Hill T, Lewicki P, Czyzewska M, Boss A. 1989. Self-perpetuating development of encoding biases in person perception. *J. Pers. Soc. Psychol.* 57:373–87

Hill T, Lewicki P, Czyzewska M, Schuller G. 1990. The role of learned inferential encoding rules in the perception of faces: effects of nonconscious self-perpetuation of a bias. *J. Exp. Soc. Psychol.* 26:350–71

Hilton JL, Darley JM. 1991. The effects of interaction goals on person perception. In *Advances in Experimental Social Psychology*, ed. MP Zanna, 24:235–67. Orlando, FL: Academic

Hilton JL, Fein S. 1989. The role of typical diagnosticity in stereotype-based judgments. *J. Pers. Soc. Psychol.* 57:501–11

Hilton JL, Klein JG, von Hippel W. 1991. Attention allocation and impression formation. *Pers. Soc. Psychol. Bull.* 17:548–59

Hilton JL, von Hippel W. 1990. The role of consistency in the judgment of stereotype-relevant behaviors. *Pers. Soc. Psychol. Bull.* 16:430–48

Hilton JL, Wittenbrink B, Gist PL. 1993. *Turning base metal into gold: stereotypes as explanatory frameworks.* Presented at Annu. Meet. Soc. Pers. Soc. Psychol., 3rd, Chicago

Hogg MA, Abrams D. 1988. *Social Identifications: A Social Psychology of Intergroup Relations and Group Processes.* London: Routledge

Islam MR, Hewstone M. 1993a. Dimensions of contact as predictors of intergroup anxiety, perceived out-group variability, and out-group attitude: an integrative model. *Pers. Soc. Psychol. Bull.* 19:700–10

Islam MR, Hewstone M. 1993b. Intergroup attributions and affective consequences in majority and minority groups. *J. Pers. Soc. Psychol.* 64:936–50

Jackson LA, Sullivan LA, Hodge CN. 1993. Stereotype effects on attributions, predictions, and evaluations: no two social judgments are quite alike. *J. Pers. Soc. Psychol.* 65:69–84

Johnson C, Mullen B. 1994. Evidence for accessibility of paired distinctiveness in distinctiveness-based illusory correlation in stereotyping. *Pers. Soc. Psychol. Bull.* 20: 65–60

Johnston L, Hewstone M. 1992. Cognitive models of stereotype change. III. Subtyping and the perceived typicality of disconfirming group members. *J. Exp. Soc. Psychol.* 28:360–86

Jost JT, Banaji MR. 1994. The role of stereotyping in system-justification and the production of false consciousness. *Br. J. Soc. Psychol.* 33:1–27

Judd CM, Park B. 1988. Outgroup homogeneity: judgments of variability at the individual and group levels. *J. Pers. Soc. Psychol.* 54:778–88

Judd CM, Park B. 1993. Definition and assessment of accuracy in social stereotypes. *Psychol. Rev.* 100:109–28

Judd CM, Ryan CS, Park B. 1991. Accuracy in the judgment of in-group and out-group variability. *J. Pers. Soc. Psychol.* 61: 366–79

Jussim L. 1991. Social perception and social reality: a reflection-construction model. *Psychol. Rev.* 98:54–73

Jussim L, Coleman LM, Lerch L. 1987. The nature of stereotypes: a comparison and integration of three theories. *J. Pers. Soc. Psychol.* 52:536–46

Jussim L, Nelson TE, Manis M, Soffin S. 1995. Prejudice, stereotypes, and labeling effects: sources of bias in person perception. *J. Pers. Soc. Psychol.* 68:228–46

Kanazawa S. 1992. Outcome or expectancy? Antecedent of spontaneous causal attribution. *Pers. Soc. Psychol. Bull.* 18: 659–68

Kashima ES, Kashima Y. 1993. Perceptions of general variability of social groups. *Soc. Cogn.* 11:1–21

Kelly C. 1989. Political identity and perceived intragroup homogeneity. *Br. J. Soc. Psychol.* 28:239–50

Klein SB, Loftus J, Trafton JG, Fuhrman RW. 1992. Use of exemplars and abstractions in trait judgments: a model of trait knowledge about self and others. *J. Pers. Soc. Psychol.* 63:739–53

Klein WM, Kunda Z. 1992. Motivated person perception: constructing justifications for desired beliefs. *J. Exp. Soc. Psychol.* 28: 145–68

Klein WM, Kunda Z. 1993. Maintaining self-serving social comparisons: biased reconstruction of one's past behaviors. *Pers. Soc. Psychol. Bull.* 19:732–39

Kleinpenning G, Hagendoorn L. 1991. Contextual aspects of ethnic stereotypes and interethnic evaluations. *Eur. J. Soc. Psychol.* 21:331–48

Kleinpenning G, Hagendoorn L. 1993. Forms of racism and the cumulative dimension of ethnic attitudes. *Soc. Psychol. Q.* 56: 21–36

Klinger MR, Beall PM. 1992. *Conscious and unconscious effects of stereotype activation.* Presented at Annu. Meet. Midwest. Psychol. Assoc., 64th, Chicago

Kraus S, Ryan CS, Judd CM, Hastie R, Park B. 1993. Use of mental frequency distributions to represent variability among members of social categories. *Soc. Cogn.* 11: 22–43

Krueger J, Clement RW. 1994. Memory-based judgments about multiple categories: a revision and extension of Tajfel's Accentuation Theory. *J. Pers. Soc. Psychol.* 67: 35–47

Krueger J, Rothbart M. 1988. Use of categorical and individuating information in making inferences about personality. *J. Pers. Soc. Psychol.* 55:187–95

Krueger J, Rothbart M. 1990. Contrast and accentuation effects in category learning. *J. Pers. Soc. Psychol.* 59:651–63

Krueger J, Rothbart M, Sriram N. 1989. Category learning and change: differences in sensitivity to information that enhances or reduces inter-category distinctions. *J. Pers. Soc. Psychol.* 56:866–75

Kunda Z. 1990. The case for motivated reasoning. *Psychol. Bull.* 108:480–98

Kunda Z, Oleson KC. 1995. Maintaining stereotypes in the face of disconfirmation: constructing grounds for subtyping deviants. *J. Pers. Soc. Psychol.* 68:565–79

Kunda Z, Sherman-Williams B. 1993. Stereotypes and the construal of individuating information. *Pers. Soc. Psychol. Bull.* 19: 90–99

Leippe MR, Eisenstadt D. 1994. Generalization of dissonance reduction: decreasing prejudice through induced compliance. *J. Pers. Soc. Psychol.* 67:395–413

Lewicki P. 1986. *Nonconscious Social Information Processing.* Orlando, FL: Academic

Linville PW, Fischer GW. 1993. Exemplar and abstraction models of perceived group variability and stereotypicality. *Soc. Cogn.* 11: 92–125

Linville PW, Fischer GW, Salovey P. 1989. Perceived distributions of the characteristics of in-group and out-group members: empirical evidence and a computer simulation. *J. Pers. Soc. Psychol.* 57: 165–88

Leyens JP, Yzerbyt VY, Schadron G. 1992. The social judgeability approach to stereotypes. In *European Review of Social Psychology,* ed. W Stroebe, M Hewstone, 3: 91–120. London: Wiley

Maass A, Milesi A, Zabbini S, Stahlberg D. 1995. Linguistic intergroup bias: differential expectancies or in-group protection? *J. Pers. Soc. Psychol.* 68:116–26

Maass A, Salvi D, Arcuri L, Semin G. 1989. Language use in intergroup contexts: the linguistic intergroup bias. *J. Pers. Soc. Psychol.* 57:981–93

Mackie DM, Allison ST, Worth LT, Asunscion AG. 1992. The generalization of outcome-biased counter-stereotypic inferences. *J. Exp. Soc. Psychol.* 28:43–64

Mackie DM, Hamilton DL, eds. 1993. *Affect,*

Cognition, and Stereotyping: Interactive Processes in Group Perception. San Diego: Academic

Macrae CN, Bodenhausen GV, Milne AB. 1994a. When one stereotype is better than two: inhibitory mechanisms in category activation. Presented at Annu. Conv. Soc. Exp. Soc. Psychol., Lake Tahoe, NV

Macrae CN, Bodenhausen GV, Milne AB, Jetten J. 1994b. Out of mind but back in sight: stereotypes on the rebound. J. Pers. Soc. Psychol. 67:808–17

Macrae CN, Hewstone M, Griffiths RJ. 1993. Processing load and memory for stereotype-based information. Eur. J. Soc. Psychol. 23:77–87

Macrae CN, Milne AB, Bodenhausen GV. 1994c. Stereotypes as energy-saving devices: a peek inside the cognitive toolbox. J. Pers. Soc. Psychol. 66:37–47

Macrae CN, Shepherd JW, Milne AB. 1992. The effects of source credibility on the dilution of stereotype-based judgments. Pers. Soc. Psychol. Bull. 18:765–75

Major B, Crocker J. 1993. Social stigma: the consequences of attributional ambiguity. See Mackie & Hamilton 1993, pp. 345–70

Manis M, Nelson TE, Shedler J. 1988. Stereotypes and social judgment: extremity, assimilation, and contrast. J. Pers. Soc. Psychol. 55:28–36

McCauley C. 1994. Stereotypes as base rate predictions: commentary on Koehler on base-rate. Psycoloquy ISSN 1055–1143

McConahay JG. 1986. Modern racism, ambivalence, and the modern racism scale. In Prejudice, Discrimination, and Racism, ed. JF Dovidio, SL Gaertner, pp. 91–125. New York: Academic

McConnell AR, Sherman SJ, Hamilton DL. 1994a. On-line and memory-based aspects of individual and group target judgments. J. Pers. Soc. Psychol. 67:173–85

McConnell AR, Sherman SJ, Hamilton DL. 1994b. Illusory correlations in the perception of groups: an extension of the distinctiveness-based account. J. Pers. Soc. Psychol. 67:414–29

McConnell AR, Sherman SJ, Hamilton DL. 1995. Target cohesiveness: implications for social information processing about groups and individuals. Presented at Annu. Meet. Midwest. Psychol. Assoc., 67th, Chicago

McGarty C, Haslam SA, Turner JC, Oakes PJ. 1993. Illusory correlations as accentuation of actual intercategory differences: evidence for the effect with minimal stimulus information. Eur. J. Soc. Psychol. 23:391–410

McKenzie-Mohr D, Zanna MP. 1990. Treating women as sexual objects: Look to the gender schematic male who has viewed pornography. Pers. Soc. Psychol. Bull. 16:296–308

Monteith M. 1993. Self-regulation of prejudiced responses: implications for progress in prejudice-reduction efforts. J. Pers. Soc. Psychol. 65:469–85

Monteith MJ, Devine PG, Zuwerink JR. 1993. Self-directed versus other-directed affect as a consequence of prejudice-related discrepancies. J. Pers. Soc. Psychol. 64:198–210

Mullen B. 1991. Group composition, salience, and cognitive representations: the phenomenology of being in a group. J. Exp. Soc. Psychol. 27:297–323

Mullen B, Johnson C. 1990. Distinctiveness-based illusory correlations and stereotyping: a meta-analytic integration. Br. J. Soc. Psychol. 29:11–28

Mullen B, Johnson C. 1995. Cognitive representation in ethnophaulisms and illusory correlation in stereotyping. Pers. Soc. Psychol. Bull. 21:420–33

Murray N, Sujan H, Hirt ER, Sujan M. 1990. The influence of mood on categorization: a cognitive flexibility interpretation. J. Pers. Soc. Psychol. 59:411–25

Nelson LJ, Miller DT. 1995. The distinctiveness effect in social categorization: You are what makes you unusual. Psychol. Sci. 6:246–49

Nelson TE, Biernat MR, Manis M. 1990. Everyday base rates (sex stereotypes): potent and resilient. J. Pers. Soc. Psychol. 59:664–75

Neuberg SL, Newsom JT. 1993. Personal need for structure: individual differences in the desire for simple structure. J. Pers. Soc. Psychol. 65:113–31

Nisbett RE, Ross L. 1980. Human Inference: Strategies and Shortcoming of Social Judgment. Englewood Cliffs, NJ: Prentice-Hall

Oakes PJ, Turner JC. 1990. Is limited information processing capacity the cause of social stereotyping? In European Review of Social Psychology, ed. W Stroebe, M Hewstone, 1:112–35. London: Wiley

Ostrom TM, Sedikides C. 1992. Out-group homogeneity effects in natural and minimal groups. Psychol. Bull. 112:536–52

Park B, Hastie R. 1987. Perception of variability in category development: instance- versus abstraction-based stereotypes. J. Pers. Soc. Psychol. 53:621–35

Park B, Judd CM. 1990. Measures and models of perceived group variability. J. Pers. Soc. Psychol. 59:173–91

Park B, Judd CM, Ryan CS. 1991. Social categorization and the representation of variability information. In European Review of Social Psychology, ed. W Stroebe, M Hewstone, 2:211–45. London: Wiley

Park B, Ryan CS, Judd CM. 1992. The role of meaningful subgroups in explaining differences in perceived variability for in-groups and out-groups. *J. Pers. Soc. Psychol.* 63: 553–67

Pendry LF, Macrae CN. 1994. Stereotypes and mental life: the case of the motivated but thwarted tactician. *J. Exp. Soc. Psychol.* 30:303–25

Perdue CW, Dovidio JF, Gurtman MB, Tyler RB. 1990. Us and them: social categorization and the process of intergroup bias. *J. Pers. Soc. Psychol.* 59:475–86

Perdue CW, Gurtman MB. 1990. Evidence for the automaticity of ageism. *J. Exp. Soc. Psychol.* 26:199–216

Pettigrew TF. 1979. The ultimate attribution error: extending Allport's cognitive analysis of prejudice. *Pers. Soc. Psychol. Bull.* 5:461–76

Quattrone GA. 1986. On the perception of a group. In *Psychology of Intergroup Relations*, ed. S Worchel, WG Austin, pp. 25–48. Chicago: Nelson-Hall

Robinson RJ, Keltner D, Ward A, Ross L. 1995. Actual versus assumed differences in construal: realism in intergroup perception and conflict. *J. Pers. Soc. Psychol.* 68: 404–17

Rojahn K, Pettigrew TF. 1992. Memory for schema-relevant information: a meta-analytic resolution. *Br. J. Soc. Psychol.* 31: 81–109

Rosenthal R, Jacobson L. 1968. *Pygmalion in the Classroom.* New York: Holt Rinehart Winston

Rothbart M. 1981. Memory processes and social beliefs. In *Cognitive Processes in Stereotyping and Intergroup Behavior*, ed. DL Hamilton, pp. 145–81. Hillsdale, NJ: Erlbaum

Rothbart M, Dawes R, Park B. 1984. Stereotyping and sampling biases in intergroup perception. In *Attitude Judgment,* ed. JR Eiser, pp. 109–34. New York: Springer-Verlag

Rothbart M, Taylor M. 1992. Category labels and social reality: Do we view social categories as natural kinds? In *Language, Interaction and Social Cognition,* ed. GR Semin, K Fiedler, pp. 11–36. London: Sage

Rubini M, Semin GR. 1994. Language use in the context of congruent and incongruent in-group behaviors. *Br. J. Soc. Psychol.* 33: 355–62

Rudman L, Borgida E. N.d. The afterglow of construct accessibility: the behavioral consequences of priming men to view women as sexual objects. *J. Exp. Soc. Psychol.* In press

Sanbonmatsu DM, Akimoto SA, Gibson BD. 1994. Stereotype-based blocking in social explanation. *Pers. Soc. Psychol. Bull.* 20: 71–81

Sanitioso R, Kunda Z, Fong GT. 1990. Motivated recruitment of autobiographical memories. *J. Pers. Soc. Psychol.* 59: 229–41

Schaller M. 1991. Social categorization and the formation of group stereotypes: further evidence for biased information processing in the perception of group-behavior correlations. *Eur. J. Soc. Psychol.* 21:25–35

Schaller M. 1992. In-group favoritism and statistical reasoning in social inference: implications for formation and maintenance of group stereotypes. *J. Pers. Soc. Psychol.* 63:61–74

Schaller M, Boyd C, Yohannes JOM. 1995. The prejudiced personality revisited: personal need for structure and formation of erroneous group stereotypes. *J. Pers. Soc. Psychol.* 68:544–55

Sears DO. 1988. Symbolic racism. In *Towards the Elimination of Racism: Profiles in Controversy,* ed. P Katz, D Taylor, pp. 53–84. New York: Plenum

Sedikides C, Anderson CA. 1994. Causal perception of intertrait relations: the glue that holds person types together. *Pers. Soc. Psychol. Bull.* 20:294–302

Sedikides C, Skowronski JJ. 1991. The law of cognitive structure activation. *Psychol. Inq.* 2:169–84

Semin GR, Fiedler K. 1988. The cognitive functions of linguistic categories in describing persons: social cognition and language. *J. Pers. Soc. Psychol.* 54:558–68

Sherman JW. 1994. *The mental representation of stereotypes and its implications for stereotype development and function.* PhD thesis. Univ. Calif., Santa Barbara

Sherman JW, Hamilton DL. 1994. On the formation of interitem associative links in person memory. *J. Exp. Soc. Psychol.* 30: 203–17

Sherman SJ, Hamilton DL, Roskos-Ewoldson DR. 1989. Attenuation of illusory correlation. *Pers. Soc. Psychol. Bull.* 15:559–71

Sherman SJ, Mackie DM, Driscoll DM. 1990. Priming and the differential use of dimensions in evaluation. *Pers. Soc. Psychol. Bull.* 16:405–18

Sidanius J. 1993. The psychology of group conflict and the dynamics of oppression: a social dominance perspective. In *Explorations in Political Psychology,* ed. S Iyengar, WJ McGuire, pp. 183–219. Durham, NC: Duke Univ. Press

Simon B, Mlicki P, Johnston L, Caetano A. 1990. The effects of ingroup and outgroup homogeneity on ingroup favoritism, stereotyping and overestimation of relative ingroup size. *Eur. J. Soc. Psychol.* 20:519–23

Skowronski JJ, Carlston DE, Isham JT. 1993. Implicit versus explicit impression formation: the differing effects of overt labeling and covert priming on memory and impressions. *J. Exp. Soc. Psychol.* 29:17–41

Smith ER. 1990. Content and process specificity in the effects of prior experiences. See Srull & Wyer 1990, pp. 1–59

Smith ER. 1991. Illusory correlation in a simulated exemplar-based memory. *J. Exp. Soc. Psychol.* 27:107–23

Smith ER. 1993. Social identity and social emotions: toward new conceptualizations of prejudice. See Mackie & Hamilton 1993, pp. 297–316

Smith ER, Stewart TL, Buttram RT. 1992. Inferring a trait from a behavior has long-term, highly specific effects. *J. Pers. Soc. Psychol.* 62:753–59

Smith ER, Zárate MA. 1992. Exemplar-based model of social judgment. *Psychol. Rev.* 99:3–21

Sniderman PM, Piazza T, Tetlock PE, Kendrick A. 1991. The new racism. *Am. J. Pol. Sci.* 35:423–47

Snyder M. 1992. Motivational foundations of behavioral confirmation. In *Advances in Experimental Social Psychology,* ed. MP Zanna, 25:67–114. Orlando, FL: Academic

Snyder M, Miene P. 1994. On the functions of stereotype and prejudice. See Zanna & Olson 1994, pp. 33–54

Snyder M, Tanke ED, Berscheid E. 1977. Social perception and interpersonal behavior: on the self-fulfilling nature of social stereotypes. *J. Pers. Soc. Psychol.* 35:656–66

Snyder ML, Kleck RE, Strenta A, Mentzer SJ. 1979. Avoidance of the handicapped: an attributional ambiguity analysis. *J. Pers. Soc. Psychol.* 37:2297–306

Spencer SJ, Fein S. 1994. *The effect of self-image threats on stereotyping.* Presented at Annu. Meet. East. Psychol. Assoc., 65th, Providence, RI

Srull TK, Wyer RS Jr. 1989. Person memory and judgment. *Psychol. Rev.* 96:58–83

Srull TK, Wyer RS Jr, eds. 1990. *Advances in Social Cognition,* Vol. 3. Hillsdale, NJ: Erlbaum

Stangor C, Duan C. 1991. Effects of multiple task demands upon memory for information about social groups. *J. Exp. Soc. Psychol.* 27:357–78

Stangor C, McMillan D. 1992. Memory for expectancy-congruent and expectancy-incongruent information: a review of the social and social developmental literatures. *Psychol. Bull.* 111:42–61

Stangor C, Sullivan L, Ford T. 1991. Affective and cognitive determinants of prejudice. *Soc. Cogn.* 9:359–80

Stephan WG, Ageyev V, Coates-Shrider L, Stephan CW, Abalakina M. 1994. On the relationship between stereotypes and prejudice: an international study. *Pers. Soc. Psychol. Bull.* 20:277–84

Stephan WG, Stephan CW. 1993. Cognition and affect in stereotyping: parallel interactive networks. See Mackie & Hamilton 1993, pp. 111–36

Stroebe W, Insko CA. 1989. Stereotype, prejudice, and discrimination: changing conceptions in theory and research. See Bar-Tal et al 1989, pp. 3–34

Stroessner SJ, Hamilton DL, Mackie DM. 1992. Affect and stereotyping: the effect of induced mood on distinctiveness-based illusory correlation. *J. Pers. Soc. Psychol.* 62:564–76

Stroessner SJ, Mackie DM. 1992. The impact of induced affect on the perception of variability in social groups. *Pers. Soc. Psychol. Bull.* 18:546–54

Stroessner SJ, Mackie DM. 1993. Affect and perceived group variability: implications for stereotyping and prejudice. See Mackie & Hamilton 1993, pp. 63–86

Swim JK. 1994. Perceived versus meta-analytic effect sizes: an assessment of the accuracy of gender stereotypes. *J. Pers. Soc. Psychol.* 66:21–36

Swim JK, Aikin KJ, Hall WS, Hunter BA. 1995. Sexism and racism: old-fashioned and modern prejudices. *J. Pers. Soc. Psychol.* 68:199–214

Tetlock PE. 1992. The impact of accountability on judgment and choice: toward a social contingency model. In *Advances in Experimental Social Psychology,* ed. MP Zanna, 25:331–76. New York: Academic

Vanbeselaere N. 1991. The different effects of simple and crossed categorizations: a result of the category differentiation process or of differential category salience? In *European Review of Social Psychology,* ed. W Stroebe, M Hewstone, 2:247–78. Chichester, Engl.: Wiley

von Hippel W, Jonides J, Hilton JL, Narayan S. 1993. Inhibitory effect of schematic processing on perceptual encoding. *J. Pers. Soc. Psychol.* 64:921–35

von Hippel W, Sekaquaptewa D, Vargas P. 1995. On the role of encoding processes in stereotype maintenance. In *Advances in Experimental Social Psychology,* ed. MP Zanna, 27:177–254. Orlando, FL: Academic

Vonk R, van Knippenberg A. 1995. Processing attitude statements from in-group and out-group members: effects of within-group and within-person inconsistencies on reading times. *J. Pers. Soc. Psychol.* 68:215–27

Weber JG. 1994. The nature of ethnocentric attribution bias: ingroup protection or enhancement? *J. Exp. Soc. Psychol.* 30:482–504

Weber R, Crocker J. 1983. Cognitive processes in the revision of stereotypic beliefs. *J. Pers. Soc. Psychol.* 45:961–77

Wegner DM. 1994. Ironic processes of mental control. *Psychol. Rev.* 101:34–52

Weiner B. 1990. On perceiving the other as responsible. *Nebr. Symp. Motiv.,* 38:165–98. Lincoln: Univ. Nebraska Press

Whitley BE. 1990. The relationship of heterosexual attributions for the causes of homosexuality to attitudes toward lesbians and gay men. *Pers. Soc. Psychol. Bull.* 16: 369–77

Wilder DA. 1993. The role of anxiety in facilitating stereotypic judgment of out-group behavior. See Mackie & Hamilton 1993, pp. 87–109

Wilder DA, Shapiro P. 1991. Facilitation of outgroup stereotypes by enhanced ingroup identity. *J. Exp. Soc. Psychol.* 27:431–52

Wilder DA, Thompson JE. 1988. Assimilation and contrast effects in the judgments of groups. *J. Pers. Soc. Psychol.* 54:62–73

Wittenbrink B. 1994. *Stereotypes as social concepts in a knowledge-based approach to categorization.* PhD thesis. Univ. Mich., Ann Arbor. 113 pp.

Wolfe CT, Spencer SJ, Fein S. 1995. *Influence of motivation on implicit stereotyping.* Presented at Annu. Conv. Am. Psychol. Assoc., 103rd, New York

Wyer RS Jr, Carlston DE. 1994. The cognitive representation of persons and events. See Wyer & Srull 1994, pp. 41–98

Wyer RS Jr, Srull TK, eds. 1994. *Handbook of Social Cognition,* Vol. 1, *Basic Processes.* Hillsdale, NJ: Erlbaum

Yee DK, Eccles JS. 1988. Parent perceptions and attributions for children's math achievement. *Sex Roles* 19:317–33

Yzerbyt VY, Schadron G, Leyens J-P, Rocher S. 1994. Social judgeability: the impact of meta-informational cues on the use of stereotypes. *J. Pers. Soc. Psychol.* 66: 48–55

Zanna MP, Olson JM, eds. 1994. *Psychology of Prejudice: The Ontario Symposium,* Vol. 7. Hillsdale, NJ: Erlbaum

Zuckerman M, Kieffer SC. 1994. Race differences in face-ism: Does facial prominence imply dominance? *J. Pers. Soc. Psychol.* 66:86–92

Annu. Rev. Psychol. 1996. 47:273–305

EXPERT AND EXCEPTIONAL PERFORMANCE: Evidence of Maximal Adaptation to Task Constraints

K. A. Ericsson and A. C. Lehmann

Department of Psychology, Florida State University, Tallahassee, Florida 32306-1051

KEY WORDS: expert performance, skill acquisition, expertise, deliberate practice, long-term working memory

ABSTRACT

Expert and exceptional performance are shown to be mediated by cognitive and perceptual-motor skills and by domain-specific physiological and anatomical adaptations. The highest levels of human performance in different domains can only be attained after around ten years of extended, daily amounts of deliberate practice activities. Laboratory analyses of expert performance in many domains such as chess, medicine, auditing, computer programming, bridge, physics, sports, typing, juggling, dance, and music reveal maximal adaptations of experts to domain-specific constraints. For example, acquired anticipatory skills circumvent general limits on reaction time, and distinctive memory skills allow a domain-specific expansion of working memory capacity to support planning, reasoning, and evaluation. Many of the mechanisms of superior expert performance serve the dual purpose of mediating experts' current performance and of allowing continued improvement of this performance in response to informative feedback during practice activities.

CONTENTS

0066-4308/96/0201-0273$08.00

INTRODUCTION

Human behavior is enormously adaptive to environmental demands. In psychology, the most important changes in behavior are attributed to learning, as are changes in cognition, brain function, and many other modifications of the human body. Some adaptive changes, such as increase in muscle volume in response to exercise, are commonly observed and are accepted as a natural result of training activities. However, recent research in developmental biology shows that physical adaptation is more far-reaching than is commonly believed. For example, the shape of the eye is affected by an individual's visual activity; the increased incidence of near-sightedness in Western cultures appears to be an adaptive reaction to watching TV, reading, and other activities requiring sustained focus on nearby objects (Wallman 1994).

The adaptability of human behavior presents a challenge to scientists who seek to identify invariant characteristics and to propose general laws that describe all forms of behavior. We suggest that the most promising approach to finding invariants and exceptions to them is to study cases of maximal adaptation and learning, such as the behavior of experts. Expert performers devote most of their lives to attaining the highest levels of performance in a highly constrained activity (Ericsson & Charness 1994, Ericsson et al 1993). They often start training at very young ages, and the duration and intensity of their sustained training far exceed the range for other activities pursued by individuals in the normal population.

VIEWS OF EXPERT PERFORMANCE

It is generally assumed that outstanding human achievements reflect some varying balance between training and experience (nurture) on one hand and innate differences in capacities and talents (nature) on the other. One view, typically associated with Galton's work (1869/1979), holds that individual differences reflect innate basic capacities that cannot be modified by training and practice. The second and more recent view, typically associated with de Groot (1946/1978) and with Chase & Simon (1973), is that experts' knowledge and task-specific reactions must have been acquired through experience. These two views define mutually exclusive domains corresponding roughly to the popular distinction between hardware and software in computer-based metaphors for human information processing.

In the view of expert performance as talent, instruction and practice are necessary but not sufficient to attain expert levels of performance. Performance increases monotonically as a function of practice toward an asymptote representing a fixed upper bound on performance. Contemporary researchers who hold this view generally assume that training can affect some of the components mediating performance but not others, and that stable, genetically determined factors constrain the ultimate level of performance. Consequently, empirical research has focused on identifying and measuring talent relevant to particular types of activity. A practical extension of this view is that, by testing individuals at a young age, one can select the most talented children and provide them with the resources for the best training. Later in this chapter we briefly review the evidence, or rather the lack of firm evidence, for the talent-based view of expert performance.

At the time de Groot (1946/1978) started his research on chess expertise, the prevailing view was that chess experts achieved their superior performance by greater than normal intellectual capacity for extensive search of alternative chess moves. However, de Groot (1946/1978) found that world-class chess players accessed the best chess moves during their initial perception of the chess position, rather than after an extensive search. This finding implied pattern-based retrieval from memory and is fundamental to Chase & Simon's (1973) and Simon & Chase's (1973) theory of expertise. Chase & Simon showed that pattern-based retrieval can account for superior selection of chess moves and exceptional memory for chess positions without violating general limits to human information processing (Newell & Simon 1972), including the limited capacity of short-term memory.

Chase & Simon (1973) proposed that the attainment by experts of many other forms of expertise, in fact "any skilled activity (e.g. football, music)" (p. 279), was the result of acquiring, during many years of experience in their domain, vast amounts of knowledge and the ability to perform pattern-based retrieval. This assertion was borne out by subsequent research on solving textbook problems in physics (Larkin et al 1980, Simon & Simon 1978). Novices, who possessed all the necessary knowledge, struggled with physics problems and retrieved formulas and computed results by working backward from the question, whereas physics experts retrieved a solution plan as part of their normal comprehension of problems. Chi et al (1982) showed that physics experts not only had more knowledge than novices but also organized it better. Experts could therefore represent physics problems in terms of the relevant theoretical principles, whereas novices' representations were based on salient surface elements. Voss et al (1983) showed that expert reasoning is specific to a domain. Their subjects, experts in domains such as chemistry and social science, lacked the special knowledge and strategies to successfully analyze a problem in political science. More recently, researchers have designed methods to elicit experts' knowledge (Cooke 1994; Hoffman 1987, 1995) and to describe its structure and organization in specific domains (Hoffman 1992, Olson & Biolsi 1991). Glaser & Chi (1988) and, more recently, Bédard & Chi (1992) and McPherson (1993a) have reviewed this knowledge-based approach to expertise. This view is consistent with theories of skill acquisition (Anderson 1983, 1993; Fitts & Posner 1967), in which knowledge is first acquired and then organized into appropriate actions that, with further practice, individuals can access automatically through pattern-based retrieval. For reviews of the important progress in the laboratory study of skill acquisition, see Proctor & Dutta (1995) and VanLehn (1989, 1996).

Following a related view, some investigators have equated expertise with the amount and complexity of knowledge gained through extensive experience of activities in a domain.[1] However, recent studies have shown that individuals with expertise defined in this manner do not necessarily exhibit performance that is superior on relevant tasks to the performance of less-experienced individuals. The dissociation between level of expertise (based on the amount of experience) and performance has been most clearly demonstrated in many types of expert decision making and judgment (Camerer & Johnson 1991). In their review, Shanteau & Stewart (1992) found that the validity and reliability of expert judgments were typically low and unrelated to the amount of experience. Furthermore, statistical regression models that combine a small number of cues usually available to experts nearly always outperform (or at least equal) expert judgment involving prediction (Dawes et al 1989). Human expert judgments are superior to such models primarily in well-defined domains with developed theories supporting reasoning, such as medicine and bridge. Several efforts have been made to distinguish additional characteristics of task domains in which expert judges display superior performance (Bolger & Wright 1992, Shanteau 1992). The availability of rapid feedback appears to be a critical factor for improvement of decision accuracy. For example, nurses screening emergency calls for medical help improve their response accuracy as a function of years of experience (Leprohon & Patel 1995).

The amount of auditors' general experience in their domain is poorly related to the accuracy of their performance (Bonner & Pennington 1991), and in this domain consensus among experts for important evaluations decreases with experience (Bédard 1991). Similarly, extensive experience in interactions with

---

[1] Amount of overall experience in a domain should be distinguished from the amount of time spent on focused activities designed to improve performance (deliberate practice), because the latter has been found to be closely related to the attained level of performance (Ericsson et al 1993).

a computer system does not automatically lead to knowledge and proficiency (Rosson 1985, see Ashworth 1992 for a review). In many domains, such as mathematics (Lewis 1981), computer programming (Doane et al 1990), and physics (Reif & Allen 1992), some of the experts failed to demonstrate superior performance on representative activities. Part of the problem is that most experts are highly specialized, and task-specific experience is a better, but still modest, predictor of performance (Bonner & Pennington 1991).

These findings raise troubling issues about the relation of experience-based expertise and consistently superior performance. We agree with other investigators (e.g. Edwards 1992, Sternberg & Frensch 1992) who assert that empirical investigations should focus on reproducible superior performance, because the analysis of its mediating mechanisms is likely to provide evidence for adaptations to task constraints.

SCOPE OF EXPERT PERFORMANCE

One of the marks of expert performers is that they can display their superior performance reliably upon demand. To achieve this control, expert performers need to master all relevant factors—including motivation. Hence, expert performers should be able to reproduce their superior performance on representative tasks presented under controlled laboratory conditions, and their performance can therefore be subject to scientific analysis.

Following Ericsson & Smith (1991a), we define expert performance as consistently superior performance on a specified set of representative tasks for a domain. The virtue of defining expert performance in this restricted sense is that the definition both meets all the requirements for carrying out laboratory studies of performance and comes close to meeting those for evaluating performance in many domains. At the same time it excludes those domains where investigators have been unable to supply a valid measure with associated demonstrations of superior performance.

In most domains, methods have evolved to reliably measure individuals' performance under standardized conditions, which make experts easy to identify. Their consistently superior performance has then been successfully reproduced and experimentally studied in the laboratory with representative tasks (see Ericsson & Charness 1994 for a review). At least in the traditional domains of expert performance, intriguing generalities have been discovered.

Age and Peak Performance

The age at which experts typically attain their highest levels of performance is closely related to their domain of expertise (Lehman 1953). In vigorous sports the age distributions for peak performance are remarkably narrow. They center in the twenties and exhibit systematic differences across different sports and activities within a given sport (Schulz & Curnow 1988, Schulz et al 1994). The highest achievements in fine motor skills and even in predominantly cognitive activities, such as chess (Elo 1965), occur most frequently for experts in their thirties (Lehman 1953). In the arts and sciences there is a close relation between the time of the most creative and unique achievements and the time of highest productivity, that is, consistent (reproducible) generation of quality products (Simonton 1988); peak ages for the most creative achievements most frequently fall in the thirties and forties. Peak ages systematically differ even across the primarily cognitive domains (Simonton 1988) and even within domains—for example, between postal and tournament chess (Charness & Bosman 1990).

The 10-Year Rule of Necessary Preparation

That experts in most domains attain their highest level of performance a decade or more after physical maturation points to the importance of extensive preparation. Simon & Chase (1973) made an even more direct claim about the necessity for intense preparation. They found that it takes chess players around ten years of preparation to attain an international level of chess skill. Even the chess prodigy Bobby Fisher needed a preparation period of nine years (Ericsson et al 1993). Simon & Chase also suggested that similar preparation is required in other domains, and subsequent studies (Bloom 1985, Hayes 1981) indicate that the 10-year rule can be generalized to several different domains, including vigorous sports. According to this rule, not even the most "talented" individuals can attain international performance without approximately 10 years of preparation; the vast majority of international-level performers have spent considerably longer.

More generally, the mere number of years of experience with relevant activities in a domain is typically only weakly related to performance (Ericsson et al 1993). Even more refined measures, such as the number of hours in chess competitions (Charness et al 1995) and the number of baseball games in the major leagues (Schulz et al 1994) only weakly predict individual differences in performance among skilled performers.

The Role of Deliberate Practice

An important reason for the weak relation between experience and performance is that many of our most common activities, such as work and competitions, play and leisure, afford few opportunities for effective learning and improvement of skill. Drawing on research on learning and skill acquisition and on the educational practices in traditional domains such as music and sports, Ericsson et al (1993) used the term deliberate practice for the individualized training activities especially designed by a coach or teacher to improve specific aspects of an individual's performance through repetition and successive refinement. To receive maximal benefit from feedback, individuals have to monitor their training with full concentration, which is effortful and limits the duration of daily training. Ericsson et al argued that the amount of deliberate practice should be closely related to the level of acquired performance.

In fact, individual differences in the amount of deliberate practice, determined from diaries and retrospective estimates, were shown to be related to the level of performance attained by expert musicians and athletes (see Ericsson et al 1993 for a review). Furthermore, the age at which elite performers started deliberate practice was systematically younger than that of less accomplished performers. An analysis of these performers' daily patterns of practice and rest indicated that their maximal amount of fully concentrated training that they could sustain every day for years without leading to exhaustion and burn-out was around four hours a day.

In many domains, knowledge of effective training procedures has accumulated over a long time, and qualified—often professional—teachers draw on this knowledge to design deliberate practice regimens for individual students. In domains such as chess, for which there is no organized system of formal training, Ericsson et al (1993) found practice activities that have the characteristics of deliberate practice and were thereby able to extend their research framework to these domains. From informal interviews with elite chess players, they learned that these players created optimal learning situations by studying published chess games for several hours every day and attempting to predict—one by one—the moves chosen by chess masters. A subsequent study confirmed that ratings of chess skill were closely related to the total amount of time chess players have devoted to the study of chess (Charness et al 1995).

Expert Performance and Talent

The belief that most anatomical and physiological characteristics are unmodifiable and thus reflect innate talent is not valid for expert performance acquired through at least a decade of intense practice. Ericsson et al (1993) and Ericsson (1990) reviewed evidence showing that observed changes in response to long-term intense training, such as the size of hearts, the number of capillaries supplying blood to affected muscles, and the metabolic properties of critical muscles (conversion of fast-twitch and slow-twitch muscles), revert to values in the normal range when athletes' training is decreased. Once many of these changes have occurred, however, they can apparently be maintained with regular training at lower frequency and duration (Shephard 1994).

There is evidence suggesting that practice at young ages when the body is developing may be necessary for certain adaptations to take place. Early training appears necessary for classical ballet students to change their joints and give them maximal turnout at the hip (Miller et al 1984). Contrary to common belief, these changes do not reflect an increased range of flexibility. The range of these dancers' movements in the opposite direction is reliably decreased compared to that of control subjects (Hamilton et al 1992). Similar results have been found for musicians (Wagner 1988). More generally, vigorous physical activity stimulates the growth of bones and joints (Bailey & McCulloch 1990, Martin & McCulloch 1987, Sammarco & Miller 1982); these adaptations, however, are restricted to those limbs that are involved in this activity. This specificity is particularly salient in unilateral activities, such as baseball pitching (King et al 1969) and racquet sports (Jones et al 1977). Many of the anatomical and physiological differences between individuals in the general population and elite athletes, dancers, and musicians can be accounted for by intense training that exposes parts of these performers' bodies to specific stimulation well outside the normal range encountered during everyday life.

Recent research has refuted earlier claims that several perceptual, motor, and cognitive capacities cannot be obtained through training and practice. With appropriate instruction (Biederman & Shiffrar 1987), college students can acquire the mysterious ability to identify the sex of chicks (Gibson 1969). World-class typists (Book 1924) and expert pianists (Keele & Ivry 1987) appear to acquire the ability to tap their fingers at a superior rate because this skill, at least in the case of pianists, is correlated with the amount of deliberate practice (Ericsson et al 1993) and does not generalize to the rate of tapping feet (Keele & Ivry 1987). The exceptional abilities of children and autistic savants can be explained by the acquisition of skills without assuming special talent at the outset (Howe 1990, Ericsson & Faivre 1988). Finally, the ability of some musicians to correctly name pitches (absolute pitch) is related to early exposure to music and the start of musical training. In their review, Takeuchi & Hulse (1993) argued that any child can acquire perfect pitch until the age of around six. Early exposure to pitch recognition activities appears sufficient to account for the development of differences in brain structure associated with perfect pitch (Schlaug et al 1995). In animals, differential morphological changes of the brain result from different types of extended practice activities (Black et al 1990).

Numerous studies of basic perceptual abilities and reaction time have not found any systematic superiority of elite athletes over control subjects (see Abernethy 1987a and Starkes & Deakin 1984 for reviews). Similarly, experts in visual medical diagnosis show no consistent advantage in basic perceptual capacities over control subjects (Norman et al 1992b). Furthermore, IQ is either unrelated or weakly related to performance among experts in chess (Doll & Mayr 1987) and music (Shuter-Dyson & Gabriel 1981); factors reflecting motivation and parental support are much better predictors of improvement (Schneider et al 1993). This is consistent with a general finding that the correlation between IQ and performance in a domain decreases over time, and after more than five years of professional experience the correlation is no longer reliable, even after appropriate statistical correction for restrictions of range (Hulin et al 1990).

Reviews of adult expert performance show that individual differences in basic capacities and abilities are surprisingly poor predictors of performance (Ericsson et al 1993, Regnier et al 1994). These negative findings, together with the strong evidence for adaptive changes through extended practice, suggest that the influence of innate, domain-specific basic capacities (talent) on expert performance is small, possibly even negligible. We believe that the motivational factors that predispose children and adults to engage in deliberate practice are more likely to predict individual differences in levels of attained expert performance.

THE STUDY OF EXPERT PERFORMANCE

Expert performance acquired over many thousands of hours of deliberate practice is unlikely to improve in response to a few hours of laboratory testing, provided that the laboratory settings faithfully reflect the tasks and constraints of the natural conditions (Ericsson & Smith 1991a). The major challenge to investigators is therefore to develop a collection of standardized laboratory tasks that capture the essential aspects of a particular type of expert performance.

Capturing the Phenomena of Expert Performance in the Laboratory

For some types of expert performance such as typing, juggling, and exceptional memory, the conditions under which these acts are performed are so standardized that they are easily reproduced in the laboratory. For other types, it is very difficult to reproduce the perceptual conditions or even to design a collection of standardized tasks that captures the essential characteristics of superior performance in a domain. The methodology for assessing specific types of expert performance in the laboratory is still emerging, and we report on investigators' solutions to these problems in different domains.

In sports, investigators discovered long ago that performance on tasks, where sports situations were represented abstractly, did not differ between various levels of athletes (see Tenenbaum & Bar-Eli 1993 for a review). Perhaps as a consequence, some of the most careful re-creations of actually occurring situations are found in sports, e.g. Helson & Pauwels (1993).

Recent advances in video and computer technology offer exciting possibilities for very high fidelity of reproduction. However, to capitalize on the control offered by laboratory studies, we recommend that investigators strive for the minimum of complexity necessary to successfully reproduce the relevant expert performance.

Analysis of Captured Expert Performance

It is important to distinguish tasks that capture the essence of expertise in a domain from other tasks in which the experts may also excel. For example, chess experts' ability to consistently select superior chess moves for arbitrary positions from chess games is a definitive feature of chess skill, whereas exceptional memory for chess positions is not.

In this first section we review only studies of expert performance captured with standardized tasks under normal or experimentally varied conditions. The cognitive processes that mediate superior performance have been examined using more traditional process data, such as reaction time, eye fixations, verbal reports (Ericsson & Simon 1993), or incidental recall. In the subsequent section we review research on a broader range of tasks that examined selected aspects of experts' performance.

EXPERT PERFORMANCE IN TRADITIONAL DOMAINS   *Chess*   The study of expert performance originated with the study of chess experts, and chess has remained the major domain for testing theories of expertise. To capture expert performance in chess, de Groot (1946/1978) identified chess positions for which he had extensively studied the consequences of various moves. He presented chess players with one of these chess positions and asked them to think aloud while selecting the best move. Comparing the think-aloud protocols of world-class players to those of good players in local chess clubs, de Groot found that both types of players engaged in extensive planning and search, but that the depth and amount of search did not differ. However, world-class players selected better moves than did the club players, who often failed to consider the best move.

From the findings that the world-class players frequently accessed the best move as one of their first possibilities in their original representation of the chess position, de Groot (1946/1978, also Chase & Simon 1973) inferred that chess masters do not generate chess moves by search but rather by cued recall from memory. Calderwood et al (1988) and Gobet & Simon (1995a) supported that claim and found that the quality of selected chess moves remained high when the time available for the search was drastically reduced.

Many studies have replicated superior move selection as a function of chess skill and have analyzed the mediating processes. For example, Charness (1981a) and Gruber (1991) found that the depth of search increased with chess skill up to the level of chess experts, although further increases in depth of search beyond that skill level have not been observed (Charness 1989, de Groot 1946/1978). Holding (1989) obtained more direct experimental evidence for improved move selection by search. He found that the amount of search and the quality of selected moves decreased when chess players had to perform a demanding secondary task while selecting a move. Holding & Reynolds (1982) found that expert chess players discovered superior moves for chess positions even when recognition-based access to moves from memory was prevented.

Both recognition-based retrieval and search appear to be important to selecting the best move (Saariluoma 1990, 1992). When confronted with a chess position, chess players retrieved potential moves on the basis of their representation of the position, where better representations allowed access to moves that were more in line with associated long-term strategic goals. The search primarily helped to evaluate alternative approaches and eliminate possible oversights and errors (Saariluoma 1992). However, even the world-class chess players studied by de Groot (1946/1978) would occasionally discover superior moves as the result of their search.

In sum, expert selection of moves in chess is mediated by retrieval of appropriate goals and moves from memory, and—if time permits—by systematic higher-level search and evaluation. Experts also exhibit superior incidental memory[2] for the examined positions (Charness 1981b, Lane & Robertson 1979).

Medicine   Along with chess, medical reasoning and diagnosis are among the traditional domains of research on expertise (see Elstein et al 1990 for a review). Typically, subjects have been instructed to think aloud or comment as they inspect information describing a case. Although medical experts receive extensive training in medical school, during internship, and within their specialty, it has been surprisingly difficult to demonstrate superior diagnostic performance for typical cases beyond the performance medical experts attained during their first year of residency (Norman et al 1992b, Schmidt et al 1990). Small but reliable differences are seen (Winkler & Poses 1993), and more recently larger differences in diagnostic accuracy as a function of medical expertise have been observed in tests of diagnostic performance for difficult cases (Norman et al 1994, Patel & Groen 1991). Recent theoretical reviews (Patel et al 1994, Schmidt et al 1990) show a consistent picture of the development of expert diagnostic performance from medical students with a lot of general medical knowledge to medical experts with structured clinical knowledge that supports the generation of accurate diagnoses.

---

[2]   A discussion of effects of aging on expert performance is outside the scope of our review and interested readers are directed to recent reviews by Ericsson & Charness (1994) and Krampe (1994).

In one of the pioneering studies of medical diagnosis, Feltovich and co-workers (1984) contrasted medical students' difficulties in retrieving their relevant knowledge with the medical experts' effortless access to their highly organized knowledge of diagnostic alternatives. More recently, Boshuizen & Schmidt (1992) showed that medical experts have acquired higher-order concepts relating clinical information to diagnostic alternatives that replace the extensive biomedical reasoning of medical students and interns. Lemieux & Bordage (1992) found that superior diagnostic performance was associated with higher-level and more refined inferences generated from the presented clinical information. Patel et al (1994) found evidence for a working memory representation based on facts that summarize clinical findings and that allowed flexible reasoning about diagnostic alternatives. This representation enabled experts to recover from initially incorrect hypotheses, evaluate diagnostic alternatives, and construct an explanation of all relevant clinical findings.

In sum, expert performance in medical diagnosis is primarily found for difficult cases that compel experts to reason extensively about diagnostic alternatives. Consistent with chess experts, medical experts have very good incidental memory for the relevant information in their domain (Hassebrock et al 1993), and the amount of information recalled typically increases with expertise (Norman et al 1989a).

Bridge   The critical task that can be isolated for an individual bridge player is playing a given hand in such a manner that the contracted number of tricks are won. With information from bidding and a given bridge hand, experts are very accurate in estimating the probability of making a particular number of tricks (the contract); amateur bridge players are more biased and show systematic overconfidence (Keren 1987). Think-aloud studies of bridge players planning to play a given bridge hand show that experts perceive problems and constraints better and plan more extensively than less skilled players (Charness 1989). After a game, incidental memory for the original bridge hands increases with bridge skill (Engle & Bukstel 1978).

Auditing   Only a small number of auditing tasks such as prediction of bankruptcy, detection of fraud, and detection of accounting mistakes, have known correct solutions (Bédard & Chi 1993). Although auditors can reliably predict bankruptcy for collections of documented cases (see Whittred & Zimmer 1985 for a review), their bankruptcy judgments for contemporary firms are problematic because these judgments are public and may themselves influence the probability of bankruptcy (Bonner & Pennington 1991). Investigators have been more successful in analyzing think-aloud protocols of the fraud detection process (Johnson et al 1991, 1992) and of the identification of deliberately seeded mistakes (Bedard & Biggs 1991a,b). Two generalizable conclusions have emerged. The amount of experience auditors have with general accounting does not predict accuracy, whereas the amount of experience with particular types of firms does, especially experience with medical firms, where the rate of fraud is comparatively high. In accord with the findings from expert medical diagnosis, the primary difficulty in successful identification of fraud is not so much the detection of isolated inconsistencies but the generation of an integrated explanation of patterns of deviations.

OTHER DOMAINS   In many domains of expertise, it is difficult to identify representative tasks with well-defined correct responses because the products generated in these domains—computer programs, research designs, and written papers—are complex. Most of the recent research on experts has been conducted in the domain of computer programming with highly experienced professionals as subjects (Adelson & Soloway 1985, Jeffries et al 1981). Experts and nonexperts have been given the same program specifications, and their subsequent design processes have been monitored with think-aloud protocols. In these studies, expert programmers, unlike novices, were found to generate an initial higher-level representation of their design (mental model) and to modify it until it met all the requirements. Only later did they proceed to a detailed design of its components. When the presented task was familiar to the experts, they often rapidly retrieved or constructed an accurate mental model (Adelson & Soloway 1985, Jeffries et al 1981), but when the task was not familiar, experts spent considerable effort generating a mental model that satisfied all the relevant constraints (Adelson & Soloway 1985, Guindon 1990). When Koubek & Salvendy (1991) monitored problem solving by expert and "super-expert" programmers on a program modification task, they found evidence not for automatization of the super-experts' performance but rather for reliance on a more general and abstract representation of the computer program than the regular experts had.

Similarly, research contrasting expert and nonexpert writers shows that experts expend more effort on planning and consider additional constraints regarding organization, structure, and intended readers than less skilled writers do (Bryson et al 1991, Flower & Hayes 1980, Kellogg 1994). Consistent with results for routine problem solving, Schraagen (1993) found that highly experienced scientists could easily generate research designs for familiar problems in their own area of research but not for problems in an unfamiliar area.

Recent research on expertise in physics (see Anzai 1991 for a review) has focused on the representation of concepts and on the externalized representation of physics problems as diagrams (Larkin & Simon 1987). In their study of novices and physics professors, Reif & Allen (1992) collected think-aloud protocols on reasoning about acceleration in many well-defined tasks. They found that the acquisition of an integrated, accurate representation of theoretical concepts is not an inevitable consequence of extended experience; even some of the professors "exhibit marked deficiencies in concept interpretation" (p. 1).

Remarkably accurate and complex reasoning has been observed in some individuals who regularly bet on horse races (Ceci & Liker 1986) and whose intelligence (IQ) was representative of the general population. Consistent with other types of expert performance, their superior predictions of races were mediated by a complex mental representation. This representation enabled them to reason about many interacting factors in order to extract relevant information about a specific horse from its performance in previous races.

EXPERT PERCEPTUAL PERFORMANCE   *Visual medical diagnosis*   In a recent review of expertise in visual diagnosis of X-rays and skin disorders, Norman and coworkers (1992a) found only modest increases in accuracy for representative X-rays beyond that of medical residents with more than one year of daily experience with X-ray diagnosis. These investigators observed distinctly superior performance by experts only on difficult cases (Lesgold et al 1988, Wolf et al 1994). For skin disorders the accuracy of diagnosis increased uniformly as a function of expertise over both easy and difficult cases (Norman et al 1989b). On the basis of think-aloud protocols Lesgold et al (1988) were able to study expert radiologists' construction of an integrated mental representation of X-rays for complex cases. These experts were able to incorporate into their mental representation unusual features, such as dislocation of organs due to previous surgery, and other information about the patient's clinical history. Norman et al (1992a) found that correct as well as incorrect clinical histories influenced both the diagnosis of X-rays and identification of consistent visual information.

Increased expertise in visual diagnosis appears to be associated with more rapid perceptual identification of abnormal features at presentation times of 0.5 s (Myles-Worsley et al 1988) and 2.0 s (Lesgold et al 1988). Experts reached their correct diagnosis of skin disorders faster than novices but took longer on their incorrect decisions (Norman et al 1989b).

Other domains   When expert judges or referees in sports are shown filmed sequences of sports events, their ability to make perceptually based judgments relevant to their specific expertise is superior to that of control subjects. Expert judges of gymnastics were better able to detect errors in gymnastic routines, but their incidental recognition memory for the performances was not different from that of novice judges (Ste-Marie & Lee 1991). Expert referees were no better than expert players and coaches in detecting that a foul had been committed in basketball, but they were more accurate in identifying the specific type of violation (Allard et al 1993). Expert coaches are better than novices in evaluating and describing filmed sequences of swimmers' swim strokes (Leas & Chi 1993) and the motor execution of shot putters (Pinheiro & Simon 1992).

EXPERT PERCEPTUAL-MOTOR PERFORMANCE   *Typing*   An expert's skill in typing can be elicited under standardized conditions with unfamiliar texts or even randomized orders of words (see Gentner 1988, Salthouse 1986 for reviews). In any particular instant, expert typists are looking well ahead in the text they are typing. The difference between the text visually fixated and the letters typed in a given instant (eye-hand span) increases with the typist's typing speed. By directing their perception ahead of the currently typed text, experts can prepare future keystrokes by moving their fingers in advance toward a desired location (Gentner 1988). The largest differences in speed between expert and novice typists are found for successive keystrokes made by fingers of different hands because experts who have had extended practice can prepare these movements in advance by overlapping movements (Gentner 1983, Salthouse 1984). When subjects are prevented from looking ahead at the text to be typed, the speed of expert typists is reduced nearly to that of novice typists (Shaffer 1973, Salthouse 1984).

Music   Expert musical performance is typically displayed in the solo perform- ance of a piece that the musician has extensively studied beforehand. A distinc- tive characteristic of expert musicians is their superior ability to reliably reproduce the timing and loudness variations in consecutive performances of the same piece (Ericsson et al 1993, Krampe 1994, MacKenzie et al 1983, Palmer 1989, Sloboda 1991). When experts are asked to violate the rules governing artistic interpretations of musical pieces (Repp 1992), the reproduci- bility of their performance declines (Clarke 1993). Furthermore, expert musi- cians can better maintain independent timing in both hands when playing music (Shaffer 1981) or tapping (Summers et al 1993) than less accomplished musi- cians.

Expert musicians have also been studied under standardized conditions in which they play (sight read) unfamiliar music. Similar to typing, individual differences in sight-reading were correlated with differences in eye-hand span (Bean 1938, Sloboda 1984). When the sight-reading of expert pianists was paced while they accompanied a solo instrument, Ericsson & Lehmann (1994) found systematic individual differences that were predicted only by relevant training opportunities in the accompaniment of choirs and soloists.

Juggling   In a task analysis of juggling, Beek (1989) found that the possible movement patterns for juggling a certain number of balls are highly constrained. This task characteristic explains the high consistency in world-class jugglers' methods and timing. From careful analysis of juggling performance, Beek found that sustained juggling is not a steady state but instead requires continuous corrections and adjustments. In some of his experiments Beek (1989) occluded parts of a juggler's visual field and found that the juggler needed to see only the apex of the ball's trajectory to maintain successful control of the juggling.

Sports   The demands on expert perceptual-motor performance in sports nearly always include requirements for speed, very precise motor responses, or both. As the level of competition increases in sports requiring speeded responses, the available time to produce responses decreases because of the greater strength and speed of elite opponents. Elite athletes have to select responses on the basis of advance perceptual cues. Even the very best cricket players cannot make any major corrections within the last 190 ms before ball contact (McLeod 1987), as shown by experimental studies in which these players had to hit pitched balls that bounced unpredictably on a rough surface. During the last 200 ms before ball contact, athletes extract very limited information, as Lamb & Burwitz (1988) demonstrated. In their experiment, athletes catching tennis balls shot by a "cannon" indoors were able to perform this task without a reliable decrement when the light was turned off during this time.

When confronted with representative situations, elite athletes can produce the required reactions faster (Helson & Pauwels 1993) and make anticipatory movements earlier than less skilled athletes (see Abernethy 1987b for a review). The temporal precision required to successfully complete an action in sports is very high, and in some types of hitting the precision may be as high as ±2 ms (McLeod & Jenkins 1991). To attain such a level of precision, athletes' motor systems can adjust the force in hitting movements as late as 50 ms prior to ball/bat contact. For example, elite table tennis players control the temporal variability in initiating a forehand drive to produce the highest timing accuracy at ball contact (Bootsma & van Wieringen 1990). In fact, for some hitting skills the expert players' backward swing phase is actually more variable than that of novices, although temporal variability at ball contact is less for experts (see Abernethy & Burgess-Limerick 1992 for a review).

In contrast to researchers in most of the other domains reviewed in this chapter, researchers in sports—with few exceptions—have not collected concurrent and retrospective verbal reports on expert performance on representative tasks. Think-aloud protocols show that expert snooker players engage in deeper planning than novices when evaluating a configuration of billiard balls (Abernethy et al 1994), and unexpected recall by expert miniature-golf players for the nature of their shots has been found to be superior to that of less skilled players (Bäckman & Molander 1986).

EXPERT MEMORY PERFORMANCE   The highest levels of memory performance have been observed in professional mnemonists. Researchers have also studied some types of expert performance, such as mental multiplication and memorization of dinner orders, in which exceptional memory is an integral part.

The pioneering research on individuals with exceptional memory was conducted by Binet (1894) who examined the performance of two subjects, Inaudi and Diamondi, on standardized memory tasks for digits. Since then, the memory performance of many exceptional individuals has been studied in the laboratory, e.g. S (Luria 1968), VP (Hunt & Love 1972), TE (Gordon et al 1984), Rajan (Thompson et al 1993), and many others (Brown & Deffenbacher 1988). Reviews of this laboratory research (Ericsson 1985, 1988) show that truly exceptional memory performance is typically restricted to a single type of material, often sequences or matrices of digits. With sufficiently rapid presentation, memory performance decreases dramatically and approaches the normal range, even for this preferred type of material. Although all of the exceptional individuals were found to have engaged in prior training and practice with their preferred material, the strongest evidence for the acquired nature of exceptional memory comes from training studies with college students.

After 50–100 h of practice on the digit-span task, several students surpassed the performance of most exceptional subjects—20 digits (Chase & Ericsson 1981, 1982). With further practice, two subjects attained the highest digit spans ever recorded: 82 (subject SF) (Chase & Ericsson 1982) and over 100 digits (subject DD) (Staszewski 1988a), respectively. They matched and surpassed the performance of the exceptional subjects when tested on the previously used memory tasks involving digit matrices, and their pattern of recall was indistinguishable from that of exceptional subjects (Ericsson & Chase 1982). Subsequently, Chase & Ericsson (1982) proposed the theory of skilled memory, which accounts for the superior memory performance of both trained and exceptional subjects. Skilled memory theory specifies how subjects can rapidly encode a particular type of material in long-term memory (LTM) by associating this material with pre-existing knowledge and patterns. Subjects maintain the accessibility of the stored information in LTM through previously generated associations between the encoded information and a reusable retrieval structure acquired during prior training. Recently Richman et al (1995) have proposed an explicit simulation model of exceptional digit-span performance that is able to reproduce virtually all aspects of DD's observable memory performance, including verbally reported information.

Chase & Ericsson (1982) proposed that if students can acquire memory skills enabling them to use LTM in memory tasks with rapid presentation rates [originally designed to measure short-term memory (STM)], then the mechanisms of skilled memory can be adapted to expand working memory in many types of expert performance. The superior memory of waiters and waitresses for drink orders (Bennett 1983) and the exceptional memory of a waiter (JC) for dinner orders (Ericsson & Polson 1988a,b) support this hypothesis and were successfully captured by laboratory analog tasks. Verbal reports and—in the case of JC—a series of experiments show that superior memory performance is mediated by acquired mechanisms consistent with skilled memory theory.

Some tasks, like multiplication or the addition of a long series of large numbers, are easy to perform with paper and pencil but difficult and very demanding of memory when carried out mentally. Expert mental calculators acquire their skill through extended, specific training on the task (Staszewski 1988b). Such experts have to retain several intermediate products that are given a distinctive memory encoding to avoid proactive interference (Chase & Ericsson 1982, Staszewski 1988b). Extended working memory in mental multiplication and abacus calculation (Hatano & Osawa 1983) was accounted for by Ericsson & Kintsch (1995) in an extension of skilled memory theory that distinguished several types of long-term working memory (LT-WM) involving different encoding methods with differential accessibility and storage characteristics.

In sum, expert memory performance is not an automatic consequence of domain-specific experience but rather requires the acquisition of specific memory skills tailored to the demands of working memory by the particular activity.

SUMMARY   Investigators have been able to capture and study in the laboratory the mechanisms that mediate expert performance in many domains. On the most general level, captured expert performance reflects many different types of complex mechanisms acquired to meet the specific demands of the tasks in a domain of expertise. Hence, traditional accounts of expert performance in terms of pattern-based, automatic retrieval of actions are insufficient and have to be extended.

In perceptual performance, experts extract new and more informative perceptual features to improve performance. To achieve high levels of perceptual-motor performance, experts must circumvent reaction-time limits for serial discrete motor responses by advance preparation and overlapping of movement production, reflected in increased eye-hand spans in typing and music. In many sports, expert levels of motor performance require remarkable timing, often within the millisecond range. This performance appears to be mediated by dynamic adjustments of the motor system as late as 50 ms prior to the critical event, such as the contact between ball and racquet. Mnemonists and trained memory experts show that speed of storage in LTM can be dramatically improved and that the limited capacity of general working memory, based on STM, can be extended in specific activities with the acquisition of domain-specific LT-WM.

Contrary to the belief that expert performance is highly automatized, most types of expert performance are mediated by reportable thoughts involving planning, reasoning, and anticipation. Even perceptual-motor activities have been successfully monitored with concurrent and retrospective verbal reports that reveal considerable planning and generation of expectations (for snooker, see Abernethy et al 1994; baseball, McPherson 1993b; tennis, McPherson & Thomas 1989; control of simulated cargo ships, Anzai 1984; other types of process control, see Ericsson & Simon 1993 for a review). That experts' incidental memory for task-relevant information is superior to that of novices also implies that most forms of expert performance remain mediated by attention-demanding cognitive processes.

Thus, the analysis of expert performance shows that experts increase their level of performance by structural changes of performance. The ability of experts to exceed usual capacity limitations is important because it demonstrates how particular acquired skills can supplant critical basic limits within a restricted and specific type of activity.

The Study of Components of Expert Performance

To test the hypothesis that expert performance is an extreme adaptation to task constraints mediated through deliberate practice, it is essential to preserve all of the relevant constraints in the tasks studied. On the other hand, the complexity of expert performance makes it desirable for investigators to identify perceptual or memory components and associated tasks in which these components can be studied separately. However, to gain useful information about the structure of components, it is important to capture the contextual demands of these components within the overall expert performance.

The problem with studying component tasks is that high performance on a given task can be attained independently of expert performance on the task as a whole. Thousands of hours of study are required to attain the skill level of chess masters. Nevertheless, Ericsson & Harris (1990) and Ericsson & Oliver (1989) showed that an individual with essentially no prior knowledge of chess could learn to recall briefly presented chess positions at a level matching that of chess masters after only 50 h of practice in memorizing chess positions. A detailed analysis of chess pieces showed that the trained subjects focused on perceptually salient pawn chains, whereas chess masters recalled the critical pieces in the center of the chess board. Hence, a chess masters' performance level can be attained in a manner that is insensitive to the constraints of extracting the most important information about the chess position.

RAPID PERCEPTION OF EXPERTS   The highly interactive nature of competitive sports and their demands for rapid and complex motor responses makes experimental investigation difficult. Hence, investigators have filmed situations in sports from the vantage point of such athletes as a receiver of a tennis serve. To assess the earliest point at which an athlete can predict where, for example, a tennis serve will land, the experimenter can prematurely stop the film sequence at various points (including points prior to the time that the server's racquet has made contact with the ball) and ask athletes to make their predictions. Usually, accuracy and RT for the decision is recorded.

Experts' superior predictions based on early perceptual cues (see Abernethy 1987b, 1991 for reviews) have been observed for the landing location of serves in badminton (Abernethy & Russell 1987b), types of serves in tennis (Goulet et al 1989), types of pitches in cricket (McLeod 1987), direction and force of shots in squash (Abernethy 1990), placement of shots on the goal in field hockey (Starkes 1987), and predictions of passes in volleyball (Wright et al 1990). Investigators have used several methods to identify which perceptual cues experts rely on for their successful predictions. One method has been to record eye fixations during the viewing of a film (see Ripoll 1991 for a review). For example, the pattern of expert tennis players' eye fixations differed from that of novices during the early phases of the tennis serve (Goulet et al 1989). Another approach has been to manipulate the frames of the film to systematically mask specific types of stimuli, such as the server's arm or racquet. For example, occluding the arm of the server degraded the accuracy of prediction in expert badminton players (Abernethy & Russell 1987a).

Investigators have found evidence for other domain-specific perceptual skills in experts, such as detecting the presence or absence of a volleyball (Allard & Starkes 1980) and counting pieces and detecting the presence of "check" in chess (Saariluoma 1985). These studies suggest that local features mediated the superiority of experts over nonexperts because the advantage in reaction time was preserved even for randomly rearranged stimuli, although the performance of both experts and novices was typically worse for those stimuli.

These findings show that not only does the speed of experts' perceptual process increase, but experts can circumvent the demand for rapid reactions by accurate anticipation based on advance perceptual cues. Furthermore, the experts' ability to accurately report anticipated outcomes refutes traditional claims that experts completely automate the execution of perceptual-motor performance.

SUPERIOR MEMORY OF EXPERTS   Experts in most domains display superior memory on unexpected recall tasks, which implies that accurate memory for important stimuli is a natural consequence of expert processing. In this section we review studies on memory performance with explicit and controlled memory tasks. In these studies, only the pioneering work on chess conforms to our

proposal that investigators first identify a component of intact expert performance and then design tasks to investigate that particular component.

In their classic study, Chase & Simon (1973) followed up de Groot's
(1946/1978) finding that chess experts' superior memory is a natural consequence of their examination of a chess position. Instructing chess players to
memorize briefly presented chess positions, Chase & Simon showed that these
players' superior recall for regular chess positions reflected chess-specific
knowledge; their recall was uniformly poor for randomly rearranged positions.
Because Chase & Simon presented the stimuli for only 5 s, they inferred that
recall reflected only storage in STM. All chess players perceived patterns of
chess pieces (chunks), but the number of chunks did not differ systematically
between experts and novices and it fell within the traditional limits of STM
(Miller 1956).[3] Chase & Simon (1973) attributed higher recall with increased
expertise to the availability of more complex patterns of chess pieces (chunks)
in LTM, where on the average each of the experts' chunks corresponded to a
larger number of pieces. Their basic finding that experts exhibited superior
memory for representative structured stimuli but not for recall of random,
unstructured stimuli was replicated in chess (see Charness 1991 for a review)
and in many other domains: bridge (Charness 1979, Engle & Bukstel 1978),
GO (Reitman 1976), Othello (Wolff et al 1984), snooker (Abernethy et al
1994), medicine (Norman et al 1989a), electronic circuit diagrams (Egan &
Schwartz 1979), computer programming (McKeithen et al 1981), dance
(Starkes et al 1987), basketball (Allard et al 1980, Allard & Burnett 1985,
Starkes et al 1994), field hockey (Starkes & Deakin 1984, Starkes 1987),
volleyball (Borgeaud & Abernethy 1987), figure skating (Deakin & Allard
1991), and football (Garland & Barry 1991).

Further research uncovered several potential exceptions. Experts' memory
is nearly always reduced for randomly rearranged stimuli but is still superior to
novices' memory. This finding held true for random chess configurations
(Lories 1987, Saariluoma 1989), process-control displays (Vicente 1992), random musical notation (Halpern & Bower 1982, Sloboda 1976), randomly
rearranged computer programs (Adelson 1981, Shneiderman 1976), unstructured game diagrams in volleyball (Allard & Burnett 1985), unstructured
stimuli in modern dance (Starkes et al 1990), and nonsense ballet movements
(Smyth & Pendleton 1994). Nor did experts show superior memory for information, such as melodies auditorily presented to musicians (Sloboda & Parker
1985), text presented to expert actors (Intons-Peterson & Smyth 1987, Noice
1993), and noncontour maps presented to map experts (Gilhooly et al 1988).

---

[3] This mechanism predicts superior memory for individuals at many different levels of skill. In
this section we therefore include some studies of subjects whose performance does not meet our
criterion for expert-level performance.

Finally, memory for medical information does not increase uniformly with expertise (Patel & Groen 1991), and for some types of information about computer programs, expert programmers recall even systematically less than novices (Adelson 1984).

We propose that experts' superior memory is not general across all types of information in a domain but reflects selective encoding of relevant information and mechanisms acquired to expand the functional capacity of the experts' working memory.

Chess   Chase & Simon (1973) gave an elegant account of the superior memory of chess experts in terms of complex chunks in STM, but this account has not been supported by subsequent research. Charness (1976) and Frey & Adesman (1976) showed that even briefly presented information is stored in LTM and not in STM. More recently, Cooke and coworkers (1993) and Gobet & Simon (1995b) extended these findings, showing that highly skilled chess players can recall substantial amounts from the comparably fast presentation of up to nine different chess positions.

Highly skilled chess players cannot only recognize isolated patterns but also construct an integrated representation of the position. This representation consists of interconnected chunks (Chi 1978) with a hierarchical structure (Freyhof et al 1992) and relations to familiar types of chess games (Cooke et al 1993, Gobet & Simon 1995b). It provides access to relevant information about appropriate moves and distinguishes memory of different chess positions in LTM. However, a highly interpreted representation does not facilitate systematic search and exploration of possible future moves. Having found that for memorized chess positions a chess master could very rapidly retrieve the piece in any location of the board, Ericsson & Oliver (in Ericsson & Staszewski 1989) proposed that chess masters have acquired a retrieval structure that mentally represents all the different locations of the chess board, and they can thereby manipulate and encode the location of individual chess pieces directly. Furthermore, Saariluoma (1989) showed that chess masters can store regular and random chess positions when each position is verbally presented as a sequence of chess pieces with their respective locations on the board. Finally, chess masters can play blindfold chess games—without a perceptually available chessboard—at close to their normal strength (Holding 1985). An experimental study by Saariluoma (1991) showed that a grand master under blindfold conditions could maintain the chess positions for 10 simultaneous chess games in memory with virtually no errors.

Recently, Ericsson & Kintsch (1995) proposed that chess experts extend their working memory capacity, acquiring long-term working memory (LT-WM) skills to support the planning and evaluation of chess positions. LT-WM is a single mechanism that accounts for experts' superior performance on memory tests for chess positions as well as for other memory-demanding activities for which Chase & Simon (1973) originally proposed a separate mechanism, namely the Mind's Eye. The empirical evidence favors an account based on LT-WM for also explaining superior memory of experts in other games with similar demands for planning, such as bridge, GO, Othello, and snooker.

Medicine   The superior memory of medical experts reflects their abilities to select critical information (Groen & Patel 1988) and to summarize relevant detailed information about patients by making higher-level inferences (Schmidt & Boshuizen 1993). Given that the criterion for expert performance is superior diagnostic accuracy, not the reproduction of presented details, the acquisition of higher-level concepts and an associated working memory system is an adaptive response to the demands of effective reasoning about alternative diagnoses. The detailed structure of the working memory of medical experts is discussed by Patel et al (1994) and Ericsson & Kintsch (1995).

Other domains   In general, analyses of representative demands of expert performance in a domain yield reasonable predictions of the superior perform-ance experts ought to display for a particular memory task. For example, the critical demand for anticipation and coordination in team sports requires that elite athletes continuously update their representation of the current situation of a game, and this skill is reflected in their superior memory for repre-sentative game situations (Allard & Starkes 1991). The important role of higher-level plans for the overall function of computer programs accounts well for expert computer programmers' superior memory for the general structure of programs and for their inferior memory for details (Adelson 1984). Expert actors (Noice 1991) study theatrical scripts to portray the integrated behavior of a character, and expert musicians create personal interpretations of music, tasks for which immediate memory for briefly presented information and rapid rote memorization are not critical constraints for these types of expert perform-ers.

Another general mechanism that mediates improvement in creation of new memory traces in LTM, especially with slower presentation rates, is the extent of associated knowledge and patterns. Expert knowledge of a domain leads to superior recall for information relevant to the domain but not for other types of information (Chiesi et al 1979, Morris et al 1985, Schneider et al 1989, Spilich et al 1979). Superior recall even for arbitrary information associated to con-cepts of the domain of expertise has been demonstrated (Bellezza & Buck 1988). It is likely that this type of effect of general knowledge can—at least partially—explain experts' superior memory even for randomly arranged ver-sions of stimuli in some domains, such as modern dance, volleyball, and music. Finally, superior memory performance can in some cases be mediated by knowledge through skilled guessing, especially when the guess is based on partially recalled information (de Groot 1966, Egan & Schwartz 1979).

Summary   The vastly superior memory of experts for briefly presented information appears to reflect memory skills and LT-WM that they acquire to support many important activities, such as planning, reasoning, and anticipation of future events. Future investigations concerning experts' superior memory should therefore carefully analyze the demands and function of memory in intact expert performance.

RELATING COMPONENTS TO CAPTURED EXPERT PERFORMANCE   Once a component of expert performance has been captured by specifically designed tasks and its structure has been successfully analyzed, it is important to relate it to the intact expert performance. Lacking complete simulation models of expert performance, investigators have relied on correlational techniques, but estimating the strength of the relation between performance on the component task and expert performance goes beyond the standard paradigm of contrasting the performance of extreme groups (experts vs novices). It requires either representative samples of performers or homogenous samples of expert performers.

In representative samples, Pfau & Murphy (1988) and Charness (1981b) found that chess ratings were reliably predicted by memory for chess positions. Pfau & Murphy (1988) found that, not surprisingly, the ability to select chess moves, the defining task for measuring expert performance, was an even better predictor. Charness (1979, 1983, 1987) found that characteristics of generating bids for a bridge hand had a modest correlation with bridge skill in a representative sample. Underwood et al (1994) were able to decompose the skill of solving crossword puzzles into a number of component tasks. Individual differences in the ability to solve crossword puzzles were then accurately predicted by performance on the tests of component skills.

CONCLUSIONS

Expert and exceptional performance is highly reproducible and, when compared with the performance of novices, has yielded the largest reliable differences observed by behavioral researchers among healthy adults. In chess, sports, and many other domains with thousands of active participants, individuals attain internationally recognized levels of exceptional performance only after spending about 10 years in intense preparation. In several domains expert performers engage in deliberate practice for around 4 h per day, a level that appears to be the maximum individuals can sustain on a daily basis for many years (see Ericsson et al 1993 for a review).

The conclusion that expert performance results from extended, deliberate practice differs from previously held ideas about the roles of talent and expertise. We have found that, with the single exception of height, current evidence for domain-specific characteristics (talent) among expert performers can be better accounted for by extended intense practice, which causes physiological, anatomical, and even neurological adaptations in the body. As for expertise, the levels of performance individuals attain after years of experience alone are much lower than those of experts who have adhered to regimens of careful training and practice.

In contrast to skilled activities that can be performed by rote, most types of expertise—even athletic performance—continue to be mediated by cognitive processes such as monitoring, planning, reasoning, and anticipating. For example, elite marathon runners report that they continuously monitor their physiological state and the effectiveness of their running, whereas novice runners deliberately think about things unrelated to their running to minimize their experience of pain (Morgan & Pollock 1977, see O'Connor 1992 for a review).

Expert performers acquire mechanisms for internally representing their current situation as a precondition for planning, reasoning, anticipating, and controlling motor production. As demands on speed and accuracy in a particular activity increase, expert performers face new learning tasks. Continued successful learning is necessary for experts to achieve a level of performance higher than their current level. For example, although many skilled typists have been able to automatize the level of performance they have already maintained (Shaffer 1975), research shows that they must commit their full attention and engage in active learning to further increase their typing speed (Book 1925a,b). Many of the mechanisms that mediate an expert's current performance also enable that expert to improve performance in response to feedback. Further analysis of the structure of expert performance and of the learning processes by which experts improve will provide investigators with the most promising information about the potential for and limits of human learning and adaptation.

ACKNOWLEDGMENTS

We wish to thank the following colleagues for their valuable comments and suggestions on earlier versions of this paper: Fran Allard, Jean Bédard, Neil Charness, Peter Delaney, Bud Fennema, Janet Grassia, David Kaufman, Geoffrey Norman, William Oliver, Caroline Palmer, Vimla Patel, Geoffrey Paull, Michael Rashotte, Pertti Saariluoma, John Shea, Herbert Simon, Fred Stephan, Rick Wagner, and Rolf Zwaan.

Literature Cited

Abernethy B. 1987a. Selective attention in fast ball sports. II. Expert-novice differences. *Aust. J. Sci. Med. Sports* 19(4):7–16

Abernethy B. 1987b. Anticipation in sport: a review. *Phys. Educ. Rev.* 10:5–16

Abernethy B. 1990. Expertise, visual search, and information pick-up in squash. *Perception* 19:63–77

Abernethy B. 1991. Visual search and decision-making in sport. *Int. J. Sport Psychol.* 22:189–210

Abernethy B, Burgess-Limerick R. 1992. Visual information for the timing of skilled movements: a review. In *Approaches to the Study of Motor Control and Learning*, ed. JJ Summers, pp. 343–84. Amsterdam/New York: Elsevier

Abernethy B, Neal RJ, Koning P. 1994. Visual-perceptual and cognitive differences between expert, intermediate, and novice snooker players. *Appl. Cogn. Psychol.* 18: 184–211

Abernethy B, Russell DG. 1987a. The relationship between expertise and visual search strategies in a racquet sport. *Hum. Mov. Sci.* 6:283–319

Abernethy B, Russell DG. 1987b. Expert-novice differences in an applied selective attention task. *J. Sport Psychol.* 9: 326–45

Adelson B. 1981. Problem solving and the development of abstract categories in programming languages. *Mem. Cogn.* 9: 422–33

Adelson B. 1984. When novices surpass experts: the difficulty of the task may increase with expertise. *J. Exp. Psychol. Learn. Mem. Cogn.* 10:484–95

Adelson B, Soloway E. 1985. The role of domain experience in software design. *IEEE Trans. Softw. Eng.* SE-11:1351–60

Allard F, Burnett N. 1985. Skill in sport. *Can. J. Psychol.* 39:294–312

Allard F, Deakin J, Parker S, Rogers W. 1993. Declarative knowledge in skilled motor performance. See Starkes & Allard 1993, pp. 95–107

Allard F, Graham S, Paarsalu ME. 1980. Perception in sport: basketball. *J. Sport Psychol.* 2:14–21

Allard F, Starkes JL. 1980. Perception in sport: volleyball. *J. Sport Psychol.* 2:22–33

Allard F, Starkes JL. 1991. Motor-skill experts in sports, dance and other domains. See Ericsson & Smith 1991b, pp. 126–52

Anderson JR, ed. 1981. *Cognitive Skills and Their Acquisition*. Hillsdale, NJ: Erlbaum

Anderson JR. 1983. *The Architecture of Cognition*. Cambridge, MA: Harvard Univ. Press

Anderson JR. 1993. Problem solving and learning. *Am. Psychol.* 48:35–44

Anzai Y. 1984. Cognitive control of real-time event-driven systems. *Cogn. Sci.* 8:221–54

Anzai Y. 1991. Learning and use of representations for physics expertise. See Ericsson & Smith 1991b, pp. 64–92

Ashworth CA. 1992. Skill as the fit between performer resources and task demands. In *Proc. 14th Annu. Cogn. Sci. Meet.*, pp. 444–49. Hillsdale, NJ: Erlbaum

Bäckman L, Molander B. 1986. Effects of adult age and level of skill on the ability to cope with high-stress conditions in a precision sport. *Psychol. Aging.* 1:334–36

Bailey DA, McCulloch RG. 1990. Bone tissue and physical activity. *Can. J. Sport Sci.* 15(4):229–39

Bean KL. 1938. An experimental approach to the reading of music. *Psychol. Monogr.* 50: 1–80

Bédard J. 1991. Expertise and its relation to audit decision quality. *Contemp. Account. Res.* 8:198–222

Bédard J, Chi MTH. 1992. Expertise. *Curr. Dir. Psychol. Sci.* 1(4):135–39

Bédard J, Chi MTH. 1993. Expertise in auditing. *Auditing* 12:1–25 (Suppl.)

Bedard JC, Biggs SF. 1991a. The effect of domain-specific experience on evaluation of management representations in analytical procedures. *Auditing* 10:77–89 (Suppl.)

Bedard JC, Biggs SF. 1991b. Pattern recognition, hypotheses generation, and auditor performance in an analytical task. *Account. Rev.* 66:622–42

Beek PJ. 1989. *Juggling Dynamics*. Amsterdam, Netherlands: Free Univ. Press

Bellezza FS, Buck DK. 1988. Expert knowledge as mnemonic cues. *Appl. Cogn. Psychol.* 2:147–62

Bennett HL. 1983. Remembering drink orders: the memory skill of cocktail waitresses. *Hum. Learn.* 2:157–69

Biederman I, Shiffrar MM. 1987. Sexing day-old chicks: a case study and expert systems analysis of a difficult perceptual-learning task. *J. Exp. Psychol. Learn. Mem. Cogn.* 13:640–45

Binet A. 1894. *Psychologie des Grands Calculateurs et Joueurs d'Echecs* [Psychology of great mental calculators and chess players]. Paris: Librairie Hachette

Black JE, Isaacs KR, Anderson BJ, Alcantara AA, Greenough WT. 1990. Learning causes synaptogenesis, whereas motor activity causes angiogenesis, in cerebellar cortex of adult rats. *Proc. Natl. Acad. Sci. USA* 87:5568–72

Bloom BS. 1985. Generalizations about talent development. In *Developing Talent in Young People*, ed. BS Bloom, pp. 507–49. New York: Ballantine. 557 pp.

Bolger F, Wright G. 1992. Reliability and validity in expert judgment. In *Expertise and Decision Support*, ed. G Wright, F Bolger, pp. 47–76. New York: Plenum

Bonner SE, Pennington N. 1991. Cognitive processes and knowledge as determinants of auditor expertise. *J. Account. Lit.* 10: 1–50

Book WF. 1924. Voluntary motor ability of the world's champion typists. *J. Appl. Psychol.* 8:283–308

Book WF. 1925a. *Learning to Typewrite*. New York: Gregg

Book WF. 1925b. *The Psychology of Skill.* New York: Gregg

Bootsma RJ, van Wieringen PCW. 1990. Timing an attacking forehand drive in table tennis. *J. Exp. Psychol. Hum. Percept. Perform.* 16:21–29

Boshuizen HPA, Schmidt HG. 1992. On the role of biomedical knowledge in clinical reasoning by experts, intermediates and novices. *Cogn. Sci.* 16:153–84

Borgeaud P, Abernethy B. 1987. Skilled perception in volleyball defense. *J. Sport Psychol.* 9:400–6

Brown E, Deffenbacher K. 1988. Superior memory performance and mnemonic encoding. See Obler & Fein 1988, pp. 191–211

Bryson M, Bereiter C, Scardamalia M, Joram E. 1991. Going beyond the problem as given: problem solving in expert and novice writers. In *Complex Problem Solving*, ed. RJ Sternberg, RA Frensch, pp. 61–84. Hillsdale, NJ: Erlbaum

Calderwood R, Klein GA, Crandall BW. 1988. Time pressure, skill and move quality in chess. *Am. J. Psychol.* 101:481–93

Camerer CF, Johnson EJ. 1991. The process-performance paradox in expert judgment: How can the experts know so much and predict so badly? See Ericsson & Smith 1991b, pp. 195–217

Ceci JS, Liker JK. 1986. A day at the races: a study of IQ, expertise, and cognitive complexity. *J. Exp. Psychol. Gen.* 115:255–66

Charness N. 1976. Memory for chess positions: resistance to interference. *J. Exp. Psychol. Hum. Learn. Mem.* 2:641–53

Charness N. 1979. Components of skill in bridge. *Can. J. Psychol.* 33:1–16

Charness N. 1981a. Search in chess: age and skill differences. *J. Exp. Psychol. Hum. Percept. Perform.* 7:467–76

Charness N. 1981b. Aging and skilled problem solving. *J. Exp. Psychol. Gen.* 110:21–38

Charness N. 1983. Age, skill, and bridge bidding: a chronometric analysis. *J. Verbal Learn. Behav.* 22:406–16

Charness N. 1987. Component process in bridge bidding and novel problem-solving tasks. *Can. J. Psychol.* 41:223–43

Charness N. 1989. Expertise in chess and bridge. See Klahr & Kotovsky 1989, pp. 183–208

Charness N. 1991. Expertise in chess: the balance between knowledge and search. See Ericsson & Smith 1991b, pp. 39–63

Charness N, Bosman EA. 1990. Expertise and aging: life in the lab. In *Aging and Cognition: Knowledge Organization and Utilization*, ed. TH Hess, pp. 343–85. Amsterdam/New York: Elsevier

Charness N, Krampe RT, Mayr U. 1995. *The importance of coaching in entrepreneurial skill domains: an international comparison of life-span chess skill acquisition.* Presented at Conf. Acquis. Expert Perform., Wakulla Springs, FL

Chase WG, Ericsson KA. 1981. Skilled memory. See Anderson 1981, pp. 141–89

Chase WG, Ericsson KA. 1982. Skill and working memory. In *The Psychology of Learning and Motivation*, ed. GH Bower, 16:1–58. New York: Academic

Chase WG, Simon HA. 1973. The mind's eye in chess. In *Visual Information Processing*, ed. WG Chase, pp. 215–81. New York: Academic

Chi MTH. 1978. Knowledge structures and memory development. See Siegler 1978, pp. 73–96

Chi MTH, Glaser R, Farr M, eds. 1988. *The Nature of Expertise.* Hillsdale, NJ: Erlbaum. 434 pp.

Chi MTH, Glaser R, Rees E. 1982. Expertise in problem solving. In *Advances in the Psychology of Human Intelligence*, ed. RS Sternberg, 1:1–75. Hillsdale, NJ: Erlbaum

Chiesi HL, Spilich GJ, Voss JF. 1979. Acquisition of domain-related information in relation to high and low domain knowledge. *J. Verbal Learn. Verbal Behav.* 18:257–73

Claessen HFA, Boshuizen HPA. 1985. Recall of medical information by students and doctors. *Med. Educ.* 19:61–67

Clarke E. 1993. Imitating and evaluating real and transformed musical performances. *Music Percept.* 10:317–42

Cooke NJ. 1994. Varieties of knowledge elicitation techniques. *Int. J. Hum.-Comput. Stud.* 41:801–49

Cooke NJ, Atlas RS, Lane DM, Berger RC. 1993. Role of high-level knowledge in memory for chess positions. *Am. J. Psychol.* 106:321–51

Dawes RM, Faust D, Meehl PE. 1989. Clinical versus actuarial judgment. *Science* 243(4899):1668–74

Deakin JM, Allard F. 1991. Skilled memory in expert figure skaters. *Mem. Cogn.* 19: 79–86

de Groot AD. 1946/1978. *Thought and Choice and Chess.* The Hague, Netherlands: Mouton

de Groot AD. 1966. Perception and memory versus thought: some old ideas and recent findings. In *Problem Solving: Research, Method and Theory,* ed. B Keinmuntz, pp. 19–50. New York: Wiley. 406 pp.

Doane SM, Pellegrino JW, Klatzky RL. 1990. Expertise in a computer operating system: conceptualization and performance. *Hum.-Comput. Interact.* 5:267–304

Doll J, Mayr U. 1987. Intelligenz und Schachleistung—eine Untersuchung an Schachexperten. [Intelligence and achievement in chess—a study of chess masters]. *Psychol. Beitr.* 29:270–89

Edwards W. 1992. Discussion: of human skills. *Organ. Behav. Hum. Decis. Process.* 53:267–77

Egan DE, Schwartz BJ. 1979. Chunking in recall of symbolic drawings. *Mem. Cogn.* 7:149–58

Elo AE. 1965. Age changes in master chess performances. *J. Gerontol.* 20:289–99

Elstein AS, Shulman LS, Sprafka SA. 1990. Medical problem solving: a ten-year retrospective. *Eval. Health Prof.* 13:5–36

Engle RW, Bukstel LH. 1978. Memory processes among bridge players of differing expertise. *Am. J. Psychol.* 91:673–89

Ericsson KA. 1985. Memory skill. *Can. J. Psychol.* 39:188–231

Ericsson KA. 1988. Analysis of memory performance in terms of memory skill. In *Advances in the Psychology of Human Intelligence,* ed. RJ Sternberg, 4:137–79. Hillsdale, NJ: Erlbaum

Ericsson KA. 1990. Peak performance and age: an examination of peak performance in sports. In *Successful Aging: Perspectives from the Behavioral Sciences,* ed. PB Baltes, MM Baltes, pp. 164–95. New York: Cambridge Univ. Press

Ericsson KA, Charness N. 1994. Expert performance: its structure and acquisition. *Am. Psychol.* 49(8):725–47

Ericsson KA, Chase WG. 1982. Exceptional memory. *Am. Sci.* 70:607–15

Ericsson KA, Faivre IA. 1988. What's exceptional about exceptional abilities? See Obler & Fein 1988, pp. 436–73

Ericsson KA, Harris MS. 1990. *Expert chess memory without chess knowledge: a training study.* Poster presented at Annu. Meet. Psychon. Soc., 31st, New Orleans, LA

Ericsson KA, Kintsch W. 1995. Long-term working memory. *Psychol. Rev.* 102: 211–45

Ericsson KA, Krampe RT, Tesch-Römer C. 1993. The role of deliberate practice in the acquisition of expert performance. *Psychol. Rev.* 100(3):363–406

Ericsson KA, Lehmann AC. 1994. The acquisition of accompanying (sight-reading) skills in expert pianists. In *Proc. 3rd Int. Conf. Music Percept. Cogn., Liege, Belgium,* ed. I Deliege, pp. 337–38. Liege, Belgium: Eur. Soc. Cogn. Sci. Music

Ericsson KA, Oliver WL. 1989. A methodology for assessing the detailed structure of memory skills. In *Acquisition and Performance of Cognitive Skills,* ed. AM Colley, JR Beech, pp. 193–215. Chichester, Engl: Wiley. 348 pp.

Ericsson KA, Polson PG. 1988a. An experimental analysis of a memory skill for dinner-orders. *J. Exp. Psychol. Learn. Mem. Cogn.* 14:305–16

Ericsson KA, Polson PG. 1988b. Memory for restaurant orders. See Chi et al 1988, pp. 23–70

Ericsson KA, Simon HA. 1993. *Protocol Analysis: Verbal Reports as Data* (Rev. ed.). Cambridge, MA: MIT Press

Ericsson KA, Smith J. 1991a. Prospects and limits in the empirical study of expertise. See Ericsson & Smith 1991b, pp. 1–38

Ericsson KA, Smith J, eds. 1991b. *Toward a General Theory of Expertise: Prospects and Limits.* Cambridge: Cambridge Univ. Press. 344 pp.

Ericsson KA, Staszewski J. 1989. Skilled memory and expertise: mechanisms of exceptional performance. See Klahr & Kotovsky 1989, pp. 235–67

Feltovich PJ, Johnson PE, Moller JH, Swanson DB. 1984. LCS: the role and development of medical knowledge in diagnostic expertise. In *Readings in Medical Artificial Intelligence,* ed. WJ Clancey, EH Shortcliffe, pp. 275–319. Reading, MA: Addison-Wesley

Fitts P, Posner MI. 1967. *Human Performance.* Belmont, CA: Brooks/Cole

Flower L, Hayes JR. 1980. The cognition of discovery: defining a historical problem. *Coll. Comp. Commun.* 31:21–32

Frey PW, Adesman P. 1976. Recall memory for visually presented chess positions. *Mem. Cogn.* 4:541–47

Freyhof H, Gruber H, Ziegler A. 1992. Expertise and hierarchical knowledge representation in chess. *Psychol. Res.* 54: 32–37

Galton F Sir. 1869/1979. *Hereditary Genius:*

An Inquiry into Its Laws and Consequences. London: Friedman

Garland DJ, Barry JR. 1991. Cognitive advantages in sports: the nature of perceptual structure. *Am. J. Psychol.* 104:211–28

Gentner DR. 1983. The acquisition of typewriting skill. *Acta Psychol.* 54:233–48

Gentner DR. 1988. Expertise in typewriting. See Chi et al 1988, pp. 1–22

Gibson EJ. 1969. *Principles of Perceptual Learning and Development*. Englewood Cliffs, NJ: Prentice Hall

Gilhooly KJ, Wood M, Kinnear PR, Green C. 1988. Skill in map reading and memory for maps. *Q. J. Exp. Psychol.* 40A:87–107

Glaser R, Chi MTH. 1988. Overview. See Chi et al 1988, pp. xv–xxviii

Gobet F, Simon HA. 1995a. The roles of recognition processes and look-ahead search in time-constrained expert problem solving: evidence from grandmaster level chess. *Psychol. Sci.* In press

Gobet F, Simon HA. 1995b. Templates in chess memory: a mechanism for recalling several boards. *Complex Information Processes, Work. pap. # 513.* Carnegie Mellon Univ., Pittsburgh, PA

Gordon P, Valentine E, Wilding J. 1984. One man's memory: a study of a mnemonist. *Br. J. Psychol.* 75:1–14

Goulet C, Bard C, Fleury M. 1989. Expertise differences in preparing to return a tennis serve: a visual information processing approach. *J. Sport Exerc. Psychol.* 11: 382–98

Groen GJ, Patel VL. 1988. The relationship between comprehension and reasoning in medical expertise. See Chi et al 1988, pp. 287–310

Gruber H. 1991. *Qualitative Aspekte von Expertise im Schach: Begriffe, Modelle, empirische Untersuchungen und Perspektiven der Expertiseforschung* [Qualitative aspects of expertise in chess: terminology, models, empirical studies, and outlooks on expertise research]. Aachen, Germany: Feenschach

Guindon R. 1990. Knowledge exploited by experts during software system design. *Int. J. Man-Mach. Stud.* 33:279–304

Halpern AR, Bower GH. 1982. Musical expertise and melodic structure in memory for musical notation. *Am. J. Psychol.* 95:31–50

Hamilton WG, Hamilton LH, Marshall P, Molnar M. 1992. A profile of the muscoloskeletal characteristics of elite professional ballet dancers. *Am. J. Sports Med.* 20:267–73

Hassebrock F, Johnson PE, Bullemer P, Fox PW, Moller JH. 1993. When less is more: representation and selective memory in expert problem solving. *Am. J. Psychol.* 106: 155–89

Hatano G, Osawa K. 1983. Digit memory of grand experts in abacus-derived mental calculation. *Cognition* 15:95–110

Hayes JR. 1981. *The Complete Problem Solver*. Philadelphia: Franklin Inst. Press

Helson W, Pauwels JM. 1993. The relationship between expertise and visual information processing. See Starkes & Allard 1993, pp. 109–34

Hoffman RR. 1987. The problem of extracting the knowledge of experts from the perspective of experimental psychology. *AI Mag.* 8(2):53–67

Hoffman RR, ed. 1992. *The Psychology of Expertise. Cognitive Research and Empirical AI.* New York: Springer. 395 pp.

Hoffman RR. 1995. Eliciting knowledge from experts: a methodological analysis. *Organ. Behav. Hum. Decis. Process.* 62:129–58

Holding DH. 1985. *The Psychology of Chess Skill.* Hillsdale, NJ: Erlbaum

Holding DH. 1989. Counting backwards during chess move choice. *Bull. Psychon. Soc.* 27:421–24

Holding DH, Reynolds RI. 1982. Recall or evaluation of chess positions as determinants of chess skill. *Mem. Cogn.* 10: 237–42

Howe MJA. 1990. *The Origins of Exceptional Abilities.* Oxford: Blackwell

Hulin CL, Henry RA, Noon SL. 1990. Adding a dimension: time as a factor in the generalizability of predictive relationships. *Psychol. Bull.* 107:328–40

Hunt E, Love T. 1972. How good can memory be? In *Coding Processes in Human Memory*, ed. AW Melton, E Martin, pp. 237–60. New York: Holt

Intons-Peterson MJ, Smyth MM. 1987. The anatomy of repertory memory. *J. Exp. Psychol.* 13:490–500

Jeffries R, Turner A, Polson P, Atwood M. 1981. The processes involved in designing software. See Anderson 1981, pp. 255–84

Johnson PE, Grazioli S, Jamal K, Zualkerman IA. 1992. Success and failure in expert reasoning. *Organ. Behav. Hum. Decis. Process.* 53:173–203

Johnson PE, Jamal K, Berryman RG. 1991. Effects of framing on auditor decisions. *Organ. Behav. Hum. Decis. Process.* 50:75–105

Jones HH, Priest JD, Hayes WC, Tichenor CC, Nagel DA. 1977. Humeral hypertrophy in response to exercise. *J. Bone Jt. Surg.* 59: 204–8

Keele SW, Ivry RI. 1987. Modular analysis of timing in motor skill. In *The Psychology of Learning and Motivation*, ed. GH Bower, 21:183–228. New York: Academic

Kellogg RT. 1994. *The Psychology of Writing.* Oxford: Oxford Univ. Press

Keren G. 1987. Facing uncertainty in the game of bridge: a calibration study. *Organ. Behav. Hum. Decis. Process.* 39:98–114

King JW, Brelsford HJ, Tullos HS. 1969. Analysis of the pitching arm of the professional baseball pitcher. *Clin. Orthop.* 67: 116–23

Klahr D, Kotovsky K, eds. 1989. *Complex Information Processing: The Impact of Herbert A. Simon.* Hillsdale, NJ: Erlbaum

Koubek RJ, Salvendy G. 1991. Cognitive performance of super-experts on computer program modification tasks. *Ergonomics* 34:1095–1112

Krampe RT. 1994. *Maintaining Excellence: Cognitive-Motor Performance in Pianists Differing in Age and Skill Level.* Berlin: Edition Sigma

Lamb KL, Burwitz L. 1988. Visual restriction in ball-catching: a re-examination of early findings. *J. Hum. Mov. Stud.* 14:93–99

Lane DM, Robertson L. 1979. The generality of levels-of-processing hypothesis: an application to memory for chess positions. *Mem. Cogn.* 7:253–56

Larkin JH, McDermott J, Simon DP, Simon HA. 1980. Models of competence in solving physics problems. *Cogn. Sci.* 4: 317–45

Larkin JH, Simon HA. 1987. Why a diagram is (sometimes) worth ten thousand words. *Cogn. Sci.* 11:65–99

Leas RR, Chi MTH. 1993. Analyzing diagnostic expertise of competitive swimmers. See Starkes & Allard 1993, pp. 75–94

Lehman HC. 1953. *Age and Achievement.* Princeton, NJ: Princeton Univ. Press

Lemieux M, Bordage G. 1992. Propositional versus structural semantic analyses of medical diagnostic thinking. *Cogn. Sci.* 16: 185–94

Leprohon J, Patel VL. 1995. Decision making strategies for telephone triage in emergency medical services. *J. Med. Decis. Making.* 15:240–53

Lesgold A, Rubinson H, Feltovich P, Glaser R, Klopfer D, Wang Y. 1988. Expertise in a complex skill: diagnosing X-ray pictures. See Chi et al 1988, pp. 311–42

Lewis C. 1981. Skill in algebra. See Anderson 1981, pp. 85–110

Lories G. 1987. Recall of random and nonrandom chess positions in strong and weak chess players. *Psychol. Belg.* 27:153–59

Luria AR. 1968. *The Mind of a Mnemonist.* New York: Avon

MacKenzie CL, Nelson-Schulz JA, Wills BL. 1983. A preliminary investigation of motor programming in piano performance as a function of skill level. In *Acquisition Of Symbolic Skills,* ed. DR Rogers, JA Sloboda, pp. 283–92. New York: Plenum

Martin AD, McCulloch RG. 1987. Bone dynamics: stress, strain and fracture. *J. Sport Sci.* 5:155–63

McKeithen KB, Reitman JS, Rueter HH, Hirtle SC. 1981. Knowledge organization and skill differences in computer programmers. *Cogn. Psychol.* 13:307–25

McLeod P. 1987. Visual reaction time and high-speed ball games. *Perception* 16: 49–59

McLeod P, Jenkins S. 1991. Timing accuracy and decision time in high-speed ball games. *Int. J. Sport Psychol.* 22:279–95

McPherson SL. 1993a. Knowledge representation and decision-making in sport. See Starkes & Allard 1993, pp. 159–88

McPherson SL. 1993b. The influence of player experience on problem solving during batting preparation in baseball. *J. Sport Exerc. Psychol.* 15:304–25

McPherson SL, Thomas JR. 1989. Relation of knowledge and performance in boys' tennis. *J. Exp. Child. Psychol.* 48:190–211

Miller EH, Callander JN, Lawhon SM, Sammarco GJ. 1984. Orthopaedics and the classical ballet dancer. *Contemp. Orthop.* 8(1):72–97

Miller GA. 1956. The magical number seven, plus or minus two: some limits on our capacity for processing information. *Psychol. Rev.* 63:81–97

Morgan WP, Pollock ML. 1977. Psychological characterization of the elite distance runner. *Ann. NY Acad. Sci.* 301:383–403

Morris PE, Tweedy M, Gruneberg MM. 1985. Interest, knowledge and the memorization of soccer scores. *Br. J. Psychol.* 76:415–25

Myles-Worsley M, Johnston WA, Simons MA. 1988. The influence of expertise on X-ray image processing. *J. Exp. Psychol. Learn. Mem. Cogn.* 14:553–57

Newell A, Simon HA. 1972. *Human Problem Solving.* Englewood Cliffs, NJ: Prentice Hall

Noice H. 1991. The role of explanations and plan recognition in the learning of theatrical scripts. *Cogn. Sci.* 15:425–60

Noice H. 1993. Effects of rote versus gist strategy on the verbatim retention of theatrical scripts. *Appl. Cogn. Psychol.* 7:75–84

Norman GR, Brooks LR, Allen SW. 1989a. Recall by expert medical practitioners and novices as a record of processing attention. *J. Exp. Psychol. Learn. Mem. Cogn.* 15: 1166–74

Norman GR, Brooks LR, Coblentz CL, Babcook CJ. 1992a. The correlation of feature identification and category judgments in diagnostic radiology. *Mem. Cogn.* 20:344–55

Norman GR, Coblentz CL, Brooks LR, Babcook CJ. 1992b. Expertise in visual diagnosis: a review of the literature. *Acad. Med. Rime Suppl.* 67:78–83

Norman GR, Rosenthal D, Brooks LR, Allen SW, Muzzin LJ. 1989b. The development of expertise in dermatology. *Arch. Dermatol.* 125:1063–68

Norman GR, Trott AD, Brooks LR, Smith EKM. 1994. Cognitive differences in clinical reasoning related to postgraduate training. *Teach. Learn. Med.* 6(2):114–20

Obler IK, Fein D, eds. 1988. *The Exceptional Brain: Neuropsychology of Talent and Special Abilities.* New York: Guilford. 522 pp.

O'Connor PJ. 1992. Psychological aspects of endurance performance. In *Endurance in Sport,* ed. RJ Shephard, PO Astrand, pp. 139–45. Boston: Blackwell

Olson JR, Biolsi KJ. 1991. Techniques for representing expert knowledge. See Ericsson & Smith 1991b, pp. 240–85

Palmer C. 1989. Mapping musical thought to musical performance. *J. Exp. Psychol. Hum. Percept. Perform.* 15:331–46

Patel VL, Arocha JF, Kaufmann DR. 1994. Diagnostic reasoning and medical expertise. In *The Psychology of Learning and Motivation,* ed. D Medin, 30:187–251. New York: Academic

Patel VL, Groen GJ. 1991. The general and specific nature of medical expertise: a critical look. See Ericsson & Smith 1991b, pp. 93–125

Pfau HD, Murphy MD. 1988. Role of verbal knowledge in chess skill. *Am. J. Psychol.* 101:73–86

Pinheiro VED, Simon HA. 1992. An operational model of motor skill diagnosis. *J. Teach. Phys. Educ.* 11:288–302

Proctor RW, Dutta A. 1995. *Skill acquisition and human performance.* Thousand Oaks, CA: Sage. 442 pp.

Regnier G, Salmela J, Russell SJ. 1994. Talent detection and development in sports. See Singer et al 1993, pp. 290–313

Reif F, Allen S. 1992. Cognition for interpreting scientific concepts: a study of acceleration. *Cogn. Instr.* 9(1):1–44

Reitman J. 1976. Skilled perception in go: deducing memory structures from inter-response times. *Cogn. Psychol.* 8:336–56

Repp B. 1992. Diversity and commonality in music performance: an analysis of timing microstructure in Schumann's "Träumerei". *J. Acoust. Soc. Am.* 95:2546–68

Richman HB, Staszewski JJ, Simon HA. 1995. Simulation of expert memory using EPAM IV. *Psychol. Rev.* 102:305–30

Ripoll H. 1991. The understanding-acting process in sport: the relationship between the semantic and the sensorimotor visual function. *Int. J. Sport Psychol.* 22:221–43

Rosson MB. 1985. The role of experience in editing. *Proc. INTERACT '84 IFIP Conf. on Hum.-Comput. Interact.,* pp. 45–50. New York: Elsevier

Saariluoma P. 1985. Chess players' intake of task-relevant cues. *Mem. Cogn.* 13:385–91

Saariluoma P. 1989. Chess players' recall of auditorily presented chess positions. *Eur. J. Cogn. Psychol.* 1:309–20

Saariluoma P. 1990. Apperception and restructuring in chess players' problem solving. In *Lines of Thought: Reflections on the Psychology of Thinking,* ed. KJ Gilhooly, MTG Keene, G Erdos, 2:41–57. London: Wiley

Saariluoma P. 1991. Aspects of skilled imagery in blindfold chess. *Acta Psychol.* 77: 65–89

Saariluoma P. 1992. Error in chess: the apperception-restructuring view. *Psychol. Res.* 54:17–26

Salthouse TA. 1984. Effects of age and skill in typing. *J. Exp. Psychol. Gen.* 13:345–71

Salthouse TA. 1986. Perceptual, cognitive, and motoric aspects of transcription typing. *Psychol. Bull.* 99:303–19

Sammarco GJ, Miller EH. 1982. Forefoot conditions in dancers. *Foot Ankle* 3(2):85–98

Schlaug G, Jäncke L, Huang Y, Steinmetz H. 1995. In vivo evidence of structural brain asymmetry in musicians. *Science* 267: 699–701

Schneider W, Bös K, Rieder H. 1993. Leistungsprognose bei jugendlichen Spitzensportlern [Prediction of performance of young elite athletes]. In *Konzentration und Leistung* [Concentration and performance], ed. J Beckman, H Strang, E Hahn, pp. 277–99. Göttingen, Ger: Hogrefe

Schmidt HG, Boshuizen HPA. 1993. On the origin of intermediate effects in clinical case recall. *Mem. Cogn.* 21:338–51

Schmidt HG, Norman GR, Boshuizen HPA. 1990. A cognitive perspective on medical expertise: theory and implications. *Acad. Med.* 65:611–21

Schneider W, Körkel J, Weinert FE. 1989. Domain-specific knowledge and memory performance: a comparison of high- and low-aptitude children. *J. Educ. Psychol.* 81: 306–12

Schraagen JM. 1993. How experts solve a novel problem in experimental design. *Cogn. Sci.* 17:285–309

Schulz R, Curnow C. 1988. Peak performance and age among superathletes: track and field, swimming, baseball, tennis, and golf. *J. Geront. Psychol. Sci.* 43:113–20

Schulz R, Musa D, Staszewski J, Siegler RS. 1994. The relationship between age and major league baseball performance: implications for development. *Psychol. Aging* 9: 274–86

Shaffer LH. 1973. Latency mechanisms in transcription. In *Attention and Performance,* ed. S Kornblum, 4:435–46. New York: Academic

Shaffer LH. 1975. Multiple attention in continuous verbal tasks. In *Attention and Performance,* ed. PM Rabbitt, S Dornic, 5: 157–67. London: Academic

Shaffer LH. 1981. Performances of Chopin, Bach, and Bartok: studies in motor programming. *Cogn. Psychol.* 13:326–76

Shanteau J. 1992. Competence in experts: the role of task characteristics. *Organ. Behav. Hum. Decis. Process.* 53:252–66

Shanteau J, Stewart TR. 1992. Why study expert decision making? Some historical perspectives and comments. *Organ. Behav. Hum. Decis. Process.* 53:95–106

Shephard RJ. 1994. *Aerobic Fitness and Health.* Champaign, IL: Human Kinetics

Shneiderman B. 1976. Exploratory experiments in programmer behavior. *Int. J. Comput. Inf. Sci.* 5:123–43

Shuter-Dyson R, Gabriel C. 1981. *The Psychology of Musical Ability.* London: Methuen. 2nd ed.

Siegler RS, ed. 1978. *Children's Thinking: What Develops?* Hillsdale, NJ: Erlbaum

Simon DP, Simon HA. 1978. Individual differences in solving physics problems. See Siegler 1978, pp. 325–48

Simon HA, Chase WG. 1973. Skill in chess. *Am. Sci.* 61:394–403

Simonton DK. 1988. *Scientific Genius: A Psychology of Science.* Cambridge: Cambridge Univ. Press

Singer RN, Murphey M, Tennant LK. 1993. *Handbook of Research on Sport Psychology.* London/New York: Macmillan. 984 pp.

Sloboda JA. 1976. Visual perception of musical notation: registering pitch symbols in memory. *Q. J. Exp. Psychol.* 28:1–16

Sloboda JA. 1984. Experimental studies in music reading: a review. *Music Percept.* 22:222–36

Sloboda JA. 1991. Musical expertise. See Ericsson & Smith 1991b, pp. 153–71

Sloboda JA, Parker HH. 1985. Immediate recall of melodies. In *Musical Structure and Cognition,* ed. I Cross, P Howell, R West, pp. 143–67. New York: Academic

Smyth MM, Pendleton LR. 1994. Memory for movement in professional ballet dancers. *Int. J. Sport Psychol.* 25:282–94

Spilich GJ, Vesonder GT, Chiesi HL, Voss JF. 1979. Text processing of domain related information for individuals with high and low domain knowledge. *J. Verbal Learn. Verbal Behav.* 18:275–90

Starkes JL. 1987. Skill in field hockey: the nature of the cognitive advantage. *J. Sport Exerc. Psychol.* 9:146–60

Starkes JL, Allard F, eds. 1993. *Cognitive Issues in Motor Expertise.* New York: Elsevier

Starkes JL, Allard F, Lindley S, O'Reilly K. 1994. Abilities and skill in basketball. *Int. J. Sport Psychol.* 25:249–65

Starkes JL, Caicco M, Boutilier C, Sevesk B. 1990. Motor recall of experts for structured and unstructured sequences in creative modern dance. *J. Sport Exerc. Psychol.* 12:317–21

Starkes JL, Deakin J. 1984. Perception in sport: a cognitive approach to skilled performance. In *Cognitive Sport Psychology,* ed. WF Straub, JM Williams, pp. 115–28. Lansing, NY: Sport Sci. Assoc.

Starkes JL, Deakin JM, Lindley S, Crisp F. 1987. Motor versus verbal recall of ballet sequences by young expert dancers. *J. Sport Psychol.* 9:222–30

Staszewski JJ. 1988a. The psychological reality of retrieval structures: an investigation of expert knowledge. *Diss. Abstr. Int.* 48: 2126B

Staszewski JJ. 1988b. Skilled memory and expert mental calculation. See Chi et al 1988, pp. 71–128

Ste-Marie DM, Lee TD. 1991. Prior processing effects on gymnastics judging. *J. Exp. Psychol. Learn. Mem. Cogn.* 17: 126–36

Sternberg RJ, Frensch PA. 1992. On being and expert: a cost benefit analysis. In *The Psychology of Expertise. Cognitive Research and Empirical AI,* ed. RR Hoffman, pp. 191–203. New York: Springer

Summers JJ, Ford SK, Todd JA. 1993. Practice effects on the coordination of the two hands in bimanual tapping task. *Hum. Mov. Sci.* 12:111–33

Takeuchi AH, Hulse SH. 1993. Absolute pitch. *Psychol. Bull.* 113:345–61

Tenenbaum G, Bar-Eli M. 1993. Decision making in sport: a cognitive perspective. See Singer et al 1993, pp. 171–92

Thompson CP, Cowan TM, Frieman J. 1993. *Memory Search by a Memorist.* Hillsdale, NJ: Erlbaum. 156 pp.

Underwood G, Deihem C, Batt V. 1994. Expert performance in solving word puzzles from retrieval cues to crossword clues. *Appl. Cogn. Psychol.* 8:531–48

VanLehn K. 1989. Problem solving and cognitive skill acquisition. In *Foundations Of Cognitive Science,* ed. MI Posner, pp. 527–79. Cambridge, MA: Bradford/MIT Press

VanLehn K. 1996. Cognitive skill acquisition. *Annu. Rev. Psychol.* 47:513–39

Vicente KJ. 1992. Memory recall in a process control system: a measure of expertise and display effectiveness. *Mem. Cogn.* 20: 356–73

Voss JF, Greene TR, Post TA, Penner BC. 1983. Problem-solving skill in the social sciences. In *The Psychology of Learning and Motivation: Advances in Research and Theory,* ed. GH Bower, 17:165–213. New York: Academic

Wagner C. 1988. The pianist's hand: anthropometry and biomechanics. *Ergonomics* 31:97–131

Wallman J. 1994. Nature and nurture of myopia. *Nature* 371:201–2

Whittred G, Zimmer I. 1985. The implications

of distress prediction models for corporate lending. *Account. Finan.* 25:1–13

Winkler RL, Poses RM. 1993. Evaluating and combining physicians' probabilities of survival in an intensive care unit. *Manage. Sci.* 39:1526–43

Wolf FM, Miller JG, Borzynski ME, Schlesinger A, Rosen DS, et al. 1994. Effects of expertise and case difficulty on the inter-pretation of pediatric radiographs. *Acad. Med.* 69:S31–S34 (Suppl.)

Wolff AS, Mitchell DH, Frey PW. 1984. Perceptual skill in the game of Othello. *J. Psychol.* 118:7–16

Wright DL, Pleasants F, Gomez-Meza M. 1990. Use of advanced visual cue sources in volleyball. *J. Sport Exerc. Psychol.* 12:406–14

Annu. Rev. Psychol. 1996. 47:307–38

TEAMS IN ORGANIZATIONS: Recent Research on Performance and Effectiveness

Richard A. Guzzo and Marcus W. Dickson

Psychology Department, University of Maryland, College Park, Maryland 20742

KEY WORDS: group dynamics, organizational change, autonomous workgroups, computer assisted groups, cockpit resource management

ABSTRACT

This review examines recent research on groups and teams, giving special emphasis to research investigating factors that influence the effectiveness of teams at work in organizations. Several performance-relevant factors are considered, including group composition, cohesiveness, and motivation, although certain topics (e.g. composition) have been more actively researched than others in recent years and so are addressed in greater depth. Also actively researched are certain types of teams, including flight crews, computer-supported groups, and various forms of autonomous work groups. Evidence on basic processes in and the performance effectiveness of such groups is reviewed. Also reviewed are findings from studies of organizational redesign involving the implementation of teams. Findings from these studies provide some of the strongest support for the value of teams to organizational effectiveness. The review concludes by briefly considering selected open questions and emerging directions in group research.

CONTENTS

0066-4308/96/0201-0307$08.00

INTRODUCTION

Scope and Objectives

For more than a decade now, psychology has enjoyed a rekindled interest in groups and teams. Chapters in previous *Annual Review of Psychology* volumes have considered group research (e.g. Levine & Moreland 1990) and organizational behavior (e.g. Wilpert 1995), but this chapter is unique because of its special focus on team performance in organizational contexts, especially in work organizations.

The literature reviewed considers, among other emphases, research conducted in organizational settings with groups or teams that must meet the demands of producing goods or delivering services. Although we review some research conducted in other than organizational settings, we emphasize studies in which the dependent variables were clearly indicative of performance effectiveness rather than studies on intragroup or interpersonal processes in groups (e.g. studies of conformity, opinion change, conflict). We also include studies of interventions made to test the efficacy of techniques intended to improve team effectiveness. Such interventions may be targeted at individual team members (e.g. enhancing member skills that are important to team performance), at teams as performing units (e.g. team development interventions), or at the organizations in which teams work. Thus, research on larger-scale organizational change efforts of which the implementation or enhancement of teams are one part of an overall change strategy is included. Lastly, we emphasize research in the 1990s, though we do refer to earlier works.

Definitional Struggles

WORK GROUP/TEAM   What is a work group? A variety of definitions have been offered (Guzzo & Shea 1992), but one we adopt owes its origins to the work of Alderfer (1977) and Hackman (1987). A "work group" is made up of individuals who see themselves and who are seen by others as a social entity, who are interdependent because of the tasks they perform as members of a group, who are embedded in one or more larger social systems (e.g. community, organization), and who perform tasks that affect others (such as customers or coworkers).

"Team" has largely replaced "group" in the argot of organizational psychology. Is this a mere matter of wording or are there substantive differences between groups and teams? For many, "team" connotes more than "group." Katzenbach & Smith (1993), for example, assert that groups become teams when they develop a sense of shared commitment and strive for synergy among members. The definition of work groups presented above, we believe, accommodates the uses of the many labels for teams and groups, including empowered teams, autonomous work groups, semi-autonomous work groups, self-managing teams, self-determining teams, self-designing teams, crews, cross-functional teams, quality circles, project teams, task forces, emergency response teams, and committees—a list that represents, but does not exhaust, available labels. Consequently, we use the labels "team" and "group" interchangeably in this review, recognizing that there may be degrees of difference, rather than fundamental divergences, in the meanings implied by these terms. We use the terms interchangeably as a convenience. The word "group" predominates in the research literature—intergroup relations, group incentives, group dynamics—and though it uses "group" as its root word, we believe the literature has great relevance for understanding virtually all forms of teams in organizations, too.

EFFECTIVENESS   There is no singular, uniform measure of performance effectiveness for groups. We prefer to define it broadly, as have Hackman (1987) and Sundstrom et al (1990). Accordingly, effectiveness in groups is indicated by (a) group-produced outputs (quantity or quality, speed, customer satisfaction, and so on), (b) the consequences a group has for its members, or (c) the enhancement of a team's capability to perform effectively in the future. Research that assesses one or more of these three aspects of effectiveness is of primary interest in this review.

Framework for the Review

We begin with recent research on several long-standing issues relevant to work-group effectiveness, including team cohesiveness, team composition and performance, leadership, motivation, and group goals. They are generic issues in the sense that they pertain to almost all teams doing almost all kinds of work. Although not the only performance-relevant research topics, they are the ones most actively investigated in recent years.

We then consider research on the performance of different kinds of groups, including cockpit crews and electronically mediated groups, as well as groups created to solve problems (quality circles, task forces) and autonomous work groups. The next section explicitly addresses teams and the organizational systems in which they are embedded and focuses on the interconnections between team and organization.

The final section offers selected conclusions and flags open questions and new directions for future research. The section concludes with a brief discussion of points of leverage for effecting change in teams.

NEW LOOKS AT LONG-STANDING ISSUES IN GROUP PERFORMANCE

Cohesiveness

Reviews of cohesiveness research have appeared in recent years (e.g. Evans & Dion 1991, Guzzo & Shea 1992). The former review found a substantial positive association between cohesion and performance while the latter offered a more qualified conclusion. Smith et al (1994) report a positive correlation between a cohesiveness-like measure of top management teams in small high-technology firms and firm financial performance. Zaccarro et al (1995) reported that highly task-cohesive military teams under high temporal urgency performed as well on a decision task as did either high task-cohesive or low task-cohesive teams under low temporal urgency, suggesting that task cohesion can improve team decision making under time pressure. The topic of cohesiveness is still very much an unsettled concern in the literature. It is certainly related to issues of familiarity, which are discussed at other points in the chapter.

Group Composition

Group composition refers to the nature and attributes of group members, and it is one of the most frequently studied group design variables. Most of the empirical research on composition and work-group performance in recent years has investigated variables associated with team effectiveness without intervening or experimenting to affect those variables. The typical model of study has been to assess the performance of existing groups or teams in organizations over time and to relate that performance to measured aspects of group composition.

Other studies investigated group composition as one of several possible design variables for groups. Group design refers to issues of staffing (who is in the group, what the group size should be), specifying the group's task and members' roles, and creating organizational support systems (e.g. training opportunities) for groups. Studies conducted with teams in organizational settings are of particular interest here.

One study that related team effectiveness to composition and other potential design variables was reported by Campion et al (1993). They studied 80 work groups in a financial services firm and found broad evidence of relationships between effectiveness and 19 design variables clustered into five categories: team job design (e.g. amount of self-management in the team), interdependence among team members, composition (especially the heterogeneity of members), intragroup processes, and contextual factors (e.g. managerial support). Campion et al found team size to be positively related to effectiveness and found heterogeneity of members' background and expertise to be unrelated or negatively related to effectiveness, depending on the specific criterion measure.

Another study examining some of the same issues was reported by Magjuka & Baldwin (1991). Here the focus was on factors that contribute to the successful implementation of team-based employee-involvement programs and the longer-term effective performance of teams in such programs. Through teams employees have voice in organizational affairs, gain access to information and address problems previously reserved for management, and take on new and varied responsibilities. On the basis of results from their national survey, Magjuka & Baldwin identified factors thought to contribute to the effectiveness with which employee involvement teams are designed and implemented. They then obtained additional data and examined relationships between these factors and effectiveness for 72 teams in two manufacturing firms. They found that larger team size, greater within-team heterogeneity (in terms of the kinds of jobs team members held), and greater access to information were positively associated with team effectiveness. The implications of these findings for designing and implementing employee involvement teams are straightforward. Other factors such as hours spent in meetings and members' wages did not relate to effectiveness.

HETEROGENEITY AND PERFORMANCE   The extent to which team effectiveness is affected by the heterogeneity among members is a complicated matter. Magjuka & Baldwin (1991) and Campion et al (1993), as noted above, offer seemingly contradictory findings. Jackson et al (1995), in their paper on diversity in organizations, reviewed and summarized empirical evidence from a number of related disciplines about the link between diversity (that is, within-group heterogeneity) and team effectiveness. Their reading of the literature is that heterogeneity is positively related to the creativity and the decision-making effectiveness of teams. Note that heterogeneity is broadly defined here and refers to the mix of personalities, gender, attitudes, and background or experience factors. For example, Bantel & Jackson (1989) found that organizational innovations in the banking industry were positively associated with heterogeneity of functional expertise among members of the top management teams of firms in that industry. Watson et al (1993) reported that, over time (15 weeks), initial performance differences between newly formed culturally homogeneous and culturally diverse groups disappeared and eventually "crossed-over," such that culturally heterogeneous groups that initially performed poorly relative to homogeneous groups later performed better than homogeneous groups on selected aspects of task performance (namely, generating alternative solutions and applying a range of perspectives in analyzing business cases). Overall, the Campion et al (1993) finding of a nil or negative association between the heterogeneity of group members' backgrounds and team effectiveness appears to be more the exception than the rule (Jackson et al 1991), though evidence supporting the value of member heterogeneity for team performance is clearest in the domains of creative and intellective tasks. The processes (cognitive, social) through which heterogenous group compositions have their effect on team performance are far from fully specified, though Jackson et al (1995) explore possible mediating processes.

Heterogeneity of members also appears to have other, performance-related consequences. Jackson et al (1991) reported that heterogeneity among members of top management teams in bank holding companies was positively related to turnover in those teams. Wiersema & Bird (1993) found similar, if stronger, results in a sample of Japanese firms. Turnover is usually thought of as dysfunctional for team effectiveness, though it is possible that the consequences of losing and replacing members could work to the advantage of teams in some circumstances.

FAMILIARITY AND PERFORMANCE   Another aspect of group composition that has recently been studied for its relationship to team performance is that of familiarity among members. Goodman & Leyden (1991) examined, over the course of 15 months, the productivity (in tons per shift) of coal-mining crews who differed in the extent to which members were familiar with each other, their jobs, and their mining environment. Results indicated that lower levels of familiarity were associated with lower levels of productivity. Watson et al (1991) studied groups who spent more than 30 hours in decision-making tasks and found that group decision-making effectiveness (relative to individual decision-making effectiveness) rose over time, a finding they attribute at least in part to the effects of increased familiarity among members. Dubnicki & Limburg (1991) found that older health-care teams tend to be more effective in certain ways, though newer teams express more vitality. Thus, some evidence indicates that teams composed of individuals who are familiar with one another carry out their work with greater effectiveness than teams composed of strangers. However, one should bear in mind that some older evidence indicates that there may be a point, perhaps two or three years after a group is formed, at which group longevity and member familiarity become detriments to group performance (Katz 1982). In the later section on cockpit crews we provide further discussion of team member familiarity.

Leadership and Group Performance

The effects on group performance of leaders' expectations of group performance were studied in a field experiment by Eden (1990a). The purpose of the intervention was to raise, through information provided by an "expert," group leaders' expectations of their group's performance in a training setting. The groups were platoons in the Israeli Defense Forces in training that lasted 11 weeks. Platoons training under leaders who held high expectations performed better on physical and cognitive tests at the end of training than did comparison platoons. This research extends prior work on the effects of expectations on performance (Eden 1990b) and indicates that such expectancy effects occur in the absence of any lowered expectations for comparison groups.

Jacobs & Singell (1993) offer a different perspective on how individual leaders can affect team performance. They examined the effects of managers (after controlling for other variables) on the won-lost record of professional baseball teams over two decades and found it was possible to identify superior managers. Superior managers were effective through at least two possible processes: by exercising excellent tactical skills or by improving the individual performances of team members.

George & Bettenhausen (1990) studied groups of sales associates reporting to a store manager and found that the favorability of leaders' moods was inversely related to employee turnover. Another study in business organizations examined the position-based power dominance of firms' chief executive officers (CEOs) and their top-management team size as predictors of firm performance (Haleblian & Finkelstein 1993). The study found that firms' performance was worse in turbulent environments when the CEO was dominant and better when top-management team size was greater.

Motivation and Group Performance

In recent years motivation in groups has received more theoretical rather than empirical attention. Much of this attention is devoted to understanding motivation at a collective (group, team) level rather than to strictly confining the motivation construct to an individual level of analysis. For example, Shamir (1990) analyzed three different forms of collectivistic work motivation: calculation (rewards or sanctions are anticipated to follow from group performance), identification (one's self-concept is influenced by membership in a group), and internalization (acceptance of group beliefs and norms as a basis for motivated behavior). Each orientation is considered viable in different circumstances. Guzzo et al (1993) introduced the concept of group potency and defined it as the group's collective belief that it can be effective. They differentiated the construct from other related constructs (e.g. collective efficacy) and reviewed evidence that the strength of this motivational belief sig-

nificantly predicted group effectiveness in customer service and other domains. Guzzo et al (1993) maintained an interest in motivation at the group
level of analysis, not at the individual level of analysis.

Individual motivation within groups also has received attention, especially
as individual motivation is related to group-level factors. Earley (1994) provided empirical evidence on the role of individualism-collectivism (a culture-
based individual difference) in shaping the impact of motivational (self-efficacy) training for individuals. Group-focused training was found to have a
stronger impact on collectivist individuals, and self-focused training was
found to have a greater impact on individualists. For Earley, a central research
question was how individual motivation is affected by the match of motivational training to the individual values of trainees. Sheppard (1993) offered an
interpretation of individual task-performance motivation in groups that drew
heavily on expectancy theory (e.g. Vroom 1964), reinterpreting within the
expectancy theory framework evidence on individual motivational deficits in
the form of social loafing and free-riding in groups.

Group Goals

Related to issues of group motivation are issues of group goals and goal-setting. Goals for group performance can take many forms: quantity, speed,
accuracy, service to others, and so on (see Brawley et al 1992 for an exploration of the types of goals set by sports teams). And the evidence is clear that,
compared with the absence of goals (or the presence of ill-defined goals),
specific, difficult goals for groups raise group performance on those dimensions reflecting the content of the goal (Weldon & Weingart 1993). That is,
goals for quantity tend to raise quantity, goals for speed tend to raise speed,
and so on.

There are occasional reports of failures of group goals to induce performance effects (see Fandt et al 1990 for an example). Despite the exceptions,
there does appear to be a strong evidentiary basis for the performance effects
of goals. In light of this, research has been redirected toward understanding the
processes through which goals have their effects. Weingart (1992), for example, examined in a laboratory experiment member effort and planning, two
possible mediators of goal effects, and found evidence indicating that member
effort mediated the impact of goal difficulty on performance. The quality of
the planning process also affected group performance in the expected direction
but was not observed to be a result of goal levels. Weldon et al (1991) and
Weingart & Weldon (1991) also provide evidence that group goals raise
member effort, but only in the former study did that effort translate into
increased group performance. Other possible mediators of the effects of group
goals include the degree of cooperation and communication they stimulate in
groups (Weldon & Weingart 1993; see also Lee 1989, Locke & Latham 1990).

Goals for group performance often coexist with goals for individual performance. When group and individual goals conflict, dysfunctions can result. However, it is not necessarily the case that even when group and individual goals are compatible the presence of both results in levels of performance higher than when either goal type exists alone. Specifically, Mitchell & Silver (1990) found that the presence of both individual and group goals resulted in performance no greater than that attained in the presence of group goals alone. Self-efficacy has also been explored in this context, with Lee (1989) showing that team goal-setting mediated the relationship between team-member self-efficacy and winning percentage among several female field hockey teams.

Other Issues

Other issues of long-standing interest because of their relationship to group performance effectiveness include feedback and communication in groups. For example, in a study of a collegiate volleyball team, de Armas Paredes & Riera-Milian (1987) found won-lost records to be related to the quality of intrateam communication. The performance effects of feedback were investigated in a study of railway work crews by Pearson (1991), who found small but statistically significant increases in productivity over time as a consequence of receiving performance feedback. The effect of task-performance feedback also was investigated by McLeod et al (1992). However, they found no significant change in task performance effectiveness attributable to such goal-referenced feedback. They also investigated the effects of feedback that concerned interpersonal processes in groups and did detect a change in the dominance behavior of individuals attributable to it.

KINDS OF GROUPS

The preceding section reviewed recent research on long-standing issues of relevance to group performance. Issues such as composition, motivation, and leadership are of near-universal importance to groups. They are relevant to many types of teams in many kinds of settings. In this section we consider recent research on particular types of groups.

Many classifications of groups into types have been offered. Hackman's (1990) book, for example, organizes its reports of groups into categories such as service (e.g. delivery) and performing (e.g. symphonic) teams. In this section we, too, specify different kinds of groups on the basis of the work they do. We do not offer the following categories as a typology that we expect to have value outside of the confines of this review. Instead, the categorizations defined below are a matter of convenience for organizing recent research literature.

Flight Crews: Teams in the Cockpit

"The crew concept" in airlines has had many names over the years. The phrase "Cockpit Resource Management" initially took hold. More recently, this focus has come to be known as "Crew Resource Management" (CRM) owing, in part, to the recognition of the importance of including persons not actually in the cockpit (e.g. controllers, flight attendants, etc) as part of the team (Lauber 1993).

CRM has been defined as "using all available resources—information, equipment, and people—to achieve safe and efficient flight operations" (Lauber 1984). The practical importance of such a program is shown in the fact that over 70% of all severe aircraft accidents between 1959 and 1989 were at least partially attributable to flight crew behavior.

In general, CRM training includes "not only optimizing the person-machine interface and the acquisition of timely, appropriate information, but also interpersonal activities including leadership, effective team formation and maintenance, problem solving and decision making, and maintaining situation awareness....It represents a new focus on crew-level (as opposed to individual-level) aspects of training and operations" (Helmreich & Foushee 1993, p. 4). Helmreich & Wilhelm (1991) noted that CRM training is generally well received by trainees and leads to positive changes in crew members' attitudes about both crew coordination and personal capabilities (or self-efficacy). However, they also acknowledge that in a small percentage of trainees there is a "boomerang effect" in which attitudes become less positive.

Related to CRM training is Line-Oriented Flight Training (LOFT), which is a broad category encompassing flight simulations conducted for several purposes (e.g. to qualify as a pilot, for training). Butler (1993) asserted that LOFT is most important as a training methodology to reinforce CRM concepts and training. This type of LOFT is called CRM LOFT, and it is ongoing, systematic flight simulation of realistic problem situations that require the type of decision-making skills and crew communication that are taught in CRM training. Wiener et al (1993) provide an excellent review of literature on CRM training and LOFT.

CRM AND CREW COMMUNICATION   Communication is one of the major areas covered in CRM training (Orlady & Foushee 1987). In the context of CRM training, communication includes such things as "polite assertiveness and participation, active listening, and feedback" (Orlady & Foushee 1987, p. 199). Though effective communication is almost universally recognized as crucial to effective flight crew performance, and CRM training is generally seen as improving communication skills of flight crew members, there is little experimental or quasi-experimental research on the effectiveness of CRM's communication training for improving outcomes. Instead, the majority of the research examines the effects of CRM training on process variables.

Effective crew coordination is in large part a function of effective crew communication, and so we note research by Stout et al (1994), though not quite a CRM-based study. Their preliminary investigations used a low-fidelity flight simulator, and they examined the interactions among two-person teams of undergraduate volunteers. They found that, when team members must act interdependently to perform effectively, increased levels of such team process and communication behaviors as providing information before it is needed, planning, asking for input, and stepping in to help others were all related to increased effectiveness. Urban et al (1995) had similar results in another non-CRM laboratory study in which they examined the impact of workload and team structure on effectiveness.

CRM AND DECISION MAKING   Diehl (1991) suggested that 50% of all accident-related errors are errors of decision. Thus, the question of whether CRM can enhance the quality of decision making in the cockpit is an important one.

Flight crews are in some ways like many other types of groups that make decisions. Power dynamics are present, and traditional group decision-making pitfalls (e.g. groupthink, risky shift) must be avoided. Flight crews are similar to other groups in that they determine what the situation is, assess available options, and choose among them.

In other ways, though, decision making in the cockpit is unlike other group-decision situations. One significant difference is that crew decision making is hierarchically managed decision making: Each member of the crew contributes his or her knowledge and opinions, and the captain is the final decision-maker. Finally, there is a great variety of expertise available in a flight crew, making flight crews perhaps more heterogeneous than many other types of decision-making groups (Orasanu 1993).

CONTEXTUAL VARIABLES   There are several contextual variables that play a role in airline crew performance and process. One of the most significant is the limited duration of flight crews' existence as a unit. In the commercial airline industry, a given flight crew will probably only work together for at most four days, and sometimes will be together for only part of one day. Indeed, commercial airline flight crews perhaps most closely resemble project teams or task forces in that they are composed of persons with expertise in a specific area (e.g. navigator, captain) and work together for a limited period of time, after which members are reassigned to other flight crews.

Because of this, CRM training and LOFT are conducted in the context of a team (all of the members of a CRM or LOFT flight crew are trainees). Further, the training is not done with the intention of strengthening that particular team, but rather with the goal of making the individuals more effective in whatever team/flight crew they find themselves.

Crews learn to develop relationships quickly (Bowers et al 1993a, Foushee et al 1986). This process can be facilitated by the standard preflight briefing. In this meeting, the captain lays out his or her expectations for the crew and states the goals of the flight (Ginnett 1993).

Finally, and most significantly, Foushee et al (1986) found that newly formed crews communicate less effectively and are more likely to have accidents than are crews that have been intact for at least a short time. This is the primary reason that Hackman (1993) recommended that the system of scheduling flight crews be modified, though he recognized that there would be strong resistance to this idea by flight crew personnel. Note that this mirrors the studies cited earlier suggesting that teams composed of individuals who are familiar with each other will in general be more effective than teams composed of people who do not know each other at all, as is often the case in newly formed cockpit crews. Indeed, the United States Army embraced this view when they mandated "battle-rostering" of crews (assigning aviation crews who work together for extended periods of time). However, recent research by Leedom & Simon (1995) suggested that battle-rostering for the long-term may lead to overconfidence—and errors—among aviators.

Leedom & Simon (1995) also noted that the underlying purpose of battle-rostering and other tactics to increase team member familiarity is to increase predictability of behavior in the team setting. They explored the effectiveness of standardized behavior-based training to improve team coordination and functioning and found that this approach led to higher levels of performance than did battle-rostering and that it did so without the potential overconfidence effects found with battle-rostering. Thus, the issue of crew structure and familiarity remains open.

A second contextual issue is the increasing level of automation in the cockpit. With new aircraft designs and the emergence of the "glass cockpit," crews face new issues of communication, interaction, and decision making. One reason for the emergence of new automation is the attempt by aircraft manufacturers to reduce human decision making as much as possible—because people too often make bad decisions (Billings 1991). Bowers et al (1993b) found in a simulator test that the addition of automation decreased the perceived workload, but this decrease in workload did not necessarily result in increased performance. In fact, in difficult situations the nonautomated crews made better decisions than the automated crews. Further, Costley et al (1989) found that there were lower communication rates in more automated aircraft, though there was no decrease in operational actions.

MILITARY FLIGHT CREWS   Although there are of course many similarities between military flight crews and commercial flight crews, there are also some significant differences between the two. Military flight crews may be significantly larger, for example, and they are likely to remain together as a unit for much longer periods of time than are commercial flight crews, owing to battle-rostering (described in the preceding section). Further, issues of rank of personnel may play a greater role in the military flight crews, and this may be at odds with the assertiveness taught in most CRM-type training. Finally, military flights in peacetime are almost always training flights of some kind, whereas commercial flights are for the purpose of transportation of cargo and passengers rather than for training (Prince & Salas 1993).

Despite those differences, CRM and LOFT-type training programs have been developed by several branches of the military (often called Air Crew Training, or ACT) (Prince & Salas 1993). These ACT programs have generally similar results to CRM training and LOFT, and the research findings from one area generally mirror those of the other. For example, the finding that there is a high correlation between CRM-type behaviors and objective and subjective measures of the effectiveness of aircrews (Povenmire et al 1989) could easily have come from either the commercial or the military air crew research programs.

Further, Prince & Salas (1993) note several similarities between military and commercial research into the origins of flight difficulties. These included problems with the exchange of information in the cockpit, the distribution and level of priority of tasks, and relationships within the crew.

It is important to note that CRM- and LOFT-type training has not yet fully taken root in the military's flying culture, and that the programs that have been developed vary from one service branch to another and from one command to another. This lack of consistency across commands and services may make full-scale adoption and acceptance of such programs more difficult to achieve in the military than in the commercial airlines.

OVERALL EFFECTIVENESS OF CRM TRAINING AND LOFT   As noted above, there is a great deal of research on the effectiveness of CRM training and LOFT, and this body of work is explored in much greater detail in Wiener et al (1993) than can be covered here.

In summary, however, compared with no training of crews in CRM, training in CRM results in more crews being rated by crew evaluators as above average and fewer being rated as below average (Helmreich et al 1990). Further, skills learned in CRM training and LOFT are often cited by pilots as playing a key role in their handling of crisis situations (e.g. National Transportation Safety Board 1990a,b).

Computer-Assisted Groups

The continuing spread of computerization has been accompanied by an expansion of research on groups that use computers in their work. This research has in large part focused on comparing computer-mediated group meetings with non-computer-mediated meetings and, where work is done by groups, on idea generation and choice making.

An interpretation and annotated bibliography of studies, especially experiments, on computer-assisted groups, is provided by Hollingshead & McGrath (1995). They identified fifty research reports over two decades yielding about 150 findings relevant to task performance in computer-mediated groups. Almost all studies were done in laboratories with ad hoc groups. Overall, Hollingshead & McGrath found that computer-mediated groups tended to be characterized by less interaction and exchange than face-to-face groups and tend to take longer in their work. Whether computer-mediated or face-to-face groups are superior in task performance (on dimensions other than speed) appears to depend on the task. Specifically, computer-mediated groups appear superior at generating ideas but face-to-face groups appear superior on problem-solving tasks and tasks requiring the resolution of conflicts (of preferences, for example). They also suggest that a large part of the effect of computer technology in groups may be due to structuring of the task imposed by the use of computer technology rather than other aspects of the electronic medium.

It is interesting to note that increased structuring of the task—whether by computers or by nontechnological means—seems to enhance group processes. Consider, for example, the "stepladder technique," in which a core group of perhaps two members make a tentative decision, and with each successive "step" a new member is added and a presentation is made of the group's current ideas, followed by a renewed discussion of the possibilities. Rogelberg et al (1992) found that groups using this highly structured process produced higher quality solutions (to a survival problem) than did groups using conventional discussion methods. Further, Hartell (1991) demonstrated that teams of undergraduates trained in and utilizing a system of Problem Identification/Verification dealt with trouble-shooting tasks more effectively than teams who were not trained.

CREATIVITY AND BRAINSTORMING   Examples of research on brainstorming can be found in the work of Gallupe, Valacich, and colleagues. Dennis & Valacich (1993) reported that electronically interacting groups (i.e. communicating via computers) produced more ideas during a brainstorming task than did nominal groups (i.e. those whose members did not interact). Gallupe et al (1991, 1992, 1994) compared face-to-face brainstorming with electronic brainstorming groups and found the latter to be superior or the equal of interacting groups.

These studies suggest that the electronic brainstorming medium reduces the extent to which the production of new ideas is blocked by such things as listening to others or waiting for a turn to speak.

Sainfort et al (1990) compared experimental groups using a computer-aided decision system, a videotape training system in conflict resolution, or no support system. They found that the computer-aided groups generated more potential solutions to the problem and perceived themselves as making greater progress than either of the other groups. Also, both technology groups (computer and videotape) were significantly more effective in solving the problem than the control group. All of this research corresponds to the conclusions of Hollingshead & McGrath (1995).

DECISION MAKING   McLeod's (1992) meta-analysis of 13 studies examined the relationship between various electronic group decision support systems and group process outcomes. It was shown that the use of electronic group support systems in group decision making leads to increases in decision quality, level of focus on task, equality of participation, and the length of time required to reach a decision. However, use of a group decision support system led to decreases in overall consensus and in satisfaction with the process and the decision.

George et al (1992) examined whether the inclusion of a facilitator among groups making decisions using an electronic meeting system would have an effect on the group process or quality of decisions made. They found that there were no differences in either group process or outcomes (i.e. decision quality) between groups that determined their own group process and those for whom the group process was determined by a facilitator. Similarly, Archer (1990) found that if the phases of a decision process in a complex business situation were organized and rational, there was no difference in decision quality between computer-mediated and face-to-face decision making.

CONTEXTUAL ISSUES   Contextual factors other than the computer programs themselves also play a role in computer-assisted groups. Valacich et al (1994) found significantly different results between groups using the same computer-mediated communication system when all members of the group were in one room as opposed to when the members were dispersed. In this case, the dispersed group generated more unique solutions and solutions of higher quality than did the proximate group.

COMMUNICATION PATTERNS   Several authors have reached similar conclusions about communication patterns in groups who communicate solely or primarily by computer. For example, Kiesler & Sproul (1992) found that communication in such groups is characterized by greater direct advocacy, greater equality of participation (even when members are of different status levels), more extreme or risky decisions, and more hostile or extreme communications (e.g. "flaming") than in face-to-face groups. Dubrovsky et al (1991) also found that social-status inequalities were less salient in groups who communicated and made decisions by electronic mail than in face-to-face groups. However, they also found that differences in influence based on differences in expertise were less pronounced in e-mail groups. They refer to these phenomena as "the equalization effect."

In some computer-mediated decision systems, communication among members is anonymous. Jessup et al (1990) reported three experiments in which they showed that when there was anonymity in the group decision-making process, members were more critical of ideas proposed, more probing in their questioning, and more likely to generate questions and ideas.

GROUP PROCESSES Sambamurthy et al (1993) found that experimental groups using a computerized group decision support system to make budget allocation decisions had better organized decision processes than did groups using a paper-and-pencil version of the decision support system and than a control group to which no decision support system was provided. However, the computerized system also appeared to reduce the thoroughness of the discussion and led to a less intensely critical decision process. Likewise, Poole et al (1993) found that use of a group-decision support system improved the organization of subjects' decision-making process but may have led to less thorough and critical discussion. Keys et al (1988) used undergraduates in a study of the effects of use of a decision-support system in a business strategy game, and found that students in the computer condition did more and better planning than those in a control condition. Aiken & Riggs (1993) examined the applicability of a group decision-support system, in which communication among group members was almost entirely electronic, to the question of group creativity. They found that groups using the group decision-support system were more productive and more satisfied with the process because of such things as increased participation, synergy, and enhanced structure.

SHORTFALLS OF COMPUTER-MEDIATED GROUP WORK Computer-mediated group work is not always superior to face-to-face interaction, however. Straus & McGrath (1994) found that the productivity (in terms of quantity but not quality) of face-to-face groups on discussion tasks exceeded that of electronically mediated groups and that this productivity difference was greatest on those tasks requiring higher levels of coordination among group members. Lea & Spears (1991) confirmed previous research that groups communicating by way of computers produce more polarized decisions than do face-to-face groups. Adrianson & Hjelmquist (1991) found less conformity and opinion change in groups using computer-mediated communication than in those using face-to-face communication and found that personality characteristics of group members were only weakly related to these communication patterns.

OTHER TECHNOLOGIES   Computers are, of course, not the only technological innovation used for group communication and decision making. More simplistic technology such as teleconferencing has also been introduced. Interestingly, the negative interpersonal interactions found in computer-based communications (e.g. "flaming," increased time to decision) appear to be absent in teleconferencing, which is much more similar to face-to-face communications. Groups making decisions via teleconferencing tend to take less time than do face-to-face groups, and members tend to perceive the leader as taking on fewer leadership roles (Rawlins 1989).

SUMMARY   Technological systems that more closely mimic face-to-face interaction (e.g. videophones and videoconferencing) are becoming more widely available, and these advances will spur new research into their use as group decision-making tools. Simultaneously, use of systems in which there is no real-time communication is also becoming more and more common (e.g. groupware, list-servers). These communication systems provide ample opportunities for research. We believe that technology-based group communication and decision-making systems will continue to thrive and that researchers will have to struggle to keep up with the pace of programmer advances and practitioner usage.

Defined Problem-Solving Groups

Some groups are created for the specific purpose of generating solutions to problems. Quality circles and task forces are two such kinds of groups.

QUALITY CIRCLES   Quality circles were developed as a means to generate ideas that, if implemented, would raise the product quality by reducing defects, error rates, and so on. Quality circles were a precursor in the United States to the more recent "total quality movement" in which many mechanisms of quality (and, more generally, productivity) improvement are implemented to foster continuous improvements in the quality of products and of services. Quality circles typically are 6–12 employees who perform related jobs and who meet to discuss problems—and opportunities—to raise the quality or productivity of their part of an organization. They generate solutions that may or may not be implemented by the organization. The introduction of quality circles usually is accompanied by training in group process (e.g. in structured techniques for diagnosing problems and brainstorming) as well as training in aspects of quality management, such as in working with statistical indicators of quality.

Although quality circles have been a popular form of groups in organizations, evidence suggests that quality circles have relatively little enduring impact on organizational effectiveness (Lawler et al 1992) and research on them has diminished. Steel et al (1990) studied quality circles over a 14-month period in a United States federal mint and found no evidence that they affected important organizational outcomes. Quality circles may sometimes be successful at generating so-called big hits early on (i.e. quality improvements that have substantial economic value to a firm) but the evidence does not indicate that quality circles can maintain such contributions over time.

TASK FORCES   Task forces are another kind of group created to solve problems. They are temporary, created with a relatively well-bounded mandate to be fulfilled. Task forces have a more limited time horizon than do quality circles; once the task is accomplished, the task force can disband. May & Schwoerer (1994) reported on the creation of task forces to develop and implement ways of reducing the incidence of cumulative trauma disorders (or CTDs) that result from repetitive, forceful movements in a meat-packing plant. (Carpal tunnel syndrome is one such disorder.) Teams were made up of 7–9 volunteers representing several functions (e.g. medical, management) and were trained in substantive issues related to CTDs. The teams appeared successful in decreasing the incidence and severity of CTDs, though the number of production days lost to injuries was unaffected. The authors of the report also presented their views on the appropriate structure, training, and support of task forces similar to those studied.

AUTONOMOUS WORK GROUPS   We use the label "autonomous work groups" as a synonym for "self-managing teams" and for "empowered teams." These are teams of employees who typically perform highly related or interdependent jobs, who are identified and identifiable as a social unit in an organization, and who are given significant authority and responsibility for many aspects of their work, such as planning, scheduling, assigning tasks to members, and making decisions with economic consequences (usually up to a specific limited value) (e.g. see Dobbelaere & Goeppinger 1993).

The concept of autonomous work groups has been in the literature for half a century. However, there was little momentum for their adoption in US workplaces until the past decade or so as firms reduced levels of management, thus giving over to lower-level employees responsibilities in the past held by management, and as firms sought new ways of increasing employee involvement and productivity. Autonomous work groups are inherent in many recent attempts to radically transform organizational work systems, a topic discussed in the next section on teams and organizational change. This section deals with research specifically targeted at autonomous work groups.

Cohen & Ledford (1994) studied a large sample of self-managing teams at different levels and in varying functions in a service organization. These self-managing teams had been in existence for two years on average. They were systematically matched against comparable traditionally managed teams. Further, teams were screened from the sample when they did not unambiguously fulfill the definition of self-management. Criteria of team effectiveness included ratings on different dimensions of performance (e.g. quality, productivity, safety) obtained from different sources (team members and higher levels of management) as well as indicators of effectiveness from company records, such as customer complaints and monetary losses due to absenteeism. Ratings indicated that self-managing teams were more effective than their comparison groups. However, no significant differences were observed on measures of effectiveness based on company records. Work-related attitudes (e.g. satisfaction) were more favorable among members of self-managing teams.

Cordery et al (1991) reported a study of autonomous work groups at a greenfield site. A greenfield site is a new physical location of work. In this study of mineral processing plants in Australia, work groups at the new plant site were compared with groups in existing sites. An important differentiating feature of the new site was that an organizational structure unlike those at any existing sites was implemented. That organizational structure "centered on the operation of autonomous work groups in the processing area" (Cordery et al 1991, p. 465). Greenfield teams in this site had decision-making responsibility for such things as allocating work, attending to administrative matters, and setting priorities, as well as having influence on hiring decisions. Their members also acquired multiple skills and worked under a pay-for-skills reward system. Traditional (nonautonomous) groups, against which autonomous work groups were compared, also existed in parts of the new plant and in the established site. The primary intervention was thus a change in the nature of group work, in the competencies of members (through multiskilling), and in groups' supporting organizational context (reward system, authority system, information availability). This intervention secondarily influenced individual inputs through its creation of multiskilled group members.

The Cordery et al (1991) data indicated that autonomous work groups were associated with more favorable employee attitudes than were traditional work groups, though this difference abated over time (measurements were made at 8 and 20 months after the greenfield start-up). However, both turnover and absenteeism were higher among members of autonomous work groups in comparison with traditional groups.

The Cordery et al (1991) study was much like an earlier study by Wall et al (1986) that contrasted autonomous work groups in greenfield and established sites engaged in food production. The earlier study also found higher turnover among employees in the greenfield site. However, the findings of these two studies contradict the report by Weisman et al (1993), who found that higher retention (i.e. lower turnover) among nurses was associated with self-management practices. A previous review of research by Beekun (1989) concluded that the use of autonomous work teams is associated with decreases in absenteeism and turnover. Other results that differed from Cordery et al (1991) were reported by Wall et al (1986), who found less evidence of positive attitudinal consequences of autonomous work groups than did the latter study. Barker's (1993) case study report noted that members of self-managing teams had lower levels of absenteeism and tardiness because the members of the teams enforced attendance and on-time norms much more strictly than managers had enforced those policies prior to the implementation of teams.

Overall there is substantial variance in research findings regarding the consequences of autonomous work groups on such measures as productivity, turnover, and attitudes. This variance may indicate that the effects of autonomous work groups are highly situationally dependent. That is, the effects of autonomous work-group practices may depend on factors such as the nature of the work force (e.g. its dominant values) and the nature of the organization (e.g. information and reward systems). Smith & Comer (1994) did address the proposition that the success enjoyed by self-organizing teams (self-organizing teams are similar to autonomous work groups) may depend on the situation. Through a laboratory experiment, Smith & Comer demonstrated that self-managing groups can be expected to be more successful in turbulent environments. This study is unique in its attempt to provide direct answers to complex questions about the "fit" of autonomous (and related forms of) work groups. Considerably more research will be required, given the number of possible factors that could moderate the impact of autonomous work groups in organizations.

TEAMS AND CHANGE IN ORGANIZATIONAL SYSTEMS

Groups are almost always embedded in larger social systems (e.g. communities, schools, business organizations). These social systems that surround teams define a major part of the context in which team performance occurs. As Levine & Moreland (1990) have pointed out, too much past research on group performance effectiveness has been devoid of attention to the linkages between group performance and aspects of the social systems in which groups are located. For theorists such as McGrath (1991), a fundamental assumption about the nature of groups is that they are partially nested within, and loosely coupled to, a surrounding social system. "Partially nested" refers to the fact that individuals often are members of more than one group and that groups may be parts of more than one social system. "Loosely coupled" refers to the fact that there are few clear, mechanistic-like connections either between groups and surrounding systems or within groups, a point similar to Guzzo & Shea's (1992) metaphor of groups being systems more like clouds than clocks. Another of McGrath's (1991) fundamental assertions about the nature of groups is that in such systems they perform multiple tasks concurrently.

There are several consequences of taking seriously the concept of the embeddedness of teams in organizations. One is that team performance effectiveness and the factors that bring it about are tied to the nature and effectiveness of the entire organization. Changes in team effectiveness can thus have consequences for change in the larger system, such as when improved performance by a team or set of teams is thought to yield greater profits for a business. Perhaps we usually think of team-organization linkages in just this way: that team performance contributes to organizational performance.

The regularity and strength of such linkages between the performance of components (individuals, teams, departments) and overall organizational effectiveness is explored in Harris (1994). That work mostly addresses the apparent paradox that investments in computer technology may bring about improvements in performance at the component level but do not necessarily translate into larger system improvements. It also raises widely applicable issues about measurement, the nature of social systems, and cross-level influences. In light of these considerations, it could be quite wrong to make the easy assumption that improvements in team performance yield gains for the whole organization.

Team-organization linkages also imply that changes in the larger social system can bring about changes in the teams situated in it. That is, one need not directly intervene into teams to change their performance: Interventions into the surrounding organizational system may bring about improved (or, if the intervention is a poor one, reduced) team performance.

The teams-in-organizational-context perspective is complex. It obscures cause-and-effect relations so perceptible from experimental studies of groups stripped of context. It implies that the effects of interventions made at one level (individual, group, organization) may reside at another level. And it implies that multiple simultaneous influences on and of teams may be taking place in these social systems. Complicated though it is, it is imperative to examine research evidence on teams and change in organizational systems.

Research evidence on teams and organizational change tends to be of a unique character. Understandably there are fewer controlled, experiment-like methods and far more case studies and surveys. This is an embodiment of a classical trade-off of rigor for relevance in research. However, there are by now quite large numbers of less-rigorous but highly relevant research reports.

It is likely that weaknesses of research design in some are at least partly compensated by strengths in the research designs of other reports.

An indication of just how many such reports exist is given by Macy & Izumi (1993). They presented the results of a meta-analysis of 131 field studies (yielding 506 effect-size estimates) of organizational change that appeared over a 30-year period. Interestingly, they encountered 1800 studies, only 131 of which provided sufficient quantitative data for their meta-analysis. (Of these 131 studies, 88.5% were published in refereed journals.) We focus first on their findings with regard to broad organizational change and then address those findings most specific to teams in organizations.

In regard to overall organizational change, Macy & Izumi (1993) found that indicators of financial performance show the greatest improvements when multiple changes are simultaneously made in aspects of organizational structure, human resource management practices, and technology. Macy & Izumi report a +0.37 correlation between the number of changes made ("action levers" in their terminology) and indicators of financial performance. Other criteria of change (e.g. employee attitudes) showed no such relationship. But of the many action levers that can be pulled in large-scale organizational change efforts, which specific ones have the greatest impact?

With effect-size measures of financial performance as dependent variables, the action levers with the greatest impact included the creation of autonomous work groups and team development interventions. Group-oriented interventions also showed evidence of improving behavioral measures of performance such as turnover and absenteeism. Other interventions showing appreciable relationships to financial indicators of organizational performance included job redesign, increased employee involvement, changes (mostly flattening) of organizational hierarchies, and changes in workflow. (Macy & Izumi 1993 suggest viewing these findings with caution owing to the sometimes small number of cases on which they are based.) Employee attitudes showed little systematic improvement with these interventions.

In summary, according to Macy & Izumi (1993): Multifaceted, system-wide organizational interventions show the most reliable positive impact on organizational effectiveness, team-oriented interventions are one of a few subsets of interventions that have the most notable effects, and team-oriented interventions affect both financial and behavioral measures of performance.

A nonquantitative, comprehensive review of research evidence on teams, organizational systems, and effectiveness was provided by Applebaum & Batt (1994). Applebaum & Blatt described alternative organizational systems in which teams are of greater or lesser significance as well as attempts to transform organizations to more team-based social systems. Historically, according to these authors, teams are significant elements in Swedish sociotechnical and Japanese lean-production models of work organization. In contrast, teams have not been emphasized in German or traditional American human resource models of organization.

With existing models of work organization such as these as a backdrop, Applebaum & Blatt (1994) examined experiments in workplace innovation in American organizations. Applebaum & Blatt draw on two lines of evidence about the use of innovative work practices and their impact. One line of evidence consists of 12 large surveys reported between 1982 and 1993. The other consists of 185 case studies.

With regard to teams, Applebaum & Blatt (1994) related that in recent years many US organizations have been experimenting with team-based work arrangements. More specifically, it was estimated in 1990 that 47% of large US companies made use of self-directed, autonomous work teams and that there was a strong growth trend in the use of such teams from 1987 to 1990 (Lawler et al 1992). Quality circles were the most frequently implemented type of team, estimated to be present in 66% of the largest companies in the United States (Lawler et al 1992). Another estimate of the popularity of teams in organizations was provided by Gordon (1992). Gordon reported that 80% of organizations with 100 or more employees used teams in some way and that 50% of employees in these organizations are members of at least one team at work.

There are, however, many variations in team-based organizational practices. In some organizations the introduction or renewed emphasis on teams represents only a small marginal change to standard operating procedures while in others the adoption of teams is a part of a large-scale attempt at radical organizational transformation. Further, in some but not all organizations the implementation of team-based work arrangements may be accompanied by changes in hiring, compensation, decision making, technology, and other processes. As Applebaum & Blatt (1994) aptly noted, in practice "teams" is one of several "commonly abused terms" (p. 72). Given this variation, the path to unambiguous conclusions about the connections between teams and organizational effectiveness is often quite hard to find. The following conclusions are offered cognizant of the caveats and qualifications required by the state of the research evidence.

Applebaum & Blatt (1994), largely on the basis of their review of case studies, concluded that there is clear evidence that team-based work arrangements bring about improved organizational performance, especially in measures of efficiency (e.g. reduced cycle times in production) and quality (e.g. fewer defects in products). Some research reports run counter to this conclusion (e.g. Robertson et al 1992). However, Applebaum & Blatt's (1994) conclusions are supported by the work of Levine & D'Andrea Tyson (1990), who examined the effects of employee participation on productivity. Levine & D'Andrea Tyson identified three forms of participation: consultative, representative, and substantive, the latter form constituting the greatest degree of participation. Consultative participation, for example, may come through the creation of quality circles, representative participation through labor-management committees, and substantive participation through autonomous work groups. Cotton (1993) also largely concurred, identifying autonomous work groups and self-determining teams as structures that provide far more participation than quality circles or various forms of representative participation. Levine & D'Andrea Tyson (1990) reviewed empirical evidence from diverse sources (e.g. organizational psychology, economics, industrial relations) and concluded that "participation *usually* leads to small, short-run improvements in performance and *sometimes* leads to significant, long-lasting improvements in performance" (p. 203, emphasis in original) and that "there is usually a positive, often small effect of participation on productivity, sometimes a zero or statistically insignificant effect, and almost never a negative effect" (pp. 203–4). Substantive participation, according to Levine & D'Andrea Tyson, is the form most likely to result in significant, long-lasting increases in productivity, and work teams are the primary means by which substantive participation is attained. Cotton (1993), too, found self-directed work teams to be "an effective way to improve employee productivity and attitudes" (p. 199) and found little evidence that consultative or representative participation has the same consequences.

A national survey of 727 US work establishments conducted in 1991 also is a source of evidence on the impact of team-based organizational arrangements (see Spaeth & O'Rourke 1994 for a description of the survey procedures). An establishment is a location of employment. Small business enterprises are more likely to have a single establishment whereas large enterprises have many. The relationship between performance and the team-based work practices was analyzed by Kalleberg & Moody (1994). They found that organizations adopting sets of practices that included teams as an important element of organization design tended to excel on several performance dimensions (e.g. employee relations, product quality) though not on the dimension of customer service. Note that in this survey performance was assessed by ratings (rather than, say, by measures of output) made by an establishment's representative, the same representative who provided other information about their establishment. Thus, in this survey, the potential exists that some part of the observed relationships are attributable to a response-response bias.

In summary, ample evidence indicates that team-based forms of organizing often bring about higher levels of organizational effectiveness in comparison with traditional, bureaucratic forms. This evidence, however, is confounded because more than one change (e.g. more than just the creation of teams) typically is implemented in studies of organizational change, and measures of effectiveness reflect more than just those contributions uniquely attributable to teams. The question "What makes teams effective?" is directly addressed by research on group composition, leadership, goal setting, and the like. In contrast, researchers on teams and organizational change ask "To what extent do teams as elements in larger social systems contribute to system effectiveness?" For many group researchers and theorists this is a rather nontraditional question. And it is a vexing question for all, although there is consistent, and sometimes quite powerful evidence that teams contribute to organizational effectiveness.

DISCUSSION

This review has sampled a wide-ranging collection of research studies on team effectiveness, focusing on work teams in organizational systems. Studies emphasized in the review are those centrally concerned with some aspect of effectiveness as a dependent variable and with changes and interventions made to influence the effectiveness with which teams perform. Rather than restating the findings in summary form, this final section considers selected issues raised by the research review. We first highlight three open issues (out of many) in team effectiveness research. Then, newer waves in team research are identified and briefly considered, including those most directly related to issues discussed in this review. Finally, we discuss "points of leverage" for intervening to affect team performance. Thoughts on future research and theorizing are offered throughout.

Open Questions

What is diversity? How does it affect team performance? These two open questions about team composition and effectiveness provide fertile soil for further research and theorizing.

DIVERSITY   Diversity refers to dissimilarity among members in terms of gender, ethnicity, race, personality, culture, and functional experience, among other things. There is evidence that team effectiveness is well-served by diverse members when teams perform cognitive, creativity-demanding tasks. This is not to say that diverse membership might not pay off in enhanced effectiveness in other task domains; rather, too little is now known to draw firm conclusions. Also, it is not known whether all forms of diversity contribute in similar portions or in similar ways to team performance on intellective tasks. In fact, there is a real need to develop theory and data on the ways in which dissimilarity among members contributes to task performance. Just as research on goal and team performance has begun to emphasize the mediating processes connecting goals and team effectiveness, research on diversity in teams should increasingly emphasize the processes that mediate its effects.

FAMILIARITY   When does familiarity help and hurt team effectiveness? Research on familiarity among coal-mining crews, cockpit crews, and other work groups shows a benefit to familiarity. That is, the greater the familiarity among members of a group, the greater their performance. However, other research indicates that too-familiar cockpit crews may, in fact, be more inclined to make errors. Perhaps the value of familiarity is time-dependent. That is, high familiarity among members (or high interpositional knowledge, as discussed by Cannon-Bowers et al 1995) may have the greatest utility early in a team's existence, perhaps by fostering the rapid appearance of coordination and integration of team members' efforts. High familiarity may have value at other times, too, such as in times of stress or high demand. However, familiarity may eventually become a liability as the lack of membership change (and thus the lack of any unfamiliar members being introduced into a team) contributes to stultification and entropy in teams. The venerable work by Katz (1982) suggested that communication within and between teams declines as teams age, thus communication may be an important mediator of the effects of familiarity.

TEAM BOUNDARIES   Where are team boundaries? The boundaries of teams are imaginary lines of demarcation separating member from outsider. Boundaries are essential to the definition of teams (Sundstrom et al 1990) and to the psychology of being a member of the in-group vs the out-group. In many instances team boundaries are reinforced by such things as uniforms and the use of space or turf. However, the boundaries of teams may at other times be quite difficult to discern. "Virtual teams"—teams whose members are connected through a network of computers—are examples of teams whose boundaries of inclusion and exclusion may be quite difficult to establish, especially if individuals may selectively join an electronic conversation for some but not all of the team's existence. But problems of establishing team boundaries are not limited to electronic groups. Vandermark (1991) and Lichtenberg et al (1990) suggested that there are benefits to including as team members persons who might traditionally have been considered on the periphery. Vandermark (1991) raised the issue with regard to the inclusion of cabin crews in the cockpit resource management training of flight crews; Lichtenberg et al (1990) raised the issue with regard to psychiatric aides and their role in teams of health-care professionals. Further, viewing teams as entities embedded in larger systems populated by individuals who are members of more than one team also can complicate the identification of team boundaries. We believe that future research is needed to clarify issues of inclusion and exclusion by virtue of team boundaries (for further discussion, see Guzzo 1996), how boundaries relate to effectiveness, and how the nature of boundaries might shape the effects of interventions intended to raise team performance.

New Waves, New Directions

We briefly consider three areas of research in which there have been recent surges of interest: electronically mediated teams, interventions for enhancing team effectiveness, and teams in the context of social systems.

ELECTRONICALLY MEDIATED TEAMS   Although the first studies of electronically mediated teams were done nearly two decades ago, the pace of research on such teams has accelerated in recent years. No doubt this is attributable to many factors, not the least of which is the decreasing expense of the technology needed for such research. And new technologies (e.g. videoconferencing, communication, and support software for groups) continually create opportunities to conduct new research. There is no doubt that electronically mediated teams will become an increasingly common feature of the organizational landscape. We therefore suggest that research on electronically mediated groups break free from the tradition of comparing those groups to face-to-face groups. Instead, future research should accept such groups on their own terms. It should focus instead on contrasting technologies and on team effectiveness under different ways of utilizing available technologies. From a practical point of view we need more research on how to maximize team effectiveness with new technologies. From a theoretical point of view we need better insights and explanations of the drivers of the dynamics of team performance and effectiveness under such technologies.

INTERVENTIONS   New ways of intervening to improve team effectiveness are in the works. Many of these are tied to a foundation of research on teamwork and effectiveness in military teams. Salas et al (1995) pointed out that, although there have been few direct tests of team-training interventions in recent research on military teams, knowledge has progressed to a point where such training interventions are now possible, grounded in workable conceptualizations of competencies and task requirements in teams. New ways of intervening are also on the horizon due to new methodologies of team research and new theoretical models of team performance (e.g. see Guzzo & Salas 1995).

TEAMS IN CONTEXT   A third notable area of expanding research interest is teams in context. The oft-cited recognition that, historically, the bulk of psychological research has examined teams in the absence of consideration of their contexts is giving way to more frequent studies of teams in naturalistic settings, such as organizations. We expect this shift to be accompanied by new theoretical emphases and insights, especially as they relate to the influence of aspects of the teams' environments. In organizations, such environmental factors could include intraorganizational factors such as reward practices and information systems, as well as extraorganizational factors such as the customer demands and business environments.

Points of Leverage

Three primary points of leverage exist for intervening to enhance team effectiveness. One is the design of the group. Design includes such things as specification of membership, of member roles and methods of their coordination, and of goals. Several studies we have reviewed concern design as a point of leverage for raising team effectiveness. Diversity of membership and size of group, for example, have been found to be related to team effectiveness, although the relationships are not completely consistent across all studies or all group tasks. The effect of goals on group performance has been more uniformly found to be positive, although even here we found one study that was an exception to the pattern of evidence. What we are calling "design" is very much like what traditional models of group performance refer to as "inputs" in the input-process-output description of group performance.

The "process" element in the traditional input-process-output model includes both social processes in groups (e.g. cohesiveness) and task processes (e.g. rules of task performance). Group process is thus a second leverage point at which interventions can be made to improve team effectiveness. Some evidence in the literature reviewed found, for example, that group cohesiveness can contribute to performance, and other studies found that structured task processes—such as the stepladder technique for group problem solving—can contribute positively to performance.

The traditional input-process-output model would be too confining if its interpretation were restricted to the idea that inputs (i.e. member characteristics, goals) fully determine group process. Inputs influence group process but may not strongly constrain it. One factor that can strongly constrain group process is the technology with which a group works, such as computers. Our review of computer-assisted groups indeed shows their process to be different (e.g. more equal but less overall member participation) from non-computer-assisted groups and that these differences may or may not result in enhanced effectiveness, depending on factors such as the task.

A third point of leverage for enhancing team effectiveness is the context. That is, team performance can be raised by changing the conditions in which teams perform. Several lines of evidence we have reviewed point to the power of the context as a driver of team effectiveness. Organizational leaders, for example, are a part of the context in which work groups perform, and leaders have been shown to influence team effectiveness. Cockpit resource management and its variations appear to have positive effects on flight crews because such interventions change the organizational context (values, culture) in which crews are formed and carry out their work. Further, large-scale organizational change efforts that change the social system of which teams are a part have been shown to enhance effectiveness. The point of leverage with the most consistent research support for affecting team performance is the context. In fact, it is probably most justifiable to conclude that the greatest changes in team effectiveness are most likely to be realized when changes in teams' organizational context are supported by the appropriate team design and process.

Literature Cited

Adrianson L, Hjelmquist E. 1991. Group processes in face-to-face and computer mediated communication. *Behav. Inf. Tech.* 10(4):281–96

Aiken MW, Riggs M. 1993. Using a group decision support system for creativity. *J. Creat. Behav.* 27(1):28–35

Alderfer CP. 1977. Group and intergroup relations. In *Improving the Quality of Work Life,* ed. JR Hackman, JL Suttle, pp. 227–96. Pallisades, CA: Goodyear

Applebaum E, Blatt R. 1994. *The New American Workplace.* Ithaca, NY: ILR

Archer NP. 1990. A comparison of computer conferences with face-to-face meetings for small group business decisions. *Behav. Inf. Tech.* 9(4):307–17

Bantel KA, Jackson SE. 1989. Top management and innovations in banking: Does composition of the top teams make a difference? *Strateg. Manage. J.* 10:107–24 (Special issue)

Barker JR. 1993. Tightening the iron cage: concertive control in self-managing teams. *Adm. Sci. Q.* 38:408–37

Beekun RI. 1989. Assessing the effectiveness of socio-technical interventions: antidote or fad? *Hum. Relat.* 47:877–97

Billings CE. 1991. Human-centered aircraft automation: a concept and guidelines. *Tech. Memo. 103885.* Moffett Field, CA: NASA-Ames Res. Cent.

Bowers CA, Braun CC, Holmes BE, Morgan BB Jr. 1993a. The development of aircrew coordination behaviors. In *Proc. Seventh Int. Symp. Aviat. Psychol.,* pp. 573–77. Columbus, OH

Bowers CA, Deaton J, Oser RL, Prince C, Kolb M. 1993b. The impact of automation on crew communication and performance. In *Proc. Seventh Int. Symp. Aviation Psychol.,* pp. 573–77. Columbus, OH

Brawley LR, Carron AV, Widmeyer WN. 1992. The nature of group goals in sports teams: a phenomenological analysis. *Sport Psychol.* 6:323–33

Butler RE. 1993. LOFT: Full-mission simula-

tion as Crew Resource Management Training. See Wiener et al 1993, pp. 231–59

Campion MA, Medsker GJ, Higgs AC. 1993. Relations between work group characteristics and effectiveness: implications for designing effective work groups. *Pers. Psychol.* 46:823–50

Cannon-Bowers JA, Tannenbaum SI, Salas E, Volpe CE. 1995. Defining competencies and establishing team training requirements. See Guzzo & Salas 1995, pp. 333–80

Cohen SG, Ledford GE Jr. 1994. The effectiveness of self-managing teams: a field experiment. *Hum. Relat.* 47:13–43

Cordery JL, Mueller WS, Smith LM. 1991. Attitudinal and behavioral effects of autonomous group working: a longitudinal field study. *Acad. Manage. J.* 34:464–76

Costley J, Johnson D, Lawson D. 1989. A comparison of cockpit communication B737–B757. In *Proc. Fifth Int. Symp. Aviat. Psychol.,* pp. 413–18. Columbus, OH

Cotton JL. 1993. *Employee Involvement.* Newbury Park, CA: Sage

de Armas Paredes M, Riera-Milian MA. 1987. Analisis de la communicacion en un equipo deportivo y su influencia en los resultados de este. [Analysis of communication in a sports team and its influence on performance.] *Bol. Psicol. Cuba* 10:37–48 (Abstr.)

Dennis AR, Valacich JS. 1993. Computer brainstorms: more heads are better than one. *J. Appl. Psychol.* 78:531–37

Diehl A. 1991. The effectiveness of training programs for preventing aircrew "error." In *Proc. Sixth Int. Symp. Aviat. Psychol.,* pp. 640–55. Columbus: Ohio State Univ.

Dobbelaere AG, Goeppinger KH. 1993. The right way and the wrong way to set up a self-directed work team. *Hum. Resour. Prof.* 5:31–35

Dubnicki C, Limburg WJ. 1991. How do healthcare teams measure up? *Healthc. Forum* 34(5):10–11

Dubrovsky VJ, Kiesler S, Sethna BN. 1991.

The equalization phenomenon: status effects in computer-mediated and face-to-face decision-making groups. *Hum.-Comput. Interact.* 6(2):119–46

Earley PC. 1994. Self or group? Cultural effects of training on self-efficacy and performance. *Adm. Sci. Q.* 39:89–117

Eden D. 1990a. Pygmalion without interpersonal contrast effects: whole groups gain from raising manager expectations. *J. Appl. Psychol.* 75:394–98

Eden D. 1990b. *Pygmalion in Management: Productivity as a Self-Fulfilling Prophecy.* Lexington, MA: Lexington Books

Evans CR, Dion KL. 1991. Group cohesion and performance: a meta-analysis. *Small Group Res.* 22:175–86

Fandt PM, Richardson WD, Conner HM. 1990. The impact of goal-setting on team simulation experience. *Simul. Gaming* 21(4): 411–22

Foushee HC, Lauber JK, Baetge MM, Acomb DB. 1986. Crew performance as a function of exposure to high-density, short-haul duty cycles. *NASA Tech. Memo. 88322.* Moffett Field, CA: NASA-Ames Res. Cent.

Gallupe RB, Bastianutti L, Cooper WH. 1991. Brainstorming electronically. *J. Appl. Psychol.* 76:137–42

Gallupe RB, Cooper WH, Grise' M-L, Bastianutti LM. 1994. Blocking electronic brainstorms. *J. Appl. Psychol.* 79: 77–86

Gallupe RB, Dennis AR, Cooper WH, Valacich JS, Bastianutti L, Nunamaker J. 1992. Electronic brainstorming and group size. *Acad. Manage. J.* 35:350–69

George JF, Dennis AR, Nunamaker JF. 1992. An experimental investigation of facilitation in an EMS decision room. *Group Decis. Negot.* 1(1):57–70

George JM, Bettenhausen K. 1990. Understanding prosocial behavior, sales performance, and turnover: a group-level analysis in a service context. *J. Appl. Psychol.* 75: 698–709

Ginnett RC. 1993. Crews as groups: their formation and their leadership. See Wiener et al 1993, pp. 71–98

Goodman PS, Leyden DP. 1991. Familiarity and group productivity. *J. Appl. Psychol.* 76:578–86

Gordon J. 1992. Work teams—How far have they come? *Training* 29:59–65

Guzzo RA, Salas E, eds. 1995. *Team Effectiveness and Decision Making in Organizations.* San Francisco: Jossey-Bass

Guzzo RA, Shea GP. 1992. Group performance and intergroup relations in organizations. In *Handbook of Industrial and Organizational Psychology,* ed. MD Dunnette, LM Hough, 3:269–313. Palo Alto, CA: Consult. Psychol. Press. 2nd ed.

Guzzo RA, Yost PR, Campbell RJ, Shea GP. 1993. Potency in groups: articulating a construct. *Br. J. Soc. Psychol.* 32(1):87–106

Guzzo RA. 1996. Fundamental considerations about workgroups. In *In Handbook of Work Group Psychology,* ed. M West. Chichester: Wiley. In press

Hackman JR. 1987. The design of work teams. In *Handbook of Organizational Behavior,* ed. JW Lorsch, pp. 315–42. Englewood Cliffs, NJ: Prentice-Hall

Hackman JR, ed. 1990. *Groups That Work and Those That Don't.* San Francisco: Jossey-Bass

Hackman JR. 1993. Teams, leaders, and organizations: new directions for crew-oriented flight training. See Wiener et al 1993, pp. 47–70

Haleblian J, Finkelstein S. 1993. Top management team size, CEO dominance, and firm performance: the moderating roles of environmental turbulence and discretion. *Acad. Manag. J.* 36:844–63

Harris DH, ed. 1994. *Organizational Linkages: Understanding the Productivity Paradox.* Washington, DC: Natl. Acad. Press

Hartel CEJ. 1991. *Improving team-assisted diagnostic decision making: some training propositions and an empirical test.* PhD thesis. Colo. State Univ., Fort Collins

Helmreich RL, Foushee HC. 1993. Why crew resource management? Empirical and theoretical bases of human factors training in aviation. See Wiener et al 1993, pp. 3–45

Helmreich RL, Wilhelm JA. 1991. Outcomes of crew resource management training. *Int. J. Aviat. Psychol.* 14:287–300

Helmreich RL, Wilhelm JA, Gregorich SE, Chidester TR. 1990. Preliminary results from the evaluation of cockpit resource management training: performance ratings of flightcrews. *Aviat. Space Environ. Med.* 576–79

Hollingshead AB, McGrath JE. 1995. Computer-assisted groups: a critical review of the empirical research. See Guzzo & Salas 1995, pp. 46–78

Jackson SE, Brett JF, Sessa VI, Cooper DM, Julin JA, Peyronnin K. 1991. Some differences make a difference: individual dissimilarity and group heterogeneity as correlates of recruitment, promotion, and turnover. *J. Appl. Psychol.* 76:675–89

Jackson SE, May KE, Whitney K. 1995. Understanding the dynamics of diversity in decision-making teams. See Guzzo & Salas 1995, pp. 204–61

Jacobs D, Singell L. 1993. Leadership and organizational performance: isolating links between managers and collective success. *Soc. Sci. Res.* 22:165–89

Jessup LM, Connolly T, Tansik DA. 1990. Toward a theory of automated group work:

the deindividuating effects of anonymity. *Small Group Res.* 21(3):333–48

Kalleberg AL, Moody JW. 1994. Human resource management and organizational performance. *Am. Behav. Sci.* 37:948–62

Katz RL. 1982. The effects of group longevity on project communication and performance. *Adm. Sci. Q.* 27:81–104

Katzenbach JR, Smith DK. 1993. The discipline of teams. *Harv. Bus. Rev.* 71:111–20

Keys B, Burns O, Case T, Wells RA. 1988. Decision support package in a business game: performance and attitudinal affects. *Simul. Games.* 19(4):440–52

Kiesler S, Sproul L. 1992. Group decision making and communication technology. *Organizational Behav. Hum. Decis. Process.* 52(1):96–123

Lauber JK. 1984. Resource management in the cockpit. *Air Line Pilot* 53:20–23

Lauber JK. 1993. Foreword. See Wiener et al 1993, pp. xv–xviii

Lawler EE, Mohrman SA, Ledford G. 1992. *Employee Involvement and TQM: Practice and Results in Fortune 5000 Companies.* San Francisco: Jossey-Bass

Lea M, Spears R. 1991. Computer-mediated communication, de-individuation and group decision-making. *Int. J. Man-Mach. Stud.* 34(2):283–301

Lee C. 1989. The relationship between goal-setting, self-efficacy, and female field hockey team performance. *Int. J. Sport Psychol.* 20(2):147–61

Leedom DK, Simon R. 1995. Improving team coordination: a case for behavior-based training. *Mil. Psychol.* 7(2):109–22

Levine DI, D'Andrea Tyson L. 1990. Participation, productivity, and the firm's environment. In *Paying For Productivity,* ed. AS Blinder, pp. 183–237. Washington, DC: Brookings Inst.

Levine JM, Moreland RL. 1990. Progress in small group research. *Annu. Rev. Psychol.* 41:585–634

Lichtenberg PA, Strzepek DM, Zeiss AM. 1990. Bringing psychiatric aides into the treatment team: an application of the Veterans Administration's ITTG model. *Gerontol. Geriatri. Educ.* 10(4):63–73

Locke EA, Latham GP. 1990. *A Theory of Goal-Setting and Task Performance.* Englewood Cliffs, NJ: Prentice Hall

Macy BA, Izumi H. 1993. Organizational change, design, and work innovation: a meta-analysis of 131 North American field studies—1961–1991. In *Research in Organizational Change and Development,* ed. W Passmore, R Woodman, 7:235–313. Greenwich, CT: JAI

Magjuka RJ, Baldwin TT. 1991. Team-based employee involvement programs: effects of design and administration. *Person. Psychol.* 44:793–812

May DR, Schwoerer CE. 1994. Employee health by design: using employee involvement teams in ergonomic job redesign. *Person. Psychol.* 47:861–76

McGrath JE. 1991. Time, interaction, and performance: a theory of groups. *Small Group Res.* 22:147–74

McLeod PL. 1992. An assessment of the experimental literature on electronic support of group work: results of a meta-analysis. *Hum.-Comput. Interact.* 7(3):257–80

McLeod PL, Liker JK, Lobel SA. 1992. Process feedback in task groups: an application of goal setting. *J. Appl. Behav. Sci.* 28: 15–41

Mitchell TR, Silver WS. 1990. Individual and group goals when workers are interdependent: effects on task strategies and performance. *J. Appl. Psychol.* 75:185–93

National Transportation Safety Board. 1990a. *Aircraft Accident Rep.: United Airlines Flight 811, Boeing 747-122, N4713U.* Honolulu, HI, Feb. 24, 1989. (*NTSB/AAR/90/01*). Washington, DC: Natl. Transp. Saf. Board

National Transportation Safety Board. 1990b. *Aircraft Accident Rep.: United Airlines Flight 232, McDonnell-Douglas DC-10-10.* Sioux Gateway Airport, Sioux City, IA, July 19, 1989. (*NTSB/AAR/90/06*). Washington, DC: Natl. Transp. Saf. Board

Orasanu JM. 1993. Decision-making in the cockpit. See Wiener et al 1993, pp. 137–72

Orlady HW, Foushee HC, eds. 1987. *Proc. of the NASA/MAC Workshop on Cockpit Resource Manage.* (*NASA Conf. Publ. 2455*). Moffett Field, CA: NASA-Ames Res. Cent.

Pearson CAL. 1991. An assessment of extrinsic feedback on participation, role perceptions, motivation, and job satisfaction in a self-managed system for monitoring group achievement. *Hum. Relat.* 44:517–37

Poole MS, Holmes M, Watson R, DeSanctis G. 1993. Group decision support systems and group communication: a comparison of decision-making in computer-supported and non-supported groups. *Commun. Res.* 20(2):176–213

Povenmire HK, Rockway M, Bunecke JL, Patton MW. 1989. Cockpit resource management skills enhance combat mission performance in B-52 simulator. In *Proc. Fifth Int. Symp. Aviat. Psychol.,* pp. 310–25. Columbus, OH

Prince C, Salas E. 1993. Training and research for teamwork in the military aircrew. See Wiener et al 1993, pp. 337–66

Rawlins C. 1989. The impact of teleconferencing on the leadership of small decision-making groups. *J. Organ. Behav. Manage.* 10(2):37–52

Robertson D, Rinehart J, Huxley C, and the CAW Research Group on CAMI. 1992.

Team concept and Kaizen: Japanese production management in a unionized Canadian auto plant. *Stud. Polit. Econ.* 39: 77–107

Rogelberg SG, Barnes-Farrell JL, Lowe CA. 1992. The stepladder technique: an alternative group structure facilitating effective group decision making. *J. Appl. Psychol.* 77:730–37

Sainfort FC, Gustafson DH, Bosworth K, Hawkins RP. 1990. Decision support system effectiveness: conceptual framework and empirical evaluation. *Organ. Behav. Hum. Decis. Process.* 45(2):232–52

Salas E, Bowers CA, Cannon-Bowers JA. 1995. Military team research: 10 years of progress. *Mil. Psychol.* 7:55–75

Sambamurthy V, Poole MS, Kelly J. 1993. The effects of variations in GDSS capabilities on decision-making processes in groups. *Small Group Res.* 24(4):523–46

Shamir B. 1990. Calculations, values, and identities: the sources of collectivistic work motivation. *Hum. Relat.* 43:313–32

Sheppard JA. 1993. Productivity loss in performance groups: a motivational analysis. *Psychol. Bull.* 113:67–81

Smith C, Comer D. 1994. Self-organization in small groups: a study of group effectiveness within non-equilibrium conditions. *Hum. Relat.* 47:553–81

Smith KA, Smith KG, Olian JD, Sims HP, O'Bannon DP, Scully J. 1994. Top management team demography and process: the role of social integration and communication. *Adm. Sci. Q.* 39:412–38

Spaeth JL, O'Rourke DP. 1994. Designing and implementing the national organizations study. *Am. Behav. Sci.* 37:872–90

Steel RP, Jennings KR, Lindsey JT. 1990. Quality circle problem solving and common cents: evaluation study findings from a United States federal mint. *J. Appl. Behav. Sci.* 26:365–81

Stout RJ, Salas E, Carson R. 1994. Individual task proficiency and team process: What's important for team functioning? *Mil. Psychol.* 6(3):177–92

Straus SG, McGrath JE. 1994. Does the medium matter? The interaction of task type and technology on group performance and members reactions. *J. Appl. Psychol.* 79: 87–97

Sundstrom E, De Meuse KP, Futrell D. 1990. Work teams: applications and effectiveness. *Am. Psychol.* 45:120–33

Urban JM, Bowers CA, Monday SD, Morgan BB Jr. 1995. Workload, team structure, and communication in team performance. *Mil.*

Psychol. 7(2):123–39

Valacich JS, George JF, Nunamaker JF, Vogel DR. 1994. Physical proximity effects on computer-mediated group idea generation. *Small Group Res.* 25(1):83–104

Vandermark MJ. 1991. Should flight attendants be included in CRM training? A discussion of a major air carrier's approach to total crew training. *Int. J. Aviat. Psychol.* 1(1):87–94

Vroom VH. 1964. *Work and Motivation.* New York: Wiley

Wall TD, Kemp NJ, Jackson PR, Clegg CW. 1986. Outcomes of autonomous work groups: a field experiment. *Acad. Manage. J.* 29:280–304

Watson WE, Kumar K, Michaelsen LK. 1993. Cultural diversity's impact on interaction process and performance: comparing homogeneous and diverse task groups. *Acad. Manage. J.* 36:590–602

Watson WE, Michaelsen LK, Sharp W. 1991. Member competence, group interaction, and group decision making: a longitudinal study. *J. Appl. Psychol.* 76:803–9

Weingart LR. 1992. Impact of group goals, task component complexity, effort, and planning on group performance. *J. Appl. Psychol.* 77:682–93

Weingart LR, Weldon E. 1991. Processes that mediate the relationship between a group goal and group member performance. *Hum. Perform.* 4:33–54

Weisman CS, Gordon DL, Cassard SD, Bergner M. 1993. The effects of unit self-management on hospital nurses' work process, work satisfaction, and retention. *Med. Care.* 31(5):381–93

Weldon E, Jehn KM, Pradhan P. 1991. Processes that mediate the relationship between a group goal and improved group performance. *J. Pers. Soc. Psychol.* 61:555–69

Weldon E, Weingart LR. 1993. Group goals and group performance. *Br. J. Soc. Psychol.* 32:307–34

Wiener EL, Kanki BG, Helmreich RL, eds. 1993. *Cockpit Resource Management.* San Francisco: Academic

Wiersema MF, Bird A. 1993. Organizational demography in Japanese firms: group heterogeneity, individual dissimilarity, and top management team turnover. *Acad. Manage. J.* 36:996–1025

Wilpert B. 1995. Organizational behavior. *Annu. Rev. Psychol.* 46:59–90

Zaccaro SJ, Gualtieri J, Minionis D. 1995. Task cohesion as a facilitator of team decision making under temporal urgency. *Mil. Psychol.* 7(2):77–93

Annu. Rev. Psychol. 1996. 47:341–70

PSYCHOLOGY IN CANADA

J. G. Adair

Department of Psychology, University of Manitoba, Winnipeg, Manitoba R3T 2N2 Canada

A. Paivio

Department of Psychology, University of Western Ontario, London, Ontario H3C 3J7 Canada

P. Ritchie

Department of Psychology, University of Ottawa, Ottawa, Ontario K1N 6N5 Canada

KEY WORDS: discipline development, Canadian psychology, history, research contributions, professional psychology

ABSTRACT

This chapter reviews how psychology in Canada evolved over half a century to become the most popular discipline in universities and a respected health-care and helping profession. The organization, journals, and funding of the scientific discipline are described. The importance of DO Hebb's research as the stimulus and foundation for discipline growth and significant research contributions to basic processes is identified. The multicultural mosaic of Canadian society and early research on second-language learning are shown to have influenced cross-cultural and social research. Canadian research contributions to basic processes and to the social and health sciences are reviewed. Although late to begin in Canada, clinical research and the profession of psychology are shown to have substantially developed over the past two decades. With large numbers of quality researchers and practitioners, psychology has a bright future in Canada.

CONTENTS

0066-4308/96/0201-0341$08.00

INTRODUCTION

Psychology is flourishing in Canada. It is the most popular discipline in universities, prominent in government and private-sector research settings, and well established among the health-care and helping professions. As a national discipline it is mature, contributing substantially to an understanding of Canadian issues and the solution of social problems, and to the international literature. Canadian psychology has acquired its favorable contemporary status over a half century of evolution and growth. Its development has been shaped by the history and structure of Canadian society, wartime influences on the discipline, and actions initiated by the Canadian Psychological Association and other professional bodies.

History and Structure of Canadian Society

Canada shares with the United States and Mexico the indigenous North American societies of aboriginal peoples and the origins of their larger non-native populations. Canada has a multicultural and bilingual political history stemming from its British and French roots as well as influences from the United States. French and English have equal status as the official languages of the federal Parliament and of the government of Canada. French, however, remains the primary working language in Quebec whereas English dominates in most of the rest of the country.

Evolution of Canadian Psychology as a Scientific Discipline

The two national traditions influenced trends and emphases that gave Canadian psychology unique characteristics within a common North American psychology, often influenced by the development of the discipline in the United States. For example, the linguistic and religious traditions of Quebec fostered an interest in applied developmental psychology that served the needs of clergy who controlled the educational system until the past quarter century. Piagetian psychology became a research focus at the Université de Montréal, even before it emerged elsewhere in North America. Because of its bilingual character, Montreal also became a center for basic and applied research in bilingualism and biculturalism, research that began at McGill University.

The development of academic psychology in English Canada, initially at the University of Toronto, was rooted in British idealistic philosophy and Wundtian psychology. This direction changed with the appointment in 1889 of James Mark Baldwin, an American, known for his work on mental development. Although not directly influenced by Baldwin, child study reemerged in the late 1920s as a research specialty at the University of Toronto (Hoff 1992).

Both world wars fostered the development of tests related to selection and training of service personnel. All major Canadian psychologists were engaged in that effort in World War II. For example, the Test Construction Committee developed a test (Ferguson 1992) of verbal and nonverbal intelligence (the M test), which became a useful selection device for all branches of the Canadian military. This experience influenced the development of ability and personality testing in Canada. Canadian psychologists also had a leading role in training nursery school teachers in Britain, in order that mothers could work in factories and participate in other war-related activities. These activities became an impetus to the advancement of child and developmental psychology in Canada, carried on initially by some of the same people who led the wartime effort (Wright 1992).

Despite its distinct origins, psychology in Canada suffered from an identity problem that persisted at least into the 1950s (MacLeod 1955). For example, it remained linked to philosophy departments in many Canadian universities beyond the end of World War II. Wartime experiences, however, aided the emergence of psychology as an independent basic and applied science.

In the early 1950s, the Canadian Psychological Association (CPA) engaged a former Canadian, Robert MacLeod of Cornell University, to conduct a critical review of Canadian psychology. The recommendations (MacLeod 1955) triggered a series of CPA-sponsored conferences, reports, and actions that have had a major influence on the development of the discipline, especially in English Canada, from 1960 to the late 1970s. A later conference (Ritchie et al 1988) examined the state of the discipline as a whole with special foci on research, service delivery, and teaching.

Canadian psychology was dominated by academic scientists well into the 1970s. As the CPA membership changed, applied psychologists began to influence the direction and decisions of the Association as well as the annual convention program. These developments motivated a group of experimental psychologists, especially those with research interests in biopsychology, neuropsychology, and cognitive psychology, to form a separate association, the Canadian Society for Brain, Behaviour, and Cognitive Science (CSBBCS) in 1989. The changes were partly influenced as well by similar developments in the United States. Some collaboration has continued in Canada between the parent organization and its experimental offshoot.

SCIENTIFIC RESEARCH

Organization of the Discipline

The research discipline is organized in three major associations at the national level. In addition to CPA and the CSBBCS, there is a provincially based Société Québécoise pour la Recherche en Psychologie (SQRP) that serves as a national association for Francophone psychologists. Like CSBBCS, it holds an annual research conference. Within CPA, there are 28 sections for subdiscipline research areas. Sections receive program time at the CPA annual meeting, present prizes to the best graduate-student papers, and publish annual newsletters.

RESEARCH CONFERENCES   In addition to the national association meetings, a number of speciality research conferences (some internationally known) are held annually in Canada. For example, the Ontario Symposium on Personality and Social Psychology has published proceedings from its conferences held for several years at the University of Western Ontario (e.g. Zanna & Olson 1994). Within experimental psychology there is a rich tradition of research conferences. The Lake Ontario Visionary Establishment (LOVE) has met annually for 24 years in Niagara Falls (around St. Valentine's Day, appropriately enough) to exchange research developments on cognition and perception. The eighth annual Vancouver Conference on Cognitive Science, in 1995, was devoted to attention. The Banff Annual Symposium in Cognitive Science (BASICS) has met under the leadership of the Universities of Calgary and Alberta with the collaboration of other Western Canadian universities for the past 14 years. The Banff International Conference on Behavioral Science holds its meetings annually on different topics. The 27th meeting, in 1995, was devoted to child abuse.

RESEARCH JOURNALS   The Canadian Psychological Association publishes three bilingual journals. The *Canadian Journal of Experimental Psychology* (*CJEP*) is the oldest of the three. Articles published in *CJEP* are almost exclusively experimental, primarily in cognition and perception, but across the full range of basic research. The journal publishes articles by non-Canadians, is frequently cited in other journals, and has been innovative in publishing original research on topics that later became popular across the discipline, such as imagery, arousal, and laterality. The *Canadian Journal of Behavioural Science* is a broad social science journal devoted to research on social, personality, developmental, clinical, and health psychology. Although many articles are pertinent to Canada, or have a cross-cultural focus, some articles by foreign authors are occasionally published. *Canadian Psychology*, a third journal, publishes generalist articles on a variety of discipline- and profession-related issues. Recent issues have been devoted to qualitative research, alternatives to classic statistical procedures, and the history of social psychology. Professional issues, such as confidentiality, regulation and accreditation, and ethics, are also frequently discussed. Although of general interest, these articles are mostly read and cited by Canadian psychologists. The *Revue Québécoise de Psychologie*, a fourth primary journal for scholarly research, is published in French by the SQRP.

HIGHER EDUCATION IN CANADA   Whereas higher education in Canada is a provincial responsibility, substantial funding is provided by the federal government. The system is an amalgam of the British, French, and American systems. A total of 59 Canadian universities have psychology programs. The undergraduate degree requires three or four years of full-time study with a concentration of courses called a major. Most universities offer a limited-enrollment Honors or Specialist degree program, which provides more intense exposure to psychology and is universally considered preparatory to graduate-degree training in English Canada. Honors programs typically conclude with a thesis based on a project designed, usually in collaboration with the faculty supervisor, and conducted by the student. Considerable pride is taken in undergraduate research training, as reflected in several well-attended undergraduate research conferences.

Forty-two universities are members of the Canadian Association for Graduate Studies (CAGS). Virtually all offer at least one graduate degree in psychology. Graduate research training typically begins with a Master's degree program, which generally includes the completion of some coursework and an independent thesis project. Usually designed as a one- or two-year program following the baccalaureate degree, the average time to completion of the master's degree is often longer (CAGS 1993). This course of study is followed by a doctoral degree program, which requires on average about five years. Most doctoral programs require some coursework in addition to the preparation and defense of a doctoral dissertation.

There were 3162 students registered in 1992 in graduate psychology programs within Canada, approximately evenly divided between the Masters and Ph.D. degree programs (CAGS 1993). About 17% were part-time students. The distribution by gender is noteworthy. The ratio of female (69%) to male (31%) graduate students in psychology is surpassed only by social work and library science among all humanities and social science disciplines within Canada. The even greater proportion of female students (78%) at the undergraduate level (Statistics Canada 1994) suggests that the proportion of female graduate students may continue to increase.

Employment prospects for academic- and research-oriented graduates in all fields have been limited in the past decade. The hiring bulge through the late 1960s and early 1970s resulted in a large faculty cohort moving through the system together. As academic-research positions became no longer available over the next decade, the number of graduates in teaching careers in under-graduate institutions and in government agencies increased, enhancing psy-chology's visibility in society. Postdoctoral fellowships have kept some in scholarly career paths, but this has not been a safety net for many. Just when some faculty began to retire, the recession and government retrenchment on funding for education quickly closed the door of opportunity. As faculty retirements accelerate in the next decade, there may yet be a period of in-creased demand and hiring.

RESEARCH FUNDING   Funding for basic psychological research in Canada comes from three major federal government granting agencies. With some advice from members of the discipline, these agencies have struck a Tri-Council agreement to divide the responsibility for funding psychologists and to govern jurisdictional disputes. The Natural Sciences and Engineering Research Council (NSERC) supports research on fundamental psychological processes; the Medi-cal Research Council (MRC) funds research by psychologists based in medical schools or research elsewhere that addresses normal and abnormal behavior, neuroscience, and health-related issues; and the Social Sciences and Humanities Research Council (SSHRC) supports research in social, personality, develop-mental, educational, and applied psychology, and in the history, philosophy, and methods of psychology. These agencies fund individual and collaborative projects following a substantial peer review procedure.

The amounts awarded to psychologists and the funding processes vary across councils. According to their most recent reports, NSERC awarded approximately $12 million annually, SSHRC awarded $4 million, and MRC awarded $1.5 million to psychological researchers. The average level of grant support to successful applicants is about $30,000 annually. Whereas grants may appear small by US standards, no overhead allowances are charged and some basic services may be provided in Canadian universities.

Within all agencies the trend has been toward more competitive adjudica-tion, with lower success rates, and slightly larger awards to fewer researchers. Within the SSHRC, increased competition has been accompanied by policy changes to render it more similar to NSERC in terms of emphasis on the investigator's publication record and on programmatic rather than short-term projects. Increasing emphasis has been placed on interdisciplinary research, partnerships with government, collaborative projects, and research themes in the national interest. The first national theme of relevance to psychologists was the aging population. Several years of special SSHRC funding led to the establishment in 1990 of the Canadian Aging Research Network (CARNET), a federally funded group of sociologists and psychologists who examine, among other topics, the effects of aging on cognitive processes.

A recent trend in government science policy is to place emphasis on research that fuels the economy and on partnerships with industry. The prolonged recession also has led to significant budget cuts to all three councils. In this climate, there is concern that basic research will not likely be so favorably treated in the years to come.

The National Health Research and Development Program, located in the federal Department of Health, is the most notable of the other national agencies that fund applied health research. Within each of the provinces, particularly in Ontario, Quebec, British Columbia, and Alberta, there also are a number of sources with limited funding. These sources are usually Health Research Councils or Mental Health or Addiction Research Foundations. Applied research is generally underfunded, but as is increasingly the case at the federal level, some areas benefit by virtue of being targeted for support. Recent examples include forensic issues and aging, as well as the development of evidence-based clinical indicators.

"CANADIANIZATION" OF THE DISCIPLINE: TEXTBOOKS AND TEACHING   The employment of a substantial number of new faculty from outside the country in the early 1970s raised concerns within all social sciences about the Canadian focus of these disciplines. These concerns were exacerbated by the lack of Canadian-written or Canadian-published textbooks, a dearth of Canadian research examples for use in the classroom, and the unavailability of relevant supplementary teaching materials. There were calls within the social sciences for the "Canadianization" of our disciplines.

Although less vocal than members of other academic disciplines, some psychologists were motivated to put together books of readings providing appropriate examples of Canadian issues and research. The first, an introductory psychology reader for Canadian students (Pressey & Zubek 1970), was followed by books of readings (Berry & Wilde 1972, Gardner & Kalin 1981, Koulack & Perlman 1973) designed to focus on what is uniquely Canadian in social research—bilingualism and second-language learning, multiculturalism, intergroup relations, and so on. The most recent of these (Earn & Towson 1986) creatively combined research reports interspersed with interviews of prominent Canadian researchers, although the latter were discontinued in a second edition.

In Francophone Canada, the lack of exposure to Canadian research was compounded by the absence of textbooks in the French language. In a first attempt to correct this problem, Bégin & Joshi (1979) edited and published the writings of eight Francophone social psychologists. In 1982, Robert (1988) published the first edition of her edited text covering basic research in experimental psychology.

Two decades after the first attempts at increased Canadian content, authored textbooks as opposed to edited compilations of past writings of social and introductory psychology for the Canadian market finally became available. A social psychology textbook (Alcock et al 1988) featured Canadian examples, research by Canadian psychologists, and special chapters addressing Canadian issues. A Canadian-authored introductory textbook soon followed (Grusec et al 1990), and an established American introductory psychology textbook (Baron 1995) was thoroughly retooled by two Canadian junior authors so that it could be called "Psychology: Canadian Edition" (Baron et al 1995).

Our overview reveals slower progress in the development of Canadian teaching materials and textbooks than those who first advocated Canadianization of the discipline might have wished or expected. Prerequisite to the development of Canadian textbooks is a sensitivity to the culture and substantial research devoted to issues of importance to the country. Over the past three decades, the number of researchers in Canada and the quality of research have increased greatly. We have contributed much to the understanding of Canadian society, as well as to the universal understanding of behavior. The current existence of a distinctively "Canadian" psychology to market commercially confirms the vitality and relevance of the discipline that we teach.

Research Emphases

Scientific research in Canada has been concentrated in universities across the country. A review of published research from 1960 to 1982, reported in Ritchie et al (1988), indicated that nearly three fourths of the publications by Canadian psychologists came from a select group of universities. Following the University of Toronto, which headed the list, were ten other universities: Alberta, British Columbia, Carleton, Dalhousie, McGill, McMaster, Queen's, Waterloo, Western Ontario, and York. A review (Endler et al 1978) of the top 100 British, Canadian, and US university departments by Social Science Citation Index (SSCI) citation counts in 1975 included ten of these universities, in addition to the University of Manitoba and the Ontario Institute for Studies in Education. The publications of psychologists in small universities and in nonacademic positions according to the 1982 survey, comprised only 10% of the total number of publications by Canadian psychologists (Ritchie et al 1988). However, the increased qualifications of scholars in these settings over the past decade has likely increased the level of their contribution.

The review of research reported in Ritchie et al (1988) also revealed a concentration of publications by Canadians within the areas of physiological psychology, animal models, cognitive processes, developmental psychology (primarily cognitive and language), and perception, in that order. With the more recent development of programs in social, clinical, health, and personality psychology and government emphasis on the social relevance of research, the pattern of Canadian research activity has changed somewhat.

RESEARCH CONTRIBUTIONS

Basic Processes

Canadian research contributions in experimental psychology cover the traditional and recent problem areas studied in other countries. Canadian psychologists have contributed to progress in such areas as neuropsychology, animal behavior, memory and cognition, and language in disproportionate degree relative to their modest numbers as evidenced by publication rates, citation counts, and the number of theoretical concepts and findings that have had a broad and lasting impact on advances in those areas. Significant contributions up to the early 1980s were reviewed by Rule, Paivio, Adair, and Mogenson at the 1984 CPA State of the Discipline Conference (Ritchie et al 1988). Here, we summarize the major early influences and selectively review more recent developments.

NEUROPSYCHOLOGY AND NEUROSCIENCE   Because of the influence of Donald Hebb at McGill University, Canadian psychologists have been leading developers of neuropsychology, behavioral neuroscience, cognitive neuroscience, and (more generally) biopsychology, areas that were traditionally included under physiological psychology. Hebb's (1949) theoretical work was initially inspired by the results of psychological tests with neurosurgery patients. His observation that patients retained much of their general intelligence despite loss of large portions of the brain led to the development of his cell assembly theory. This theory in turn motivated pioneering studies of the effects of early environmental stimulation on later emotional, perceptual, and intellectual development. A fundamental theoretical assumption, the Hebb synapse rule, currently forms the basis of almost all neural network models of learning and memory in that the rule is used to determine weightings of the connection points. Either directly, or indirectly through his students, Hebb influenced neurological sciences in terms of basic knowledge as well as clinical applications in the treatment and rehabilitation of neurological patients.

The greatest impact on brain research in Canada stemmed from the serendipitous discovery at McGill that septal stimulation could reinforce a variety of responses. The discovery (see Milner 1991) was made in 1954 by James Olds, who had gone to McGill for postdoctoral research experience under Hebb, and Peter Milner, one of Hebb's students. Psychologists in Canada and elsewhere subsequently sought to identify neurochemical substrates for brain stimulation reward (e.g. Phillips et al 1989, Wise 1989) and relations between stimulation of septal and hypothalamic centers and such metabolic processes as hunger and thirst. PM Milner (1991) has reviewed recent developments in this area.

Brenda Milner, another of Hebb's students, pioneered research on memory functions of the hippocampus and other cognitive functions subserved by different brain regions. For example, tests of patients with unilateral lesions revealed left hemisphere–right hemisphere distinctions in processing verbal and nonverbal material in memory tasks (see Milner 1980). Her work inspired intensive research by Canadians on hippocampal functions and functional laterality of the brain in general. For example, O'Keefe & Nadel (1978) highlighted the role of the hippocampus in spatial memory, a function investigated more recently in relation to food caching behavior of different species (e.g. Sherry 1992). Vanderwolf, long recognized for his systematic research on the relations between slow wave activity in the hippocampus and behavioral activity, recently proposed that experience-dependent changes in neural connectivity occur in many different brain systems rather than exclusively in the hippocampus (Vanderwolf & Cain 1994).

In the 1960s, Kimura used dichotic listening tasks with normal subjects to demonstrate a left-hemisphere advantage in processing speech and a right-hemisphere advantage in processing melodies. Lateralized presentation of visual materials has yielded comparable asymmetries, which have been used to support different theoretical accounts of the phenomena (see Bryden 1982). Bryden (1982) uncovered experimental artifacts associated with procedures used in this area and provided new information on factors (e.g. handedness and sex differences) related to functional asymmetries. Kimura (e.g. 1993) has focused recently on neuromotor mechanisms in speech and manual communication, as well as on sex differences and hormonal factors in brain asymmetries in cognitive tasks. Hampson and McGlone are among the Canadian contributors to these areas (see Kimura 1993). Others have intensively investigated developmental and neurological factors associated with individual differences in handedness and functional asymmetries (e.g. Porac 1993, Witelson & Nowakowski 1991). Canadian researchers also have clarified the role of the corpus callosum in interhemispheric transfer (e.g. Lassonde et al 1990).

Goddard's discovery in the 1970s of kindling (seizures produced by repeated low-level stimulation), thought to influence long-term potentiation, is one of the candidates for the physiological basis of the Hebb synapse (see Goddard 1980). However, subsequent research by Canadians (e.g. Cain et al 1992) has revealed interpretive problems. A particularly notable contribution to both science and practice is the neural gating theory of pain developed in the 1960s by Melzack and Wall (see Melzack 1993).

Canadian neuropsychologists have contributed significantly to the understanding of a variety of clinical disorders. B Milner's research in particular set the stage for subsequent studies of amnesia (e.g. Moscovitch et al 1986, Tulving 1995). Other prominent topics, including aphasia, learning and reading disabilities, stuttering, head injuries, sleep disorders, and disorders of the motor system, have been exhaustively reviewed by Fuerst & Rourke (1995).

The strength of Canadian contributions in neuropsychology is reflected in the first comprehensive textbook of human neuropsychology written by two third-generation students of Hebb, who are themselves active contributors to research in this area. Now in its third edition (Kolb & Whishaw 1990), the book has been translated into several languages and is used worldwide. Pinel (1990), a research contributor to the understanding of brain mechanisms and behavior, wrote a highly regarded textbook on biopsychology, now in its second edition.

ANIMAL BEHAVIOR   Hebb's theory stimulated pioneering behavioral studies of the effects of early experience on emotional and cognitive development of animals. This Hebbian tradition is being carried on by Tees (e.g. Tees & Buhrmann 1990) among others. Key areas of classical and instrumental conditioning research in Canada include conditioning of drug reactions to external stimuli (e.g. Stewart 1992), consummatory and aversive reactions to taste stimuli (e.g. Delamater et al 1986), and discriminative learning using complex stimulus arrays (Honig 1992). Progress has been made in the study of social learning in animals (e.g. Galef 1990) and of animal memory as inferred from food caching and foraging behavior in different species (e.g. Phillips et al 1991, Roberts 1992, Sherry 1992, Shettleworth 1992).

MOTIVATION AND EMOTION   Early theoretical contributions to motivation and emotion by Canadian researchers, including Malmo's work in physiological and behavioral arousal, Amsel's theory of the motivational effects of frustration, Berlyne's emphasis on conflict and arousal in the motivation of directed thinking, and Bindra's theory of motivation based on "central motivational states" were reviewed (see Ritchie et al 1988). White & Milner (1992) have reviewed more recent psychobiological approaches to conditioned motivation and related problems.

ATTENTION AND PERCEPTION   Vision has been the most researched perceptual modality in Canada as it has elsewhere, but notable contributions encompass other modalities as well. Dodwell (1992) reviewed and updated his influential theoretical work on pattern recognition and other problems in visual perception. Macmillan & Creelman (1991) reviewed signal detection theory and methods as applied to different modalities. Bregman (1990) expanded his earlier work

on auditory streaming to auditory scene analysis, which yields auditory analogues of Gestalt principles for vision. A widely adopted textbook on sensation
and perception by Canadian psychologists Coren, Ward, and Enns (1994)
includes references to their research on efferent processes in visual perception,
psychophysical scaling, and visual attention.

Scientific advances have been made in such areas as stereoscopic perception (e.g. Hess & Wilcox 1994, Regan et al 1990), perceived vs imagined
movement (Friedman & Harding 1990), haptic perception (e.g. Lederman et al
1988), information processing and psychophysical models of vision (e.g. Di
Lollo & Dixon 1988), the relation between visual perception and action (e.g.
Goodale & Milner 1992), and the effects of the orientation of letters and other
visual patterns on recognition speed (e.g. Jolicoeur 1992). Alternative interpretations have been proposed for the McCollough effect, one based on classical
conditioning (Allan & Siegel 1993) and the other on adaptation-level theory
(Dodwell & Humphrey 1993). The sensory deprivation research pioneered by
Zubek, a student of Hebb, has been applied to studies of isolation in polar
regions (Suedfeld 1991) and to some therapeutic effects of restricted environmental stimulation.

Earlier Canadian contributions to research on attention include work on
vigilance, processing flexibility revealed by requiring people to stop an already initiated ballistic response, and attentional processes in visual field
asymmetries. More recent reviews by Canadians cover their own research and
that of others on attentional processes in dichotic listening (Bryden & Mondor
1991), attentional mechanisms across species (Baker & Mercier 1989), and
shifts in visual attention (see Wright 1994).

MEMORY AND COGNITION   Memory has long been one of the most active
research topics in Canada, spanning several decades and resulting in many
notable empirical and theoretical contributions. The distinction between short-
term and long-term memory was strongly supported by B Milner's neuropsychological studies with amnesic patients. Craik & Lockhart were responsible
for the levels of processing hypothesis, recognized as the most influential
theoretical view of memory in more than 25 years (for a recent retrospective,
see Lockhart & Craik 1990). Tulving introduced the episodic-semantic memory
distinction and many other original ideas that he has incorporated into a general
model of memory systems and processes (Tulving 1983, 1995). For almost 30
years, Paivio's dual coding theory provided an impetus for research on many
aspects of cognitive functioning, especially on imagery and memory (Paivio
1995). Murdock has contributed original mathematical models of associative
and other aspects of memory (e.g. Murdock 1993). Canadians also pioneered
the distinction between implicit (or priming) memory and explicit memory (e.g.
Graf & Schacter 1985, Jacoby & Dallas 1981). A variety of specific memory

phenomena have been inventively clarified—for example, organization of memory (e.g. Begg 1982, Tulving 1983), conditions under which cues facilitate and interfere with retrieval (e.g. Runquist 1983), and the so-called generation effect (Slamecka & Graf 1978).

The dual coding approach to cognitive functioning emphasizes the independent but interrelated activity of two modality specific systems, one based on nonverbal imagery and the other on verbal processes (Paivio 1991). An alternative computational approach also emerged in Canada, beginning as a critique of mental imagery in the 1970s and expanding subsequently to embrace cognition more generally (Pylyshyn 1984).

Specific topics that have been or are becoming prominent in Canadian cognitive research include symbolic comparisons of stimuli on various attributes (e.g. size or brightness of remembered objects), concept learning (Brooks 1987), problem solving and reasoning (e.g. Gick & Paterson 1992, Thompson 1995), the associative basis of arithmetic skills (e.g. Campbell & Clark 1989), and gender and other individual differences in cognitive abilities (e.g. Robert & Morin 1993).

LANGUAGE AND COMMUNICATION   Canadians have made unique contributions to research on language, especially bilingualism. An applied experiment (Lambert & Tucker 1972) showed that children from monolingual English homes became fluently bilingual as a result of education in a French-language immersion program. The experiment influenced the development of similar programs throughout Canada and elsewhere. In the 1960s, Gardner and Lambert initiated an extensive program of research on motivational and attitudinal factors in second-language learning (see Gardner 1991). Bilingual memory and cognition (including a bilingual version of dual coding theory) and neuropsychological factors in bilingualism are among the topics that have been systematically studied in Canada since the 1950s (see Reynolds 1991). Lambert (1991) has summarized and evaluated much of the research for which his work was the initial impetus.

Canadian researchers have also advanced our understanding of such language-related phenomena as semantic priming effects on word recognition and naming tasks (e.g. Besner & Smith 1992, Masson 1995), the Stroop effect (MacLeod 1991), reading and language processing (e.g. Henderson et al 1993, Levy & Burns 1990), models of metaphor processing (e.g. Katz 1992), and cognitive and language development (reviewed below under Developmental Psychology).

Social and Health Sciences

Although late-starting in Canada, psychological research in the social and health subdisciplines has developed rapidly to a level of visible national and international contribution. Substantial research has been conducted by Canadian psychology, not only on many current topics and issues that are investigated in other countries but also in areas that uniquely reflect the particular culture and values of the country.

SOCIAL PSYCHOLOGY   No single person determined the course of development of Canadian social psychology the way Hebb did for experimental psychology. However, Lambert's research on bilingualism and second language learning (discussed above in the section "Language and Communication"), established a Canadian tradition of social research with a focus on culture and language. In addition to contemporary research on communication and attitudinal factors affecting second-language learning, the cultural diversity of Canada provides an impetus for research on immigrants' adaptation to their new culture (e.g. Dompierre & Lavellée 1990, Sayegh & Lasry 1993) and the acculturation process (e.g. Lalonde & Cameron 1993). As a consequence of our multicultural society, the research of many social psychologists focuses on prejudice (Zanna & Olson 1994), ethnic identities (Aboud & Doyle 1993), and perceived discrimination (Dion et al 1992). Gardner has shown how stereotypes serve positive functions as well as providing the basis for prejudice; Taylor's research (e.g. Taylor et al 1990) has shown that minority-group members often feel that their group, but not themselves, is the target of discrimination.

There is also extensive Canadian research that may be described as more universalistic cognitive and experimental social psychology. Zanna's applications of dissonance theory to issues of attitude formation and change (Zanna & Sande 1987) and Ross's (1989) work on autobiographical memory have been influential. Current Canadian research on attribution theory (Olson 1988), loneliness (Perlman & Joshi 1987), close relationships (Fehr & Russell 1991), self-esteem (Campbell 1990), social cognition and language (Hoffman & Tchir 1990), and intrinsic motivation (Vallerand & Bissonnette 1992) are other examples.

CROSS-CULTURAL PSYCHOLOGY   Canada's diverse population and its national policy of multiculturalism provides a veritable laboratory for cross-cultural studies. Research comparing different cultural subgroups within Canada is more common than research comparing cultures across countries. The distinction between comparative studies of cultures and the ethnic study focus of social psychology is often blurred. Most prominent is the work of Berry, who has contributed extensively to both the theory and methodology of cross-cultural psychology. His recent evaluation with Kalin (Berry & Kalin 1995) of the effects of a national policy of multiculturalism within Canada demonstrates in a number of ways its benefits. More traditional cross-cultural research is found in the comparisons of the rules of address among Koreans and Korean-Canadians (Kroger et al 1984). Canadian research has also contributed to the understanding of processes involved in the development of indigenous psychologies in other cultures (Adair et al 1993, Kim & Berry 1993).

Within Canada, cross-cultural research has evolved over the years. Although some research addresses French-English differences (e.g. Clément & Noels 1992), more recent studies have concentrated on comparing ethnic minorities (e.g. Lortie-Lussier et al 1986) to the majority population. Native and Arctic Inuit groups have received some attention (e.g. Corenblum & Annis 1993); however, the amount of such cross-cultural research is minimal compared with the greater share of research devoted to immigrant groups.

PERSONALITY, INDIVIDUAL DIFFERENCES, AND THEIR MEASUREMENT   There are a number of excellent personality researchers across Canada. Endler (Endler & Magnusson 1976) is one of the leading proponents of the person-situation interactional approach to personality. His interactional model and measures of anxiety, stress, and coping styles have had a significant impact on personality theory and research. Altemeyer's (1994) research and writings have revived and revised the concept of the Authoritarian personality with a greatly improved measure of right-wing authoritarianism. Wiggins has proposed a circumplex model of personality (Wiggins & Broughton 1991). Paulhus' research (Paulhus & Reid 1991) on self-presentation has reexamined socially desirable responding and self-deception. Lefcourt's work on locus of control (Lefcourt et al 1984) and Sorrentino's research on the uncertainty orientation motive (Sorrentino et al 1992) are examples of other Canadian personality research.

Jackson (1985) is one of psychology's leading psychometricians and contributors to personality measurement. His *Personality Research Form* (PRF), based on Henry Murray's list of needs, was developed using an elaborate series of empirical and statistical methodologies to produce a test with a high level of psychometric sophistication. This instrument, which has impressively high reliability and validity, is widely used and forms the basis for extensive personality research. In addition, Jackson has published the *Jackson Personality Inventory*, and the *Jackson Vocational Interest Survey*, both high-quality instruments.

DEVELOPMENTAL PSYCHOLOGY   Developmental psychology in Canada had early and distinguished beginnings. Research on the developmental processes at the Child Study Institute at Toronto (see Wright & Myers 1982) and the social learning theory approach of Walters and Park at Waterloo laid the foundation for considerable infant, child, and adolescent research for years to come. Current developmental research is diverse, with only a sampling of some contemporary contributions noted here. Among outstanding cognitive developmental research is the work of Case (e.g. 1985) on intellectual development, Olson and others on the child's developing beliefs about mind (e.g. Astington et al 1988), and Siegel (1993) on reading and learning disabilities. Sensory and perceptual development have been examined with specific reference to color vision (Maurer 1987), sound and music (Schneider et al 1990), and in cross-language speech perception (Werker 1992).

Within social and personality development, there is substantial current attention focused on the development of social and interpersonal skills. For example, Rubin's work (Rubin et al 1989) on sociability and social withdrawal of children is well known. Grusec (1991) has studied ways of socializing concerns for other members of the family, and both Lytton (Lytton & Romney 1991) and Serbin (Serbin & Sprafkin 1986) have examined the differential socialization and salience of gender typing of boys and girls. The atypical child who is rejected, aggressive, or antisocial has been the focus of an impressive program of research (some of it longitudinal) and treatment at the Research Unit on Children's Psycho-Social Maladjustment at the Université de Montréal (Vitaro & Tremblay 1994). Eaton (Eaton & Yu 1989) has charted activity level as an index of temperament from fetus through childhood.

RESEARCH ON AGING   For several decades, there has been a strong tradition of research into the cognitive aspects of aging. Studies in the 1950s and 1960s by Inglis and Schonfield showed declines in learning, free recall, and short-term memory with aging, and seemed to identify retrieval as a major problem for the elderly. Contemporary Canadian research continues this early work with studies on age differences in memory (see Craik & Jennings 1992), text comprehension (Hultsch & Dixon 1984), and prospective memory (Dobbs & Rule 1987). Other aspects of cognitive aging that have been studied in Canada include age-related performance differences on various skills (Charness & Bosman 1992), differences between normal aging and persons afflicted with Alzheimer's disease or frontal lobe lesions (Moscovitch & Winocur 1992), and communication style and effectiveness (Arbuckle & Gold 1993, Ryan & Laurie 1990).

Although less of a tradition, there is considerable recent social research in Canada on the aging population. Much of this work is interdisciplinary. Prominent among psychological contributions has been the work on the happiness and well-being of the aged in and out of institutionalized care (Stones & Kozma 1989). Special funding for research on aging enabled interdisciplinary centers to be established at a number of universities, which bodes well for future contributions.

HISTORY AND PHILOSOPHY OF PSYCHOLOGY   Canadian psychologists have a strong interest and record of contributions to the history and philosophy of psychology. An early tradition of historical research was begun by Wright &

Myers (1982), who carefully documented the history of the discipline in Canada, and the impetus for theoretical and philosophical work was provided by the Center for Advanced Study in Theoretical Psychology, established at the University of Alberta by Royce (1975). Notable contemporary contributions include the work of Danziger (1990) on the historical origins of psychological research methodology, Minton's (1988) analysis of Terman's career and contributions to intelligence testing, and recent analyses of the history of social psychology (Collier et al 1991, Lubek et al 1992). The philosophy and theory of psychology also receive considerable attention in Canada (Stam et al 1987).

FORENSIC AND CORRECTIONAL PSYCHOLOGY   Applied research on forensic and correctional psychology has been exceptionally strong in Canada. Hare's pioneering research on psychopathy is internationally recognized, and his Psychopathy Checklist (Hare et al 1990), probably the most widely used instrument for assessing its presence in criminal populations, has been recently revised into a brief screening device for forensic clinicians. Considerable research also has been devoted to defining and assessing competency to stand trial (e.g. Roesch et al 1993).

   Correctional rehabilitation within and outside the institution, with particular attention to sexual offenders (Marshall 1994) and inmates of maximum security psychiatric institutions, has been another research focus (Rice et al 1991). Dutton et al (1994) have sytematically studied the perpetrators of spousal abuse and family violence. By far the greatest number of studies in Canada have been devoted to the factors influencing eyewitness memory and testimony. This topic has captured the attention of many social psychologists, and some of the leading research has been conducted in Canada (Lindsay et al 1991, Yuille & Tollestrup 1990).

CLINICAL/HEALTH RESEARCH   Although introduced belatedly in Canada, clinical research has accelerated over the last two decades. Early contributions were limited to the work of a few individuals, such as Meichenbaum's (1977) theory and approach of cognitive behavior modification. As the numbers of clinical researchers increased in Canada, their work became more focused and programmatic. Although research into schizophrenia (Nicholson & Neufeld 1993) and alcohol addiction (Pihl et al 1993) was an early and continuous focus of Canadian clinical research, a number of researchers have begun to study depression (Costello 1993, Dobson & Shaw 1987), with particular attention to the variables underlying its emergence, such as dependency and self-criticism (Zuroff et al 1990), and perfectionism (Hewitt & Flett 1993), and to the variables influencing the prognosis of its treatment (Segal et al 1992). In recent years, a number of clinical researchers have begun to focus on the anxiety disorders (Rachman & Maser 1988), including research on social anxiety (Meleshko &

Alden 1993), panic attacks (Cox et al 1994), and their cognitive-behavioral treatments (Cote et al 1994). A similar trend in research topics is found in addiction research. Gambling addiction, a disorder of the current decade, is currently being researched by Ladouceur et al (1994). Bowers (1982) has made significant contributions to our understanding of hypnosis and to its application in therapy. Indeed, the developing strength of the clinical research community in Canada bodes well for its future contribution to the clinical literature and treatment.

Health research, although less broadly developed in Canada, is marked by several noteworthy contributions. Melzack's (1993) extensive research on pain, especially his formulation of the gate control theory, has substantially influenced research on the human response to all forms of pain. Other Canadian research has focused on the expression of pain (Craig et al 1994) and its management (McGrath et al 1992) in both children and adults. Related research has documented the long-term effects of chronic illness on infant-mother attachment (Goldberg 1988) and on the quality of life of adults (Devins & Seland 1987). In quite a different area, Polivy & Herman (1985) have sorted out some of the contributions of external stimulation and internal restraints to eating disorders and their treatment, and Pliner (1994) has aided our understanding of reactions to novel foods. Several Canadian-authored books (Bakal 1992, Genest & Genest 1987) have reviewed the field of health psychology.

OTHER CANADIAN RESEARCH   The foregoing survey of research contributions to several broad subdisciplines provides a snapshot of Canadian psychology yet omits reference to many researchers working on other topics. There are large numbers of Canadian researchers working on, for example, industrial/organizational psychology, gender and women's issues, hypnosis, statistics and methodology, and a host of other topics. Although the space here does not permit their review, the work is substantial and important to Canadian psychology and beyond. Similarly, this review has focused on contributions to the research literature. A great deal of applied research that has contributed to Canadian society has been reviewed elsewhere (Rule & Adair 1984).

PROFESSIONAL PSYCHOLOGY IN CANADA

Development

Dobson & Dobson (1993) provide the most comprehensive source on professional psychology in Canada, covering the full scope of applied services (clinical/health, counseling, forensic, industrial/organizational, school, and nontraditional) as well as training and regulatory issues. Canadian psychology's development as a profession is distinct from its evolution as a discipline.

The conflicts between the two and proposed resolutions are captured in the major discipline reviews of the past four decades (Appleby & Rickwood 1968, Berlyne et al 1971, Bernhardt 1961, Ferguson 1977, MacLeod 1955, Ritchie et al 1988, Webster 1967).

In earlier decades, the debate focused on whether an applied vocation was legitimate. In the absence of a cohesive national strategy, professional psychology developed piecemeal. Paradoxically, Canadian contributions to foundational and applied knowledge have been strong. A partial explanation for this derives from the conditions of being the world's largest country geographically but with a relatively small population and having a confederal political system in which the provinces are constitutionally accorded primary responsibility for education and health services. Combined with cultural and linguistic factors, the challenge of any national undertaking in Canada is formidable. Therefore, the historic, political, and cultural context of the profession's emergence must also be evaluated (Ritchie & Sabourin 1992).

Events internal to the discipline also determined the particular circumstances that characterize the history of Canadian professional psychology. In particular, the CPA failed to support the development of psychology as an applied profession after World War II. CPA largely distanced itself from provincial efforts to establish psychology as a human services profession well into the 1970s. CPA then began a slow, difficult shift toward involvement in professional issues. Although the results have been mixed, some promise is seen in the functional-structural approach to the unity of psychology recently adopted by CPA (Ritchie & Sabourin 1992).

Organization

The nature and activities of contemporary professional organizations in Canada have been comprehensively described (Craig 1993) and historically reviewed (Wright 1971). There are two types. The first is regulatory, i.e. those organizations with a primary public protection mandate, with statutory authority to regulate the admission and practice of psychologists offering services to the public. Responsibility for the regulation of the profession is accorded to the provinces and territories by the Canadian constitution. The second type is societal, i.e. those with a primary mission to advance and protect the discipline and profession. Some regulatory bodies serve dual regulatory and societal functions. At the national level, organizations are federations of provincial/territorial and national bodies, or membership-based societal associations.

PROVINCIAL ORGANIZATIONS   Professional psychology is formally organized in all 10 Canadian provinces and in one of the two territories. Approximately 10,000 psychologists are legally recognized to practice psychology in Canada. Provincial/territorial regulatory bodies admit according to defined eligibility criteria. They also discipline psychologists for infractions of ethical and practice standards and may conduct mandatory or voluntary peer review or offer continuing education.

The historical absence of a cohesive strategy for the development of professional psychology in Canada had a great impact on the issue of varying levels of entry to practice. Some provinces/territories admit psychologists on the basis of the master's degree while others require the doctorate. Despite periodic intentions to resolve this problem, organized psychology has been unable to do so. However, the resolution may soon be at hand. In 1994, the federal, provincial, and territorial governments concluded a wide-ranging accord (The Agreement on Internal Trade) that proposes to eliminate internal barriers to the free mobility of regulated professionals. This may give the profession five years to resolve this matter before governments impose a solution.

The provincial/territorial societal bodies have been vital agents in the advancement of professional psychology in Canada, and they remain central to its future viability. Provincial/territorial associations engage in a wide range of advocacy and lobbying as well as provide direct benefits (e.g. preferred rates for various commercial services). They typically organize an annual meeting and continuing education activities and offer other supports to maintaining competence.

NATIONAL ORGANIZATIONS   The Canadian Psychological Association is the oldest national organization, having been created by 38 founding members in 1939. With approximately 3000 full members and fellows, plus 1000 student and other affiliates, it is currently the largest psychological association in Canada. CPA offers primary support to the professional and scientific communities in six areas: (a) communications through its three journals, annual convention, and quarterly newsletter; (b) accreditation of doctoral programs and internships; (c) sponsorship of various insurance services and member benefits; (d) development and promulgation of a code of ethics (CPA 1991), as well as guidelines and standards of practice; (e) advocacy pertinent to practitioners and scientists; (f) 28 sections and a smaller number of less formally organized interest groups that provide a focal point for concentrated attention in all the major subdiscipline branches of applied psychology.

The CPA Code of Ethics (CPA 1991) and its Companion Manual (CPA 1992) merit particular mention. The Code is being studied across the world in the development or revision of ethics codes and standards (e.g. Pettifor 1995). Among its distinguishing characteristics (Sinclair 1993) are: adherence to a clear conceptual framework (ethical decision-making); the articulation of explicit values, organized around four core principles (respect for the dignity of persons, responsible caring, integrity in relationships, and responsibility to society); and its pertinence to pedagogic, professional, and scientific activities. The CPA Code has been adopted by most of the provincial/territorial bodies regulating psychologists.

The Council of Provincial Associations of Psychologists (CPAP) brings together all provincial/territorial regulatory and societal bodies (Wand 1990). As a catalyst, CPAP ensures that provincial/territorial concerns are considered by other national organizations.

CPAP was the moving force in the creation of the Canadian Register of Health Service Providers in Psychology (CRHSPP) in 1985. It was established to facilitate enhanced public access to psychological health services, to offer continuing professional education, and to conduct research. Approximately 3000 psychologists are currently listed in the Canadian Register. Eligibility criteria are based on specified training and experience requirements and on statutorily based recognition as a psychologist. CRHSPP's recent focus on the prevention and treatment of psychological factors associated with coronary heart disease draws extensively on Canadian and international research in health psychology. It also generated the most extensive program of continuing professional education ever undertaken in Canadian psychology. Characterizing psychology's emergence as a major health profession in Canada, CRHSPP is increasingly recognized by governments, insurance companies, and quality assurance agencies (Craig 1993).

APPLIED TRAINING AND ACCREDITATION   In their review of applied graduate level training in Canada, Dobson & Dobson (1993) identified 88 graduate programs in professional psychology spanning 16 different domains. There are 57 at the doctoral level, whereas 31 are terminal master's programs. The authors caution that this is an underestimate of master's programs because most doctoral programs include a master's component.

Doctoral programs have generally adopted a scientist-practitioner orientation, while terminal master's programs are often purely practice-oriented. Doctoral programs vary in the emphasis they place on applied skill development, but they are more similar in the emphasis they place on research related training outcomes. The prospect of having doctoral programs with a primary objective to train practitioners for careers of service has been long debated in Canada (Dobson & King 1995, Ritchie et al 1988, Webster 1967). However, an American-style professional school, within or outside a university, has yet to be established. Changes in the Canadian health-care system and renewed pressures on universities to produce graduates with high-level applied skills may influence this issue in the future.

Of the 16 domains identified by Dobson & Dobson (1993), clinical psychology is the largest field of applied graduate education. In these programs, there is a clear preference for the scientist-practitioner model in Anglophone universities (Conway 1984, Dobson & Dobson 1993), whereas Francophone programs in Québec are more practitioner oriented (Granger 1984). Educational psychology programs make up the second largest category, but this designation is often more administrative than substantive. Educational psychology programs are as likely to offer training in broader areas, including counseling and clinical, as they are to offer training in areas more narrowly associated with applied learning and school psychology. Training specific to school psychology was reviewed by Holmes (1993), whereas Hiebert & Uhlemann (1993) addressed training in counseling psychology, the third largest domain. The remaining domains cover a wide range of fields in applied psychology, with noteworthy concentrations in neuropsychology, industrial/organizational psychology, and community/applied social psychology.

Doctoral programs and internships in clinical psychology, counseling psychology, and neuropsychology may apply for accreditation. Doyle et al (1993) reviewed the history, development, and the current criteria and practices of accreditation in Canada. Accreditation is directed by a panel within CPA, whose Board remains responsible for all policy matters. A Memorandum of Agreement between CPA and the American Psychological Association enables programs and internships to apply for joint accreditation. There are 14 CPA-accredited (13 joint APA-CPA) programs and 23 CPA-accredited internships (15 joint).

PROFESSIONAL PSYCHOLOGY SERVICES   Consistent with the diversity of graduate training in professional psychology, a vast array of psychological services is provided to the Canadian public. The scope of psychology's professional applications was comprehensively surveyed by Martin and colleagues for the last full-scale state of the discipline review (Ritchie et al 1988). Recent articles delineate specific components of health psychology (Hearn & Evans 1993), clinical psychology (Hunsley & Lefebvre 1990), and counseling psychology (Hiebert & Uhlemann 1993). Fuerst & Rourke (1995) assess the full scope of human neuropsychology research in Canada, much of it conducted concurrently with the provision of clinical neuropsychological services.

Increasingly, the traditional delineations of clinical, counseling, and health psychologies are being subsumed under the broader designation of health service psychology. This was precipitated in Canada by psychology's emergence as a major health-care profession in the past decade. The advent of the CRHSPP also prompted a more generic affiliation with health care. Psychologists are offering a wide variety of traditional and innovative services to an ever expanding pool of recipients in diverse private and public settings. For example, Hearn & Evans (1993) identified 65 areas serviced by general hospital psychologists alone. The full range of contemporary theoretical orientations is found among clinical services in Canada, although recent data suggest that cognitive-behavioral and behavioral approaches are the most prevalent theoretical orientations (Hunsley & Lefebvre 1990, Warner 1991).

Canada's health-care system is undergoing an intense period of reform and renewal, engendering disruption and dislocation in the short term, as well as opportunity in the long term. Professional psychology's strengths in applied research and its skills in prevention, diagnosis, and treatment are likely to enhance its potential value to a Canadian society striving to balance sustainable affordability with a traditional commitment to high-quality health services.

Among other areas of psychological practice in Canada, school psychology provides extensive services, although it has developed largely in isolation from the rest of Canadian professional psychology (Holmes 1993). Emerging areas of strength are industrial/organizational psychology (Cronshaw 1993) and forensic psychology (Pollock & Webster 1993). The emergence of nontraditional applications has also been assessed from a Canadian perspective (Wilson 1993).

Future

A recent national conference devoted to professional psychology (Dobson & King 1995) heralded a new era in its maturation. A global portrait of professional psychology's current preoccupations and the means it has identified to secure its future were delineated at the 1994 National Conference on Professional Psychology (Dobson & King 1995). A repeated refrain of the conference was "moving the markers." The almost 50 principles and the several dozen action plans adopted by the conference provide a conceptual framework and a clear path with which to "move the markers."

At the conference, preparing professional psychologists for marketplace expectations was established as a legitimate training goal. Graduate education would be more focused on entrepreneurial skills and would become more market oriented. The doctoral degree was reaffirmed as the level of entry to practice as a professional psychologist, although it was agreed that training models could vary in their relative emphasis on practice and research.

The challenges faced by Canadian professional psychology are similar to those in many other countries. Limited resources, a small critical mass of service providers and applied scientists, underdeveloped organizational infrastructure, greater accountability to a public increasingly skeptical of professionals generally, consumerism, health-care reform, and fiscal constraints are not unique to Canada. Some of the particularities of this country's history, demographics, and sociopolitical system nonetheless give these issues a distinctly national character. Following two decades of rapid expansion, Canadian professional psychology was revitalized by the recent conference and its strong vision of the discipline's scientific and applied utility to Canadian society. Responding constructively to Canadians' expectations of psychologists in a time of increasing fiscal restraint requires attentiveness to the needs of Canadian society. The profession's capacity for creativity and flexibility, while remaining faithful to its scientific rigor and service-oriented values, will be mediated by its ability to develop greater cohesion as an organized profession.

RETROSPECT AND PROSPECT

Psychology in Canada is similar in most respects to psychology elsewhere, especially in the United States. Its uniqueness reflects its English-French linguistic duality and cultural diversity. Its beginnings as a discipline in the 1930s, followed by its emerging identity and growth in the years after World War II, provided a base for its rapid development with the expansion of higher education in the 1960s. In the years following, psychology expanded throughout Canada to encompass all of the scientific specialties found elsewhere. Its special strength as a science is in the quality researchers to be found in universities and other settings; as a profession it is strong and vital in each of the ten provinces. The tensions between scientific and professional psychology are present, as they are in other countries, but are beginning to evolve into new forms of collaboration. Given the quality of its researchers and practitioners, and provided that adequate private and public funding are secured, psychology has a bright future in Canada.

ACKNOWLEDGMENTS

The authors wish to acknowledge the assistance of Dr. F. I. M. Craik, Dr. Kenneth Dion, and Dr. Keith Dobson, who read and commented on an earlier draft of this chapter. We would like to also thank the many colleagues with whom we have had discussions in the preparation of the chapter.

Literature Cited

Aboud FE, Doyle AB. 1993. The early development of ethnic identity and attitudes. In *Ethnic Identity: Formation and Transmission Among Hispanics and Other Minorities,* ed. ME Bernal, GP Knight, pp. 47–59. Albany: State Univ. NY

Adair JG, Puhan BN, Vohra N. 1993. Indigenization of psychology: empirical assessment of progress in Indian research. *Int. J. Psychol.* 28:149–69

Alcock JE, Carment DW, Sadava SW. 1988. *A Textbook of Social Psychology.* Scarborough, Ont.: Prentice-Hall

Allan LG, Siegel S. 1993. McCollough effects as conditioned responses: reply to Dodwell and Humphrey. *Psychol. Rev.* 100:183–203

Altemeyer B. 1994. Reducing prejudice in right-wing authoritarians. See Zanna & Olson 1994, pp. 131–48

Appleby MH, Rickwood J. 1968. *Psychology in Canada. Special Study #3*. Ottawa: Sci. Counc. Can.

Arbuckle TY, Gold DP. 1993. Aging, inhibition, and verbosity. *J. Geront.* 48:225–32

Astington JW, Harris PL, Olson DR, eds. 1988. *Developing Theories of Mind*. Cambridge: Cambridge Univ. Press

Bakal DA. 1992. *Psychology and Health*. New York: Springer-Verlag. 2nd ed.

Baker AG, Mercier P. 1989. Attention, retrospective processing and cognitive representations. In *Contemporary Learning Theory: Pavlovian Conditioning and the Status of Traditional Learning Theory*, ed. SB Klein, RR Mowrer, pp. 85–116. Hillsdale, NJ: Erlbaum

Baron RA. 1995. *Psychology*. Boston: Allyn & Bacon. 3rd ed.

Baron RA, Earhard B, Ozier M. 1995. *Psychology: Canadian Edition*. Scarborough, Ont.: Allyn-Bacon

Begg I. 1982. Imagery, organization, and discriminative processes. *Can. J. Psychol.* 36:273–90

Bégin G, Joshi P. 1979. *Psychologie Sociale*. Québec: Laval Univ. Press

Berlyne DE, Black AH, Berry RG, Douglas VI. 1971. *The future of Canadian psychology. Rep. Can. Psychol. Assoc. Sci. Counc. Can*. Ottawa: Sci. Counc. Canada

Bernhardt KS, ed. 1961. *Training for Research in Psychology*. Toronto: Univ. Toronto Press

Berry JW, Kalin R. 1995. Multicultural and ethnic attitudes in Canada: an overview of the 1991 national survey. *Can. J. Behav. Sci.* 27:301–20

Berry JW, Wilde GJS. 1972. *Social Psychology: The Canadian Context*. Toronto: McClelland & Stewart

Besner D, Smith MC. 1992. Models of word recognition: when observing the stimulus yields a clearer view. *J. Exp. Psychol.: Learn. Mem. Cogn.* 18:468–72

Bregman AS. 1990. *Auditory Scene Analysis: The Perceptual Organization of Sound*. Cambridge, MA: MIT Press

Bowers KS. 1982. The relevance of hypnosis for cognitive-behavioral therapy. *Clin. Psychol. Rev.* 2:67–78

Brooks LR. 1987. Decentralized control of categorization: the role of prior processing episodes. In *Concepts and Conceptualization*, ed. U Neisser, pp. 141–74. Cambridge: Cambridge Univ. Press

Bryden MP. 1982. *Laterality: Functional Asymmetry in the Intact Brain*. New York: Academic

Bryden MP, Mondor TA. 1991. Attentional factors in visual field asymmetries. *Can. J. Psychol.* 45:427–47

Cain DP, Boon F, Hargreaves E. 1992. Evidence for different neurochemical contributions to long term potentiation and to kindling and kindling-induced potentiation: role of NMDA and urethane-sensitive mechanisms. *Exp. Neur.* 116:330–38

Campbell JD. 1990. Self-esteem and clarity of the self-concept. *J. Pers. Soc. Psychol.* 59:538–49

Campbell JID, Clark JM. 1989. The time course of error priming in number-fact retrieval: evidence for excitatory and inhibitory mechanisms. *J. Exp. Psychol.: Learn. Mem. Cogn.* 15:920–29

Canadian Association for Graduate Studies. 1993. *Statistical Report 1993*. Ottawa: Can. Assoc. Grad. Stud.

Canadian Psychological Association. 1991. *Canadian Code of Ethics for Psychologists*. Old Chelsea, Québec: Can. Psychol. Assoc.

Canadian Psychological Association. 1992. *Companion Manual to the Canadian Code of Ethics for Psychologists*. Old Chelsea, Québec: Can. Psychol. Assoc.

Case R. 1985. *Intellectual Development: Birth to Adulthood*. Orlando, FL: Academic

Charness N, Bosman EA. 1992. Human factors and age. See Craik & Salthouse 1992, pp. 495–551

Clément R, Noels KA. 1992. Towards a situated approach to ethnolinguistic identity: the effects of status on individuals and groups. *J. Lang. Soc. Psychol.* 11:203–32

Collier G, Minton HL, Reynolds G. 1991. *Currents of Thought in American Social Psychology*. New York: Oxford

Conway J. 1984. Clinical psychology training in Canada: its development, current status and the prospects for accreditation. *Can. Psychol.* 25:177–91

Coren S, Ward LM, Enns JT. 1994. *Sensation and Perception*. Fort Worth, TX: Harcourt Brace. 5th ed.

Corenblum B, Annis RC. 1993. Development of racial identity in minority and majority children: an affect discrepancy model. *Can. J. Behav. Sci.* 25(4):499–521

Costello CG, ed. 1993. *Symptoms of Depression*. New York: Wiley

Cote G, Gauthier JG, Laberge B, Cormier HJ, Plamondin J. 1994. Reduced therapist contact in the cognitive behavioral treatment of panic disorder. *Behav. Ther.* 25:123–45

Cox BJ, Pirenfeld DM, Swinson RP, Norton GR. 1994. Suicidal ideation and suicide attempts in panic disorder and social phobia. *Am. J. Psychiatr.* 151:882–87

Craig KD. 1993. The organization of professional psychology in Canada. See Dobson & Dobson 1993, pp. 11–45

Craig KD, Hadjistavropoulos HD, Grunau RVE, Whitfield MF. 1994. A comparison of two measures of facial activity during pain in the newborn child. *J. Pediatr. Psychol.* 19:305–18

Craik FIM, Jennings JM. 1992. Human memory. See Craik & Salthouse 1992, pp. 51–110

Craik FIM, Salthouse TA, eds. 1992. *The Handbook of Aging and Cognition.* Hillsdale, NJ: Erlbaum

Cronshaw SF. 1993. Modern developments in the profession of Industrial/Organizational psychology. See Dobson & Dobson 1993, pp. 351–89

Danziger K. 1990. *Constructing the Subject: Historical Origins of Psychological Research.* New York: Cambridge Univ. Press

Delamater AR, LoLordo M, Berridge KC. 1986. Control of fluid palatability by exteroceptive Pavlovian signals. *J. Exp. Psychol.: Anim. Behav. Process.* 12:143–52

Devins GM, Seland TP. 1987. Emotional impact of multiple sclerosis: recent findings and suggestions for future research. *Psychol. Bull.* 101:363–75

Di Lollo V, Dixon P. 1988. Two forms of persistence in visual information processing. *J. Exp. Psychol.: Hum. Percept. Perform.* 14:671–81

Dion KL, Dion KK, Pak AW. 1992. Personality-based hardiness as a buffer for discrimination-related stress in members of Toronto's Chinese community. *Can. J. Behav. Sci.* 24:517–36

Dobbs AR, Rule BG. 1987. Prospective memory and self-reports of memory abilities in older adults. *Can. J. Psychol.* 41:209–22

Dobson KS, Dobson DJG, eds. 1993. *Professional Psychology in Canada.* Toronto: Hogrefe & Huber

Dobson KS, King MC, eds. 1995. *The Mississauga Conference on Professional Psychology.* Ottawa: Can. Psychol. Assoc.

Dobson KS, Shaw BF. 1987. Specificity and stability of self-referent encoding in clinical depression. *J. Abnorm. Psychol.* 96:34–40

Dodwell PC. 1992. Perspectives and transformations. *Can. J. Psychol.* 46:510–38

Dodwell PC, Humphrey GK. 1993. What is important about McCollough effects? Reply to Allan and Siegel. *Psychol. Rev.* 100:347–50

Dompierre S, Lavallée M. 1990. Degré de contact et stress acculturatif dans le procéssus d'adaptation des refugiés africains. (Degree of contact and acculturative stress in the adaptation process of African refugees.) *Int. J. Psychol.* 25(4):417–37

Doyle AB, Edwards H, Robinson RW. 1993. Accreditation of doctoral training programmes and internships in professional psychology. See Dobson & Dobson 1993, pp. 77–106

Dutton DG, Saunders K, Starzomski A, Bartholomew K. 1994. Intimacy-anger and insecure attachment as precursors of abuse in intimate relationships. *J. Appl. Soc. Psychol.* 24:1367–86

Earn B, Towson S. 1986. *Readings in Social Psychology: Classic and Canadian Contributions.* Peterborough, Can.: Broadview

Eaton WO, Yu AP. 1989. Are sex differences in child motor activity level a function of sex differences in maturational status? *Child Dev.* 60(4):1005–11

Endler NS, Magnusson D. 1976. Toward an interactional psychology of personality. *Psychol. Bull.* 83(5):956–74

Endler NS, Rushton JP, Roediger HL III. 1978. Productivity and scholarly impact (citations) of British, Canadian, and U.S. departments of psychology 1975. *Am. Psychol.* 33:1064–82

Fehr B, Russell JA. 1991. The concept of love viewed from a prototype perspective. *J. Pers. Soc. Psychol.* 60:425–38

Ferguson GA, ed. 1977. *Report of the Vancouver Conference on the Organ. and Represent. of Psychol. in Can.* Ottawa: Can. Psychol. Assoc..

Ferguson GA. 1992. Psychology in Canada 1939–1945. *Can. Psychol.* 33:697–705

Friedman A, Harding CA. 1990. Seeing versus imagining movement in depth. *Can. J. Psychol.* 44:371–83

Fuerst KB, Rourke BP. 1995. Human neuropsychology in Canada: the 1980s. *Can. Psychol.* 36:12–45

Galef BG Jr. 1990. A historical perspective on recent studies of social learning about foods by Norway rats. *Can. J. Psychol.* 44:311–29

Gardner RC. 1991. Attitudes and motivation in second language learning. See Reynolds 1991, pp. 43–63

Gardner RC, Kalin R. 1981. *A Canadian Social Psychology of Ethnic Relations.* Toronto: Methuen

Genest M, Genest S. 1987. *Psychology and Health.* Champaign, IL: Research

Gick ML, Paterson K. 1992. Do contrasting examples facilitate schema acquisition and analogical transfer? *Can. J. Psychol.* 46:539–50

Goddard GV. 1980. Component properties of the memory machine: Hebb revisited. In *The Nature of Thought,* ed. PW Jusczyk, RM Klein, pp. 231–47. Hillsdale, NJ: Erlbaum

Goldberg S. 1988. Risk factors in infant-mother attachment. *Can. J. Psychol.* 42:173–88

Goodale MA, Milner AD. 1992. Separate visual pathways for perception and action. *Trends Neurosci.* 15:20–25

Gormezano I, Wasserman EA, eds. 1992. *Learning and Memory: The Behavioral and Biological Substrates.* Hillsdale, NJ: Erlbaum

Graf PC, Schacter DL. 1985. Implicit and explicit memory for new associations in normal and amnesic subjects. *J. Exp. Psychol.: Learn. Mem. Cogn.* 11:501–18

Granger L. 1984. Comment on Conway. *Can. Psychol.* 25:205

Grusec JE. 1991. Socializing concern for others in the home. *Dev. Psychol.* 27:338–42

Grusec JE, Lockhart RS, Walters GC. 1990. *Foundations of Psychology.* Mississauga, Can.: Copp, Clark, Pitman

Hare RD, Harpur TJ, Hakstian AR, Forth AE, Hart SD, Newman JP. 1990. The revised psychopathy checklist: reliability and factor structure. *Psychol. Assess.* 2(3): 338–41

Hearn MT, Evans DR. 1993. Applications of psychology to health care. See Dobson & Dobson 1993, pp. 247–84

Hebb DO. 1949. *The Organization of Behavior.* New York: Wiley

Henderson JM, Singer M, Ferreira F, eds. 1993. Reading and language processing. *Can. J. Exp. Psychol.* 47:129–465 (Special issue)

Hess RF, Wilcox LM. 1994. Linear and nonlinear filtering in stereopsis. *Vis. Res.* 18: 2431–38

Hewitt PL, Flett GL. 1993. Dimensions of perfectionism, daily stress, and depression: a test of the specific vulnerability hypothesis. *J. Abnorm. Psychol.* 102:58–65

Hiebert B, Uhlemann MR. 1993. Counselling psychology: development, identity, issues. See Dobson & Dobson 1993, pp. 285–312

Hoff TL. 1992. Psychology in Canada one-hundred years ago: James Mark Baldwin at the University of Toronto. *Can. Psychol.* 33:683–94

Hoffman C, Tchir MA. 1990. Interpersonal verbs and dispositional adjectives: the psychology of causality embodied in language. *J. Pers. Soc. Psychol.* 58:765–78

Holmes B. 1993. Issues in training and credentialling in school psychology. See Dobson & Dobson 1993, pp. 123–46

Honig WK. 1992. Emergent properties of complex arrays. See Honig & Fetterman 1992, pp. 301–21

Honig WK, Fetterman JG, eds. 1992. *Cognitive Aspects of Stimulus Control.* Hillsdale, NJ: Erlbaum

Hultsch DF, Dixon RA. 1984. Memory for text materials in adulthood. In *Life-span Development and Behavior,* ed. PB Bates, OG Brian Jr, 6:77–108. New York: Academic

Hunsley J, Lefebvre M. 1990. A survey of the practices and activities of Canadian clinical psychologists. *Can. Psychol.* 31:350–58

Jackson DN. 1985. Computer-based personality testing. *Comput. Hum. Behav.* 1:255–64

Jacoby LL, Dallas M. 1981. On the relationship between autobiographical memory and perceptual learning. *J. Exp. Psychol.: Gen.* 110:306–40

Jolicoeur P. 1992. Orientation congruency effects in visual search. *Can. J. Psychol.* 46: 280–305

Katz AN. 1992. Psychological studies in metaphor processing: extensions to the placement of terms in semantic space. *Poet. Today* 13:607–32

Kim U, Berry J. 1993. *Indigenous Psychologies: Research and Experience in Cultural Contexts.* Newbury Park, CA: Sage

Kimura D. 1993. *Neuromotor Mechanisms in Human Communication.* New York: Oxford Univ. Press

Kolb B, Whishaw I. 1990. *Fundamentals of Human Neuropsychology.* New York: Freeman. 3rd ed.

Koulack D, Perlman D, eds. 1973. *Readings in Social Psychology: Focus on Canada.* Toronto: Wiley

Kroger RO, Wood LA, Kim U. 1984. Are the rules of address universal? III. Comparison of Chinese, Greek, and Korean usage. *J. Cross-Cult. Psychol.* 15:273–84

Ladouceur R, Boisvert J-M, Dumont J. 1994. Cognitive-behavioral treatment for adolescent pathological gamblers. *Behav. Modif.* 18:230–42

Lalonde RN, Cameron JE. 1993. An intergroup perspective on immigrant acculturation with a focus on collective strategies. *Int. J. Psychol.* 28:57–74

Lambert WE. 1991. "And then add your two cents' worth." See Reynolds 1991, pp. 217–49

Lambert WE, Tucker GR. 1972. *Bilingual Education in Children: The St. Lambert Experiment.* Rowley, MA: Newbury House

Lassonde M, Ptito M, Lepore F. 1990. La plasticité du système calleux. *Can. J. Psychol.* 44:166–79

Lederman SJ, Browse SJ, Klatzky RL. 1988. Haptic processing of spatially distributed information. *Percept. Psychophys.* 44: 222–32

Lefcourt HM, Martin RA, Saleh WE. 1984. Locus of control and social support: interactive moderators of stress. *J. Pers. Soc. Psychol.* 47:378–89

Levy BA, Burns KI. 1990. Reprocessing text: contributions from conceptually driven processes. *Can. J. Psychol.* 44:465–82

Lindsay RC, Lea JA, Nosworthy GJ, Fulford JA, Hector J, et al. 1991. Biased lineups: sequential presentation reduces the problem. *J. Appl. Psychol.* 76:796–802

Lockhart RS, Craik FIM. 1990. Levels of processing: a retrospective commentary on a framework for memory research. *Can. J. Psychol.* 44:87–112

Lortie-Lussier M, Fellers GL, Kleinplatz PJ. 1986. Value orientations of English, French, and Italian Canadian children: continuity of the ethnic mosaic? *J. Cross-Cult. Psychol.* 17:283–99

Lubek I, Minton HJ, Apfelbaum E. 1992. Social psychology and its history. *Can. Psychol.* 33(3):521–661 (Special issue)

Lytton H, Romney DM. 1991. Parents' differential socialization of boys and girls: a meta-analysis. *Psychol. Bull.* 109(2): 267–96

MacLeod CM. 1991. Half a century of research on the Stroop effect: an integrative review. *Psychol. Bull.* 109:163–203

MacLeod RB. 1955. *Psychology in Canadian Universities and Colleges.* Ottawa: Can. Soc. Sci. Res. Counc.

Macmillan NA, Creelman CD. 1991. *Detection Theory: A User's Guide.* Cambridge: Cambridge Univ. Press

Marshall WL. 1994. Treatment effects on denial and minimization in incarcerated sex offenders. *Behav. Res. Ther.* 32:559–64

Masson EJ. 1995. A distributed memory model of semantic priming. *J. Exp. Psychol.: Learn. Mem. Cogn.* 21:3–23

Maurer D. 1987. Emergence of the ability to discriminate a blue from gray at one month of age. *Can. J. Psychol.* 44:147–56

McGrath PJ, Humphreys P, Keene D, Goodman JT, Lascelles MA, et al. 1992. The efficacy and efficiency of a self-administered treatment for adolescent migraine. *Pain* 49:321–24

Meichenbaum D. 1977. *Cognitive-Behavior Modification.* New York: Plenum

Meleshko KG, Alden LE. 1993. Anxiety and self-disclosure: toward a motivational model. *J. Pers. Soc. Psychol.* 64:1000–9

Melzack R. 1993. Pain: past, present and future. *Can. J. Psychol.* 47:615–29

Milner B. 1980. Complementary functional specializations of the human cerebral hemispheres. In *Nerve Cells, Transmitters, and Behavior,* ed. R Levi-Montalcini, pp. 601–25. Vatican City: Pontif. Acad. Sci.

Milner PM. 1991. Brain stimulation reward: a review. *Can. J. Psychol.* 45:1–36

Minton HL. 1988. *Lewis M. Terman: Pioneer in Psychological Testing.* New York: NY Univ. Press

Moscovitch M, Winocur G. 1992. The neuro psychology of memory and aging. See Craik & Salthouse 1992, pp. 315–72

Moscovitch M, Winocur G, McLachlan D. 1986. Memory as assessed by recognition and reading time in normal and memory-impaired people with Alzheimer's disease and other neurological disorders. *J. Exp. Psychol.: Gen.* 115:331–47

Murdock BB. 1993. TODAM2: a model for the storage and retrieval of item associative, and serial-order information. *Psychol. Rev.* 100:183–203

Nicholson IR, Neufeld RW. 1993. Classification of the schizophrenias according to symptomatology: a two-factor model. *J. Abnorm. Psychol.* 102:259–70

O'Keefe J, Nadel L. 1978. *The Hippocampus as a Cognitive Map.* Oxford: Claredon

Olson JM. 1988. Misattribution, preparatory information, and speech anxiety. *J. Pers. Soc. Psychol.* 54(5):758–76

Paivio A. 1991. Dual coding theory: retrospect and current status. *Can. J. Psychol.* 45: 255–87

Paivio A. 1995. Imagery and memory. In *The Cognitive Neurosciences,* ed. MS Gazzaniga. Cambridge, Mass: MIT Press

Paulhus DL, Reid DB. 1991. Enhancement and denial in socially desirable responding. *J. Pers. Soc. Psychol.* 60(2):307–17

Perlman D, Joshi P. 1987. The revelation of loneliness. *J. Soc. Behav. Pers.* 2(2): 63–76

Pettifor JL. 1995. The Canadian Code of Ethics for Psychologists: the Challenge of Ethical Decision-Making in a Moral Context. *Eur. Congr. Psychol. IV,* Athens

Phillips AG, Blaha CD, Fibiger HC. 1989. Neurochemical correlates of brain-stimulation reward measured by ex vivo and in vivo analyses. *Neurosci. Biobehav. Rev.* 13:99–104

Phillips DP, Ryon J, Danilchuk W, Fentress JC. 1991. Food caching in captive coyotes: sterotypy of action sequence and spatial distribution of cache sites. *Can. J. Psychol.* 45:83–91

Pihl RO, Peterson JB, Lau MA. 1993. A biosocial model of the alcohol-aggression relationship. *J. Stud. Alcohol* 11:128–39

Pinel JPJ. 1990. *Biopsychology.* Boston, MA: Allyn Bacon

Pliner P. 1994. Development of measures of food neophobia in children. *Appetite.* 23: 147–63

Polivy J, Herman CP. 1985. Dieting and binging: a causal analysis. *Am. Psychol.* 40: 193–201

Pollock JL, Webster BD. 1993. Psychology and the law: the emerging role of forensic psychology. See Dobson & Dobson 1993, pp. 391–412

Porac C. 1993. Are age trends in adult hand preference best explained by developmental shifts or generational differences? *Can. J. Exp. Psychol.* 47:697–713

Pressey AW, Zubek JP. 1970. *Readings in General Psychology: Canadian Contributions.* Toronto: McClelland & Stewart

Pylyshyn ZW. 1984. *Computation and Cognition.* Cambridge, MA: MIT Press

Rachman S, Maser JD, eds. 1988. *Panic: Psychological perspectives.* Hillsdale, NJ: Erlbaum

Regan DM, Frisby JP, Poggio GF, Schor CM, Tyler CW. 1990. The perception of stereodepth and stereomotion: cortical mechanisms. In *Visual Perception,* ed. L Spillman. New York: Academic

Reynolds AG, ed. 1991. *Bilingualism, Mul-*

ticulturalism, and Second Language Learning: The McGill Conference in Honour of Wallace E. Lambert. Hillsdale, NJ: Erlbaum

Rice ME, Quinsey VL, Harris GT. 1991. Sexual recidivism among child molesters released from a maximum security psychiatric institution. J. Consult. Clin. Psychol. 59(3):381–86

Ritchie PL-J, Hogan TP, Hogan TV, eds. 1988. Psychology in Canada: The State of the Discipline, 1984. Ottawa: Can. Psychol. Assoc.

Ritchie PL-J, Sabourin ME. 1992. Sous un même toit: Canada's functional-structural approach to the unity of psychology. Int. J. Psychol. 27:311–25

Robert M. 1988. Fondements et étapes de la recherche scientifique en psychologie. St-Hyacinthe, Can.: Edisem. 3rd. ed.

Robert M, Morin P. 1993. Gender differences in horizontality and verticality representation in relation to the initial position of the stimuli. Can. J. Exp. Psychol. 47: 507–22

Roberts WA. 1992. Foraging by rats on a radial maze: learning, memory, and decision rules. See Gormezano & Wasserman 1992, pp. 7–23

Roesch R, Ogloff JR, Golding SL. 1993. Competency to stand trial: legal and clinical issues. Appl. Prevent. Psychol. 2:43–51

Ross M. 1989. Relation of implicit theories to the construction of personal histories. Psychol. Rev. 96:341–57

Royce JR. 1975. Psychology is multi-: methodological, variate, epistemic, world view, systemic, paradigmatic, theoretic, and disciplinary. Nebr. Symp. Motiv. 23:1–63

Rubin KH, Hymel S, Mills RS. 1989. Sociability and social withdrawal in childhood: stability and outcomes. J. Pers. 57(2): 237–55

Rule BG, Adair J. 1984. Contributions of psychology as a social science to Canadian society. Can. Psychol. 25:52–58

Runquist WN. 1983. The generality of the effects of cue structure similarity on cue discrimination and recall. Can. J. Psychol. 37: 484–97

Ryan EB, Laurie S. 1990. Evaluations of older and younger adult speakers: influence of communication effectiveness and noise. Psychol. Aging 5(4):514–19

Sayegh L, Lasry JC. 1993. Immigrants' adaptation in Canada: assimilation, acculturation, and orthogonal cultural identification. Can. Psychol. 34:98–109

Schneider BA, Morrongiello BA, Trehub SE. 1990. Size of critical band in infants, children, and adults. J. Exp. Psychol.: Hum. Percept. Perf. 16:642–52

Segal ZV, Shaw BF, Vella DD, Katz R. 1992. Cognitive and life stress as predictors of relapse in remitted unipolar depressed patients: a test of the congruency hypothesis. J. Abnorm. Psychol. 101:26–36

Serbin LA, Sprafkin C. 1986. The salience of gender and the process of sex typing in three- to seven-year-old children. Child Dev. 57(5):1188–99

Sherry DF. 1992. Landmarks, the hippocampus, and spatial search in food-storing birds. See Honig & Fetterman 1992, pp. 185–201

Shettleworth SJ. 1992. Spatial memory in hoarding and nonhoarding tits (Paridae). See Gormezano & Wasserman 1992, pp. 25–44

Siegel LS. 1993. Phonological processing deficits as the basis of a reading disability. Dev. Rev. 13(3):246–57

Sinclair C. 1993. Codes of ethics and standards of practice. See Dobson & Dobson 1993, pp. 167–200

Slamecka NJ, Graf P. 1978. The generation effect: delineation of a phenomenon. J. Exp. Psychol.: Hum. Learn. Mem. 4: 592–604

Sorrentino RM, Hewitt EC, Raso-Knott PA. 1992. Risk-taking in games of chance and skill: informational and affective influences on choice behavior. J. Pers. Soc. Psychol. 62:522–33

Stam HJ, Rogers TB, Gergen KJ, eds. 1987. The Analysis of Psychological Theory: Metapsychological Perspectives. Washington, DC: Hemisphere

Statistics Canada. 1994. Universities: Enrollment and Degrees 1991. Ottawa: Minist. Ind. Sci. Technol.

Stewart J. 1992. Conditioned stimulus control of the expression of sensitization of the behavioral activating effect of opiate and stimulant drugs. See Gormezano & Wasserman 1992, pp. 129–51

Stones MJ, Kozma A. 1989. Happiness and activities in later life: a propensity formulation. Can. Psychol. 30:526–37

Suedfeld P. 1991. Polar psychology: an overview. Environ. Behav. 23:653–65

Taylor DM, Wright SC, Moghaddam FM, Lalonde RN. 1990. The personal/group discrimination discrepancy: perceiving my group, but not myself, to be a target for discrimination. Pers. Soc. Psychol. Bull. 16:254–62

Tees RC, Buhrmann K. 1990. The effect of early experience on water maze spatial learning and memory in rats. Dev. Psychobiol. 23:427–39

Thompson VA. 1995. Conditional reasoning: the necessary and sufficient conditions. Can. J. Exp. Psychol. 49:1–58

Tulving E. 1983. Elements of Episodic Memory. New York: Oxford Univ. Press

Tulving E. 1995. Organization of memory: quo vadis? In The Cognitive Neurosciences, ed.

MS Gazzaniga. Cambridge, MA: MIT Press

Vallerand RJ, Bissonnette R. 1992. Intrinsic, extrinsic, and amotivational styles as predictors of behavior: a prospective study. *J. Pers.* 60:599–620

Vanderwolf CH, Cain DP. 1994. The behavioral neurobiology of learning and memory: a conceptual reorientation. *Brain Res. Rev.* 19:264–97

Vitaro F, Tremblay RE. 1994. Impact of a prevention program on aggressive children's friendships and social adjustment. *J. Abnorm. Child Psychol.* 22:457–75

Wand B. 1990. *The Council of Provincial Associations of Psychologists: 1967–1990.* Ottawa: Counc. Prov. Assoc. Psychol.

Warner RE. 1991. A survey of theoretical orientations of Canadian clinical psychologists. *Can. Psychol.* 32:525–28

Webster EC, ed. 1967. *The Couchiching Conference on Professional Psychology in Canada.* Montréal: Can. Psychol. Assoc.

Werker JF. 1992. Cross-language speech perception: developmental change does not involve loss. *Speech Perception and Word Recognition*, ed. J Goodman, HC Nusbaum, pp. 95–120. Cambridge, MA: MIT Press

White NM, Milner PM. 1992. The psychobiology of reinforcers. *Annu. Rev. Psychol.* 43: 443–71

Wiggins JS, Broughton R. 1991. A geometric taxonomy of personality scales. *Eur. J. Pers.* 5:343–65

Wilson RF. 1993. Nontraditional applications of professional psychology. See Dobson & Dobson 1993, pp. 413–29

Wise RA. 1989. Opiate reward: sites and substrates. *Neurosci. Biobehav. Rev.* 13: 129–33

Witelson SF, Nowakowski RS. 1991. Left out axons make men right: a hypothesis for the origin of handedness and functional asymmetry. *Neuropsychologia.* 29:327–33

Wright MJ. 1971. The psychological organizations of Canada. *Can. Psychol.* 15:112–31

Wright MJ. 1992. Women ground-breakers in Canadian Psychology: World War II and its aftermath. *Can. Psychol.* 33:675–82

Wright MJ, Myers CR. 1982. *History of Academic Psychology in Canada.* Toronto: Hogrefe

Wright RD, ed. 1994. Shifts of visual attention. *Can. J. Psychol.* 48:151–338 (Special issue)

Yuille JC, Tollestrup PA. 1990. Some effects of alcohol on eyewitness memory. *J. Appl. Psychol.* 75:268–73

Zanna MP, Olson JM, eds. 1994. *The Psychology of Prejudice: The Ontario Symposium on Personality and Social Psychology.* Hillsdale, NJ: Erlbaum

Zanna M, Sande G. 1987. The effects of collective actions on the attitudes of individual group members: a dissonance analysis. In *Social Influence: The Ontario Symposium 5,* ed. MP Zanna, JM Olson, CP Herman, pp. 151–63

Zuroff DC, Igreja I, Mongrain M. 1990. Dysfunctional attitudes, dependency, and self-criticism as predictors of depressive mood states: a 12-month longitudinal study. *Cogn. Ther. Res.* 14:315–26

Annu. Rev. Psychol. 1996. 47:371–400

METHODOLOGICAL ISSUES IN PSYCHOPATHOLOGY RESEARCH

K. J. Sher and T. J. Trull

Department of Psychology, 210 McAlester Hall, University of Missouri-Columbia, Columbia, Missouri 65211

KEY WORDS: analogue research, specificity, research design, diagnosis, statistics

ABSTRACT

We present an overview of methodological issues involved in conducting psychopathology research, including conceptual, analytic, and interpretive considerations. Research issues germane to structured diagnostic interviewing, comorbidity of mental disorders, and ascertainment and sampling are reviewed. Further, the problem of specificity (with respect to disorder, to differential deficit, and to time) is discussed. Specific issues concerning risk vs protective factors, conducting research with special populations, and the continuity of abnormal and normal functioning are highlighted. Finally, various analogue strategies (human subclinical syndromes, experimental study of "pathological" processes in normals, animal models, and computer simulations) are critiqued. Our review documents many of the impressive methodological developments that have emerged in this field, and we hope our review stimulates additional research that exploits recent methodological advances.

CONTENTS

0066-4308/96/0201-0371$08.00

INTRODUCTION

Research into the causes, correlates, and consequences of psychopathology is becoming an increasingly sophisticated endeavor. Rather than providing a systematic empirical or theoretical review of substantive research areas (but see Clark et al 1995, Dodge 1993, Fowles 1992, Widiger & Trull 1991, Zinbarg et al 1992) the present review is intended as an overview of methodological issues that are frequently encountered in conducting and interpreting the results of research investigations. We contend that recent methodological developments provide important tools that hold promise for progress in many areas of psychopathology research.

CONCEPTUALIZATION AND OPERATIONALIZATION OF DISORDER

Much psychopathology research focuses on identifying unique features that characterize individuals from diagnostic groups and on investigating factors or mechanisms that lead to the development of disorder. Although various alternatives are available (e.g. Berner et al 1992), most psychopathology researchers have accepted the various conceptualizations and definitions of mental disorder that are offered by the chief architects of the major diagnostic systems, and most research reports are based on the *Diagnostic and Statistical Manual of Mental Disorders* (DSM) (American Psychiatric Association 1994), i.e. DSM-III (APA 1980), DSM-III-R (APA 1987), and DSM-IV (APA 1994).

At the heart of the DSM is the conceptual definition of what constitutes a mental disorder, based largely on the proposal of Spitzer & Endicott (1978a). The current DSM-IV definition includes the notion of dysfunction within the individual, as well as distress, disability, and disadvantage. Recently, the validity of the DSM and Spitzer & Endicott definitions has been challenged on both conceptual and logical grounds (e.g. Wakefield 1992a,b, 1993).

Despite the elusive nature of a totally satisfying conceptual definition of disorder, current definitions of mental disorder remain viable working constructs for psychopathology research. The development of explicit operational criteria for defining specific disorders represents perhaps the most significant development in psychopathology research in the past twenty years.

DIAGNOSTIC ASSESSMENT TECHNOLOGY

Historically, unstructured clinical interviews were used to assign mental disorder diagnoses to subjects. However, the reliability and, by implication, the validity of this method has been shown to be poor (Matarazzo 1983, Ward et al 1962). In fact, part of the resurgence of interest in the diagnosis and classification of mental disorders can be attributed to the introduction of structured diagnostic interviews [e.g. the *Diagnostic Interview Schedule* (DIS) (Robins et al 1991a) and the *Structured Clinical Interview for DSM-IV* (SCID) (First et al 1995)] and semistructured diagnostic interviews [e.g. the *Structured Interview for DSM-IV Personality* (SIDP-IV) (Pfohl et al 1995) and the *Schedule of Affective Disorders and Schizophrenia* (SADS) (Spitzer & Endicott 1978b)]. Structured and semistructured methods have several advantages over unstructured ones (Rogers 1995): (*a*) they result in relatively higher interrater reliability, (*b*) they allow continuous (vs categorical) ratings of psychopathology, (c) they reduce both information and criterion variance that is often related to disagreement among interviewers, and (d) they result in a much more comprehensive assessment of a wide range of psychopathological symptoms.

Diagnostic Interviews: Research Issues

Below we discuss strengths, as well as weaknesses, of structured diagnostic interviews.

RELIABILITY AND STABILITY OF DIAGNOSES   Interrater reliability is a chief concern for researchers employing structured interviews. However, interrater reliability is *not* solely a function of the diagnostic interview itself. Its level of interrater reliability is also influenced by the quality of the interviewers/raters, as well as the ability of the subjects to report accurately and consistently the symptoms they are experiencing. Thus, interrater reliability should be assessed in every study, regardless of previous findings. Poorly trained or inconsistent interviewers/raters can make even the best structured interview look weak.

The stability of diagnoses derived from structured interviews has also been the focus of research. For example, those individuals given a lifetime diagnosis of a specific mental disorder would be expected to receive the same lifetime diagnosis at a later point in time (Robins 1985, Vandiver & Sher 1991). However, the results show that respondents tend to report, on average, fewer lifetime symptoms of psychopathology at retest, resulting in lower prevalence rates for lifetime diagnoses at the second interview (Robins 1985). Using the DIS, Wells et al (1988) and Vandiver & Sher (1991) found that lifetime diagnoses were not particularly durable over a one-year time frame across a variety of Axis I disorders.

What factors influence this instability? Several possibilities have been proposed (Goodwin & Sher 1993, Robins 1985). 1. Subjects may feel it unnecessary to repeat what they reported previously. 2. This effect may be primarily attributable to the unreliable reporting of symptoms by subjects who are closest to the diagnostic threshold (Rice et al 1992, Robins et al 1982, Vandiver & Sher 1991). The categorical nature of diagnosis leads to the somewhat inaccurate perception of instability because even small changes in the report of these close-to-threshold subjects result in a change in diagnostic status. 3. Respondents may become bored or fatigued during retest and fail to accurately report lifetime symptoms (Bromet et al 1986). 4. Respondents may respond negatively to screening questions regarding the presence of symptoms in order to avoid follow-up probe questions (Semler et al 1987). 5. Subjects may be inconsistent in choosing the period of time within which the most "severe" symptoms occurred such that fewer total symptoms for a disorder are reported at retest (Semler et al 1987). 6. Variations in mood at the time of assessment over time could lead to inconsistent reporting of lifetime symptoms because of mood congruency effects on recall (Goodwin & Sher 1993).

SOURCE OF DIAGNOSTIC DATA   Traditionally, researchers have treated the subjects' responses to structured interview questions as the most valid sources of information. Given the potential threats to the reliability and validity of structured interview data noted above, however, it seems prudent to employ supplemental data from sources in addition to subjects' responses to structured interview questions. The use of collateral information may be especially important for personality (Axis II) disorders (Zimmerman 1994). Unlike Axis I symptoms, features of personality disorder are assumed to be both long-standing and generally cross-situational. Further, acceptance of a patient's self-report of personality disorder symptoms assumes some degree of introspection and self-awareness of the impact that the patient's cognitive and interpersonal style has on others (Zimmerman 1994). Therefore, a knowledgeable informant might be particularly helpful to employ.

Comparisons of personality disorder ratings based on patient interviews and informant interviews find poor agreement between the two sources (Riso et al 1994, Tyrer et al 1979, Zimmerman et al 1988). The cause of this apparent discrepancy is unclear and could be attributable to subjects' minimizing or denying symptoms, to subjects' lack of introspection and self-awareness, to informants' sensitivity to subclinical symptoms of psychopathology, and informants having "an axe to grind." Two recent studies (Chapman et al 1994, Kendler et al 1991) suggest yet another possibility: that the diagnostic status of *informants* influences the data they provide on targeted subjects.

Although many investigators have found discrepancies among data provided by different sources of diagnostic information, few researchers have offered guidelines or suggestions regarding how best to integrate the diagnostic information. Zimmerman (1994) advocated the use of clinical judgment in combining Axis II diagnostic information from patients and informants, whereas others (Piacentini et al 1992, Reich & Earls 1987) have provided more explicit guidelines.

LAY INTERVIEWERS VS CLINICIANS   One ongoing debate concerns the relative merits and disadvantages of employing lay vs clinician interviewers in psychopathology research. Some diagnostic interviews (e.g. the DIS) have been developed such that they can be administered by lay interviewers. Employing lay interviewers is less costly in both time and expense. In addition, lay interviewers may have fewer preconceptions regarding the comorbidity of symptoms and diagnoses. Clinicians with biases regarding which symptoms or disorders often co-occur might provide ratings that matched their model of psychopathology rather than those that accurately reflected the respondent's psychological state. On the other hand, experienced clinicians are likely to be more familiar with the diagnostic system and the full array of psychopathology symptoms, and to be better able to formulate additional probes and questions aimed at clarifying responses of patients (Spitzer 1983).

Comparisons of lay-administered DIS diagnoses with clinician diagnoses indicate that the two types of raters show low agreement (Anthony et al 1985, Folstein et al 1985). Whether this indicates a lack of validity for lay interviewers or clinicians is unclear because there is no psychopathology gold standard (Robins 1985). Regardless, several researchers clearly view these results as an indictment of lay-administered diagnostic interviews (Coyne 1994, Spitzer 1983). While some interviews were developed so that lay persons could administer them, nothing about the interviews themselves requires that they be administered by a nonclinician (Widiger et al 1995), and the related issues of type of *interview* and type of *interviewers* are typically confounded. At present there is no consensus regarding the ultimate validity of clinician vs lay interviewers.

Laboratory Findings

As noted in a recent review (Widiger & Trull 1991), laboratory findings (e.g. biochemical assays, pharmacological challenges, psychophysiological assessment, cognitive assessments, neuroimaging, genotyping) hold promise for increasing the precision of diagnosis as is the case in clinical medicine. The development of specific markers for various mental disorders is of great importance not only for answering basic questions about their nature but for the applied question of how to increase the sensitivity and specificity of our diagnostic procedures.

COMORBIDITY

In both community and clinical samples, rates of comorbidity (i.e. the co-occurrence of two or more mental disorder diagnoses within one individual) are substantial (Clark et al 1995, Kessler et al 1994, Lilienfeld et al 1994, Robins et al 1991b). Although the use of the term "comorbidity" in psychopathology research has been questioned for conceptual reasons, researchers continue to encourage exploration of comorbidity patterns in order to better understand the nature of mental disorders (Robins 1994, Rutter 1994a, Spitzer 1994, Widiger & Ford-Black 1994).

There are several possible models for understanding comorbidity (Docherty et al 1986, Widiger & Trull 1991). For simplicity's sake, we consider the situation in which only two mental disorder diagnoses co-occur. First, comorbidity may indicate that one disorder causes the other. Second, both disorders may be coeffects or consequences of a common cause or disease process. Third, mutual (reciprocal) causality may lead to comorbidity. Fourth, the co-occurrence of two disorders may be a chance result attributable to the high base rates of both disorders in a particular setting. Finally, two disorders may co-occur because the criteria sets for these disorders overlap (i.e. they share the same criteria).

From a research perspective, comorbidity presents several problems. First, comorbidity (depending on the model above that best describes it) may pose a challenge to the assumption that two disorders are unique and distinct entities worthy of separate diagnostic status. If two disorders frequently occur together but rarely occur alone, then the benefits of studying each disorder separately may be questioned. Second, to the extent that comorbidity is present in one's sample, multiple syndromes (and possibly multiple patterns or combinations of disorders) are being studied. This situation makes it more difficult to interpret the results of a study because the effects that are observed can not be attributed solely to the target disorder being studied. Finally, comorbidity complicates interpretations of longitudinal data because different patterns of comorbidity may emerge over time *within* individuals.

Widiger & Shea have (1991) outlined several options for addressing the comorbidity issue in research: (*a*) employ exclusionary criteria in a study such that one disorder will take diagnostic precedence over another, (*b*) add differentiating criteria aimed at successfully making a differential diagnosis between two disorders, and (*c*) remove from consideration criteria that are shared by two disorders. Although each proposed solution would decrease the comorbidity rates between two disorders, there are problems with each (see Widiger & Shea 1991).

Two additional approaches might be considered. One approach involves studying only so-called pure types of individuals—those without any additional diagnoses. Although on the surface this approach has some appeal, it will result in studying an unrepresentative subsample, limiting the generalizability of the findings. Another approach involves statistically controlling for comorbidity in the study via regression techniques (Trull & Sher 1994). Although this approach is useful in identifying unique features of a disorder, important but common features will not necessarily be identified.

GENERAL RESEARCH DESIGN ISSUES

Ascertainment and Sampling

Despite the importance of sampling in psychopathology research, there are surprisingly few general discussions of the issues and implications related to sampling choices (but see Henry 1990, Verhulst & Koot 1992). Most studies of psychopathology employ nonprobability samples, often based primarily on convenience (e.g. volunteers from the community, specific clinical settings). Although nonprobability sampling is convenient and often the only feasible strategy, it compromises the external validity of the findings and is vulnerable to various types of selection bias.

In probability sampling (e.g. simple random sampling, systematic sampling, stratified sampling, cluster sampling, or multistage sampling), each member of the population has a nonzero probability of being selected for further study (but the probability of selection may not be the same for all members of the population). If the probabilities for selection are unequal, then it is necessary to weight cases accordingly before calculating *population* estimates (e.g. levels of association between variables) (Henry 1990). The major advantages of probability sampling are greater external validity and the availability of analytic methods for estimating possible selection bias and error. Of course, probability sampling is more time and resource intensive.

One choice confronting the psychopathology researcher is whether to sample clinical (i.e. presenting for treatment) or nonclinical subjects. Clinical subjects are crucial to investigations of the course of treated disorder. However, several features of clinical samples may adversely affect studies of etiology and disorder development. First, the assessment of clinical subjects for factors believed to be related to the etiology of a disorder may mistakenly reveal the consequences of the disorder rather than the origins (e.g. see Mednick & McNeil 1968). Further, clinical subjects who receive a particular diagnosis may be atypical and unrepresentative of the population of individuals who meet criteria for the diagnosis. The most dysfunctional or severe cases are overrepresented in clinical samples (Cohen & Cohen 1984), and comorbidity is greater among clinical subjects (Berkson 1946).

Aside from the representativeness of the sample, researchers must be cognizant that results from a study (e.g. prevalence rates, comorbidity rates and patterns, associations between putative risk factors and disorder) can change, often dramatically, as a function of the ascertainment source. Patterns of results that vary as a function of the sample employed have recently been demonstrated in mental retardation (Borthwick-Duffy 1994), depression (Henderson 1994), alcohol use disorders (Mezzich et al 1991), and in twin studies of psychopathology (Torgersen 1987). Additional potential ascertainment biases have been discussed recently as well (Curtis & Gurling 1990, Hsu 1989, Kendler & Eaton 1988, Schwartz & Link 1989).

The Problem of Specificity

A central issue that cuts across much research in psychopathology is that of specificity. Three broad domains of specificity are critical to the study of psychopathology: (a) specificity with respect to syndrome/diagnosis, (b) specificity with respect to differential correlates of a disorder or "differential deficit," and (c) specificity with respect to time (i.e. the temporal parameters describing the functional relations between a disorder and a covariate of interest).

SPECIFICITY WITH RESPECT TO DISORDER OR SYNDROME AND THE COMPOSITION OF CONTROL GROUPS   A first step in establishing that a given variable is associated with a diagnosis is the demonstration that individuals suffering from a given disorder differ from individuals not so affected. However, the selection of controls in psychopathology research involves numerous considerations. In the most common design employed in psychopathology research, individuals with a given disorder ("cases") are compared with individuals who do not have the disorder ("controls"). Although the optimal controls for a given study vary as a function of the disorder and the specific hypotheses under investigation, several general issues warrant comment. First, the selection and description of controls require as much consideration as that given to cases. It is likely that inconsistencies across similar studies are as attributable to differences among control groups as to differences among groups of cases (Iacono 1991). Differences between cases and controls not of primary interest to the investigator could statistically account for the association between diagnostic status and the variable of interest. Whether these third variables should be controlled (e.g. by exclusion criteria, matching, or regression-based statistical controls) is, however, not a straightforward question. Iacono (1991), Garber & Hollon (1991), and Meehl (1970, 1971) have noted that decisions concerning the control of third-variables require models of the structural relations among all of the variables (i.e. diagnostic status, "nuisance" variables, outcomes) under investigation. Thus, demonstration that controlling for a "nuisance" variable eliminates a bivariate effect of interest should not be taken to mean that the uncontrolled effect should be discounted (see Baron & Kenny 1986).

Nevertheless, in many studies potential confounds exist that could artifactually produce associations that lack theoretical meaning. There are numerous ways that individuals diagnosed with a given disorder might differ from controls (e.g. hospitalization, medication status, social class, comorbidity) and the proper handling of each of these will depend upon the nature of the study. Whatever strategy is employed, however, it is important to note that some commonly used techniques for equating cases and controls can have deleterious effects on the validity of case/control comparisons (Chapman & Chapman 1973a).

An increasingly recognized problem concerns the use of controls that have more stringent exclusionary criteria applied to them than cases (Schwartz & Link 1989). Also, varying levels of exclusionary criteria applied to controls have been shown to affect the estimates of the prevalence of disorder in their first-degree relatives in family studies (e.g. Tsuang et al 1988). Thus, there are converging lines of evidence that the sampling of controls in cross-sectional studies should follow established epidemiological principles (e.g. Kelsey et al 1986, Rothman 1986, Schlesselmann 1982) as described by Schwartz & Link (1989).

In a related vein, several recent reports (Coryell & Zimmerman 1987, Halbreich et al 1989, Olson et al 1993) have noted that so-called normal volunteers in psychopathology studies (even after passing an initial screening for psychopathology) manifest relatively high rates of psychopathology and family history of psychopathology. This phenomenon suggests that these normal controls be as systematically assessed as cases in order that similar exclusions on psychopathological criteria could be applied to both cases and controls and the diagnostic composition of controls can be thoroughly reported. However, it does not follow that the detection of significant psychopathology should *necessarily* result in exclusion from the control group.

Often researchers are interested in identifying how individuals with a specific disorder differ from one or more groups of individuals with other disorders. However, comparisons of a diagnostic group with a "normal" control group yields relatively little information concerning specificity (Garber & Hollon 1991). This is a central issue to many areas of psychopathology research because it has been consistently demonstrated that certain variables ranging from biochemical, to neurophysiological, to personological, to environmental are associated with multiple and clinically diverse disorders.

Garber & Hollon (1991, pp. 132–33) make the useful distinction between narrow and broad forms of specificity and their implications for the selection of control groups. They state (p. 153):

> [T]he contrast of interest is between a specific nosological entity and some higher order category to which it belongs (broad specificity) versus that entity and other specific nosological entities that belong to that same higher order category (narrow specificity)....Diagnostically heterogeneous controls that are homogeneous with respect to the larger category of interest are typically to be preferred when comparing a specific nosological entity and some superordinate category (broad specificity). Diagnostically homogeneous controls are to be preferred when specific contrasts between distinct nosological entities within a broader category are desired (narrow specificity).

Garber & Hollon's (1991) recommendations concerning specificity designs can be difficult to implement in the context of significant comorbidity within either the target or control diagnostic groups because their recommendations appear to be based on the assumption of relatively pure categories. Although one could subtype a target disorder on the basis of comorbidity and employ these additional diagnostic groupings in a specificity design, the number of diagnostically distinct comorbidity types can be quite large and the resulting sample sizes quite small, making traditional group contrasts unwieldy.

As noted earlier, one could sidestep the comorbidity system by employing only "pure" (noncomorbid) subjects in each diagnostic grouping. However, this approach can be problematic with respect to external validity concerns, and if comorbidity is associated with the severity of a disorder, "pure" groups are more likely to evidence less severe variants of the disorder being studied. It may, in some cases, be helpful to think of diagnoses as variables rather than as distinct homogeneous entities and examine unique effects within the context of linear models (Trull & Sher 1994). From this perspective, specificity tests would involve testing for differences among the regression coefficients associated with each diagnosis.

SPECIFICITY WITH RESPECT TO NATURE OF DEFICIT OR "DIFFERENTIAL DEFICIT"
Often researchers are interested in determining the extent to which individuals with a given diagnosis show a specific, as opposed to a generalized, deficit. In order to infer strongly that these individuals are particularly impaired on a specific ability, researchers had often compared their performance on a test assessing the specific ability to a (theoretically relevant) control test. More than twenty years ago, Chapman & Chapman (1973a,b) showed that unless the tasks being compared were first matched on their discriminating power, it is hazardous to infer a differential deficit based on differential test performance. Chapman & Chapman (1978, 1983, 1985a) later proposed that an experimental and control task can be considered to be matched on their discriminating power when their

true score variances (i.e. the product of the observed score variance and the reliability of the task) are equated in a representative sample. Some of the earlier recommendations of the Chapmans have been challenged because of a lack of attention to construct validation issues and because attempts to match tests in the ways suggested by the Chapmans could result in a "confounding [of] the hypothetical processes being compared" (Knight 1987, p. 6). However, the basic validity of the insight concerning the importance of true score variance is difficult to refute.

Structural equation models with latent variables (e.g. see Bollen 1989, Loehlin 1992, von Eye & Clogg 1994) have great potential utility for addressing questions involving differential correlates of a disorder and have been underutilized in psychopathology research. Latent variable models are particularly well suited for distinguishing between general and specific effects. First, a general effect can be modeled by postulating a direct path from the latent variable (e.g. general cognitive ability assessed by multiple observed variables) to a criterion (e.g. the presence or absence of a diagnosis). Second, we can test if a specific component of this general ability is significantly related to the criterion by assessing the significance of a "residual" path from the error ("uniqueness") of the manifest variable to the criterion (see Bentler 1990, Hoyle & Smith 1994, Newcomb 1994). This residual path represents an effect from that component of the specific ability (or other attribute) that is unshared with the general ability (or other attribute). The basic logic can be extended to higher-order factor models where the residual path would be from the "disturbance" (i.e. the error at the factor level) of a lower-order factor to the criterion (Stacy et al 1991).

Although we are not aware of published examples, structural equation models with latent variables can, in principle, be used to address concerns about the equivalence of true score variances between two or more tests. For example, matched tests could be modeled as latent variables in a large nonclinical sample.

More informative, but more difficult with the sample sizes typically available to psychopathology researchers, is a type of multigroup analysis termed "structured means analysis" (Byrne et al 1989). That is, multiple tasks could be modeled as latent variables in separate samples of both a target (e.g. subjects with a specific disorder) and one or more control populations. In addition to modeling covariances, means of the latent variables are also estimated. Cross-group equality constraints can then be used to test hypotheses concerning the equivalence of the error structure, factor structure, and mean performance across groups (see Hoyle & Smith 1994). In addition to testing differences in the pattern of means across groups, the analysis also includes assessment of the comparability of the factor structure (and thus, construct equivalence across groups). The concerns regarding the equivalence of true score variance are not rendered moot by this approach. However, in principle, the analysis provides all of the relevant information for assessing the psychometric validity issues raised by the Chapmans.

SPECIFICITY WITH RESPECT TO TIME   Research on psychopathology often attempts to identify markers of both broad-band and relatively specific forms of psychological disorders. The concept of *marker* has been applied to a wide range of individual difference variables that are hypothesized to relate to the prediction, diagnosis, and consequences of disorder. We explicitly exclude the term genetic marker, which has a narrower meaning and does not imply covariation in the general population.

Types of markers: conceptual distinctions   On the basis of conceptual and methodological grounds, various authors have proposed a number of ways of subtyping markers on the basis of their time-bound functional relations with respect to disorder (e.g. see Nuechterlein 1990, Nuechterlein & Dawson 1984, Zubin et al 1985). Most distinguish at least three types: *vulnerability markers* (i.e. detectable prior to the onset of disorder), *episode* or *state markers* (i.e. detectable only during symptomatic periods), and *residual markers* (i.e. detectable only after an episode). Another type of marker discussed in the literature concerns *invulnerability* or *protective markers,* discussed briefly in the section "Distinguishing Risk and Protective Factors."

It seems likely that many potential marker variables will have vulnerability, episode, and residual components. As recently noted by Rutter (1994b) in a related context, "the biological expectation is for neither change nor stability but rather for a complex mixture of the two, both of which need to be accounted for" (p. 932). In the following discussion, we broaden the usage of the term "marker" to include a range of covariates of disorder. This is because the analytic issues are quite general and need not refer to personal attributes and, indeed, can be extended to a discussion of ostensibly environmental variables such as life events.

Issues in the analysis of longitudinal data   Because of the mixture of change and stability, research on markers is best served by longitudinal data. Recent developments in longitudinal research methodology provide a useful set of tools for researchers interested in disentangling the temporal patterns of relationship between a psychopathological construct (e.g. diagnosed disorder, score on a symptom measure) and another variable. The numerous important strengths of prospective, longitudinal designs in studying psychopathology have been highlighted recently by a number of authors (e.g. Farrington 1991, Loeber & Farrington 1994, Pickles 1993, Rutter 1994b, Verhulst & Koot 1992, Wierson & Forehand 1994) and include the ability to: (*a*) resolve the temporal aspects of disorder (i.e. onset, duration, termination) and predictor variables of interest, (*b*) resolve directionality of associations, and (*c*) study individual growth (trajectories of behavior problems) over time, among others.

In those situations where two or more constructs are measured at the same point in time on two or more occasions, cross-lagged panel models with latent variables are being increasingly used to study the reciprocal relations between two or more latent variables over time (e.g. Hays et al 1994, Smith et al 1995). Advantages of these models include the ability to model the extent to which changes in one variable prospectively predict changes in another variable [e.g. Nuechterlein's (1990) "mediating" vulnerability], to measure factorial invariance of the construct over time, and to model the covariances between contemporaneous disturbance terms where disturbances are the latent error variables at the factor level. This latter feature of the design is particularly important in that it serves as a type of control for the linear effect of unmeasured "third variables" that might produce a spurious correlation between study variables at later waves of assessment.

One limitation of traditional autoregressive, cross-lagged models is the failure to model the persistence of disorders or other constructs. That is, the model resolves variables at the level of measurement occasion, but the tendency to diagnose or experience symptoms over time, although modeled via stability paths, does not constitute a latent variable itself, and so can neither predict other variables nor be predicted by them. A relatively new class of latent variable models that decompose each measurement occasion into a state and trait component (latent state-trait models, e.g. Steyer et al 1992) appear to be particularly useful for both quantifying disorder (or symptom) persistence and for distinguishing state and trait markers. Although there have been few applications of this technique to psychopathology research (but see Steyer et al 1989, 1990), the technique appears to hold great promise for prospective psychopathology research. Recently, Kenny & Zautra (1995) have extended the basic state-trait decomposition approach to the univariate case.

Another important class of latent variable models relevant for studying psychological disorders in longitudinal context (especially for investigating the predictors of course of symptoms) are those that model differential growth (i.e. change) over time (e.g. McArdle & Epstein 1987, Meredith & Tisak 1990, Muthen 1991). Several recent studies of psychopathology have used this general technique (e.g. Patterson 1993, Stoolmiller et al 1993). A related innovation in the analysis of longitudinal data is the development of a class of techniques referred to as hierarchical linear models (HLM) or random regression models (RRM) (see Arnold 1992, Bryk & Raudenbush 1987, Gibbons et al 1993 for informative overviews of these techniques). Among the strengths of these designs, beyond modeling differential growth, are that they are useful for partitioning trait and state dependence, allow for the inclusion of subjects who fail to provide data at all measurement occasions (and thus minimize attrition bias), and permit the inclusion of both temporally static (e.g. sex) and time-dependent covariates (e.g. life events) (Gibbons et al 1993). Although most of the work on HLM has focused on continuous data, these models have been extended to the case of binary outcomes (e.g. Gibbons & Hedeker 1994) and so could be applied to categorical diagnoses. Applications of HLM to psychopathology research are beginning to appear in the literature (e.g. Lahey et al 1995, Raudenbush & Chang 1993, Tate & Hokanson 1993).

Many of the statistical techniques described above were originally developed to analyze data using continuous variables. However, it appears that most of these techniques have counterparts for dichotomous categorical variables such as psychiatric diagnoses in both manifest and latent variable models (e.g. Hagenaars 1990, Muthen 1992). In addition, other techniques for analyzing categorical variables in prospective designs are particularly well suited for studying the development and course of a number of behavior problems (e.g. see Ellickson et al 1992, Graham et al 1991, Langenbucher & Chung 1995, Singer & Willett 1991, Willett & Singer 1993, Wood et al 1994).

Application of the techniques for analyzing longitudinal data have other limitations. Because of low base rates, assembling sufficiently large cohorts of individuals with manifest disorder can be difficult, and the investigation of many questions requires large sample sizes. Moreover, many disorders are relatively rare, and additional inclusion criteria (e.g. "first-episode" cases) can make case-finding difficult. This problem is further compounded in etiological studies where predictors of the onset of new cases are studied because samples must be sufficiently large to yield enough cases for analysis as the sample passes through its period of risk. Potential solutions include the conduct of high-risk studies (Mednick & McNeil 1968, but see Sher 1991) and the use of overlapping cohort or "accelerated" longitudinal designs (Raudenbush & Chang 1993, Stanger et al 1994). Although cross-sectional and "follow-back" (e.g. archival) longitudinal analyses can often provide important insights and tests of hypotheses, for a large class of research questions there is no substitute for prospective data.

Conceptual and Empirical Overlap Among Ostensibly Distinct Constructs

In conducting research on psychopathology, great care must be taken to guard against artifactually demonstrating relations caused by unintended or unwanted overlap of conceptually distinct constructs. (One aspect of this general concern was discussed in the earlier section on comorbidity.) In a highly instructive review of methodological issues in research on life stress, social support, personality, and psychopathology, Monroe & Steiner (1986) illustrated a number of methodological challenges to research in this area. First, these authors pointed to substantial measurement overlap among all of these constructs. For example, disorder can be indicated by loss of social interest; life stress can be indicated by loss of important social ties; personality can be indicated by affiliative tendencies; and social support can be indicated by the extent, quality, and utilization of social networks. The associations among these constructs weaken as controls for measurement overlap are introduced. Second, even if measurement overlap is recognized, conceptual problems can remain. For example, many symptoms or situations (e.g. a distressed marital relation) can legitimately be viewed as fundamental to two or more alternative constructs (e.g. both a significant stressor and a social support deficit). In addition, both personality and psychopathology can influence the amount and kind of stressors and social support experienced as well as determine reactivity to events. Although there are no simple solutions to many of these difficulties, Monroe & Steiner (1986) noted that attention to measurement overlap confounds, prospective designs that control for preexisting disorder, consideration of alternative models of causation, and fine-grained analyses can aid in drawing more valid inferences.

Distinguishing Risk vs Protective Factors

Although much research on psychopathology attempts to identify risk factors that have direct effects on outcomes, the identification of variables (e.g. "protective" factors) that interact with risk variables to moderate (e.g. attenuate) their effects is an important goal (see Rutter 1987). Such interactive or moderating effects are key to theories of "stress buffering" (Monroe & Steiner 1986) and diathesis-stress models of psychopathology (Fowles 1992).

While it is often desirable to hypothesize interactions of interest and test for them in studies, Luthar & Zigler (1991) have noted that significant interactions are the exception rather than the rule in research on risk and protective factors. As McClelland & Judd (1993) note, detecting interactions in field (as opposed to experimental) studies is made difficult by the low power occasioned by both the joint distribution of the predictor variables and the forms of interaction that are likely to be obtained. For example, stress-diathesis and stress-buffering theories would not be expected to produce cross-over interactions, the type of interaction most easily detected. Although in some cases that approximate extreme-groups designs (e.g. when samples are divided on the basis of diagnostic group or risk status) power can be increased, the resulting estimates of model fit are likely to be overestimates (see previous discussion on sampling).

Rejecting the utility of interactive concepts because they are difficult to demonstrate and yield only small increments in model fit seems short-sighted. An extensive discussion of the issues of testing for moderation in multiple regression can be found in Aiken & West (1991). Latent variable extensions are described by Kenny & Judd (1984), and Cole (1993) provided a useful example of these techniques.

Cross-Cultural, Gender, and Special Population Issues

There has been increased recognition for the need to include women and minorities in clinical research of all types in recent years. Indeed, such inclusion is nearly mandatory for research grants supported by the National Institutes of Health (NIH 1994). The requirement increases our understanding of the relation between gender and race/ethnicity and health outcomes.

This emphasis involves additional considerations. Cross-cultural researchers (e.g. Rogler 1989) discuss how "culturally sensitive" research in psychopathology requires attention at every stage of the research process. Indeed, some argue that care must be taken to avoid assuming that the concepts developed in the context of one culture are not inappropriately applied to another, the so-called "category fallacy" (Good & Good 1986). Validity concerns are quite general, and cross-cultural experts stress the need for great care in adapting research questions and the technologies for studying them across cultures (e.g. Lewis-Fernandez & Kleinman 1994). Marsella & Kameoka (1989) described several different domains where lack of "equivalence" can jeopardize the validity of cross-cultural comparisons. These include linguistic equivalence, conceptual equivalence, scale equivalence, and norm equivalence. Factorial invariance (e.g. Hoyle & Smith 1994), that is the equivalence of factor structure, must also be considered.

Concepts relevant to an understanding of culture are often desirable to include. For example, Rogler (1989) described how individual differences in acculturation—"the complex process whereby the behaviors and attitudes of a migrant group change toward those of the host society as a result of exposure to a cultural system that is substantially different" (p. 298)—can moderate the relation between cultural variables and outcomes.

Research that examines differences in the prevalence of disorder across gender or ethnic groups involves yet additional considerations. Between-group differences in prevalence can result from sampling bias because members of one group may be particularly likely to be under- or overrepresented in a particular setting (e.g. a clinic, the criminal justice system). Additional biases can result from diagnostic criteria sets that are differentially sensitive to members of one gender or ethnicity, or assessment instruments that are similarly differentially sensitive. These and related issues are discussed by Adebimpe (1994), Westermeyer (1988), and Widiger & Spitzer (1991).

Continuity of Abnormal and Normal Functioning and Taxometric Methods

Due, perhaps, to the influence of the categorical nature of diagnostic systems for mental disorders, many psychopathology researchers assume (either implicitly or explicitly) that individuals who meet diagnostic criteria for a particular mental disorder are *qualitatively* different from individuals who do not receive the diagnosis. One's stance on this issue is important because it influences the sampling strategy employed as well as the statistical analyses utilized. For example, if one assumes a continuity between abnormal and normal functioning, it then becomes possible to sample individuals who may not meet diagnostic criteria for a particular disorder. In contrast, the assumption of qualitative differences among individuals will dictate that only individuals who are "diagnosable" are of primary interest.

The empirical determination of whether a construct is categorical or dimensional is a complicated undertaking (Gangestad & Snyder 1985, 1991; Grayson 1987; Grove & Andreasen 1986; Hicks 1984; Kendell 1975; Meehl 1992). Many investigators have attempted to address the categorical vs dimensional status of diagnostic constructs by utilizing *factor analysis* and *cluster analysis*. Bimodality/multimodality methods (Kendell 1975, Mendelsohn et al 1982, Moldin et al 1987) have also been used. Each of these methods, however, has serious problems (Aldenderfer & Blashfield 1984, Grove & Andreasen 1986, Meehl 1979, Morey 1988), and the general consensus is that none of them is likely to be useful in solving the modality issue. Other methods have been developed that may have value, although they too have limitations.

Several investigators have used *mixture analysis* to demonstrate the categorical distinctiveness of disorders, examining the distribution of scores to determine whether the distribution is best described by more than one component distribution (suggesting the presence of clinical types) (Cloninger et al 1985, Daniel et al 1991, Davis et al 1988, Harvey et al 1990, Sweeney et al 1993). Although this technique has an advantage over the simple examination of a distribution for bimodality in that it can identify more than two types, a number of other potential difficulties with the mixture analysis approach have been identified (Grayson 1986, Grove & Andreasen 1989).

Another approach is *latent class analysis* (LCA), which has been referred to as a categorical data analog to factor analysis (Young 1982). In LCA, both observed and unobserved variables are assumed to be categorical in nature, and there are no assumptions regarding the distributional form of the variables in the latent class model (unlike mixture analysis). Several studies have utilized LCA to assess whether diagnostic constructs represent latent classes or categories in the areas of schizophrenia (Castle et al 1994, Young et al 1982) and depression (Eaton et al 1989, Young et al 1986). One potential limitation of LCA is the number of variables that can be employed in the analysis. Because the model attempts to account for the distribution of cases across all possible response patterns for the observed variables, utilizing a large number of variables may prove unwieldy.

Finally, Meehl & Golden (1982) have developed *taxometric methods*, including *maximum covariance analysis* (MAXCOV), specifically for the purpose of detecting the existence of a latent class variable. (See Golden 1991; Grove & Meehl 1993; Meehl 1973, 1992, 1995; and Meehl & Yonce 1994 for overviews of MAXCOV and other taxometric procedures.) A number of recent studies have used MAXCOV and related procedures to identify latent psychopathological taxa (e.g. Erlenmeyer-Kimling et al 1989, Golden 1982, Grove et al 1987, Harris et al 1994, Haslam & Beck 1994, Korfine & Lenzenweger 1995, Lenzenweger & Korfine 1992, Trull et al 1990, Tyrka et al 1995).

In summary, mixture analysis, LCA, and the taxometric methods developed by Meehl & Golden (1982) have some usefulness. However, even these methods have their limitations. For example, recently Golden (1991) argued that they may potentially lead to spurious findings. Clearly, comparisons of the performance of different methods with large data sets (which should include truly categorical variables) and with Monte Carlo samples is necessary to evaluate the strengths and weaknesses of these methods.

ANALOGUE RESEARCH STRATEGIES

Much research relevant to an understanding of human psychopathology involves so-called analogue research. The broad label of analogue research encompasses numerous approaches to studying psychopathological phenomena, including the use of nonclinical individuals manifesting various degrees of psychological symptoms (i.e. subclinical or subsyndromal approaches), the experimental study of "pathological" processes in normals, various animal models of psychopathology, and computer simulations of psychopathological phenomena. In this section, we provide a selective overview of the potential value, pitfalls, and issues surrounding these approaches.

Human Subclinical Syndromes

A commonly used analogue method employs human subjects who exhibit subclinical psychopathology (i.e. they do not reach diagnostic threshold). Syndromes that have received the most focus include depression (Abramson et al 1978, Coyne & Gotlib 1983, Depue & Monroe 1978, Gotlib 1984), psychosis-proneness and schizophrenia-spectrum disorders (Chapman & Chapman 1985b, 1987; Chapman et al 1994; Lenzenweger et al 1991), anxiety disorders (e.g. Sher et al 1983), and more recently, borderline personality disorder (Trull 1995).

A controversy over the value of subclinical analogue research on depression has surfaced (Coyne 1994, Kendall & Flannery-Schroeder 1995, Tennen et al 1995a,b; Vredenburg et al 1993; Weary et al 1995). On the one hand, Vredenburg et al argued that the use of college students as analogues for depressed patients may be advantageous for a number of important reasons. These include homogeneity of the college environment, academic demands and other stressors that may be relevant to the development of depressive symptoms, and the lower rates of comorbidity and previous treatment for depression in this college population. On the other hand, Coyne noted that few of these analogue studies include measures that assess all features included in the criteria set for major depressive disorder and typically do not assess the duration of symptoms. Furthermore, distressed college students are both younger and less depressed than patients with a diagnosis of major depressive disorder, and the quality of their relationships and the stressors they experience are different from those of clinically depressed subjects.

Relatedly, Tennen et al (1995a) observed that previous guidelines offered for the conduct of analogue studies of depression (Kendall et al 1987) have largely gone unheeded. Kendall & Flannery-Schroeder (1995) noted that the comparability of the correlates of depression in college students and clinic patients is largely untested. In response, Weary et al (1995) asserted that the criticisms aimed at paper-and-pencil measures of depression may be exaggerated, and the preference for a structured diagnostic interview over a self-report inventory should be critically examined.

This debate will likely continue. What is needed to address at least some of these issues are studies that examine whether individuals who score above a cutoff on self-report screening measures exhibit significant degrees of dysfunction and resemble the clinical patients who meet diagnostic criteria for the disorder in question. Several recent studies focusing on depression (Gotlib et al 1995, Sherbourne et al 1994) and borderline personality disorder (Trull 1995) suggest similar levels of dysfunction in particular domains for subclinical and "diagnosed" subjects. One issue is clear: Generalization from subclinical to clinical populations may be hazardous, and care must be taken to characterize carefully the phenomena under investigation in studies of subclinical subjects.

Experimental Study of "Pathological" Processes in Normals

Another approach to studying psychopathology involves the experimental manipulation of some aspect of the environment, experimental task demands, or neurochemistry in order to assess whether such a manipulation can induce psychopathological signs or symptoms in "normal" subjects. While ethical concerns constrain the severity of signs and symptoms that can be induced, this general approach can be used to study a range of both etiological variables and psychopathological phenomena. As with all modeling ventures, external validity cannot be readily assumed. However, the experimental approach can yield high internal validity (strong inferences) concerning cause-effect relations within the bounds of the experiment, and thus is an important strategy in psychopathology research.

The nature of these experimental investigations is broad and ranges from the study of environmental factors to pharmacological factors. At the environmental end of the continuum, researchers have studied the effects of non-contingent aversive stimulation on motivation and emotion (Mineka & Hendersen 1985), the effects of different types of conditioned and unconditioned stimuli on fear acquisition (e.g. Ohman & Soares 1993), and the effects of viewing so-called traumatic imagery on cognitive processing (Horowitz 1975), to name just a few.

Investigations can target specific psychological processes where the interest is not so much on environmental determinants of behavior but rather intraindividual psychological processes. For example, studies of mood induction procedures bear on various cognitive theories of depression (Clark 1983, Martin 1990). Studies of the effects of diminished attention on language production (Barch & Berenbaum 1994) inform researchers interested in determining the extent to which a single deficit (i.e. limited attention) might explain other deficits (i.e. language production) in schizophrenia.

Pharmacological challenges have been used in a number of different ways to study psychopathological processes. First, they have been used to study the effects of specific neurotransmitter systems on mood, physiology, and behavior in normal individuals (e.g. Malaspina et al 1994). If naturally occurring derangement of some neuropharmacologic system is posited to lead to signs and symptoms of disorder, then experimentally altering the system in certain ways could lead to specific deficits or symptoms. In addition, studying the effects of drugs of abuse in "normal" individuals can provide valuable insights concerning their addictive properties and the conditions governing their varied effects (e.g. Steele & Josephs 1990).

Because experimental analogue research is limited to inducing relatively mild symptoms of transient duration, there will probably always be a generalizability gap between experimentally induced phenomena and the clinical disorder or symptom being modeled. Nevertheless, the ability to unambiguously attribute causation in an experimental paradigm makes this type of analogue research a valuable research strategy.

Animal Models

Although many human behaviors are difficult if not impossible to model fully in animals, animal models are not as severely constrained by practical and ethical concerns, and they permit control of genetic and environmental variables, the use of invasive and toxic techniques, and detailed study of mechanism. Although many have argued that there is no single, compelling model for any specific form of psychopathology, animal models play an important role in contemporary research.

Some have argued that for a model to be a valid analog of the human disorder, a set of comprehensive criteria must be met. For example, Abramson & Seligman (1977) developed four criteria that should be used to evaluate the adequacy of models (both human and animal): (*a*) description of the essential features of the disorder's causes, preventives, and cure; (*b*) convincing similarity of symptoms between the model and the target disorder; (*c*) similarity of physiology, cause, cure, and prevention; and (*d*) characterization of the specific syndrome (narrow or broad) being modeled. As noted by Mineka & Zinbarg (1991), criteria such as these can be overly restrictive, and a number of useful "mini-models" have been developed that can shed light on selected aspects of a disorder (e.g. cause, symptomatology, physiology, treatment, prevention). Moreover, models can serve an important heuristic function, and thus even patently invalid models can still be of considerable heuristic value if they lead to important questions or prediction (Overmier & Patterson 1988).

There appear to be a number of naturally occurring behavior disorders seen in veterinary practice that may have relevance to a number of human conditions ranging from stereotypic disorders (e.g. excessive grooming), aggression, mood disorders, anxiety disorders, eating disorders, hyperactivity, and sleep disorders (Stein et al 1994). Most of these behavior disorders in animals, however, have yet to be exploited as models of human psychopathology (but see Rapoport et al 1992). Instead, researchers have tended to use a wide variety of experimental manipulations to induce specific signs and symptoms or more complex syndromes in animals that have some similarity to human psychopathologic phenomena. Further, for many human disorders multiple types of animal models have been developed. For example, in the area of alcoholism, modeling approaches have ranged from environmental manipulations such as schedules of reinforcement (e.g. Riley & Wetherington 1989) to selective breeding for alcohol preference (e.g. Li et al 1993). Contemporary approaches to modeling depression range from a variety of (social) "separation" models, to stress models (e.g. learned helplessness, "behavioral despair"), to brain-damage models (e.g. bilateral lesions of the olfactory bulbs) (Richardson 1991, Willner 1991). Selective breeding techniques have also been used (e.g. Overstreet 1986). Although not technically a model of depression, drug-induced locomotor sensitization and "kindled" seizures have been very influential regarding theories on mechanisms underlying recurrent affective disorders (e.g. Post & Weiss 1989). Animal models of schizophrenia have primarily involved pharmacologic manipulations such as the administration of psychostimulants (especially dopamine agonists) and hallucinogens (e.g. McKinney 1988). Animal models of various anxiety disorders range from direct administration of centrally acting anxiogenic agents such as beta-carbolines (e.g. Meng & Drugan 1993) to models based on stress-induced hypothermia in mice and ultrasonic vocalization in rat pups following isolation from their mother and/or littermates (e.g. Olivier et al 1994), to a variety of learning models (e.g. Kandel 1983, Mineka & Zinbarg 1991). Indeed, at present, animal models may present the most powerful approach for simultaneously characterizing genetic vulnerability, environmental stressors, and their effects on neurochemistry and behavior (e.g. Shanks et al 1991). It seems likely that in the next few years, progress in molecular and behavior genetics will permit the characterization of the effects of both single and multiple specific genes on behavior and their neurochemical mediation (Crabbe et al 1994, Plomin et al 1994, Takahashi et al 1994).

Computer Simulation

For more than twenty years (see Colby 1975) computer simulation techniques using both traditional symbolic reasoning approaches and, more recently, connectionist concepts have been developed to model various aspects of psychopathology, e.g. schizophrenic speech (Garfield & Rapp 1994), interactional styles (DeGiacomo et al 1990), REM sleep latency and depression (MacLean et al 1983), and information processing deficits in psychosis (Hoffman 1987). Hoffman & McGlashan (1993) have shown how connectionist models can be used to describe a range of symptoms and their developmental courses in purported subtypes of schizophrenia. Although computer simulations have not yet had a major impact in the study of psychopathology, they have the potential of integrating psychological processes and neurophysiology and can be useful for generating hypotheses and facilitating insights about basic mechanisms and commonalities across seemingly disparate phenomena. Further, simulation models force researchers to formalize their theoretical notions and examine them for internal coherence and explanatory power (see Cohen et al 1992, Hoffman 1992).

CONCLUDING COMMENT

In this brief review, we have sought to highlight those issues and approaches most central to the general area of psychopathology research. However, given space limitations, several topics of general interest (e.g. high-risk research, developmental issues) could not be systematically covered, and many specialized topics, each of which have their own set of methodological issues, are discussed only in passing (e.g. assessing cognitive functions, pharmacological challenges, animal models). However, we believe that our review documents many of the impressive methodological developments that have occurred in recent years. Unfortunately, many of these developments have not been effectively disseminated to the research community, and our hope is that greater attention to many of the general methodological points discussed in this review will lead to improved conduct and analysis of primary research investigations. Our review points to a number of areas where available methods remain problematic (e.g. diagnosis technology); attention to the issues identified to date should lead to further methodological advances.

ACKNOWLEDGMENTS

Preparation of this chapter was supported in part by grant AA7231 from the National Institute on Alcohol Abuse and Alcoholism to Kenneth J. Sher.

Literature Cited

Abramson LY, Seligman MEP. 1977. Modeling psychopathology in the laboratory: history and rationale. In *Psychopathology: Experimental Models,* ed. JD Maser, MEP Seligman, pp. 1–26. San Francisco: Freeman

Abramson LY, Seligman MEP, Teasdale JD. 1978. Learned helplessness in humans: critique and reformation. *J. Abnorm. Psychol.* 87:49–74

Adebimpe VR. 1994. Race, racism, and epidemiology surveys. *Hosp. Comm. Psychiatr.* 45:27–31

Aiken LS, West SG. 1991. *Multiple Regression: Testing and Interpreting Interactions.* Newbury Park, CA: Sage

Aldenderfer MS, Blashfield RK. 1984. *Cluster Analysis.* Beverly Hills, CA: Sage

American Psychiatric Association. 1980. *Diagnostic and Statistical Manual of Mental Disorders.* Washington, DC: Am. Psychiatr. Assoc. 3rd ed.

American Psychiatric Association. 1987. *Diagnostic and Statistical Manual of Mental Disorders.* Washington, DC: Am. Psychiatr. Assoc. 3rd ed. Rev.

American Psychiatric Association. 1994. *Diagnostic and Statistical Manual of Mental Disorders.* Washington, DC: Am. Psychiatr. Assoc. 4th ed.

Anthony JC, Folstein M, Romanoski AJ, Von Korff MR, Nestadt GE, et al. 1985. Comparison of the Lay Diagnostic Interview Schedule and standardized psychiatric diagnosis. *Arch. Gen. Psychiatr.* 42:667–75

Arnold CL. 1992. An introduction to hierarchical linear models. *Meas. Eval. Couns. Dev.* 25:58–90

Barch D, Berenbaum H. 1994. The relationship between information processing and language production. *J. Abnorm. Psychol.* 103:241–50

Baron R, Kenny DA. 1986. The moderator-mediator variable distinction in social psychological research: conceptual, strategic, and statistical considerations. *J. Pers. Soc. Psychol.* 51:1173–82

Bentler PM. 1990. Latent variable structural models for separating specific from general effects. In *Research Methodology: Strengthening Causal Interpretations of Nonexperimental Data,* ed. L Sechrest, E Perrin, J Bunker, pp. 61–83. Rockville, MD: Dep. Health Hum. Serv.

Berkson J. 1946. Limitations of the application of fourfold table analysis to hospital data. *Biometr. Bull.* 2:47–53

Berner P, Gabriel E, Hatschnig H, Kieffer W, Koehler K, et al. 1992. *Diagnostic Criteria for Functional Psychoses.* Cambridge: Cambridge Univ. Press. 2nd ed.

Bollen KA. 1989. *Structural Equations with Latent Variables.* New York: Wiley

Borthwick-Duffy SA. 1994. Epidemiology and prevalence of psychopathology in people with mental retardation. *J. Consult. Clin. Psychol.* 62:17–27

Bromet EJ, Dunn LO, Connell MM, Dew MA, Schulberg HC. 1986. Long-term reliability of diagnosing lifetime major depression in a community sample. *Arch. Gen. Psychiatr.* 43:435–40

Bryk AS, Raudenbush SW. 1987. Application of hierarchical linear models to assessing change. *Psychol. Bull.* 101:147–58

Byrne BM, Shavelson RJ, Muthen B. 1989.

Testing for the equivalence of factor co-variance and mean structures: the issue of partial measurement invariance. *Psychol. Bull.* 105:456–66

Castle DJ, Sham PC, Wessely S, Murray RM. 1994. The subtyping of schizophrenia in men and women: a latent class analysis. *Psychol. Med.* 24:41–51

Chapman LJ, Chapman JP. 1973a. *Disordered Thought in Schizophrenia.* New York: Appleton-Century-Crofts

Chapman LJ, Chapman JP. 1973b. Problems in the measurement of cognitive deficit. *Psychol. Bull.* 79:380–85

Chapman LJ, Chapman JP. 1978. The measurement of differential deficit. *J. Psychiatr. Res.* 14:303–11

Chapman LJ, Chapman JP. 1983. Reliability and the discrimination of normal and pathological groups. *J. Nerv. Ment. Dis.* 171:658–61

Chapman LJ, Chapman JP. 1985a. Methodological problems in the study of differential deficits in retarded groups. In *Current Topics in Human Intelligence,* Vol. 1, *Research Methodology,* ed. DK Detterman, pp. 141–53. New York: Guilford

Chapman LJ, Chapman JP. 1985b. Psychosis proneness. In *Controversies in Schizophrenia,* ed. M Alpert, pp. 157–74. New York: Guilford

Chapman LJ, Chapman JP. 1987. The search for symptoms predictive of schizophrenia. *Schizophr. Bull.* 13:497–503

Chapman TF, Mannuzza S, Klein DF, Fyer AJ. 1994. Effects of informant mental disorder on psychiatric family history data. *Am. J. Psychiatr.* 151:574–79

Clark D. 1983. On the induction of depressed mood in the laboratory: evaluation and comparison of the Velten and musical procedures. *Adv. Behav. Res. Ther.* 5:27–49

Clark LA, Watson D, Reynolds S. 1995. Diagnosis and classification of psychopathology: challenges to the current system and future directions. *Annu. Rev. Psychol.* 46: 121–53

Cloninger CR, Martin RL, Guze SB, Clayton PJ. 1985. Diagnoses and prognosis in schizophrenia. *Arch. Gen. Psychiatr.* 42: 15–25

Cohen JD, Targ E, Servan-Schreiber D, Spiegel D. 1992. The fabric of thought disorder: a cognitive neuroscience approach to disturbances in the processing of context in schizophrenia. In *Cognitive and Clinical Disorders,* ed. DJ Stein, JE Young, pp. 99–127. New York: Academic

Cohen P, Cohen J. 1984. The clinician's illusion. *Arch. Gen. Psychiatr.* 41:1178–82

Colby KM. 1975. *Artificial Paranoia: A Computer Simulation Model of Paranoid Processes.* New York: Pergamon

Cole D. 1993. Models of cognitive mediation and moderation in child depression. *J. Abnorm. Psychol.* 102:271–81

Coryell WH, Zimmerman M. 1987. HPA-axis abnormalities in psychiatrically well controls. *Psychiatr. Res.* 20:265–73

Coyne JC. 1994. Self-reported distress: analog or ersatz depression? *Psychol. Bull.* 116: 29–45

Coyne JC, Gotlib IH. 1983. The role of cognition in depression: a critical appraisal. *Psychol. Bull.* 94:472–505

Crabbe JC, Belknap JK, Buck KJ. 1994. Genetic and animal models of alcohol and drug abuse. *Science* 264:1715–23

Curtis D, Gurling H. 1990. Unsound methodology in investigating a pseudoautosomal locus in schizophrenia. *Br. J. Psychiatr.* 156: 415–16

Daniel DG, Goldberg TE, Gibbons RD, Weinberger DR. 1991. Lack of a bimodal distribution of ventricular size in schizophrenia: a gaussian mixture analysis of 1056 cases and controls. *Biol. Psychiatr.* 30: 887–903

Davis JM, Koslow SH, Gibbons RD, Maas JW, Bowden CL, et al. 1988. Cerebrospinal fluid and urinary biogenic amines in depressed patients and healthy controls. *Arch. Gen. Psychiatr.* 45:705–17

DeGiacomo P, Pierri G, Lefons E, Mich L. 1990. A technique to simulate human interaction: relational styles leading to a schizophrenic communication pattern and back to normal. *Acta Psychiatr. Scand.* 82: 413–19

Depue RA, Monroe SM. 1978. Learned helplessness in the perspective of the depressive disorders: conceptual and definitional issues. *J. Abnorm. Psychol.* 87:3–20

Docherty JP, Fiester SJ, Shea T. 1986. Syndrome diagnosis and personality disorder. *Am. Psychiatr. Assoc. Annu. Rev.* 5:315–55

Dodge KA. 1993. Social-cognitive mechanisms in the development of conduct disorders and depression. *Annu. Rev. Psychol.* 44:559–84

Eaton WW, Dryman A, Sorenson A, McCutcheon A. 1989. DSM-III major depressive disorder in the community: a latent class analysis of data from the NIMH Epidemiologic Catchment Area program. *Br. J. Psychiatr.* 155:48–54

Ellickson PL, Hays RD, Bell RM. 1992. Stepping through the drug use sequence: longitudinal scalogram analysis of initiation and regular use. *J. Abnorm. Psychol.* 101: 441–51

Erlenmeyer-Kimling L, Golden RR, Cornblatt BA. 1989. A taxometric analysis of cognitive and neuromotor variables in children at risk for schizophrenia. *J. Abnorm. Psychol.* 98:203–8

Farrington DP. 1991. Longitudinal research strategies: advantages, problems, and prospects. *J. Am. Acad. Child Adol. Psychiatr.* 30:369–74

First MB, Spitzer RL, Gibbon M, Williams JBW. 1995. Structured Clinical Interview for DSM-IV Axis I Disorders—Patient Edition (SCID-I/P, Version 2.0). New York: Bimetr. Res. Dep.

Folstein MF, Romanoski AJ, Nestadt G, Chahal R, Merchant A, et al. 1985. Brief report on the clinical reappraisal of the Diagnostic Interview Schedule carried out at the Johns Hopkins site of the Epidemiological Catchment Area Program of the NIMH. *Psychol. Med.* 15:809–14

Fowles DC. 1992. Schizophrenia: diathesis-stress revisited. *Annu. Rev. Psychol.* 43: 303–36

Gangestad S, Snyder M. 1985. "To carve nature at its joints": on the existence of discrete classes in personality. *Psychol. Rev.* 92:317–49

Gangestad S, Snyder M. 1991. Taxonomic analysis redux: some statistical considerations for testing a latent class model. *J. Pers. Soc. Psychol.* 61:141–46

Garber J, Hollon SD. 1991. What can specificity designs say about causality in psychopathology research? *Psychol. Bull.* 110: 129–36

Garfield DAS, Rapp C. 1994. Application of artificial intelligence principles to the analysis of "crazy" speech. *J. Nerv. Ment. Dis.* 182:205–11

Gibbons RD, Hedeker D. 1994. Application of random-effects probit regression models. *J. Consult. Clin. Psychol.* 62:285–96

Gibbons RD, Hedeker D, Elkin I, Waternaux C, Kraemer HC, et al. 1993. Some conceptual and statistical issues in analysis of longitudinal psychiatric data: application to the NIMH treatment of depression collaborative research program dataset. *Arch. Gen. Psychiatr.* 50:739–50

Golden RR. 1982. A taxometric model for the detection of a conjectured latent taxon. *Multivariate Behav. Res.* 17:389–416

Golden RR. 1991. See Grove & Cicchetti 1991, pp. 259–94

Good B, Good MD. 1986. The cultural context of diagnosis and therapy: a view from medical anthropology. In *Mental Health Research in Minority Communities: Development of Culturally Sensitive Training Programs,* ed. MR Miranda, HHL Kitano, pp. 1–27. Rockville, MD: NIMH

Goodwin AH, Sher KJ. 1993. Effects of induced mood on diagnostic interviewing: evidence for a mood and memory effect. *Psychol. Assess.* 5:197–202

Gotlib IH. 1984. Depression and general psychopathology in university students. *J. Abnorm. Psychol.* 93:19–30

Gotlib IH, Lewinsohn PM, Seeley JR. 1995. Symptoms versus a diagnosis of depression: differences in psychosocial functioning. *J. Consult. Clin. Psychol.* 63:90–100

Graham JW, Collins LM, Wugalter SE, Chung JK, Hansen WB. 1991. Modeling transitions in latent stage-sequential processes: a substance use prevention example. *J. Consult. Clin. Psychol.* 59:48–57

Grayson D. 1986. Assessment of evidence for a categorical view of schizophrenia. *Arch. Gen. Psychiatr.* 43:712–13

Grayson D. 1987. Can categorical and dimensional views of psychiatric illness be distinguished? *Br. J. Psychiatr.* 151:355–61

Grove WM, Andreasen NC. 1986. See Millon & Klerman 1986, pp. 347–62

Grove WM, Andreasen NC. 1989. Quantitative and qualitative distinctions between psychiatric disorders. In *The Validity of Psychiatric Diagnosis,* ed. LN Robins, JE Barrett, pp. 127–41. New York: Raven

Grove WM, Andreasen NC, Young MA, Endicott J, Leller MB, et al. 1987. Isolation and characterization of a nuclear depressive syndrome. *Psychol. Med.* 17:471–84

Grove WM, Cicchetti D, eds. 1991. *Thinking Clearly about Psychology,* Vol. 1, *Personality and Psychopathology.* Minneapolis: Univ. Minn. Press

Grove WM, Meehl PE. 1993. Simple regression-based procedures for taxometric investigations. *Psychol. Rep.* 73:707–37

Hagenaars JA. 1990. *Categorical Longitudinal Data.* Newbury Park, CA: Sage

Halbreich U, Bakhai Y, Bacon KB, Goldstein S, Asnis GM, et al. 1989. The normalcy of self-proclaimed "normal volunteers." *Am. J. Psychiatr.* 146:1052–55

Harris GJ, Rice ME, Quinsey VL. 1994. Psychopathy as a taxon: evidence that psychopaths are a discrete class. *J. Consult. Clin. Psychol.* 62:387–97

Harvey I, McGuffin D, Williams M, Toone BK. 1990. The ventricle-brain ratio (VBR) in functional psychoses: an admixture analysis. *Psychiatr. Res.: Neuroimaging Suppl.* 35:61–69

Haslam N, Beck AT. 1994. Subtyping major depression: a taxometric analysis. *J. Abnorm. Psychol.* 103:686–92

Hays RD, Marshall GN, Wang EYI, Sherbourne CD. 1994. Four-year cross-lagged associations between physical and mental health in the medical outcomes study. *J. Consult. Clin. Psychol.* 62:441–49

Henderson AS. 1994. Does aging protect against depression? *Soc. Psychiatr. Psychiatr. Epidemiol.* 29:107–9

Henry GT. 1990. *Practical Sampling.* Newbury Park, CA: Sage

Hicks LE. 1984. Conceptual and empirical analysis of some assumptions of an explicitly typological theory. *J. Pers. Soc. Psychol.* 46:1118–31

Hoffman RE. 1987. Computer simulations of

neural information processing and the schizophrenia-mania dichotomy. *Arch. Gen. Psychiatr.* 44:178–88

Hoffman RE. 1992. Attractor neural networks and psychotic disorders. *Psychiatr. Ann.* 22:119–24

Hoffman RE, McGlashan TH. 1993. Parallel distributed processing and the emergence of schizophrenic symptoms. *Schizophr. Bull.* 19:119–40

Horowitz MJ. 1975. Intrusive and repetitive thoughts after experimental stress: a summary. *Arch. Gen. Psychiatr.* 32:1457–63

Hoyle RH, Smith GT. 1994. Formulating clinical research hypotheses as structural equation models: a conceptual overview. *J. Consult. Clin. Psychol.* 62:429–40

Hsu LM. 1989. Random sampling, randomization, and equivalence of contrasted groups in psychotherapy outcome research. *J. Consult. Clin. Psychol.* 57:131–37

Iacono WG. 1991. See Grove & Cicchetti 1991, pp. 430–50

Kandel ER. 1983. From metapsychology to molecular biology: explorations into the nature of anxiety. *Am. J. Psychiatr.* 140: 1277–93

Kelsey J, Thompson DW, Evans AS. 1986. *Methods in Obsevational Epidemiology.* New York: Oxford Univ. Press

Kendall PC, Flannery-Schroeder EC. 1995. Rigor, but not rigor mortis, in depression research. *J. Pers. Soc. Psychol.* 68:892–94

Kendall PC, Hollon SD, Beck AT, Hammen CL, Ingram RE. 1987. Issues and recommendations regarding the use of the Beck Depression Inventory. *Cogn. Ther. Res.* 11: 289–99

Kendell R. 1975. *The Role of Diagnosis in Psychiatry.* Oxford: Blackwell

Kendler KS. 1990. The super-normal control group in psychiatric genetics: possible artifactual evidence for coaggregation. *Psychiatr. Genet.* 1:45–53

Kendler KS, Eaton WW. 1988. The proband method in psychiatric epidemiology: a bias associated with differences in family size. *Acta Psychiatr. Scand.* 77:511–14

Kendler KS, Silberg JL, Neale MC, Kessler RC, Heath AC, et al. 1991. The family history method: Whose psychiatric history is measured? *Am. J. Psychiatr.* 148:1501–4

Kenny DA, Judd CM. 1984. Estimating the nonlinear and interactive effects of latent variables. *Psychol. Bull.* 90:201–10

Kenny DA, Zautra A. 1995. The trait-state-error model for multiwave data. *J. Consult. Clin. Psychol.* 63:52–59

Kessler RC, McGonagle KA, Zhao S, Nelson CB, Hughes M, et al. 1994. Lifetime and 12-month prevalence of DSM-III-R psychiatric disorders in the United States. *Arch. Gen. Psychiatr.* 51:8–19

Knight RA. 1987. Relating cognitive processes

to symptoms: a strategy to counter methodological difficulties. In *Positive and Negative Symptoms in Psychosis: Description, Research, and Future Directions,* ed. PD Harvey, EE Walker, pp. 1–29. Hillsdale, NJ: Erlbaum

Korfine L, Lenzenweger MF. 1995. The taxonicity of schizotypy: a replication. *J. Abnorm. Psychol.* 104:26–31

Lahey BB, Loeber R, Hart E, Frick PJ, Applegate B, et al. 1995. Four-year longitudinal study of conduct disorder in boys: patterns and predictors of persistence. *J. Abnorm. Psychol.* 104:83–93

Langenbucher JW, Chung T. 1995. Onset and staging of DSM-IV alcohol dependence using mean age and survival-hazard methods. *J. Abnorm. Psychol.* 104:346–54

Lenzenweger MF, Cornblatt BA, Putnick M. 1991. Schizotypy and sustained attention. *J. Abnorm. Psychol.* 100:84–89

Lenzenweger MF, Korfine L. 1992. Confirming the latent structure and base rate of schizotypy: a taxometric analysis. *J. Abnorm. Psychol.* 101:567–71

Lewis-Fernandez R, Kleinman A. 1994. Culture, personality, and psychopathology. *J. Abnorm. Psychol.* 103:67–71

Li TK, Lumeng L, Doolittle DP. 1993. Selective breeding for alcohol preference and associated responses. *Behav. Genet.* 23: 163–70

Lilienfeld SO, Waldman ID, Israel AC. 1994. A critical examination of the use of the term and concept of "comorbidity" in psychopathology research. *Clin. Psychol. Sci. Pract.* 1:71–83

Loeber R, Farrington DP. 1994. Problems and solutions in longitudinal and experimental treatment studies of child psychopathology and delinquency. *J. Consult. Clin. Psychol.* 62:887–900

Loehlin JC. 1992. *Latent Variable Models: An Introduction to Factor, Path, and Structural Analysis.* Hillsdale, NJ: Erlbaum. 2nd ed.

Luthar S, Zigler E. 1991. Vulnerability and competence: a review of research on resilience in childhood. *Am. J. Orthopsychiatr.* 61:6–22

MacLean A, Cairns J, Knowles JB. 1983. REM latency and depression: computer simulations based on the results of phase delay of sleep in normal subjects. *Psychiatr. Res.* 9:69–79

Malaspina D, Colemann EA, Quitkin M, Amador XF, Kaufmann CA, et al. 1994. Effects of pharmacologic catecholamine manipulation on smooth pursuit eye movements in normals. *Schizphr. Res.* 13: 151–60

Marsella AJ, Kameoka VA. 1989. Ethnocultural issues in the assessment of psychopathology. In *Measuring Mental Illness: Psy-*

chometric Assessment for Clinicians. The Clinical Practice Series, No. 8, ed. S Wetzler, pp. 231–56. Washington, DC: Am. Psychiatr. Press

Martin M. 1990. On the induction of mood. Clin. Psychol. Rev. 10:669–97

Matarazzo JD. 1983. The reliability of psychiatric and psychological diagnosis. Clin. Psychol. Rev. 3:103–45

McArdle JJ, Epstein D. 1987. Latent growth curves with developmental structural equation models. Child Dev. 58:110–33

McClelland GH, Judd CM. 1993. Statistical difficulties of detecting interactions and moderator effects. Psychol. Bull. 114: 376–90

McKinney WT. 1988. Models of Mental Disorders: A New Comparative Psychiatry. New York: Plenum

Mednick SA, McNeil TF. 1968. Current methodology in research on the etiology of schiozophrenia: serious difficulties which suggest the use of the high-risk-group method. Psychol. Bull. 70:681–93

Meehl PE. 1970. Nuisance variables and the ex post facto design. In Minnesota Studies in the Philosophy of Science, ed. M Radner, S Winokur, 4:373–402. Minneapolis: Univ. Minn. Press

Meehl PE. 1971. High school yearbooks: a reply to Schwartz. J. Abnorm. Psychol. 77: 143–48

Meehl PE. 1973. MAXCOV-HITMAX: a taxonomic search for loose genetic syndromes. In Psychodiagnosis: Selected Papers, pp. 200–24. Minneapolis: Univ. Minn. Press

Meehl PE. 1979. A funny thing happened to us on the way to the latent entities. J. Pers. Assess. 43:563–81

Meehl PE. 1992. Factors and taxa, traits and types, differences of degree and differences in kind. J. Pers. 60:117–74

Meehl PE. 1995. Bootstraps taxometrics: solving the classification problem in psychopathology. Am. Psychol. 50:266–75

Meehl PE, Golden RR. 1982. Taxometric methods. In Handbook of Research Methods in Clinical Psychology, ed. P Kendall, J Butcher, pp. 127–81. New York: Wiley

Meehl PE, Yonce LJ. 1994. Taxometric analysis. I. Detecting taxonicity with two quantitative indicators using means above and below a sliding cut (MAMBAC procedure). Psychol. Rep. 74:1059–1274

Mendelsohn GA, Weiss DS, Feimer NR. 1982. Conceptual and empirical analysis of the typological implications of patterns of socialization and femininity. J. Pers. Soc. Psychol. 42:1157–70

Meng ID, Drugan RC. 1993. Sex differences in open-field behavior in response to the beta-carboline FG 7142 in rats. Physiol. Behav. 54:701–5

Meredith W, Tisak J. 1990. Latent curve analysis. Psychometrika 55:107–22

Mezzich AC, Arria AM, Tarter RE, Moss H, Van Thiel DH. 1991. Psychiatric comorbidity in alcoholism: importance of ascertainment source. Alcohol. Clin. Exp. Res. 15:893–98

Millon T, Klerman GL, eds. 1986. Contemporary Directions in Psychopathology: Toward the DSM-IV. New York: Guilford

Mineka S, Hendersen RW. 1985. Controllability and predictability in acquired motivation. Annu. Rev. Psychol. 36:495–529

Mineka S, Zinbarg R. 1991. Animal models of psychopathology. In Clinical Psychology: Historical and Research Foundations, ed. CE Walker, pp. 51–86. New York: Plenum

Moldin SO, Gottesman II, Erlenmeyer-Kimling L. 1987. Searching for the psychometric boundaries of schizophrenia: evidence from the New York High-Risk study. J. Abnorm. Psychol. 96:354–63

Monroe SM, Steiner SC. 1986. Social support and psychopathology: interrelations with preexisting disorder, stress, and personality. J. Abnorm. Psychol. 95:29–39

Morey LC. 1988. The categorical representation of personality disorder: a cluster analysis of the DSM-III-R features. J. Abnorm. Psychol. 97:314–21

Muthen B. 1991. Analysis of longitudinal data using latent variable models with varying parameters. In Best Methods for the Analysis of Change: Recent Advances, Unanswered Questions, Future Directions, ed. L Collins, J Horn, pp. 1–17. Washington, DC: Am. Psychol. Assoc.

Muthen B. 1992. Latent variable modeling in epidemiology. Alcohol Health. Res. World 16:286–92

National Institutes of Health. 1994. NIH Guidelines on the inclusion of women and minorities as subjects in clinical research. NIH Guide 23(10), Mar. 11., P.T. 34

Newcomb MD. 1994. Drug use and intimate relationships among women and men: separating specific from general effects in prospective data using structural equation models. J. Consult. Clin. Psychol. 62: 463–76

Nuechterlein KH. 1990. Methodological considerations in the search for indicators of vulnerability to severe psychopathology. In Event Related Brain Potentials: Basic Issues and Applications, ed. JW Rohrbaugh, R Parasuramn, R Johnson Jr, pp. 364–73. New York: Oxford Univ. Press

Nuechterlein KH, Dawson ME. 1984. A heuristic vulnerability/stress model of schizophrenic episodes. Schizophr. Bull. 10: 300–12

Ohman A, Soares JJ. 1993. On the automatic nature of phobic fear: conditioned electrodermal responses to masked fear-relevant stimuli. *J. Abnorm. Psychol.* 102: 121–32

Olivier B, Molewijk E, van Oorschot R, van der Poel G, Zethof T, et al. 1994. *Eur. Neuropsychopharmacol.* 4:93–102

Olson SC, Bornstein RA, Schwarzkopf SB, Nasrallah HA. 1993. Are controls in schizophrenia research "normal"? *Annu. Clin. Psychiatr.* 5:1–5

Overmier JB, Patterson J. 1988. Animal models of human psychopathology. In *Animal Models of Psychiatirc Disorders,* ed. P Simon, P Soubrie, D Widlocher, 1:1–35. Basel: Karger

Overstreet DH. 1986. Selective breeding for increased cholinergic function: development of a new animal model of depression. *Biol. Psychiatr.* 21:49–58

Patterson GR. 1993. Orderly change in a stable world: the antisocial trait as chimera. *J. Consult. Clin. Psychol.* 61:911–19

Pfohl B, Blum N, Zimmerman M. 1995. *Structured Interview for DSM-IV Personality (SIDP-IV).* Iowa City, IA: Dep. Psychiatr.

Piacentini JC, Cohen P, Cohen J. 1992. Combining discrepant diagnostic information from multiple sources: Are complex algorithms better than simple ones? *J. Abnorm. Child Psychol.* 20:51–63

Pickles A. 1993. Stages, precursors and causes in development. In *Precursors and Causes in Development and Psychopathology,* ed. DF Hay, A Angold, pp. 23–49. Chichester: Wiley

Plomin R, Owen MJ, McGuffin P. 1994. The genetic basis of complex human behavior. *Science* 264:1733–39

Post RM, Weiss SRB. 1989. Non-homologous animal models of affective disorders: clinical relevance of sensitization and kindling. In *Animal Models of Depression,* ed. GF Koob, CL Ehlers, DJ Kupfer, pp. 30–54. Boston: Birkhauser

Rapoport JL, Ryland DH, Kriete M. 1992. Drug treatment of canine acral lick: an animal model of obsessive-compulsive disorder. *Arch. Gen. Psychiatr.* 48:517–21

Raudenbush SW, Chang W-S. 1993. Application of a hierarchical linear model to the study of adolescent deviance in an overlapping cohort design. *J. Consult. Clin. Psychol.* 61:941–51

Reich W, Earls F. 1987. Rules of making psychiatric diagnoses in children on the basis of multiple sources of information: preliminary strategies. *J. Abnorm. Child Psychol.* 15:601–16

Rice JP, Rochberg N, Endicott J, Lavori PW, Miller C. 1992. Stability of psychiatric diagnoses: an application to the affective disorders. *Arch. Gen. Psychiatr.* 49:824–30

Richardson JS. 1991. Animal models of depression reflect changing views on the essence and etiology of depressive disorders in humans. *Prog. Neuro-psychopharmacol. Biol. Psychiatr.* 15:199–204

Riley AL, Wetherington CL. 1989. Schedule-induced polydipsia: Is the rat a small furry human? (An analysis of an animal model of human alcoholism.) In *Contemporary Learning Theories: Instrumental Conditioning Theory and the Impact of Biological Constraints on Learning,* ed. SB Klein, RR Mowrer, pp. 205–36. Hillsdale, NJ: Erlbaum

Riso LP, Klein DN, Anderson RL, Ouimette PC, Lizardi H. 1994. Concordance between patients and informants on the Personality Disorder Examination. *Am. J. Psychiatr.* 151:568–73

Robins LN. 1985. Epidemiology: reflections on testing the validity of psychiatric interviews. *Arch. Gen. Psychiatr.* 42:918–24

Robins LN. 1994. How recognizing "comorbidities" in psychopathology may lead to an improved research nosology. *Clin. Psychol. Sci. Pract.* 1:93–95

Robins LN, Helzer JE, Ratcliff KS, Seyfried W. 1982. Validity of the Diagnostic Interview Schedule, version II: DSM-III diagnoses. *Psychol. Med.* 12:855–70

Robins LN, Locke BZ, Regier DA. 1991b. An overview of psychiatric disorders in America. In *Psychiatric Disorders in America,* ed. LN Robins, DA Regier, pp. 328–66. New York: Free Press

Robins LN, Cottler LB, Keating S. 1991a. *NIMH Diagnostic Interview Schedule, Version III—Revised (DIS-III-R): Question by Question Specifications.* St. Louis: Washington Univ. Sch. Med.

Rogers R. 1995. *Diagnostic and Structured Interviewing: A Handbook for Psychologists.* Odessa, FL: Psychol. Assess. Resour.

Rogler LH. 1989. The meaning of culturally sensitive research in mental health. *Am. J. Psychiatr.* 146:296–303

Rothman KJ. 1986. *Modern Epidemiology.* Boston: Little, Brown

Rutter M. 1987. Psychosocial resilience and protective mechanisms. *Am. J. Orthopsychiatr.* 57:316–31

Rutter M. 1994a. Comorbidity: meanings and mechanisms. *Clin. Psychol. Sci. Pract.* 1: 100–3

Rutter M. 1994b. Beyond longitudinal data: causes, consequences, changes, and continuity. *J. Consult. Clin. Psychol.* 62:928–40

Schlesselmann J. 1982. *Case Control Studies: Design, Conduct, and Analysis.* New York: Oxford Univ. Press

Schwartz S, Link BG. 1989. The 'well control' artifact in case/control studies of specific psychiatric disorders. *Psychol. Med.* 19: 737–42

Semler G, Witchen HU, Joschke K, Zaudig M, von Geiso T, et al. 1987. Test-retest reliability of a standardized psychiatric interview (DIS/CIDI). *Eur. Arch. Psychiatr. Neurol. Sci.* 236:214–22

Shanks N, Zalcman S, Zacharko RM, Anisman H. 1991. Alterations of central norepinephrine, dopamine and serotonin in several strains of mice following acute stressor exposure. *Pharmacol. Biochem. Behav.* 38: 69–75

Sher KJ. 1991. *Children of Alcoholics: A Critical Appraisal of Theory and Research.* Chicago: Univ. Chicago Press

Sher KJ, Frost RO, Otto R. 1983. Cognitive deficits in compulsive checkers: an exploratory study. *Behav. Res. Ther.* 21: 357–63

Sherbourne CD, Wells KB, Hays RD, Rogers W, Burnam MA, Judd LL. 1994. Subthreshold depression and depressive disorder: clinical characteristics of general medical and mental health specialty outpatients. *Am. J. Psychiatr.* 151:1777–84

Singer JD, Willett JB. 1991. Modeling the days of our lives: using survival analysis when designing and analyzing longitudinal studies of duration and the timing of events. *Psychol. Bull.* 110:288–90

Smith GT, Goldman MS, Greenbaum PE, Christiansen BA. 1995. Expectancy for social facilitation from drinking: the divergent paths of high-expectancy and low-expectancy adolescents. *J. Abnorm. Psychol.* 104:32–40

Spitzer RL. 1983. Psychiatric diagnosis: are clinicians still necessary? *Comp. Psychiatr.* 24:399–411

Spitzer RL. 1994. Psychiatric "co-occurrence": I'll stick with "comorbidity." *Clin. Psychol. Sci. Pract.* 1:88–92

Spitzer RL, Endicott J. 1978a. Medical and mental disorder: proposed definition and criteria. In *Critical Issues in Psychiatric Diagnosis*, ed. RL Spitzer, DF Klein, pp. 15–39. New York: Raven

Spitzer RL, Endicott J. 1978b. *Schedule of Affective Disorders and Schizophrenia.* New York: Biometr. Res. 3rd ed.

Stacy AW, Newcomb MD, Bentler PM. 1991. Personality, problem drinking, and drunk driving: mediating, moderating, and direct effect models. *J. Pers. Soc. Psychol.* 60: 795–811

Stanger C, Achenbach TM, Verhulst FC. 1994. Accelerating longitudinal research on child psychopathology: a practical example. *Psychol. Assess.* 6:102–7

Steele CM, Josephs RA. 1990. Alcohol myopia: its prized and dangerous effects. *Am. Psychol.* 45:921–33

Stein DJ, Dodman NH, Borchelt P, Hollander E. 1994. Behavioral disorders in veterinary practice: relevance to psychiatry. *Comp. Psychiatr.* 35:275–85

Steyer R, Ferring D, Schmitt MJ. 1992. States

and traits in psychological assessment. *Eur. J. Psychol. Assess.* 8:79–98

Steyer R, Macjen A-M, Schwenkmezger P, Buchner A. 1989. A latent state-trait anxiety model and its application to determine consistency and specificity coefficients. *Anxiety Res.* 1:281–99

Steyer R, Schwenkmezger P, Auer A. 1990. The emotional and cognitive components of trait anxiety: a latent state-trait anxiety model. *Pers. Individ. Diff.* 11:125–34

Stoolmiller M, Duncan T, Bank B, Patterson GR. 1993. Some problems and solutions in the study of change: significant patterns in client resistance. *J. Consult. Clin. Psychol.* 61:920–28

Sweeney JA, Clementz BA, Escobar MD, Li S, Pauler DK, et al. 1993. Mixture analysis of pursuit eye-tracking dysfunction in schizophrenia. *Biol. Psychiatr.* 34:331–40

Takahashi JS, Pinto LH, Vitaterna MH. 1994. Forward and reverse genetic approaches to behavior in the mouse. *Science* 264: 1724–33

Tate RL, Hokanson JE. 1993. Analyzing individual status and change with hierarchical linear models: illustration with depression in college students. *J. Pers.* 61:181–206

Tennen H, Hall JA, Affleck G. 1995a. Depression research methodologies in the *J. Pers. Soc. Psychol.: a* review and critique. *J. Pers. Soc. Psychol.* 68:870–84

Tennen H, Hall JA, Affleck G. 1995b. Rigor, rigor mortis, and conspiratorial views of depression research. *J. Pers. Soc. Psychol.* 68:895–900

Torgersen S. 1987. Sampling problems in twin research. *J. Psychiatr. Res.* 21:385–90

Trull TJ. 1995. Borderline personality disorder features in nonclinical young adults. 1. Identification and validation. *Psychol. Assess.* 7:33–41

Trull TJ, Sher KJ. 1994. Relationship between the five-factor model of personality and Axis I disorders in a nonclinical sample. *J. Abnorm. Psychol.* 103:350–60

Trull TJ, Widiger TA, Guthrie P. 1990. Categorical versus dimensional status of borderline personality disorder. *J. Abnorm. Psychol.* 99:40–48

Tsuang MT, Fleming JA, Kendler KS, Gruenberg AS. 1988. Selection of controls for family studies. *Arch. Gen. Psychiatr.* 45: 1006–8

Tyrer P, Alexander MS, Cicchetti D, Cohen MS, Remington M. 1979. Reliability of a schedule for rating personality disorders. *Br. J. Psychiatr.* 135:168–74

Tyrka AR, Cannon TD, Haslam N, Mednick SA, Schulsinger F, et al. 1995. The latent structure of schizotypy. I. Premorbid indicators of a taxon of individuals at risk for schizophrenia-spectrum disorders. *J. Abnorm. Psychol.* 104:173–83

Vandiver T, Sher KJ. 1991. Temporal stability of the Diagnostic Interview Schedule. *Psychol. Assess.* 3:277–81

Verhulst FC, Koot HM. 1991. Longitudinal research in child and adolescent psychiatry. *J. Am. Acad. Child Adol. Psychiatr.* 30: 361–68

von Eye A, Clogg CC, eds. 1994. *Latent Variables Analysis: Applications for Developmental Research.* Thousand Oaks, CA: Sage

Vredenburg K, Flett GL, Krames L. 1993. Analogue versus clinical depression: a critical reappraisal. *Psychol. Bull.* 113: 327–44

Wakefield JC. 1992a. The concept of mental disorder: on the boundary between biological facts and social values. *Am. Psychol.* 47:373–88

Wakefield JC. 1992b. Disorder as harmful dysfunction: a conceptual critique of DSM-III-R's definition of mental disorder. *Psychol. Rev.* 99:232–47

Wakefield JC. 1993. Limits of operationalization: a critique of Spitzer and Endicott's (1978) proposed operational criteria for mental disorder. *J. Abnorm. Psychol.* 102: 160–72

Ward CH, Beck AT, Mendelson M, Mock JE, Erbauch JK. 1962. The psychiatric nomenclature. *Arch. Gen. Psychiatr.* 7:198–205

Weary G, Edwards JA, Jacobson JA. 1995. Depression research methodologies in the *J. Pers. Soc. Psychol.:* a reply. *J. Pers. Soc. Psychol.* 68:885–91

Wells KB, Burnam MA, Leake B, Robins LN. 1988. Agreement between face-to-face and telephone administered versions of the depression section of the NIMH Diagnostic Interview Schedule. *J. Psychiatr. Res.* 22: 207–20

Westermeyer J. 1988. National differences in psychiatric morbidity: methodological issues, scientific interpretations and social implications. *Acta Psychiatr. Scand.* 344: 23–31 (Suppl.)

Widiger TA, Ford-Black MM. 1994. Diagnoses and disorders. *Clin. Psychol. Sci. Pract.* 1:84–87

Widiger TA, Mangine S, Corbitt EM, Ellis CG, Thomas GV. 1995. *Personality Disorder Interview—IV: A Semistructured Interview for the Assessment of Personality Disorders.* Odessa, FL: PAR

Widiger TA, Shea T. 1991. Differentiation of Axis I and Axis II disorders. *J. Abnorm. Psychol.* 100:399–406

Widiger TA, Spitzer RL. 1991. Sex bias in the diagnosis of personality disorders: conceptual and methodological issues. *Clin. Psychol. Rev.* 11:1–22

Widiger TA, Trull TJ. 1991. Diagnosis and clinical assessment. *Annu. Rev. Psychol.* 42:109–33

Wierson M, Forehand R. 1994. Introduction to special section: the role of longitudinal data with child psychopathology and treatment: preliminary comments and issues. *J. Consult. Clin. Psychol.* 62:883–86

Willett JB, Singer JD. 1993. Investigating onset, cessation, relapse, and recovery: why you should, and how you can, use discrete-time survival analysis to examine event occurrence. *J. Consult. Clin. Psychol.* 61: 952–65

Willner P. 1991. Animal models of depression. In *Behavioral Models in Psychopharmacology: Theoretical, Industrial and Clinical Perspectives,* ed. P Willner, pp. 91–125. Cambridge: Cambridge Univ. Press

Wood PK, Sher KJ, von Eye A. 1994. Conjugate methods in configural frequency analysis. *Biometr. J.* 36:387–410

Young MA. 1982. Evaluating diagnostic criteria: a latent class paradigm. *J. Psychiatr. Res.* 17:285–96

Young MA, Scheftner WA, Klerman GL, Andreasen NC, Hirschfeld R. 1986. The endogenous sub-type of depression: a study of its internal construct validity. *Br. J. Psychiatr.* 148:257–67

Young MA, Tanner MA, Meltzer HY. 1982. Operational definitions of schizophrenia: What do they identify? *J. Nerv. Ment. Dis.* 170:443–47

Zimmerman M. 1994. Diagnosing personality disorders: a review of issues and research methods. *Arch. Gen. Psychiatr.* 51:225–45

Zimmerman M, Pfohl B, Coryell W, Stangl D, Corenthal C. 1988. Diagnosing personality disorder in depressed patients: a comparison of patient and informant interviews. *Arch. Gen. Psychiatr.* 45:733–37

Zinbarg RE, Barlow DH, Brown TA, Hertz RM. 1992. Cognitive-behavioral approaches to the nature and treatment of anxiety disorders. *Annu. Rev. Psychol.* 43: 235–67

Zubin J, Steinhauer SR, Day R, van Kammen DP. 1985. Schizophrenia at the crossroads: a blueprint for the 80s. *Compr. Psychiatr.* 26:217–40

Annu. Rev. Psychol. 1996. 47:401–29

THE SOCIAL STRUCTURE OF SCHOOLING

Sanford M. Dornbusch, Kristan L. Glasgow, and I-Chun Lin

Department of Sociology, Stanford University, Stanford, California 94305-2047

KEY WORDS: mass education, stratification, professional bureaucracy, teaching conditions, tracking

ABSTRACT

The term *social structure* refers to a relatively enduring pattern of social arrangements or interrelations within a particular society, organization, or group. This chapter reviews how the social structure of the larger society and the organizational structure of schools affect the educational process within American schools. The institutional context of schooling is first discussed. The ideology of mass education, social stratification, status attainment, credentialism, and the emphasis on ability differences are considered. The focus then shifts to the organizational structure of schools, beginning with a discussion of the external social context for school organization. Attention is given to professionalism and bureaucracy, institutional forms of organization, decentralized control, and community influences. Finally, the internal structure of school organization is considered: teachers' working conditions, status differences among students, and curriculum tracking. Throughout, the emphasis is on ways in which social structure influences what is taught in school, how it is taught, and what is learned.

CONTENTS

0066-4308/96/0201-0401$08.00

INTRODUCTION

This review examines the ways in which social structural contexts affect the educational process: namely, what is taught in school, how it is taught, and what is learned. The term *social structure* refers to a relatively enduring pattern of social arrangements or interrelations within a particular society, organization, or social group. Thus, social structure may take different forms depending on the level of social organization.

We specifically focus on how the social structure of the larger society and the organizational structure of schools affect the educational process within primary and secondary schools in the United States. At the societal level, social structure is expressed in institutional form, consisting of an integrated pattern of social ideology, norms, and roles. At the organizational level, social structure is embodied both by the external context within which an organization operates and by the internal coordinating mechanisms that give rise to the organization's visible form.

Our review of the social structure of schooling is limited to those properties of institutional and organizational structure that have significant effects on the educational process. As we describe select aspects of these structural forms, we attempt to show how they are related to various educational outcomes. The interdependent relation between social structures and the behavior of actors (individual or corporate) has long been a central concern of the social sciences. In an educational setting, the interactions among school administrators, teachers, counselors, parents, and students are governed in part by the social structures in which they participate.

We begin by describing the institutional context of schooling and focus specifically on the ideology of mass education, social stratification, and individual differences in ability. The review then shifts to the organizational structure of schools and examines the external social context within which schools operate. Particular attention is given to professionalism and bureaucracy, institutional forms of organization, decentralized control, and community influences. We then consider the internal structure of school organization, which includes teachers' working conditions, status differences among students in the classroom, and the system of curriculum tracking.

THE INSTITUTIONAL CONTEXT OF SCHOOLING

The Ideology of Mass Education

All over the world, schooling has been identified as a key component of the nation-state. It is striking that even countries without the resources to pay for a system of mass education often incorporate the right to education in their constitutions (Kurian 1982). Because education is viewed as a part of modernity, it is ringingly endorsed even in places where it is largely unavailable. This general acceptance of education as a central ideological component of the state helps to create a worldwide, somewhat standardized, and highly rationalized system of schooling (Benavot et al 1991).

As new nations seek to replicate the characteristics of schooling in developed societies, similarities of structure become normative. While there is some variability across countries, that all schools should have certain features is taken for granted. For example, administrators serve as coordinators of school activities, students are grouped by grade level, most teachers lecture, students are expected to listen to their teachers, and students are tested on their knowledge of the prescribed curriculum. There are more similarities than differences in the structures of schools across national boundaries, even though nations differ in the extent to which they implement mass education (Ramirez & Meyer 1980).

A central goal of mass education is the development of a properly trained and socialized citizenry. As Boli et al (1985, p. 149) noted, "It is surprising how consistently educational systems attempt to build collective society by enhancing individual development." The ideology of mass education embraces the notion that all students, regardless of position in the larger social order, shall receive sufficient education to participate fully as citizens and workers.

The American educational system, for example, attempts to extend educational opportunity to as many people as possible (Karabel 1977, Salomone et al 1982). Turner (1960) described the US educational model as *contest mobility;* individuals compete with others on an equal footing and distinguish themselves with respect to their own merits. With contest mobility, no rigid criteria define excellence, nor are there specified ages or grades at which "winners" are selected. Students who have not done well have an opportunity to win in other contests.

By contrast, the English educational system has standards and methods by which gifted individuals are quickly identified and then cultivated for assimilation into the elite community. The British system of *sponsored mobility,* unlike the American contest model, stipulates that students follow rules defined by the elite (Turner 1960). Whereas the sponsored mobility model aims to identify gifted youth early in life, the American system of contest mobility is more compatible with the ideology of mass education.

The educational transformations in the United States around 1910 and after World War II represent the first national effort to realize the goal of mass education (Karabel 1977, Trow 1977). Between 1910 and 1940, secondary schools were transformed from elite to mass institutions. Under the new structure of public schooling, admission to high school was open and tuition was free, which allowed universal access to secondary education. As a result, secondary-school attendance during this period rose from 15% to more than

70% for youth 14 to 17. By comparison, in 1993 more than 80% of Americans graduated from high school (Census Bureau 1994). Ironically, there has been increased emphasis on a national "drop-out" problem as the proportion of graduates increases (Rumberger 1987).

A second transformation that took place after World War II ushered in a similar shift within American colleges and universities. At this time, the nation witnessed the burgeoning of the community-college system, a system that attempted to provide educational opportunity at the college level for everyone. Whereas only 2% of Americans were college graduates in 1900, 22% are now (Census Bureau 1975, 1994). Another indicator of the success of mass education in the United States is that the proportion of African-Americans who are college graduates (12.0%) is greater than the proportion of college graduates (9.5%) in Great Britain as a whole (Government Statistical Service 1994, Census Bureau 1994).

It is precisely the ideal of mass education that makes debates about educational inequality so politically charged. In an elite system of schooling, achievement differences among social classes or ethnic groups are assumed. In a system of mass education, group differences in achievement are seen as a glaring problem (Mickelson 1987). The ideology underpinning mass education implies that equality in educational opportunities leads to equality in educational outcomes, but this expectation has not been realized. At the federal level, $7 billion were distributed to schools in 1993 as part of the continuing attempt to reduce achievement disparities across social classes and ethnic groups (Census Bureau 1994). It should be noted, however, that although group differences in achievement remain large, these massive expenditures are believed to have slightly narrowed the achievement gap (Congress of the United States 1986). Thus once again, the ideology of mass education has shaped the educational system and influenced the extent to which social groups gain access to different levels of education.

Social Stratification and Schooling

The relation of educational achievement to social stratification is intricate. On one hand, education is viewed as a mechanism for inheritance. In agrarian societies, for instance, land and livestock are passed from generation to generation. In this way parents transmit their wealth to their children. In urban industrial societies, however, few parents have the capacity to give large amounts of capital to their offspring. Accordingly, the primary way in which parents aid their children economically is to invest in their education.

On the other hand, education is viewed as vital to social mobility. The less privileged are urged to pursue higher education to reach high-status professional and managerial positions. Thus, education is seen as a vehicle both for the inheritance of privilege and for improving the status of those of humble origin.

We briefly consider below some general perspectives on the relation between stratification and education. The topic is important, for the impact of stratification on learning begins in the earliest grades and persists over the long term (Entwisle & Alexander 1993). We then turn to empirical research on status attainment and credentialism. The research findings reported are interpretable in various ways. Consequently, no particular perspective is clearly refuted or supported.

APPROACHES TO STRATIFICATION AND SCHOOLING   Two classic theoretical perspectives in sociology address the link between schooling and social stratification—functionalism and conflict theory. The functional approach views the primary task of schools as one of preparing individuals for occupations in a knowledge-based society. It assumes that the needs of the society determine the behavior of individuals and the distribution of rewards. This perspective is usually interpreted as placing an emphasis on mobility processes rather than on the perpetuation of inequality (Karabel & Halsey 1977).

According to the functional perspective, schools perform two key tasks in modern society. First, schools teach the cognitive skills necessary to perform occupations that require increasingly sophisticated technical knowledge. Second, schools attempt to provide a rational means of selecting persons in order that the most able and motivated persons are sorted into the highest status positions (Davis & Moore 1945). According to Collins (1977), this perspective is based on three basic premises. First, the increase in the number of skills requirements needed to perform many occupations is the result of ongoing technological change; second, formal education equips individuals either with general capacities for learning or with specific skills required for more technical occupations; and third, the rise of educational requirements is a consequence of technological demands that have resulted in a larger proportion of the population completing more years of schooling.

Unlike the functional perspective, the conflict approach views the educational system as an arena for competition among status groups. Conflict theorists, both neo-Weberian and neo-Marxist, emphasize the role of schooling in sustaining a system of structured inequality (Karabel & Halsey 1977). Because social class of origin strongly influences the quality and extent to which an individual is educated, conflict approaches tend to emphasize the perpetuation of existing patterns of inequality rather than social mobility.

The neo-Weberian conflict perspective views educational systems as largely dedicated to perpetuating status cultures (tastes, mannerisms, linguistic style). Employers choose employees on the basis of educational credentials that indicate membership in a status culture compatible with that of the organization. Therefore, conflict theorists maintain that educational systems are shaped by conflicting interests rather than by society's functional needs (Collins 1977, Karabel & Halsey 1977).

According to the neo-Marxist conflict approach, schooling serves as a device for social control and for legitimating power differentials. Schools reproduce the values and personality characteristics necessary for a compliant and efficient labor force (Hurn 1978). Schools serving predominantly working-class communities impart different values (discipline, loyalty, and commitment to the established order) and emphasize different personal qualities (punctuality, docility, and compliance) compared with schools serving high-status communities (Bowles 1977, Bowles & Gintis 1976). In this approach, cognitive skills have a relatively small role in the reproduction of inequality (Karabel & Halsey 1977).

There have been empirical tests of the neo-Marxist perspective, but they are inconclusive. Bills (1983) found no support for the predictions of social class differences in noncognitive socialization. Oakes (1982) found, however, that student attitudes were distributed across curriculum tracks in ways consistent with the ideas of Bowles & Gintis (1976). She reported that students in the low track see themselves as inadequate in school but do not blame the school for their current low position. Such findings suggest the importance of further testing of conflict theories in general.

One hypothesized mechanism by which inequality is reproduced by status groups is through the transmission of *cultural capital*, defined as a form of symbolic wealth consisting of elite knowledge, dispositions, and skills (Bourdieu 1977). Bourdieu argued that individuals located at the top of the class structure maintain their position of advantage by transmitting elite knowledge or ideas directly to their children. Thus cultural capital is an additional form of inherited wealth. Privileged children are familiar with topics valued by the elite that schools do not directly teach but for which schools do reward students.

The cultural-capital hypothesis asserts that there is a direct relation between family background and cultural capital, that cultural capital is directly related to academic rewards, and that the effect of family background on academic rewards is indirect, through cultural capital (Katsillis & Rubinson 1990). Research testing these relations has produced inconsistent results. Katsillis & Rubinson (1990) found an association between parents' social class and children's cultural capital in Greece, but there was no link between cultural capital and educational achievement. In a contrary set of findings, data from research in the United States indicated that cultural capital was less tied to parental background than Bourdieu suggested and yet was significantly related to the grades and educational attainment of white high school students (DiMaggio

1982, DiMaggio & Mohr 1985). Cultural capital may be important, but its mechanism of transmission is unclear.

SCHOOLING AND THE STATUS ATTAINMENT PROCESS   The status-attainment perspective examines the effects of social origin on educational and occupational attainments. Specifically, the Wisconsin models of status attainment examine the relative impact of family background, significant others, and academic aptitude and achievement upon individuals' entrance into educational and occupational structures (Sewell & Hauser 1975, Sewell et al 1969). In general, these models show that socioeconomic status indirectly affects educational and occupational attainments through parental and peer influences and educational aspirations (Jencks & Crouse 1983). The Wisconsin approach has been criticized for excluding various structural factors (Kerckhoff 1976). An external structural factor not considered by the approach is the social origins of teachers themselves, which have been found to influence their reactions to the status of their students. Low-status and minority students do less well with high-status teachers, and test scores are depressed with increasing pupil-teacher distance scores (Alexander et al 1987).

Whether schooling serves predominantly as a vehicle for social mobility or as a mechanism for the reproduction of social inequality is not easily determined. The evidence generated through the study of status attainment models can be interpreted as supporting either position. On one hand, the results suggest that status attainment in the United States is a meritocratic process, because individuals with social origins that place them at a disadvantage can overcome those disadvantages through schooling. Yet the results also show that the advantages held by individuals with higher social origin contribute to later attainment. For this reason, schools are often criticized for not using more meritocratic procedures and for not eliminating the effects of family status on future life chances (Hallinan 1988).

Although schooling is clearly not the only factor contributing to occupational attainment (Jencks 1972), parents nevertheless emphasize education for their children. Education is the most important factor subject to parental influence. Even the parents of low-status children care a great deal about education, though they are often portrayed as not caring about it. In reality, these parents view schooling as the only legitimate path of social mobility for their children. Indeed, low-status parents' concern about the educational performance of their children is usually equal to or greater than the concern of high-status parents (Ritter et al 1993).

CREDENTIALISM   If the performance of increasingly complex jobs is contingent upon higher levels of education, then the cognitive skills learned in school should be related to measures of occupational performance, income, and status.

The empirical evidence, however, suggests that educational credentials, rather than cognitive skills, predict future earnings and occupational status (Hurn 1978). Credentials, then, are the critical link between schooling and the occupational structure. As the proportion of the population with higher levels of education grows, the educational credentials required for entrance into particular classes of occupations rise correspondingly. This increase in educational requirements is independent of the complexity of the occupation (Hurn 1978).

One reason credentialism exists is that it simplifies the lives of personnel managers. Educational background is used to shrink the pool of qualified applicants. Yet, reliance upon education as a sorting mechanism can be inappropriate. Berg (1970) has noted that better-educated candidates do not necessarily perform better on the job than those with less education; indeed, he reports the opposite result among sales personnel.

Educational credentials are increasingly important in acquiring class standing and securing employment (Hout 1988, Useem 1986). Higher education and even advanced degrees have become prerequisites for numerous high-status occupations. The increasing emphasis on credentials is not support for viewing education as either reproducing inequality or fostering mobility. Individuals may attain high educational degrees either as the result of inherited advantage or as a product of mobility.

In recent years, income disparities between the better- and less-educated have markedly increased. The payoff for higher education has never been greater, while graduation from high school no longer brings substantial economic returns (Hout 1988). The result is increasing importance for the distinction in secondary schools between curricula that are college-preparatory and those that do not lead to higher education. In this age of credentialism, students in lower educational tracks in high school are even more unlikely to achieve occupationally. The discussion of tracking in the section "The Internal Structure of School Organization" later in this review takes on greater importance because of the increasing societal emphasis on higher education.

The Ideological Emphasis on Ability

Within the institutional context of schooling, there are national differences in the emphasis on ability or effort. American schools focus on individual differences in student ability, whereas Asian schools emphasize student effort (Bennett 1987, Rohlen 1983). Stevenson (1990), for example, has shown that Asian schools are organized to encourage high math performance by all students; Asian educators believe that few students are too low in ability to learn the material in math curriculum. Teachers in Asian schools, asked to define the essence of good teaching, report clarity of presentation as the primary characteristic. By contrast, American teachers say the essence of good teaching is understanding individual differences among students. American teachers, unlike Asian teachers, expect variability in performance that is a product of differences in ability. Yet students in Asian schools exhibit not only higher average performance in mathematics but lower variability in math perform-ance compared with American students (Stevenson 1990).

The ideological emphasis on ability is consonant with the stress on public testing and measurement in American schools. A result of this ability empha-sis is that individual students are more often called on, praised, or disciplined in class in the United States than they are in Japan. American students are, therefore, more aware of their own level of ability than they would be in a more group-oriented setting (Rosenholtz & Simpson 1984).

Grading is influenced by the ability/effort trade-off. Grading in the United States emphasizes ability, with separate grades sometimes awarded for effort. But Japanese teachers prefer to grade on improvements in measured ability that indicate an increase in effort (Holloway 1988).

The ideological emphasis on ability within the institutional context of American schools also has consequences for the organization of curricula. The later section in the review entitled "Curriculum Tracking" highlights the leg-acy of this emphasis on ability. Let us now turn our attention to social structure as it more directly impinges on the organization of schools.

THE ORGANIZATIONAL STRUCTURE OF SCHOOLS

In the previous section we examined a number of institutional structures within American society and their relation to various aspects of the schooling process. Those same institutional forms also have implications for structures at different levels of social organization, including organizational structure. In this section, we focus on how the organizational structure of American schools affects what is taught in primary and secondary grades, how it is taught, and what is learned.

The organizational structure of schools must be examined from two related points of view. First, schools are organizations embedded in an external social context that facilitates or constrains the extent to which organizational goals are successfully realized. Second, internal structures within a school help shape its visible organizational form. Thus, in the discussion that follows, we demonstrate the ways in which critical aspects of the educational process are affected by factors in both the external and internal organizational structures of schools.

The External Context of School Organization

SCHOOLS AS PROFESSIONAL BUREAUCRACIES   Two of the most common forms of organization in Western industrial societies are professions and bureaucracies. American schools show characteristics that embody aspects of each of these two forms of organizational structure.

In some respects, schools resemble traditional bureaucratic organizations. There are clear hierarchies of authority, specific job descriptions for each organizational position (superintendent, principal, teacher), specific role expectations for the incumbents of these positions, and the positions are supposed to be filled according to merit (Bidwell 1965, Bidwell & Quiroz 1991). Yet, as we shall see, schools seldom function in ways that fit the bureaucratic model.

School personnel also operate as professionals (Hurn 1978). Teachers and, to a lesser degree, school librarians and counselors are assigned professional status. Teachers are licensed by the state and are believed to have internalized sufficient knowledge to deal with the active task of teaching (Dornbusch & Scott 1975). As professionals, they are given considerable discretion in developing and implementing classroom activities (Bidwell & Quiroz 1991). Therefore, most schools operate as a mixed form—a professional bureaucracy. School personnel are professionals operating within the context of a hierarchical bureaucracy (Hall 1972).

Schools have most of the disadvantages and few of the advantages of both bureaucracies and professions. Hierarchical superiors, such as principals, have few sanctions with which to control teachers, and unions fight to further restrict the principal's decision-making power. The most critical task performed by schools, instruction, is only loosely coupled with the school's administrative processes (Bidwell & Quiroz 1991, Weick 1976).

Pay, for example, is almost never distributed on the basis of merit in American public schools (Choy et al 1993). Unions argue that differential rewards would be based on favoritism by administrators rather than on the quality of teacher performance (Cramer 1983, Spillane 1987). Some decision-making in high schools is allocated to department heads, but they have little power over teachers and serve mainly to deflect the principal's attempts to influence department policies (Worner 1993). Thus, bureaucratic control over teachers is limited.

In addition, teachers do not perform in ways that fit the model of professionalism. Professionals, at least to a limited extent, are supposed to control one another and oppose control exerted by those outside the profession. But teachers generally do not trust one another. This is partially a product of lack of faith in their own professional education (Choy et al 1993, Stuck 1984). Because teachers believe they gain little practical knowledge in teacher-training schools (Digest of Education Statistics 1994), their professional socialization does not provide a basis for shared evaluative standards. Peer control of standards is almost nonexistent among teachers (Dornbusch & Scott 1975).

SCHOOLS AS INSTITUTIONAL ORGANIZATIONS   Schools often fail to meet expected curricular goals. To avoid a crisis in confidence, schools strive to create an external appearance of legitimacy in the eyes of community members, the school board, and state and federal agencies (Sergiovanni 1994). Schools have developed ways to prevent close inspection of their technical core. Accordingly, schools are seen as institutional rather than as technical organizations (Meyer & Rowan 1977).

The structure of an institutional organization is shaped by the rules and beliefs taken for granted in the society and is only loosely tied to the technical tasks performed by the organization (Bidwell 1965, March & Olsen 1976, Weick 1976). Explanations of organizational structure have shifted in recent years from an emphasis on the organization's production technology to the organization's response to environmental pressures. Environmental explanations of organizational structure are well suited for educational organizations because such organizations have a weak or diffuse technological base (Hannaway 1993, Levin 1993). Institutional organizations are evaluated in terms of their adherence to institutional rules and beliefs rather than on the quality of their performance (DiMaggio & Powell 1983).

Therefore, there is little supervision or evaluation of the details of instruction and learning in schools. The activities within each grade or within each school are given prima facie support by other units (Meyer & Rowan 1977). The sixth-grade teacher, for example, will accept new students who have completed fifth grade, even though the teacher may have only a vague idea of what students learned in the previous year. A student who transfers from one school to another is usually assigned to a similar grade level, with little attempt on the part of the new teacher(s) to determine the academic material learned at the previous school. Individual classrooms and schools are thus buffered from one another. In a mutually supportive state of ignorance, school personnel often don't know and don't want to know what happens in other classrooms and schools (Rosenholtz 1991).

DECENTRALIZED CONTROL   The federal political system in the United States grants considerable power to states and local authorities. In that federal context, the educational system similarly grants substantial autonomy to local school districts and schools. There are roughly 15,000 school districts, ranging in size from a single small community containing several hundred students to a large collection of urban communities containing up to a million students (Digest of Education Statistics 1994). Education in the United States is truly decentralized.

At the head of most school districts is an elected school board, which theoretically exercises control over the local schools. School boards seek to develop educational goals that are shared by most of the families in the community they serve. The elected school board members are, however, generally not educators. Each superintendent of schools, therefore, has considerable autonomy in exercising authority (Greene 1992).

In a similar fashion, educators continue to control the operation of the school despite parental empowerment (Wong 1994). Regardless of the extent to which school boards and parents are supposed to exercise control over the educational process, administrators and teachers continue to determine the curriculum and the methods of instruction.

Given the decentralized authority granted to school districts, it is not difficult in the United States to find a few school districts to adopt an educational innovation. Yet it is correspondingly difficult to achieve widespread diffusion of a successful innovation (Cuban 1992). It takes much effort to overcome inertia across thousands of separate school districts.

Ideologically, decentralization is the norm for school organization. Since 1980, however, the proportion of school administrators in central offices has increased, indicating that decentralization has decreased (Ornstein 1989). Along with increased funding from the states and federal government comes external political pressure. Hannaway (1993) emphasized the role of political environments as determinants of organizational structure. The greater the political pressure, the more likely it is that control will be centrally held. Thus, there is a negative relation between the level of political pressure and the influence of local principals and teachers on school policy.

COMMUNITY   One might think that our knowledge of community effects would be soundly grounded in empirical research. Unfortunately, there are serious methodological problems in carrying out community research (Jencks & Mayer 1988, Steinberg 1995). In addition, there are differences in the definition of community that range from the neighborhood (a residential unit), to the school district (an administrative unit), to groups that share a common set of values and norms (a functional or value community), and to groups that exchange information and resources (social networks) (Wynn et al 1987). The empirical generalizations presented here rest on a surprisingly limited research base owing to methodological and definitional issues that have made knowledge less cumulative.

Communities differ in the socioeconomic and ethnic mix of their inhabitants, and those differences are related to differences in the quality of the schools in each community. Indeed, the single best predictor of differences among schools in the average level of academic performance is the socioeconomic status of the families who reside in the community (McPartland & McDill 1982). The greater the proportion of families with high socioeconomic status and the lower the proportion of disadvantaged minorities, the more likely that the typical student will do well (Coleman 1966). Further evidence that external factors outside the school can offset internal school processes was provided by a study that showed differences in math achievement among poor white and black children in the early grades arose during the summers when school was out. These poor children in Baltimore did as well in mathematics as better-off children when school was in session (Entwisle & Alexander 1992). During the summer, school processes are not present to counteract the effects of differences in family and community resources.

Middle-class and upper-class families demand quality education that will permit and encourage their children to attend four-year colleges. In low-status and minority communities, families exert less pressure on school personnel. For reasons outside the scope of this review, less-educated parents in the low-status groups have difficulty translating their general support for education into specific behaviors (Ritter et al 1993). The typical lack of external community pressure in low-status and minority communities results in their schools having weaker standards and demanding less effort and learning from their students (Massey et al 1975). It has been shown, however, that school programs can successfully increase parental involvement by disadvantaged parents (Epstein & Dauber 1991).

But schools with ethnic minorities and lower social classes in the local community do not necessarily lack shared values and standards (Rubenstein et al 1985). For example, regardless of ethnic and class heterogeneity, small schools are more likely to have shared values and to form a value community (Coleman & Hoffer 1987). In addition, the mix of ethnicity and social class in the community is only a weak predictor of the level of communal organization in the school. If a school of any socioeconomic level operates as if it were a functional community with shared values, then teachers' satisfaction is greater and the level of student misconduct is lower (Bryk & Driscoll 1988). The relative success of Roman Catholic and private schools, compared with public schools, in educating disadvantaged students has been attributed to these parochial and private schools drawing from functional communities with shared values (Coleman & Hoffer 1987).

Living in a disadvantaged minority community, with corresponding low demands for academic effort and achievement in school, is a powerful barrier to students' success in school. For instance, advantaged African-American families (having some college education or both natural parents present) have children who do not perform much better in school than African-American children from less-educated families or from single-parent families. This finding is related to the effects on student success of living in a community with a substantial proportion of minorities. Living in such a community depresses the school performance of students from advantaged non-Hispanic white and African-American families. This process, equally present in both ethnic groups, harms African Americans more because a larger proportion of African Americans live in communities with large numbers of minority residents (Dornbusch et al 1991). In this set of findings we can observe the importance of interactions between the community context and individual-level variables (Bronfenbrenner 1986)

Social networks within communities supply parents and students with the information they need to choose courses, understand track assignments, and generally act as advocates for their children. Research findings generally portray a pattern of information flow that places low-status students at a considerable disadvantage. They lack social capital, which is defined as participation in interpersonal networks that provide needed information and resources (Bourdieu 1977, Coleman 1988, Stanton-Salazar & Dornbusch 1995).

The parents of disadvantaged students have less understanding of the processes of schooling and less security in dealing with school personnel (Useem 1992). The teachers of such students usually do not make up for this lack of parental information. For example, teachers of classes that contain a high proportion of minority students know less about college entrance requirements and correspondingly have less information to communicate about that important issue than do teachers with few minority students in their classes (Carrasco 1988). In a study of Mexican-American high school students, one third reported never getting academic information from school personnel, and only 19% of the information networks described by these adolescents included any school personnel (Stanton-Salazar & Dornbusch 1995).

Research on social networks shows the relatively greater flow of academic information to middle-class groups. For example, middle-class parents often learn from their friends and acquaintances rather than from the school about the track to which their adolescent is assigned (Useem 1992). Among Mexican-American adolescents who used their parents and extended kin as sources of information, only the students with middle-class kin were aided by their information networks (Stanton-Salazar & Dornbusch 1995).

Much of the difference in parents' information about children's classroom and school activities can be attributed to the composition of the parents' social networks. The networks of middle-class parents consist of other parents from the school community. The social contacts of working-class parents, by contrast, tend to be limited to relatives in the area. These parents seldom socialize with other parents from their children's school and, consequently, do not obtain information that can be used to build a strong family-school link (Lareau 1987).

Social-class differences in children's leisure time activities also affect the information flow to parents about school. Lareau (1987) found the activities of working-class children tended to be informal (e.g. bike riding, watching television, playing with neighborhood children). Middle-class children, on the other hand, were more likely to be enrolled in formal after-school activities (e.g. swim lessons, arts and crafts lessons, soccer). Parents would sometimes stay to watch these activities, which provided an opportunity to interact with other parents of students in the same school. Discussions would often center on the reputations of teachers and the academic progress of children. Thus, the characteristics of social networks tended to reduce the flow of school-related information to parents from the lower socioeconomic groups and increase it to parents of higher status (Lareau 1987).

We have reviewed some aspects of external social structure that influence forms of school organization. We now shift our attention to aspects of the internal structure of schools that also affect the learning process.

The Internal Structure of School Organization

WORKING CONDITIONS FOR TEACHING   Teachers tend to perceive, believe, and act in accordance with the structures, policies, and traditions of their workplace. As organizational members, teachers define the conditions of their work according to a shared set of assumptions about the kinds of attitudes and behaviors that are appropriate to the school setting. Teachers' subjective perceptions of their working conditions—namely, what should be performed, how it should be performed, and what represents successful performance—are strongly influenced by the internal structural arrangements of the school (Rosenholtz 1991).

One of the clearest changes in internal structural arrangements is the shift from the elementary school to the middle school, junior high school, or high school. In the elementary school context, a single teacher instructs a single group of students for the entire day. In the secondary school context, each class period brings a different group of students to each teacher. The teacher in secondary school typically has a hundred or more students each day. This structural difference generates corresponding changes in the nature of teacher-student relations, as well as in the opportunities for parental contacts.

For example, Midgley et al (1988) found that middle school teachers, in comparison with elementary school teachers, trust students less and seek to exercise more control and discipline over their students. Secondary school teachers also have neither the time nor the resources to closely monitor the performance of each student and to keep parents informed of ways in which they can assist their child. It is not surprising that, under these changed conditions, collaborative relations between parents and schools weaken as students move into adolescence (Eccles & Harold 1993).

Thus, students in secondary schools have more distant relations to their teachers, and their parents are less likely to act as advocates or collaborators. If the transition to the more impersonal environment occurs at an earlier grade, the multiple life changes experienced by adolescents reaching puberty result in persistent declines in self-esteem and academic performance, especially for females (Lord et al 1994). The larger the number of stressful life changes, the more negative the outcomes (Simmons et al 1987).

The importance of working conditions is further evidenced by the oft-reported lack of commitment of teachers to their work. In general, low commitment in any job is linked to disaffection with the workplace, absenteeism, and leaving an occupation (Johns & Nicholson 1982, Marcus & Smith 1985). The same interrelations apply within the occupation of teaching (Rosenholtz 1991), with commitment linked to increased student learning (Kushman 1992).

The lack of professional status and the low economic rewards of teaching have chilling effects on the recruitment, performance, and retention of highly qualified teachers. One third of teachers would change jobs if they could, and one sixth of new teachers do so within their first year (Digest of Education Statistics 1994). The size and technical sophistication of the research literature on teacher burnout is another indicator of low commitment (Conley et al 1989, Friedman 1991, Sarros & Sarros 1987). Because organizational conditions within schools often reduce teachers' commitment to their work, efforts to recruit academically talented individuals to the occupation are often unsuccessful (Rosenholtz & Simpson 1990).

The commitment of novice teachers is affected more by different organizational conditions than is the commitment of experienced teachers. Novice teachers, less able to cope with such noninstructional issues as student misconduct, are more influenced by the level of organizational support for these boundary tasks. The commitment of experienced teachers, by contrast, is more affected by the level of organizational support for core instructional tasks. These teachers have already learned how to manage boundary issues (Rosenholtz & Simpson 1990).

A key element of working conditions for teachers is the system of teacher evaluation. Evaluation systems have two related objectives. The first is to control or modify the behavior of organizational participants, and the second is to determine the distribution of rewards and sanctions within the organization. Evaluation systems are based on the assumption that the behavior of participants will be affected by the evaluations they receive. This expectation is realized, however, only when the evaluation system is perceived as sound (Roper & Hoffman 1986).

A soundly based system of evaluation has four defining features: (*a*) the criteria for evaluation are clearly established, (*b*) the criteria are regarded as relevant to what is performed or produced, (*c*) the performance to be evaluated has been adequately sampled, and (*d*) the participant believes that a favorable evaluation may be attained by exerting a sufficient amount of effort (Dornbusch & Scott 1975).

Teachers' working conditions often do not provide an appropriate context for soundly based evaluations of their performance. Teaching activities often take place in isolation, removed from direct observation by colleagues or school administrators (Dreeben 1973, Lortie 1975, Rosenholtz 1991). Teachers are infrequently evaluated by either principals or teaching colleagues (Natriello 1984). Coupled with the relative isolation of teaching, an unsound system of evaluation leaves the process of instruction largely uncontrolled by either the profession or the school administration.

There are few organizational supports for teachers developing professional interchanges with one another. Rosenholtz (1991) identified a number of social organizational conditions within schools that either facilitate or inhibit efforts to create a system of faculty collaboration. Requests for and offers of collegial advice and assistance are less likely to be made when teachers are uncertain about classroom technology and about their own instructional practices. When the outcomes of work are highly unpredictable and nonroutine, teachers are more likely to interpret requests for assistance as evidence of their inadequate performance. Under such conditions, help-seeking behavior may be stigmatizing and may cause individuals to avoid situations of self-disclosure (Rosenholtz 1991).

The extent to which teaching goals are shared within a school also contributes to the likelihood of collegial assistance being requested or provided. When teaching goals are shared and teachers seek ways of achieving these goals, there is much greater opportunity for faculty collaboration (Rosenholtz 1991). A shared school purpose helps to define help-seeking behavior as normative and appropriate.

The lack of visibility of teaching school personnel means that the sample of teacher's performances available to fellow teachers is limited. Collegial evaluation cannot proceed behind closed doors. The visibility of teachers to one another, as in team teaching, is necessary for collegial evaluation (Dornbusch & Scott 1975). Current organizational arrangements within schools discourage evaluation by fellow professionals and the development of a professional self-image (Roper & Hoffman 1986).

The working conditions of teachers form an unsupportive environment, and poor working conditions are associated with less learning by elementary school students (Pallas et al 1987). Teachers are sufficiently disenchanted with the organization of their work that they report student expressions of gratitude as their greatest source of satisfaction (Cohen et al 1976). Equally indicative of an inadequate organizational environment is the paradoxical finding that teachers who receive more negative evaluations from the principal express more satisfaction with the principal. Any feedback, even negative, is preferable to the usual lack of evaluation of their teaching (Dornbusch & Scott 1975). Good teaching occurs despite the organizational structure within schools, not because of it.

STATUS PROBLEMS WITHIN THE CLASSROOM   Problems of dominance and non-participation in classroom work groups are often the result of status differences and the performance expectations attached to those differences (Cohen & Lotan 1994). Status differences are the product of socially perceived and agreed-upon differences in social rankings. Status characteristics theory is a performance-based approach to informal status problems that explains how, and under what conditions, status processes organize task-related interaction (Berger et al 1977).

Associated with each state of a status characteristic are differential evaluations of honor, esteem, desirability, and expectations for task performance. Performance expectations refer to the inferred capacity of individuals to make useful task contributions. These evaluations and expectations are properties of the structural relations between actors, not of the actors themselves (Berger et al 1980).

The classroom is a multicharacteristic setting where students often possess more than one status characteristic. Cohen (1986) identified three general categories of status that may become salient in this setting: social, academic, and peer status. Social status refers to the ascribed characteristics students bring into the classroom. Indicators of social status include race, ethnicity, gender, and social class (Cohen 1982, Leal 1985, Lockheed et al 1983). Attached to each state (high- or low-ranking) of these characteristics is a diffuse general expectation for competence or incompetence on a wide variety of tasks.

Academic status is locally created within the classroom (Cohen 1986). Indicators of academic status include perceived reading ability (Rosenholtz 1985, Tammivaara 1982), perceived academic ability (Hoffman & Cohen 1972), and sociometric rankings of who is the best in math and science (Cohen et al 1988). Given its relevance to everyday classroom activities, academic status is the most powerful status characteristic operating in the classroom.

Peer status is locally created within children's informal social relationships and becomes more important as children move from elementary school to middle school and high school. Two frequently used indicators of peer status are popularity and attractiveness (Webster & Driskell 1983). Other criteria for peer rankings include athletic skill and elements of personal style, such as dress (Cohen & Lotan 1994).

According to status characteristics theory, when actors are collectively engaged in a valued task, they utilize salient status information to form initial expectations of their own and others' task performance. Group members then behave so as to confirm the underlying structure of performance expectations. Behavior that is consistent with expectations maintains these expectations, and these in turn act as self-fulfilling prophecies to guide subsequent behavior (Berger et al 1980, Entwisle & Webster 1973). An informal status hierarchy emerges as the group members exchange deference for expected superior task contributions.

Classroom indicators of status effects include differential rates of task-related interaction and initiation toward the teacher. Educators would be less concerned about these differences if status problems did not affect learning. The extent to which students talk and work together is positively associated with learning math and science concepts (Cohen 1986, Cohen et al 1988).

Many current efforts to reform the organization of instruction target structural sources of inequality within and across classrooms, such as ability grouping and tracking. Cooperative learning, for example, has been widely recommended as a means of managing academic heterogeneity in untracked classrooms. Although such classroom innovations are designed to reduce inequality, it is in these very settings that informal status orders develop and maintain inequality.

Opportunities for classroom participation and learning quickly become stratified in these cooperative settings, with low-status students less likely to speak out and seek needed help than their high-status classmates. If status problems remain untreated, they effectively create new sources of inequality to replace those eliminated by curricular reforms. Using status characteristics theory as a guide, Elizabeth Cohen and her colleagues have developed a number of interventions to counteract the process of status generalization (for a complete discussion, see Cohen 1993). Classroom status interventions are pedagogical techniques for reducing inequalities in task participation within heterogeneous work groups. Students in the classroom are viewed as possessing multiple types of abilities, and feedback from the teacher emphasizes the contribution to the group task from students who otherwise would have low status. Such interventions not only reduce status problems within the classroom, but they also lead to increased learning by students who otherwise would be considered less competent.

CURRICULUM TRACKING   Given the impact of higher education on later occupational attainment, the links between secondary and higher education cannot be overlooked. Though higher education per se is not discussed, we do note how the structure of tracking in secondary schools makes students either eligible or ineligible for enrollment in four-year colleges and universities.

Most American public schools use some form of ability grouping or tracking (Oakes et al 1992). While the practice of tracking is largely confined to secondary schools, ability grouping occurs in both primary and secondary schools. Slavin (1987) distinguished between-class grouping (e.g. "honors," "advanced," "regular," "basic," or "remedial" classes) from within-class grouping (e.g. high and low reading or math groups in a single class).

Tracks refer to sequences of required courses (e.g. college-preparatory, general, or vocational tracks in American high schools). For any given track, students must complete a certain number of academic courses, the content of which varies by track level. The instructional practices of teachers take into account the composition of each class in terms of ability, thus fostering differences in the instructional agenda (Dreeben & Barr 1988). Although secondary schools are moving away from rigid tracking practices, alternative grouping plans effectively preserve their existence (Oakes et al 1992). In place of formally defined tracks, for example, some schools assign students to ability groups or course-levels on a subject-by-subject basis. Because students tend to be placed in instructional groups that are at a similar level across courses (Gamoran 1987), this alternative tends to reproduce distinct curriculum tracks.

The structural features of tracking systems differ across schools on such dimensions as the number of tracks available, criteria for track assignment, selectivity, flexibility, and mobility (Gamoran 1992, Oakes 1985, Rosenbaum 1976). Across secondary schools in the United States, for example, the number of students in the academic (college-preparatory) track ranges from 10% to 70%, with an average of 35% (Kilgore 1991).

Curriculum tracking, particularly in mathematics and science courses, structures the organization of teaching in secondary schools throughout the United States (Kerckhoff 1986, Oakes et al 1992). Tracking is based upon the ideology of individual differences in ability. Educators generally assume that reducing heterogeneity of students with respect to ability better enables students to progress at a rate commensurate with their capacities (Oakes 1987, Slavin 1990). Curriculum tracks and ability groups attempt to minimize heterogeneity by grouping students with similar capacities and interests into separate programs of instruction, which ostensibly facilitate learning for all students.

Researchers who have made attempts to identify the determinants of track assignments have traditionally viewed tracking from diverse perspectives. Supporters of tracking portray it as a benign meritocratic practice, one that creates homogeneous instructional groups within a heterogeneous student population. They cite students' prior school achievements, ability levels (as measured in standardized test scores), and aspirations as the primary bases for track or ability group assignment. Secondary analyses on large samples of American high school students show that, in general, prior school achievement is the strongest determinant of track placement (Heyns 1974, Oakes et al 1992). Garet & Delany (1988) reviewed five large-scale national survey studies on high school curriculum tracking and concluded that four of the studies show that the direct effect of ability on placement is larger than the direct effect of socioeconomic status.

Critics of the meritocratic view, however, view it as a mechanism for perpetuating social class and ethnic divisions. They contend that tracking provides greater learning opportunities for those students who are already socially advantaged. They are quick to point out that schools overestimate their ability to assess student ability. Alexander et al (1978) claimed that there is considerable slippage in curriculum sorting, with students of equal ability, motivation, and past performance often assigned to different curricula. Many students, particularly those in the middle level of ability, are misassigned (Dornbusch 1994).

Misassignment often has negative long-term consequences. Among students who aspire to graduate from a four-year college and whose math performance is above the national average, a substantial proportion are assigned to lower-track math and science courses that make their enrollment in a four-year college impossible. Such misassignment is more likely among students in disadvantaged minorities and from families with low parental education (Dornbusch 1994).

This critical perspective suggests that students are, to a large extent, selected and sorted with respect to their social origins (e.g. family socioeconomic status, race, or ethnicity). Oakes et al (1991), for example, found that Asian students were more likely to be assigned to advanced courses than were Hispanic students with whom their test scores were equivalent. In general, a disproportionate number of low-socioeconomic-status and disadvantaged minority students occupy the lower-ability and noncollege tracks (National Center for Educational Statistics 1985, Oakes et al 1992, Persell 1977, Vanfossen et al 1987).

Gamoran & Mare (1989), however, found that, among blacks and non-blacks who are equal on other characteristics, the assignment process favors blacks over nonblacks. Other studies have also found that tracking practices favor blacks (Oakes et al 1992). A possible explanation is that most blacks, as a result of poverty, residential segregation, and discrimination, performed poorly in school long before they entered high school. For those blacks who performed relatively well, an attempt may be made to redress the imbalance through more favorable track assignment.

Another perspective that combines elements of the previous positions posits that the independent contributions of social origin and ability cannot readily be disentangled. Measures of student achievement, ability, and even choice are imbued with social-class biases (Oakes 1985, Persell 1977). This view suggests a de-emphasis of either the meritocratic or status inequality perspective in favor of the study of the role of intervening social processes in program assignments.

Research guided by this view of intervening social processes has examined the impact of parental influences on initial track assignment in secondary schools. Students of average ability from advantaged families are more likely to be assigned to higher tracks because of actions by their parents (Baker & Stevenson 1986; Useem 1991, 1992). The well-documented positive association between parental socioeconomic status and placement in more advanced courses or tracks is partially explained by the tendency of well-educated parents to be more effective managers of their children's schooling (Lareau 1987; Useem 1991, 1992).

Other studies have examined the actions of counselors when dealing with students of differing social status. Counselors tend to place students with advantaged social origins into higher-level tracks or ability groups, in comparison with less-advantaged students with similar academic profiles (Cicourel & Kitsuse 1963, Rosenbaum 1976).

Structural factors also affect patterns of course enrollment. The organization of curricula across schools and differences in the composition of student populations shape course-placement patterns (Garet & Delany 1988). When the proportion of minorities and low-status students in a school is high, the lower-track program is larger, and the higher-track program is less rigorous (Oakes et al 1992).

The slightly better performance of minority students in Roman Catholic schools may be partially because of the structure of tracking within those schools. Compared to noncollege tracks in public high schools, Catholic schools place greater academic demands on students in noncollege tracks and require more rigorous coursework and a greater number of academic courses (Coleman et al 1982). After controlling for background characteristics of the students, Catholic schools place more students into the college-preparatory track than do public schools (Oakes 1987, Lee & Bryk 1988, Camarena 1990, Hoffer et al 1985). This tendency of Catholic schools to assign more students to the academic track may be a function of their lack of financial resources. They are unlikely to have enough money to create a variegated curriculum that includes, for example, vocational courses.

Academic performance is influenced by differences in the educational resources available to students in different tracks (Oakes 1987). Teachers of lower-track classes are themselves lower in ability and experience, and they set lower academic standards for their students compared with standards set by teachers of higher-track classes (Gamoran & Berends 1987; Oakes 1985, 1987; Dornbusch 1994). More competent and experienced teachers are usually assigned to higher tracks and ability groups (Ball 1981, Finley 1984, Rosenbaum 1976). Relative to lower-tracked students, college-preparatory students have greater access to science laboratories (National Center for Educational Statistics 1985), better class materials, and career/school guidance services (Rosenbaum 1976).

Given the differential allocation of resources by track, field studies have found that more learning occurs in higher tracks (Oakes 1985, Rosenbaum 1980). Studies using national survey data have corroborated these findings, even after controlling for family background, prior achievement, race, and gender (Kerckhoff 1986, Shavit & Featherman 1988, Vanfossen et al 1987). Tracking produces differential gains in achievement—higher-track students gain at the expense of those in the lower track (Kerckhoff 1986, Oakes 1987, Vanfossen et al 1987). The achievement gap between tracks is particularly large in math and science (Gamoran 1987).

By selecting and sorting students into different programs of instruction, curriculum tracking produces socially significant classifications—ability group or track membership—to which others may differentially respond. Track or ability group placement may be perceived by teachers, counselors, and students as a proxy for competence. That is, in the absence of information to suggest otherwise, placement may serve as a major indicator of a student's overall academic competence. Rothbart et al (1971) demonstrated experimentally that generalized labels of academic competence affect patterns of teacher-student interaction. Videotaped interactions revealed that teachers spent more time attending to students who were randomly labeled as having greater academic ability than to students randomly labeled as having less ability.

Tracked students are often differentially characterized by their teachers. Students occupying the lower tracks are stereotyped as "thick," "unresponsive," and "slow," whereas higher-tracked students are seen as "sharp" and "bright" (Finley 1984, Schwartz 1981). These stereotypic conceptions may influence the performance expectations teachers form for their students. Tuckman & Bierman (1971), for example, inferred from year-end placement recommendations that ability group placements affected teachers' expectations. In their study, high school and junior high school students were randomly selected into the next higher-ability group, while comparable students remained in their assigned lower-ability group as controls. At the end of the year, teachers recommended 54% of the randomly selected students in the higher group remain at that level, but only 1% of the comparison students were recommended for placement into the higher group in the next year.

Academically tracked students report more positive treatment by their teachers than do students from either the general or vocational track (Dornbusch 1994, Vanfossen et al 1987). On the basis of interviews with fifty high school seniors in the Boston area, Rosenbaum (1976, p. 179) concluded that "even when noncollege-track students get the same teachers as college-track students, they do not get as much attention, concern, or effort from their teachers." During class discussions, elementary school teachers ignore the responses of students in lower groups but encourage students in higher groups to formulate the correct answer (Schwartz 1981).

The labeling of students with respect to track positions splits their attitudes into proschool and antischool sentiments (Gamoran & Berends 1987, Oakes 1985). Students occupying higher-track levels evidence more favorable attitudes toward themselves and their schoolwork. This attitudinal difference is likely to be reinforced and perpetuated as students initiate and maintain within-track friendships (Hallinan & Williams 1989). Given such findings, it is not surprising that college-tracked students express higher educational expectations than students tracked for other destinations (Rosenbaum 1980, Vanfossen et al 1987).

As early as first grade, instructional differences among within-class ability groups produce differences in learning (Dreeben & Gamoran 1986, Pallas et al 1994). At the secondary school level, students' participation in the college-preparatory track has a significant positive effect on their academic achievements in high school and on college enrollment, even after controlling for background characteristics and prior school achievement (Hotchkiss & Dorsten 1987, Rosenbaum 1980). Thus, the structure of tracking in elementary and secondary schools affects the educational possibilities of students and, as a result, their occupational opportunities. For above-average students, specifically those in the 50th to 80th percentile on math achievement, assignment to a lower track in secondary school leads to a permanent loss of educational potential. When assigned to the lower track, these students work less hard and learn less despite their high ability. They are likely never to be reassigned to the college-preparatory track (Dornbusch 1994). The resulting loss of talent is a national tragedy.

CONCLUSION

This review is addressed to psychologists interested in education. Although psychologists focus on many areas of education, they tend to study specific interactions among teachers, counselors, and students. Sociologists, on the other hand, are more likely to examine larger societal and organizational structures. The interactions of individuals and small groups are influenced by the contexts in which they operate. The intention here is to inform educational psychologists about some of the larger social structures that constrain small-group and individual behavior within schools. Knowledge of schooling will be best advanced by overcoming existing disciplinary boundaries and linking levels of analysis.

Literature Cited

Alexander KL, Cook MA, McDill EL. 1978. Curriculum tracking and educational stratification. *Am. Sociol. Rev.* 43:47–66

Alexander KL, Entwisle DR, Thompson MS. 1987. School performance, status relations, and the structure of sentiment: bringing the teacher back in. *Am. Sociol. Rev.* 52:665–82

Baker DP, Stevenson DL. 1986. Mothers' strategies for children's school achievement: managing the transition to high school. *Sociol. Educ.* 59(1):156–66

Ball SJ. 1981. *Beachside Comprehensive: A Case-Study of Secondary Schooling.* New York: Cambridge Univ. Press

Benavot A, Cha YK, Kamens D, Meyer JW, Wong S. 1991. Knowledge for the masses: world models and national curricula. *Am. Sociol. Rev.* 56(1):85–100

Bennett WJ. 1987. Implications for American education. In *Japanese Education Today,* ed. CH Dorfman, pp. 69–71. Washington, DC: US Dep. Educ.

Berg IE, with Gorelick S. 1970. *Education and Jobs: The Great Training Robbery.* New York: Praeger

Berger J, Fisek MH, Norman RZ, Zelditch M. 1977. *Status Characteristics and Social Interaction: An Expectation States Approach.* New York: Elsevier

Berger J, Rosenholtz SJ, Zelditch M. 1980. Status organizing processes. *Annu. Rev. Sociol.* 6:479–508

Bidwell CE. 1965. The school as a formal organization. In *Handbook of Organizations,* ed. JB March, pp. 972–1022. Chicago: Rand McNally

Bidwell CE, Quiroz PA. 1991. Organizational control in the high school workplace: a theoretical argument. *J. Res. Adolesc.* 1: 211–29

Bills DB. 1983. Social reproduction and the Bowles-Gintis thesis of a correspondence between school and work settings. In *Research in Sociolology of Education and Socialization,* ed. AC Kerckhoff, 4:185–210. Greenwich, CT: JAI

Boli J, Ramirez FO, Meyer JW. 1985. Explaining the origins and expansion of mass education. *Comp. Educ. Rev.* 29(2):145–70

Bourdieu P. 1977. Cultural reproduction and social reproduction. See Karabel & Halsey 1977, pp. 487–511

Bowles S. 1977. Unequal education and the reproduction of the social division of labor. See Karabel & Halsey 1977, pp. 137–53

Bowles S, Gintis H. 1976. *Schooling in Capitalist America.* New York: Basic

Bronfenbrenner U. 1986. Ecology of the family as a context for human development: research perspectives. *Dev. Psychol.* 22:723–42

Bryk AS, Driscoll ME. 1988. *The High School as Community: Contextual Influences, and Consequences for Students and Teachers.* Madison, WI: Natl. Cent. Eff. Second. Sch.

Camarena M. 1990. Following the right track: a comparison of tracking practices in public and Catholic schools. In *Curriculum Differentiation in U.S. Secondary Schools: Interpretative Studies,* ed. R Page, L Valli, pp. 159–82. Albany: State Univ. NY Press

Carrasco JA. 1988. *The flow of college-related information for students in high school settings: an organizational perspective.* PhD thesis. Stanford Univ., Stanford, CA. 182 pp.

Census Bureau. 1975. *Historical Statistics of the United States, Colonial Times to 1970.* Washington, DC: US Dep. Commer.

Census Bureau. 1994. *Statistical Abstract of the United States. 1994.* Washington, DC: US Dep. Commer.

Choy SP, Bobbitt SA, Henke RR, Medrich EA, Horn LJ, Lieberman J. 1993. *America's Teachers: Profile of a Profession.* Berkeley, CA: MPR Assoc. 205 pp.

Cicourel AV, Kitsuse JI. 1963. *The Educational Decision-makers.* Indianapolis: Bobbs Merrill

Cohen EG, Deal TE, Meyer JW, Scott WR. 1976. *Organization and Instruction in Elementary Schools: First Results.* Stanford, CA: Stanford Cent. Res. Dev. Teach. 317 pp.

Cohen EG. 1982. Expectation states and interracial interaction in school settings. *Annu. Rev. Sociol.* 8:209–35

Cohen EG. 1986. On the sociology of the classroom. In *The Contribution of the Social Sciences to Education Policy and Practice,* ed. M Lockheed, J Hannaway, pp. 127–62. Berkeley, CA: McCutchan

Cohen EG. 1993. From theory to practice: the development of an applied research program. In *Theoretical Research Programs: Studies in the Growth of Theory,* ed. J Berger, M Zelditch Jr, pp. 385–415. Stanford, CA: Stanford Univ. Press

Cohen EG, Lotan RA. 1994. *Complex instruction and status problems in the untracked middle school.* Presented at Annu. Meet. Am. Educ. Res. Assoc., New Orleans

Cohen EG, Lotan RA, Catanarite L. 1988. Can expectations for competence be altered in the classroom? In *Status Generalization: New Theory and Research,* ed. M Webster, M Foschi, pp. 27–54. Stanford, CA: Stanford Univ. Press

Coleman JS. 1966. *Equality of Educational*

Opportunity. Washington, DC: US Dep. Health, Educ., Welf.

Coleman JS. 1988. Social capital in the creation of human capital. *Am. J. Sociol.* 94: S95–S120

Coleman JS, Hoffer T. 1987. *Public and Private High Schools: The Impact of Communities.* New York: Basic

Coleman JS, Kilgore SB, Hoffer T. 1982. Public and private schools. *Society* 19(2):4–9

Collins R. 1977. Functional and conflict theories of educational stratification. See Karabel & Halsey 1977, pp. 118–36

Congress of the United States. 1986. *Trends in Educational Achievement. CBO Study.* Washington, DC: Congr. Budg. Off.

Conley SC, Bacharach SB, Bauer S. 1989. The school work environment and teacher career dissatisfaction. *Educ. Adm. Q.* 25(1): 58–81

Cramer J. 1983. Merit pay: challenge of the decade. *Curric. Rev.* 22(5):7–10

Cuban L. 1992. What happens to reforms that last? The case of the junior high school. *Am. Educ. Res. J.* 29(2):227–51

Davis K, Moore WE. 1945. Some principles of stratification. *Am. Sociol. Rev.* 10:242–49

Digest of Education Statistics. 1994. Washington, DC: Natl. Cent. Educ. Stat.

DiMaggio PJ. 1982. Cultural capital and school success: the impact of status culture participation on the grades of US high school students. *Am. Sociol. Rev.* 47: 189–201

DiMaggio PJ, Mohr J. 1985. Cultural capital, educational attainment, and marital selection. *Am. J. Sociol.* 90(6):1231–61

DiMaggio PJ, Powell WW. 1983. The iron cage revisited: institutional isomorphism and collective rationality in organizational fields. *Am. Sociol. Rev.* 48:147–60

Dornbusch SM, 1994. *Off the track.* Presidential Address. Presented at Biennial Meet. Sociol. Res. Adolesc., San Diego

Dornbusch SM, Ritter PL, Steinberg L. 1991. Community influences on the relation of family statuses to adolescent school performance: differences between African Americans and non-Hispanic whites. *Am. J. Educ.* 99(4):543–67

Dornbusch SM, Scott WR. 1975. *Evaluation and the Exercise of Authority.* San Francisco: Jossey-Bass

Dreeben R. 1973. The school as workplace. In *Second Handbook of Research on Teaching,* ed. RWM Travers, pp. 450–73. Chicago: Rand McNally

Dreeben R, Barr R. 1988. Classroom composition and the design of instruction. *Sociol. Educ.* 61:129–42

Dreeben R, Gamoran A. 1986. Race, instruction, and learning. *Am. Sociol. Rev.* 51: 660–69

Eccles JS, Harold RD. 1993. Parent-school in-volvement during the early adolescent years. *Teach. Coll. Rec.* 94:568–87

Entwisle DR, Alexander KL. 1992. Summer setback: race, poverty, school composition, and mathematics achievement in the first two years of school. *Am. Sociol. Rev.* 57: 72–84

Entwisle DR, Alexander KL. 1993. Entry into school: the beginning school transition and educational stratification in the United States. *Annu. Rev. Sociol.* 19:401–23

Entwisle DR, Webster M. 1973. Status factors in expectation raising. *Sociol. Educ.* 46: 115–26

Epstein JL, Dauber SL. 1991. School programs and teacher practices of parental involvement in inner-city elementary and middle schools. *Elem. Sch. J.* 91:289–305

Finley MK. 1984. Teachers and tracking in a comprehensive high school. *Sociol. Educ.* 57:233–43

Friedman IA. 1991. High- and low-burnout schools: school culture aspects of teacher burnout. *J. Educ. Res.* 84(6):325–33

Gamoran A. 1987. The stratification of high school learning opportunities. *Sociol. Educ.* 59:185–98

Gamoran A. 1992. The variable effects of high school tracking. *Am. Sociol. Rev.* 57: 812–28

Gamoran A, Berends M. 1987. The effects of stratification in secondary schools: synthesis of survey and ethnographic research. *Rev. Educ. Res.* 57:415–35

Gamoran A, Mare RD. 1989. Secondary school tracking and educational inequality: compensation, reinforcement, or neutrality? *Am. J. Sociol.* 94:1146–83

Garet MS, Delany B. 1988. Students, courses, and stratification. *Sociol. Educ.* 61:61–77

Government Statistical Service. 1994. *Social Trends.* London: Cent. Stat. Off., Gov. Stat. Serv.

Greene KR. 1992. Models of school board policy-making. *Educ. Adm. Q.* 28(2):220–36

Hall RH. 1972. *Organizations: Structure and Process.* Englewood Cliffs, NJ: Prentice-Hall

Hallinan MT. 1988. Equality of educational opportunity. *Annu. Rev. Sociol.* 14:249–68

Hallinan MT, Williams RA. 1989. Interracial friendship choices in secondary schools. *Am. Sociol. Rev.* 54:67–78

Hannaway J. 1993. Political pressure and decentralization in institutional organizations of school. *Sociol. Educ.* 66:147–63

Heyns B. 1974. Social selection and stratification within schools. *Am. J. Sociol.* 79: 1434–51

Hoffer T, Greeley AM, Coleman JS. 1985. Achievement growth in public and Catholic schools. *Sociol. Educ.* 58:74–97

Hoffman D, Cohen EG. 1972. *An exploratory study to determine the effects of general-*

ized *performance expectations upon activity and influence of students engaged in a group simulation game.* Presented at Annu. Meet. Am. Educ. Res. Assoc., Chicago

Holloway SD. 1988. Concepts of ability and effort in Japan and the United States. *Rev. Educ. Res.* 58(3):327–45

Hotchkiss L, Dorsten L. 1987. Curriculum effects on early post high school outcomes. In *Research on Sociology of Education and Socialization,* ed. RG Corwin, 7:191–219. Greenwich, CT: JAI

Hout M. 1988. The American occupational structure in the 1980's. *Am. J. Sociol.* 93: 1358–1400

Hurn C. 1978. *The Limits and Possibilities of Schooling: An Introduction to the Sociology of Schooling.* Boston: Allyn & Bacon

Jencks C. 1972. *Inequality.* New York: Harper & Row

Jencks C, Crouse J, Mueser P. 1983. The Wisconsin model of status attainment: a national replication with improved measures of ability and aspiration. *Sociol. Educ.* 56: 3–19

Jencks C, Mayer S. 1988. *The Social Consequences of Growing Up in a Poor Neighborhood.* Northwestern Univ., Cent. Urban Aff. Policy Res., Evanston, IL

Johns G, Nicholson N. 1982. The meaning of absence: new research strategies for theory and research. In *Research in Organizational Behavior,* ed. BM Straw, LL Cummings, 4:127–72. Greenwich, CT: JAI

Karabel J. 1977. Community colleges and social stratification: submerged class conflict in American higher education. See Karabel & Halsey 1977, pp. 232–54

Karabel J, Halsey AH. 1977. Educational research: a review and interpretation. See Karabel & Halsey 1977, pp. 1–85

Karabel J, Halsey AH, eds. 1977. *Power and Ideology in Education.* New York: Oxford Univ. Press

Katsillis J, Rubinson R. 1990. Cultural capital, student achievement, and educational reproduction: the case of Greece. *Am. Sociol. Rev.* 55(2):270–79

Kerckhoff A. 1976. The status attainment process: socialization or allocation? *Soc. Forces* 55:368–81

Kerckhoff A. 1986. Effects of ability grouping in British secondary schools. *Am. Sociol. Rev.* 51:842–58

Kilgore SB. 1991. The organizational context of tracking in schools. *Am. Sociol. Rev.* 56: 189–203

Kurian GT. 1982. *Encyclopedia of the Third World.* New York: Facts on File. Rev. ed.

Kushman JW. 1992. The organizational dynamics of teacher workplace commitment: a study of urban elementary and middle schools. *Educ. Adm. Q.* 28(1):5–42

Lareau A. 1987. Social class differences in family school relationships: the importance of cultural capital. *Sociol. Educ.* 60: 73–85

Leal A. 1985. *Sex inequalities in classroom interaction: an evaluation of an intervention.* PhD thesis. Stanford Univ., Stanford, CA

Lee VE, Bryk AS. 1988. Curriculum tracking as mediating the social distribution of high school achievement. *Sociol. Educ.* 62: 78–94

Levin B. 1993. School response to a changing environment. *J. Educ. Adm.* 31:4–21

Lockheed ME, Harris AM, Nemcef WP. 1983. Sex and social influence: Does sex function as a status characteristic in mixed-sex groups of children? *J. Educ. Psychol.* 75: 877–86

Lord SE, Eccles JS, McCarthy KA. 1994. Surviving the junior high school transition: family processes and self-perceptions as protective and risk factors. *J. Early Adolesc.* 14:162–99

Lortie D. 1975. *Schoolteacher: A Sociological Analysis.* Chicago: Univ. Chicago Press

March J, Olsen J. 1976. *Ambiguity and Choice in Organizations.* Oslo: Universitetsforlaget

Marcus PM, Smith CB. 1985. Absenteeism in an organizational context. *Work Occup.* 12: 251–68

Massey GC, Scott M, Dornbusch SM. 1975. Racism without racists: institutional racism in urban schools. *Black Schol.* 7:10–19

McPartland JM, McDill EL. 1982. Control and differentiation in the structure of American education. *Sociol. Educ.* 55:77–88

Meyer JW, Rowan B. 1977. Institutionalized organizations. *Am. J. Sociol.* 83:340–63

Mickelson RA, 1987. Education and the struggle against race, class and gender inequality. *Hum. Sociol.* 11(4):440–64

Midgley C, Feldlaufer H, Eccles JS. 1988. The transition to junior high school: beliefs of pre- and post-transition teachers. *J. Youth Adolesc.* 17:543–62

National Center for Educational Statistics. 1985. *High School and Beyond: An Analysis of Course-Taking Patterns in Secondary Schools as Related to Student Characteristics. Rep. No. NCES 85–206.* Washington, DC: USGPO

Natriello G. 1984. Teachers' perceptions of the frequency of evaluation and assessments of their effort and effectiveness. *Am. Educ. Res. J.* 21:579–95

Oakes J. 1982. Classroom social relationships: exploring the Bowles and Gintis hypothesis. *Sociol. Educ.* 55:197–212

Oakes J. 1985. *Keeping Track: How Schools Structure Inequality.* New Haven, CT: Yale Univ. Press

Oakes J. 1987. Tracking in secondary schools:

a contextual perspective. *Educ. Psychol.* 22:129–53

Oakes J, Gamoran A, Page RN. 1992. Curriculum differentiation: opportunities, outcomes, and meanings. In *Handbook of Research on Curriculum*, ed. PW Jackson, pp. 570–608. New York: Macmillan

Oakes J, Selvin MJ, Karoly L, Guiton G. 1991. *Educational Matchmaking: Toward a Better Understanding of Curriculum and Tracking Decisions.* Santa Monica, CA: Rand

Ornstein AC. 1989. Centralization and decentralization of large public school districts. *Urban Educ.* 24:233–35

Pallas AM, Entwisle DR, Alexander KL, Cadigan D. 1987. Children who do exceptionally well in first grade. *Sociol. Educ.* 60: 257–71

Pallas AM, Entwisle DR, Alexander KL, Stluka MF. 1994. Ability group effects: instructional, social, or institutional? *Sociol. Educ.* 67:27–46

Persell C. 1977. *Education and Inequality.* London: Collier MacMillan

Ramirez FO, Meyer JW. 1980. The social construction of the modern world system. *Annu. Rev. Soc.* 6:369–99

Ritter PL, Mont-Reynaud R, Dornbusch SM. 1993. Minority parents and their youth: concern, encouragement, and support for school achievement. In *Families and Schools in a Pluralistic Society*, ed. NF Chavkin, pp. 107–19. Albany: State Univ. NY Press

Rohlen T. 1983. *Japan's High Schools.* Berkeley: Univ. Calif. Press

Roper SS, Hoffman DE. 1986. Collegial support for professional improvement: the Stanford collegial evaluation program. *Or. Sch. Stud. Counc. Bull.* 29:1–22

Rosenbaum JE. 1976. *Making Inequality: The Hidden Curriculum of High School Tracking.* New York: Wiley

Rosenbaum JE. 1980. Track misperceptions and frustrated college plans: an analysis of the effects of tracks and track perceptions in the National Longitudinal Survey. *Sociol. Educ.* 53:74–88

Rosenholtz SJ. 1985. Modifying status expectations in the traditional classroom. In *Status, Rewards, and Influence: How Expectations Organize Behavior*, ed. J Berger, M Zelditch. San Francisco: Jossey-Bass

Rosenholtz SJ. 1991. *Teachers' Workplace: The Social Organization of Schools.* New York: Teachers Coll. Press

Rosenholtz SJ, Simpson C. 1984. The formation of ability conceptions: developmental trend or social construction? *Rev. Educ. Res.* 54:31–63

Rosenholtz SJ, Simpson C. 1990. Workplace conditions and the rise and fall of teachers'

commitment. *Sociol. Educ.* 63:241–57

Rothbart M, Dalfen S, Barrett R. 1971. Effects of teacher's expectancy on student-teacher interaction. *J. Educ. Psychol.* 62:49–54

Rubinstein R, Kelly J, Maines D. 1985. The interdisciplinary background of community psychology: the early roots of an ecological perspective. *Am. Psychol. Assoc. Div. Comm. Psychol. Newsl.* 18(3):10–14

Rumberger RW. 1987. High school dropouts: a review of issues and evidence. *Rev. Educ. Res.* 57:101–21

Salomone RC, Ryan FA, Tollett KS, Levin HM, Glazer N, et al. 1982. The federal role in increasing equality of educational opportunity. *Harvard Educ. Rev.* 52(4): 419–59

Sarros JC, Sarros AM. 1987. Predictors of burnout among school teachers. *J. Educ. Adm.* 25(2):216–30

Schwartz F. 1981. Supporting or subverting learning: peer group patterns in four tracked schools. *Anthropol. Educ. Q.* 12: 99–121

Sergiovanni TJ. 1994. Organizations or communities? Changing the metaphor changes the theory. *Educ. Adm. Q.* 30(2):214–26

Sewell WH, Haller AO, Portes A. 1969. The educational and early occupational attainment process. *Am. Sociol. Rev.* 34:82–92

Sewell WH, Hauser RM. 1975. *Education, Occupation, and Earnings.* New York: Academic

Shavit Y, Featherman DL. 1988. Schooling, tracking, and teenage intelligence. *Sociol. Educ.* 61:42–51

Simmons RG, Burgeson R, Carlton-Ford S, Blyth DA. 1987. The impact of cumulative change in early adolescence. *Child Dev.* 58:1220–34

Slavin RE. 1987. Ability grouping and student achievement in elementary schools: a best-evidence synthesis. *Rev. Educ. Res.* 57: 293–336

Slavin RE. 1990. Achievement effects of ability grouping in secondary schools: a best-evidence synthesis. *Rev. Educ. Res.* 60: 471–99

Spillane RR. 1987. Why Bud Spillane is making merit pay a test of leadership. *Exec. Educ.* 9(7):20–21

Stanton-Salazar RD, Dornbusch SM. 1995. Social capital and the reproduction of inequality: information networks among Mexican-origin high school students. *Sociol. Educ.* 68:116–35

Steinberg L. 1995. Problems and promises of community research. *Sociol. Res. Adolesc. Newsl.* Winter

Stevenson HW. 1990. *Making the Grade in Mathematics.* Reston, VA: Natl. Counc. Teach. Math.

Stuck AF. 1984. *Cognitive development: a perspective for teacher development.* Presented at Annu. Meet. Am. Educ. Res. Assoc.

Tammivaara JS. 1982. The effects of task structure on beliefs about competence and participation in small groups. *Sociol. Educ.* 55:212–22

Trow M. 1977. The second transformation of American secondary education. See Karabel & Halsey 1977, pp. 105–18

Tuckman BW, Bierman M. 1971. *Beyond Pygmalion: Galatea in the schools.* Presented at Annu. Meet. Am. Educ. Res. Assoc., New York

Turner R. 1960. Sponsored and contest mobility and the school system. *Am. Sociol. Rev.* 25(6):855–67

Useem EL. 1991. Student selection into course sequences in mathematics: the impact of parental involvement and school policies. *J. Res. Adolesc.* 1(3):231–50

Useem EL. 1992. Middle schools and math groups: parents' involvement in children's placement. *Sociol. Educ.* 5:263–79

Useem M. 1986. Pathways to top corporate management. *Am. Sociol. Rev.* 51(2): 184–200

Vanfossen BE, Jones JD, Spade JZ. 1987. Curriculum tracking and status maintenance. *Sociol. Educ.* 60:104–22

Webster M, Driskell JE. 1983. Beauty as status. *Am. J. Sociol.* 89:140–65

Weick K. 1976. Educational organizations as loosely coupled systems. *Adm. Sci. Q.* 21: 1–19

Wong K. 1994. Linking governance reform to schooling opportunities for the disadvantaged. *Educ. Adm. Q.* 30:153–77

Worner GWB. 1993. The instructional leadership team: a new role for the department head. *Natl. Assoc. Second. Sch. Princ. Bull.* 77(553):37–45

Wynn J, Richman H, Rubinstein RA, Littell J. 1987. *Communities and Adolescents: An exploration of Reciprocal Supports.* A report prepared for WT Grant Found. Comm. Work, Fam., Citizsh: Youth Am. Futur. Chapin Hall Cent. Child. Univ. Chicago

Annu. Rev. Psychol. 1996. 47:431–59

ORIGINS AND EARLY DEVELOPMENT OF PERCEPTION, ACTION, AND REPRESENTATION

Bennett I. Bertenthal

Department of Psychology, University of Virginia, Charlottesville, Virginia 22903

KEY WORDS: perceptual development, motor development, conceptual development, cognitive development, sensorimotor development, perception-action, representation

ABSTRACT

Research relevant to the origins and early development of two functionally dissociable perceptual systems is summarized. One system is concerned with the perceptual control and guidance of actions, the other with the perception and recognition of objects and events. Perceptually controlled actions function in real time and are modularly organized. Infants perceive where they are and what they are doing. By contrast, research on object recognition suggests that even young infants represent some of the defining features and physical constraints that specify the identity and continuity of objects. Different factors contribute to developmental changes within the two systems; it is difficult to generalize from one response system to another; and neither perception, action, nor representation qualifies as ontogenetically privileged. All three processes develop from birth as a function of intrinsic processing constraints and experience.

CONTENTS

INTRODUCTION

Recent findings on the perceptual, motor, and conceptual competencies of young infants challenge long-held beliefs about early development. According to most classical developmental theories (Baldwin 1906, Bruner 1973, Piaget 1952), newborns are endowed with only a very simple repertoire of sensorimotor behaviors that are gradually integrated and internalized. The capacity for representation and conceptualization is presumed to emerge from this developmental process. It is not clear, however, that this position is still tenable. Indeed, the capacity for representation may be available at birth or soon thereafter (Carey & Gelman 1991; Eimas 1994; Leslie 1988; Karmiloff-Smith 1992; Mandler 1988, 1992; Mounoud 1993; Spelke 1994).

This new view requires a reconceptualization of the developmental relations among perception, action, and representation. Most models of perceptual processing now suggest that different sensory inputs converge into a unified representation that precedes both thought and action (Marr 1982, Ungerleider & Mishkin 1982). This monolithic view of perception suggests that assessing what is perceived is independent of whether the response measure is based on an action or a perceptual judgment. From a developmental perspective, this view implies that evidence for representation of objects should be manifested by thought and action at the same age. It is now apparent, however, that this view is obsolete. The paradigmatic case for this assertion is the conflicting and contradictory evidence on object permanence. Most infants do not reach for an object hidden by an occluder until they are 8–9 months old (Butterworth 1982). This failure to recover the hidden object is interpreted as evidence that infants do not think about objects that are not perceptually present (Piaget 1954). Nevertheless, infants as young as 3 months old show evidence that they represent the continuity and solidity of objects—at least when the test of object permanence demands nothing more than a visual fixation by the infant (Baillargeon 1987, Diamond 1991, Spelke et al 1992). In order to eliminate these confusions and contradictions in the literature we must adopt a new framework for understanding the early perceptual, motor, and cognitive development of infants.

An intriguing possibility is suggested by Goodale & Milner (1992), who propose that the visual system is divided into two functionally dissociable pathways. One is concerned primarily with the perceptual control and guidance of actions, the other primarily with the perception and recognition of objects and events. This dichotomy resembles the one advanced previously by

Ungerleider & Mishkin (1982) that the visual brain consists of two systems, a "what" and a "where" system. It is nevertheless different, because the emphasis is not on the input side of visual processing but the output side or the responses elicited by the visual information. "What" vs "how," not "what" vs "where," best captures this functional dissociation.

This functional dissociation between control and recognition represents the departure point for the current review. Although virtually all the evidence for this dissociation is based on neurophysiological findings with monkeys and neuropsychological findings with human adults, it is plausible that this dissociation is present early in development, given that the proposed division of labor maps onto different neural pathways that are all developing within the first year (Johnson 1990). One may speculate that this functional dissociation is not limited to visual processing, but extends to other modalities as well.

A brief review of the processing differences between these two perceptual systems will clarify further why behaviors mediated by the perceptual control system are functionally dissociable from behaviors mediated by the object recognition system.

1. Object recognition includes processes that make contact with information perceived at some prior time and stored in some representational form. Successful recognition depends on both how the visual scene is parsed and on the representational format of the stored information. By contrast, the perception and control of actions is directed toward present information and, if anything, includes a prospective view toward information in order to offset delays produced by neural transmission and the inertia of body segments.

2. The second difference is related to the first and involves the coordinate system for perceiving objects. Perception of objects involves an allocentric or world-based coordinate system such that displacements are seen relative to a stable or constant world. By contrast, acting on an object requires that the object be referenced egocentrically—i.e. relative to the effector system involved in the action (Paillard 1991).

3. A third difference concerns the coding and preservation of modality-specific information. Objects are typically specified by multimodal sources of input, but the information is stored in a modality-specific format. This provision is necessary to explain how observers recognize specific features of objects, such as its color or pitch, as well as the covariation between features specified both within and between modalities. By contrast, perceptual information is represented by the action system in an amodal format comprised of body-scaled information. This format transforms all sensory inputs into the appropriate muscle synergies necessary for producing coordinated actions in response to local conditions. It is thus not essential to represent the modality of the sensory input, because the function of this information is the same regardless of its source.

4. The last processing difference concerns the role of awareness in the perception of information. Objects that are not consciously processed are neither recognized nor stored for future recall. Recognition requires that observers direct their attention toward selected objects and know when they are perceiving the relevant information. Conversely, information necessary for detecting self-motion and controlling other actions operates without any necessary awareness by the observer. For example, patients with brain lesions who are unable to recognize objects are nevertheless able to reach for these objects and to anticipate their size and shape correctly while reaching (Goodale et al 1991, Weiskrantz et al 1974).

In the remainder of this chapter, I summarize recent research relevant to the development of these two perceptual systems, noting that different factors contribute to developmental changes within the two systems, that it is difficult to generalize from one response system to another, and that neither perception, action, nor representation qualifies as ontogenetically privileged. All three processes develop from birth as a function of intrinsic processing constraints and experience.

PERCEPTUAL CONTROL OF ACTIONS

All spatially coordinated behaviors, such as visual tracking, reaching, and sitting, require that perceptual information and action are coupled. In the words of James Gibson (1979), "We must perceive in order to move, but we must also move in order to perceive" (p. 223). Perceptual information relevant to the regulation of movements includes spatio-temporal patterns of optic flow at a moving eye, haptic patterns of joint, muscle, and skin deformations, and so on. All of this information changes in ways that are lawfully related to the properties of the environment and the action itself. For example, reaching for an object is guided by perceptual information that changes as the reach is executed. These perceptual changes modulate the effectors to insure that the reach is successful (Jeannerod 1994). Similarly, perceptual information is necessary to maintain postural equilibrium, but again the information changes as the posture is adjusted in response to that information (Howard 1986). From this perspective it is arbitrary and misleading to conceptualize perception and action as independent processes. It is more parsimonious to view these two processes as opposite poles of a functional unit or action system, along the lines suggested by Reed (1982, 1989).

Newborn Actions Are Spatially Coordinated

When are perception and action first coupled? Until recently, the answer to this question was dominated by Piaget's (1952) view of sensorimotor development. He asserted that perceptions and actions are initially independent processes that are coordinated gradually with experience. The implication of this proposal is that the early behavior of the neonate is essentially random and insensitive to contextual information. Recent research suggests that some rethinking of this extreme position is necessary.

During the past decade, researchers have observed that newborn infants are capable of performing many actions that are regulated by perceptual information. For example, newborn infants orient to sound (Clifton et al 1981, Muir & Field 1979, Zelazo et al 1984), scan differently in different stimulus conditions (Haith 1980), visually track moving targets (Bloch & Carchon 1992, Kremenitzer et al 1979), increase the frequency of hand-to-mouth contacts following oral delivery of a sucrose solution (Blass et al 1989, Rochat et al 1988), and show hand extensions toward a visible moving object (Trevarthen 1984, von Hofsten 1982). Of course, these behaviors are fragile and inconsistent, which explains why they were overlooked for quite some time. Subtle changes in posture or stimulus parameters are often sufficient to disrupt these coordinated behaviors. For example, Roucoux et al (1983) have shown that neonates sometimes experience difficulty in tracking objects visually because of the instability of their trunks, which do not yet move independently of their heads.

It thus appears that newborns enter the world prepared to perceptually regulate actions that are essential to the survival and adaptation of the neonate. An intriguing suggestion is that behaviors practiced in the womb show an advantage at birth (von Hofsten 1993). For example, proprioceptive guidance of the hand to the mouth is readily observed in neonates (Butterworth & Hopkins 1988, Rochat et al 1988). Furthermore, Butterworth & Hopkins (1988) report that the mouth is more likely to remain open during arm movements when the hand goes directly to the mouth rather than first touching other portions of the face. Soon after birth, this response is observed more frequently prior to feeding than following feeding (Lew & Butterworth 1995). Taken together, these findings suggest significant specificity in the coordination of hand and mouth at birth.

The evidence for the coupling of perception and actions at birth should not be misconstrued as suggesting that these systems are fully developed or that new couplings will not emerge. Contemporary theorists emphasize that development involves a confluence of factors that include neural and biomechanical changes as well as environmental and task factors (Newell 1986, Savelsbergh & van der Kamp 1993, Thelen 1995). Practice and experience with a specific action system contribute to its development. Some of the best examples involve behaviors traditionally viewed as motor skills, such as posture and gait (Sveistrup & Woollacott 1995, Thelen & Ulrich 1991).

One reason that practice and experience are not sufficient to capture the process of developmental change is that the infant is also changing in body proportions and neural connectivity. For example, Banks (1988) reports that the optical components of the eye are still growing at birth, the photoreceptors will mature and migrate during the first few months, and the dendritic arborization of the central visual pathways will continue to develop for some time. These changes inform us that the resolution and projective structure of the visual image will improve with development. Likewise, the perception of spatial layout and of the relative depths and distances of objects will improve with development (Yonas & Owsley 1987).

It is perhaps even more important to point out that oculomotor functioning will show significant improvement during early development. Saccadic localization of stationary and moving targets involves a direct mapping between retinal location and neuromuscular stimulation of the relevant eye muscles. Initially, this localization process is imprecise and involves multiple saccades before the target is foveated (Aslin & Salapatek 1975). No doubt some experience is necessary to learn the precise relation between the neural pulse duration and saccade magnitude necessary for rotating the eye to the correct position. It is still somewhat surprising that the calibration process requires over four months to complete, especially when estimates suggest that infants make between 3 million and 6 million eye movements by 3.5 months of age (Haith et al 1988). One especially intriguing hypothesis about this lengthy process is that the mapping of retinal locus onto an oculomotor command is constrained by the changing distribution of photoreceptors in the retina (Aslin 1988). It is thus necessary for the infant to adapt continually to this changing sensorimotor relation during early development.

This last example illustrates especially well that actions are spatially coordinated from birth but become better tuned or coordinated as a function of neural development and experience. Although the process by which perceptuomotor behaviors develop is rarely investigated, researchers have begun to recognize that motor skills are not only products of this developmental process, but are intimately involved in the process itself.

Reciprocity Between Action and Perception

Perceptual control of behavior depends on the detection of the relevant perceptual information as well as the functionality of the actions available to infants. As simple actions such as visual tracking or sucking are practiced and repeated, they become better coordinated and controlled, and perceptual information is detected with increasing specificity. An excellent example of these changes is revealed by research on the minimum audible angle necessary for detection of the direction of a sound source. In this task infants are expected to turn their heads to the right or left of midline if they are capable of localizing the sound (Ashmead et al 1987, Morrongiello 1988). Ashmead et al (1991) summarize the data from a number of studies to show that the minimum detectable difference decreases rapidly between 8 and 24 weeks of age and then continues to decrease more gradually through 80 weeks of age. It is noteworthy that the most rapid improvement occurs during and just following the time that infants are developing independent control of their heads (Bayley 1969).

The preceding example is an excellent illustration of the reciprocity that exists between action and perception in development. As new actions become available, new opportunities for exploring the fit between the self and the environment emerge (Adolph et al 1993a). Another example of this proposal is associated with the development of crawling or self-produced locomotion. Perceptual guidance is necesary to assure movement without collisions on a safe and sturdy surface of support (Gibson & Schmuckler 1989).

Bertenthal & Campos (1990) report that perceptual sensitivity to objects and surfaces changes significantly following some experience with crawling. For example, Campos et al (1992) report a series of studies showing that precrawling infants show no evidence of fear (as indexed by heart rate acceleration) when lowered onto the deep side of a visual cliff (simulating an apparent drop-off in height), whereas crawling infants show a significant degree of fear. Fear is also shown by precrawling infants if they are given sufficient experience with self-locomotion in baby-walkers. Apparently, such experience with perceptual guidance of self-locomotion changes infants' perceptual appreciation of an apparent cliff. Precrawling infants do not show fear of heights not because they cannot perceive depth (Yonas & Owsley 1987) but because they do not yet need to coordinate the perception of surfaces with their direction of heading.

Similar findings are reported by Gibson et al (1987), who tested crawling and newly walking infants on their mode of locomotion on two surfaces varying in rigidity (plywood vs waterbed). Infants capable of upright locomotion differentially explored the two surfaces and chose to walk only on the rigid surface. Crawling infants did not show different behavior on the two surfaces. In more recent research, Adolph et al (1993b) report that newly walking infants, but not crawling infants, differentiate between inclined and declined surfaces by choosing a more stable posture, such as sitting or crawling backwards, when traversing the down-sloping surface.

Another compelling example of the reciprocity between perception and the development of new actions is offered by Bushnell & Boudreau (1993). Adults detect many different properties of objects, such as size, texture, weight, hardness, and temperature, from haptic explorations (Lederman & Klatzky 1987). Some of these properties, such as size and temperature, demand minimal control of the hand and fingers, whereas other properties, such as weight and shape, require much greater control. Bushnell & Boudreau reviewed the ages at which infants first discriminate different object properties and concluded that the sequence corresponds to developmental changes in the control of the hand and fingers. For example, infants detect size within the first few months, but texture, temperature, and hardness are not detected until around 6 months of age, and weight and shape are not detected until even later. Although the evidence for this claim is still incomplete, alternative interpetations (e.g. that these observations result from differential exposure to different object properties) are unlikely, given the ecology of the infant's environment.

New perceptions and new actions are related through a dynamic process involving the selection of new behaviors in response to new sources of variability in the organism and in the environment (Bertenthal et al 1994, Manoel & Connolly 1995; Thelen 1989, 1995). Consider the coordination of the limbs during forward prone progression. Most infants crawl with their abdomens on the ground before crawling on hands-and-knees. Once they develop sufficient strength to support themselves on hands-and-knees they briefly show many different patterns of interlimb coordination before converging on a pattern of moving diagonally opposite limbs simultaneously (Freedland & Bertenthal 1994). The selection of this specific pattern is a function of perceiving the optimal coordinative structure to insure balance while minimizing the expenditure of energy.

Another example related to the development of crawling experience involves the spatial coding of a hidden object. Numerous studies report that crawling infants show improved localization of objects following a displacement of the infant or the object (Bremner & Bryant 1985, Horobin & Acredolo 1986). Precrawling infants tend to code the location of an object with a body-centered frame of reference, presumably because this coding is initially necessary for successful orientation to the object. With the emergence of crawling, infants show a transitional period during which their responses vary. Eventually, they learn to update their initial spatial coding in response to the perceived displacement (Bai & Bertenthal 1992).

Thelen and colleagues offer additional examples of how the development of new actions, such as infant stepping, emerge following periods of increased variability (Thelen & Ulrich 1991, Ulrich et al 1991). Overall, this research suggests that perceptuomotor development is an emergent process in which a goal-directed organism seeks stable outcomes to specific tasks.

Perception Is Prospective

Our actions, like those of all animals, are coupled to the spatial layout and demand perceptual guidance and control (Lee 1993). In locomotion, for example, we must make contact with some surfaces while avoiding others. In general, it is necessary to control actions prospectively and not retrospectively (i.e. following feedback from the action) in order to insure smooth and safe movement (von Hofsten 1993). The inertia of the limbs and the time lags of neural conduction demand some anticipation of future actions (Haith 1994, von Hofsten 1993). Information needed for the specification of upcoming events is available in the optic and acoustic arrays and is used for controlling future actions. As adults, we readily appreciate the temporal component in the control of actions. For example, we know that it is necessary to be in the right place at the right time to catch a ball, meet a person, or give a lecture. Recent findings in the literature reveal some remarkable examples of future-oriented behavior by infants.

One of the earliest examples of prospective behavior is seen in the development of smooth visual pursuit of moving targets. In order to track an object smoothly it is necessary to anticipate its future position: The programming of eye movements takes time. Shea & Aslin (1990) presented infants with 2° white squares that moved at a range of fixed velocities between 3 and 12 degrees per second. They reported that the pursuit system is clearly functional by 7 weeks of age and suggested that slower speeds and larger targets could be detected at younger ages. This suggestion is consistent with the findings of other investigators (Bloch & Carchon 1992, Kremenitzer et al 1979, Roucoux et al 1983), who report brief segments of smooth pursuit in newborns and one-month-old infants. The success of pursuit tracking at such young ages is especially impressive when it is recognized that eye movements may also have to compensate for unrelated head movements. In studies where the head was unrestrained during testing, young infants tracked a moving target with a combination of head and eye movements (Daniel & Lee 1990, Regal et al 1983, Roucoux et al 1983).

Another eye movement paradigm that shows early evidence of future-oriented behavior is the visual expectation paradigm pioneered by Haith (1993): Infants observe small pictures that alternate between the left and right of the center of the screen. After a few repetitions, 2- and 3-month-old infants begin to show anticipatory fixations to the location of the appearance of the next picture, even when the timing and location of the alternation patterns become more complex (Canfield & Haith 1991, Wentworth & Haith 1992). It thus appears that even very young infants can learn quickly how to control the location of their fixations in order to explore the changing pattern of information available in their visual world.

One of the most remarkable examples of prospective behavior by infants involves their reaching for moving objects. Von Hofsten (1983) studied infants' reaching for stationary and moving objects and reported that they began to contact objects in both conditions at the same age. By 18 weeks of age, infants could catch an object moving at 30 cm/s, and by 8 months infants could catch objects moving at 125 cm/s. In this study, a reach did not correspond to a simple reflex response. The objects were contacted at various locations along their trajectory, and the aiming and timing errors were quite small. These observations suggest that the infants were sucessfully controlling their reaches by extrapolating from the trajectories of the objects and modulating their motor responses. This modulation is a complex process involving the perception of both passive and active forces that vary from one reach to the next (Zernicke & Schneider 1993). In a related study, Robin et al (1995) observed 5- and 7.5-month-old infants reaching for a horizontally moving object. Infants usually reach with their ipsilateral hand for a stationary object (Perris & Clifton 1988). In this study, infants shifted to reaching with their contralateral hand when the object was moving, which increased the time available to intercept the target. Kinematic measures, such as velocity and duration of arm movements, converged with those reported by von Hofsten to suggest that infants aimed their reaches in anticipation of the future position of the moving object.

Prospective behaviors are also evidenced when infants learn to posturally compensate for a loss of balance (Bertenthal et al 1995, von Hofsten 1993), lean toward objects that are out of reach (McKenzie et al 1993, Rochat & Goubet 1995, Yonas & Hartman 1993), anticipate the size, shape, and orientation of objects that they are attempting to grasp (Lockman et al 1984, von Hofsten & Ronnqvist 1988), and guide their locomotion around obstacles (Gibson & Schmuckler 1989, Schmuckler & Gibson 1989). One interpretation of all of these findings is that infants become successful across tasks as they develop the capacity to represent future events. The problem with this cognitive interpretation is that it ignores developmental differences attributable to the coordination of different motor skills. A more parsimonious interpretation is that the prospective behavior displayed by infants is not contingent on a central representation but rather emerges piecemeal from the specific experiences that infants encounter through their actions. It is thus the dynamic interplay between actions and outcomes that fosters the development of prospective control. As infants experience new tasks that demand greater control, the precise timing of their actions will improve.

Perception Is Multimodal

In most situations, the perceptual information available for controlling actions is multimodal. Consider, for example, the control of posture during independent stance. Posture is specified by proprioceptive, vestibular, and visual flow information (Lishman & Lee 1973). It is a goal-directed behavior, even if it is not consciously controlled (Howard 1986). The individual's goal is to position the head and body relative to gravity and the surface of support. When a perturbation of this position is sensed, a postural compensation is initiated. One reason that this perceptuomotor response is so successful is that it is specified by multiple and redundant sensory inputs. This redundancy increases the likelihood of detection by even young infants who show rapid development of this perceptual-motor response.

Much of the research on the development of postural control tests infants in a "moving room." In this paradigm, the infant sits or stands on a stationary floor while the walls and ceiling move forward and backward. This movement produces visual information congruent with the head moving in the opposite direction. If the optical flow is perceived as specifying self-motion (as opposed to object motion), then the infant will show a postural compensation that varies with age and experience (Bertenthal & Rose 1995).

Lee & Aronson (1974) were the first to show that independently standing infants compensate posturally in a directionally appropriate manner in response to such visual flow information. Others subsequently demonstrated that optical flow information restricted to the peripheral portions of the visual field was sufficient to induce postural compensations (Bertenthal & Bai 1989, Stoffregen et al 1987). Additional evidence for the coupling between vision and posture was reported by Butterworth & Hicks (1977) and Bertenthal & Bai (1989), who showed that infants who could sit independently also responded with postural compensations of their trunk when tested in the moving room. It appears that an even earlier form of this coupling is present at birth. Jouen (1990) reported that newborn infants show postural compensations of their head when stimulated by an optical flow pattern of blinking lights located in the periphery of the visual field.

In the moving room paradigm postural compensations are induced by visual information, but it would be misleading to suggest that the response is controlled exclusively by visual inputs. Postural sway is specified visually by optical flow information, but it is also specified by more proximal stimulation from muscles, joints, and the inner ear. Studies involving mechanical perturbations of a platform reveal that somatosensory and vestibular systems also induce postural responses (Hirschfeld & Forrsberg 1994, Woollacott & Sveistrup 1994). Developmental changes in postural control involve learning to regulate the amount of force to compensate for the perceived displacement. Bertenthal et al (1995) studied infants during the period when they are learning to sit without support. They report that the compensatory forces necessary to maintain postural equilibrium become more precisely scaled to the perceived displacement of the trunk between 5 and 9 months of age. Performance improves not only because compensatory postural responses are more finely modulated, but also because the perceived displacements are detected more rapidly and precisely.

How do infants learn that different sources of sensory input are equivalent and converge on the same motor response? If sensory information is first represented in a modality-specific format, then it would appear necessary for infants to learn the relations between different sensory inputs, such as vision and touch. Indeed, this form of learning to coordinate different modalities is the bedrock of Piaget's (1954) theory of sensorimotor development. Yet current evidence suggests that this form of associative learning is unnecessary.

An alternative proposal is that all sensory inputs related to self-produced actions are represented in a common amodal format that maps directly onto an appropriate pattern of muscle activations (Lee 1993, Warren 1990). Such a common format is thought to insure that all sources of sensory information are transformed into the same body-scaled information necessary for modulating the motor response synergies involved in the performance of coordinated movements (Bertenthal & Rose 1995, Savelsbergh & van der Kamp 1993). For example, when an individual detects that support is perturbed, it is not important to determine which sensory input channel specified this loss of balance. The goal is simply to restore equilibrium, and this involves scaling the compensatory forces to the perceived displacement.

Another example of the equivalence of different sensory inputs for controlling actions involves the development of reaching. Historically, the prevailing view has been that reaching is initially visually guided (Bushnell 1985, Piaget 1952, White et al 1964), but more recent studies show that infants reach readily and accurately in the dark for sounding as well as luminous objects (Clifton et al 1991, Clifton et al 1994, Stack et al 1989). In one study (Clifton et al 1993), infants between 6 and 25 weeks of age were tested longitudinally to determine whether they required sight of their hands when beginning to reach for, contact, and grasp objects. Each session included trials of objects presented in the light and trials of glowing and sounding objects presented in complete darkness. The results revealed little variation as a function of experimental condition. Overall, infants first contacted the object in both conditions at comparable ages (light 12.3 weeks; dark 11.9 weeks), and they first grasped the object in the light at 16.0 weeks and in the dark at 14.7 weeks. Infants could not see their hands or arms in the dark; their early success in contacting the glowing and sounding objects indicates that proprioceptive information was sufficient to guide reaching. It thus appears that no single source of sensory information (e.g. visual, proprioceptive, or vestibular) is privileged in initially guiding actions.

Some of the most dramatic evidence for the amodal representation of sensory inputs is revealed by studies of neonatal imitation. Meltzoff & Moore (1983, 1989, 1994) and many others (see Anisfeld 1991 for a review) have shown convincingly that newborn infants imitate specific facial gestures (e.g. mouth opening) produced by an adult model. Such gestures cannot be visually guided because they involve movements that the infant cannot see—i.e. movement of the infant's own face. The correspondence between the perceived facial gesture and action by the newborn suggests that visual information concerning the adult's face is perceived amodally in a format that maps directly onto the appropriate muscle activation patterns (Meltzoff & Moore

1994). Currently, this claim remains fairly controversial because it necessitates the detection of a correspondence between the visual perception of the actions of a model and the proprioceptive perception of one's own actions. No complete explanation for this matching has yet been presented, although the spatiotemporal coding of the model's gestures may provide more specific information than assumed by most investigators (Bertenthal & Pinto 1993).

In sum, actions are most often guided by multimodal information. This redundancy may help to explain why the perception and control of adaptive behaviors, such as reaching, sitting, and walking, develop rapidly once the necessary muscle synergies are available. Moreover, the availability of multiple sources of information for modulating actions in response to local conditions increases the consistency, stability, and flexibility of any adaptive behavior.

Perception Is Context Specific

Recent theoretical and empirical advances in the study of motor control and coordination highlight that actions are a product of multiple factors including physical, physiological, and energetic components (Freedland & Bertenthal 1994, Goldfield 1993, Manoel & Connelly 1995, Thelen 1995, Turvey 1990). A principal implication of this view is that the same actions will not necessarily be observed in different contexts. For example, Grenier (1981) reported that reaching movements by newborns are much better coordinated when the head is stabilized than when it is unsupported. This finding is especially important because it emphasizes that context involves not only external factors, but also the ways in which different body segments are configured and interact. Zernicke & Schneider (1993) show explicitly that the forces responsible for moving limb segments are a function both of active forces (produced by muscle contractions) and of passive forces (corresponding to gravity and the inertial forces from the other moving body parts). Thus, it is apparent that there exist multiple constraints that determine whether or not an action will be performed in a specific context.

This contextual specificity is illustrated by the finding that newborn infants perform alternating step-like movements when held upright with their feet on a support surface. Within a few months, these movements disappear, presumably because they are inhibited by the development of higher-level cortical structures (Zelazo 1984). Curiously, however, similar movements are still observed in babies lying on their stomachs or backs (Thelen & Fisher 1982). These findings may be explained by a simple biomechanical calculation showing that more energy is needed to lift a leg to full flexion while upright than while supine. Although gravity is a constant force in the environment, it only becomes a constraint after the newborn period when infants begin experiencing rapid weight gains that decrease the ratio of muscle to subcutaneous fat in the legs. Experimental manipulations that changed the weight of the leg or the resistance of the leg to flexion (e.g. submerging infants in torso-deep water) showed that the presence or absence of stepping was systematically related to the biomechanical constraints of the situation (Thelen et al 1984, Thelen et al 1987). This simulation of developmental change highlights the important contribution of contextual variables.

The development of reaching in different postures is another example of the context specificity of motor control. Coordinated reaching is only possible in the context of a stable body posture (von Hofsten 1993, Paillard 1991). When infants incapable of sitting without support (22–26 weeks of age) are placed in a fully supported posture (e.g. supine or reclined), they tend to reach for objects with both hands (Rochat & Senders 1991, Rochat 1992). By contrast, infants capable of sitting without support (28–38 weeks of age) reach with one hand, regardless of their posture. The younger infants also reach with one hand when placed in a seated position, because they must compensate for a loss of balance by recruiting the other hand to help stabilize themselves in this position. Note that in this case infants shift to a different response because the task is different, not because they have undergone a change in neural or muscular control. The selection of a more stable response induced by behavior becoming more variable in a new situation or task appears to represent one of the few general processes in the development of new actions (Freedland & Bertenthal 1994, Manoel & Connolly 1995, Thelen 1995).

Additional evidence suggests that perception-action couplings are relatively specific and thus do not generalize to similar actions. For example, Rochat & Senders (1991) report a progression in hand-mouth coordination from bimanual action organized in mirror image symmetry toward an asymmetrical involvement of the hands. This same progression is repeated when infants begin to visually explore objects that are grasped, even though bimanual reaching is less flexible or functional. Likewise, visual control of a sitting posture does not generalize to visual control of a standing posture (Bertenthal & Bai 1989, Woollacott & Sveistrup 1994). It appears that infants must learn to modulate or control each new motor response de novo, even if the perceptual information (e.g. optical flow specifying self-motion) is readily processed.

There is an important moral to this section. It is misleading and contradictory to ascribe a specific perceptual skill to an infant based on one task. Performance is based on multiple factors; seemingly insignificant variables, such as postural stability or orientation, produce profound effects. Moreover, the presence or absence of the skill in question will also depend on the specific motor response necessary for performing the task. For this reason, researchers are well advised not to discuss these perceptual skills independent of the task or response assessed. A better approach is to determine whether the perceptual information is transformed into the appropriate motor response synergies, and to specify all the factors that contribute to this process. This strategy shifts the focus from assessing onset of perceptual skills to understanding how these skills develop.

OBJECT PERCEPTION AND RECOGNITION

The recognition system is distinguished from the perception-action system primarily by the fact that recognition is defined with reference to the past. If I recognize a student or a friend, for example, some immediately perceived information must match some previously stored information. Although theorists (Biederman 1987, Marr 1982, Rock 1984) offer little consensus on the representational format of this information, it is reasonably certain that the stored information is not an exact copy of the perceived scene. Logical and functional imperatives dictate that storing all the available information in the scene is neither necessary nor useful for specific tasks. The ordinary environment consists of a hierarchical nesting of information at multiple scales ranging from large objects, such as mountains and trees, to very small objects, such as leaves and cells; it is rich in structure and consists of places, surfaces, layouts, people, animals, etc. From any point of observation, a plenum of structured information is available, including the texture and composition of individual surfaces, the arrangement of those surfaces in the spatial layout, and the binding of some into distinct objects. What is perceived and recognized depends on the intentions and goals of the observer. The task of recognizing a book is the same regardless of its orientation, position, or location relative to the observer. It is thus unlikely that information about the spatial properties of the book will be stored for purposes of book-recognition, because these will change with the position of the observer. Unlike the perception-action system, which is viewer-centered, the recognition system encodes and stores those properties that are invariant across multiple perspective transformations of the object.

In this section, we review evidence that recognition begins at birth and that infants are endowed with perceptual decoding principles that exploit some of the most important regularities in the physical world. (This discussion is restricted to the processing of visual information because such information is most relevant to the proposed functional dissociation that guides this review.) These principles are initially available in implicit form and guide perception by constraining or privileging certain interpretations of the visual scene. As infants perceive the same information repeatedly, the stored representations derived from these experiences become increasingly rich and abstract (Eimas 1994). Perceptual and conceptual knowledge blend together in this framework, because stored representations are accessible for both recognition and reasoning (Spelke 1994).

Newborn Recognition of Objects

The traditional view is that infants are endowed with very simple capacities to look at objects—capacities that enable them to perceive the world piecemeal via fleeting images (e.g. Piaget 1954). This view acknowledges that recognition of some kind occurs early in life, but it is of a kind linked to previously produced actions and not to stored information about the world. Such a proposal is generally consistent with the development of those behaviors associated with the aforementioned perception-action system, but it does not generalize at all to the development of the object recognition system. Nevertheless, recent studies on object recognition reveal evidence of very early representation, beginning with recognition memory in neonates (Slater et al 1984, 1990a,b).

The habituation paradigm is foundational to the study of perceptual recognition by infants (Bornstein 1985) and thus deserves a brief overview. In this paradigm infants are presented with a specific stimulus for a number of trials until their attention declines. One reason that infants' attentiveness declines over trials is presumably that as they develop a stored representation of the stimulus it becomes less interesting. The encoding and storage of stimulus information are tested by presenting a novel stimulus following some criterion decrease in responding. If the infant's decline in responsiveness occurred because the first stimulus became familiar, then a novel stimulus should reinitiate responsiveness. Conversely, the novel stimulus should not produce an increase in responsiveness if the previous decline was simply a function of fatigue. Note that the sensitivity of this paradigm with very young infants is attributable to requiring only very simple responses, such as visual fixation.

The finding that neonates habituate to visual displays is provocative because it confirms that they begin to store perceptual information from their first encounters with the world. It is not necessarily the case, however, that this information is stored beyond the period of the study. Recently, Rovee-Collier (1995) introduced the concept of a "time window" to explain when and how new information would be integrated into memory. In essence, this theory predicts that repeated encounters with the same information over short periods increase the likelihood of long-term retention of that information.

Studies of neonates' face recognition capabilities suggest that the time window is functional from birth. Bushnell et al (1989) showed that neonates look longer at their mothers' faces than at strangers' faces, even when olfactory information was controlled by masking the odor of the mother. Walton et al (1992) reported that this preference was also observed when the faces were video recorded. More recently, Pascalis et al (1995) replicated this finding but showed that this preference was extinguished when women wore head scarves. The authors suggest that neonates store a representation of their mothers' faces in which the hairline and outer contour play a prominent role. This finding is consistent with the evidence that very young infants are biased toward the perception of low spatial frequencies, i.e. large-scale pattern information (Banks & Dannemiller 1987). As the spatial resolution of the visual system improves, infants respond more to the internal features of the face (de Schonen & Mathivet 1989, Morton & Johnson 1991).

These findings converge to show that infants begin to store frequently repeated perceptual information from birth. Presumably, this information is functionally significant and engages the infants' attention much more than other information available to them. Although the mother is typically specified by multimodal information, it is intriguing to find that neonates show recognition of modality-specific information. This finding is consistent with other evidence that perceptual information is stored in a modality-specific format by the recognition system (Bertenthal & Rose 1995). Less clear is the organization of the perceptual information stored by the neonate. We addresss this issue in the next section.

Implicit Knowledge of Objects

Before visual information is stored by infants, they must bind and/or segment it into units likely to be perceived when the same information is presented again. The complexity of most visual scenes makes this a formidable task for young infants. The infant's visual world may include a wide variety of objects ranging from blankets and stuffed animals to people, machines, and furniture. Most objects are not completely visible: Portions are occluded, boundaries are not always delineated, and the projective structure of this information changes continuously as infants and objects move. The first task for the infant is to ascertain which surfaces and features in the optic array comprise objects distinct from other objects.

Object segmentation is readily accomplished by adult observers, who organize the visual scene based on perceptual grouping principles, physical knowledge of objects, and past experience (Needham & Baillargeon 1995). Such grouping principles apply across many different contexts and situations. Recent research suggests that even young infants apply some of these same processes when viewing the visual world. For example, Spelke & van de Walle (1993) report that 3-month-old infants perceive two objects as distinct if they are separated in depth or move independently. By contrast, young infants do not perceive boundaries between objects that are stationary and adjacent, even if the objects differ in color, texture, and form. It is suggested that infants' perception of the spatial layout follows two specific principles or processing constraints. In essence, these principles assert that surfaces are perceived as connected if, and only if, they move together (principle of contact) or lie on a single object (principle of cohesion).

Additional studies reveal that young infants perceive the unity of partially occluded objects when the visible parts are seen to move together in a rigid fashion (henceforth referred to as "rigid motion") (Baillargeon 1987, Craton & Yonas 1990, Kellman et al 1986, Johnson & Nanez 1995, Slater et al 1990b). In an early study by Kellman & Spelke (1983), 4-month-old infants were repeatedly presented with a vertically oriented rod that moved horizontally back and forth behind a block that occluded the center of the rod. Once infants became habituated to this event, they were presented on alternating trials with two novel displays—a complete rod and a broken rod consisting of two collinear segments separated by a gap in the middle. Infants showed a significant increase in visual attention to the broken rod but not to the complete rod, suggesting that they perceived the previously presented partially occluded rod as a unitary object. Later studies revealed that any rigid translation of the partially occluded rod enabled 4-month-old infants to perceive the visible portions as unified (Kellman et al 1986); on the other hand, static grouping principles such as good continuation, collinearity, and similarity of texture or color were not sufficient to suggest unity (Kellman & Spelke 1983).

As infants grow older they begin to exploit additional regularities of the physical world in the process of segmenting objects. Needham & Baillargeon (1995) review a number of recent findings showing that infants by 8 months of age employ featural properties, such as color and shape, and physical constraints, such as the impenetrability of surfaces, to help them interpret ambiguous arrangements of objects in the visual scene. Their findings also suggest an important caveat to interpreting age-related changes in object segmentation. When infants were given prior experience with the objects that were displayed during the experiment, the correct perceptual response was shown at 4.5 months instead of at 8 months of age. Apparently, object segmentation processes interact with past experience when infants perceptually organize a visual scene.

The interplay between perceptual grouping processes and past experience is also illustrated by research on infants' perception of biological motions (Bertenthal 1993). These motions are depicted by points of light moving as if attached to the major joints and head of a person walking. Adult observers, who do not recognize static displays of such point-lights in any consistent way, recognize the moving point-lights as depicting a human form in less than 0.5 s (Johansson 1973, Bertenthal & Pinto 1994). Three- and five-month-old infants discriminate these same moving point-light displays from ones in which the temporal patterning of the lights are perturbed (Bertenthal et al 1987, Proffitt & Bertenthal 1990). It is conjectured that multiple processing constraints, including stored knowledge of the human form, contribute to the interpretation of these point-light displays (Bertenthal 1993, Bertenthal & Pinto 1994). This conjecture is supported by findings showing that 5-month-old infants do not discriminate point-light displays depicting unfamiliar objects, such as a four-legged spider, from a perturbed version (Bertenthal & Pinto 1993).

At a general level, the point-light display is similar to the partially occluded rod because both depict unitary objects that are more or less occluded. Nevertheless, an important difference between the displays is that the visible segments of the rod move rigidly, whereas the point-lights do not. The contact principle proposed by Spelke & van de Walle (1993; see above) exploits the rigid motions of spatially separated surfaces to organize the visual scene. In the case of biological motions, this principle will not suffice. Note that the object motions in these two displays correspond to very different categories of knowledge (i.e. physical vs biological), suggesting that different processing principles may be associated with different core domains (Leslie 1988, Carey & Spelke 1994).

One of the most important reasons that the preceding decoding principles appear so generalizable is that they mirror the physical constraints governing an object's behavior (Spelke et al 1992). A similar conclusion is reached by Shepard (1994) based on his research on adult perception of apparent motions. In the absence of any physically presented motion, the perceived path of an apparent motion is underspecified and must therefore reflect certain organizing principles in the visual system. Shepard contends that the visual system selects a particular motion from among the infinite set of possible motions according to the constraints of kinematic geometry, which govern the relative motions of rigid objects, or of local parts of nonrigid objects, during brief moments. According to Shepard, these physical constraints represent some of the most pervasive properties about the world that have endured throughout evolution; thus, natural selection should have favored genes that internalized these constraints as processing principles.

Computational research investigating infants' perception of structure from motion offers some additional support for the internalization of those physical constraints that contribute to the perception of objects. When perspective information is excluded from the display, a transforming 2-dimensional projection of a 3-dimensional stimulus is underdetermined. It is thus necessary for observers to implement additional processing constraints, such as a rigidity assumption, in order to extract a unique structure from the projection (Marr 1982). Arterberry & Yonas (1988) tested infants' perception of structure from motion by testing them with a 2-dimensional projection of a sphere filled with a random distribution of elements. When viewed statically, the 2-dimensional image appears ambiguous, but as soon as the elements begin to rotate, a rigid form is perceived—as long as the image is interpreted as the projection of a 3-dimensional rigid object. Arterberry & Yonas showed that infants as young as 4 months of age perceive 3-dimensional forms from 2-dimensional projections that change over time. Similar findings are presented by Kellman (1984) and Kellman & Short (1987). Collectively, these findings suggest that young infants are sensitive to some of the same processing constraints used by adults for perceiving 3-dimensional objects.

Explicit Knowledge of Objects

Theoretical opinion is divided over whether the processing constraints discussed above are induced from early perceptual experiences or correspond to innate cognitive representations of the physical world (Baillargeon 1993, 1995; Karmiloff-Smith 1992; Leslie 1988; Mandler 1988, 1992; Spelke 1994). In either case, an abstract representation of some kind guides the perception of objects by 3 months of age or younger. Moreover, recent findings suggest that these representations not only guide perception but also provide an early foundation for reasoning about the world. In other words, these abstract representations about the motions of objects are accessible to infants as explicit knowledge (Baillargeon 1993, 1995; Leslie 1988; Spelke et al 1992).

The principal evidence for this knowledge derives from occlusion studies in which inferences are required because the entire event is not visible. For example, Spelke et al (1992) tested 2.5–4.5-month-old infants' reasoning about the continuity and solidity of objects by habituating them to various events. In one experiment, an initially visible ball was dropped behind a screen and then the screen was raised to reveal the ball on the floor of the stage. After infants became habituated to this event, a brightly colored surface was added above the floor, the screen was lowered to cover both surfaces, and then the ball was dropped again. On alternating trials the screen was raised to reveal a ball on the new surface or on the floor of the stage. Adult observers reason that the former event is (covert manipulation aside) impossible because it would require the ball to pass through or jump over the upper surface. Such movements would violate both the continuity principle of objects (i.e. objects follow one continuous path over space and time) and the solidity principle (i.e. the parts of distinct objects may never coincide in place and time). Apparently, infants appreciate these principles, because they paid considerably more visual attention to the impossible event than to the possible event. Additional experiments by Spelke et al (1992) and by Baillargeon (1993) converge to show that young infants reason about the continuity and solidity of objects involved in simple physical events.

Certain other physical concepts, such as gravity and inertia, are not understood by infants until close to the end of their first year (Spelke et al 1992, Spelke et al 1994). This finding highlights an important difference between the perception-action system and the object-recognition system. Research on young infants' reaching for moving targets (reviewed above) suggests that they are implicitly sensitive to gravity and inertia by 5 to 6 months of age;

otherwise, it is difficult to imagine how they could successfully anticipate the future position of moving targets. This implicit knowledge is not generaliz able, however, because it is encapsulated in the action and is thus not repre- sented in a format accessible by the cognitive system. By contrast, knowledge about gravity and inertia that is represented by the object-recognition system will generalize across situations once it is stored as a representation.

The conclusion that young infants reason about physical events is contested by some theorists (e.g. Fischer & Biddell 1991, Oakes & Cohen 1995, Siegler 1993). In evaluting this research, it is important to distinguish between the evidence for infants' reasoning and the conclusion that these results reflect innate theories of the physical world. The empirical evidence that reasoning occurs is much more defensible than the evidence for an innate core of knowl- edge, especially because most studies of infants' physical reasoning focus on infants 3 months old or older. Resolution of this issue requires an explanation of how core knowledge about the physical world (e.g. about the continuity and solidity of objects) develops from perceptual information (Spelke 1994). This is a daunting requirement, but preliminary ideas are beginning to appear in the literature.

Baillargeon (1995) suggests that the development of physical knowledge reflects a highly constrained learning mechanism that processes the available perceptual information. Regrettably, the details of this learning mechanism are vague, although some of the predictions are not. Baillargeon claims that in- fants first learn to encode the causal properties of a physical event, such as a collision, at a very simple level and then begin to encode both qualitative and quantitative variables about the event. For example, a series of experiments by Kotovsky & Baillargeon (reviewed in Baillargeon 1995) reveals that 2.5- month-old infants expect a stationary object to be displaced when hit by a moving object, but it is not until 5.5–6.5 months of age that infants recognize that a stationary object should be displaced further by a larger than by a smaller moving object. It is conjectured that infants will begin to encode other variables, such as mass, speed, and distance, following additional experience with relevant events (Baillargeon 1995).

Object Recognition Is Domain Specific

An important implication of the preceding theory is that infants' knowledge of physical events develops piecemeal and not all at once. Some object proper- ties, such as size, are more easily detected than others, such as mass, and thus conceptual knowledge of the physical world develops gradually as it is tutored by experience. A related developmental trend is that infants appear to use spatio-temporal information to specify the identity of objects prior to individu- ating these objects on the basis of featural information (Cohen & Oakes 1993, Xu & Carey 1995). Even though infants are sensitive by 6 to 7 months of age to launching events and other events involving spatio-temporal continuity (Baillargeon 1993, Leslie & Keeble 1987, Oakes 1995), recent evidence suggests that they do not detect the individuating properties of objects in these dynamic events until 10 to 12 months of age (Xu & Carey 1995). Evidence for this latter conclusion is somewhat suspect, however, because infants can perceptually categorize certain basic kinds of objects by 3 months of age (Quinn & Eimas 1986). Perceptual categorization requires that infants both distinguish between and generalize about objects based on specific features; thus, these categorization findings suggest that young infants do represent identifying features of objects.

The apparent discrepancy between the findings cited aboved may be explained by noting that evidence for perceptual categorization of objects prior to 10 months of age is restricted primarily to animate objects, such as people and animals (Eimas & Quinn 1994, Eimas et al 1994, Quinn & Eimas 1986, Quinn et al 1993). By contrast, studies investigating infants' knowledge of object motions and causal interactions involve inanimate objects, such as cars and blocks (e.g. Baillargeon 1995, Leslie 1988, Oakes & Cohen 1995). Recent neuropsychological evidence suggests that adults represent and perceptually process living and nonliving things differently (Farah 1992). In general, living things are represented holistically whereas nonliving things are represented by the relations among their parts. The origins of these differences may be present early in development, a possibility that would help to explain the finding of different representations for animate and inanimate objects by infants.

Although such a reconciliation between findings is somewhat speculative, it is certainly consistent with recent proposals that conceptual knowledge is present early and organized by core principles of domain-specific knowledge—e.g. people, objects, number (Cary & Spelke 1994, Wellman & Gelman 1992). One explanation for early differences that emerge between core domains follows from the proposal by Eimas (1994) that categorical knowledge emerges from a progressive abstraction of the stored perceptual information. Presumably, the perceptual properties that are initially encoded and stored differ as a function of the task being performed along with these processes, and thus initial knowledge about people and objects will differ because our early interactions with these entities are so different.

CONCLUSIONS

The research discussed in this review is noteworthy for many reasons, but three are highlighted. First, recent findings on newborns reveal that they are considerably more competent than once believed. Neonates are endowed with much more than reflexes or fixed action patterns. Their actions are goal directed and spatially coordinated, even though they lack consistency and are often obscured by other factors, such as posture. Also, neonates show recognition memory from birth, and by 3 months of age infants reason about events that are perceptually occluded. During the first year of life, these actions and representations become more accessible and more generalizable, but the clear message from the recent research is that the representations available to infants are not directly a function of the coordination and internalization of actions.

Second, this review was organized by the proposal that perception and action and object recognition and representation are functionally dissociable processes that follow different developmental trajectories. Although it is premature to offer specific predictions based on this proposal, it is possible to offer a few generalizations regarding the development of both systems.

The findings on the development of perception and action concur with the earlier characterization of the perceptual control system as functioning in real time with little explicit reference to past experience. Perceptually controlled actions are modularly organized and not represented in a form that is recalled or used to guide the production of other responses. It is sufficient that infants perceive where they are and what they are doing. All that matters is the present fit between the infant and the environment. Past experience does of course contribute to the development of these systems in the form of perceptual learning. With exploration of their own actions and the environment, infants show increasing sensitivity to perceptual changes and finer control of actions that are guided by this information. In essence, then, learning is implicit or procedural; it is elicited by context, not by recall of explicit information about how to coordinate sensorimotor behaviors.

By contrast, research on the development of object recognition confirms that even young infants represent defining features and physical constraints that specify the unity and boundedness of objects. It is significant that these defining properties, such as structure from rigid motions, are invariant across perspective transformations. This invariance increases the likelihood that objects are recognized in new orientations and contexts. The representations necessary for object recognition are organized as domain-specific concepts that accumulate new perceptual information over time. Perceptual experience is the principal engine by which representations become more abstract and differentiated. These representations not only guide perceptual processing, but also are available in explicit form to guide infants' reasoning about the most fundamental and frequently encountered properties of their world.

The third and last conclusion emerging from this review concerns the generalizability of specific research findings. It is always advisable to exercise caution when generalizing between different contexts and measures (Thelen 1995), and the current review offers new reasons for such caution. As discussed repeatedly in this review, competencies manifested by one response system, such as eye movements, are not necessarily manifested by another system, such as reaching, at the same age. An additional complication becomes evident when inferring conceptual competencies, e.g. object permanence, from various response measures, because the development of conceptual knowledge and systems are mediated by dissociable processes that follow independent developmental trajectories. Thus, the development of a specific response measure could easily lag behind or otherwise misrepresent the development of a specific concept.

The proposed functional dissociation between perceptuomotor and object recognition processes is not meant to imply that these two processing systems are completely independent. Clearly, thought and action interact at some level, and developmental changes in one system surely affect the other. An important research task for the future is to investigate when and how new representations and actions are coordinated in the process of development.

Literature Cited

Adolph KE, Eppler MA, Gibson EJ. 1993a. Development of perception of affordances. *Adv. Infancy Res.* 8:51–98

Adolph KE, Eppler MA, Gibson EJ. 1993b. Crawling versus walking infants' perception of affordances for locomotion over sloping surfaces. *Child Dev.* 64:1158–74

Anisfeld M. 1991. Review: neonatal imitation. *Dev. Rev.* 11:60–97

Ashmead DH, Clifton RK, Perris EE. 1987. Precision of auditory localization in human infants. *Dev. Psychol.* 23:641–47

Ashmead DH, Davis DL, Whalen T, Odom RD. 1991. Sound localization and sensitivity to interaural time differences in human infants. *Child Dev.* 62:1211–26

Aslin RN. 1988. Anatomical constraints on oculomotor development: implications for infant perception. In *The Minnesota Symposia on Child Psychology: Perceptual Development in Infancy*, ed. A Yonas, pp. 67–104. Hillsdale, NJ: Erlbaum

Aslin RN, Salapatek P. 1975. Saccadic localization of visual targets by the very young human infant. *Percept. Psychophys.* 17: 293–302

Arterberry ME, Yonas A. 1988. Infants' sensitivity to kinetic information for three-dimensional object shape. *Percept. Psychophys.* 44:1–6

Bai DL, Bertenthal BI. 1992. Locomotor status and the development of spatial search skills. *Child Dev.* 63:215–26

Baillargeon R. 1987. Object permanence in 3.5- and 4.5-month-old infants. *Dev. Psychol.* 23:655–64

Baillargeon R. 1993. The object concept revisited: new directions in the investigation of infants' physical knowledge. In *Carnegie Symposium on Cognition: Visual Perception and Cognition in Infancy*, ed. CE Granrud, pp. 265–315. Hillsdale, NJ: Erlbaum

Baillargeon R. 1995. A model of physical reasoning in infancy. *Adv. Infancy Res.* In press

Baldwin JM. 1906. *Mental Development in the Child and the Race.* New York: Macmillan

Banks MS. 1988. Visual recalibration and the development of contrast and optical flow perception. In *The Minnesota Symposia on Child Psychology: Perceptual Development in Infancy*, ed. A Yonas, pp. 145–96. Hillsdale, NJ: Erlbaum

Banks MS, Dannemiller JL. 1987. Infant visual psychophysics. In *Handbook of Infant Perception. Vol. 1: From Sensation to Perception*, ed. P Salapatek, L Cohen, pp. 115–84. Orlando: Academic

Bayley N. 1969. *Bayley Scales of Infant Development.* New York: Psychological Corp.

Bertenthal BI. 1993. Perception of biomechanical motions by infants: intrinsic image and knowledge-based constraints. In *Carnegie Symposium on Cognition: Visual Perception and Cognition in Infancy*, ed. C Granrud, pp. 175–214. Hillsdale. NJ: Erlbaum

Bertenthal BI, Bai DL. 1989. Infants' sensitivity to optical flow for controlling posture. *Dev. Psychol.* 25:936–45

Bertenthal BI, Campos JJ. 1990. A systems approach to the organizing effects of self-produced locomotion during infancy. *Adv. Infancy Res.* 6:51–98

Bertenthal BI, Campos JJ, Kermoian R. 1994. An epigenetic perspective on the development of self-produced locomotion and its consequences. *Curr. Dir. Psychol. Sci.* 5: 140–45

Bertenthal BI, Pinto J. 1993. Dynamical constraints in the perception and production of human movements. See Thelen & Smith 1993, pp. 209–39

Bertenthal BI, Pinto J. 1994. Global processing of biological motions. *Psychol. Sci.* 5: 221–25

Bertenthal BI, Proffitt DR, Kramer SJ. 1987. The perception of biomechanical motions. *J. Exp. Psychol.: Hum. Percept. Perform.* 23:171–78

Bertenthal BI, Rose JL. 1995. Two modes of perceiving the self. In *The Self in Infancy: Theory and Research,* ed. P Rochat. In press

Bertenthal BI, Rose JL, Bai DL. 1995. Perception-action coupling in the development of visual control of posture. *J. Exp. Psychol.: Hum. Percept. Perform.* In press

Biederman I. 1987. Recognition-by-components: a theory of human image understanding. *Psychol. Rev.* 94:115–47

Blass EM, Fillion TJ, Rochat P, Hoffmeyer LB, Metzger MA. 1989. Hand-mouth coordination in neonates. *Dev. Psychol.* 25: 963–75

Bloch H, Carchon I. 1992. On the onset of eye-head coordination in infants. *Behav. Brain Res.* 49:85–90

Bornstein MH. 1985. Habituation of attention as a measure of visual information processing in human infants: summary, systematization, and synthesis. In *Measurement of Audition and Vision in the First Year of Postnatal Life: A Methodological Overview,* ed. G Gottlieb, NA Krasnegor, pp. 253–300. Norwood, NJ: Ablex

Bremner JG, Bryant PE. 1985. Active movement and development of spatial abilities in infancy. In *Children's Searching: the Development of Search Skill and Spatial Representation,* ed. HM Wellman, pp. 53–72. Hillsdale, NJ: Erlbaum

Bruner J. 1973. *Beyond the Information Given: Studies in the Psychology of Knowing.* New York: Norton

Bushnell E. 1985. The decline of visually guided reaching during infancy. *Infant Behav. Dev.* 8:139–55

Bushnell EW, Boudreau JP. 1993. Motor development and the mind: the potential role of motor abilities as a determinant of aspects of perceptual development. *Child Dev.* 64:1005–21

Bushnell IWR, Sai F, Mullin JT. 1989. Neonatal recognition of the mother's face. *Br. J. Dev. Psychol.* 7:3–15

Butterworth G. 1982. Object permanence and identity in Piaget's theory of infant cognition. In *Infancy and Epistemology: An Evaluation of Piaget's Theory,* ed. G Butterworth, pp. 137–69. New York: St. Marten's

Butterworth G, Hicks L. 1977. Visual proprioception and postural stability in infancy: a developmental study. *Perception* 5:255–63

Butterworth GE, Hopkins B. 1988. Hand-mouth coordination in the newborn baby. *Br. J. Dev. Psychol.* 6:303–14

Campos JJ, Bertenthal BI, Kermoian R. 1992. Early experience and emotional development: the emergence of fear of heights. *Psychol. Sci.* 3:61–64

Canfield RL, Haith MM. 1991. Young infants' visual expectations for symmetric and asymmetric stimulus sequences. *Dev. Psychol.* 27:198–208

Carey S, Gelman R, eds. 1991. *The Epigenesis of Mind: Essays on Biology and Cognition.* Hillsdale, NJ: Erlbaum

Carey S, Spelke ES. 1994. Domain specific knowledge and conceptual change. *Domain-specificity in Cognition and Culture,* ed. L Hirschfeld & S Gelman, pp. 169–200. New York: Cambridge Univ. Press

Clifton RK, Morrongiello BA, Kulig JW, Dowd JM. 1981. Developmental changes in auditory localization in infancy. In *Development of Perception,* Vol. 1, *Psychobiological Perspectives,* ed. R Aslin, J Alberts, M Petersen, pp. 141–60. New York: Academic

Clifton RK, Muir DW, Ashmead DH, Clarkson MG. 1993. Is visually guided reaching in early infancy a myth? *Child Dev.* 64:1099–110

Clifton R, Rochat P, Litovsky R, Perris E. 1991. Object representation guides infants' reaching in the dark. *J. Exp. Psychol.: Hum. Percept. Perform.* 17:323–29

Clifton R, Rochat P, Robin D, Berthier N. 1994. Multimodal perception in the control of infant reaching. *J. Exp. Psychol.: Hum. Percept. Perform.* 20:876–86

Cohen LB, Oakes LM. 1993. How infants perceive a simple causal event. *Dev. Psychol.* 29:421–33

Craton L, Yonas A. 1990. The role of motion in infant perception of occlusion. In *The Development of Attention: Research and Theory,* ed. J Enns, pp. 21–46. Amsterdam: Elsevier

Daniel BM, Lee D. 1990. Development of looking with head and eyes. *J. Exp. Child Psychol.* 50:200–16

de Schonen S, Mathivet E. 1989. First come

first served. A scenario about development of hemispheric specialization in face recognition during infancy. *Eur. Bull. Cogn. Psychol.* 9:3–44

Diamond A. 1991. Neurophysiological insights into the meaning of object concept development. See Carey & Gelman 1991, pp. 67–110

Eimas PD. 1994. Categorization in early infancy and the continuity of development. *Cognition* 50:83–93

Eimas PD, Quinn PC. 1994. Studies on the formation of perceptually based basic-level categories in young infants. *Child Dev.* 65: 903–17

Eimas PD, Quinn PC, Cowan P. 1994. Development of exclusivity in perceptually based categories of young infants. *J. Exp. Child Psychol.* 58:418–31

Farah MJ. 1992. Is an object an object an object? Cognitive and neuropsychological investigations of domain specificity in visual object recognition. *Curr. Dir. Psychol. Sci.* 1:164–69

Fischer KW, Bidell T. 1991. Constraining nativist inferences about cognitive capacities. See Carey & Gelman 1991, pp. 199–236

Freedland RL, Bertenthal BI. 1994. Developmental changes in interlimb coordination: transition to hands-and-knees crawling. *Psychol. Sci.* 5:26–32

Gibson JJ. 1979. *The Ecological Approach to Visual Perception.* Boston: Houghton-Mifflin

Gibson EJ, Riccio G, Schmuckler MA, Stoffregen TA, Rosenberg D, Taormina J. 1987. Detection of the traversability of surfaces by crawling and walking infants. *J. Exp. Psychol.: Hum. Percept. Perform.* 13: 533–44

Gibson EJ, Schmuckler MA. 1989. Going somewhere: an ecological and experimental approach to development of mobility. *Ecol. Psychol.* 1:3–25

Goldfield EC. 1993. Dynamic systems in development: action systems. See Thelen & Smith 1993, pp. 51–70

Goodale MA, Milner AD. 1992. Separate visual pathways for perception and action. *Trends Neurosci.* 15:20–25

Goodale MA, Milner AD, Jakobson LS, Carey DP. 1991. A neurological dissociation between perceiving objects and grasping them. *Nature* 349:154–56

Grenier A. 1981. 'Motoricité libérée' par fixation manuelle de la nuque au cours des premières semaines de la vie ['Liberated movements' by manual fixation of the neck during the first weeks of life]. *Arch. Fr. Pediatr.* 38:557–61

Haith MM. 1980. *Rules that Babies Look By: The Organization of Newborn Visual Activity.* Hillsdale, NJ: Erlbaum

Haith MM. 1993. Future-oriented processes in infancy: the case of visual expectations. In *Carnegie Symposium on Cognition: Visual Perception and Cognition in Infancy,* ed. CE Granrud, pp. 235–64. Hillsdale, NJ: Erlbaum

Haith MM. 1994. Visual expectations as the first step toward the development of future-oriented processes. In *The Development of Future-Oriented Processes,* ed. MH Haith, JB Benson, RJ Roberts, BF Pennington, pp. 11–38. Chicago: Univ. Chicago Press. In press

Haith MM, Hazan C, Goodman GS. 1988. Expectation and anticipation of dynamic visual events by 3.5-month-old babies. *Child Dev.* 59: 467–79

Hirschfeld H, Forssberg H. 1994. Epigenetic development of postural responses for sitting during infancy. *Exp. Brain Res.* 97: 528–40

Horobin K, Acredolo L. 1986. The role of attentiveness, mobility history and separation of hiding sites on Stage IV behavior. *J. Exp. Child Psychol.* 41:114–27

Howard IP. 1986. The perception of posture, self-motion, and the visual vertical. In *Handbook of Perception and Human Performance.* Vol. 1: *Sensory Processes and Perception,* ed. KR Boff, L Kaufman, JP Thomas, 18:1–62. New York: Wiley

Jeannerod M. 1994. Object oriented action. In *Insights into the Reach to Grasp Movement,* ed. KMB Bennett, U Castiello, pp. 3–15. Amsterdam: Elsevier

Johansson G. 1973. Visual perception of biological motion and a model for its analysis. *Percept. Psychophys.* 14:201–11

Johnson MH. 1990. Cortical maturation and the development of visual attention in early infancy. *J. Cogn. Neurosci.* 2:81–95

Johnson SP, Nanez JE. 1995. Young infants' perception of object unity in two-dimensional displays. *Infant Behav. Dev.* 18: 133–43

Jouen F. 1990. Early visual-vestibular interactions and postural development. In *Sensory-Motor Organization and Development in Infancy and Early Childhood,* ed. H Bloch, BI Bertenthal, pp. 199–216. Dordrecht: Kluwer

Karmiloff-Smith A. 1992. *Beyond Modularity.* Cambridge, MA: Bradford/MIT Press

Kellman PJ. 1984. Perception of three-dimensional form by human infants. *Percept. Psychophys.* 36:353–58

Kellman PJ, Short K. 1987. Development of three-dimensional form perception. *J. Exp. Psychol.: Hum. Percept. Perform.* 13: 545–57

Kellman PJ, Spelke ES. 1983. Perception of partly occluded objects in infancy. *Cogn. Psychol.* 15:483–524

Kellman PJ, Spelke ES, Short KR. 1986. Infant perception of object unity from translatory motion in depth and vertical translation. *Child Dev.* 57:72–86

Kremenitzer JP, Vaughan HG, Kurtzberg D. Dowling K. 1979. Smooth-pursuit eye movements in the newborn infant. *Child Dev.* 50:442–48

Lederman SJ, Klatzky RL. 1987. Hand movements: a window into haptic object recognition. *Cogn. Psychol.* 19:342–68

Lee DN. 1993. Body-environment coupling. In *Ecological and Interpersonal Knowledge of the Self,* ed. U Neisser, pp. 68–88. Cambridge: Cambridge Univ. Press

Lee DN, Aronson E. 1974. Visual proprioceptive control of standing in human infants. *Percept. Psychophys.* 15:529–32

Leslie AM. 1988. The necessity of illusion: perception and thought in infancy. *Thought Without Language,* ed. L Weiskrantz, pp. 185–210. Oxford: Clarendon

Leslie AM, Keeble S. 1987. Do six-month-old infants perceive causality? *Cognition* 25: 265–88

Lew A, Butterworth G. 1995. The effects of hunger on hand-mouth coordination in newborn infants. *Dev. Psychol.* 31: 456–63

Lishman JR, Lee DN. 1973. The autonomy of visual kinaesthesis. *Perception* 2:287–94

Lockman JJ, Ashmead DH, Bushnell EW. 1984. The development of anticipatory hand orientation during infancy. *J. Exp. Child Psychol.* 37:176–86

Mandler JM. 1988. How to build a baby: on the development of an accessible representational system. *Cogn. Dev.* 3:113–36

Mandler JM. 1992. How to build a baby: II. Conceptual primitives. *Psychol. Rev.* 99: 587–604

Manoel Ede J, Connolly KJ. 1995. Variability and the development of skilled actions. *Int. J. Psychophysiol.* In press

Marr D. 1982. *Vision.* San Francisco, CA: Freeman

McKenzie BE, Skouteris H, Day RH, Hartman B, Yonas A. 1993. Effective action by infants to contact objects by reaching or leaning. *Child Dev.* 64:415–29

Meltzoff AN, Moore MK. 1983. Newborn infants imitate adult facial gestures. *Child Dev.* 54:702–9

Meltzoff AN, Moore MK. 1989. Imitation in newborn infants: exploring the range of gestures imitated and the underlying mechanisms. *Dev. Psychol.* 25:954–62

Meltzoff AN, Moore MK. 1994. Imitation, memory, and the representation of persons. *Infant Behav. Dev.* 17:83–100

Morrongiello BA. 1988. Infants' localization of sounds in the horizontal plane: estimates of minimum audible angle. *Dev. Psychol.* 24:8–13

Morton J, Johnson M. 1991. CONSPEC and CONLERN: a two process theory of infant face recognition. *Psychol. Rev.* 98:164–81

Mounoud P. 1993. The emergence of new skills: dialectic relations between knowledge systems. See Savelsbergh 1993, pp. 13–46

Muir D, Field J. 1979. Newborn infants orient to sounds. *Child Dev.* 50:431–36

Needham A, Baillargeon R. 1995. Object segregation in infancy. *Adv. Infancy Res.* In press

Newell KM. 1986. Constraints on the development of coordination. In *Motor Development in Children: Aspects of Coordination and Control,* ed. MG Wade, HTA Whiting, pp. 341–60. Boston: Martinus Nijhoff

Oakes LM. 1994. Development of infants' use of continuity cues in their perception of causality. *Dev. Psychol.* 30:869–79

Oakes LM, Cohen LB. 1990. Infant perception of a causal event. *Cogn. Dev.* 5:193–207

Oakes LM, Cohen LB. 1995. Infants' perception of causality. *Adv. Infancy Res.* In press

Paillard J. 1991. Motor and representational framing of space. In *Brain and Space,* ed. J. Paillard, pp. 163–82. New York: Oxford Univ. Press

Pascalis O, de Schonen S, Morton J, Deruelle C, Fabre-Grenet M. 1995. Mother's face recognition by neonates: a replication and an extension. *Infant Behav. Dev.* 18: 79–85

Perris E, Clifton R. 1988. Reaching in the dark toward sound as a measure of auditory localization in infants. *Infant Behav. Dev.* 11: 473–92

Piaget J. 1952. *The Origins of Intelligence in Children.* New York: Int. Univ. Press

Piaget J. 1954. *The Construction of Reality in the Child.* New York: Basic Books

Proffitt DR, Bertenthal BI. 1990. Converging operations revisited: assessing what infants perceive using discrimination measures. *Percept. Psychophys.* 41:1–12

Quinn PC, Eimas PD. 1986. On categorization in early infancy. *Merrill-Palmer Q.* 32: 331–63

Quinn PC, Eimas PD, Rosenkrantz SL. 1993. Evidence for representations of perceptually similar natural categories by 3-month-old and 4-month-old infants. *Perception* 22:463–75

Reed ES. 1982. An outline of a theory of action systems. *J. Motor Behav.* 14:98–134

Reed ES. 1989. Changing theories of postural development. In *The Development of Posture and Gait across the Lifespan,* ed. M Woollacott, A Shumway-Cook, pp. 3–24. Columbia: Univ. S. Carolina Press

Regal DM, Ashmead DH, Salapatek P. 1983. The coordination of eye and head movements during early infancy: a selective review. *Behav. Brain Res.* 10:133–39

Robin D, Berthier N, Clifton R. 1995. Infants'

predictive reaching for moving objects in the dark. *Dev. Psychol.* In press

Rochat P. 1992. Self-sitting and reaching in 5–8 month old infants: the impact of posture and its development on early eye-hand coordination. *J. Motor Behav.* 24:210–20

Rochat P, Blass EM, Hoffmeyer LB. 1988. Oropharyngeal control of hand-mouth coordination in newborn infants. *Dev. Psychol.* 24:459–63

Rochat P, Goubet N. 1995. Development of sitting and reaching in 5- to 6-month-old infants. *Infant Behav. Dev.* 18:53–68

Rochat P, Senders SJ. 1991. Active touch in infancy: action systems in development. In *Newborn Attention: Biological Constraints and the Influence of Experience,* ed. MJ Weiss, PR Zelazo, pp. 412–42. Norwood, NJ: Ablex

Rock I. 1984. *The World of Perception.* New York: W. H. Freeman

Roucoux A, Culee C, Roucoux M. 1983. Development of fixation and pursuit eye movements in human infants. *Behav. Brain Res.* 10:133–39

Rovee-Collier C. 1995. Time windows in cognitive development. *Dev. Psychol.* 51: 147–69

Savelsbergh GJP, ed. 1993. *The Development of Coordination in Infancy.* Amsterdam: Elsevier

Savelsbergh GJP, van der Kamp J. 1993. The coordination of infant's reaching, grasping, catching and posture: a natural physical approach. See Savelsberg 1993, pp. 289–317

Schmuckler MA, Gibson EJ. 1989. The effect of imposed optical flow on guided locomotion in young walkers. *Br. J. Dev. Psychol.* 7:193–206

Shea SL, Aslin RN. 1990. Oculomotor responses to step-ramp targets by young human infants. *Vision Res.* 30:1077–92

Shepard RN. 1994. Perceptual-cognitive universals as reflections of the world. *Psychon. Bull. Rev.* 1:2–28

Siegler RS. 1993. Commentary: cheers and lamentations. In *Carnegie Symposium on Cognition: Visual Perception and Cognition in Infancy,* ed. CE Granrud, pp. 333–44. Hillsdale, NJ: Erlbaum

Slater A, Mattock A, Brown E. 1990. Size constancy at birth: newborn infants' responses to retinal and real size. *J. Exp. Child Psychol.* 49:314–22

Slater A, Morison V, Rose D. 1984. Habituation in the newborn. *Infant Behav. Dev.* 7:183–200

Slater A, Morison V, Somers M, Mattock A, Brown E, Taylor D. 1990b. Newborn and older infants' perception of partly occluded objects. *Infant Behav. Dev.* 13:33–49

Spelke E. 1994. Initial knowledge: six suggestions. *Cognition* 50:431–45

Spelke ES, Breinlinger K, Macomber J, Jacobson K. 1992. Origins of knowledge. *Psychol. Rev.* 99:605–32

Spelke ES, Katz G, Purcell SE, Ehrlich SM, Breinlinger K. 1994. Early knowledge of object motion: continuity and inertia. *Cognition* 51:131–76

Spelke ES, Van de Walle G. 1993. Perceiving and reasoning about objects: insights from infants. In *Spatial Representation,* ed. N Eilan, W Brewer, R McCarthy, pp. 132–61. Oxford: Blackwell

Stack D, Muir D, Sherriff F, Roman J. 1989. Development of infant reaching in the dark to luminous objects and "invisible sounds." *Perception* 18:69–82

Stoffregen TA, Schmuckler MA, Gibson EJ. 1987. Use of central and peripheral optical flow in stance and locomotion in young walkers. *Perception* 16:113–19

Sveistrup H, Woollacott MH. 1995. Can practice modify the developing automatic postural response. *Child Dev.* In press

Thelen E. 1989. Self-organization in developmental processes: can systems approaches work? In *The Minnesota Symposia on Child Psychology: Systems in Development,* ed. M Gunnar, E Thelen, pp. 77–117. Hillsdale, NJ: Erlbaum

Thelen E. 1995. Motor development: a new synthesis. *Am. Psychol.* 50:79–95

Thelen E, Fisher DM. 1982. Newborn stepping: an explanation for a 'disappearing' reflex. *Dev. Psychol.* 18:760–75

Thelen E, Fisher DM, Ridley-Johnson R. 1984. The relationship between physical growth and a newborn reflex. *Infant Behav. Dev.* 7:479–93

Thelen E, Skala KD, Kelso JAS. 1987. The dynamic nature of early coordination: evidence from bilateral leg movements in young infants. *Dev. Psychol.* 23: 179–86

Thelen E, Smith L, eds. 1993. *Dynamical Systems in Development.* Vol. 2: *Applications.* Cambridge, MA: Bradford Books

Thelen E, Ulrich BD. 1991. Hidden skills: a dynamic systems analysis of treadmill stepping during the first year. *Monogr. Soc. Res. Child Dev.* (Ser. No. 223) 56:1

Trevarthen C. 1984. How control of movement develops. In *Human Motor Actions: Bernstein Reassessed,* ed. HTA Whiting, pp. 223–61. Amsterdam: Elsevier

Turvey MT. 1990. Coordination. *Am. Psychol.* 4:938–53

Ulrich BD, Jensen JL, Thelen E. 1991. Stability and variation in the development of infant stepping: implications for control. In *Adaptability of Human Gait,* ed. AE Patla, pp. 145–64. Amsterdam: Elsevier

Ungerleider LG, Mishkin M. 1982. Two cortical visual systems. In *Analysis of Visual Behavior,* ed. DJ Ingle, MA Goodale, RJW

Mansfield, pp. 549–86. Cambridge, MA: MIT Press

von Hofsten C. 1982. Eye-hand coordination in newborns. *Dev. Psychol.* 18:450–61

von Hofsten C. 1983. Catching skills in infancy. *J. Exp. Psychol.: Hum. Percept. Perform.* 9:75–85

von Hofsten C. 1993. Prospective control: a basic aspect of action development. *Hum. Dev.* 36:253–70

von Hofsten C, Ronnqvist L. 1988. Preparation for grasping an object: a developmental study. *J. Exp. Psychol.: Hum. Percept. Perform.* 14:610–21

Walton GE, Bower NJA, Bower TGR. 1992. Recognition of familiar faces by newborns. *Infant Behav. Dev.* 15:265–69

Warren W. 1990. The perception-action coupling. In *Sensory-Motor Organization and Development in Infancy and Early Childhood,* ed. H Bloch, BI Bertenthal, pp. 23–38. Dordrecht: Kluwer

Wellman HM, Gelman SA. 1992. Cognitive development: foundational theories of core domains. *Annu. Rev. Psychol.* 43:337–75

Weiskrantz L, Warrington E, Sander MD, Marshall J. 1974. Visual capacity in the hemianopic field following restricted occipital ablation. *Brain* 97:709–29

Wentworth N, Haith MM. 1992. Event-specific expectations of 2- and 3-month-old infants. *Dev. Psychol.* 28:842–50

White B, Castle P, Held R. 1964. Observations on the development of visually-directed reaching. *Child Dev.* 35:349–64

Woollacott MH, Sveistrup H. 1994. The development of sensorimotor integration underlying posture control in infants during the transition to independent stance. In *Interlimb Coordination: Neural, Dynamical and Cognitive Constraints,* ed. SP Swinnen, J Massion, H Heuer, pp. 371–89. San Diego: Academic

Xu F, Carey S. 1995. Infants' metaphysics: the case of numerical identity. *Cogn. Psychol.* In press

Yonas A, Hartman B. 1993. Perceiving the affordance of contact in 4- and 5-month-old infants. *Child Dev.* 64:298–308

Yonas A, Owsley C. 1987. Development of visual space perception. In *Handbook of Infant Perception.* Vol. 1: *From Sensation to Perception,* ed. P Salapatek, L Cohen, pp. 80–122. Orlando: Academic

Zelazo PR, Brody LR, Chaikan H. 1984. Neonatal habituation and dishabituation of head turning to rattle sounds. *Infant Behav. Dev.* 7:311–21

Zelazo PR 1984. "Learning to walk": recognition of higher-order influences? *Adv. Infancy Res.* 3:251–60

Zernicke RF, Schneider K. 1993. Biomechanics and developmental neuromotor control. *Child Dev.* 64:982–1004

Annu. Rev. Psychol. 1996. 47:461–84
Copyright © 1996 by Annual Reviews Inc. All rights reserved

AUDITORY PSYCHOPHYSICS AND PERCEPTION

Ira J. Hirsh

Central Institute for the Deaf and Departments of Psychology and of Speech and Hearing, Washington University, St. Louis, Missouri 63110

Charles S. Watson

Departments of Speech and Hearing Sciences and of Psychology, Indiana University, Bloomington, Indiana 47405

KEY WORDS: hearing, psychoacoustics, auditory perception

ABSTRACT

In this review of auditory psychophysics and perception, we cite some important books, research monographs, and research summaries from the past decade. Within auditory psychophysics, we have singled out some topics of current importance: Cross-Spectral Processing, Timbre and Pitch, and Methodological Developments.

Complex sounds and complex listening tasks have been the subject of new studies in auditory perception. We review especially work that concerns auditory pattern perception, with emphasis on temporal aspects of the patterns and on patterns that do not depend on the cognitive structures often involved in the perception of speech and music.

Finally, we comment on some aspects of individual differences that are sufficiently important to question the goal of characterizing auditory properties of the typical, average, adult listener. Among the important factors that give rise to these individual differences are those involved in selective processing and attention.

CONTENTS

0066-4170/96/0101-0461$08.00

461

INTRODUCTION

Fechner's so-called inner and outer psychophysics are today represented in audition by (*a*) the relations between auditory behavior and correlated physiological observations, mostly in the cochlea and auditory nerve, and (*b*) the relations between auditory responses and properties of stimulus sounds. In this review, we deal primarily with the latter because the former are richly represented in the biological and neuroscience literature.

Auditory psychophysics or psychoacoustics has been concerned with measures of absolute sensitivity, masking, and discrimination between sounds that differ in frequency content, intensity, duration, and spatial location. After a century of work, psychophysical methods are more precise (mostly through the application of signal-detection theory), and attention has turned toward complex sounds—sounds that contain many components simultaneously and sequentially and that are more representative of sounds in a natural or speech-filled acoustic environment.

The past two decades have also seen a growing interest in auditory perception, a development that, in contrast with the history in visual perception, has been long delayed. From the 1930s, of course, there were considerable advances in our understanding of the auditory perception of speech (see Miller & Eimas 1995) and, to a lesser degree, of music. Now, however, we find several books and many articles on this more complex aspect of hearing, the scope of which extends beyond the auditory perception of speech and music.

We note three important trends in psychoacoustic research in these recent decades. First, after a century-old preoccupation with pitch and other frequency-related dimensions as the principal features of auditory processes, the important role of time and time-varying properties in the stimulus has become clear. Temporal relations have been clear enough in their application to speech perception, but now it is becoming evident that such temporal relations are a necessary component of auditory perception in general.

Second, in spite of a traditional goal of psychophysics to reveal characteristics of the average adult listener, experimenters have in recent years shown results for individual listeners. These data on individual listeners challenge the notion of the typical observer. The dependence of these differences on properties of the stimulus, the psychophysical methods used, and the amount of training on a task may predict the form of an account of individual differences in sensory processes or capabilities, and also in listeners' proclivities in responding in a variety of auditory tasks.

Third, the important research on speech perception (see Miller & Eimas 1995) and on the psychology of music (see McAdams & Bigand 1993) has been developed in light of the characteristics of speech (or music) as a part of a general language system, including remembered rules and structures. Such cognitive processes have not always been clearly distinguished from auditory perceptual processes.

In previous recent volumes of the *Annual Review of Psychology,* hearing has been described as follows:

In Volume 30, Trahiotis & Robinson (1979) wrote on auditory psychophysics, emphasizing pitch perception, intensity perception, auditory nonlinearities, and binaural hearing.

In Volume 34, McFadden & Wightman (1983) wrote on relations between normal and pathological hearing.

In Volume 38, de Boer & Dreschler (1987) wrote on spectrotemporal representation of signals.

In Volume 40, Teas (1989) wrote on auditory physiology.

In Volume 42, Middlebrooks & Green (1991) wrote on sound localization, and Krumhansl (1991) wrote on music psychology.

In Volume 46, Miller & Eimas (1995) wrote on speech perception.

In the present chapter, we bring the reader up to date on some of these topics, largely through books and other secondary sources. In somewhat greater detail, we focus on three psychoacoustic topics: profile analysis, "comodulation masking release" (CMR), and pitch and timbre.

In addition, we address more general areas such as auditory perception and individual differences. Our literature sources are principally from the past decade.

Contemporary Psychophysics

Several good summaries of contemporary work in auditory psychophysics are available (Green 1988a, Handel 1989, Moore 1989). We note especially the book edited by Yost, Popper, and Fay (1993), in which the field is addressed in chapters, each written by an expert or two. In the chapter "Auditory Intensity Discrimination" (Green 1993a) are discussions of classical intensity discrimination, loudness, signal-detection tasks, profile analysis, and comodulation masking release (see "Cross-Spectral Processing" in this review). In the chapter "Frequency Analysis and Pitch Perception" (Moore 1993) are discussions of frequency selectivity, auditory filters, psychophysical tuning curves, masking, and psychophysics of complex tones. "Time Analysis" (Viemeister & Plack 1993) considers temporal resolution—the microtime of acoustic carrier frequencies and the macrotime of modulating waveforms. The temporal dependencies of masking and of the auditory filter as well as temporal integration are treated extensively. "Sound Localization" (Wightman & Kistler 1993; see also Middlebrooks & Green 1991) addresses this still active area of investigation, with recent findings going quite beyond the traditional interaural differences in time of arrival and intensity of sound in the space around a listener. Of particular interest have been the acoustical properties of the outer ear and of the head. The vexing problem of extending principles of localization, which are based on simple tones, to complex sounds is treated by Hafter et al (1988). The chapter "Auditory Perception" (Yost & Sheft 1993) discusses the roles of spectral profile, timbre, harmonicity, pitch, and binaural and temporal factors in determining sound sources. (See also Hartmann 1988.) Finally, "Auditory Scene Analysis" (Bregman 1993) is a briefer version of Bregman's earlier study (1990).

We do not review these areas that have been so well and recently reviewed by others.

As this chapter was being completed, another excellent book on hearing appeared (Moore, 1995), which contains 12 chapters by different expert authors.

RECENT INTRODUCTORY TEXTS   Luce (1993) has crafted an impressive book, *Sound and Hearing*. Intended for undergraduates (bright ones), it contains the best introduction to acoustics to appear in quite some time. Numerous graphs and equations contribute to a systematic presentation. The topics concerned with hearing include both behavioral and physiological literatures, and again quantitative approaches serve to organize and filter the psychoacoustic information. Signal-detection theory, along with other theoretical material, is presented clearly. Whereas complex signals are dealt with, complex perceptual processes are not.

It is difficult to classify Handel's (1989) excellent *Listening*. Intended to be a textbook, it covers a broad spectrum from acoustics to auditory cognitive processes. It also may be considered a research monograph in places where the author connects his text with experimental findings and perceptual theory—for example, about timbre, dynamic patterns, and breaking the acoustic stream into events. When experiments are missing, he does not fail to maintain a consistent story that remains clear and reasonable.

In addition, revisions of previous texts have appeared—by Gelfand (second edition, 1990), Moore (third edition, 1989) and Yost (third edition, 1994—a revision of Yost & Nielsen 1985).

RESEARCH MONOGRAPHS   Green's monograph (1988b) on profile analysis addresses the discrimination of spectra through psychophysical experiments in which the intensity of one component in a group of multicomponent tones is manipulated.

Another group of books departs from traditional psychoacoustic studies and considers auditory perception and cognition. Bregman (1990) sets forth in extenso his auditory scene analysis and stream segregation. Several of these books consist of edited summaries of papers given at conferences, e.g. Cazals et al (1992) and McAdams & Bigand (1993). A report from a panel of contributors (CHABA 1989) attacks the problems of complexity, both of the acoustic stimulus and of the auditory responses. Dowling & Harwood (1986), Jones & Holleran (1992), Tighe & Dowling (1993), and Aiello (1994) move beyond perception into a cognitive realm, with examples and theories taken from music and music theory.

AUDITORY PSYCHOPHYSICS—SELECTED TOPICS

Cross-Spectral Processing

The latest general review of psychoacoustic research in the *Annual Review of Psychology* (de Boer & Dreschler 1987) briefly introduced two new classes of experiment: profile analysis (Spiegel et al 1981) and what later was termed comodulation masking release (CMR) (Hall et al 1984). Such experiments have in common the listener's use of information distributed over many critical bands (CB) in detecting a narrow-band signal. The large number of subsequent experiments on profiles and CMR have not led to a rejection of the critical-band theory, which has been the foundation of most auditory theories since Fletcher's (1940) germinal paper on that topic. But they have made it clear that listeners can monitor the output of more than one CB simultaneously and thereby can achieve better performance than they would by listening only to the CB containing the signal. Although de Boer & Dreschler (1987) observed that, "Appealing as the concept of profile analysis might be for auditory theory, it probably does not play an important part in everyday sound analysis," the recognition and discrimination of vowels on the basis of spectral peaks (formants) do not accord with that conclusion.

PROFILE ANALYSIS   The fundamental observation in profile experiments is that the detection of an increment in the level of a sinusoid can be made easier by the presence of other, nonincremented, uniform-level sinusoids. In typical profile experiments, the standard stimulus consists of as few as 3 and up to more than 30 equal-level sinusoids presented simultaneously for about 100 ms. The nontarget or contextual components may be distributed over a few hundred to several thousand Hz. The listener's task is to compare that uniform-spectrum sound to one that is identical except for an increment in level that is (or is not) added to one of these components. Whereas classical intensity-discrimination experiments have required listeners to compare the levels of successively presented stimuli, in this task an increment in one component of a profile might be detected by comparing it to the other simultaneously presented components (or it may be perceived as a different quality). There remains, of course, an element of sequential comparison in the profile task, because listeners are clearly basing their judgments on a difference in the spectral shapes of the complex with and without the level increment added to a single component. The correctness of Green's (1988b) interpretation (simultaneous comparisons) is made clear by the roving-level control procedure commonly used by Green and his collaborators (e.g. Green et al 1983, 1987; Spiegel et al 1981). The stimuli are randomly varied in overall level by as much as 40 dB within a trial so that the absolute level of the components bears little or no information, and the listeners' judgments can only be based on spectral shape.

Another informative way in which profile discrimination differs from sequential intensity discrimination is in the effects of interstimulus interval. In the traditional sequential-comparison intensity-discrimination tasks, increasing the time between the stimuli to be compared can drastically reduce the accuracy of the discrimination. Green et al (1983) showed that similar delay—out to a maximum of 8 s—between the comparison stimuli in a profile task yielded only very slight reduction in discrimination thresholds. It is more difficult to remember the absolute level of a tone or of a tone complex than to recall whether a profile was categorized as "bumpy" or "bumpless." The difference in the apparent resistance of the memory for the two classes of experiments suggests, in terms of the theory of trace- vs context-coding in auditory memory (Durlach & Braida 1969), that the profiles are examples of context-coding. In still older terms, the difference recalls the distinction between prothetic and metathetic continua, differences characterized by "more than" compared with "different from" (Stevens 1975, p. 13). The distinctions of sound quality vs level, trace- vs context-coding, metathetic vs prothetic continua, categorical vs noncategorical perception, etc, appear to have some commonality among their referents, but this variety of loosely similar terminology and associated theories seems to represent a problem in need of a solution.

In addition to the basic observations mentioned earlier, several other systematic findings have been reported about these interesting profile stimuli. One finding is that the phase relations among both target and contextual components seem to have no effect on performance, except in cases of intercomponent intervals substantially less than a critical band. Another is that the thresholds vary systematically with the number of components in the profile, generally decreasing as more nontarget components are added (Bernstein & Green 1988). The generality of the latter result has been questioned by Henn & Turner (1990), who reported no significant decrease in the average thresholds for five subjects as the number of profile components was increased. Kidd et al (1991) noted that Henn & Turner's procedure differed in several ways from that of most earlier profile experiments. One difference was that Henn & Turner trained the subjects initially without the within-trial roving stimulus levels and, possibly as a consequence, measured much lower thresholds than previously reported for three-component profiles. Green (1992) also pointed out that a common problem in failures to replicate the effects of profile experiments is that some subjects have thresholds so high they are almost certainly discriminating on the basis of changes in overall level rather than spectral shape. Although enough independent profile experiments have now been published that virtually no doubt remains about the authenticity of the major effects, it is troublesome that perhaps as many as half of the otherwise normal listeners tested cannot seem to make the basic profile discriminations, at least without extremely lengthy training.

Another unexplained finding in profile experiments is that the components closer to the edges of the overall power spectrum have higher thresholds, and this bowl-like relation appears to be at least partly dependent on relative rather than absolute frequency (Green et al 1987, Green & Mason 1985). No basis in the stimulus or in peripheral processing mechanisms seems to account for this result. By default it may depend on the distribution of auditory attention. An excellent review and discussion of profile research is included in Green (1993a).

The systematic study of profile discrimination seems entirely consistent with the recent interest in stimuli more representative of sounds that the auditory system probably had to identify in the course of its evolution. Although most naturally occurring sounds combine both spectral and temporal signatures, it is nevertheless important to determine and explain the limits of listeners' abilities to recognize sounds on the basis of spectral shapes. Studies, for example, of vowel (formant) discrimination under minimal-uncertainty conditions report performance similar to that obtained in profile experiments (e.g. Kewley-Port & Watson 1994). The profile- and formant-discrimination tasks both employ stimuli that consist of sets of simultaneous, fixed-frequency sinusoids, which are discriminated on the basis of changes in the level of one or more of their components.

Although profile research remains mainly an empirical endeavor, Green (1988b) has applied the multiple-channel model developed by Durlach et al (1986) with some success, meaning the data are generally consistent with decisions based on the level of the target tone minus the mean level of the nontarget tones. The multiple-channel model, however, does not account for most of the other profile effects discussed earlier in this section. An alternative theory would be to estimate the pitch of the profiles, on the basis of the "envelope weighted average instantaneous frequency" (EWAIF) proposed by Feth (1974). However, that model does not seem applicable to stimuli as broad in their bandwidth as are most profiles.

COMODULATION MASKING RELEASE   Comodulation masking release (CMR), like profile analysis, is a demonstration that listeners can and do benefit from information broadly distributed across the spectrum in detecting signals whose energy is restricted to a narrow frequency band. Unlike profile analysis, however, in which the information used by the listener is limited to the form of the power spectrum, in CMR listeners exploit stimulus variation in the time domain.

Another series of studies also reflects the importance of temporal modulations, especially coherent ones, in processing complex sounds. These studies of "Modulation Detection Interference" (MDI) concern a listener's ability to detect a change in the temporal pattern of a sound, which is disrupted if other sounds have a similar temporal structure. As in the case of CMR, these studies reflect the use of information across several critical bands. But in MDI, performance is degraded because the listener cannot avoid broad-band listening, even when it is not to his advantage (see Yost & Sheft 1994, for a review).

The original CMR experiment by Hall et al (1984) employed a broadband noise (0–10 kHz) that was multiplied by a low-frequency band of noise (0–50 Hz). A traditional band-narrowing experiment was then conducted using this noise, for which random fluctuations in its envelope were highly correlated ("comodulated") throughout its bandwidth. The signal was a 300-ms 1-kHz tone, with 50-ms rise and decay times. In contrast with a control condition using unprocessed random noise, which showed uniform thresholds for detection of the signal for all bandwidths exceeding a critical bandwidth (roughly 100–150 Hz), thresholds for the comodulated noise were similar to those for the random noise below a critical bandwidth but decreased systematically as the bandwidth was increased to 1 kHz. The maximum reduction of the thresholds for the comodulated noise, compared with the random noise, was about 10 dB. This improvement in threshold, or CMR, has now been the subject of a large number of experiments generally aimed at understanding the mechanisms by which listeners are able to use across-CB temporal comparisons to enhance the detection of a signal in a single CB. In the same article, Hall et al described an experiment showing that the temporal information utilized in achieving a release from masking could be presented in the CB immediately adjacent to that containing the signal or in a single CB as much as 300 Hz above or below the signal frequency, in all cases yielding 5–6 dB of CMR. More recent experiments on CMR have commonly used from one to several bands of noise ("flanking bands") located from one to several CBs above or below the band of noise containing the signal (e.g. Wright & McFadden 1990). In some experiments either (a) these flanking bands and the signal band are modulated with a common envelope, the "correlated" or "comodulated" condition; (b) all of the flanking bands share an envelope but the signal band is incoherently modulated from those flanking bands, the "uncorrelated condition"; or (c) each band is independently modulated, the "all-uncorrelated" condition. Wright & McFadden intermixed these conditions within trial blocks. They concluded that the absence of any large effect of this form of trial-to-trial uncertainty implies that the listeners do not have to choose among several condition-specific listening strategies.

Several theories have been proposed to explain the CMR, and some experimental support has been found for most of them. No theory is yet able to account for all CMR effects. Perhaps earliest was the theory that the envelope fluctuations remote from the signal frequency served to identify regions (dips or troughs in the envelope) where the signal-to-noise ratio was highest and to which the listener therefore attended (Buus 1985, Hall 1986). This explanation was supported by the demonstration that brief signals are more detectable when they are positioned in the valleys of sinusoidally amplitude-modulated (SAM) noise in a CMR task than when they are at the peaks, and also that phase-incoherent placement of the signals yields still higher thresholds (Moore et al 1990).

Another theoretical explanation of CMR is that the listener detects the reduction in the correlation between the envelopes of the signal band and those of the flanking bands, resulting from the introduction of the signal (Cohen & Schubert 1987, Green 1992, Richards 1987). Hall & Grose (1988) provided a partial test of both models by comparing the detection of a single sinusoidal signal presented in the center of three bands to conditions in which signals were present in two or all three of the bands. The results were more consistent with the correlation-decorrelation hypothesis than they were with valley-listening. Actual measures, however, of the correlation between samples of the noises with and without signals did not provide a convincing fit to the correlation-detection hypothesis. The data were somewhat more consistent with a version of the Durlach-Braida (1963) equalization-cancellation model for the detection of signals presented in dichotic listening conditions.

Timbre vs Pitch

The auditory attributes of pitch and loudness appear to be unidimensional and extend from low to high or from soft to loud. In contrast, timbre is a more qualitative attribute and includes several dimensions (Plomp 1970). Useful summaries of work on timbre are found in Moore (1989, pp. 229–33), Handel (1989, pp. 226–63), and Rasch & Plomp (1982, pp. 12–24).

The classical view of timbre holds that different timbres result from different distributions of amplitudes of the harmonic components of a complex tone in a steady state. That quality that permits a listener to identify the instruments of an orchestra, however, involves also dynamic features of the sound (Moore 1989, pp. 232–33), as had been shown earlier by Grey (1977), by Grey & Moorer (1977), and by Risset & Wessel (1982), particularly for onset characteristics. The tones of different instruments do not begin in the same manner, and further, not all of the harmonics of different instruments rise at the same rate.

Extending the work of Kendall (1986), Iverson & Krumhansl (1993) have assessed the relative importance of the onset and the "remainder," or steady state, by asking listeners to judge the similarity of different orchestral-instrument tones. Applying a multidimensional-scaling technique to results for complete tones, for 80-ms onsets, and for remainders (tones without the onset), they found that both the temporal and spectral information was available in all three types of tone samples. These results were not consistent with earlier work that relied on identification of instruments as opposed to judgments of similarity.

Beyond the domain of musical tones, timbre has become almost a synonym for "quality." One problem is that one of the many adjectives used by listeners to describe different timbres is "pitchlike." Singh (1987) demonstrated that there is an intimate relation, even a tradeoff, between pitch and timbre in certain tasks involving tone sequences. Pitt (1994) reported that listeners are less accurate in judging the similarity of pitches of tones with different timbres than they are in judging the similarity of pitches of tones with the same timbre. Further, although Bregman's (1990) early studies of stream segregation were concerned with the pitch relations among the notes in a sequence, Singh & Hirsh (1992) found that streaming could also be observed across same-pitch notes with different timbres. It is widely accepted these days (Moore 1993) that pitch can be mediated both by different parts of the spectrum and by the temporal structure of the waveform. No wonder then that timbral differences in spectral patterns are confused with spectral pitch.

Methodological Developments

Although no effort has been made in recent years to catalog the broad range of modifications of standard psychophysical procedures used to study particular auditory abilities, we mention two methodological variants, both directed at increasing psychophysical efficiency. Green (1993b) has developed a maximum-likelihood technique by which a stimulus dimension can be sampled with high efficiency and that yields valid threshold estimates in as few as a dozen trials, using a yes-no (single-interval) procedure. This method appears to have promise for studies of large stimulus domains in which stimuli yielding greater-than-chance but less-than-perfect detection or discrimination performance cannot be readily estimated on any a priori basis. Naturally, there is no magic in this method, and multiple estimates are still required to achieve the reliabilty desired in most experiments.

Another procedure, resurrected from the dark ages of psychophysical history, is the method of adjustment. Digital synthesis of complex stimuli makes it possible to present stimuli repeatedly, while allowing listeners to vary some discrete spectral-temporal component in order to achieve a specified perceptual goal (e.g. to make the entire complex perceptually equal to an invariant one that is presented alternately). When the observers are able to vary a spectral or temporal portion of a complex stimulus it appears possible to achieve narrowed attentional focus on those stimulus details considerably faster—sometimes in minutes rather than hours—than when observers are trained to attend to them in a forced-choice adaptive procedure (Turner et al 1994, Watson et al 1976). The interpretation of different threshold estimates obtained under adjustment and forced-choice discrete-trial procedures is problematic, as noted by Turner et al. One solution is to use the adjustment procedure to achieve narrowed attentional focus and to then quickly switch to a forced-choice procedure. The accuracy of discrimination achieved through the adjustments may then be shown to carry over to performance under the more interpretable forced-choice method. Although this is a complicated way to achieve the desired end, a reduction by an order of magnitude of the time required to approach asymptotic performance might make this approach worth considering.

AUDITORY PERCEPTION

While perceptual studies in the field of vision have been numerous and fruitful, auditory perception has been a strong area of research only during the past few decades (see Yost & Watson 1987). To be sure, interest in the perception of speech and music has been strong for much of this century, but, owing to the unique aspects of speech and music, a major emphasis has been placed on the cognitive facets of linguistic and musical structures without an accompanying concern for perception that is uniquely auditory (Julesz & Hirsh 1972). This observation is curious in view of the importance accorded by the early Gestalt psychologists to auditory as well as visual examples of so-called organized perceptual processes—for example, von Ehrenfels's demonstration of the recognizability of a melody under transposition (when the "elements" are changed but the *Gestaltqualität* or melodic structure remains). Interest has now shifted from sensory processes to perception of auditory patterns and patterns of patterns.

What is perceived? There is disagreement about the referent of an auditory percept. Moore (1989) and Yost & Sheft (1993) suggested that we perceive "objects," but it is not clear whether by "object" they mean a tangible, space-occupying object such as a violin, or an abstract object of perception. Julesz & Hirsh (1972) and Handel (1989) favor the term "event," a pattern across an interval of time. Bregman (1990) and Yost (1992) suggest "images" and "scenes of images." Hartmann (1988), on the other hand, suggested "entities" as a less encumbered term. The important notion is that an acoustic entity, even one imbedded in other such entities, gives rise to an auditory entity, which in turn may permit identification of the acoustic source, such as a particular voice. But many acoustic patterns are identified as patterns (a brief melody, for example) without reference to an objectlike source.

The most persistent and resistant problem concerns the ability of listeners to process separately several acoustic signals sounding simultaneously. The signal combination provides a very complex singular pressure waveform that if looked at via spectrograph or oscillograph is a meaningless jumble. The most peripheral part of the auditory system encodes frequency and frequency bands over time, but how does the listener separate the voice signal from the baby's cry, from the truck outside, and so on? A cognitive approach (McAdams 1993) suggests that the listener imposes knowledge of meaningful structures on the acoustic jumble in order to hold together stimulus aspects that belong together. A more ecological approach (Gaver 1993) suggests that biologically or environmentally significant streams are so held together because of those significances. A more purely perceptual approach (Bregman 1990, 1993), motivated by principles of grouping and of belongingness from Gestalt psychology, puts the responsibility on features of the acoustic patterns themselves. Finally, there is the possibility some of the necessary stream segregation is accomplished in peripheral sensory processes (Duda et al 1990, Meddis & Hewitt 1992, Patterson 1987, Patterson et al 1992).

Auditory Patterns

Auditory events or entities, whether brief or prolonged, may be said to comprise auditory patterns. On the acoustical or stimulus side, such patterns range from simple to complex. Hirsh (1988) suggested a hierarchy from single sounds in a steady state, to single sounds with a changing state, to sound sequences, to concurrent sequences. CHABA (1989, pp. 23–27) made similar suggestions. Hartmann (1988), Bregman (1990), and Yost (1992), seeking single dimensions that controlled segregation and integration of single sounds into larger entities, listed variables like onset and offset times, temporal modulation, duration, spectral content, level and location in space, in addition to more general features like context, musical training, and selective attention.

Contemporary research has not yielded a suitable definition or theory about auditory patterns. To be sure, we have plenty of definitions and theories about the patterns of speech and music, but the dimensions we use come more from linguistic or music theory than from the dimensions of auditory perception.

Temporal Perception

The auditory system can respond quickly to changes in the acoustic stimulus. The literature on temporal resolution is well reviewed and interpreted by Viemeister & Plack (1993). The chapter addresses minimal detectable separation between brief sounds, mostly through gap-detection studies; the temporal modulation transfer function; the influence of spectrum on temporal resolution; the influence of temporal relations in masking (see the section in this review on "Comodulation Masking Release"); and temporal integration.

Time also serves as an important dimension in which auditory patterns are formed. Judgments of the temporal order of events are critical. Warren (1993) has reviewed his own studies and related work by others. When the listener's task is to discriminate the order AB from BA, thresholds can be in the 1–2 ms range for pairs of brief events. To make it possible for the listener to report whether A or B came first in such pairs, 20 ms is sufficient (Rosen & Howell 1987). If the listener must give verbal responses to name the order of events in longer sequences or if the order is continuously recycled, longer onset separations are required.

Judged order for a single sequence can be disrupted by the presence of a second sequence. Order relations in either of two such streams depend upon the rate of events and frequencies involved (Bregman 1990, 1993). The basic observation out of which grew auditory stream segregation and scene analysis, summarized in these recent Bregman references, concerns sequences of pitches. At moderate rates with a relatively narrow range of pitches, a listener reports hearing a single line of pitches. When, however, some of the pitches are in a high range and others are in a low range and the rate of alternation is higher, listeners report hearing two concurrent pitch lines.

RHYTHMIC PATTERNS   A special aspect of temporal perception is rhythm, the structure of a series of temporal intervals between the onsets of sounds in a sequence. Rhythmic patterns are among the oldest subjects in auditory psychophysics, and work on them is summarized by Handel (1989, pp. 383–459) and by Jones & Yee (1993). A sequence of equally timed sound onsets has no necessary rhythmic structure except for that imposed by a listener. The stimulus structure emerges from the interplay of different onset intervals relative to an underlying "beat." Listeners can discriminate, recognize, or imitate such rhythmic patterns. Time alone can serve as the basis for forming such patterns, as in the case of drums. Changes in frequency or intensity are not necessary to the rhythmic pattern, but such changes elaborate the patterns with markings or accents. Listeners' sensitivity to the time of occurrence of elements within rhythmic and arrhythmic sequences has been demonstrated by Hirsh et al (1990) and by Monahan & Hirsh (1990).

Paul Fraisse has summarized his large body of work on time and rhythm (Deutsch 1982). His reliance on Gestalt principles of grouping and of common fate to explain the various structures in rhythmic patterns, with their meters and beats, is supplemented by notions of expectancy and anticipation (Fraisse 1984). Similar lines are found in the beat-based theory of Povel & Essens (1985) and in the emphasis on expectancy of Jones (see Jones & Yee 1993).

OTHER TEMPORAL PATTERNS   Most natural sources generate waveforms with temporal patterns of modulation of amplitude and frequency. The auditory processing of these modulations, undoubtedfly useful for integration and segregation of sound sources, has recently been reviewed by Darwin & Carlyon (1995). Temporal sequences either of discrete tonal components or even of individual brief segments of a burst of "frozen noise" can be resolved with accuracy rivaling, or often exceeding, that with which listeners can hear out similarly fine acoustic details of speech. At least in this restricted sense, speech processing is clearly not a special auditory ability. To be sure, familiarity with word-length tonal sequences is essential if small changes in the frequency, duration, or intensity of individual components are to be detected (Watson 1987). When a new tonal sequence is presented on each trial, even after many hours of training and as many as 10,000 trials, discrimination thresholds are often elevated by more than one order of magnitude. Kidd & Watson (1992) found that discrimination performance under such conditions of high stimulus uncertainty was strongly predictable by the proportion of the total duration of the tonal pattern that was represented by the target component (the tone subject to change in the discrimination task). The just-detectable increment in the frequency of a 25-ms component of a 100-ms tonal sequence is thus roughly the same as that of a 100-ms component of a 400-ms sequence, or a 250-ms component of a 1-s sequence. This result contrasts sharply with frequency discrimination for single tones. In the range of frequencies used in the tonal patterns (below 3 kHz), the absolute duration of isolated tones is a strong determinant of the size of the frequency-discrimination threshold for durations between 6 and 200 ms, although above 200 ms the thresholds are essentially constant (Moore 1973). The proportion of the total duration of a complex pattern that is occupied by a particular component has also been shown to strongly predict the detectability of segments of frozen noise, which are common to two-noise bursts presented in sequence (Fallon-Coble & Robinson 1992). The similarity between the effects of proportional duration for bursts of Gaussian noise and those for tonal sequences is sufficiently strong to make it appear that the proportional-duration rule may be general for the discrimination of a wide range of unfamiliar sounds.

Lutfi (1993) has developed a model of pattern discrimination that is applicable to tonal sequences and to a variety of other complex stimuli: "Component discriminability in an unfamiliar tone pattern (profile or sequence) is a linearly increasing function of the component's relative entropy (CoRE) in the pattern. Ancillary: The threshold for detection of a change decreases by one order of magnitude (factor of 10) for each one bit increase in CoRE." This model successfully describes discrimination performance in a number of tonal-pattern studies by Watson and various coworkers in which the dimension subject to variation was the frequency, duration, or intensity of single target tones. The success with which this model fits a wide range of discrimination experiments is strongly dependent on the assumption that the weight assigned to the target tone (as well as the weights for all other tones) varies with the square of the amplitude-duration product for that tone. Given this assumption, the predictions of the CoRE model should be in general agreement with the proportional-target-tone-duration rule described in the preceding section (Kidd & Watson 1992). In fact, it fits a broad range of experimental data somewhat more accurately than does that empirical rule.

A much more restricted model of temporal sequence discrimination has been proposed by Sorkin (1990). It successfully describes a variety of cases in which arrhythmic temporal sequences of tones differ only in the durations of the intercomponent gaps. If listeners are presented with two arrhythmic sequences of tones, frequency-pattern discrimination is dependent on the complexity of the sequence of intervals (Sorkin 1987). Further, such temporally jittered patterns can be discriminated in the temporal domain (Sorkin 1990). But when the overall time of the sequence is compressed or expanded, such a model is not invariant with overall time (Sorkin & Montgomery 1991). Two facts are noteworthy in this line of research. One is that random variation in the temporal spacing of components of a tonal sequence when the frequencies of the components remain fixed has a surprisingly strong degrading effect on pattern discriminability. The other fact is that Sorkin's model, based simply on the temporal correlation between the patterns to be discriminated (and limited by an assumed internal temporal noise with a standard deviation of about 15 ms), does an excellent job of predicting the variation in discrimination for a wide range of gap-sequence correlations.

INDIVIDUAL DIFFERENCES

The study of individual differences has received considerably less attention than the performance of average normal adult listeners, with subject-to-subject differences in performance often treated as a close relation to measurement error. Nevertheless, reliable individual differences do characterize populations of so-called normal subjects tested in a wide range of sensory, motor, and intellectual tasks. In some cases, as in individual differences in the ability to hear out the details of complex auditory patterns, the range of thresholds in discrimination performance can be as large as or even larger than the effects of the primary relevant stimulus parameters (e.g. Johnson et al 1987; Watson 1987, p. 272). Many reports of large individual differences in the discrimination or detection abilities of audiometrically normal listeners have come from studies of temporal masking (e.g. McFadden & Wright 1990) and of localization (e.g.Wenzel et al 1993). Neff & Dethlefs (1995) analyzed data from a large number of her earlier studies in which listeners had been highly trained to detect signals in the presence of uncertain-frequency maskers and in which individual differences in thresholds as large as 20–25 dB were commonly reported. On the basis of an imposing array of data she rejected her earlier hypothesis of two classes of listeners [also proposed by McFadden & Wright (1990) for temporal masking] in favor of a single broad distribution of abilities.

A troublesome problem in the study of individual differences in auditory capabilities is that investigations of spectral and temporal discrimination using a wide variety of nonspeech sounds have with only a few exceptions failed to report any strong correlations between so-called psychoacoustic abilities and speech perception by normal-hearing listeners (Era et al 1986, Espinoza-Varas & Watson 1988). This situation led to the suggestion that individual differences in speech recognition abilities under difficult listening conditions (e.g. with masking noise), despite similar spectral and temporal acuity, may best be explained by central factors in speech processing (Watson 1991, Watson et al 1992). This hypothesis has been proposed in the past, but the supporting evidence has been modest at best. One piece of contrary evidence is the failure of the difference scores on the test for Speech Perception in Noise (SPIN) (recognition of words high in predictability minus recognition of words low in predictability) to reflect individual differences in language abilities or any significant individual differences in the ability to employ contextual cues (Bilger et al 1984, Owen 1981). Other attempts to confirm the role of individual differences in central or top-down processing mechanisms in speech recognition have sought correlations between various intellectual or linguistic skills and speech recognition. Several studies have reported small but significant correlations between measures of cognitive skill and speech recognition (e.g. Era et al 1986, van Rooijj et al 1989). Others have found modest correlations (0.5–0.6) between tests of general intellectual ability and performance on auditory psychophysical tests (Raz et al 1987, B Watson 1991). The uncertainty about the relations between sensory and intellectual or cognitive measures may reflect in part the range of intellectual demands of different psycho-physical methods. In support of a central-processing-efficiency explanation of individual differences in speech processing is a significant correlation (r > 0.5–0.6) between the ability to recognize speech under degraded listening conditions and the ability to read lips in the absence of any auditory input (Brink 1974, Watson et al 1992).

In an earlier chapter in this series, McFadden & Wightman (1983) wrote of the need for systematic test-battery studies of the "interrelations among the various auditory abilities in both normal and hearing-impaired listeners." Few such studies have been conducted since they made that recommendation, while reasons to do them have accumulated. For example, controversies concerning typical listeners' abilities to discriminate profile stimuli (see section on "Pro-file Analysis" in this review) have largely involved the range of individual abilities to perform in those experiments. When small numbers of subjects are used in a profile experiment, it appears that the only way to collect reasonably homogeneous data is to pretest larger groups of listeners and reject those who cannot, without lengthy training, discriminate on the basis of small differences in spectral shape (Green 1988b, p. 94; Henn & Turner 1990; Kidd et al 1991).

Various studies of the auditory performance of young children and even of infants in a wide variety of listening tasks have been made available in a conference proceedings edited by Werner & Rubel (1992). As these editors note in their introduction, "even in the simplest psychoacoustic tasks, such as the detection of a sound in quiet, infants and children exhibit what might be interpreted as auditory deficits compared to young adults." The results of many recent investigations suggest a continuous reduction in psychophysical thresholds starting around age 2 and continuing to age 5, or even to age 10 or 11 in some cases, after which adult-like performance is achieved. Specific examples include a 12–13 dB reduction in the masked threshold for tones, with an almost linear decrease between six months and ten years of age (Schneider et al 1989); the minimum audible angle in spatial localization decreases from about 27° at two months of age to 5–6° at 20 months and is nearly at adult levels of 2–3° for five-year-old subjects (Clifton 1992). The majority of recent developmental studies of auditory capabilities, however, have not traced changing performance from infancy to young adulthood but instead have simply compared infant performance with that of adults, which leaves considerable uncertainty about the time course of the developmental changes.

Two contributions to the volume edited by Werner & Rubel describe inter-nal-noise models that assume a central or decision-process noise, the power of which diminishes over the course of childhood (Viemeister & Schlauch 1992, Wightman & Allen 1992). In the absence of strong neurophysiological evi-dence of auditory-system development over this same period, there appears to be no simple way to decide between these general maturational models and theories that treat the developmental trends as though grounded in changes in the auditory system (e.g. Schneider & Trehub 1992, Werner 1992).

Some of these individual differences across developmental ages may be related to "central auditory processing disorder" (CAPD), a diagnostic category used by many clinicians to denote children who perform poorly on a variety of tests of the perception of complex sounds, both speech and non-speech, in the absence of other evidence of auditory deficits. [Research on CAPD has recently been summarized in Katz et al (1992). See also critical evaluations by Rees (1981) and Humes et al (1992).] Large-scale epidemiological studies must be conducted before meaningful relations, if such exist, can be shown to relate auditory-processing deficits either to language development or to the general academic success of special children who currently carry the CAPD label.

SELECTIVE PROCESSING

Auditory Attention

The concept of selective auditory attention to particular sounds or to selected spectral or temporal portions of complex sounds has been the subject of many investigations over the past decade or so. Considered in subjective terms, learning to direct attention to some particular aspect of a sound can lead the listener to report that a spectral-temporal region becomes more salient or stands out from its acoustic background. In some cases, such as those studied by Bregman (1990) and others concerned with auditory-stream segregation, the perceptual experience is quite similar to certain experiences with visual displays, in which one part is seen as "figure" and the remainder as "ground." Psychophysical correlates of selective auditory attention include evidence from "streaming" experiments that certain (within-figure) portions of complex sounds are processed more accurately than others. If some spectral-temporal portions of a complex sound can be shown to have a stronger influence on psychophysical judgments than others, to which the listener is also capable of responding, this might be considered objective evidence of the "distribution of auditory attention." When the listener is either trained or "cued" to respond preferentially to one sound out of a catalog or to one spectral-temporal part of a complex sound (Darwin & Carlyon 1995), evidence of enhanced processing of the trained, or cued, stimuli is an objective correlate of what is commonly meant by "selective attention." It is not identical to phenomenological attention, of course, because psychophysical evidence of selective processing does not presuppose claims by the listener that one sound, or part of a sound, seems more salient than others. In this section, experimental evidence relevant to psychophysically defined selective auditory attention is discussed; phenomenologically or subjectively defined attention is considered either explicable in these terms or beyond the scope of current methods of investigation.

Green noted over 30 years ago (1964) that a powerful way to test the predictions of theories, or models, of auditory processing was to analyze responses to individual stimuli or parts of individual stimuli, which he referred to as "molecular" psychophysics in contrast with the "molar" psychophysics of average responses made to average stimuli. A systematic method for deriving evidence of selective attention from "molecular" experiments has been developed by Berg (1989), who refers to this method as "conditional on a single stimulus" (COSS). COSS analyses can be employed for any component of a sound for which there is some variation from trial to trial. Thus, for example, Berg & Green (1990) introduced 0.5–2.0 dB of trial-to-trial random fluctuation in the levels of each component of 11-tone profile stimuli. The subjects' task was to detect an increment in the level of a midfrequency profile component in a two-alternative forced-choice procedure. Their responses were analyzed in relation to the trial-by-trial levels of each of the individual 11 tonal frequencies, which yielded a picture of the spectral weights employed by each listener in arriving at his or her responses. In this study, listeners who based most of their response variance on the weight assigned to the target tone achieved much lower thresholds than listeners whose "attentional" weights were distributed over several nontarget tonal components as well as to the target tone. In general, this procedure shows considerable promise for direct tests of models that include assumptions about single-band, multiband, or "off-frequency" listening, and it also provides an orderly approach to explaining individual differences among listeners in a more principled manner than by accusing some of them of having high levels of internal noise or of "failing to attend."

Another approach to selective listening, noted earlier in this section, is to train, or cue, the listener to attend to some particular aspect of the waveform presented at a given instant. A much-replicated training experiment was devised by Greenberg & Larkin (1968), who taught listeners to detect an 1100–Hz tone in a broadband Gaussian noise background, using a two-alternative forced-choice procedure. After the listeners had learned to detect the 1100–Hz tone, "probe" signals ranging from 500 to 1700 Hz were presented in lieu of it on a low percentage of the trials at the level required to achieve about 80% correct with the original signal. The result was a surprisingly narrow band around 1100 Hz (roughly a CB in width) within which performance diminished from a maximum at 1100 Hz to near chance. Although this result might be interpreted as the listeners simply failing to respond to noticeably off-frequency signals, Scharf et al (1987) demonstrated that this was not the case. They informed their listeners that on some percentage of the trials signals of other frequencies would be presented, a procedure that only slightly affected the "attentional-band" outcome.

Dai et al (1991) replicated this finding and extended it to target frequencies from 250 to 4000 Hz. They found that the width of the attentional band was close to the CB at 1000 Hz and higher but only half that width at 250 and 500 Hz. Psychometric functions for probe frequencies more than a CB away from a 1000-Hz target tone were depressed by about 7.0 dB, compared to sensitivity for the test tone. This suggests either that the skirts of the attentional bands do not fall off at a constant rate or, more likely, that listeners are always giving some weight to activity in multiple bands. Hafter et al (1993), sampling a range from 750 to 3000 Hz, showed that the attentional focus can be varied from trial to trial by presenting a cue in advance of the trial to indicate the signal frequency. Narrow attentional bands were found using the Greenberg-Larkin probe procedure and were only slightly wider than those in single-band experiments.

CONCLUSION

The areas of psychoacoustics and auditory perception are well represented in recent books and monographs. A bridge is being formed between the psychophysics of simple sounds and the processing of complex sounds. The latter is enabling further relations to be made to more cognitive aspects of auditory perception, especially attention and individual differences. We can anticipate a fruitful expansion in the next decade of auditory sensory and perceptual theory.

ACKNOWLEDGMENTS

Preparation of this chapter was supported by the Research Department, Central Institute for the Deaf; and by grants NIH/NINCD DC00250 and AFSOR F49620-92-J-0506 to Indiana University. The authors thank William Yost for helpful suggestions.

Literature Cited

Aiello R, ed. 1994. *Musical Perceptions.* New York: Oxford. 290 pp.

Atkinson RC, Herrnstein RJ, Lindzey G, Luce RD, eds. 1988. *Stevens' Handbook of Experimental Psychology,* Vol. 1. New York: Wiley. 905 pp.

Berg B. 1989. Analysis of weights in multiple observation tasks. *J. Acoust. Soc. Am.* 86: 1743–46

Berg B, Green DM. 1990. Spectral weights in profile listening. *J. Acoust. Soc. Am.* 88: 758–66

Bernstein LB, Green DM. 1988. Detection of changes in spectral shape: uniform vs. nonuniform background spectra. *Hear. Res.* 32:157–65

Bilger RC, Nuetzel JM, Rabinowitz WM, Rzeczkowski C. 1984. Standardization of a test of speech perception in noise. *J. Speech Hear. Res.* 27:32–48

Bregman AS. 1990. *Auditory Scene Analysis.* Cambridge, MA: MIT Press. 783 pp.

Bregman AS. 1993. Auditory scene analysis: hearing in complex environments. See McAdams & Bigand 1993, pp. 10–36

Brink B. 1974. Experience concerning audiovisual tests utilized at a school for the deaf. In *Scandinavian Audiology*, Suppl. 4, *Visual and Audio-Visual Perception of Speech*, ed. H Birk Nielsen, E Kampp, pp. 210–21. Stockholm, Sweden: Almquist & Wiksell

Buus S. 1985. Release from masking caused by envelope fluctuations. *J. Acoust. Soc. Am.* 78:1958–65

Cazals Y, Demany K, Horner K, eds. 1992. *Auditory Physiology and Perception. Advanced Bioscience,* Vol. 83, Oxford: Pergamon

CHABA (Committee on Hearing, Bioacoustics, and Biomechanics). 1989. *Classification of Complex Nonspeech Sounds.* Washington, DC: Natl. Acad. Press. 88 pp.

Clifton R. 1992. The development of spatial hearing in human infants. See Werner & Rubel 1992, pp. 135–57

Cohen MF, Schubert ED. 1987. The effect of cross-spectrum correlation on the detectability of a noise signal. *J. Acoust. Soc. Am.* 81:721–23

Darwin CJ, Carlyon RP. 1995. Auditory grouping. In *BCJ Moore(Ed) Hearing*, ed. BCJ Moore, pp. 387–424. San Diego: Academic

Dai H, Scharf B, Buus S. 1991. Effective attenuation of signals in noise under focussed attention. *J. Acoust. Soc. Am.* 89:2837–42

de Boer E, Dreschler WA. 1987. Auditory psychophysics: spectrotemporal representation of signals. *Annu. Rev. Psychol.* 38:181–202

Deutsch D, ed. 1982. *The Psychology of Music.* New York: Academic. 542 pp.

Dowling WJ, Harwood DL. 1986. *Music Cognition.* Orlando, FL: Academic. 258 pp.

Duda R, Lyon RF, Slaney M. 1990. Correlograms and the separation of sounds. In *IEEE Conference on Signals, Systems and Computers*, 1:457–61. San Jose: Maple Press

Durlach NI, Braida LD. 1963. Equalization and cancellation theory of binaural masking level differences. *J. Acoust. Soc. Am.* 35:1206–18

Durlach NI, Braida LD. 1969. Intensity perception. I. Preliminary theory of intensity resolution. *J. Acoust. Soc. Am.* 46:372–83

Durlach NI, Braida LD, Ito Y. 1986. Toward a model for discrimination of broadband signals. *J. Acoust. Soc. Am.* 80:63–72

Era P, Jokela J, Qvarnberg Y, Heikkinen E. 1986. Pure-tone thresholds, speech understanding, and their correlates in samples of men of different ages. *Audiology* 25:338–52

Espinoza-Varas B, Watson CS. 1988. Low commonality between tests of auditory discrimination and of speech perception. *J. Acoust. Soc. Am.* 84(Suppl. 1):S143

Fallon-Coble S, Robinson DE. 1992. Discriminability of bursts of reproducible noise. *J. Acoust. Soc. Am.* 92:2630–35

Feth LL. 1974. Frequency discrimination of complex periodic tones. *Percept. Psychophys.* 15:375–78

Fletcher H. 1940. Auditory patterns. *Rev. Mod. Phys.* 12:47–65

Fraisse P. 1984. Perception and estimation of time. *Annu. Rev. Psychol.* 35:1–36

Gaver WW. 1993. What in the world do we hear? An ecological approach to auditory event perception. *Ecol. Psychol.* 5:1–29

Gelfand SA. 1990. *Hearing: An Introduction to Psychological and Physiological Acoustics.* New York: Dekker. 2nd ed. 535 pp.

Green DM. 1964. Consistency of auditory detection judgments. *Psychol. Rev.* 71:392–407

Green DM. 1988a. Audition: psychophysics and perception. See Atkinson et al 1988, pp. 327–76

Green DM. 1988b. *Profile Analysis: Auditory Intensity Discrimination.* New York: Oxford

Green DM. 1992. On the similarity of two theories of comodulation masking release. *J. Acoust. Soc. Am.* 91:1769

Green DM. 1993a. Auditory intensity discrimination. See Yost et al 1993, pp. 13–55

Green DM. 1993b. A maximum-likelihood method for estimating thresholds in a yes-no task. *J. Acoust. Soc. Am.* 93:2096–2105

Green DM, Kidd G Jr, Picardi M. 1983. Successive versus simultaneous comparison in auditory intensity discrimination. *J. Acoust. Soc. Am.* 73:639–43

Green DM, Mason CR. 1985. Auditory profile analysis: frequency, phase and Weber's law. *J. Acoust. Soc. Am.* 77:1155–61

Green DM, Onson ZA, Forrest TG. 1987. Frequency effects in profile analysis and detecting complex spectra changes. *J. Acoust. Soc. Am.* 81:692–99

Greenberg GZ, Larkin WD. 1968. Frequency-response characteristic of auditory observers detecting signals of a single frequency in noise: the probe-signal method. *J. Acoust. Soc. Am.* 44:1513–23

Grey JM. 1977. Multidimensional perceptual

scaling of musical timbres. *J. Acoust. Soc. Am.* 61:1270–77

Grey JM, Moorer JA. 1977. Perceptual evaluations of synthesized musical instrument tones. *J. Acoust. Soc. Am.* 62:454–62

Hafter ER, Buell TN, Richards VM. 1988. Onset coding in lateralization: its form, site and function. In *Auditory Function: Neurobiological Bases of Hearing,* ed. GW Edelman, WE Gall, WM Cowan, pp. 647–76. New York: Wiley

Hafter ER, Schlauch RS, Tang J. 1993. Attending to auditory filters that were not stimulated directly. *J. Acoust. Soc. Am.* 94: 743–47

Hall JW III. 1986. The effect of across-frequency differences in masking level on spectro-temporal pattern analysis. *J. Acoust. Soc. Am.* 79:781–87

Hall JW III, Grose JH. 1988. Comodulation masking release: evidence for multiple cues. *J. Acoust. Soc. Am.* 84:1669–75

Hall JW III, Grose JH. 1990. Comodulation masking release and auditory grouping. *J. Acoust. Soc. Am.* 88:119–25

Hall JW III, Haggard MP, Fernandes MA. 1984. Detection in noise by spectro-temporal pattern analysis. *J. Acoust. Soc. Am.* 76: 50–56

Handel S. 1989. *Listening: An Introduction to the Perception of Auditory Events.* Cambridge, MA: MIT Press. 597 pp.

Hartmann WM. 1988. Pitch perception and the organization and integration of auditory entities. In *Auditory Function: Neurobiological Bases of Hearing,* ed. GW Edelman, WE Gall, WM Cowan, pp. 623–45. New York: Wiley

Henn CC, Turner CW. 1990. Pure-tone increment detection in harmonic and inharmonic backgrounds. *J. Acoust. Soc. Am.* 88: 126–31

Hirsh IJ. 1988. Auditory perception and speech. See Atkinson et al 1988, pp. 377–408

Hirsh IJ, Monahan CB, Grant KW, Singh PG. 1990. Studies in auditory timing. I. Simple patterns. *Percept. Psychophys.* 47:215–26

Humes L, Christopherson L, Cokely C. 1992. Central auditory processing disorders in the elderly: fact or fiction? See Katz et al 1992, pp. 141–49

Iverson P, Krumhansl CL. 1993. Isolating the dynamic attributes of musical timbre. *J. Acoust. Soc. Am.* 94:2595–603

Johnson DM, Watson CS, Jensen JK. 1987. Individual differences in auditory capabilities. *J. Acoust. Soc. Am.* 81:427–38

Jones MR, Holleran S, eds. 1992. *Cognitive Bases of Musical Communication.* Washington, DC: Am. Psychol. Assoc. 284 pp.

Jones MR, Yee W. 1993. Attending to auditory events: the role of temporal organization. See McAdams & Bigand 1993, pp. 69–112

Julesz B, Hirsh IJ. 1972. Visual and auditory perception: an essay of comparison. In *Human Communication: A Unified View,* ed. EE David, P Denes, pp. 283–340. New York: McGraw-Hill

Katz J, Stecker NA, Henderson D, eds. 1992. *Central Auditory Processing: A Transdisciplinary View.* St. Louis, MO: Mosby

Kendall RA. 1986. The role of acoustic signal partitions in listener categorization of musical phrases. *Music Percept.* 4:185–214

Kewley-Port D, Watson CS. 1994. Formant-frequency discrimination for isolated English vowels. *J. Acoust. Soc. Am.* 95: 485–96

Kidd G Jr, Mason CR, Uchanski RM, Brantley MA, Shah P. 1991. Evaluation of simple models of auditory profile analysis using random reference spectra. *J. Acoust. Soc. Am.* 90:1340–54

Kidd GR, Watson CS. 1992. The "proportion-of-the-total-duration rule" for the discrimination of auditory patterns. *J. Acoust. Soc. Am.* 92:3109–18

Krumhansl CL. 1991. Music psychology: tonal structures in perception and memory. *Annu. Rev. Psychol.* 42:277–303

Luce RD. 1993. *Sound & Hearing: A Conceptual Introduction.* Hillsdale, NJ: Erlbaum. 322 pp., Demonstration CD

Lutfi RA. 1993. A model of auditory pattern analysis based on component-relative-entropy. *J. Acoust. Soc. Am.* 94:748–58

McAdams S. 1993. Recognition of sound sources and events. See McAdams & Bigand 1993, pp. 146–98

McAdams S, Bigand E, eds. 1993. *Thinking in Sound: The Cognitive Psychology of Human Audition.* New York: Oxford. 354 pp.

McFadden D, Wightman FL. 1983. Audition: some relations between normal and pathological hearing. *Annu. Rev. Psychol.* 34: 95–128

McFadden D, Wright BA. 1990. Temporal decline of masking and comodulation detection differences. *J. Acoust. Soc. Am.* 88: 711–24

Meddis R, Hewitt MJ. 1992. Modeling the identification of concurrent vowels with different fundamental frequencies. *J. Acoust. Soc. Am.* 91:233–45

Middlebrooks JC, Green DM. 1991. Sound localization by human listeners. *Annu. Rev. Psychol.* 42:135–59

Miller JL, Eimas PD. 1995. Speech perception: from signal to word. *Annu. Rev. Psychol.* 46:467–92

Monahan CB, Hirsh IJ. 1990. Studies in auditory timing. II. Rhythmic patterns. *Percept. Psychophys.* 47:227–42

Moore BCJ. 1973. Frequency difference limens for short tones. *J. Acoust. Soc. Am.* 54:610–19

Moore BCJ. 1989. *An Introduction to the Psy-*

chology of Hearing. New York: Academic. 350 pp. 3rd ed.

Moore BCJ. 1993. Frequency analysis and pitch perception. See Yost et al 1993, pp. 56–115

Moore BCJ, ed. 1995. *Hearing.* New York: Academic. 468 pp. 2nd ed.

Moore BCJ, Glasberg BR, Schoonevelt GP. 1990. Across-channel masking and co-modulation masking release. *J. Acoust. Soc. Am.* 87:1683–94

Neff DL, Dethlefs TM. 1995. Individual differences in simultaneous masking by random frequency maskers. *J. Acoust. Soc. Am.* 98: 125–34

Owen JH. 1981. Influence of acoustical and linguistic factors on the SPIN test difference scores. *J. Acoust. Soc. Am.* 70:678–82

Patterson RD. 1987. A pulse ribbon model of monaural phase perception. *J. Acoust. Soc. Am.* 82:1560–86

Patterson RD, Robinson K, Holdsworth J, McKeown D, Zhang C, Allerhand L. 1992. Complex sounds and auditory images. See Cazals et al 1992, pp. 429–46

Pitt MA. 1994. Perception of pitch and timbre by musically trained and untrained listeners. *J. Exp. Psychol.: Hum. Percept. Perform.* 20:976–86

Plomp R. 1970. Timbre as a multidimensional attribute of complex tones. In *Frequency Analysis and Periodicity Detection in Hearing,* ed. R Plomp, GF Smoorenberg, pp. 397–411. Leiden: Sijthoff

Povel DJ, Essens P. 1985. Perception of temporal patterns. *Music Percept.* 2:411–40

Rasch RA, Plomp R. 1982. The perception of musical tones. See Deutsch 1982, pp. 1–24

Raz N, Willerman L, Yama M. 1987. On sense and senses: intelligence and auditory information processing. *Pers. Individ. Diff.* 8: 201–10

Rees N. 1981. Saying more than we know: Is auditory processing disorder a meaningful concept? In *Central Auditory and Language Disorders in Children,* ed. RW Keith, pp. 94–120. Houston, TX: College-Hill

Richards VM. 1987. Monaural envelope correlation perception. *J. Acoust. Soc. Am.* 82: 1621–30

Risset J-C, Wessel DL. 1982. Exploration of timbre by analysis and synthesis. See Deutsch 1982, pp. 25–88

Rosen S, Howell P. 1987. Is there a natural sensitivity at 20 ms in relative tone-onset-time continua? See Schouten 1987, pp. 199–209

Scharf B, Quigley S, Aoki C, Peachey N, Reeves A. 1987. Focused attention and frequency selectivity. *Percept. Psychophys.* 42:215–23

Schneider BA, Trehub SE. 1992. Sources of developmental change in auditory sensitivity. See Werner & Rubel 1992, pp. 3–46

Schneider BA, Trehub SE, Morrongiello BA, Thorpe LA. 1989. Developmental changes in masked thresholds. *J. Acoust. Soc. Am.* 86:1733–42

Schouten MEH, ed. 1987. *The Psychophysics of Speech Perception.* Boston: Martinus Nijhoff. 488 pp.

Singh PG. 1987. Perceptual organization of complex-tone sequences: a tradeoff between pitch and timbre? *J. Acoust. Soc. Am.* 82:886–99

Singh PG, Hirsh IJ. 1992. Influence of spectral locus and F0 changes on the pitch and timbre of complex tones. *J. Acoust. Soc. Am.* 92:2650–61

Sorkin RD. 1987. Temporal factors in the discrimination of tonal sequences. *J. Acoust. Soc. Am.* 82:1218–26

Sorkin RD. 1990. Perception of temporal patterns defined by tonal sequences. *J. Acoust. Soc. Am.* 87:1695–1701

Sorkin RD, Montgomery DA. 1991. Effect of time compression and expansion on the discrimination of tonal patterns. *J. Acoust. Soc. Am.* 90:846–57

Spiegel MF, Picardi MC, Green DM. 1981. Signal and masker uncertainty in intensity discrimination. *J. Acoust. Soc. Am.* 70: 1015–19

Stevens SS. 1975. *Psychophysics: Introduction to Its Perceptual, Neural and Social Prospects,* ed. G Stevens. New York: Wiley. 329 pp.

Teas DC. 1989. Auditory physiology: present trends. *Annu. Rev. Psychol.* 40:405–29

Tighe TJ, Dowling WJ, eds. 1993. *Psychology and Music: The Understanding of Melody and Rhythm.* Hillsdale, NJ: Erlbaum. 228 pp.

Trahiotis C, Robinson DE. 1979. Auditory psychophysics. *Annu. Rev. Psychol.* 30:31–61

Turner CW, Horwitz AR, Souza PE. 1994. Forward- and backward-masked intensity discrimination measured using forced-choice and adjustment procedures. *J. Acoust. Soc. Am.* 96:221–26

van Rooij JCGM, Plomp R, Orlebeke JF. 1989. Auditive and cognitive factors in speech perception by elderly listeners. I. Development of a test battery. *J. Acoust. Soc. Am.* 86:1294–307

Viemeister NF, Plack CJ. 1993. Time analysis. See Yost et al 1993, pp. 116–54

Viemeister NF, Schlauch RS. 1992. Issues in infant psychoacoustics. See Werner & Rubel 1992, pp. 191–209

Warren RM. 1993. Perception of acoustic sequences: global integration and temporal resolution. See McAdams & Bigand 1993, pp. 37–68

Watson BU. 1991. Some relationships between

intelligence and auditory discrimination. *J. Speech Hear. Res.* 34:621–7

Watson CS. 1987. Uncertainty, informational masking and the capacity of immediate auditory memory. See Yost & Watson 1987, pp. 267–77

Watson CS. 1991. Auditory perceptual learning and the cochlear implant. *Am. J. Otol.* 12:73–79 (Suppl.)

Watson CS, Kelly WJ, Wroton HW. 1976. Factors in the discrimination of tonal patterns. II. Selective attention and learning under various levels of stimulus uncertainty. *J. Acoust. Soc. Am.* 60:1176–86

Watson CS, Qiu WW, Chamberlain M. 1992. Correlations between auditory and visual speech processing ability: evidence for a modality-research independent source of variance. *J. Acoust. Soc. Am.* 92:2385 (Abstr.)

Wenzel EM, Arruda M, Kistler DJ, Wightman FL. 1993. Localization using non-individualized head-related transfer functions. *J. Acoust. Soc. Am.* 94:111–23

Werner LA. 1992. Interpreting development in psychoacoustics. See Werner & Rubel 1992, pp. 47–88

Werner LA, Rubel EW, eds. 1992. *Developmental Psychoacoustics.* Washington, DC: Am. Psychol. Assoc.

Wightman F, Allen P. 1992. Individual differences in auditory capability among preschool children. See Werner & Rubel 1992, pp. 113–33

Wightman FL, Kistler DJ. 1993. Sound localization. See Yost et al 1993, pp. 155–92

Wright BA, McFadden D. 1990. Uncertainty about the correlation among temporal envelopes in two comodulation conditions. *J. Acoust. Soc. Am.* 88:1339–50

Yost WA. 1992. Auditory image perception and analysis. *Hear. Res.* 56:8–19

Yost WA. 1994. *Fundamentals of Hearing.* San Diego: Academic. 326 pp. 3rd ed.

Yost WA, Nielsen DW. 1985. *Fundamentals of Hearing.* New York: Holt, Rinehart, Winston. 269 pp. 2nd ed.

Yost WA, Sheft SS. 1993. Auditory perception. See Yost et al 1993, pp. 193–236

Yost WA, Sheft S. 1994. Modulation detection interference: across-spectral processing and auditory grouping. *Hear. Res.* 79: 48–59

Yost WA, Watson CS, eds. 1987. *Auditory Processing of Complex Sounds.* Hillsdale, NJ: Erlbaum. 328 pp.

Yost WA, Popper AN, Fay RR, eds. 1993. *Human Psychophysics.* New York: Springer-Verlag. 243 pp.

Annu. Rev. Psychol. 1996. 47:485–512

ENVIRONMENTAL PSYCHOLOGY 1989–1994

Eric Sundstrom

Department of Psychology, University of Tennessee, Knoxville, Tennessee 37916

Paul A. Bell

Department of Psychology, Colorado State University, Fort Collins, Colorado 80523

Paul L. Busby

Department of Psychology, University of Tennessee, Knoxville, Tennessee 37916

Cheryl Asmus

Department of Psychology, Colorado State University, Fort Collins, Colorado 80523

KEY WORDS: architectural research, ecological psychology, environmental design, environmental psychology, physical environment

ABSTRACT

A review of research and theory on transactions between people and physical environments emphasizes new contributions to theory and empirical research published in major journals of environmental psychology, 1989–1994. Theories focused on arousal, load, stress, privacy-regulation, behavior settings, and transactional analysis; new theory increasingly incorporated situational and contextual variables. Empirical research emphasized field settings over the laboratory and employed increasingly diverse methods, populations, and cultures. Environmental design studies integrated scientific and applied goals through post-occupancy evaluation. New findings concerned features of residences, work places, hospitals, schools, prisons, and larger community environ-

0066-4308/96/0201-0485$08.00

ments. New studies also addressed environmental stressors (e.g. temperature, noise); effects of attitudes and behaviors on conservation, crime, pollution, and hazards; and issues for neighborhoods, public places, and natural environments. Directions for the future include integrated theory to guide research, more design experiments, and development of conventions for case studies.

CONTENTS

INTRODUCTION

Environmental psychology examines relationships between people and their physical environments (e.g. Bell et al 1990, Gifford 1994). This review appears less than three decades after publication of the first textbook of environmental psychology (Proshansky et al 1970) and less than one decade after release of the *Handbook of Environmental Psychology* (Stokols & Altman 1987). Our purpose here is to describe progress in environmental psychology since the last review in the *Annual Review of Psychology* (Saegert & Winkel 1990). Focusing mainly on research published from 1989 through 1994, we review empirical studies in the field's major journals, emphasizing new findings and contributions during the past six years.

Our first section discusses trends in publication, research, and theory. Subsequent sections summarize new findings about various types of physical settings, proceeding from smaller to larger size, and from individual to social-psychological to organizational and community levels of analysis. The second section addresses built environments of relatively small size—residences—and then examines buildings occupied by private organizations and public institutions—work places, hospitals, schools, and prisons. A third section addresses larger community environments and reviews new research on environmental stressors, environmental attitudes and behaviors such as those related to conservation, and issues related to neighborhoods and public places. The fourth section explores natural environments and restorative settings. We conclude by summarizing developments in the field during the past six years and suggesting directions for the future.

RECENT TRENDS

Publication

In the past six years publication in environmental psychology steadily expanded. The empirical research stream continued to flow in the field's primary journals—*Environment and Behavior* and *Journal of Environmental Psychology*—and in *Journal of Architectural and Planning Research, Architecture and Behavior, Human Ecology,* and *Population and Environment.* Environmental psychologists published occasionally in social psychology journals, such as *Journal of Personality and Social Psychology,* and in community psychology journals such as *American Journal of Community Psychology.*

Expansion continued in edited series as well. Altman's *Human Behavior and the Environment* series added volumes on intellectual traditions (Altman & Christensen 1990), place attachment (Altman & Low 1992), and women and the environment (Altman & Churchman 1994). Zube and Moore's newer *Advances in Environment, Behavior, and Design* added two volumes (1989, 1991), and another is planned. Cambridge University Press's edited series gained volumes on human territoriality (Taylor 1988), public space (Carr et al 1992), natural environments (Kaplan & Kaplan 1989), and applications of environment-behavior research (Cherulnik 1993). Other edited volumes addressed design interventions (Prieser et al 1991), environment and cognition (Gärling & Evans 1991), housing (Arias 1993), isolated environments (Harrison et al 1991), settings for children (Weinstein & David 1990), and theories of environmental psychology (Walsh et al 1992).

A trend in edited collections favored retrospective analyses. These focused on careers of scholars (Altman & Christensen 1990), influential design-research projects (Cherulnik 1993), facility programming (Sanoff 1989), and evaluation of the built environment (Wener 1989). Similar retrospectives appeared in journals (Barker 1990, Gump 1990, Schoggen 1990).

Research

Research in environmental psychology has encompassed individuals, interpersonal relationships, groups, organizations, communities, and even cultures, and their complex relationships with environmental factors. Empirical studies examined environmental variables ranging from *ambient conditions*—temperature, sound, lighting, and air quality—to architectural features of buildings and neighborhoods, to built and natural features of entire communities and regions. The research emphasized individual and interpersonal levels of analysis and examined attitudes and cognitions about the environment more often than it incorporated direct measures or manipulations of objective, physical characteristics of the environment. Examples of studies that used objective measures include Christensen et al (1992), Edwards et al (1994), and Novaco et al (1990).

Four trends appeared in empirical studies cited in this review: 1. More research was conducted in field settings than in laboratories. 2. We see efforts toward cumulative knowledge in studies that replicate or extend earlier work (e.g. Brown 1992, Haggard & Werner 1990, Shaw & Gifford 1994). 3. Empirical studies reflected diverse methods, settings, and populations. Particularly salient is the variety of cultures represented. 4. Researchers were multidisciplinary; perhaps only half were based at universities in traditional departments of psychology.

Environmental psychology maintained its dual orientation to research and application and proceeded further toward integrating them (Farbstein & Kantrowitz 1991, Groat & Despres 1991). Researchers conducted hypothesis-testing studies in controlled settings (e.g. Veitch et al 1991), and practitioners applied research findings in facility programming (Sanoff 1989), design (Lang 1991, Prieser et al 1991), and post-occupancy evaluation (Prieser et al 1988, Wener 1989). The clearest integration appeared in *environmental design research* (e.g. Wisner et al 1991), which uses experimental or quasi-experimental interventions in natural settings to improve environmental design and to test scientific hypotheses. A typical project begins with a background analysis, development of behavioral goals, and identification of environment-behavior relationships. In the design phase the goals are translated into specific environmental features. The new design is introduced into part or all of the setting, and measurements are collected before and after renovation for post-occupancy evaluation and for tests of hypotheses. Cherulnik (1993) described 13 classic examples, including the unpublished, oft-cited quasi-experiment at the

Seattle and Los Angeles Federal Aviation Administration offices by Dennis Green, Walter Kleeman, Sam Sloan, and Robert Sommer that tested the effects of employees' participation in the re-design of their offices on subsequent satisfaction with features of their work environments.

Theory

Environmental psychologists reiterated the difficulty of developing theory on a topic as vast as the physical environment (Ittelson 1989, Kaminski 1989). Even so, theory advanced during the past six years. New theories incorporated detailed analyses of context (Michelson 1994, Wicker 1992), using smaller and more situation-specific units (Walsh et al 1992). One new theory examined the process of design itself (Lang 1991). Others integrated small-scale, proximal environments with large-scale, distal environments (Schoggen 1989) and linked environmental features with interpersonal relationships (Peterson 1992) and cultural patterns (Altman et al 1992). Some theories integrated multiple processes, such as the model by Bell et al (1990) that linked objective and subjective environmental features, perceptions, arousal and stress, coping and adaptation, and aftereffects.

Despite progress in development of theory, environmental psychologists remained far from consensus on a unified theoretical approach, and instead took a variety of approaches. Among theories that guided research, six appeared most influential:

AROUSAL   Psychophysiological arousal is well established as a process that mediates influences of environmental features such as sound and temperature. The *arousal hypothesis* predicts optimum performance and satisfaction under conditions of moderate arousal, depending on task complexity and other factors (Thayer 1989). Biner et al (1989) found students' preferences for lighting scenarios consistent with predictions of the arousal hypothesis. Extensions of the hypothesis suggest that through arousal, high temperature increases the likelihood of violence, though the nature of the relationship remains in debate (Anderson 1989, Bell 1992).

ENVIRONMENTAL LOAD   The *overload hypothesis* assumes that humans have a finite capacity for processing stimuli and information and predicts that we cope with sensory or information overload through (among other responses) selective attention and ignoring low-priority inputs. Consistent with the hypothesis, a laboratory experiment by Smith (1991) showed that 78dB(A) noise led to reduced performance by college students in a letter writing task but not in a letter-search task. Loewen & Suedfeld (1992) found that masking sound mitigated the performance deficit produced by office noise but added to arousal.

Veitch (1990) extended the arousal hypothesis to individual differences and reported better reading comprehension in noisy conditions by individuals with internal locus of control, and better reading comprehension in quiet conditions by individuals with external locus of control.

STRESS AND ADAPTATION   Previous research and theory associated extremes of temperature, sound, and other environmental variables with physiological and psychological stress and with coping and adaptive behaviors that reduce stress or its impact. Environmental stress research of the last six years examined prolonged exposures (e.g. Hedge 1989) and post-traumatic outcomes (Rubonis & Bickman 1991) including chronic illness and psychological impairment. Such findings reinforce the need for theoretical distinction of acute and chronic environmental stress (e.g. Baum et al 1990, Baum & Fleming 1993, Hobfoll 1991).

PRIVACY-REGULATION   Research on privacy, spatial behavior, crowding, and territoriality together suggests a human tendency to seek optimum social interaction, partly through use of the physical environment (Altman 1993). *Privacy regulation theory* suggests that when a person fails to achieve the subjective, optimum level of social contact for the situation, the resulting stress motivates coping behavior, which may rely on the physical setting (Brown 1992). Consistent with the theory, Haggard & Werner (1990) found that students who temporarily occupied a laboratory setting rejected intrusions more often when the chair arrangement delineated their work area than when it did not. Block & Garnett (1989) reported higher satisfaction among college students who worked on complex tasks in private rather than nonprivate settings.

ECOLOGICAL PSYCHOLOGY AND BEHAVIOR SETTING THEORY   The classic theory by Roger Barker and colleagues analyzes environments in terms of *behavior settings:* "small scale social systems composed of people and physical objects configured in such a way as to carry out a routinized program of activities with specifiable time and place boundaries" (Wicker 1992, p. 166). The July 1990 issue of *Environment and Behavior* reviews the history of ecological psychology. Analysis of a recent worker survey supported the predictions of behavior setting theory (Wicker & August 1995). Extensions of the theory have focused on specific settings (Schoggen 1989), such as gas stations (Sommer & Wicker 1991), and on what Wicker (1992) called a "sense-making" model—based on naturalistic research that addresses occupants' understandings of the context.

TRANSACTIONAL APPROACH   In a substantial extension of privacy regulation theory, Altman (1993) and colleagues (e.g. Brown et al 1992, Werner et al 1992) elaborated their *transactional* approach, which treats the physical environment as a potential context for social interaction that can support, constrain, symbolize, and confer meaning upon various aspects of social relationships. This holistic, systems-oriented analysis incorporates multiple levels and facets, variation over time, and cyclical processes. It describes social relationships and physical settings in terms of *dialectics,* or tensions between opposing influences. (Dialectics are also central to Lawrence's 1989 theory.) Related, cross-cultural research examined such practices as courtship and weddings (Altman et al 1992, Werner et al 1993).

BUILT ENVIRONMENTS

Residences

RESIDENTIAL PREFERENCE AND SATISFACTION   Previous research consistently found the housing type most preferred, especially in North America, is a single-family home away from a central city. Recent surveys also examined populations outside North America. Amerigo & Aragones (1990) found preferences among women who lived in council housing in Madrid, Spain, closely tied to their attachment to the neighborhood and to the nature of their relationships with neighbors. Kaitilla (1993) found residents of public housing in West Taraka, Papua New Guinea, dissatisfied with the small size of their housing units and with designs of kitchen, toilet, and bath. Kaitilla (1994) studied the Bumbu squatter settlement of Papua New Guinea and observed that availability of desirable building materials was important in construction of dwellings and satisfaction with them. Housing preference and satisfaction were also studied in Venezuela (Wiesenfeld 1992), Australia (Purcell 1991, Smith 1994), Turkey (Imamoğlu & Imamoğlu 1992), Sweden (Lindberg et al 1992), Canada (Cooper & Rodman 1994), the United States (Anthony et al 1990), and England (Shoul 1993). Themes apparent in the research included the importance of adequate space, convenient location for services, sense of security associated with distance from inner cities, attachment to neighborhood and people, and environmental support for changing work and family roles.

Among individuals with disabilities, Cooper & Rodman (1994) found that control over social aspects of housing was more important than control over physical aspects in predicting satisfaction. Components important in the home, such as protection and self-identity, are also important to the homeless (Bunston & Breton 1992). Researchers have conducted preference/satisfaction surveys across age spans. Devlin (1994) found that US children preferred ranch and colonial style houses as well as mobile homes, Quonset huts, and geodesic domes; adults preferred farm, Tudor, Neo-French, and split-level styles. Lindberg et al (1992) found that preferences across the life span were influenced by comfort, freedom, well-being, and togetherness. Structural adequacy and maintenance quality were found to be the best predictors of satisfaction among a sample of elderly residents (Christensen et al 1992). Among Turkish elderly, Imamoğlu & Imamoğlu (1992) found residential satisfaction correlated with proximity to towns and metropolises, for reasons related to attachment to dwellings and people (including extended family), preferences for same-age interactions, and attitudes toward institutional living. For teenage children and adults, having a disabled elderly relative live in the same home was associated with decreased satisfaction (Pruchno et al 1993).

Other trends in research on residences concern the changing role of women and the rise of single parenting. Hasell & Peatross (1990) discussed correlations between changing gender role patterns (e.g. more women working outside the home, more men taking on domestic chores) and changes in housing between 1945 and 1985 in the United States, which included a doubling of the size of the master bedroom (from 162 to 332 square feet) and an increase in the ratio of master bedroom/bath to total space from 15.5% to 22.8%. Smith (1994) also studied gender roles in relation to housing configurations; among the major findings was that women placed heavier emphasis on personal control than did men. Ahrentzen et al (1989) found that fully employed mothers spent more time than fathers in rooms with other family members. People who work at home may make adjustments among roles and space to manage conflict (Ahrentzen 1990). James (1989) found evaluations of housing negatively correlated with salience of marital role for women, not for men.

A major preference-satisfaction study by Paulus et al (1991) compared US Army families in apartment and mobile home parks. Satisfaction was high in both settings because of perceived choice, expectation of improved future conditions, and contrast with past housing. Those satisfied with mobile homes especially emphasized low noise levels, low perceived crime risk, more distance between units, more privacy, and compatibility of housing with raising children. Those satisfied with apartments cited attractiveness, other people in the complex, convenience of services, fire and weather safety (e.g. feeling safer in case of a tornado), and adequacy of recreation facilities.

HOUSING DESIGN FEATURES   In one study on attitudes toward windows, students at a US university saw skylights as desirable in family rooms, living rooms, and kitchens but not as desirable as windows in the same types of rooms (Butler & Biner 1990). Building materials (brick, concrete block, weathered wood, stucco, flagstone, wooden shingles) were associated with perceived social identity of homeowners (Sadalla & Sheets 1993). Another study in the United States found farm and Tudor styles rated most desirable and Mediterranean and saltbox styles as least desirable (Nasar 1989). Kent (1991) reported cultural variation in partitioning of space; Kent (1990) reviewed use of space and design features.

RESIDENTIAL CROWDING   A study in Bangkok, where population density is four times greater than in comparable Western cities, found a nonlinear relationship between household density and *crowding* (experience of stress in high density conditions), indicating a ceiling effect: Increasing household density was associated with increments in crowding only up to a point (Edwards et al 1994). High density and crowding correlated with dissatisfaction in Italian homes (Bonnes et al 1991). Studies of crowded homes in India and the United States found social hassles associated with psychological symptoms of distress and ill health (Evans et al 1989, Lepore et al 1991a) and found that perceived control and social support mediated these links (Evans & Lepore 1993; Lepore et al 1991b, 1992). While seeking privacy may be a common response to distress (Newell 1994), satisfaction with privacy appeared distinct from satisfaction with space (Oseland & Donald 1993). On the other hand, a study of group residences also found solitude an aversive experience, for reasons unrelated to environment (Brown 1992). In Japan, Omata (1992) described how people cope with limited space by not entertaining at home.

PLACE ATTACHMENT   Research increasingly focused on psychological attachment to places, often in the context of home and neighborhood (Altman & Low 1992). Residential satisfaction was often tied to place attachment. Studies examined attachment over time as people moved from one place to another (Bih 1992, Burt 1993, Feldman 1990, Lucca-Irizarry & Pacheco 1992, Michelson 1992). Mazumdar & Mazumdar (1993) reported how religious rituals can enhance place attachment. In Berne, Switzerland, Fuhrer & Kaiser (1993) found lower mobility associated with higher attachment to homes and vehicles. Brown & Perkins (1992) analyzed cases of disrupted attachment.

Workplaces

Emerging issues for research in the workplace included stress and health in the workplace (Evans et al 1994, Hedge 1989), physical settings for work groups (Sundstrom & Altman 1989) and collaboration (Becker 1991), electronic communications in groups (Fulk 1993), and the role of computers in collaborative work (Olson 1989) and organizations (Becker 1988). Another emerging topic concerned home-based work, particularly among women (Ahrentzen 1989, Christensen 1988). Ahrentzen (1990, 1992) identified conflicts inherent in home-based work. Case examples (Christensen 1989, 1993) suggested that successful home work requires physical space arranged compatibly with home workers' management of time, social relations, self-identity, and potentially conflicting demands (Christensen 1994).

Research also addressed ambient conditions such as lighting and sound. A simulation study by Katzev (1992) found no adverse effects of a 50% reduction in illumination on clerical workers' mood or performance. A field study of office workers found higher satisfaction, better environmental control, and fewer complaints in offices with under-floor ventilation than conventional systems (Hedge et al 1993). In a field study of office workers at multiple sites, Sundstrom et al (1994) found more than half disturbed by noise and found disturbance correlated with dissatisfaction with the environment and job, but not self- or supervisor-rated performance. Quasi-experimental analysis after relocation or renovation revealed declining environmental and job satisfaction concurrent with increasing noise, and increasing environmental satisfaction concurrent with decreasing noise.

WINDOWS   A laboratory experiment briefly placed office workers in various combinations of window size and amount of sunlight and found no differences in preference or satisfaction but found self-rated tension highest in conditions of most and least sunlight (Boubekri et al 1991). Butler & Biner (1989) found an unexpected preference among students for no windows or small windows in some places, such as computer workrooms. Research on indoor windows between rooms revealed favorable attitudes and differing perceptions: Secretaries expected loss of privacy; students saw potential for social interaction (Biner et al 1991). Biner et al (1993) found secretaries unwilling to trade items like plants or pictures for indoor windows.

ENCLOSURE AND PRIVACY   Oldham (1988) reported increased ratings of privacy and office satisfaction and decreased crowding associated with decreased density and increased enclosure; individual stimulus screening ability was related to perceptions of crowding. Oldham et al (1991) found that office employees who scored high on stimulus screening and did complex jobs in low-density areas showed greatest productivity and satisfaction. Among secretaries, Duvall-Early & Benedict (1992) found a closeable door and "co-worker not visible" associated with perceived privacy, which in turn correlated with job satisfaction.

FACETS OF WORK ENVIRONMENTS   Couch & Nimran (1989) asked managers to name features of their office environments that facilitated or inhibited performance; facilitators included supportive social interaction, inhibitors included distractions, and ambient sound and temperature were named in both categories. Carlopio & Gardner (1992) found bank employees' satisfaction associated with having a personal computer and an ergonomic chair, among other factors. Mazumdar (1992) recounted anecdotal cases of environmental "deprivation" after office renovation, which elicited reactions by workers such as shame, social withdrawal, and filing of lawsuits. Ornstein (1992) found students able to infer from photos of reception rooms messages about the organizations' consideration and control. In a post-occupancy evaluation of an office renovation, Spreckelmeyer (1993) found workers' satisfaction related to participation in designing the renovations.

Hospitals, Clinics, and Rehabilitation Settings

Despite increasing complexity of hospitals and calls for research (Shumaker & Pequegnat 1989), few studies of health-care settings appeared in the past six years. One study focused on practices of secluding patients (Morrison 1990). Among critical-care nurses, Topf (1989) found resistance to noise-induced stress greatest by those with low noise sensitivity and high commitment. Case studies examined treatment center design (Gifford & Martin 1991) and entryway and access variables (Cherulnik 1993). Design interventions in residential settings for mental patients demonstrated that interaction among patients increased following partitioning of sleeping rooms and introduction of *sociopetal* arrangements, in which chairs are grouped within comfortable conversation distance facing toward one another (Cherulnik 1993). A design intervention by Devlin (1992) in psychiatric wards created home-like conditions that were associated with decreased stereotypy (e.g. head banging) but not the increased interaction often found after adding sociopetal seating.

Schools

In a 1-year study of the effects of elementary school lighting, Kuller & Lindsten (1992) found windowless classrooms with fluorescent lighting associated with undesirable biochemical changes not found in classrooms with natural lighting. A laboratory study found no differences between conventional and full-spectrum fluorescent lighting on college students' performance and mood (Boray et al 1989). Cohen & Trostle (1990) reported that among school children, girls preferred more intense color arrangements, more multidimensional shapes, brighter lighting, and more complex scenic arrangements than did boys. Weinstein & Pinciotti (1988) evaluated a playground design intended to promote constructive play and reported increases in active and pretend play and decreases in organized games, uninvolved behavior, and roughhousing.

Reinforcing the well-established association of classroom performance and seating among college students, Brooks & Rebeta (1991) found that compared with men, women sat closer to the instructor, made better grades, and missed fewer classes; distance from the front correlated positively with absence and inversely with grades. Hillmann et al (1991) reported higher self-esteem among college students seated in the front third of a classroom; these students received better grades, participated more, missed fewer classes, and scored higher on an achievement test than those in the back of the room. Wong et al (1992) evaluated Sommer's (1974) "soft classroom," which was designed to promote interaction through carpet-covered bench seating arranged in a semi-circle. As before, observations revealed more voluntary participation and more student-to-student interaction in the "soft" classroom than in traditional class-rooms of similar size.

In a study of transitions by new college students to new school environ-ments, Lakey (1989) found perceived social support higher in suite-style than in corridor style dormitories, where students felt more anxious and saw others as less likely to help. Yamamoto et al (1992) reported that after leaving college for new jobs, students replaced some social contacts but continued to rely on family networks.

Prisons

Prison research examined inmates' perceptions of the environment (Ajdukovic 1990) but focused mainly on population density and housing design. Physi-ological signs of stress were found lower among inmates living in single cells than in dormitories (Ostfeld et al 1987, Schaeffer et al 1988). Adverse reac-tions by inmates correlated with the number of inmates per housing unit; fewer adverse reactions occurred in subdivided than unsubdivided dormitories (Pau-lus 1988). Wener & Keys (1988) found prison density associated with per-ceived crowding and found higher rates of sick call among prisoners exposed previously to high density conditions than among prisoners who had resided in lower density conditions. In a prison redesign project that applied lessons from research (Farbstein 1986), decentralized suites were associated with more positive outcomes than were conventional arrangements (Wener et al 1985, also in Cherulnik 1993).

Extreme Living Environments

Recent studies examined human adaptations to extreme living conditions such as outer space and Antarctica (reviewed by Harrison et al 1991, Suedfeld 1991, Ursin et al 1991). Some studies described how native and nonnative peoples adapt. For example, Inuit settlements near Nome, Alaska, were usually found close to roads and water and far from hills (Burger & Gochfeld 1991), and much upheaval occurred as the Inuit of Canada adapted to modern changes (Goehring & Stager 1991). Visitors to polar regions face risks to their physical and mental health because of isolation, leading researchers to call them ICE (Isolated and Confined Environments). Carrere & Evans (1994) observed four trends in an Antarctic ICE. 1. Individuals chose to spend much time alone, and design features that helped to increase or decrease social interaction were valued. 2. Design flexibility to provide a variety of work and leisure activities was desired. 3. Individual and group personalization was prevalent. 4. Evaluation of the quality of the environment remained neutral. Others noted the importance of comfort with group interactions for coping in ICEs (Kahn & Leon 1994, Koschyev et al 1994, Leon 1991, Leon et al 1991). Successful coping with environmental extremes may have long-term benefits in the form of reduced physical health risks (Palinkas 1991).

ENVIRONMENTAL INFLUENCES IN THE COMMUNITY

Physical Environmental Stressors

NOISE   Studies found noise a major source of annoyance in a variety of settings. Levy-Leboyer & Naturel (1991) reported neighborhood noise especially troublesome if it occurred at night and could have been avoided; evidence that the perpetrator of the intrusive noise is unconcerned made it more annoying, as did perceived loss of control. Hopkins (1994) found noise a significant problem in shopping malls.

AIR POLLUTION   Past research found lower socioeconomic groups most likely to live in areas with high air pollution (Mukherjee 1993). However, Napton & Day (1992) found predominantly middle-class residents in highly polluted areas in Texas, mostly affiliated with petrochemical industries, where choice of neighborhood was largely dictated by proximity to work. Even low levels of SO_2 were associated with slower reaction time, reduced concentration, and lower psychological well-being in Bavaria (Bullinger 1989). Other studies found people with emotion-oriented coping styles less annoyed by foul odors than were people with problem-oriented coping styles (Cavalini et al 1991, Steinheider & Winneke 1993). In contrast, a laboratory study by Baron (1990) found beneficial effects of pleasant scents. Students exposed to perfume, cologne, and air freshener previously found to elicit positive attitudes set higher goals, adopted more efficient strategies in clerical work, made more concessions during negotiations, and showed less inclination to avoid conflict or use competitive strategies for dealing with future conflict than did members of a control group. Males exposed to pleasant scent had higher self-efficacy than those not exposed to the scents.

HEAT AND VIOLENCE   Debate continued over the relationship between ambient temperature and incidence of human violence, including whether a relationship exists (Rotton 1993a,b), and whether violence increases linearly with rising temperature (Anderson 1989, Anderson & DeNeve 1992) or increases to a point of moderate discomfort and then decreases with extreme discomfort at higher temperatures (the *negative affect-escape model of aggression;* Bell 1992). Data analysis techniques and control of extraneous variables remained issues in the debate (Cohn 1990, 1993, Simpson & Perry 1990). Reifman et al (1991) found professional baseball players more likely to be hit by wild pitches as temperature increased. Ruback & Pandey (1992) found passengers on Indian rickshaws less bothered by heat when given information about its sensory and emotional effects, which increased their perceived control. Rotton et al (1990) studied walking speed as a function of ambient temperature and found that pace was sometimes more rapid in cool settings and at other times more rapid in warm settings.

Attitudes About the Environment

ENVIRONMENTAL CONCERN   Studies demonstrating concern about environmental issues accompanied growth of the environmental movement (Krause 1993). Lyons & Breakwell (1994) found that knowledge of science predicted environmental concern, but others found little relationship of environmental concern with environmental knowledge (Arcury 1990) or sociodemographic variables (Samdahl & Robertson 1989, Scott & Willits 1994, Syme & Nancarrow 1992). Among predictors of environmental concern, authoritarianism showed a strong, inverse relationship (Schultz & Stone 1994). Other studies found women higher than men on environmental concern but found men more likely to be environmental activists (Baldassare & Katz 1992, Mohai 1991, Schahn & Holzer 1990, Stern et al 1993). Inconsistent findings appeared on racial differences in environmental concern (Adeloa 1994, Taylor 1989). Ecocentric vs anthropocentric value orientations predicted environmental concern and behavior in one study (Thompson & Barton 1994), but attempts to predict environmental behavior from environmental attitudes continue to yield disappointing results (Oskamp et al 1991).

PERCEIVED ENVIRONMENTAL RISK   Environmental psychologists showed increasing interest in perception of risk from toxic exposure, natural and human-caused disaster, ozone depletion and global warming, and injury in built and natural settings (Slovic 1987, also Ewert 1994, Vaughan 1993). Perceived risk was strongly associated with reduced neighborhood satisfaction (Baba & Austin 1989, Gärling & Gärling 1990). In a study by Grieshop & Stiles (1989) over 25% of California respondents said they had suffered illness from pesticide exposure, yet many of those who perceived the risk still used pesticides. Much work examines perceived risk associated with nuclear power (Earle & Cvetkovich 1990, MacGill 1989, Maharik & Fischhoff 1993, Reicher et al 1993). Perceived nuclear risk increased following the 1986 accident at the Chernobyl reactor (Drottz-Sjoberg & Sjoberg 1990, Midden & Verplanken 1990, Peters et al 1990, Renn 1990, van der Pligt & Midden 1990, Verplanken

1989). A new tool—the Environmental Appraisal Inventory (EAI)—assesses perceived threat to self, threat to environment, and perceived control over environmental hazards (Fridgen 1994, Schmidt & Gifford 1989).

Preserving the Environment

COMMONS DILEMMA   Hardin's (1968) description of self-interested abuse of a shared environment spawned many laboratory simulations of the *commons dilemma* in which individuals harvest from a shared resource (Fusco et al 1991, Gifford & Wells 1991). The dilemma is that short-term self-interest (making large harvests from the shared resource) is harmful to long-term group interest, because collective short-term self-interest destroys the commons. Research has sought solutions that encourage individual conservative harvests to preserve the commons in the long run. Recent results confirmed and extended past research. Trusting others to conserve emerged as an extremely important factor in willingness to conserve (Mosler 1993, Parks 1994). Rewards for cooperative behavior and punishments for selfish behavior were found beneficial in preserving the commons (Bell et al 1989, Birjulin et al 1993, Harvey et al 1993). Division of the commons into individual territories—the privatization strategy—also helped preserve the commons in laboratory simulations. Such a territorial/privatization solution eliminates the commons and is impractical for some resources, but it also eliminates the need for intricate systems of reward and punishment (Martichuski & Bell 1991). Outside the laboratory, privatization showed promise for preserving low-income housing (Leavitt & Saegert 1989). Debate continues on privatization and group rules (Feeny et al 1990).

CONSERVATION BEHAVIOR   Strategies for promoting recycling, energy conservation, and anti-littering behavior continued to draw research interest, as reviewed in the March 1995 issue of *Environment and Behavior* (also DeYoung 1993). Waste source reduction—not producing waste in the first place—clearly has the most beneficial impact on the environment (DeYoung et al 1993). Educational efforts had least impact on pro-environmental behavior (Thompson & Stoutemyer 1991). Recycling knowledge predicted recycling behavior (Gamba & Oskamp 1994, Granzin & Olsen 1991, Vining & Ebreo 1990), but using a person designated as a neighborhood block leader who coordinated and encouraged recycling improved recycling behavior over mere educational strategies (Burn 1991, Hopper & Nielsen 1991). Individual personal belief (Axelrod & Lehman 1993) and commitment to recycling predicted long-term recycling behavior (Wang & Katzev 1990), as did perceived personal benefit (Oskamp et al 1994). Individual and group norms can reduce littering (Cialdini et al 1990), as can shame and embarrassment (Grasmick et al 1991). Howenstine

(1993) found that failure to recycle was associated with indifference, location issues, and household nuisance.

Wayfinding

Recent research examined design features that facilitate cognitive mapping of environments, the role of cognitive maps in finding one's way through them—*wayfinding*—and factors that influence wayfinding (Gärling 1989; Gopal et al 1989; Hirtle & Hudson 1991; Holding 1992, 1994; Kitchin 1994; Leiser & Zilbershatz 1989; O'Neill 1991a; Rovine & Weisman 1989; Sadalla & Montello 1989; Wood & Beck 1989). Peponis et al (1990) introduced the concept of a *search structure* in which properties of layouts combine with navigation rules to determine exploration patterns. O'Neill (1991c, 1992) found lower complexity of layout associated with increased architectural legibility, which in turn correlated with improved wayfinding. O'Neill (1991b) found that signage improved wayfinding, especially in less complex floorplans. Adults are clearly better than children at giving orienting directions, though children improve with age (Blades & Medlicott 1992, Rutland et al 1993). However, cognitive mapping and wayfinding pose special problems for the elderly (Lipman 1991), with a notable exception for elderly hunters (Hill 1992). Among elderly adults, verbal directions and studying maps improved wayfinding more than did either watching videotapes or receiving verbal directions with instructions to form a mental image of the setting (Kirasic & Mathes 1990). Having to realign a map mentally as opposed to aligning it in hand with the floorplan makes wayfinding especially difficult for the elderly (Aubrey & Dobbs 1990, Warren & Scott 1993).

Environment and Crime

Researchers continued to identify environmental contributors to and barriers against crime. One study examined environmental factors in convenience store robberies (D'Alessio & Stolzenberg 1990). Another examined the role of perceived risk of victimization (Brantingham & Brantingham 1993). Brown & Harris (1989) tested predictions related to territoriality and found that the more severe the territorial intrusion in a burglary, the more difficult the long-term coping by the victim. Brown & Bentley (1993) found that burglars were especially wary of signs that residents would show territorial concern. Canter & Larkin (1993) reported that 87% of sexual offenders operated close to their home base. Perkins et al (1992) found territorial functioning, architectural "defensible space" features, and signs of social and physical disorder related to crime and fear of crime. Perkins et al (1993) reported similar findings. MacDonald & Gifford (1989) reported that signs of territorial defense indicated to convicted burglars that a residence contained things worth stealing. Shaw & Gifford (1994) found residents' and burglars' assessments of vulnerability to burglary inversely related to "surveilability" and positively related to presence of actual barriers. Other studies found fear of crime greatest in places seen as providing refuge for criminals or limiting escape by potential victims (Day 1994, Fisher & Nasar 1992, Loewen et al 1993, Nasar & Fisher 1993).

Commuting Stress

Research on commuting stress by Novaco et al (1990, 1991) found both subjective and objective impedance to be significant predictors of commuter stress, which manifested in both physical and psychological health outcomes. Hanson et al (1994) found longer commutes among women in two US counties, who took jobs further from home than men (perhaps reflecting their lower power or status). Other research found symptoms of stress among public transit drivers (Carrere et al 1991, Evans & Carrere 1991).

Coping with Disaster

Natural and human-caused disasters may have many consequences, including loss of resources, impedance of daily activities, disruption to home and neighborhood, and changes in perception of risk (Hutchins & Norris 1989, Laska 1990). In examining adaptive responses to disasters, Hobfoll's (1991) *conservation of resources stress theory* posits that the speed and extent of loss or preservation of resources (possessions, loved ones, community services) predicts adaptive efficiency in response to disaster. Baum et al (1992) found that compared with victims of a flood, victims of a toxic waste dump were more anxious, depressed, and alienated and less able to do challenging tasks. Consequences to their resources continued into the future, while flood victims' consequences were sooner past. Other human-caused technological catastrophes showed a similar pattern, in which longer-lasting consequences to victims' resources correlated with more adverse aftereffects (Baum & Fleming 1993, Green et al 1990).

Museums

Research on the way people explore museums, in combination with principles of environmental psychology, has guided the design of museums and modifications intended to change the experience of the museum visitor (Loomis 1987). Bitgood & Loomis (1993) summarized current applications. Studies found the museum experience influenced by the type and size of labels (Bitgood & Patterson 1993), availability of comfortable places (Hood 1993), front-end evaluation of exhibit designs (Miles & Clarke 1993, Screven 1990), and maps. Recent evidence suggests that museums can relieve stress and attentional fatigue (Kaplan et al 1993).

NATURAL ENVIRONMENTS

Natural settings have been the focus of much research in environmental psychology. Several recent studies suggested that preferences for natural scenes with greenery and water may be universal (Herzog 1989, 1992; Herzog & Bosley 1992; Hull & Revell 1989; Schroeder 1991; Yang & Brown 1992; Zube 1991). Sebba (1991) suggested that most adults identify the most significant places in childhood as being outdoors. Adding vegetation to built environments enhanced aesthetic value in some but not all settings (Hull & Harvey 1989, Joardar 1989, Orland et al 1992, Sheets & Manzer 1991). One study found that joint experiences in natural settings benefited human groups (Ewert & Heywood 1991).

Why are natural environments so highly valued? Recent research suggests that viewing natural scenery stimulates the parasympathetic nervous system and has a calming effect on people under stress (Hartig et al 1991, Ulrich et al 1991). Ulrich (1993) theorized that such effects may even have an evolutionary basis in that natural selection may have favored those who can relax in a natural setting—the *biophilia hypothesis*. Kaplan et al (1993) noted that a visit to a museum or similar setting can also have restorative effects on stressed individuals. Kaplan & Kaplan (1989) proposed that prolonged attention to a task leads to *directed attention fatigue,* which is relieved in natural environments.

CONCLUSIONS

Advances

Environmental psychology advanced in many areas from 1989 through 1994. We identified six themes:

1. Multiple theories. Environmental psychology's theories expanded, addressed more contextual factors, and increasingly spanned individual, interpersonal, organizational, community, and cultural levels of analysis. Research was guided by theories on arousal, stress, privacy regulation, behavior settings, and the transactional approach. Environmental psychology has yet to embrace a unified theory.
2. Field research. Natural settings predominated in empirical research, which used methods ranging from systematic observation and interviews to design interventions and detailed case studies. Laboratory experiments appeared less common than in the past.
3. Cumulative knowledge. Though some studies represented one-time efforts, others built on previous work. Examples of cumulative research included

studies of vulnerability to residential burglaries and responses to environmental disaster.

4. Applied orientation. Environmental psychology kept a focus on designing settings that promote occupants' goals, often in environmental design research.
5. Interdisciplinary collaboration. The field maintained its multidisciplinary roots. Perhaps only half of the studies in this review came from university-based researchers in traditional departments of psychology.
6. Cross-cultural focus. Environmental psychology maintained an international character through data from a variety of cultures and a focus of research on cross-cultural differences and commonalties.

Future Directions

In the *Annual Review of Psychology* chapter on environmental psychology in 2002 we expect to read that trends of 1989 to 1994 continued: Rising volume of research in natural settings, integration of research and practice, greater diversity of researchers and settings. We hope to read of advances in three specific areas:

1. Stronger theory. In the past six years theories became more differentiated and integrative, perhaps forming the basis for a more unified theoretical approach to guide future research and practice. Current theories suggest potential elements of a unified theory: systems principles; integration of psychological processes like arousal and stress with social-psychological, social, and cultural processes; ecological analysis; and others.
2. Environmental design research. Many classic studies of environmental psychology involved design experiments, which we hope will become more common. Such projects could increasingly serve both the applied and the scientific goals of environmental psychology.
3. Case studies. As the literature of case studies and design experiments expands, the field needs methodological conventions, a shared vocabulary, and accepted models for reporting case studies. We hope to see progress on these in the 2002 review.

Literature Cited

Adeloa FO. 1994. Environmental hazards, health, and racial inequality in hazardous waste distribution. *Environ. Behav.* 26: 99–126

Ahrentzen S. 1989. A place of peace, prospect, and of P.C.: the home as office. *J. Archit. Plan. Res.* 6:271–89

Ahrentzen S. 1990. Managing conflict by managing boundaries: how professional home-workers cope with multiple roles at home. *Environ. Behav.* 22:723–52

Ahrentzen S. 1992. Home as a workplace in the lives of women. See Altman & Low 1992, pp. 113–38

Ahrentzen S, Levine D, Michelson W. 1989. Space, time, and activity in the home: a gender analysis. *J. Environ. Psychol.* 9: 69–102

Ajdukovic D. 1990. Psychosocial climate in correctional institutions. *Environ. Behav.* 22:420–32

Altman I. 1993. Dialectics, physical environments, and personal relationships. *Comm. Monogr.* 60:26–34

Altman I, Brown BB, Staples B, Werner CM. 1992. A transactional approach to close relationships: courtship, weddings and place-making. See Walsh et al 1992, pp. 193–241

Altman I, Christensen K, eds. 1990. *Human Behavior and the Environment: Advances in Theory and Research,* Vol. 11. *Environment and Behavior Studies: Emergence of Intellectual Traditions.* New York: Plenum. 392 pp.

Altman I, Churchman AS, eds. 1994. *Human Behavior and the Environment: Advances in Theory and Research,* Vol. 13. *Women and the Environment.* New York: Plenum. 340 pp.

Altman I, Low SM, eds. 1992. *Human Behavior and the Environment: Advances in Theory and Research,* Vol. 12. *Place Attachment.* New York: Plenum. 314 pp.

Amerigo M, Aragones I. 1990. Residential satisfaction in council housing. *J. Environ. Psychol.* 10:313–25

Anderson CA. 1989. Temperature and aggression: ubiquitous effects of heat on occurrence of human violence. *Psychol. Bull.* 106:74–96

Anderson CA, DeNeve KM. 1992. Temperature, aggression, and negative affect escape model. *Psychol. Bull.* 111:347–51

Anthony KH, Weidemann S, Chin Y. 1990. Housing perceptions of low-income single parents. *Environ. Behav.* 22:147–82

Arcury TA. 1990. Environmental attitude and environmental knowledge. *Hum. Organ.* 49:300–4

Arias EG, ed. 1993. *The Meaning and Use of Housing: International Perspectives, Approaches and their Applications.* Aldershot: Avebury

Aubrey JB, Dobbs AR. 1990. Age and sex differences in the mental realignment of maps. *Exp. Aging Res.* 16:133–39

Axelrod LJ, Lehman DR. 1993. Responding to environmental concerns: What factors guide individual action? *J. Environ. Psychol.* 13:149–59

Baba Y, Austin DM. 1989. Neighborhood environmental satisfaction, victimization, and social participation as determinants of perceived neighborhood safety. *Environ. Behav.* 21:763–80

Baldassare M, Katz C. 1992. The personal threat of environmental problems as predictor of environmental practices. *Environ. Behav.* 24:602–16

Barker RG. 1990. Recollections of the Midwest Psychological Field Station. *Environ. Behav.* 22:503–13

Baron RA. 1990. Environmentally induced positive affect: its impact on self-efficacy, task performance, negotiation, and conflict. *J. Appl. Soc. Psychol.* 20:368–84

Baum A, Fleming I. 1993. Implications of psychological research on stress and technological accidents. *Am. Psychol.* 48:665–67

Baum A, Fleming I, Israel A, O'Keeffe MK. 1992. Symptoms of chronic stress following a natural disaster and discovery of a human-made hazard. *Environ. Behav.* 24: 347–72

Baum A, O'Keeffe MK, Davidson LM. 1990. Acute stressors and chronic response: the case of traumatic stress. *J. Appl. Soc. Psychol.* 20:1643–54

Becker F. 1988. Managing innovation: computer and organizational ecology. In *Handbook of Human-Computer Interaction,* ed. M Helander, pp. 1107–17. Amsterdam: Elsevier

Becker F. 1991. Workplace planning, design, and management. Toward a new paradigm. See Zube & Moore 1991, pp. 115–51

Bell PA. 1992. In defense of the negative affect escape model of heat and aggression. *Psychol. Bull.* 111:342–46

Bell PA, Fisher JD, Baum A, Greene TE. 1990. *Environmental Psychology.* Fort Worth, TX: Holt, Rinehart & Winston. 3rd ed.

Bell PA, Petersen TR, Hautaluoma JE. 1989. The effect of punishment probability on overconsumption and stealing in a simulated commons. *J. Appl. Soc. Psychol.* 19: 1483–95

Bih H. 1992. The meaning of objects in environmental transitions: experiences of Chinese students in the United States. *J. Environ. Psychol.* 12:135–47

Biner P, Butler D, Fischer A, Westergren A. 1989. An arousal optimization model of lighting level preferences: an interaction of social situation and task demands. *Environ. Behav.* 21:3–16

Biner P, Butler D, Lovegrove T, Burns R. 1993. Windowlessness in the workplace: a reexamination of the compensation hypothesis. *Environ. Behav.* 25:205–27

Biner P, Butler D, Winsted D. 1991. Inside windows: an alternative to conventional windows in office and other settings. *Environ. Behav.* 23:359–82

Birjulin AA, Smith JM, Bell PA. 1993. Monetary reward, verbal reinforcement, and harvest strategy of others in the commons dilemma. *J. Soc. Psychol.* 133:207–14

Bitgood SC, Loomis RJ. 1993. Introduction: environmental design and evaluation in museums. *Environ. Behav.* 25:683–97

Bitgood SC, Patterson DD. 1993. The effects of gallery changes on visitor reading and object viewing time. *Environ. Behav.* 25: 761–81

Blades M, Medlicott L. 1992. Developmental differences in the ability to give route directions from a map. *J. Environ. Psychol.* 12:175–85

Block L, Garnett S. 1989. Performance and satisfaction in private versus nonprivate work settings. *Environ. Behav.* 21:277–97

Bonnes M, Bonaiuto M, Ercolani, AP. 1991. Crowding and residential satisfaction in the urban environment: a contextual approach. *Environ. Behav.* 23:531–52

Boray PF, Gifford R, Rosenblood L. 1989. Effects of warm white, cool white and full spectrum fluorescent lighting on simple cognitive performance, mood and ratings of others. *J. Environ. Psychol.* 9:297–308

Boubekri M, Hulliv R, Boyer L. 1991. Impact of window size and sunlight penetration on office workers' mood and satisfaction: a novel way of assessing sunlight. *Environ. Behav.* 23:474–93

Brantingham PL, Brantingham PJ. 1993. Nodes, paths and edges: considerations on the complexity of crime and the physical environment. *J. Environ. Psychol.* 13:3–28

Brooks C, Rebeta J. 1991. College classroom ecology: the relation of sex of student to classroom performance and seating preference. *Environ. Behav.* 23:305–13

Brown BB. 1992. The ecology of privacy and mood in a shared living group. *J. Environ. Psychol.* 12:5–20

Brown BB, Altman I, Werner CM. 1992. Close relationships in the physical and social world: dialectic and transactional analyses. *Communication Yearbook,* ed. S Deetz, 15:509–22. Newbury Park, CA: Sage

Brown BB, Bentley DL. 1993. Residential burglars judge risk: the role of territoriality. *J. Environ. Psychol.* 13:51–61

Brown BB, Harris PB. 1989. Residential burglary victimization: reactions to the invasion of a primary territory. *J. Environ. Psychol.* 9:119–32

Brown BB, Perkins DD. 1992. Disruptions in place attachment. See Altman & Low 1992, pp. 279–304

Bullinger M. 1989. Psychological effects of air pollution on healthy residents—a time series approach. *J. Environ. Psychol.* 9: 103–18

Bunston T, Breton M. 1992. Homes and homeless women. *J. Environ. Psychol.* 12: 149–62

Burger J, Gochfeld M. 1991. The effect of mi-cro habitat on Inuit habitat selection in Nome, Alaska. *Environ. Behav.* 23: 680–703

Burn SM. 1991. Social psychology and the stimulation of recycling behaviors: the block leader approach. *J. Appl. Soc. Psychol.* 21:611–29

Burt CDB. 1993. Concentration and academic ability following transition to university: an investigation of the effects of homesickness. *J. Environ. Psychol.* 13:333–42

Butler DL, Biner PM. 1989. Effects of setting on window preferences and factors associated with those preferences. *Environ. Behav.* 21:17–31

Butler DL, Biner PM. 1990. A preliminary study of skylight preferences. *Environ. Behav.* 22:119–40

Canter D, Larkin P. 1993. The environmental range of serial rapists. *J. Environ. Psychol.* 13:63–69

Carlopio J, Gardner D. 1992. Direct and interactive effects of the physical work environment on attitudes. *Environ. Behav.* 24: 579–601

Carr S, Francis M, Rivlin LG, Stone AM. 1992. *Public Space.* New York: Cambridge Univ. Press

Carrere S, Evans GW. 1994. Life in an isolated and confined environment: a qualitative study of the role of the designed environment. *Environ. Behav.* 26:707–41

Carrere S, Evans GW, Palsane MN, Rivas M. 1991. Job strain and occupational stress among public transit workers. *J. Occup. Psychol.* 64:305–16

Cavalini PM, Koeter-Kemmerling LG, Pulles MPJ. 1991. Coping with odour annoyance and odour concentrations: three field studies. *J. Environ. Psychol.* 11:123–42

Cherulnik PD. 1993. *Applications of Environment-Behavior Research: Case Studies and Analysis.* New York: Cambridge Univ. Press

Christensen DL, Carp FM, Cranz GL, Wiley JA. 1992. Objective housing indicators as predictors of the subjective evaluations of elderly residents. *J. Environ. Psychol.* 12: 225–36

Christensen K, ed. 1988. *The New Era of Home-Based Work.* Boulder, CO: Westview

Christensen K. 1989. Home-based clerical work: no simple truth; no single reality. *Homework,* ed. E Boris, C Daniels, pp. 183–97. Urbana, IL: Univ. Ill. Press

Christensen K. 1993. Eliminating the journey to work. *Full Circles: Geographies of Women over the Life Course,* ed. C Katz, J Monk, pp. 55–87. London: Routledge

Christensen K. 1994. Working at home: frameworks of meaning. See Altman & Churchman 1994, pp. 133–66

Cialdini RB, Reno RR, Kallgren CA. 1990. A

focus theory of normative conduct: recycling the concept of norms to reduce littering in public places. *J. Pers. Soc. Psychol.* 58:1015–26

Cohen S, Trostle S. 1990. Young children's preferences for school-related physical-environmental setting characteristics. *Environ. Behav.* 22:753–66

Cohn EG. 1990. Weather and violent crime: a reply to Perry and Simpson, 1987. *Environ. Behav.* 22:280–94

Cohn EG. 1993. The prediction of police calls for service: the influence of weather and temporal variables on rape and domestic violence. *J. Environ. Psychol.* 13:71–83

Cooper M, Rodman MC. 1994. Accessibility and quality of life in housing cooperatives. *Environ. Behav.* 26:49–70

Couch A, Nimran V. 1989. Perceived facilitators and inhibitors of work performance in an office environment. *Environ. Behav.* 21: 206–26

D'Alessio S, Stolzenberg L. 1990. A crime of convenience: the environment and convenience store robbery. *Environ. Behav.* 22: 255–271

Day K. 1994. Conceptualizing women's fear of sexual assault on campus: a review of causes and recommendations for change. *Environ. Behav.* 26:742–65

Devlin AS. 1992. Psychiatric ward renovation: staff perception and patient behavior. *Environ. Behav.* 24:66–84

Devlin AS. 1994. Children's housing style preferences: regional, socioeconomic, sex, and adult comparisons. *Environ. Behav.* 26:527–59

DeYoung R. 1993. Changing behavior and making it stick: the conceptualization and management of conservation behavior. *Environ. Behav.* 25:485–505

DeYoung R, Duncan A, Frank J, Gill N, Rothman S, et al. 1993. Promoting source reduction behavior: the role of motivational information. *Environ. Behav.* 25:70–85

Drottz-Sjoberg BM, Sjoberg L. 1990. Risk perception and worries after the Chernobyl accident. *J. Environ. Psychol.* 10:135–49

Duvall-Early K, Benedict J. 1992. The relationships between privacy and different components of job satisfaction. *Environ. Behav.* 24:670–79

Earle TC, Cvetkovich G. 1990. What was the meaning of Chernobyl? *J. Environ. Psychol.* 10:169–76

Edwards JN, Fuller TD, Sermsri S, Vorakitphokatorn S. 1994. Why people feel crowded: an examination of objective and subjective crowding. *Popul. Environ.* 16: 149–73

Evans GW, Carrere S. 1991. Traffic congestion, perceived control, and psychophysiological stress among urban bus drivers. *J. Appl. Psychol.* 76:658–63

Evans GW, Johansson G, Carrere S. 1994. Psychosocial factors and the physical environment: inter-relations in the workplace. *Int. Rev. Ind. Organ. Psychol.* 9:1–29

Evans GW, Lepore SJ. 1993. Household crowding and social support: a quasi-experimental analysis. *J. Pers. Soc. Psychol.* 65:308–16

Evans GW, Palsane MN, Lepore SJ, Martin J. 1989. Residential density and psychological health. *J. Pers. Soc. Psychol.* 57: 994–99

Ewert A. 1994. Playing the edge: motivation and risk taking in a high-altitude wildernesslike environment. *Environ. Behav.* 26: 3–24

Ewert A, Heywood J. 1991. Group development in the natural environment: expectations, outcomes, and techniques. *Environ. Behav.* 23:592–615

Farbstein J. 1986. *Correctional Facility Planning and Design*. New York: Van Nostrand Reinhold

Farbstein J, Kantrowitz M. 1991. Design research in the swamp: toward a new paradigm. See Zube & Moore 1991, pp. 297–318

Feeny D, Berkes F, McCay BJ, Acheson JM. 1990. The tragedy of the commons: twenty-two years later. *Hum. Ecol.* 18: 1–19

Feldman RM. 1990. Settlement-identity: psychological bonds with home place in a mobile society. *Environ. Behav.* 22: 183–229

Fisher BS, Nasar JL. 1992. Fear of crime in relation to three exterior site features: prospect, refuge, and escape. *Environ. Behav.* 24:35–65

Fridgen C. 1994. Human disposition toward hazards: testing the environmental appraisal inventory. *J. Environ. Psychol.* 14: 101–11

Fuhrer U, Kaiser FG. 1993. Place attachment and mobility during leisure time. *J. Environ. Psychol.* 13:309–21

Fulk J. 1993. Social construction of communication technology. *Acad. Manage. J.* 36: 921–50

Fusco ME, Bell PA, Jorgensen MD, Smith JM. 1991. Using a computer to study the commons dilemma. *Simul. Games* 22:67–74

Gamba RJ, Oskamp S. 1994. Factors influencing community residents' participation in community curbside recycling programs. *Environ. Behav.* 26:587–612

Gärling A, Gärling T. 1990. Parents' residential satisfaction and perceptions of children's accident risk. *J. Environ. Psychol.* 10:27–36

Gärling T. 1989. The role of cognitive maps in spatial decisions. *J. Environ. Psychol.* 9: 269–78

Gärling T, Evans GW, eds. 1991. *Environ-*

ment, Cognition, and Action. New York: Oxford

Gifford R. 1994. Environmental psychology. *Encyclopedia of Hum. Behav.* 2:265–77

Gifford R, Martin M. 1991. A multiple sclerosis center program and post-occupancy evaluation. See Prieser et al 1991, pp. 197–222

Gifford R, Wells J. 1991. FISH: a commons dilemma simulation. *Behav. Res. Methods Instrum. Comput.* 23:437–41

Goehring B, Stager JK. 1991. The intrusion of industrial time and space in the Inuit lifeworld. *Environ. Behav.* 23:666–79

Gopal S, Klatzky RL, Smith TR. 1989. Navigator: a psychologically based model of environmental learning through navigation. *J. Environ. Psychol.* 9:309–31

Granzin KL, Olsen JE. 1991. Characterizing participants in activities protecting the environment: a focus on donating, recycling and conservation behaviors. *J. Public Policy Mark.* 10:1–27

Grasmick HG, Bursik RJ Jr, Kinsey KA. 1991. Shame and embarrassment as deterrents to noncompliance with the law: the case of an antilittering campaign. *Environ. Behav.* 23: 233–51

Green BL, Grace MC, Lindy JD, Gleser GC, Leonard AC, Kramer TL. 1990. Buffalo Creek survivors in the second decade: comparison with unexposed and nonlitigant groups. *J. Appl. Soc. Psychol.* 20:1033–50

Grieshop JI, Stiles MC. 1989. Risk and home-pesticide users. *Environ. Behav.* 21: 699–716

Groat LN, Despres C. 1991. The significance of architectural theory for environmental design research. toward a new paradigm. See Zube & Moore 1991, pp. 3–52

Gump PV. 1990. A short history of the Midwest Psychological Field Station. *Environ. Behav.* 22:436–57

Haggard LM, Werner CM. 1990. Situational support, privacy regulation, and stress. *Basic Appl. Soc. Psychol.* 11:313–37

Hanson S, Pratt G, Mattingly D, Gilbert M. 1994. Women, work, and metropolitan environments. See Altman & Churchman 1994, pp. 227–53

Hardin G. 1968. The tragedy of the commons. *Science* 162:1243–48

Harrison AA, Clearwater YA, McKay CP, eds. 1991. *From Antarctica to Outer Space: Life in Isolation and Confinement.* New York: Springer-Verlag

Hartig T, Mang M, Evans GW. 1991. Restorative effects of natural environment experience. *Environ. Behav.* 23:3–26

Harvey ML, Bell PA, Birjulin AA. 1993. Punishment and type of feedback in a simulated commons dilemma. *Psychol. Rep.* 73: 447–50

Hasell MJ, Peatross FD. 1990. Exploring con-

nections between women's changing roles and house forms. *Environ. Behav.* 22:3–26

Hedge A. 1989. Environmental conditions and health in offices. *Int. Rev. Ergon.* 3:87–110

Hedge A, Michael AT, Parmelee S. 1993. Reactions of office workers and facilities managers to underfloor task ventilation in offices. *J. Arch. Plan. Res.* 10:203–18

Herzog TR. 1989. A cognitive analysis of preference for urban nature. *J. Environ. Psychol.* 9:27–43

Herzog TR. 1992. A cognitive analysis of preference for urban spaces. *J. Environ. Psychol.* 12:237–48

Herzog TR, Bosley PJ. 1992. Tranquility and preference as affective qualities of natural environments. *J. Environ. Psychol.* 12: 115–27

Hill KA. 1992. Spatial competence of elderly hunters. *Environ. Behav.* 24:779–94

Hillmann RB, Brooks CI, O'Brien J. 1991. Differences in self-esteem among college freshmen as a function of classroom seating-row performance. *Psychol. Rec.* 41: 315–20

Hirtle SC, Hudson J. 1991. Acquisition of spatial knowledge for routes. *J. Environ. Psychol.* 11:335–45

Hobfoll SE. 1991. Traumatic stress: a theory based on rapid loss of resources. *Anxiety Res.* 4:187–97

Holding CS. 1992. Clusters and reference points in cognitive representations of the environment. *J. Environ. Psychol.* 12: 45–55

Holding CS. 1994. Further evidence for the hierarchical representation of spatial information. *J. Environ. Psychol.* 14:137–47

Hood MG. 1993. Comfort and caring: two essential environmental factors. *Environ. Behav.* 25:710–24

Hopkins J. 1994. Orchestrating an indoor city: ambient noise inside a megamall. *Environ. Behav.* 26:785–812

Hopper JR, Nielsen JM. 1991. Recycling as altruistic behavior: normative and behavioral strategies to expand participation in a community recycling program. *Environ. Behav.* 23:195–220

Howenstine E. 1993. Market segmentation for recycling. *Environ. Behav.* 25:65–91

Hull RB, Harvey A. 1989. Explaining the emotion people experience in suburban parks. *Environ. Behav.* 21:323–45

Hull RB, Revell GRB. 1989. Cross-cultural comparison of landscape scenic beauty evaluations: a case study in Bali. *J. Environ. Psychol.* 9:177–91

Hutchins GL, Norris FH. 1989. Life change in the disaster recovery period. *Environ. Behav.* 21:33–56

Imamoğlu EO, Imamoğlu V. 1992. Housing and living environments of the Turkish elderly. *J. Environ. Psychol.* 12:35–43

Ittelson WH. 1989. Notes on theory in environment and behavior research. See Zube & Moore 1989, pp. 71–83

James K. 1989. Family-role salience and environmental cognition. *J. Environ. Psychol.* 9:45–55

Joardar SD. 1989. Use and image of neighborhood parks: a case of limited resources. *Environ. Behav.* 21:734–62

Kahn PM, Leon GR. 1994. Group climate and individual functioning in an all-women Antarctic expedition team. *Environ. Behav.* 26:669–97

Kaitilla S. 1993. Satisfaction with public housing in Papua New Guinea: the case of West Taraka housing scheme. *Environ. Behav.* 25:514–45

Kaitilla S. 1994. Urban residence and housing improvement in a Lae squatter settlement, Papua New Guinea. *Environ. Behav.* 26: 640–68

Kaminski G. 1989. The relevance of ecologically oriented conceptualizations of theory building in environment and behavior research. See Zube & Moore 1989, pp. 3–36

Kaplan R, Kaplan S. 1989. *The Experience of Nature: A Psychological Perspective.* New York: Cambridge Univ. Press

Kaplan S, Bardwell LV, Slakter DB. 1993. The museum as a restorative environment. *Environ. Behav.* 25:725–42

Katzev R. 1992. The impact of energy-efficient office lighting strategies on employee satisfaction and productivity. *Environ. Behav.* 24:759–78

Kent S. 1990. *Domestic Architecture and the Use of Space: An Interdisciplinary Cross-Cultural Study.* Cambridge: Cambridge Univ. Press

Kent S. 1991. Partitioning space: cross-cultural factors influencing domestic spatial segmentation. *Environ. Behav.* 23:438–73

Kirasic KC, Mathes EA. 1990. Effects of different means of conveying environmental information on elderly adults' spatial cognition and behavior. *Environ. Behav.* 22: 591–607

Kitchin RM. 1994. Cognitive maps: What are they and why study them? *J. Environ. Psychol.* 14:1–19

Koscheyev VS, Roschina NA, Makhov VV. 1994. Psychophysiological characteristics related to the functional state of the Soviet-American Arctic Bering Bridge Expedition. *Environ. Behav.* 26:166–78

Krause D. 1993. Environmental consciousness: an empirical study. *Environ. Behav.* 25: 126–42

Kuller R, Lindsten C. 1992. Health and behavior of children in classrooms with and without windows. *J. Environ. Psychol.* 12: 305–17

Lakey B. 1989. Personal and environmental antecedents of perceived social support developed at college. *Am. J. Comm. Psychol.* 17:503–19

Lang J. 1991. Design theory from an environment and behavior perspective: toward a new paradigm. See Zube & Moore 1991, pp. 53–101

Laska SB. 1990. Homeowner adaptation to flooding: an application of the general hazards coping theory. *Environ. Behav.* 22: 320–57

Lawrence RJ. 1989. Structuralist theories in environment-behavior-design research. See Zube & Moore 1989, pp. 37–70

Leavitt J, Saegert S. 1989. *From Abandonment to Hope: Community-Households in Harlem.* New York: Columbia Univ. Press

Leiser D, Zilbershatz A. 1989. The Traveller: a computational model of spatial network learning. *Environ. Behav.* 21:435–63

Leon GR. 1991. Individual and group process characteristics of polar expedition teams. *Environ. Behav.* 23:723–48

Leon GR, Kanfer R, Hoffman RG, Dupre L. 1991. Interrelationships of personality and coping in a challenging extreme situation. *J. Res. Pers.* 25:357–71

Lepore SJ, Evans GW, Palsane MN. 1991a. Social hassles and psychological health in the context of chronic crowding. *J. Health Soc. Behav.* 32:357–67

Lepore SJ, Evans GW, Schneider ML. 1991b. Dynamic role of social support in the link between chronic stress and psychological distress. *J. Pers. Soc. Psychol.* 61:899–909

Lepore SJ, Evans GW, Schneider ML. 1992. Role of control and social support in explaining the stress of hassles and crowding. *Environ. Behav.* 24:795–811

Levy-Leboyer C, Naturel V. 1991. Neighbourhood noise annoyance. *J. Environ. Psychol.* 11:75–86

Lindberg E, Hartig T, Garvill J, Gärling T. 1992. Residential-location preferences across the life span. *J. Environ. Psychol.* 12: 187–98

Lipman PD. 1991. Age and exposure differences in acquisition of route information. *Psychol. Aging* 6:128–33

Loewen LJ, Steel GD, Suedfeld P. 1993. Perceived safety from crime in the urban environment. *J. Environ. Psychol.* 13:323–31

Loewen LJ, Suedfeld P. 1992. Cognitive and arousal effects of masking office noise. *Environ. Behav.* 24:381–95

Loomis RJ. 1987. *Museum Visitor Evaluation: New Tool for Management.* Nashville, TN: Am. Assoc. State Local Hist.

Lucca-Irizarry N, Pacheco AM. 1992. Intercultural encounters of Puerto Rican migrants. *Environ. Behav.* 24:226–38

Lyons E, Breakwell GM. 1994. Factors predicting environmental concern and indifference in 13- to 16-year-olds. *Environ. Behav.* 26:223–38

MacDonald JE, Gifford R. 1989. Territorial cues and defensible space theory: the burglar's point of view. *J. Environ. Psychol.* 9:193–205

MacGill SM. 1989. Public perceptions of science: what Seascale said about the Black Report. *J. Environ. Psychol.* 9:133–55

Maharik M, Fischhoff B. 1993. Contrasting perceptions of the risks of using nuclear energy sources in space. *J. Environ. Psychol.* 13:243–50

Martichuski DK, Bell PA. 1991. Reward, punishment, privatization, and moral suasion in a commons dilemma. *J. Appl. Soc. Psychol.* 21:1356–69

Mazumdar S. 1992. "Sir, please do not take away my cubicle": the phenomenon of environmental deprivation. *Environ. Behav.* 24:691–722

Mazumdar S, Mazumdar S. 1993. Sacred space and place attachment. *J. Environ. Psychol.* 13:231–42

Michelson W. 1994. Everyday life in contextual perspective. See Altman & Churchman 1994, pp. 17–42

Michelson W. 1992. Meeting the demands of real-world complexity. *Environ. Behav.* 24: 260–67

Midden CJH, Verplanken B. 1990. The stability of nuclear attitudes after Chernobyl. *J. Environ. Psychol.* 10:111–19

Miles R, Clarke G. 1993. Setting off on the right foot: front-end evaluation. *Environ. Behav.* 25:698–709

Mohai P. 1991. Men, women, and the environment: an examination of the gender gap in environmental concern and activism. *Soc. & Nat. Res.* 5:1–19

Morrison P. 1990. The use of environmental seclusion in psychiatric settings. *J. Environ. Psychol.* 10:353–62

Mosler HJ. 1993. Self-dissemination of environmentally-responsible behavior: the influence of trust in a commons dilemma game. *J. Environ. Psychol.* 13:111–23

Mukherjee BN. 1993. Public response to air pollution in Calcutta proper. *J. Environ. Psychol.* 13:207–30

Napton ML, Day FA. 1992. Polluted neighborhoods in Texas: Who lives there? *Environ. Behav.* 24:508–26

Nasar JL. 1989. Symbolic meanings of house styles. *Environ. Behav.* 21:235–57

Nasar JL, Fisher B. 1993. 'Hot spots' of fear and crime: a multi-method investigation. *J. Environ. Psychol.* 13:187–206

Newell PB. 1994. A systems model of privacy. *J. Environ. Psychol.* 14:65–78

Novaco RW, Kliewer W, Broquet A. 1991. Home environmental consequences of commute travel impedence. *Am. J. Comm. Psychol.* 19:881–909

Novaco RW, Stokols D, Milanesi L. 1990. Objective and subjective dimensions of travel impedence as determinants of commuting stress. *Am. J. Comm. Psychol.* 18:231–57

Oldham GR. 1988. Effects of changes in workspace partitions and spatial density on employee reactions: a quasi-experiment. *J. Appl. Psychol.* 73:253–58

Oldham GR, Kulik CT, Stepina LP. 1991. Physical environments and employee reactions: effects of stimulus-screening skills and job complexity. *Acad. Manage. J.* 34: 929–38

Olson MH, ed. 1989. *Technological Support for Work Group Collaboration*. Hillsdale, NJ: Erlbaum

Omata K. 1992. Spatial organization of activities of Japanese families. *J. Environ. Psychol.* 12:259–67

O'Neill MJ. 1991a. A biologically based model of spatial cognition and wayfinding. *J. Environ. Psychol.* 11:299–320

O'Neill MJ. 1991b. Effects of signage and floor plan configuration on wayfinding accuracy. *Environ. Behav.* 23:553–74

O'Neill MJ. 1991c. Evaluation of a conceptual model of architectural legibility. *Environ. Behav.* 23:259–84

O'Neill MJ. 1992. Effects of familiarity and plan complexity on wayfinding in simulated buildings. *J. Environ. Psychol.* 12: 319–27

Orland B, Vining J, Ebreo A. 1992. The effect of street trees on perceived values of residential property. *Environ. Behav.* 24: 298–325

Ornstein S. 1992. First impressions of the symbolic meanings connoted by reception area design. *Environ. Behav.* 24:85–110

Oseland N, Donald I. 1993. The evaluation of space in homes: a facet study. *J. Environ. Psychol.* 13:251–61

Oskamp S, Harrington MJ, Edwards TC, Sherwood DL, Okuda SM, Swanson DC. 1991. Factors influencing household recycling behavior. *Environ. Behav.* 23:494–519

Oskamp S, Williams R, Unipan J, Steers N, Mainieri T, Kurland G. 1994. Psychological factors affecting paper recycling by businesses. *Environ. Behav.* 26:477–503

Ostfeld AM, Kasl SV, D'Atri DA, Fitzgerald EF. 1987. *Stress, Crowding, & Blood Pressure in Prison*. Hillsdale, NJ: Erlbaum

Palinkas LA. 1991. Effects of physical and social environments on the health and well-being of Antarctic winter-over personnel. *Environ. Behav.* 23:782–99

Parks CD. 1994. The predictive ability of social values in resource dilemmas and public goods games. *Pers. Soc. Psychol. Bull.* 20: 431–38

Paulus PB. 1988. *Prison Crowding: A Psychological Perspective*. New York: Springer-Verlag

Paulus PB, Nagar D, Camacho LM. 1991. Environmental and psychological factors in reactions to apartments and mobile homes. *J. Environ. Psychol.* 11:143–61

Peponis J, Zimring C, Choi YK. 1990. Finding the building in wayfinding. *Environ. Behav.* 22:555–90

Perkins DD, Meeks JW, Taylor RB. 1992. The physical environment of street blocks and resident perceptions of crime and disorder: implications for theory and measurement. *J. Environ. Psychol.* 12:21–34

Perkins DD, Wandersman A, Rich RC, Taylor RB. 1993. The physical environment of street crime: defensible space, territoriality and incivilities. *J. Environ. Psychol.* 13: 29–49

Peters HP, Albrecht G, Hennen L, Stegelmann HU. 1990. 'Chernobyl' and the nuclear power issue in West German public opinion. *J. Environ. Psychol.* 10:121–34

Peterson DR. 1992. Interpersonal relationships as a link between person and environment. See Walsh et al 1992, pp. 127–55

Prieser WFE, Rabinowitz ET, White ET. 1988. *Post-Occupancy Evaluation.* New York: Van Nostrand Reinhold

Prieser WFE, Vischer JC, White ET, eds. 1991. *Design Intervention: Toward a More Humane Architecture.* New York: Van Nostrand Rinehold

Proshansky H, Ittelson W, Rivlin L, eds. 1970. *Environmental Psychology.* New York: Holt, Rinehart & Winston. 690 pp.

Pruchno RA, Dempsey NP, Carder P, Koropeckyj-Cox T. 1993. Multigenerational households of caregiving families: negotiating shared space. *Environ. Behav.* 25:349–66

Purcell AT. 1991. The effects of depth of processing, typicality and affect on recognition memory for instances of single detached houses. *J. Environ. Psychol.* 11:163–77

Reicher S, Podpadec P, Macnaghten R, Brown R, Eiser JR. 1993. Taking the dread out of radiation? Consequences of and arguments over the inclusion of radiation from nuclear power production in the category of the natural. *J. Environ. Psychol.* 13:93–109

Reifman AS, Larrick RP, Fein S. 1991. Temper and temperature on the diamond: the heat-aggression relationship in major league baseball. *Pers. Soc. Psychol. Bull.* 17:580–85

Renn O. 1990. Public response to the Chernobyl accident. *J. Environ. Psychol.* 10: 151–67

Rotton J. 1993a. Atmospheric and temporal correlates of sex crimes: Endogenous factors do not explain seasonal differences in rape. *Environ. Behav.* 25:625–42

Rotton J. 1993b. Geophysical variables and behavior: LXXIII. Ubiquitous errors: a reanalysis of Anderson's (1987) "temperature and aggression." *Psychol. Rep.* 73:259–71

Rotton J, Shats M, Standers R. 1990. Tempera-

ture and pedestrian tempo: walking without awareness. *Environ. Behav.* 22:650–74

Rovine MJ, Weisman GD. 1989. Sketch-map variables as predictors of wayfinding performance. *J. Environ. Psychol.* 9:217–32

Ruback RB, Pandey J. 1992. Very hot and really crowded: quasi-experimental investigations of Indian "tempos." *Environ. Behav.* 24:527–54

Rubonis AV, Bickman L. 1991. Psychological impairment in the wake of disaster. *Psychol. Bull.* 109:384–99

Rutland A, Custance D, Campbell RN. 1993. The ability of three- to four-year-old children to use a map in a large-scale environment. *J. Environ. Psychol.* 13:365–72

Sadalla EK, Montello DR. 1989. Remembering changing in direction. *Environ. Behav.* 21: 346–63

Sadalla EK, Sheets VL. 1993. Symbolism in building materials: self-presentational and cognitive components. *Environ. Behav.* 25: 155–80

Saegert S, Winkel GH. 1990. Environmental psychology. *Annu. Rev. Psychol.* 41: 441–77

Samdahl DM, Robertson R. 1989. Social determinants of environmental concern: specification and test of the model. *Environ. Behav.* 21:57–81

Sanoff H. 1989. Facility programming. See Zube & Moore 1989, pp. 239–86

Schaeffer M, Baum A, Paulus P, Gaes G. 1988. Architecturally mediated effects of social density in prison. *Environ. Behav.* 20:3–19

Schahn J, Holzer E. 1990. Studies of individual environmental concern: the role of knowledge, gender, and background variables. *Environ. Behav.* 22:767–86

Schmidt FN, Gifford R. 1989. A dispositional approach to hazard perception: preliminary development of the Environmental Appraisal Inventory. *J. Environ. Psychol.* 9: 57–67

Schoggen P. 1989. *Behavior Settings.* Stanford, CA: Stanford Univ. Press

Schoggen P. 1990. Early days at the Midwest Psychological Field Station. *Environ. Behav.* 22:458–67

Schroeder HW. 1991. Preference and meaning of arboretum landscapes: combining quantitative and qualitative data. *J. Environ. Psychol.* 11:231–48

Schultz PW, Stone WF. 1994. Authoritarianism and attitudes toward the environment. *Environ. Behav.* 26:25–37

Scott D, Willits FK. 1994. Environmental attitudes and behavior: a Pennsylvania survey. *Environ. Behav.* 26:239–60

Screven CG. 1990. Uses of evaluation before, during and after exhibit design. *ILVS Rev.: J. Visit Behav.* 1:36–66

Sebba R. 1991. The landscapes of childhood:

the reflections of childhood's environment in adult memories and in children's attitudes. *Environ. Behav.* 23:395–422

Shaw KT, Gifford R. 1994. Residents' and burglars' assessment of burglary risk from defensible space cues. *J. Environ. Psychol.* 14:177–94

Sheets VL, Manzer CD. 1991. Affect, cognition, and urban vegetation: some effects of adding trees along city streets. *Environ. Behav.* 23:285–304

Shoul M. 1993. The spatial arrangements of ordinary English houses. *Environ. Behav.* 25:22–69

Shumaker SA, Pequegnat W. 1989. Hospital design, health providers, and the delivery of effective health care. See Zube & Moore 1989, pp. 161–99

Simpson M, Perry JD. 1990. Crime and climate: a reconsideration. *Environ. Behav.* 22:295–300

Slovic P. 1987. Perception of risk. *Science* 236:280–85

Smith AP. 1991. Noise and aspects of attention. *Br. J. Psychol.* 82:313–24

Smith SG. 1994. The psychological construction of home life. *J. Environ. Psychol.* 14:125–36

Sommer R. 1974. *Tight Spaces.* Englewood Cliffs, NJ: Prentice-Hall

Sommer R, Wicker AW. 1991. Gas station psychology: the case for specialization in ecological psychology. *Environ. Behav.* 23:131–49

Spreckelmeyer KF. 1993. Office relocation and environmental change: a case study. *Environ. Behav.* 25:181–204

Steinheider B, Winneke G. 1993. Industrial odours as environmental stressors: exposure-annoyance associations and their modification by coping, age, and perceived health. *J. Environ. Psychol.* 13:353–63

Stern PC, Dietz T, Kalof L. 1993. Value orientations, gender, and environmental concern. *Environ. Behav.* 25:322–48

Stokols D, Altman I, eds. 1987. *Handbook of Environmental Psychology.* New York: Wiley. 1654 pp.

Suedfeld P. 1991. Polar psychology: an overview. *Environ. Behav.* 23:653–65

Sundstrom E, Altman I. 1989. Physical environments and work-group effectiveness. In *Research in Organizational Behavior,* ed. LL Cummings, B Staw, 11:175–209. Greenwich, CT: JAI

Sundstrom E, Town JP, Osborn D, Rice RW, Konar E, Brill M. 1994. Office noise, satisfaction, and performance. *Environ. Behav.* 26:195–222

Syme GJ, Nancarrow BE. 1992. Predicting public involvement in urban water management and planning. *Environ. Behav.* 24:738–58

Taylor DE. 1989. Blacks and the environment:

toward an explanation of the concern and action gap between blacks and whites. *Environ. Behav.* 21:175–205

Taylor RB. 1988. *Human Territorial Functioning.* New York: Cambridge Univ. Press

Thayer RE. 1989. *The BioPsychology of Mood and Arousal.* New York: Oxford Univ. Press

Thompson SC, Stoutemyer K. 1991. Water use as a commons dilemma: the effects of education that focuses on long-term consequences and individual action. *Environ. Behav.* 23:314–33

Thompson SCG, Barton MA. 1994. Ecocentric and anthropocentric attitudes toward the environment. *J. Environ. Psychol.* 14:149–57

Topf M. 1989. Sensitivity to noise, personality hardiness, and noise-induced stress in critical care nurses. *Environ. Behav.* 21:717–33

Ulrich RS. 1993. Biophilia, biophobia, and natural landscapes. *The Biophilia Hypothesis,* ed. SR Kellert, EO Wilson, pp. 73–137. Washington, DC: Island Press

Ulrich RS, Simons RF, Losito BD, Fiorito E, Miles MA, Zelson M. 1991. Stress recovery during exposure to natural and urban environments. *J. Environ. Psychol.* 11:201–30

Ursin H, Bergan T, Collet J, Endresen IM, Lugg DJ, et al. 1991. Psychobiological studies of individuals in small, isolated groups in the Antarctic and in space analogues. *Environ. Behav.* 23:766–81

van der Pligt J, Midden CJH. 1990. Chernobyl: four years later: attitudes, risk management and communication. *J. Environ. Psychol.* 10:91–99

Vaughan E. 1993. Individual and cultural differences in adaptation to environmental risks. *Am. Psychol.* 48:673–80

Verplanken B. 1989. Beliefs, attitudes, and intentions toward nuclear energy before and after Chernobyl in a longitudinal within-subjects design. *Environ. Behav.* 21:371–92

Veitch JA. 1990. Office noise and illumination effects on reading comprehension. *J. Environ. Psychol.* 10:209–17

Veitch JA, Gifford R, Hine DW. 1991. Demand characteristics and full-spectrum lighting effects on performance and mood. *J. Environ. Psychol.* 11:87–95

Vining J, Ebreo A. 1990. What makes a recycler? A comparison of recyclers and non-recyclers. *Environ. Behav.* 22:55–73

Walsh WB, Craik KH, Price RH, eds. 1992. *Person-Environment Psychology: Models and Perspectives.* Hillsdale, NJ: Erlbaum

Wang TH, Katzev RD. 1990. Group commitment and resource conservation: two field experiments on promoting recycling. *J. Appl. Soc. Psychol.* 20:265–75

Warren DH, Scott TE. 1993. Map alignment in travelling multisegment routes. *Environ. Behav.* 25:643–66

Weinstein CS, David TG, eds. 1990. *Spaces for Children: The Built Environment and Child Development.* New York: Plenum

Weinstein CS, Pinciotti P. 1988. Changing a schoolyard: intentions, design decisions, and behavioral outcomes. *Environ. Behav.* 20:345–71

Wener RE. 1989. Advances in evaluation of the built environment. See Zube & Moore 1989, pp. 287–313

Wener RE, Frazier W, Farbstein J. 1985. Three generations of evaluation and design of correctional facilities. *Environ. Behav.* 17:71–95

Wener RE, Keys C. 1988. The effects of changes in jail population densities on crowding, sick call, and spatial behavior. *J. Appl. Soc. Psychol.* 18:852–66

Werner CM, Altman I, Brown BB. 1992. A transactional approach to interpersonal relations: physical environment, social context and temporal qualities. *J. Soc. Personal Relat.* 9:297–324

Werner CM, Altman I, Brown BB, Ginat J. 1993. Celebrations in personal relationships: a transactional/dialectical perspective. In *Social Context and Relationships,* ed. S Duck, pp. 109–38. Newbury Park, CA: Sage

Wicker AW. 1992. Making sense of environ-ments. See Walsh et al 1992, pp. 157–92

Wicker AW, August RA. 1995. How far should we generalize? The case of a workload model. *Psychol. Sci.* 6:39–44

Wiesenfeld E. 1992. Public housing evaluation in Venezuela: a case study. *J. Environ. Psychol.* 12:213–23

Wisner B, Stea D, Kruks S. 1991. Participatory and action research methods. See Zube & Moore 1992, pp. 271–95

Wong CY, Sommer R, Cook EJ. 1992. The soft classroom 17 years later. *J. Environ. Psychol.* 12:337–43

Wood D, Beck R. 1989. Janine Eber maps London: individual dimensions of cognitive imagery. *J. Environ. Psychol.* 9:1–26

Yamamoto T, Sawada H, Minami H, Ishii S, Inoue W. 1992. Transition from the university to the workplace. *Environ. Behav.* 24:189–205

Yang BE, Brown TJ. 1992. A cross-cultural comparison of preferences for landscape styles and landscape elements. *Environ. Behav.* 24:471–507

Zube EH. 1991. Environmental psychology, global issues, and local landscape research. *J. Environ. Psychol.* 11:321–34

Zube EH, Moore GT, eds. 1989. *Advances in Environment, Behavior, and Design,* Vol. 2. New York: Plenum. 350 pp.

Zube EH, Moore GT, eds. 1991. *Advances in Environment, Behavior, and Design,* Vol. 3. New York: Plenum. 339 pp.

Annu. Rev. Psychol. 1996. 47:513–39

COGNITIVE SKILL ACQUISITION

Kurt VanLehn

Learning Research and Development Center, University of Pittsburgh, Pittsburgh, Pennsylvania 15260

KEYWORDS: cognitive skill acquisition, problem solving, acquisition, practice effects, transfer

ABSTRACT

Cognitive skill acquisition is acquiring the ability to solve problems in intellectual tasks, where success is determined more by subjects' knowledge than by their physical prowess. This review considers research conducted in the past ten years on cognitive skill acquisition. It covers the initial stages of acquiring a single principle or rule, the initial stages of acquiring a collection of interacting pieces of knowledge, and the final stages of acquiring a skill, wherein practice causes increases in speed and accuracy.

CONTENTS

0066-4308/96/0201-0513$08.00

INTRODUCTION

When an individual acquires the ability to solve problems in intellectual tasks, where success is determined more by the subject's knowledge than by his or her physical prowess, the individual has acquired a cognitive skill. Frequently studied tasks include solving algebraic equations and word problems, college physics problem solving, computer programming, medical diagnosis, and electronic troubleshooting. Researchers in cognitive skill acquisition study how people learn to accomplish such complex, knowledge-intensive tasks and how they become experts in their fields.

A Brief History

Cognitive skill acquisition has its historical roots in the study of problem solving. Research on problem solving began early in this century with the study of what makes problems difficult to solve (Duncan 1959). In the 1960s, researchers began studying the process of solving a problem. Subjects solved multistep puzzles while explaining their reasoning aloud. Transcriptions of their commentaries, called *verbal protocols,* provided the empirical foundations for developing computational models of problem solving. Newell & Simon (1972) introduced most of the important theoretical concepts, including problem spaces, search trees, and production systems.

Because problem-solving research emphasized the process of moving from one intermediate state to another until one finally arrives at a solution, researchers preferred to use tasks where most intermediate states were physical states. In the Tower of Hanoi, for instance, subjects try to move a pyramidal stack of disks from one peg to another by moving one disk at a time according to certain restrictions. Solving the puzzle requires many movements of disks and thus subjects' intermediate states are exposed. Problems that are solved with a single physical action were seldom studied.

During the 1960s, two related fields developed. In *decision making,* researchers studied people making a choice under circumstances of uncertainty, and in *reasoning* they studied people drawing a conclusion from a combination of mental inferences. In a sense, decision making and reasoning are also forms of problem solving. However, their methodological and theoretical concerns have remained distinct from those of problem solving, perhaps because most subjects' intermediate states when performing these activities are mental and not physical.

In the 1970s, researchers of problem solving became interested in how subjects solved problems requiring much more knowledge than the simple puzzle problems that were used in the 1960s. They studied problems in chess, physics, mathematics, computer programming, medical diagnosis, and many other fields. Although one could tell subjects in a few minutes everything they needed to know to solve a puzzle, obtaining the solution of even an easy problem in a knowledge-rich task domain such as physics requires many hours of preparatory training.

The exploration of knowledge-rich problem solving began by contrasting the performance of experts and novices. One robust finding is that experts can sort problems into categories according to features of their solutions, whereas novices can only sort problems using features of the problem statement itself. As discussed by Ericsson & Lehmann (this volume), this and many other findings can be explained by assuming that whenever mental planning of solutions is possible (e.g. because all the information required to solve problems is present in the initial state), then experts typically develop the ability to plan solutions in memory. This often requires the ability to envision sequences of intermediate states; accordingly, experts develop impressive mnemonic powers, but only for intermediate states that they typically encounter.

In the 1980s, many researchers began studying how people acquire expertise. Researchers initially focused on the role of practice in the development of expertise. Phenomena that were often associated with motor skills, such as the power-law of practice and the identical elements model of transfer, were found to be important with cognitive skills as well. Most of the recent work has focused on the role of instruction during the early stages of skill acquisition, in particular on the role of examples. In this literature, an *example* is a problem whose solution is given to the student, along with the solution's derivation. Examples appear to play a central role in the early phases of cognitive skill acquisition.

Because reviews of the early days of problem solving and cognitive skill acquisition are available (VanLehn 1989, Kahney 1993), as well as reviews of expertise (Ericsson & Lehmann, this volume) and instructional considerations (Glaser & Bassok 1989, Voss et al 1995), this review focuses exclusively on recent work in cognitive skill acquisition. Because there is much material to cover and simply listing the major findings would make it impossible to assimilate them all, a loose framework has been provided.

A Framework for Reviewing Cognitive Skill Acquisition

Fitts (1964) distinguished three phases of motor skill acquisition. His *early, intermediate,* and *late* phases also aptly describe the course of cognitive skill acquisition.

During the early phase of cognitive skill acquisition, the subject is trying to understand the domain knowledge without yet trying to apply it. This phase is dominated by reading, discussion, and other general-purpose information acquisition activities which lie outside the scope of this review. Most investigations of cognitive skill acquisition do not collect observations during the early phase.

The intermediate phase begins when students turn their attention to solving problems. Before they begin solving problems themselves, they often study a few problems that have already been solved (called examples henceforth). Examples may be printed in a textbook or presented by a teacher. As they solve problems, students may refer back to the textbook or ask a teacher for help, but their primary focus is on solving problems. This kind of activity differentiates the intermediate phase from the early phase, where the primary focus is on studying expository instructional material.

When subjects enter the intermediate phase, they have some relevant knowledge for solving problems but certainly not all of it. They also may have acquired some misunderstandings. Thus, the first order of business for problem solvers is to correct these flaws in the domain knowledge. (For lack of a better word, *flaw* will be used to stand both for missing knowledge and for incorrect knowledge.) The second order of business is to acquire heuristic, experiential knowledge that expedites problem solving.

Eventually, students remove all the flaws in their knowledge and can solve problems without conceptual errors, although they may still make unintended errors, or slips (Norman 1981). This capability signals the end of the intermediate phase and the beginning of the late phase. During the late phase, students continue to improve in speed and accuracy as they practice, even though their understanding of the domain and their basic approach to solving problems does not change. Practice effects and transfer are the main research issues in this phase.

This three-phase chronology is an idealization. The boundaries between phases are not as sharp as the description suggests. Moreover, instruction on a cognitive skill is divided into courses, topics, chapters, and sections. Students are introduced to a component of the skill, given substantial practice with it, then moved on to the next component. Thus, at any given time, students may be in the late phase with respect to some components of their skill but in other phases with respect to other components. Nonetheless, it is useful to make the three-phase distinction because different empirical phenomena characterize each phase.

This review covers the intermediate and final phases. However, much more work has been done on the intermediate phase than on the final phase; as a result, the review of intermediate phase research is split into two parts. The first part covers studies where students learned only a single principle. These studies focused on the basic processes of assimilating a new principle, retrieving it from memory during problem solving, and applying it. The second part covers studies in which students learned many principles. Following this two-part discussion of the intermediate phase is a section on the late phase.

THE INTERMEDIATE PHASE: LEARNING A SINGLE PRINCIPLE

Before beginning this discussion on learning a single principle, some general remarks about the intermediate phase are necessary.

Perhaps the most ubiquitous finding about the intermediate phase is the importance of examples. Studies of students in a variety of instructional situations have shown that students prefer learning from examples rather than learning from other forms of instruction (e.g. Chi et al 1989, Lefevre & Dixon 1986, Pirolli & Anderson 1985). Students learn more from studying examples than from solving the same problems themselves (Carroll 1994, Cooper & Sweller 1987). A three-year program in algebra was completed in two years by students who only studied examples and solved problems without lectures or other direct instruction (Zhu & Simon 1987). Because of the importance of examples, most research on the intermediate phase has used instructional material where examples are prominent. Sometimes, the instruction consists only of examples, and students must infer the general principles themselves.

Most research has been focused on students solving problems alone. There is some research on learning from a tutor, which is covered at the end of this section. Learning by solving problems in small groups has not been studied much by cognitive skill acquisition researchers.

Learning a Single Principle: Introduction

Much work on the intermediate phase has concentrated on learning material that is about the size of a single principle, where a principle is the sort of thing that a textbook states in a colored box and discusses for several pages. Often the instruction includes an example illustrating the application of the principle. Example 1 is taken from Catrambone (1994b) and illustrates an elementary probability principle that is often used in cognitive skill acquisition research. Knowledge of the principle includes not only the permutation formula but also the meaning of the variables n and r and the kinds of problems to which this formula applies. The convergence-of-forces idea employed to solve Duncker's famous X-ray problem is another commonly used principle. One can generally teach a subject a rudimentary version of a principle in an hour or less, in contrast with teaching a rudimentary version of a whole cognitive skill, which might take days or months.

Example 1: A problem solved with the permutation principle

Problem: The supply department at IBM has to make sure that scientists get computers. Today, they have 11 IBM computers and 8 IBM scientists requesting computers. The scientists randomly choose their computer but do so in alphabetical order. What is the probability that the first 3 scientists alphabetically will get the lowest, second lowest, and third lowest serial numbers, respectively, on their computers?

Solution: The equation needed for this problem is

$$\frac{1}{n*(n-1)*...*(n-r+1)}.$$

This equation allows one to determine the probability of the above outcome occurring. In this problem, n = 11 and r = 3. The 11 represents the number of computers that are available to be chosen while the 3 represents the number of choices that are being focused on in this problem. The equation divides the number of ways the desired outcome could occur by the number of possible outcomes. So, inserting 11 and 3 into the equation, we find that the overall probability is

$$\frac{1}{11*10*9} = \frac{1}{990}.$$

All the experiments discussed in this section have a similar format. Subjects are trained, typically by studying a booklet. The training material almost always includes examples and may consist only of examples. Solving the test problems is sometimes called *analogical problem solving* because it involves finding an analogy (correspondence) between the example and the problem.

After the training (and sometimes after a distractor task), the subjects are given problems to solve. The problems can be easily solved using the principle but are difficult to solve without it. Applying a principle or example consists of retrieving it, placing its parts into correspondence with parts of the problem (e.g. in the case of the permutation principle, deciding what *n* and *r* are), and drawing inferences about the problem and its solution on the basis of the problem's correspondence with the principle or example. After applying the principle or example, subjects may generalize it. Each of these processes—retrieval, mapping, application, and generalization—are discussed in turn.

Retrieval

There appear to be two kinds of retrieval: *spontaneous* and *deliberate*. Deliberate retrieval often occurs after subjects are given a hint (e.g. "The examples you studied earlier will help you solve this problem") or when the experiment simulates an instructional situation where students expect earlier material to be relevant to solving problems (Brown & Kane 1988). Spontaneous retrieval or *reminding,* as it is more commonly known, occurs when the experimenter hides the relationship between the training and testing phases of the experiment (typically by telling students that they are participating in two different experiments). This experimental paradigm explores why education so often creates "inert" knowledge in students—they can recall the knowledge when given explicit cues but they fail to apply it outside the classroom (Bransford et al 1989).

A strong but obvious effect is that deliberate retrieval is vastly more successful than reminding. Many more subjects can retrieve a principle or example after a hint than before one (e.g. Gick & Holyoak 1980).

When reminding does occur, it often is triggered by surface similarities between the problem and a training example (e.g. Catrambone & Holyoak 1989; Holyoak & Koh 1987; Ross 1984, 1987, 1989). For instance, subjects are likely to be reminded of the IBM example (Example 1) more by a problem that mentions Microsoft programmers designing computer software than by the car mechanics problem (see Example 2), even though the car mechanics problem has the same mathematical structure as the IBM example. Subjects can be reminded by structural similarities, but only when the training emphasizes the underlying structure of the examples and the test problems are reworded to emphasize their deep structure (Catrambone & Holyoak 1989).

Example 2: A problem with the same deep structure as the IBM problem

Southside High School has a vocational car mechanics class in which students repair cars. One day there are 15 students and 18 cars requiring repairs. The cars are assigned to students in order of the severity of their damages (the car in the worst shape goes first), but the student to work on the car is randomly chosen. What is the probability that the 6 cars in the worst shape are worked on by the 6 students with the highest grades, in order of their grades (i.e. the student with the highest grade working on the worst car, etc)?

Although superficial reminding seems to be the population norm, it is less common among students with high mathematics SAT scores (Novick 1988, Novick & Holyoak 1991). Moreover, deliberate retrieval, particularly in instructional situations, is often guided by structural similarity (Faries & Reiser 1988).

Mapping

The mapping process puts parts of the principle or example into correspondence with parts of the problem. For instance, in order to use Example 1 as a model for solving a new problem, subjects must find values for n and r, which in turn requires finding objects corresponding to the IBM scientists and computers.

Subjects are easily misled by surface similarities into using the wrong correspondence (mapping). For instance, Ross (1989) found that most subjects solved Example 2 by replacing IBM scientists with mechanics and computers with cars. This matches the superficial characteristics of the objects, but it produces an incorrect solution to the problem.

Application

In some cases, subjects' solving of the problem is almost finished after they have put the principle or example into correspondence with the problem. For instance, once subjects have mapped the car mechanics problem to the IBM example, the only remaining tasks are to substitute 15 for n and 6 for r in the permutation formula and to do the arithmetic. However, applying the principle or example can be much more involved (Novick & Holyoak 1991). For instance, when an example is complex, subjects usually refer back to it many times when solving a problem (e.g. Pirolli & Anderson 1985, Reed et al 1994, VanLehn 1995a). They appear to use a variety of strategies for deciding whether to refer to the example and to attempt the next step without help (VanLehn 1995a).

Generalization

Problems and examples contain information that is not causally or logically related to their solution. In the IBM example, the nature of the particular objects being chosen (IBM computers) is irrelevant. Such information comprises the surface features mentioned earlier in this section. As noted then, surface features can play a strong role in retrieval and mapping. Their role in application has not yet been established but is likely to be strong as well.

Generalization is the process of modifying one's understanding of an example or principle in such a way that surface information does not play a role in retrieval, mapping, and application. Generalization allows one to apply the principle or example to more problems.

A variety of instructional methods for encouraging generalization have been tried. Gick, Holyoak, and others have found that simply augmenting the example with an explanation of the principle behind it resulted in little generalization. Using two examples was also ineffective. What does work, however, is using two examples and some sort of highlighting device that encourages subjects to compare two examples and find their common structure (Catrambone & Holyoak 1989, Cummins 1992, Gick & Holyoak 1983, Ross & Kennedy 1990). Generalization causes subjects to be reminded of examples on the basis of structural features instead of just surface features and to be fooled less by surface features during mapping.

These results strongly suggest that generalization is not an automatic process, as was assumed in earlier theories of cognitive skill acquisition (e.g. Anderson 1983). Although protocol-taking experiments would be necessary to confirm this suggestion, it is likely that subjects must actively decide which propositions in an example are structural and which are superficial. Alternatively, subjects can probably be told which aspects of an example are general (cf Ahn et al 1992).

As one would predict from basic properties of memory, deciding that some propositions in an example are superficial does not erase them from memory, nor does building a generalization from comparison of two examples erase the examples from memory (Bernardo 1994, Novick & Holyoak 1991).

Summary

Overall, superficial reasoning is the norm in problem solving, but subjects can be induced to use deeper reasoning under certain circumstances. Left to their own devices, subjects typically just encode examples and principles in memory, where they languish until retrieved deliberately or via spontaneous, superficial association. Once retrieved, an example or principle is applied by just "plugging in" superficially similar objects and "copying" the resulting solutions. Subjects can use more structural features in spontaneous retrieval and mapping, but they must first be induced to generalize the examples, which seems to require using multiple examples and directing the subjects to find their commonalities.

On the other hand, when subjects suspect or are told that examples they have seen might help them solve their problem, their retrieval is often based on structural features. That is, they search memory or the textbook for examples whose solution might help them.

THE INTERMEDIATE PHASE: LEARNING MULTIPLE PRINCIPLES

Mastering a cognitive skill often requires learning more than one principle, as well as many other pieces of knowledge that one would hesitate to call principles per se. For instance, a physics student must learn facts, such as the units for measuring force (Newtons) and mass (grams). There are even borderline cases: Is the knowledge that mass is not the same thing as weight a principle? Learning a cognitive skill also requires learning heuristics that will help one select the right combination of principles for solving a problem.

Much of what has been observed in the study of single-principle learning probably applies to the learning of all these types of knowledge. The processes of retrieval (both spontaneous and deliberate), mapping, application, and generalization probably characterize the acquisition of minor principles (e.g. that mass and weight are different), heuristics, and other generalizations. Factual knowledge may be too simple for mapping and generalization to apply.

However, as the quantity and complexity of the material to be learned increases, one can expect to see effects that cannot be observed when studying the acquisition of single principles. This section focuses on such phenomena.

Transfer

When an example requires the use of multiple principles in its solution, then it is possible to study an interesting type of transfer. First, students are trained with examples and problems that use two or more principles in a certain combination; then they are tested on problems that require using the principles in a different combination. For instance, consider the two algebra examples shown on the top two lines of Table 1. Their solutions require the use of two principles: removing a term by subtracting it from both sides of an equation, and removing a coefficient by dividing both sides of the equation by it. These same principles can be used to solve the problems shown on the last two lines of Table 1, but they must be used in a different combination from the one used in the examples. If a student trained on the two examples can solve the two problems, then a certain rather constrained type of transfer is obtained.

However, such transfer is rarely observed. Cooper & Sweller (1987) found that many eighth-grade students trained with multiple versions of the two examples in Table 1 could not solve the problems shown on the last two lines of the table. On the other hand, the students had no difficulty solving problems, such as $ac + g = h$, that could be solved by copying the solution of the training examples. Similar lack of transfer has been found many times (Catrambone 1994b, Reed et al 1985, Sweller & Cooper 1985).

Note that this kind of transfer is different from the generalization discussed in the preceding section, where copying the examples' solution was all that was expected of the subjects. Generalizing the examples shown in the top two lines of Table 1 will enable subjects to solve problems such as $ac + g = h$ but not the ones shown in the bottom of Table 1.

Catrambone (1994a,b) showed that modifying the examples' solutions in order to highlight the application of each principle significantly increased transfer. Training that required students to draw contrasts among pairs of examples in order to see individual principle applications was less successful (Catrambone & Holyoak 1990, 1987).

Even when principle applications are not highlighted, principle-based transfer can occur, but it requires a large number of examples and above-average students (Cooper & Sweller 1987). This suggests that some students study examples differently from others—the topic of the next section.

Table 1   Examples and problems of solving equations for a

$$ab + f = g \Rightarrow ab = g - f \Rightarrow a = (g - f)/b$$
$$b(a + f) = g \Rightarrow a + f = g/b \Rightarrow a = (g/b) - f$$
$$m(ac + b) = k$$
$$f(a + b) + w = g$$

Strategy Differences in Learning from Examples

Examples are commonly used in two ways. Students study examples before solving problems, or they refer back to examples when they are in the midst of solving a problem. For each of these two activities, learning appears to be strongly affected by the students' strategies for studying examples and for referring back to them. Let us first consider the activity of studying examples before solving problems.

Chi et al (1989) found that students who explained examples thoroughly to themselves learned much more than students who merely read examples through. Chi et al had nine college students first study four introductory chapters from a college physics textbook until they could pass exams on each chapter. This ensured that all students had the necessary prerequisite knowledge for understanding the target chapter. The target chapter taught students about forces and Newton's laws. The students read the target chapter, studied three examples, and solved 19 problems. Protocols were taken during the example-studying and problem-solving phase. Students were classified on the basis of a median split of their problem-solving scores into Good and Poor learners. When protocols of the example-studying phase were analyzed, Good learners were found to utter more self-explanations than Poor learners. A *self-explanation* is any inference about the example that goes beyond the information presented in the example. For instance, given the line $F_{ax} = -F_a \cos(30°)$, a good student might say, "So F_{ax} must be the leg of the right triangle, and F_a is the hypotenuse...yep. What's that minus sign doing there?" Poor students often just read the line or paraphrase it, then move on to the next line.

Chi & VanLehn (1991) analyzed the content of the students' self-explanations. The results suggested that self-explanations were derived in two different ways. One was by deduction from knowledge acquired earlier while reading the text part of the chapter, usually by simply applying a general principle to information in the current example statement. The second was by generalizing and extending the example statement. These inferences helped to fill gaps in students' knowledge, most often by providing necessary technical details that were not discussed in the text.

VanLehn et al (1992) constructed a computer model of the example-studying and problem-solving process. In order to solve problems correctly, the model required the use of approximately 60 rules. The rules represented major principles, minor principles, facts, and technical details (e.g. how to determine whether the sign of a vector's component is positive or negative). Fewer than half of the rules were mentioned in the textbook.[1] The other rules were learned by the model as it studied the examples, but only if it self-explained them. The

---

[1]   Other investigators who have formalized textbook knowledge have also found that textbooks leave out many crucial details (e.g. Psotka et al 1988, section 1).

model accounted for the aggregate results from the Chi et al (1989) study as well as for the performance of individual subjects (VanLehn & Jones 1993). Error patterns and other analyses were also consistent with the hypothesis that most of the benefit from self-explanation comes from filling in gaps in subjects' knowledge (VanLehn & Jones 1995).

The self-explanation effect is quite general. Self-explaining examples in a variety of task domains improves learning (Brown & Kane 1988, Ferguson-Hessler & de Jong 1990, Lovett 1992, Pirolli & Bielaczyc 1989, Pirolli & Recker 1994, Pressley et al 1992). Self-explaining expository text (Chi et al 1994) and hyper-text (Recker & Pirolli 1995) instead of examples also enhances learning. Most importantly, students can be trained to self-explain, and this improves their learning dramatically (Bielaczyc et al 1994, Bielaczyc & Recker 1991, Chi et al 1994). However, self-explanation only affects the initial acquisition of knowledge and not subsequent improvement with practice (Pirolli & Recker 1994).

Several of these studies also found a self-monitoring effect (Chi et al 1989, Pirolli & Recker 1994). Both good and poor students tended to spontaneously utter assessments of their understanding. However, poor students tended to utter uniformly positive self-assessments (e.g. "Yep. That makes sense") even though their subsequent performance indicated that they really did not understand the material. On the other hand, good students tended to monitor their understanding more accurately and frequently noted failures to understand (e.g. "Wait. I don't see how they got that"). Accuracy in self-monitoring appears to be correlated with learning.

Up to this point, I have discussed different strategies for studying examples before solving problems. However, students also refer to examples as they solve problems, and in this circumstance correlations between learning and strategies may also be found. Both Good and Poor learners refer to examples during problem solving (Chi et al 1989), though they refer more often to the first few problems than to later problems (Pirolli 1991, Reed et al 1994). What matters is the way students refer to examples. Protocol analyses (Chi et al 1989; VanLehn 1995a,b) and latency analyses (Pirolli & Recker 1994) suggest that poor learners maximize their use of problem solving by analogy: They refer to an example as soon as they notice that it is relevant and copy as much of its solution as possible. On the other hand, good learners minimize their use of analogies to examples: They refer to the example only when they get stuck solving a problem and need some help. That is, good solvers prefer to solve problems by themselves, whereas poor solvers prefer to adapt an example's solution.

After solving a problem, subjects often reflect on the solution. Pirolli & Recker (1994) found that Good and Poor learners both reflected on half the problems they solve, but what they said about them was different. Poor learners usually just paraphrased the solution. Good learners tried to abstract general solution methods, often by comparing the current problem's solution to the solutions of earlier problems.

In all these studies, the criteria for learning included performance on problems that could not be solved by merely copying the example solutions. Thus, learning requires the kind of transfer discussed in the previous section entitled "Transfer." Strategy effects may not show up on single-principle experiments (covered in "The Intermediate Phase: Learning a Single Principle") because learning (generalization) is assessed on the basis of problems that students can solve by copying solutions.

In short, learners seem to use different studying strategies that allow them to trade off effort and likelihood of learning. Some students exert considerable time and energy in self-explaining examples and/or by trying to solve problems without copying the examples; these students often learn more. Other students exert less effort by merely reading the examples through and/or by copying example solutions; they learn less. As the saying goes: No pain, no gain.

Learning Events

Knowledge of a complex skill is composed of many pieces. Some of this knowledge is of principles, some is of examples or generalizations thereof, and some is of technical details, heuristics, and other information that could be relevant in solving a problem. The studies reviewed in the section "The Intermediate Phase: Learning a Single Principle" suggest that learning a single principle requires attention, both during the early phase (studying a booklet, typically) and during the intermediate phase as the principle is retrieved, mapped, applied, and generalized. Moreover, it appears that generalization of an example also requires attention—it is not an automatic process nor a mere by-product of applying the example to solve a problem. This in turn suggests that during the intermediate phase of complex skill acquisition, students acquire new pieces of domain knowledge one at a time and take time off from problem solving or example studying to attend to the discovery of new pieces of knowledge and perhaps to generalization as well.

This hypothesis is consistent with several studies of transfer. For instance, Bovair et al (1990) taught subjects sequences of simple text-editing commands. Each command had several steps, such as pressing a function key (copy, delete, move, etc), checking a prompt, selecting some text, and pressing the enter key. They represented each command's procedure with a set of rules. Across commands, some rules were identical, some were analogous, and some appeared in only one command. They trained subjects on all commands, varying the order in which the commands were taught. For each order, they calculated the number of new rules to be learned for each command, the number of rules that were identical to rules learned earlier, and the number of rules that were only analogous to rules learned earlier. They found that the training time was a linear function of the number of new rules and the total number of rules. There was a 23-s cost for each rule because the subject had to execute every rule of the command, regardless of whether that rule had already been learned. However, each new rule to be learned required a substantial additional amount of time—about 30 s. This suggests that learning a new rule requires taking time off from executing the familiar parts of a procedure. There was no cost in training time for learning rules that were analogous to rules learned earlier, which suggests generalization of these rules was quite easy. Singley & Anderson (1989) also found, using text editing, programming, and mathematical task domains, that training time was a function of the number of new rules to be learned.

If learning a new principle or other piece of knowledge does take time away from executing familiar knowledge, then *learning events* during problem solving may be observed, wherein a subjects briefly switches attention from solving the problem to reasoning about the domain knowledge itself. Learning events should also be found during other instructional activities, such as self-explanation. As it turns out, learning events can be observed via detailed protocol analysis.

Learning events were first observed in discovery-learning situations, wherein students were given very little instruction and had to discover the principles of a domain during the course of solving problems in it. Karmiloff-Smith & Inhelder (1975) observed discrete changes in children's procedures for balancing blocks on a beam and explained them as miniature discoveries—learning events. Kuhn & Phelps (1982) also noted discrete changes in college students' experiment-design strategies and assumed that they were due to learning events. Siegler & Jenkins (1989) observed children shifting their strategies for adding by counting on their fingers and coined the term "learning event" for the brief episodes where the changes occurred. VanLehn (1991) showed that all the changes in strategy observed as a subject solved the Tower of Hanoi puzzle seemed to appear during learning events.

Discovery learning is rarely used to teach a cognitive skill. Instead, students typically access examples, textbooks, and sometimes teachers or peers. However, instructional material is almost always incomplete. As discussed briefly in the section "Strategy Differences in Learning from Examples," roughly half the pieces of information required to solve problems were not mentioned in the college textbook used in the Chi et al (1989) study. When faced with incomplete instructional material, students need to discover the missing information for themselves. VanLehn (1995c) analyzed the Chi et al (1989) protocols and observed learning events in students in most of the places where information that was missing from the instruction was required for solving problems and explaining examples.

In all these studies, learning events were characterized by long pauses or verbal signs of confusion. (All the studies were based on verbal protocols.) Subjects rarely announced their discoveries in a clear fashion. Even when probed, their explanations were seldom coherent (Siegler & Jenkins 1989). Nonetheless, their problem-solving behaviors changed.

As an illustration of a learning event, consider a physics student quoted in VanLehn (1995c). The student did not know that weight is a kind of force, so he could not figure out how to find the weight of an object, even though he had calculated that the force of gravity on the object was 160 pounds. After pausing and complaining a bit, he recalled the textbook equation $F = (W/g)a$ and performed the totally unjustified substitution of g for a, thus deriving the equation $F = W$, which he interpreted as meaning that the object's weight is equal to the force of gravity on it. Amazingly, he had discovered the missing correct principle via a specious derivation. He said, "Right? Is that right? Okay. Um, so I'm going to get 160 pounds. That's the force. Yeah. It kind of makes sense 'cause they, they weigh you in pounds, don't they? That's force." The learning event consisted of reaching an impasse, using purely syntactic algebraic symbol manipulation to hypothesize a new principle (that weight is the force of gravity on an object), and then supporting the principle with the fact that pounds is a unit of force and that Americans express weight in pounds. However, this is not the end of the story. On the next occasion where the subject could use the principle, he failed to do so. This resulted in a units error, which he detected while checking his answer. That reminded him of his new principle (he said, "Oh, wait a minute! Oh, hold the bus. Hold the bus!"), but after a brief pause he decided the principle didn't apply. However, after he had failed to find another explanation for the units error, he changed his mind and decided the principle did apply. In short, learning a principle in the context of problem solving is much like learning in one of the single-principle experiments reviewed earlier. One may not be reminded of it immediately, but when one deliberately searches memory the new principle can be retrieved. Yet retrieval of a new principle is not enough. One often has to deliberate about its generality before applying it. Presumably, this deliberation causes generalization.

Learning events can be analyzed in terms of three characteristics:

1. What provoked the student to switch attention from the main task to learning? In the illustration, reaching an impasse provoked the physics student to try to derive a new principle. In some situations, most learning events were triggered by impasses (VanLehn 1991, 1995c). However, when the student already has a correct, operational solution procedure, improvements to the procedure are triggered by some kind of "noticing" process (Siegler & Jenkins 1989, VanLehn 1991), which can be modeled (Jones & VanLehn

1994) but which is still not well understood. After solving a problem, some students deliberately reflect on its solution in order to uncover its overall plan or basic idea (Recker & Pirolli 1995, VanLehn 1989).

2. What kind of reasoning went on during the learning event? In the illustration, the student used both algebraic symbol manipulation and common-sense reasoning to derive his new principle. Such educated guesses seem often to be based on causal attribution heuristics (Lewis 1988) or overgeneralizations (VanLehn 1995c). However, students often use less constrained forms of induction (VanLehn 1995c), in which case one can observe the prototypicality effects usually found in concept formation experiments (Lewis & Anderson 1985).

3. How easily retrieved is the new principle, and how general is it? Advocates of discovery learning often hope that because students discover principles by themselves, the principles will be easily retrieved and adequately general. As illustrated above, this does not seem to be the case. Principles acquired during learning events are often difficult to retrieve and seem to require deliberate attention before they are general enough (Kuhn & Phelps 1982, Siegler & Jenkins 1989, VanLehn 1995c).

Progress on understanding learning events has been slow because it is difficult to distinguish learning events from ordinary problem solving even in the protocols of the most talkative subjects. It has been necessary to have a strong theory of the kind of knowledge that can be learned and a long enough period of observation that one can see slow changes in the usage of individual pieces of knowledge. Nonetheless, the observations to date support the general hypothesis that learning a cognitive skill consists of learning a large number of small pieces of knowledge (including principles, technical details, heuristics, etc) and that for each one, learning consists of a series of learning events that construct and generalize that piece of knowledge.

Learning from a Computer Tutor

The discussion of the intermediate phase up to this point has assumed that the learner has no one to talk to and only written materials to refer to. While this constraint simplifies the observation of learning, it makes the instructional situation somewhat atypical of real-world situations where learners can obtain help by raising their hands, picking up the phone, or walking down the hall to a colleague's office. As a first step toward understanding cognitive skill acquisition "in the wild," researchers have studied students learning from a very taciturn tutor, namely, a computer.

When the tutor selects problems for the student to solve, a simple policy is to continue giving the student problems until the student has reached mastery. *Mastery* can be defined as answering the most recent N problems with a score higher than M. Some computer tutors (e.g. Anderson et al 1995) can monitor the usage of individual principles or steps and thus implement a policy that keeps assigning problems until each has been mastered. Varying the thresholds of mastery for individual pieces of knowledge can accurately predict errors (Corbett et al 1995). Tutoring based on mastery generally results in higher scores on posttests than tutoring based on fixed problem sets (e.g. Anderson et al 1989). This suggests that different students learn at different rates, which in turn is consistent with students' use of different studying strategies (see the section "Strategy Differences in Learning from Examples"), different kinds of reasoning during learning events (see "Learning Events"), and perhaps other factors as well.

Perhaps the most hotly debated issue in the use of computer tutors concerns the control of feedback on errors. The current technology enables students to use the computer as scratch paper. Instead of simply entering their answers to problems, as early computer tutors required, students today can enter all their work. This allows the computer to detect errors soon after they are committed. Many tutors inform the student as soon as an error is detected and prevent them from going on until the error is corrected. Although such feedback makes the tutor easier to build, one wonders what effect it has on learning. Lewis & Anderson (1985) found that immediate feedback that forced students to correct an error before moving on was superior to delayed feedback, but the effect was quite small. Anderson et al (1995) contrasted four feedback policies: (a) no feedback, (b) feedback when the student asked for it, (c) immediate feedback that notified the student as soon as an error was made but that did not force the student to correct the error, and (d) immediate feedback that forced immediate correction of the error. In conditions (b) and (c), students were forced to answer the problem correctly before being allowed to continue to the next problem. In condition (d), the feedback also insured that they answered the problem correctly. Only the no-feedback condition, (a), did not force students to correct their mistakes. On posttest measures of learning, students in the no-feedback condition did worse than students in the three feedback conditions, and no significant differences were found among the three feedback conditions. Thus, it appears that neither the timing of feedback nor its control (student vs machine) makes much difference in whether a student eventually acquires the target knowledge. However, if feedback is completely removed, then students are often unable to correct flaws in their knowledge on their own.

This result is consistent with the studies of learning events, which suggest that constructing or modifying a principle is a deliberate process that is often triggered when students find out they have made a mistake. It should not matter when students learn that they have made a mistake as long as they are able to locate the missing or incorrect knowledge and fix it.

Although control of feedback does not seem to affect the basic learning process, there are other aspects of immediate feedback that warrant consideration by the instructional designer. Lewis & Anderson (1985) found that delayed-feedback subjects were much better than immediate-feedback subjects at detecting their own errors. This makes sense, because the immediate-feedback subjects had no opportunity to detect their own errors during training. Anderson et al (1995) found that feedback that forced students to correct their errors immediately caused them to complete their training much faster than feedback that let students choose when to correct their errors. Apparently, students sometimes waste time going down garden paths when they are given the freedom to do so. If instruction is limited to a fixed amount of time, this can hurt their learning.

In the feedback studies just discussed, tutors only notified students of their errors. They did not point out why the students' actions were incorrect nor what they should have done instead. This pedagogy is called *minimal feedback*. Several studies have contrasted minimal feedback with feedback designed to be more helpful. Feedback that is designed to get students to infer the correct action increases their learning rate substantially, compared with minimal feedback (Anderson et al 1989, Mark & Greer 1995, McKendree 1990).

However, adding more help that focuses on what the student did wrong does not appear to offer any advantages (Sleeman et al 1989). That is, if the feedback is "The right thing to do here is X," then it does little good to add "You did Y instead. Y is wrong because...." This finding is consistent with studies showing that more errors are caused by missing knowledge rather than incorrect knowledge (VanLehn 1990, 1995c). Missing knowledge often results in students arriving at an impasse. Rather than seeking help, they often invent an expedient repair that allows them to continue but risks getting the problem wrong (VanLehn 1990). Moreover, they often repair the same impasse in different ways on different occasions (VanLehn 1990). Thus it comes as no surprise that students do not need much convincing to abandon the particular repair that resulted in their receiving negative feedback.

Although tutoring does provide a different context for learning, the same basic learning processes appear to occur within this context as well as in passive, example-studying instructional situations. However, because learning is based on noticing flaws (i.e. both incomplete and incorrect knowledge) and repairing them, computer tutoring can make learning substantially more efficient by helping students to detect their flaws (via feedback), rectify them (via help), and improve the generality and accessibility of their new knowledge (by practicing it until mastery is reached).

THE FINAL PHASE: PRACTICE EFFECTS

The intermediate phase is officially concluded when students can produce error-free performances. However, learning does not end at this point. Continued practice causes increases in speed and accuracy. This section reviews these phenomena.

The Power Law of Practice and Other General Effects

Perhaps the most ubiquitous finding about the third phase of learning is the famous power law of practice. The time needed to do a task decreases in proportion to the number of trials raised to some power. In an influential review, Newell & Rosenbloom (1981) found that the power law applies to simple cognitive skills as well as to perceptual motor skills. Several studies of complex cognitive skills (e.g. Anderson et al 1989, Anderson & Fincham 1994) found that the speed of applying individual components of knowledge increased according to a power law, thus indicating that practice benefits those components rather than the skill as a whole. Accuracy also increases according to a power law, at least on some tasks (Anderson & Fincham 1994, Logan 1988).

Several theories of the power law have been advanced. Anderson (1993) claimed that the speedup is due to two mechanisms: Knowledge is converted from a slow format (declarative knowledge) into a fast format (procedural knowledge), and the speed of individual pieces of procedural knowledge also increases with practice. Newell & Rosenbloom (1981) and Newell (1990) claimed that small, general pieces of knowledge are gradually composed together (chunked) to form large, specific pieces of knowledge, thus allowing the same task to be accomplished by applying fewer pieces of knowledge. Logan (1988) advanced a theory of the speedup based on instances and reviewed several other proposals.

With substantial practice, individuals' perceptual motor skills can sometimes become *automatic*. Automatic processing is fast, effortless, autonomous, and unavailable to conscious awareness (Logan 1988). One study, using a dual task paradigm, showed that different parts of a complex cognitive skill (troubleshooting digital circuits) became automatic after differing amounts of practice (Carlson et al 1990). However, the skill as a whole never became as automatic as driving one's car, despite substantial practice (347 problems) with only three circuits.

It is likely that other effects known to occur with perceptual motor skills also occur with cognitive skills (e.g. massed vs distributed practice, warm-up effects, randomized vs blocked practice). Proctor & Dutta (1995) reviewed research on many types of skill and found several general effects.

Replacing Mental Calculations by Memory Retrieval

Some cognitive skills are deterministic calculations, in which case answers to problems are completely and uniquely determined by the inputs of the problems. Mental arithmetic calculations are examples of such deterministic calculations. If subjects are given enough practice with a particular input, then they eventually just retrieve the output from memory rather than mentally calculate it. This fairly uncontentious phenomenon has been found with a number of simple mental tasks (Anderson & Fincham 1994, Healy & Bourne 1995, Logan 1988) as well as with deterministic subprocedures of complex tasks (Carlson et al 1990). Not only do subjects report this change in strategy, but they are much faster in responding to practiced inputs than unpracticed ones.

The change in strategy from calculation to retrieval could be taken as an explanation for power-law increases in speed and accuracy. However, Rickards (reported in Healy & Bourne 1995) had subjects report after each trial whether they had calculated the answer or retrieved it. Subjects' latencies in the calculation trials fit one power curve well, and latencies in the retrieval trials fit a second curve well, but the fit of a power law curve to subjects' latencies in all trials was poor. Logan (1988) also found evidence for two power curves. Thus, it appears that power-law learning mechanisms operate separately on both the mental calculation and the retrieval strategies. This hypothesis is also consistent with a study by Carlson & Lundy (1992), who found, using relatively complicated mental calculations, that subjects sped up rapidly when given the same inputs repeatedly, thus promoting use of retrieval. When the inputs varied, thus blocking the retrieval strategy, they still sped up, albeit more slowly. The two effects were additive. Thus, it appears that changing from a calculation strategy to a direct retrieval strategy is not in itself a sufficient explanation for the power law of practice.

Transfer of the Benefits of Practice

Although "transfer" has many meanings, it is used in this section to mean the savings in learning on one task (the transfer task) due to earlier training on a different task (the training task). Transfer is expressed as a ratio: the time saved in learning the transfer task divided by the time spent learning the training task. Thus, if practicing the training task for 20 hours yields an equivalent improvement on the transfer task, namely 20 hours of practice on the transfer task, then the ratio is 20/20, or 100% transfer. If practicing the training task for 20 hours only saves 5 hours of practice on the transfer task, then the ratio is 5/20, or 25%. If prior practice with the training task makes no difference in how long it takes to learn the transfer task, then there is no transfer. If practice on the training task increases the time to learn the transfer task, then there is negative transfer. Singley & Anderson (1989, chapter 1) discussed several ways to measure transfer.

One major, albeit uncontroversial, finding is that the degree of transfer can be predicted by the number of pieces of knowledge shared between the training and transfer tasks (e.g. Bovair et al 1990, Singley & Anderson 1989). As mentioned earlier, practice affects individual pieces of knowledge and not the skill as a whole. When practice on the training task speeds up certain subskills, use of such subskills continues to be fast when used in the transfer task.

However, there are sometimes limits to the amount of transfer one can obtain, even when a substantial amount of knowledge is shared between tasks. These limits occur because practice can change subjects' strategies for solving problems. Suppose that practice causes subjects to change from strategy A to strategy B on the training task, and from strategy A to strategy C on the transfer task. A little training on the training tasks will affect only strategy A, which is shared with the transfer task. Thus, T hours of practice on the training task will save T hours of practice on the transfer task. However, this only occurs when T is less than the amount of practice time that will cause subjects to shift from strategy A to B. Let us suppose this shift occurs after about 25 hours of practice. When T exceeds 25, then subsequent practice only affects strategy B, which is not shared with the transfer task. Thus, vast amounts of training will only save 25 hours of practice on the transfer task; therefore the amount of transfer is $25/T$. Thus, when T is less than 25, then transfer is T/T or 100%, but when T is greater than 25, transfer is only $25/T$, which approaches zero as practice on the training task increases. In short, the more practice on the training task, the less transfer.

One practice-induced strategy change, discussed earlier in "Replacing Mental Calculations by Memory Retrieval," occurs when subjects use direct memory retrieval instead of mental calculations. As Logan (1988) and Carlson et al (1990) have demonstrated, this is one way that practice can cause a decrease in transfer. Suppose the training task is to master a mental algorithm with one set of inputs and the transfer task is to master the same algorithm with a different set of inputs. As long as the subject continues to use the algorithm during training, the effects of that training should transfer. However, as the subject starts to use direct memory retrieval instead of executing the algorithm, increasing the time spent in training will not reduce the time to master the transfer task beyond a certain point. Thus, practice decreases the amount of transfer.

The practice-driven decrease in transfer can also be caused by weaning the subjects from the instructional material, which is another kind of strategy change. As discussed in the section "The Intermediate Phase: Learning a Single Principle," subjects in the intermediate phase of their training often refer to the instructional materials (usually the examples) as they solve problems. However, the frequency of these references declines with practice, and eventually subjects no longer refer to the instructional materials. Suppose the training and transfer tasks share some of their instructional materials (e.g. the examples). Even a little practice on the training task familiarizes subjects with the shared instructional materials and thus saves them time in learning the transfer task. However, with increasing practice on the training task, subjects gain no further benefit on the transfer task. Thus, more practice causes less transfer. This effect has been found in a variety of cognitive skills (Anderson & Fincham 1994, Singley & Anderson 1989). Anderson and his colleagues call this phenomena the *use specificity* of transfer and consider it prime evidence for the distinction between declarative and procedural knowledge.

Suppose the training task is actually a part of the transfer task, for instance, as mental addition is a part of mental multiplication. Intuitively, it seems that transfer should be high regardless of whether the training task is practiced for minutes or for days. However, this does not seem to be the case. For relatively small amounts of practice, the amount of overlap between tasks accurately predicts the amount of transfer (Bovair et al 1990, Singley & Anderson 1989). However, when the training task is practiced for hundreds of trials, only a few trials of practice on the transfer task are saved, even though the training task is arguably a part of the transfer task (Frensch & Geary 1993). Needless to say, more research is required on this important point, because whole educational systems are founded on the premise that training on basic skills facilitates learning practical skills that employ the basic skills as subprocedures. Frensch & Geary's result suggests that training basic skills past a certain point is wasteful.

In short, a great deal of practice on one task (the training task) helps subjects perform that task, but it usually only saves them moderate amounts of time in learning a second task (the transfer task). In fact, the head start that they get on learning the second task after a great deal of practice on the first task is about the same as the head start they would get if they only practiced the first task a moderate amount. The degree of transfer observed and how it varies with practice on the first task depend on exactly what is shared between the tasks and on when practice causes changes in problem-solving strategies.

Negative Transfer

Negative transfer occurs when the training task interferes with learning the transfer task and slows the learning down. For instance, mastering one text editor often seems to interfere with learning a similar text editor that has different commands.

The amount of transfer seems to be inversely proportional to the amount of practice on the transfer task. Using text editors designed to interfere with one another during learning, Singley & Anderson (1989) showed that negative transfer occurs mostly during the early stage of learning the transfer task. If learners learn the transfer task by receiving immediate feedback whenever they do something wrong (including exercising habits carried over from the training task), then they rapidly acquire the correct responses. On the other hand, uncorrected responses (e.g. ones that are merely inefficient and not incorrect) persist and can cause negative transfer even in the later stages of learning the transfer task.

As discussed in the preceding section, "Transfer of the Benefits of Practice," it is often the case that one gets the same time savings in learning the transfer task regardless of the amount of practice on the training task beyond a certain minimum. It would be interesting to determine whether this were true of negative transfer as well. That is, would moderate amounts of training delay the learning of the transfer task as much as vast amounts of training? To put it colloquially, is negative transfer the result of bad ideas, bad habits, or both?

THE FRONTIERS OF COGNITIVE SKILL ACQUISITION RESEARCH

Cognitive skill acquisition research started with simple knowledge-lean puzzle tasks, moved on to problems (such as Example 1) that can be solved with a single principle from a knowledge-rich task domain, and most recently has focused on chapter-sized slices of a knowledge-rich task domain. The next step in this progression is to study the acquisition of even larger pieces of knowledge, such as a whole semester's worth of physics or programming. Some early work along these lines has been done wherein students learned from a tutoring system (e.g. Anderson et al 1995), but these studies have examined acquisition of only the procedural aspects of the skill. The next step would be to examine how concepts, mental models, and factual knowledge evolve together with the more procedural aspects.

Research on cognitive processing during the intermediate phase of skill acquisition can be conveniently divided, as it was in this review, into research on the acquisition of a single principle and research on the acquisition of collections of principles and other knowledge. The single-principle research seems to have answered many of the initial questions concerning retrieval, mapping, and generalization. The remaining areas of uncertainty lie with application. It is likely that students use the same diverse set of methods for applying principles as they use for drawing analogies to complex written examples (VanLehn 1995a).

Learning from examples has been the focus of research on the intermediate phase of acquisition for complex, chapter-sized pieces of knowledge. However, most studies have focused only on passive forms of instruction, where the student studies written material with no help from a teacher, peer, or tutor.

The next step would be to find out how students learn from more interactive forms of instruction. For instance, when students receive feedback, it seems plausible that poor learners merely change their answer without thinking about why they got it wrong, whereas good learners try to find and repair the flaw in their knowledge that caused the error.

The final phase of skill acquisition has become a battle ground for some of the major theoretical questions of the day. The controversy between instance-based (e.g. Logan 1988), procedural-declarative (Anderson 1993), and other theories of memory has been mentioned already. The debate over implicit learning (e.g. Berry & Broadbent 1984) also bears most strongly on the final phase.

The first responsibility of researchers of cognitive skill acquisition ought to be to account for the differences between experts and novices. Surprisingly, they have not done so yet. Ericsson & Lehmann (this volume) argue that in many task domains, experts can mentally plan solutions to problems that novices can only solve concretely. For instance, Koedinger & Anderson (1990) found that expert geometers plan solutions to geometry proof problems using abstract, diagramatic schemas. Even when a proof consists of dozens of lines, the plan might have only one or two schema applications. The experts are able to do such planning in working memory. Novices, on the other hand, build proofs a line at a time, writing down conclusions as they go. The ability to rapidly plan solutions seems to develop rather quickly (Carlson et al 1990).

As Koedinger & Anderson point out, no existing model of skill acquisition, including Anderson's ACT*, can account for the acquisition of domain-specific planning skill. Existing models have concentrated on explaining the power law of practice and the increasing specificity of transfer. These models employ mechanisms that convert knowledge into ever more specific forms. In contrast, the development of planning skill calls for converting knowledge into more abstract forms. The field of Artificial Intelligence has produced many computationally sufficient mechanisms for abstraction. What our science needs is empirical work that discriminates among the many possible ways that planning could develop. For instance, are novices held back by a lack of knowledge of planning schemas, or do they know the schemas but cannot apply them mentally because of working-memory limitations?

ACKNOWLEDGMENTS

The preparation of this chapter was supported by the Cognitive Sciences Division of the Office of Naval Research under grant N00014-92-J-1945. I gratefully acknowledge the comments of Micki Chi and Patricia Albacete.

Literature Cited

Ahn W-K, Brewer WF, Mooney RJ. 1992. Schema acquisition from a single example. *J. Exp. Psychol.: Learn. Mem. Cogn.* 18(2): 391–412

Anderson JR. 1983. The Architecture of Cognition. Cambridge, MA: Harvard Univ. Press

Anderson JR. 1993. *Rules of the Mind.* Hillsdale, NJ: Erlbaum

Anderson JR, Conrad FG, Corbett AT. 1989. Skill acquisition and the LISP tutor. *Cogn. Sci.* 14(4):467–505

Anderson JR, Corbett AT, Koedinger KR, Pelletier R. 1995. Cognitive tutors: lessons learned. *J. Learn. Sci.* 4(2):167–207

Anderson JR, Fincham JM. 1994. Acquisition of procedural skills from examples. *J. Exp. Psychol.: Learn. Mem. Cogn.* 20(6): 1322–40

Bernardo ABI. 1994. Problem-specific information and the development of problem-type schemata. *J. Exp. Psychol.: Learn. Mem. Cogn.* 20(2):379–95

Berry EC, Broadbent DE. 1984. On the relationship between task performance and associated verbalizable knowledge. *Q. J. Exp. Psychol.* 36A:209–31

Bielaczyc K, Pirolli P, Brown AL. 1994. Training in self-explanation and self-regulation strategies: investigating the effects of knowledge acquisition activities on problem-solving. *Cogn. Instr.* In press

Bielaczyc K, Recker M. 1991. Learning to learn: the implications of strategy instruction in computer programming. In *The International Conference on the Learning Sciences,* ed. L Birnbaum, pp. 39–44. Charlottesville, VA: Assoc. Adv. Comp. Educ.

Bovair S, Kieras DE, Polson PG. 1990. The acquisition and performance of text-editing skill: a cognitive complexity analysis. *Hum.-Comput. Interact.* 5:1–48

Bransford JD, Franks JJ, Vye NJ, Sherwood RD. 1989. New approaches to instruction: because wisdom can't be told. In *Similarity and Analogical Reasoning,* ed. S Vosniadou, A Ortony, pp. 470–97. New York: Cambridge Univ. Press

Brown AL, Kane M. 1988. Preschool children can learn to transfer: learning to learn and learning from example. *Cogn. Psychol.* 20: 493–523

Carlson RA, Khoo BH, Yaure RG, Schneider W. 1990. Acquisition of a problem-solving skill: levels of organization and use of working memory. *J. Exp. Psychol.: Gen.* 110(2):193–214

Carlson RA, Lundy D. 1992. Consistency and restructuring in learning cognitive procedural sequences. *J. Exp. Psychol.: Learn. Mem. Cogn.* 19(1):127–41

Carroll WM. 1994. Using worked examples as an instructional support in the algebra classroom. *J. Educ. Psychol.* 86(3): 360–67

Catrambone R. 1994a. The effects of labels in examples on problem solving transfer. In *Proceedings of the Sixteenth Annual Conference of the Cognitive Science Society,* ed. A Ram, K Eiselt, pp. 159–64. Hillsdale, NJ: Erlbaum

Catrambone R. 1994b. Improving examples to improve transfer to novel problems. *Mem. Cogn.* 22(5):606–15

Catrambone R, Holyoak KJ. 1987. Transfer in problem solving as a function of the procedural variety of training examples. In *Proceedings of the Ninth Annual Conference of the Cognitive Science Society,* ed. E Hunt, pp. 36–49. Hillsdale, NJ: Erlbaum

Catrambone R, Holyoak KJ. 1989. Overcoming contextual limitations on problem-solving transfer. *J. Exp. Psychol.: Learn. Mem. Cogn.* 13(6):1147–56

Catrambone R, Holyoak KJ. 1990. Learning subgoals and methods for solving probability problems. *Mem. Cogn.* 18(5): 593–603

Chi MTH, Bassok M, Lewis M, Reimann P, Glaser R. 1989. Self-explanations: how students study and use examples in learning to solve problems. *Cogn. Sci.* 15: 145–82

Chi MTH, de Leeuw N, Chiu M-H, LaVancher C. 1994. Eliciting self-explanations improves understanding. *Cogn. Sci.* 18: 439–77

Chi MTH, VanLehn K. 1991. The content of physics self-explanations. *J. Learn. Sci.* 1: 69–105

Cooper G, Sweller J. 1987. Effects of schema acquisition and rule automation on mathematical problem-solving transfer. *J. Educ. Psychol.* 79(4):347–62

Corbett AT, Anderson JR, O'Brien AT. 1995. Student modeling in the ACT programming tutor. In *Cognitively Diagnostic Assessment,* ed. PD Nichols, SF Chipman, RL Brennan, pp. 19–42. Hillsdale, NJ: Erlbaum

Cummins DD. 1992. Role of analogical reasoning in the induction of problem categories. *J. Exp. Psychol.: Learn. Mem. Cogn.* 18(5):1103–24

Duncan CP. 1959. Recent research on human problem solving. *Psychol. Bull.* 56(6): 397–429

Ericsson KA, Lehmann AC. 1996. Expert and exceptional performance: evidence of maximal adaptation to task constraints. *Annu. Rev. Psychol.* 47:513–39

Faries J, Reiser B. 1988. Access and use of previous solutions in a problem solving situation. In *Proceedings of the Tenth Annual Conference of the Cognitive Science Society,* ed. V Patel, G Groen, pp. 433–39. Hillsdale, NJ: Erlbaum

Ferguson-Hessler M, de Jong T. 1990. Studying physics texts: differences in study processes between good and poor solvers. *Cogn. Instr.* 7:41–54

Fitts PM. 1964. Perceptual-motor skill learning. In *Categories of Human Learning,* ed. AW Melton, pp. 243–85. New York: Academic

Frensch P, Geary DC. 1993. Effects of practice on component processes in complex mental addition. *J. Exp. Psychol.: Learn. Mem. Cogn.* 19(2):433–56

Gick M, Holyoak KJ 1980. Analogical problem solving. *Cogn. Psychol.* 12:306–55

Gick M, Holyoak KJ. 1983. Schema induction and analogical transfer. *Cogn. Psychol.* 15: 1–38

Glaser R, Bassok M. 1989. Learning theory and the study of instruction. *Annu. Rev. Psychol.* 40:631–36

Healy AF, Bourne LE. 1995. *Learning and Memory of Knowledge and Skills: Durability and Specificity.* Thousand Oaks, CA: Sage

Holyoak KJ, Koh K. 1987. Surface and structural similarity in analogical transfer. *Mem. Cogn.* 15(4):332–40

Jones RM, VanLehn K. 1994. Acquisition of children's addition strategies: a model of impasse-free, knowledge-level learning. *Mach. Learn.* 16(1–2):11–36

Kahney H. 1993. *Problem Solving: Current Issues.* Buckingham: Open Univ. Press. 2nd ed.

Karmiloff-Smith A, Inhelder B. 1975. If you want to get ahead, get a theory. *Cognition* 3(1):195–212

Koedinger K, Anderson JR. 1990. Abstract planning and perceptual chunks: elements of expertise in geometry. *Cogn. Sci.* 14: 511–50

Kuhn D, Phelps E. 1982. The development of problem-solving strategies. *Adv. Child Dev. Behav.* 17:1–44

Lefevre J, Dixon P. 1986. Do written instructions need examples? *Cogn. Instr.* 3:1–30

Lewis C. 1988. Why and how to learn why: analysis-based generalization of procedures. *Cogn. Sci.* 12(2):211–56

Lewis MW, Anderson JR. 1985. Discrimination of operator schemata in problem solving: learning from examples. *Cogn. Psychol.* 17:26–65

Logan GD. 1988. Toward an instance theory of automatization. *Psychol. Rev.* 95(4): 492–527

Lovett MC. 1992. Learning by problem solving versus by examples: the benefits of generating and receiving information. In *Proceedings of the Fourteenth Annual Conference of the Cognitive Science Society,* ed. JK Kruschke, pp. 956–61. Hillsdale, NJ: Erlbaum

Mark MA, Greer JE. 1995. The VCR tutor: effective instruction for device operation. *J. Learn. Sci.* 4(2):209–46

McKendree J. 1990. Effective feedback content for tutoring complex skills. *Hum.-Comput. Interact.* 5:381–413

Newell A. 1990. *Unified Theories of Cognition.* Cambridge, MA: Harvard Univ. Press

Newell A, Rosenbloom P. 1981. Mechanisms of skill acquisition and the law of practice. In *Cognitive Skills and Their Acquisition,* ed. JR Anderson, pp. 1–56. Hillsdale, NJ: Erlbaum

Newell A, Simon HA, eds. 1972. *Human Problem Solving.* Englewood Cliffs, NJ: Prentrice-Hall

Norman DA. 1981. Categorization of action slips. *Psychol. Rev.* 88(1):1–15

Novick LR. 1988. Analogical transfer, problem similarity and expertise. *J. Exp. Psychol.: Learn. Mem. Cogn.* 14:510–20

Novick LR, Holyoak KJ. 1991. Mathematical problem solving by analogy. *J. Exp. Psychol.: Learn. Mem. Cogn.* 17(3):398–415

Pirolli P. 1991. Effects of examples and their explanations in a lesson on recursion: a production system analysis. *Cogn. Instr.* 8(3):207–60

Pirolli P, Anderson JR. 1985. The role of learning from examples in the acquisition of recursive programming skills. *Can. J. Psychol.* 39:240–72

Pirolli P, Bielaczyc K. 1989. Empirical analyses of self-explanation and transfer in learning to program. In *Proceedings of the Eleventh Annual Conference of the Cognitive Science Society,* ed. GM Olson, EE Smith, pp. 450–57. Hillsdale, NJ: Erlbaum

Pirolli P, Recker M. 1994. Learning strategies and transfer in the domain of programming. *Cogn. Instr.* 12(3):235–75

Pressley M, Wood E, Woloshyn V, Martin V, King A, Menke D. 1992. Encouraging mindful use of prior knowledge: attempting to construct explanatory answers facilitates learning. *Educ. Psychol.* 27:91–109

Proctor RW, Dutta A. 1995. *Skill Acquisition and Human Performance.* Thousand Oaks, CA: Sage

Psotka J, Massey LD, Mutter SA. 1988. *Intelligent Tutoring Systems: Lessons Learned.* Hillsdale, NJ: Erlbaum

Recker M, Pirolli P. 1995. Modeling individual differences in students' learning strategies. *J. Learn. Sci.* 4(1):1–38

Reed SK, Dempster A, Ettinger M. 1985. Usefulness of analogous solutions for solving algebra word problems. *J. Exp. Psychol.: Learn. Mem. Cogn.* 11:106–25

Reed SK, Willis D, Guarino J. 1994. Selecting examples for solving word problems. *J. Educ. Psychol.* 86(3):380–88

Ross B. 1984. Remindings and their effects in learning a cognitive skill. *Cogn. Psychol.* 16:371–416

Ross B. 1987. This is like that: the use of earlier problems and the separation of similarity effects. *J. Exp. Psychol.: Learn. Mem. Cogn.* 13:629–39

Ross B. 1989. Distinguishing types of superficial similarities: different effects on the access and use of earlier problems. *J. Exp. Psychol.: Learn. Mem. Cogn.* 15(3): 456–68

Ross B, Kennedy P. 1990. Generalizing from the use of earlier examples in problem solving. *J. Exp. Psychol.: Learn. Mem. Cogn.* 16(1):42–55

Siegler RS, Jenkins E. 1989. *How Children Discover New Strategies.* Hillsdale, NJ: Erlbaum

Singley M, Anderson JR. 1989. *The Transfer of Cognitive Skill.* Cambridge, MA: Harvard Univ. Press

Sleeman D, Kelley AE, Martinak R, Ward RD, Moore JL. 1989. Studies of diagnosis and remediation with high school algebra students. *Cogn. Sci.* 13:551–68

Sweller J, Cooper G. 1985. The use of worked examples as a substitute for problem solving in learning algebra. *Cogn. Instr.* 2: 59–89

VanLehn K. 1989. Problem solving and cognitive skill acquisition. In *Foundations of Cognitive Science,* ed. M Posner, pp.

526–79. Cambridge, MA: MIT Press

VanLehn K. 1990. *Mind Bugs: The Origins of Procedural Misconceptions.* Cambridge, MA: MIT Press

VanLehn K. 1991. Rule acquisition events in the discovery of problem solving strategies. *Cogn. Sci.* 15(1):1–47

VanLehn K. 1995a. Analogy events: how examples are used during problem solving. *Tech. Rep. LRDC-ONR-92-1.* Univ. Pittsburgh, Pittsburgh, PA

VanLehn K. 1995b. Looking in the book: the effects of example-exercise analogy on learning. *Tech. Rep. LRDC-ONR-92-2.* Univ. Pittsburgh, Pittsburgh, PA

VanLehn K. 1995c. Rule learning events in the acquisition of a complex skill. *Tech. Rep. LRDC-ONR-92-3.* Univ. Pittsburgh, Pittsburgh, PA

VanLehn K, Jones RM. 1993. Learning by explaining examples to oneself: a computational model. In *Cognitive Models of Complex Learning,* ed. SF Chipman, A Meyrowitz, pp. 25–82. Boston, MA: Kluwer

VanLehn K, Jones RM. 1995. Is the self-explanation effect caused by learning rules, schemas or examples? *Tech. Rep. LRDC-ONR-92-4.* Univ. Pittsburgh, Pittsburgh, PA

VanLehn K, Jones RM, Chi MTH. 1992. A model of the self-explanation effect. *J. Learn. Sci.* 2(1):1–59

Voss JF, Wiley J, Carretero M. 1995. Acquiring intellectual skills. *Annu. Rev. Psychol.* 46:155–81

Zhu X, Simon HA. 1987. Learning mathematics from examples and by doing. *Cogn. Instr.* 4(3):137–66

Annu. Rev. Psychol. 1996. 47:541–61

ATTACHMENT AND SEPARATION IN YOUNG CHILDREN

Tiffany Field

Touch Research Institute, University of Miami School of Medicine, P.O. Box 016820, Miami, Florida 33101

KEY WORDS: psychobiological attunement, stress and coping

ABSTRACT

Attachment theory is criticized for being based on momentary stressful situations, for being limited to behaviors that occur with the primary attachment figure, for including only overt behaviors in its paradigm, and for failing to consider multiple attachments at different stages of life. A model of psychological attunement is then presented and supported by several studies documenting behavioral, physiological, and biochemical responses to separations from parents and peers.

CONTENTS

INTRODUCTION

Attachment and separation have traditionally been studied in the context of mother-infant and mother-child dyads. However, more recent research sug-

0066-4308/96/0201-0541$08.00

gests the existence of bonds similar to those in mother-infant and mother-child dyads, between peers and between individuals of different ages both in humans (Field 1985) and in nonhuman primates (Reite & Capitanio 1984). Thus, attachment is increasingly considered a life-span phenomenon (Antonucci 1976, Field 1985). The physiological responses accompanying the major attachment behaviors—smiling and crying—are, in fact, independent of parenthood, age, and sex (Frodi 1985). Attachment is also considered a near-universal process. In this regard, Petrovich & Gewirtz (1985) have raised two important questions. What is the evolutionary explanation for the remarkable behavioral similarity among phylogenetically related or distantly related organisms? Why are there important behavior differences between phylogenetically related species? As an example of the latter question, they discuss the work of Cullen (1957) showing that certain cliff-nesting gulls, kittiwakes, do not learn to identify their offspring because their offspring must remain in the nest to survive. In contrast, ground-nesting gulls closely related to kittiwakes must learn to recognize their offspring because their offspring wander from the nest.

An example of cultural variation in human attachment behavior is provided by Tronick et al (1985). Although the Westernized version of attachment involves a single caregiver and its offspring, multiple caregiver attachments occur in other cultures, such as that of the Efe pygmies of Zaire. The mother is not the first to hold the newborn. Instead, the newborn is passed among several other women. Further, although the infant is constantly held and fed on demand, it is often fed by other lactating women. As a result, the infants were noted to develop multiple attachments. Tronick et al interpreted these multiple attachments as adaptive for the infant's growth and group participation. The growth advantage for the small Efe newborn is that multiple nursing mothers can provide mature milk, which is richer than the colostrum of the infant's biological mother. In this way fluid balance is maintained and growth is accelerated.

Cultural and ecological variation might explain much of the variance in attachment behavior, although individual differences have also been noted within the same cultural and ecological niches. These differences may have their origins in genetic, prenatal, or early environment variations.

Individual Differences

Bowlby's (1969) seminal model of attachment was a normative one that did not deal with individual differences in attachment behavior, although Bowlby (1978) subsequently extended his model to include this variable. Mary Ainsworth (1967) facilitated the study of individual differences by devising what has been labeled the strange situation paradigm and a system for classifying individual differences in infants' responses to reunions with their mothers following brief separations. Differences in infants' responses were documented, and these were then related to behaviors of the mothers such as their sensitivity and responsiveness to infant signals during their earlier interactions. The paradigms for studying attachments in human infants (Ainsworth) and also in infant monkeys (the Harlows and their students) inspired dozens of studies. Most of these early studies were limited to the description of overt behavior.

More recently, studies enabled by improved monitoring devices have investigated subtle individual differences in biological mechanisms.

The Bowlby-Ainsworth Model of Attachment

Bowlby (1969) described the behaviors of infants and young children who were in residential nurseries and hospital wards and therefore separated from their mothers. The children who had experienced a secure relationship with their mothers showed a predictable behavior sequence during their separations. The sequence has three phases which Bowlby called protest, despair, and detachment. The initial phase (protest) began almost immediately and lasted a few hours to a week or more. Children in this phase appeared distressed, crying loudly, throwing themselves about, and looked eagerly toward any sight or sound that could be their missing mother. Some children clung to a nurse as a substitute. During the despair phase, the children showed increasing helplessness. They were withdrawn, physically active, and cried only intermittently. This was a quiet state and sometimes was mistaken for recovery. The phase of detachment was often welcomed because the children showed more interest in their surroundings, often smiled, and were sociable. When the children's mothers visited, however, they remained remote and apathetic.

Ainsworth (1967) and her colleagues studied attachment behavior experimentally during a series of brief laboratory sequences labeled the "strange situation" and, as stated above, attended to differences in the infants' behaviors. This situation starts with the mother and infant together in a strange room with toys and proceeds through a series of different experiences, each lasting about three minutes. First, a female stranger joins the mother and infant. Then, the mother leaves the infant with the stranger. Then the mother returns. Next, the mother leaves the infant alone, and after a brief interval the stranger returns. Finally, the mother returns. The infants are given an attachment classification on the basis of their avoidant, enthusiastic, or variable responses to the mother's return.

Although the data reviewed by Bowlby (1969) and the strange situation studies by Ainsworth and her colleagues convincingly demonstrate a special attachment to the mother on the part of the infant, at least in the North American cultures, the model of attachment derived from these data has some limitations. First, in this model attachment is based on behaviors that occur during momentary separations (stressful situations) rather than during nonstressful situations. A broader understanding of attachment requires observation of how the mother and infant interact and what they provide for each other during natural, nonstressful situations. The strange situation paradigm may simply be tapping individual differences in the children's coping with momentary stress. What children do as the mother leaves and how they greet her when she returns may provide less insight into the functional significance of attachment than the way mother and child relate to each other when they are together and not stressed. An illustration of the problem with using the child's response to separation from and return of the mother is that among children who are attached to their mothers as evidenced, for example, by their harmonious interactions together, some seem to have difficulty making transitions. These children cling to their mothers when they are dropped off at nursery school, and they ignore their mothers when they are picked up after school (Field et al 1984a). Both the clinging and the ignoring behaviors result in a classification of these children as having an attachment disorder. In addition, most young children following a more prolonged separation (three days instead of three minutes) reject their mothers rather than greet them and seek physical contact (Field & Reite 1984). This behavioral pattern implies either that most children have attachment disorders or that valid classification can only be made following a very unnatural, ecologically strange three-minute situation.

A second problem with the model is that, as in a circular process, attachment has been defined on the basis of those behaviors directed to the person referred to as the attachment figure during an impending separation (such behaviors as crying and clinging) and following reunion (proximity-seeking and greeting behaviors).

A third problem is that the list of attachment behaviors is limited to those that occur with the primary attachment figure, typically the mother. However, other attachments are not necessarily characterized by those same behaviors. For example, infants do not necessarily cling to peers or siblings, follow them, or cry during an impending departure, nor do they typically run to and cling to them as they return, yet infants are unquestionably attached to peers and siblings such that they lose sleep and become fussy when they are separated from their peers (Field et al 1984b).

A fourth limitation of the attachment model is that the behavior list only includes overt behaviors. Data reviewed below in this chapter show that physiological changes also accompany separations and reunions and may suggest alternative explanations for the attachment/separation phenomena.

A fifth consideration is that in the models and the data presented by Bowlby and Ainsworth, the mother is viewed as the primary attachment figure. Although both authors acknowledge that other attachments may occur, the mother is treated as the primary attachment object, and the father and other members of the family are considered only secondary attachment figures.

However, multiple, simultaneous attachments may occur between the child and the mother, father, and siblings that may also be considered primary attachments, particularly in families where fathers and siblings share in the caregiving. As in infancy, multiple attachments may occur simultaneously throughout adulthood; for example, to a spouse and friend, as well as to one's children. That raises a sixth problem: In the model, attachment is confined to the infancy and early childhood period, ending, as noted by Bowlby, during puberty. It does not consider attachments that occur during adolescence (the first love), during adulthood (spouses and lovers), and during later life (the strong attachments noted between friends in retirement). Some may claim that the recently designed Adult Attachment Interview acknowledges adult attachment. However, it is not focused on adult attachments to other adults. Rather, it is a memory-based instrument used to assess adults' attachments to their parents during childhood.

A parsimonious model of attachment would need to accommodate *multiple attachments* to a *variety of figures* at *different stages of life*. We have used a more psychobiological approach in formulating a model that focuses on the relationship between two individuals and what they share and what might then be missing when they are separated. In this model (Field 1985), attachment is viewed as a relationship that develops between two or more organisms as they become attuned to each other, each providing the other meaningful stimulation and arousal modulation. The loss of this important source of stimulation and arousal modulation, which occurs in separation, invariably results in behavioral and physiological disorganization. Both this model and the Bowlby-Ainsworth model will be considered throughout as I review the data on attachment and separation.

PHYSIOLOGICAL DATA ON SEPARATION

Physiological data recorded during the separations of young primates and children from their mothers confirm the biphasic response to separation noted by Bowlby (1969) as protest and despair, which is a period of agitation, followed by a period of depression. The primate data are based on mother-infant pigtail and bonnet monkey separations monitored by surgically implanted telemetry (Laudenslager et al 1982, Reite & Capitanio 1984, Reite et al 1981b, Reite & Snyder 1982). Generally, in these studies behavioral agitation was followed by depression during the separation period. Shortly after the separation, the infants exhibited agitation characterized by increased motor activity and frequent distress vocalizations. Depressed behaviors typically emerged shortly thereafter and persisted throughout the separation period. The infants moved more slowly than normal, and their play behavior was diminished. Sleep disturbances were characterized by decreased rapid eye movement

(REM) sleep as well as by increased arousals and time spent awake. The agitated behavior that occurred immediately after separation was accompanied by increased heart rate and body temperature followed by decreases in these values to below baseline (Reite et al 1978).

In addition to behavioral and physiological disorganization, altered cellular immune responses were noted in the separated pigtail monkeys by Reite et al (1981a) and in the squirrel monkeys by Coe et al (1985). For example, during the separation of two pigtail monkeys who had been reared together, an altered cellular immune response occurred (Reite et al 1981a). At five weeks following reunion, the cellular immune response of both monkeys was still slightly depressed. Pigtail infants separated from their mothers also experienced persistent separation effects. For example, although heart rate tended to return to baseline and arrhythmias tended to disappear following the infants' reunion with their mothers, the altered cardiac activity persisted for some infant monkeys (Seiler et al 1979). In another study, persistent decreases in infant heart rate and body temperature were noted following reunion with the mother (Reite & Snyder 1982). Thus, the effects of these separations often persisted even after reunion with an attachment figure such as the mother or a peer. Similar data have been reported for hospitalized preschool children who were receiving chemotherapy for childhood cancer (Hollenbeck et al 1980). The disorganizing effects of separation generally paralleled those reported for primates. Behaviorally, the children first showed agitation and then depression, as manifested by their play behavior, behaviors that were paralleled by changes in body temperature and heart rate.

Stress and Coping with Separation

SEPARATION IN INFANTS AND CHILDREN   In a study of preschool children's responses to separation from the mother during the birth of another child (Field & Reite 1984), agitated behavior and physiology during the period of the mother's hospitalization were observed. Depression then followed in the children after the mother's return from the hospital. In the Field & Reite study, play sessions were videotaped, night-time sleep was time-lapse videotaped, and the parents were administered questionnaires on changes in their child's behaviors. Increases in negative affect, activity level, heart rate, night wakings, and crying characterized the period of the mother's hospitalization as one of agitation for the children (see Figures 1 and 2). Longer periods of deep sleep at this stage were interpreted as conservation-withdrawal (as if withdrawing from stimulation to conserve energy) (see Figure 2). Following the mother's return, decreases were observed in positive affect, activity level, heart rate, and active sleep, suggestive of depression (see Figures 1–3). Changes reported by the parents included greater clinging and aggressive behaviors, eating and toileting prob-

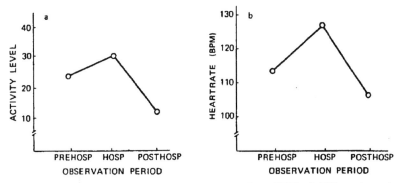

Figure 1 Mean activity level and heart rate in beats per minute (BPM) of children prior to their mother's hospitalization (PREHOSP), during hospitalization (HOSP), and following her return from the hospital (POSTHOSP) (from Field & Reite 1984).

lems, and disturbed sleep and illnesses that persisted following the mother's return from the hospital (Figure 4). Examples of the child's disturbance were revealed in parents' comments that the child "wanted to be rocked and held," "reverted to baby talk, whining, and screaming for attention," and "threatened to run a truck across the baby's head." Elevated tonic heart rate in the children during the mother's hospitalization and depressed heart rate following her return may have been mediated by the activity level changes, as in somatic coupling of activity and heart rate (Obrist 1981). These elevated levels have in turn been attributed to sympathetic adrenergic activation (Breese et al 1973). More prolonged periods of deep sleep during this phase may be the result of conservation-withdrawal noted to follow stress in infants and young children (Emde et al 1971, Engel & Schmale 1972).

Decreased activity, depressed heart rate, and shorter periods of active sleep, together with flat affect following the mother's return may suggest depression. Depressed children have less active sleep (Kupfer et al 1979), and depression can be alleviated by depriving subjects of REM sleep (Vogel 1979). The decrease in active sleep may be a homeostatic coping mechanism.

Depressed activity and heart rate are commonly reported when individuals are in situations in which they are helpless, such as an avoidance task in which human subjects have no control, situations in which adrenergic influences are minimal (Obrist et al 1978). Bradycardia, associated with situations of helplessness, has also been attributed to parasympathetic activation or vagal tone (McCabe & Schneiderman 1983). The arrival of a new sibling; a less active, tired mother; and changes in children's play interactions with their mother may have been viewed by the children in the Field & Reite (1984) study as situations over which they had very little control. The depressed behavior may

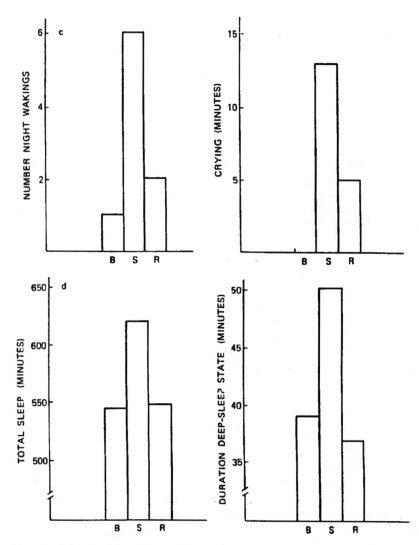

Figure 2 Children's night wakings, crying, total sleep time, and duration of deep-sleep stages during recordings for baseline (B), separation period (S), and following reunion (R).

have been exacerbated in these children by the arrival of the new sibling and an altered relationship with the mother.

Heightened levels of arousal may stimulate the sympathetic adrenergic system, resulting in agitated behavior. This behavior is typically associated with active coping, in this case with attempting to recall the mother. Agitation during separation may occur because of heightened arousal in the absence of

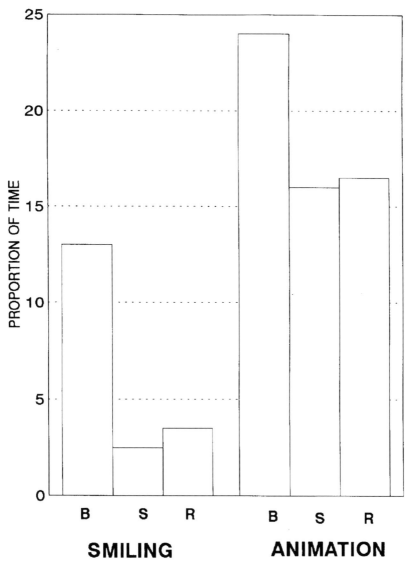

Figure 3 Proportion of mother-child play time in which smiling and animation were observed in the child during videorecordings for baseline (B), separation period (S), and following reunion (R).

the child's principal arousal modulator, the mother. Depression may emerge as the separation continues because of the child's failure to bring the mother back and of a lack of stimulation ordinarily provided by the mother. The depression may be an adaptive homeostatic mechanism offsetting the effects of sympa-

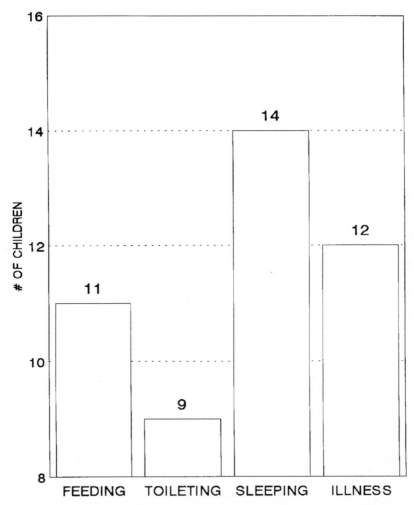

Figure 4   Number of children who experienced feeding, toileting and sleeping changes, and illness during the separation-reunion period.

thetic arousal, or it may result from inadequate amounts of stimulation and limited beta-adrenergic activity. Confounds in the Field & Reite (1984) study on separation effects were the changed relationship between the mother and first-born because of the arrival of the new sibling, the exhaustion of the mother, and very frequently the postpartum depression of the mothers themselves. These confounds, coupled with the concern generated by data showing that repeated separations had cumulative effects on monkey infants, led us to perform a study looking at repeated separations of children from mothers going on conference trips (Field 1991). Although the preschool children in the study showed similar separation behavior as when the mothers went to the hospital, they did not continue to show depression-related behavior after their mothers returned. In addition, the first trip had the worst effect, and the effects were not cumulative. Perhaps it is not surprising that because of their cognitive coping skills, the children were able to adapt to that stress.

PEER SEPARATIONS   A surprising finding for many attachment researchers is that early peer separations also are distressing for young children. A peer separation that occurs naturally and with some frequency results from the transfer of children to new schools. In a recent study, Field (1984) observed preschool children who had been together for three to four years and who were transferring to new schools. The observations were made during a two-week period prior to the separation from their classmates (Field 1984). The children who were leaving the school, as opposed to those who were staying, showed increases (compared with baseline observations three months earlier) in fantasy play, physical contact, negative statements and affect, fussiness, activity level, tonic heart rate, and illness, as well as changes in eating and sleeping patterns (see Figures 5–8). In addition to the changes in play behavior and in vegetative functions, the children's drawings of themselves manifested agitation and disorganization. The drawings included distorted facial and body parts and sad faces (see Figure 8).

The anticipatory reactions to separation by these children appeared to mimic the immediate responses to peer separations by young monkeys (Reite et al 1981b). They were also very similar to the behaviors noted in young children immediately following the hospitalization of their mothers for the birth of another child (Field & Reite 1984). In these studies, the increase in fussiness, negative affect, aggressive behavior, physical activity level, and tonic heart rate are suggestive of agitation. Although changes in eating patterns were variable, with some children eating more and others eating less, sleep disturbances uniformly involved more frequent night wakings, crying, and delayed onset of sleep. Increased illness during the children's separations is consistent with reports of changes in the immune system of young primates during mother and peer separations (Reite et al 1981a, Reite & Snyder 1982).

Separation stress occurs when peers even as young as 15 months are separated (Field et al 1984b). In the Field et al study, 15-month-old infants were transferred, following 14 months in an infant nursery, to a toddler nursery, and 24-month-old infants were graduated from a toddler nursery to a preschool nursery. Many of the same behavior changes occurred during the week immediately preceding the transfer and the week following the transfer. These included increased inactivity, negative affect, fussiness, and changes in eating and sleep behaviors. Nap-time sleep became more irregular with longer laten-

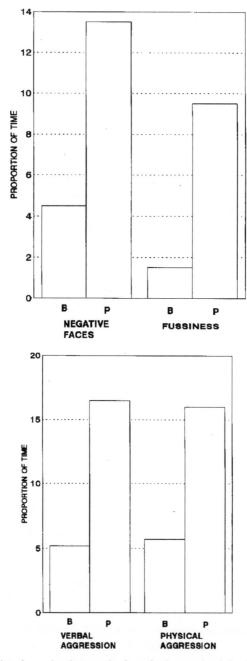

Figure 5   Proportion of peer-play-time negative faces, fussiness, and verbal and physical aggression occurring during the baseline (B) and preseparation (P) observation periods.

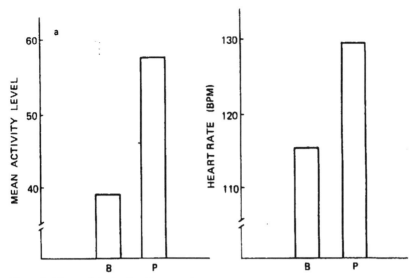

Figure 6 Mean activity level and heart rate in beats per minute (BPM) of children during peer play for the baseline (B) and preseparation (P) observation periods.

cies to sleep and more frequent arousals during nap time. In addition, erratic feeding patterns were noted as well as more frequent illness. A comparison between those infants and toddlers who were transferred to the new nurseries without close friends and those who were transferred with close friends suggested that transferring with close friends may buffer the stressful effects of the separation. Thus, the data from this group of studies are a poignant demonstration of the disorganizing effects of mother and peer separations on both the behavior and physiology of young monkeys and children.

Biological Markers and Mechanisms in Animal Models

Panksepp et al (1985) have advanced a model for attachment based upon opiate systems and derived from data on very diverse species including chicks, guinea pigs, and dogs. Because the social-separation state was similar to opioid withdrawal in their studies, opiate receptor agonists were expected to reduce separation distress. The opioid agonists Panksepp et al tested did alleviate separation distress, and when they blocked opioid receptors by naloxone, separation distress increased. They then evaluated the specificity of the opioid effects using a variety of agonists and antagonists for cholinergic, noradrenergic, dopaminergic, and serotonergic receptor systems. Only clonidine (which alleviates opiate withdrawal symptoms in humans) approached the level of efficacy of opioids.

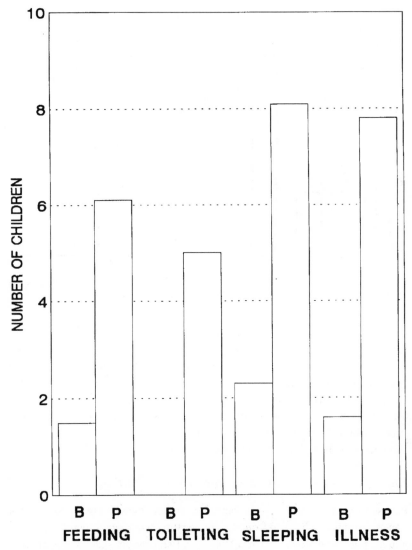

Figure 7 Number of children who experienced feeding, toileting, sleeping, and illness problems during the baseline (B) and preseparation (P) observation periods.

In another model, Kraemer (1985) postulated that early social deprivation may exert its effects through deprivation-induced (or denervation-induced) supersensitivity, possibly of noradrenergic systems. Isolated rodents, for example, become hyperactive when placed in a novel environment. This hyperactivity can be prevented by antidepressant agents. Kraemer stated that "the

Figure 8 Examples of self-drawings made prior to the departure of children attending new schools.

behavioral effects of antidepressant agents in previously isolated subjects may be due to their ability to reduce isolation-induced supersensitivity of cortical systems with noradrenergic inputs" (p. 152).

Coe et al (1985) have presented a separation model in which they argue that an acute response to separation may be adaptive, but data on sustained separations suggest that prolonged cortisol elevations can adversely affect the immune system (at least in squirrel monkeys). Sustained elevations of cortisol and the absence of behavioral symptoms may be a manifestation of depression not unlike the sustained elevations of cortisol frequently noted in depression.

Applications to the Human Infant

In Bowlby's (1969) descriptions, protest was typically followed by despair during the child's separation from its mother. The data reviewed in this chapter on the separations of young primates and young children confirm a biphasic response to separation with an agitated period typically followed by a period of depression. In the studies by Reite and his colleagues on infant monkeys, infants exhibited an agitation reaction that included increased motor activity, frequent distress vocalizations, and elevated heart rate and body temperature immediately after the separation. This agitation reaction was typically followed by depressed behavior and decreases to below baseline in both heart rate and body temperature. Similarly, in the Field & Reite (1984) study on children's separations from their mothers during hospitalization for the birth of another child, agitated behavior occurred immediately following the separation, with increases in negative affect, activity level, heart rate, night wakings, and crying. Following the mother's return, decreases were noted in these measures, suggestive of depression.

Moves to new places were the only separation situations that did not result in a biphasic process of agitation followed by depression. For example, less depression was noted in separated monkeys moved away from their social group to an isolation cage (Reite 1983), and infants, toddlers, and preschoolers apparently did not experience depression when they were moved to a new classroom (Field et al 1984b) or a new school (Field 1984). In the study on infant monkeys, only approximately 15% of the infants became depressed when they were separated from both their mothers and their social group and placed in isolation, while as many as 80% of the monkeys became depressed if they remained in their social group without their mother (Reite 1983). Reite speculated that the pigtail infants who were separated from both their mother and peers and placed in isolation did not show behavioral and physiological depression perhaps because isolation is a fearful experience. Fear may counteract the expected decrease in beta-adrenergic activity typically associated with depression.

Remaining after separation in an environment that reminds the infant of its mother may be more distressing for the infant than moving to a different environment. The children who were leaving their peers for a new school (Field 1984) did not appear to experience the biphasic process of agitation followed by depression. The anxiety related to attending a new school and making new friends may have offset any expected depression. The stress of joining a new group may have compounded the separation stress, thus sustaining the agitated behavior and physiology. New stresses may present active coping opportunities for the departing children, while the remaining children may feel "stuck" in a passive coping or helpless situation of continually being reminded of their missing peers by those environmental features associated with them.

Coe & Levine (1983) have suggested that the absence or unpredictability of reinforcement under conditions where reinforcement has been continuously present will lead to a stress response. Similar to several other researchers, he has designated control or the ability to make a coping response as the primary mechanism in dealing with stress and the lack of control associated with helplessness (Seligman 1975, Weiss 1971a,b).

These propositions suggest that separation may be stressful to the infant and young child because of the loss of a major source of reinforcement; reinforcement is typically provided by the mother in the form of adequate stimulation and arousal modulation. Loss of control, feedback, and predictability, which are clearly important features of their interaction (Field 1978), could also occur during separation. An active coping response of the infant in the separation situation might be either to seek stimulation and reinforcement from other members of the group (as a substitute for mother) or to temporarily withdraw from interactions with the group and become inactive.

We have argued elsewhere (Field 1985) that separation distress occurs primarily because the infant has lost its primary source of stimulation and arousal modulation. Aunts in the case of infant monkeys and fathers in the case of human children may serve as substitute caregivers. However, they may not be as effective as the mother in providing stimulation and arousal modulation because they are typically not as familiar with the child's individual needs for stimulation and arousal modulation. Thus, a monkey or human infant, already highly agitated because of the absence of the mother, may become even more agitated during any attempts made by substitute caregivers to provide stimulation and arousal modulation. In this case, the most adaptive response for the infant may be to withdraw and remain inactive in order to avoid the stimulation of others or the stimulation of its own activity. Depressed activity or conservation-withdrawal may continue at least until physiological equilibrium is restored or until conspecifics have become familiar with the individual's unique stimulation and arousal modulation needs. In this model, temporary depression and inactivity may be seen as adaptive behavior for warding off the highly stimulating behavior of other members of the group at a time when the infant is vulnerable to heightened arousal levels due to the absence of its primary arousal modulator, the mother.

Depression also serves as a period of physiological recuperation from the previous agitation phase. Depression, helplessness, and passive coping, however, are often considered unhealthy experiences that may contribute to disease and death. This may especially be the case when depression is experienced for prolonged periods. However, in the short term depression, helplessness, and passive coping may be the only immediately effective coping mechanisms available to the young organism separated from an attachment figure. Temporary depression or conservation-withdrawal may serve as effective coping mechanisms until physiological equilibrium is restored and the mother returns, or an effective substitute attachment figure becomes available.

PSYCHOBIOLOGICAL ATTUNEMENT: AN ALTERNATIVE ATTACHMENT MODEL

Research on attachment has been conducted in the separation context, and the proposed psychobiological mechanisms and theories of attachment have been inferred from separation effects. An attachment model derived from research on mother-infant separation effects is not only limited because it pertains to only one type of attachment but also because separation models do not specify what is ordinarily present in a relationship that is then missing during separation. Further, the disorganizing effects of the separation often persist following reunion of the attached pair. Thus, separation per se is not the only disruption to an attachment bond. As Field (1985, pp. 415–16) has noted:

> A better understanding of the process may require the study of multiple kinds of attachments at different life stages and may include both overt and physiological behaviors that occur when attached individuals are both together and apart....Attachment might instead be viewed as a relationship that develops between two or more organisms as their behavioral and physiological systems become attuned to each other. Each partner provides meaningful stimulation for the other and has a modulating influence on the other's arousal level. The relationship facilitates an optimal growth state that is threatened by changes in the individuals or their relationship or by separation and the behavioral and physiological disorganization that ensue. Thus, attachments are psychobiologically adaptive for the organization, equilibrium and growth of the organism. Because the organism's behavioral repertoire, physiological makeup, and growth needs are an integrated multivariate complex that changes developmentally, multiple and different types of attachments are experienced across the lifespan.

In a similar vein, Reite & Capitanio (1985) suggested that "attachment in fact represents a neurobiologically based and mediated biobehavioral system one of whose major functions is to promote the development and regulation (or modulation) of psychobiological synchrony between organisms" (p. 224). Support for this model comes from different species. In separated rats given substitute milk and heat, physiological and behavioral effects of separation persisted (Hofer 1981). Hofer suggested "a view of the mother as an eternal physiological regulating agent controlling autonomic cardiovascular balance by the level of milk she supplies." Similarly, simulated maternal licking of rat pups reversed the growth hormone deficits associated with separation (Kuhn et al 1978). In human neonates, maternal caretaking and sleep-wake activity cycles became synchronized only in the presence of a consistent caregiver (Sander et al 1970). Similarly, behavior and heart rate of slightly older infants and mothers share a common variance during early interactions (Lester et al 1982) and during later strange situation sessions (Donovan & Leavitt 1985). This synchrony does not happen during interactions with strangers (Yogman et al 1983). Married couples share behavioral and heart-rate rhythms during interactions (Levenson & Gottman 1984) as well as cycling of cortisol levels (Lundberg et al 1981).

One of the most salient examples, perhaps, is that provided by Reite & Capitanio (1985) on infant monkey peers. The heart rates of two attached pigtail infants who had been reared together were highly correlated. This relationship decreased during separation. Following reunion the correlations of their heart rates and body temperatures returned to baseline. In contrast, heart rate and body temperature were not correlated in two mother-reared monkeys who were not attached to each other. Similarly, time spent in delta sleep was highly correlated for the attached pair but not for the unfamiliar peers. Although Reite & Capitanio offered these data as tentative evidence for the potency of reciprocal entrainment of rhythms in attached individuals who are attached, these investigators also raised important empirical questions: "If attachment facilitates synchrony of rhythms between individuals, is this central to attachment, a precondition for attachment, an outcome of attachment, or an epiphenomenon?" (p. 243). These questions offer future directions for research on the psychobiology of attachment and separation.

ACKNOWLEDGMENTS

This research was supported by an NIMH Research Scientist Award (#MH00331) and an NIMH Research Grant (#MH46586) to Tiffany Field.

Literature Cited

Ainsworth MDS. 1967. *Infancy in Uganda: Infant Care and the Growth of Love.* Baltimore: Johns Hopkins Press

Antonucci T. 1976. Attachment: a life-span concept. *Hum. Dev.* 19:135–42

Bowlby J. 1969. *Attachment and Loss,* Vol 1. *Attachment.* New York: Basic Books

Breese GR, Smith RD, Mueller RA, Howard JL, Prange AJ, et al. 1973. Induction of adrenal catecholamine synthesizing enzymes following mother-infant separation. *Nature New Biol.* 246:94–96

Coe CL, Levine S. 1983. Biology of aggression. *Bull. Am. Acad. Psychiatr. Law* 2: 131–48

Coe CL, Wiener SG, Rosenberg LT, Levine S. 1985. Endocrine and immune responses to separation and natural loss in nonhuman primates. See Reite & Field 1985, pp. 163–97

Cullen E. 1957. Adaptions in the Kittiwake to cliff-nesting. *Ibis* 99:275–302

Donovan WL, Leavitt AL. 1985. Cardiac responses of mothers and infants in Ainsworth's strange situation. See Reite & Field 1985, pp. 130–42

Emde RN, Harmon RJ, Metcalf D, Koenig KL, Wagonfeld S. 1971. Stress and neonatal sleep. *Psychosom. Med.* 33:491–97

Engel GL, Schmale AH. 1972. Conservation-withdrawal: a primary regulatory process for organismic homeostasis. In *Ciba Found. Symp. 8. Physiology, Emotion and Psychosomatic Illness.* Amsterdam: Elsevier

Field T. 1978. The three R's of infant-adult interactions: rhythms, repertories and responsivity. *J. Pediatr. Psychol.* 3:131–36

Field T. 1984. Peer separation of children attending new schools. *Dev. Psychol.* 20:786–92

Field T. 1985. Attachment as psychobiological attunement: being on the same wavelength. See Reite & Field 1985, pp. 455–80

Field T. 1991. Young children's adaptations to repeated separations from their mothers. *Child Dev.* 62:539–47

Field T, Gewirtz JL, Cohen D, Garcia R, Greenberg R, Collins K. 1984a. Leavetakings and reunions of infants, toddlers, preschoolers and their parents. *Child Dev.* 55:628–35

Field T, Reite M. 1984. Children's responses to separation from mother during the birth of another child. *Child Dev.* 55:1308–16

Field T, Vega-Lahr N, Jagadish S. 1984b. Separation stress of nursery infants and toddlers graduating to new classes. *Infant Behav. Dev.* 7:277–84

Frodi A. 1985. Variations in parental and non-parental response to early infant communication. See Reite & Field 1985, pp. 351–68

Hofer MA. 1981. Toward a developmental basis for disease predisposition: the effects of early maternal separation on brain, behavior and cardiovascular system. In *Brain, Behavior and Bodily Disease,* ed. H Weiner, MA Hofer, AJ Stunkard, pp. 209–28. New York: Raven

Hollenbeck AR, Susman EJ, Nannis ED, Strope BE, Hersh SP, et al. 1980. Children with serious illness: behavioral correlates of separation and isolation. *Child Psychiatr. Hum. Dev.* 11:3–11

Kraemer GW. 1985. Effects of differences in early social experience on primate neurobiological-behavioral development. See Reite & Field 1985, pp. 135–62

Kuhn CM, Butler SR, Schanberg SM. 1978. Selective depression of serum growth hormone during maternal deprivation in rat pups. *Science* 201:1034–36

Kupfer DJ, Coble P, Kane J, Petti T, Connors CK. 1979. Imipramine and EEG sleep in children with depressive symptoms. *Psychopharmacology* 60:117–23

Laudenslager ML, Reite M, Harbeck RJ. 1982. Suppressed immune response in infant monkeys associated with maternal separation. *Behav. Neural Biol.* 36:40–48

Lester BM, Hoffman J, Brazelton TB. 1982. *Spectral analysis of mother-infant interaction in term and preterm infants.* Presented at meeting of ICIS, Int. Conf. Inf. Stud., Austin, Tex.

Levenson RW, Gottman JM. 1985. Physiological and affective predictors of changes in relationship satisfaction. *J. Pers. Soc. Psychol.* 49:85–94

Lundberg U, de Chateau P, Winberg J, Frankenhaeuser M. 1981. Catecholamine and cortisol excretion patterns in three-year-old children and their parents. *J. Hum. Stress* 10:3–11

McCabe P, Schneiderman N. 1985. Psychophysiological reactions to stress. In *Behavioral Medicine: The Biosocial Approach,* ed. N Schneiderman, J Tapp. Hillsdale, NJ: Erlbaum

Obrist PA. 1981. *Cardiovascular Psychophysiology.* New York: Plenum

Obrist PA, Gaebelein CJ, Teller ES, Langer AW, Grignolo A, et al. 1978. The relationship among heart rate, carotid dP/dt and blood pressure in humans as a function of the type of stress. *Psychophysiology* 15:102–15

Panksepp J, Siviy M, Normansell LA. 1985. Brain opioids and social emotions. See Reite & Field 1985, pp. 3–50

Petrovich SB, Gewirtz JL. 1985. The attachment learning process and its relation to cultural and biological evolution: proximate and ultimate considerations. See Reite & Field 1985, pp. 51–92

Reite M. 1983. Development of attachment and depression. Presented at Bienn. Meet. Soc. Res. Child Dev., Detroit

Reite M, Capitanio JP. 1984. Child abuse: a comparative and psychobiological perspective. Presented at Conf. on Biosoc. Perspect. Child Abuse. Negl., Soc. Sci. Res. Counc.

Reite M, Capitanio JP. 1985. On the nature of social separation and social attachment. See Reite & Field 1985, pp. 223–58

Reite M, Field T, eds. 1985. Psychobiology of Attachment and Separation. New York: Academic

Reite M, Harbeck R, Hoffman A. 1981a. Altered cellular immune response following peer separation. Life Sci. 29:1133-36

Reite M, Short R, Kaufman IC, Stynes AJ, Pauley JD. 1978. Heart rate and body temperature in separated monkey infants. Biol. Psychiatr. 13:91–105

Reite M, Short R, Seiler C, Pauley JD. 1981b. Attachment, loss and depression. J. Child Psychol. Psychiatr. 22:141–69

Reite M, Snyder DS. 1982. Physiology of maternal separation in a bonnet macaque infant. Am. J. Primatol. 2:115–20

Sander LW, Stechler G, Burns P, Julia N. 1970. Early mother-infant interaction and 24-hour patterns of activity and sleep. J. Acad. Child Psychiatr. 9:103-23

Seiler C, Cullen JS, Zimmerman J, Reite M. 1979. Cardiac arrhythmia in infant pigtail monkeys following maternal separation. Psychophysiology 16:103–35

Seligman MEP. 1975. Learned Helplessness: On Depression, Development and Death. San Francisco: Freeman

Tronick EZ, Winn S, Morelli GA. 1985. Multiple caretaking in the context of human evolution: Why don't the Efe know the western prescription for child care? See Reite & Field 1985, pp. 292–322

Vogel GW. 1979. A motivational function of REM sleep. In The Functions of Sleep, ed. L Cohen, R Sterman, pp. 320–38. New York: Academic

Weiss JM. 1971a. Effects of coping behavior in different warning signal conditions on stress pathology in rats. J. Comp. Physiol. Psychol. 77:1–13

Weiss JM. 1971b. Effects of coping behavior with and without a feedback signal on stress pathology in rats. J. Comp. Physiol. Psychol. 77:22–30

Yogman MW, Lester BM, Hoffman J. 1983. Behavioral and cardiac rhythmicity during mother-father-stranger infant social interaction. Pediatr. Res. 17:872–76

Annu. Rev. Psychol. 1996. 47:563–92

COVARIANCE STRUCTURE ANALYSIS: Statistical Practice, Theory, and Directions

Peter M. Bentler

Department of Psychology, University of California, Los Angeles, Box 951563, Los Angeles, California 90095-1563

Paul Dudgeon

Department of Psychology, University of Melbourne, and National Health & Medical Research Council Schizophrenia Research Unit, Mental Health Research Institute, Royal Park Hospital, Parkville, Victoria 3052 Australia

KEY WORDS: multivariate analysis, structural modeling, latent variables, LISREL, EQS

ABSTRACT

Although covariance structure analysis is used increasingly to analyze nonexperimental data, important statistical requirements for its proper use are frequently ignored. Valid conclusions about the adequacy of a model as an acceptable representation of data, which are based on goodness-of-fit test statistics and standard errors of parameter estimates, rely on the model estimation procedure being appropriate for the data. Using analogies to linear regression and anova, this review examines conditions under which conclusions drawn from various estimation methods will be correct and the consequences of ignoring these conditions. A distinction is made between estimation methods that are either correctly or incorrectly specified for the distribution of data being analyzed, and it is shown that valid conclusions are possible even under misspecification. A brief example illustrates the ideas. Internet access is given to a computer code for several methods that are not available in programs such as EQS or LISREL.

0066-4308/96/0201-0563$08.00

CONTENTS

INTRODUCTION

Most psychological data are multivariate in nature. An important approach to understanding such data is to develop and evaluate a model of how the data might have been generated. In the case of experiments, the explanatory variables are design variables whose values are controlled. By their nature, these variables are presumed to be understood. The dependent variables, on the other hand, typically are best understood with help of a model. If interest lies primarily in the means of these variables, the standard linear model and its statistical implementation via analysis of variance (anova) or its multivariate version provide good insight. Of course, assumptions need to be made, such as independence of observations, linearity and additivity of effects, homogeneity of variances, normally distributed errors, etc. There is substantial agreement on the performance characteristics of these methods when the assumptions are met, as well as, to a lesser extent, on the consequences of violation of assumptions. The same cannot be said for methods in the analysis of nonexperimental data. This chapter addresses some of the consequences of violation of assumptions in covariance structure analysis, and relates a few results to the comparable situation from anova or regression. Although most of the results reviewed here are very old, they have not yet permeated the practice of covariance structure analysis.

Nonexperimental data are inherently more difficult to analyze and understand because various variables may have different effects and directions of influence, their effects may not be independent, observed variables may be influenced by unmeasured latent variables, omitted variables may bias the observed effects, and so on. To understand such influences, typically one considers a general linear structural model for a p-variate vector of variables $\underset{\sim}{x}$

as $\underset{\sim}{x} = A\xi$, where the matrix $A = A(\gamma)$ is a function of a basic vector γ of parameters, and the underlying k $(k \geq p)$ generating variables ξ may represent measured, latent, or residual variables (e.g. Anderson 1994, Bentler 1983a, Satorra 1992). In typical applications of anova, one can assume the model is correct, and the statistical problem is to isolate true nonzero (i.e. significant) effects from zero effects. In contrast, in nonexperimental contexts the basic model setup itself may be a source of contention. That is, the matrix A or its parameters γ may be misspecified; an inappropriate or incomplete set of variables ξ may be hypothesized; or the moments, i.e. means or covariances, of these ξ variables may be incorrectly specified. Hence an important part of the methodology involves evaluating the quality of the model as a representation of the data. The standard questions of parameter significance are important only if the model itself is plausible. In this chapter we review issues in model and parameter evaluation, though we accept the basic model setup, which, of course, in some contexts may itself be questioned. For example, one could question the linearity assumption or the absence of nonlinear or interaction terms (e.g. Jöreskog & Yang 1995, Kenny & Judd 1984, Mooijaart & Bentler 1986), though the most popular model variants assume simple linear relations among variables. Nonlinear relations arise naturally with categorical data models (e.g. Jöreskog 1994; Lee et al 1992, 1995; Muthén 1984), but for simplicity we deal only with continuous variable models. Other interesting questions, such as causality (see e.g. Bullock et al 1994, Sobel 1995, Steyer 1993), equivalent models (e.g. Bekker et al 1994, Lee & Hershberger 1990, MacCallum et al 1993), or model modification (e.g. MacCallum et al 1992) also are not addressed.

As just noted, under a linear structural model, understanding the observed variables $\underset{\sim}{x}$ hinges on understanding the parameters γ and the generating variables ξ. In practice, one is satisfied with knowing how the means and the covariances (i.e. variances and correlations) among the $\underset{\sim}{x}$ variables are generated. Under the model, this requires estimating and testing for significance the parameters γ and the means and covariances of the generating ξ variables. That is, if the means and covariances among the $\underset{\sim}{x}$ variables are given by μ and Σ, an appropriate model would be based on a more basic set of parameters θ, such that $\mu = \mu(\theta)$ and $\Sigma = \Sigma(\theta)$. The q parameters in θ represent elements of γ as well as the intercepts, regression coefficients, or variances and covariances of the ξ variables. Specific versions of such models are given by the equations of the confirmatory factor analysis (Jöreskog 1969, Lockhart 1967), factor analytic simultaneous equation (Jöreskog & Sörbom 1993, Wiley 1973), Bentler & Weeks (1980), or RAM (McArdle & McDonald 1984) models. These models have a wide range of application, from individual growth modeling (Willett & Sayer 1994) to decomposition of trait and method variance (e.g. Dudgeon 1994). They can be taken as mean and covariance structure models (e.g. Browne & Arminger 1995, Satorra 1992), though more general models, in which higher-order moments are also of concern, have been developed (Bentler 1983a) but are only rarely studied (Mooijaart 1985, Mooijaart & Bentler 1986).

In this review we concentrate on the most typical applications, those of covariance structure models. In such models, μ is unstructured and hence can be estimated (in practice, at the sample mean), which allows the parameters of the covariance structure, $\Sigma = \Sigma(\theta)$, to be treated separately. Covariance structure models have become extremely popular in psychology and other social sciences since the previous *Annual Review* chapter on this topic (Bentler 1980). Widely known computer programs, such as LISREL (Jöreskog & Sörbom 1993), EQS (Bentler 1995, Bentler & Wu 1995a,b), and others (see Browne & Arminger 1995, pp. 241–42; Ullman 1995), have made the models easily accessible to applied researchers, and good general introductory texts on the topic now exist (e.g. Bollen 1989, Byrne 1994, Dunn et al 1993, Hoyle 1995, Loehlin 1992). Steiger (1994) and Faulbaum & Bentler (1994) provide perspective overviews. A new journal, *Structural Equation Modeling,* covers recent developments.

As noted above, covariance structure models are typically motivated by linear models in hypothesized variables ξ. The distribution of the ξ variables affects the distributions of the measured variables $\underset{\sim}{x}$. Typically, one assumes that ξ and hence $\underset{\sim}{x}$ are multivariate normally distributed. This assumption simplifies the statistical theory. A test of the model structure and of hypotheses on particular parameters thus are easy to obtain. However, in practice, the normality assumption will often be incorrect. For example, Micceri (1989) reported that among 440 large-sample achievement and psychometric measures taken from journal articles, research projects, and tests, all were significantly nonnormally distributed. Yet, as noted by Breckler (1990) and Gierl & Mulvenon (1995), practitioners generally do not bother to evaluate this very strong assumption and simply accept normal theory statistics as if the data were normal. As a result, conclusions that are drawn about model adequacy (from the goodness-of-fit test statistic) and parameters (from z-statistics based on standard errors) are often liable to be incorrect as well. This is an alarming state of affairs in view of the increasing reliance on covariance structure models for understanding relationships among nonexperimental data.

It is not that there are no alternatives to normal theory statistics. Several have been developed and have been available for some time in certain computer programs, especially in EQS. Others have been developed but are not yet available to applied researchers. In general, software publishers have fallen substantially behind the theoretical developments. For example, a distribution-free test [see Equation (10) below] developed by Browne about 15 years ago (Browne 1982, 1984) is not available in any extant computer program, including Browne's own program RAMONA (Browne et al 1994). Similarly, a test based on heterogeneous kurtosis theory was published a half decade ago (Kano et al 1990), yet it has not been incorporated into any programs, including Bentler's EQS program. Several other valuable statistics are similarly unavailable. Therefore, in addition to reviewing and discussing the alternatives, we provide a high-level code that can be accessed via the Appendix to implement some of the newer statistics.

THE MODELING PROCESS

Two aspects of the modeling process are important in understanding judgments about the adequacy of models and the significance of parameters. One, as touched on already, is the distributional assumptions made about the variables forming the model—this is the main focus of the review. The other is more fundamental to the process itself and has to do with models being approximate rather than exact representations. We examine this aspect briefly now because it places the first in a broader context. Consider the most popular covariance structure model, the confirmatory factor model. In this model, $\underset{\sim}{x} = \Lambda \xi + \epsilon$ explains the measured variables $\underset{\sim}{x}$ as a linear combination with weights Λ of common factors ξ and unique variates ("errors") ϵ. Factors are allowed to correlate with covariance matrix $\mathcal{E}(\xi\xi') = \Phi$, errors are uncorrelated with factors, i.e. $\mathcal{E}(\xi\epsilon') = 0$, and various error variates are uncorrelated and have a diagonal covariance matrix $\mathcal{E}(\epsilon\epsilon') = \Psi$. As a result, $\Sigma = \Sigma(\theta) = \Lambda\Phi\Lambda' + \Psi$, and the elements of θ are the unknown free parameters in the Λ, Φ, and Ψ matrices. The distribution of the variables ξ and ϵ is an important part of the specification of the model, but these are typically unknown and only the distribution of the measured variables $\underset{\sim}{x}$ is available for evaluation. As shown below, misspecification of the distribution of $\underset{\sim}{x}$ affects inferences on the null hypothesis $\Sigma = \Sigma(\theta)$ as well as on θ. Although assuring that the parameters in θ are identified is not a minor matter, to avoid getting sidetracked on this important problem we assume that uniqueness of parameter specification is not an issue so that for two possibly different parameter vectors θ_1 and θ_2, $\Sigma(\theta_1) = \Sigma(\theta_2) \Rightarrow \theta_1 = \theta_2$. Thus equality of the two covariance matrices implies equality of the parameters that generate them.

Let S represent the $p \times p$ sample covariance matrix obtained from $\underset{\sim}{x}' (=x_1,...,x_p)$ variables, each independently observed $N = n + 1$ times. There are situations in which the assumption of independent observations is implausible, in which case special methods are needed (see e.g. Lee 1990, Muthén & Satorra 1989, Weng & Bentler 1995). However, independence generally can be reasonably assumed, and we can estimate the values of the parameters in θ from S and in some circumstances test the fit of the model $\Sigma(\theta)$, by minimizing some scalar function $F = F[S, \Sigma(\theta)]$, which indicates the discrepancy between

S and the covariance matrix $\Sigma(\theta)$ reproduced from the fitted model. Discrepancy functions have the following properties: (*a*) the value of F will be greater than or equal to zero; (*b*) F will only equal zero if $\Sigma(\theta) = \mathbf{S}$; and (*c*) F must be twice differentiable with respect to both **S** and $\Sigma(\theta)$. The parameter estimates, signified by $\hat{\theta}$, are obtained at the minimum of F, signified by $\hat{F} = F[\mathbf{S}, \Sigma(\hat{\theta})]$, where the matrix $\Sigma(\hat{\theta})$ (or more conveniently signified by $\hat{\Sigma}$) indicates the covariance matrix reconstructed from the estimated parameters of the specified model. Normal theory maximum likelihood (ML) and generalized least squares (GLS) provide typical examples of discrepancy functions. For now, it is not important to give the full expression for these functions; they are given later in the paper.

A primary aim of covariance structure analysis is to specify enough restrictions in $\Sigma(\theta)$ so that, substantively, it becomes a sufficiently simple and acceptable representation for the theoretical or interpretative issue being investigated (McDonald 1989). Technically, also, the model should improve precision, i.e. reduce variance in the parameter estimator, at the expense of little or no bias in the estimator (de Leeuw 1988, Kano et al 1993). Even in the implausible situation in which we know the population covariance matrix Σ, say Σ_0, the onus would still be on us to specify some simplifying model $\Sigma(\theta_0)$ for representing the relationships in that matrix, otherwise "there is no point in using a model" (McDonald 1989, p. 101). Although in reality we employ a sample covariance matrix **S** as a consistent estimator of Σ_0, it is useful to consider briefly this implausible situation, for it helps make the problem of choosing a discrepancy function clear. Ideally, we would like to define a unique set of parameter values θ_0 for our structural model such that

$$\Sigma(\theta_0) = \Sigma_0. \tag{1}$$

This implies that for our known population covariance matrix we also (implausibly) know the true model that generated the covariance matrix. In this instance all overidentifying restrictions in the model are correctly specified, and as a consequence these restrictions (and therefore the model) hold exactly. If we fit this model to Σ_0, then at the minimum of the ML, GLS, or any other function meeting the three requirements just defined, we would find that

$$F\left[\Sigma_0, \Sigma\left(\hat{\theta}_0\right)\right] = 0 \tag{2}$$

and therefore $\hat{\theta}_0 = \theta_0$.

In reality we will never know $\Sigma(\theta_0)$. But let us still continue to assume that we know Σ_0. Then in these circumstances the results in Equation (2) will no longer necessarily hold. Although we could fit some hypothesized model $\Sigma(\theta_\phi)$ with different parameters θ_ϕ by minimizing some function $F[\Sigma_0, \Sigma(\theta_\phi)]$, the conjectured true model $\Sigma(\theta_\phi)$ would not necessarily equal the actual true

$\Sigma(\theta_0)$. While we still regard the set of true parameter values θ_0 as the value of θ_ϕ acquired at the minimum, $\Sigma(\theta_\phi)$ would in all probability be an approximation to $\Sigma(\theta_0)$. Because the ideal defined by (1) no longer necessarily occurs, we would now find that

$$F\left[\Sigma_0, \Sigma(\hat{\theta}_\phi)\right] \geq 0, \tag{3}$$

although this relationship would almost invariably be a strict inequality. More importantly, we would also find that the values of both the (approximated) true parameters in $\hat{\theta}_\phi$ and the minimum discrepancy function value $F[\Sigma_0, \Sigma(\hat{\theta}_\phi)]$ would vary according to the particular discrepancy function used.[1]

In practice we estimate our models from the sample covariance matrix S rather than fit them to Σ_0, and this introduces additional discrepancies besides that arising from (3). Cudeck & Henly (1991) provide a very good discussion of the various forms of discrepancy involved in fitting models (see also Browne & Cudeck 1993 for ways to evaluate those discrepancies). While the details of Cudeck and Henly's paper are outside our present scope, the important point to be made here about the modeling process is that the choice of a discrepancy function will influence the assessment of models and parameter estimates not only because we work with sample data that are often nonnormal, but also because the null hypothesis (1) never holds. As such, our models are only approximate rather than exact representations of the reality being envisaged. A statistical basis for making an appropriate choice is therefore needed.

Test Statistic on Model Hypotheses

If we make the right choice of discrepancy function, and if the modeling assumptions are correct and the sample size is large enough, then at the minimum, $T = n\hat{F}$ is distributed under the null hypothesis (1) as a goodness-of-fit χ^2 variate with $(p^* - q)$ degrees of freedom,[2] where $p^* = p(p + 1)/2$. T can be used as a test statistic to evaluate the null hypothesis. The null hypothesis is rejected if T exceeds a critical value in the χ^2 distribution at an α-level of

---

[1] This can be shown easily by fitting any model in LISREL or EQS and saving the reproduced covariance matrix (it does not have to be a particularly good fit). If we then refit the same model, but now to the reproduced covariance matrix rather than to the sample covariance matrix, then the fitting function value will always be zero and the parameter estimates and standard errors will be the same for, say, ML or GLS estimation. If we change the model slightly to some different specification of parameters, but still use the reproduced covariance matrix, then the fitting function value, the parameter estimates, and the standard errors will vary according to ML or GLS estimation.

[2] More generally, the degrees of freedom are further increased by one for each independent equality restriction that might be imposed (Lee & Bentler 1980), but for simplicity in this paper we assume that there are no equality restrictions.

significance. Otherwise, the model cannot be rejected, and the null hypothesis is accepted.

Because a numerical value for T is computed and printed out by all computer programs, there is a strong tendency to treat it as a χ^2 variate whether or not that is its actual distribution. In fact, except for unusual circumstances associated with the specialized "asymptotic robustness theory" (see below), when T is based on the assumption of multivariate normality of variables but the data are not normal (the typical case in practice as noted above), T will not be χ^2 distributed. As a result, incorrect conclusions about model adequacy often are obtained. And, as shown by Hu et al (1992), asymptotic robustness theory is not robust to violation of its assumptions, so it cannot be used to justify an inappropriate choice of fit function and test statistic.

Statistics on Parameter Hypotheses

Once a model null hypothesis is accepted, typical practice involves interpreting the relative size and significance levels of particular parameter estimates $\hat{\theta}_i$ to see if they differ significantly from zero. Typically, this involves evaluating the hypothesis $\theta_i = 0$ using the statistic $Z = (\hat{\theta}_i - \theta_i) / \text{SE}(\hat{\theta}_i)$, where the denominator is an estimate of the standard error. In practice, computer programs calculate this standard error estimate from the square root of the appropriate element from the inverse of the "information matrix." Unfortunately, aside from tests on regression coefficients that may be correct due to asymptotic robustness theory—which cannot be relied upon to apply to a given data analysis situation—this is the correct expression only when the distributional assumption used in defining the discrepancy function is correct. Thus, tests of parameters based on z will be incorrect in the typical case where a normal theory method is used, but the data are not normal. As a result, incorrect substantive conclusions about the meaning of a model may well be drawn. The situation is the same when sets of parameters are evaluated simultaneously using the Wald test (e.g. Bentler & Dijkstra 1985; Dijkstra 1981, Theorem 8; Lee 1985). Similar problems occur when missing parameters are evaluated using the Lagrange Multiplier test (e.g. Bentler 1995). Satorra (1989) provides an excellent general discussion.

To gain some insight into this situation, consider the regression model $y = X\beta + \epsilon$ with dependent variable y and fixed design matrix X. When the errors ϵ are independent, normal, and homoscedastic, as in typical applications of anova, the information matrix of $\hat{\beta}$ is proportional to $(X'X)$. Thus the standard errors of $\hat{\beta}$ are given, up to a constant that involves sample size, by the square roots of the diagonal elements of the inverse $(X'X)^{-1}$ of this information matrix. These are the standard errors given by available regression and anova programs. Unfortunately, when the assumptions are not true, this formula does not give the correct standard errors (see, e.g. Arminger 1995). It is likely that many applications of regression thus give incorrect tests on parameters, as do many covariance structure applications. We shall use the regression analogy several times.

Theoretical or Empirical Robustness to Violation of Assumptions

We see, then, that the typical requirements for a covariance structure statistic to be trustworthy under the null hypothesis $\Sigma = \Sigma(\theta)$ are that the parameters of the model are identified; the observations or scores for different subjects are independent; the sample size is very large; and either a discrepancy function consistent with the actual distribution of variables is optimized, or a method of model and parameter testing is chosen that is robust to violation of certain of these assumptions. Unfortunately, these several conditions are often difficult to meet in practice. As noted above, we do not discuss identification or independence; we simply assume these conditions since they can often be arranged by design. The other points bear some discussion prior to developing the technical details.

Sample size turns out to be critical because all of the statistics known in covariance structure analysis are "asymptotic," that is, are based on the assumption that N becomes arbitrarily large. Since this situation can rarely be obtained, except perhaps by large national testing services and censuses, it becomes important to evaluate whether N may be large enough in practice for the theory to work reasonably well. Different data and discrepancy functions have different robustness properties with respect to sample size. Basically, sample size requirements increase as data become more nonnormal, models become larger, and more assumption-free discrepancy functions are used (e.g. Chan et al 1995, Chou et al 1991, Curran et al 1994, Hu et al 1992, Muthén & Kaplan 1992, West et al 1995, Yung & Bentler 1994).

In principle, if one matches a discrepancy function to the distribution of variables, the resulting T and z test statistics should be well behaved. However, some of these functions cannot be applied with large models because the computational demands are simply too heavy. Also, some provide test statistics that do not work well except at impractically large sample sizes. Thus alternatives have been developed that may potentially work in more realistic sized samples, i.e. be robust to violation of the asymptotic sample size requirement of all known methods. Unfortunately, not much is known about their actual performance in practice. These topics are discussed below.

Ideally, one could specify conditions under which even the technically wrong method could lead to correct statistical inferences. This is the hope of researchers who use normal theory methods when their data are nonnormal. The only known theoretical justification for such a practice is that of asymptotic robustness (e.g. Browne 1987), which we illustrate but do not review in detail. Anderson & Amemiya (1988) and Amemiya & Anderson (1990) found, for example, that the asymptotic χ^2 goodness-of-fit test in factor analysis can be insensitive to violations of the assumption of multivariate normality of both common and unique factors, if all factors are independently distributed and the elements of the covariance matrices of common factors are all free parameters. With an additional condition of the existence of the fourth-order moments of both unique and common factors, Browne & Shapiro (1988) and Mooijaart & Bentler (1991) also demonstrated the robustness of normal theory methods in the analysis of a general class of linear latent variate models. Satorra & Bentler (1990, 1991) obtained similar results for a wider range of discrepancy functions, estimators, and test statistics. Browne (1990) and Satorra (1992) extended this theory to mean and covariance structure models, and Satorra (1993) to multiple samples. Unfortunately, asymptotic robustness theory cannot be relied upon in practice, because it is practically impossible to evaluate whether its conditions are met. Thus we cannot use this theory to avoid taking a more detailed look at the statistics of covariance structure analysis, to which we now turn.

STATISTICS BASED ON CORRECTLY SPECIFIED DISTRIBUTIONS

Ideally, there would be many classes of multivariate distributions that are realistic and practical models for data analysis, but this is not the case (Olkin 1994). In covariance structure analysis, only three types of specific distributions have been considered: multivariate normal, elliptical, and heterogeneous kurtotic. In this section we provide basic definitions for these cases and define the test statistics and parameter estimator covariance matrices that result from the correct specification of distributional forms.

To simplify matters, we note that the distribution of the data induces a distribution of the sample statistics under consideration in covariance structure analysis, namely the distribution of the elements of the sample covariance matrix $\mathbf{S}$. Hence, we can focus on the distribution of $\mathbf{S}$ instead of, or in addition to, the distribution of the raw data. Since $\mathbf{S}$ contains redundant elements, we need only be concerned with the nonduplicated elements. Let $\underset{\sim}{s}$ and $\sigma(\theta)$ be p^* $\times 1$ column vectors formed from the nonduplicated elements of $\mathbf{S}$ and $\Sigma(\theta)$, respectively. We are interested in the asymptotic distribution of $\sqrt{n}[\underset{\sim}{s} - \sigma(\theta)]$. We shall assume that typical regularity conditions hold and that the model is correct, so that asymptotically $\sqrt{n}[\underset{\sim}{s} - \sigma(\theta)]$ is multivariate normally distributed with a mean of zero and a covariance matrix given by

$$\text{acov}\{\sqrt{n}[\underset{\sim}{s} - \sigma(\theta)]\} = \Gamma.$$

(4)

The notation "acov" means asymptotic covariance, i.e. as n becomes arbitrarily large. It implies that the covariance matrix of the data $\underset{\sim}{s}$, based on a sample of size N, is given by Γ/n, where the divisor reflects the typical reduction of variances with increasing sample size. Now the specific form of Γ, that is, the detailed mathematical expressions for the elements of this matrix, depends upon the distribution of the variables $\underset{\sim}{x}$ that are being modeled. Let us abstractly consider these matrices to be given by Γ_N, Γ_E, and Γ_{HK} for normal, elliptical, and heterogeneous kurtotic distributions. Explicit expressions are given below.

Note that any specific discrepancy function $F[S, \Sigma(\theta)]$ applied to a covariance structure model is associated with two matrices:

1. $\hat{W}$, which is a consistent and unbiased estimator of some population weight matrix W having the property that, except possibly for a constant, the matrix of expected values of the second derivatives is given by

$$\mathcal{E}\left(\frac{\partial^2 F}{\partial\theta\partial\theta'}\bigg|_{\theta=\sigma}\right) = W. \tag{5}$$

This could be called the information matrix (adopting a standard usage from maximum likelihood theory) for a saturated model. W is fixed by the estimation method chosen, that is, the specific discrepancy function $F[S, \Sigma(\theta)]$ to be optimized. Although data may be used to estimate W, via $\hat{W}$, this matrix does not necessarily depend on the actual distribution of the data variables $\underset{\sim}{x}$, which may be different from that assumed.

2. Γ, the true covariance matrix of the sample covariances, which depends on the actual distribution of the data. Under specific distributions, this can be denoted as Γ_N, Γ_E, or Γ_{HK}, depending on the actual distribution of the variables that generates the sample $\underset{\sim}{s}$. Although there is a single true (typically unknown) Γ, different choices of estimators (e.g. $\hat{\Gamma}_N$) imply different discrepancy functions.

As a result, to be more precise, we shall now define the particular discrepancy function chosen for analysis as $F[(S, \Sigma(\theta)) \mid W, \Gamma]$. With this notation, following Browne (1984) we can define a discrepancy function for a correctly specified distribution as one in which $W = \Gamma^{-1}$, i.e. the class of functions $F[(S, \Sigma(\theta)) \mid W = \Gamma^{-1}, \Gamma]$. These functions are called asymptotically optimal by Satorra (1989). For all such functions and data, test statistics have a simple form.

If we estimate θ so as to minimize $F[(S, \Sigma(\theta)) \mid W = \Gamma^{-1}, \Gamma]$, at the minimum we have $F[(S, \Sigma(\hat{\theta})) \mid W = \Gamma^{-1}, \Gamma]$. For such correctly specified discrepancy functions, if the sample size is large enough, under the model hypothesis we have

$$T = n\hat{F} = nF\left[\left(\mathbf{S}, \Sigma(\hat{\theta})\right) \mid \mathbf{W} = \Gamma^{-1}, \Gamma\right] \sim \chi^2_{(p*-q)}. \tag{6}$$

Thus there exists a simple test of the model. In addition, the estimators $\hat{\theta}$ are asymptotically efficient, i.e. have the smallest possible sampling variances among estimators using the same information from the data. The covariance matrix of $\hat{\theta}$ is given by the inverse of the optimal information matrix (adopting this name from ML theory), namely

$$\mathrm{acov}(\hat{\theta}) = \left[\varepsilon\left(\frac{\partial^2 F}{\partial\theta\partial\theta'}_{\mid\theta=\theta_o}\right)\right]^{-1} = n^{-1}\left(\Delta'\Gamma^{-1}\Delta\right)^{-1}, \tag{7}$$

where $[\Delta = (\partial\sigma[\theta]/\partial\theta')_{\mid\theta=\theta_o}]$ is the matrix of partial derivatives of the model with respect to the parameters. Standard errors are then the square roots of the diagonal elements of (7). In practice, consistent estimators of the matrices in (7) are used.

To make (7) a bit more intuitive, consider again the linear regression model. For that model, the covariance matrix of the residual ϵ, up to a constant, is $\Gamma = \mathbf{I}$, and with $\Delta = \mathbf{X}$, the matrix in (7) is proportional to $(\mathbf{X}'\mathbf{X})^{-1}$. This is the usual result, but it also holds more generally. Suppose in regression that the covariance matrix of the ϵ is Γ, not $\mathbf{I}$, and that GLS with weight matrix Γ^{-1} is used rather than least-squares estimation. Then the covariance matrix of the estimator is (7), i.e. proportional to $(\mathbf{X}'\Gamma^{-1}\mathbf{X})^{-1}$. However, as we shall see, when the distribution of variables is misspecified, (7) does not give the covariance matrix of $\hat{\theta}$. Unfortunately, in practice, researchers seem to use Equation (7) whether or not it is the correct formula to use.

STATISTICS BASED ON MISSPECIFIED DISTRIBUTIONS

Now we consider the more general case, in which the discrepancy function used in an analysis is misspecified, yet we desire to compute correct statistics. We define a misspecified function as one in which $\mathbf{W} \neq \Gamma^{-1}$, i.e. the class of functions $F[(\mathbf{S},\Sigma(\theta)) \mid \mathbf{W} \neq \Gamma^{-1}, \Gamma]$. Perhaps the most typical example is one in which $\mathbf{W} = \Gamma_N^{-1}$, but $\Gamma \neq \Gamma_N$. That is, a normal theory method is used, but the data are not normally distributed. In such a case, (6) and (7) do not hold. Specifically, T is not χ^2 distributed, and the matrix (7) is not relevant nor computed. It also means that the estimator generally is not asymptotically efficient, i.e. it will not have the smallest possible sampling variability. This might be an argument for using discrepancy functions that are correctly specified, but this may be impractical. As noted by Bentler & Dijkstra (1985), Dijkstra (1981), Shapiro (1983), and especially by Satorra & Bentler (1986,

1988, 1994), the general distribution of T is in fact not χ^2, but rather a mixture

$$T \xrightarrow{\mathcal{L}} \Sigma_1^{df} \alpha_i \tau_i, \tag{8}$$

where α_i is one of the df (degrees of freedom) nonnull eigenvalues of the matrix $\mathbf{U}\Gamma$, τ_i is one of the df independent χ_1^2 variates, and, when there are no constraints on free parameters,

$$U = W - W\Delta(\Delta'W\Delta)^{-1}\Delta'W \tag{9}$$

is the residual weight matrix under the model and the weight matrix $\mathbf{W}$ used in the estimation.[3] Even though the distribution (8) has been known for over a decade, its usage has been considered impractical, and to our knowledge, the test statistic (8) was first used in covariance structure analysis by Bentler (1994). It is not available in any extant program.

Another test statistic that should hold generally, yet has not become available in any program, is the general quadratic form test statistic of Browne (1984, Proposition 4, Equation 2.20). Unlike tests based on T (see Equation 6), the test statistic

$$T_{QF} = n\hat{F}_{QF} = n\left[\underline{s} - \sigma(\hat{\theta})\right]' \hat{\mathbf{U}}_\Gamma \left[\underline{s} - \sigma(\hat{\theta})\right], \tag{10}$$

is $\chi^2_{p^*-q}$ distributed. Here, $\hat{\mathbf{U}}_\Gamma$ is given by the matrix defined in (9), and i$\mathbf{W} = \hat{\Gamma}^{-1}$s based on the asymptotically distribution free (ADF—see Equation 14 below) estimated weight matrix. This test statistic can be used without any assumption that the matrix $\hat{\mathbf{W}}$ used in a minimum discrepancy function (see Equation 5) has been correctly specified. Browne (1984, p. 82) noted that although Equation (10) is theoretically correct, it lacked empirical investigation. Remarkably, this is still true today. Its chief appeal lies in it enabling the more tractable ML or GLS estimation methods to be employed for obtaining the parameter estimates. Whether (10) suffers from the problems of poor performance in small samples, like the ADF test statistic (see below), is unknown but is certainly a possibility. As noted by Browne (1984, p. 70), Bentler's (1983b) linearized ADF estimator yields a χ^2 test that is an alternative to (10). It is the default ADF method and statistic in EQS.

Although not strictly relevant to this section, we should note that a version of the quadratic form test statistic based on that of Browne (1984) was developed by Bentler for use with normal theory least-squares estimation. Since the

---

[3] The arrow in Equation 8 indicates that as sample size increases indefinitely, the distribution of T becomes equivalent to the distribution of the right-hand side term..

typical test statistic (6) is not available, he used a variant of (10) based on normal theory, namely, where

$$T_{NQF} = n\hat{F}_{NQF} = n\left[\underline{s} - \sigma(\hat{\theta})\right]' \hat{U}_{\Gamma_N}\left[\underline{s} - \sigma(\hat{\theta})\right], \tag{11}$$

and $\hat{U}_{\Gamma_N}$ is given by the matrix defined in (9) with $W = \hat{\Gamma}_N^{-1}$ based on the normal theory estimated weight matrix. Applied to least-squares estimation, this test has been in EQS and its documentation since 1989 (Bentler 1995). Similar tests hold, of course, for elliptical and heterogeneous kurtotic distributions by suitable use of $W = \hat{\Gamma}_E^{-1}$ or $W = \hat{\Gamma}_{HK}^{-1}$. Tests of this form also were discussed by Satorra & Bentler (1990). Satorra & Bentler (1994) showed in a small study that the test could work quite well. Of course, tests such as (11) require correct distributional specification, which Browne's test (10) was designed to avoid.

Under the correct model, but with distributional misspecification, the matrix (7) also does not describe the variability of the estimator $\hat{\theta}$. The correct large-sample covariance matrix is given by

$$\text{acov}(\hat{\theta}) = n^{-1}(\Delta'W\Delta)^{-1}(\Delta'W\Gamma W\Delta)(\Delta'W\Delta)^{-1}. \tag{12}$$

This covariance matrix has been known to be the correct covariance matrix of the estimator for almost 15 years (e.g. Arminger & Schoenberg 1989; Bentler 1983a; Bentler & Dijkstra 1985; Browne 1982, 1984; Chamberlain 1982; Dijkstra 1981; Shapiro 1983; see also Kano 1993), but even today it seems to be computed only in the EQS and LINCS (Schoenberg & Arminger 1990) programs. In EQS, where (12) has been available since 1989, it is known as the "robust" covariance matrix. In contrast, by default extant programs calculate

$$\text{acov}(\hat{\theta}) = n^{-1}(\Delta'W\Delta)^{-1}, \tag{13}$$

which is the inverse of the information matrix. Even though (13) does not give correct standard errors, it is the formula used in typical practice, e.g. in ML estimation without normal data.

Emphasizing again the parallel to linear regression with $y = X\beta + \epsilon$, the information matrix (13) does not give the covariance matrix of the least-squares estimator $\hat{\beta}$ if $\text{cov}(\epsilon)$ is not proportional to I. The correct covariance matrix is given by (12), with $W = I$ (due to least-squares estimation), $\Delta = X$, and Γ as the true covariance matrix of the ϵ. More generally, if $\hat{\beta}$ is the generalized least-squares estimator based on the incorrect assumption that $\text{cov}(\epsilon) = W^{-1}$, the information matrix formula (13) does not give the standard errors, whereas (12) does.

Although the tests (8) and (10) and the covariance matrix (12) define statistics that are always correct, regardless of the distribution of variables, they are not the only options, nor necessarily the best options in any given situation. Chou et al (1991), Chou & Bentler (1995), and Finch et al (1995) did find the robust covariance matrix to give good estimates of sampling variability. Bentler (1994) found the mixture test (8) performed very well in most instances, but was destroyed by a certain type of nonnormality. The source of good or poor performance is not understood, but it is clear from the formulas that poor estimates of Γ may make these statistics behave badly in practice. Since the various results summarized in this paper rely on large-sample theory, it is also possible that these statistics can be outperformed in small samples by other methods. Additional research is clearly needed.

If the distributional assumption is correct so that $\mathbf{W} = \Gamma^{-1}$, the robust covariance matrix given in (12) reduces to the usual inverse of the information matrix as given in both (7) and (13). More generally, the standard error estimates obtained from (13) cannot be smaller than those of (12), because the difference between (12) and (13) is nonnegative definite. This means that using the usual and incorrect information matrix expression (13) under distributional misspecification will understate the variability of the estimator. This bias can be substantial, as was clearly shown by Finch et al (1995). In practice, this would make the parameter estimates appear to be more significant in z-statistics than they really are. We now review the test statistics used in practice and point to some problems and potentials.

SOME SPECIFIC TEST STATISTICS

If a distribution-free method can be used, the results will be optimal because the discrepancy function would then always be correctly specified. This is the ideal situation introduced into covariance structure analysis by the ADF method of Browne (1982) and the minimum distance method of Chamberlain (1982), which are identical. They proposed minimizing the quadratic form discrepancy function $F_{QD} = [\underline{s} - \sigma(\theta)]'\hat{\mathbf{W}}[\underline{s} - \sigma(\theta)]$ in which $\mathbf{W} = \Gamma^{-1}$ without any assumption on the distribution of variables. To implement this, an old result was used, namely that

$$\Gamma_{ij,kl} = \sigma_{ijkl} - \sigma_{ij}\sigma_{kl}, \tag{14}$$

where

$$\sigma_{ijkl} = \mathbf{E}(x_{ti} - \mu_i)(x_{tj} - \mu_j)(x_{tk} - \mu_k)(x_{tl} - \mu_l)$$

is the fourth-order multivariate moment of variables x_i about their means μ_i, ανδ σ_{ij} is an element of Σ. In practice, sample moment estimators

$$s_{ijkl} = N^{-1}\Sigma_1^N (x_{ti} - \bar{x}_i)(x_{tj} - \bar{x}_j)(x_{tk} - \bar{x}_k)(x_{tl} - \bar{x}_l)$$

and

$$s_{ij} = n^{-1}\Sigma_1^N \left(x_{ti} - \bar{x}_i \right)\left(x_{tj} - \bar{x}_j \right)$$

are used to consistently estimate σ_{ijkl} and σ_{ij} to provide the elements of $\hat{\mathbf{W}}$. Alternative ADF estimators, based on linearization, also are available (Bentler 1983a,b, Bentler & Dijkstra 1985). The ADF methods for the first time provided a way of attaining the $\chi2$ test of model fit (6) without an assumption on the distribution of variables; they also provided for optimal and correct standard errors via (7). The standard ADF method is now available in most structural modeling programs under various names: arbitrary distribution generalized least squares (AGLS) in EQS and weighted least squares (WLS) in LISREL. EQS gives the linearized ADF method by default.

Unfortunately, this great theoretical advance has not proven to be practically useful. Although the χ^2 test of model fit (6) is in principle always available via $T_{\text{ADF}} = n\hat{F}_{\text{QD}}$, the sample size may need to be impractically large for the theory to work well in practice. For example, in the simulation study of Hu et al (1992), at the smallest sample sizes the ADF test statistic virtually always rejected the true model, and sometimes 5000 cases were needed to yield nominal rejection rates. Discouraging results are typical (Chan et al 1995, Chou & Bentler 1995, Chou et al 1991, Curran et al 1994, Muthén & Kaplan 1992). Yung & Bentler (1994) proposed some computationally intensive modifications to the ADF test statistic, which improve but do not fully cure its performance deficiency.

At the most restrictive end of the distributional continuum, the ML discrepancy function based on the assumed normality of variables is

$$F_{\text{ML}} = \log|\Sigma| - \log|\mathbf{S}| + tr(\mathbf{S}\Sigma^{-1}) - p.$$

As shown by Browne (1974), for this discrepancy function

$$\Gamma = \Gamma_N = 2K'_p(\Sigma \otimes \Sigma)K_p,$$

where K_p is a transition matrix of known 0, 1/2, or 1 values that reduces the $p^2 \times p^2$ matrix $(\Sigma \otimes \Sigma)$ to order p^*, and $\otimes$ is the Kronecker product. Although it is not obvious, implicitly $\mathbf{W} = \Gamma_N^{-1}$, so, if the data are truly multivariate normal $T_{\text{ML}} = \hat{F}_{\text{ML}}$ meets (6). But if the data are not normal, T_{ML} is generally not a χ^2 variate (though it may be so, e.g. via asymptotic robustness theory). Assuming T_{ML} to be a χ^2 variate is the typical mistake in applications of covariance structure analysis. The vices and virtues of the ML statistics are shared by normal theory GLS statistics based on minimizing $F_{\text{GLS}} = .5tr\{[\mathbf{S} - \Sigma(\theta)] \mathbf{V}^{-1}\}^2$. If the data are non-normal, this function is always incorrectly specified, and (6) cannot be guaranteed to hold. However, if the data are normal, this function may or may not be correctly specified, depending on the choice of the weight matrix $\mathbf{V}$. The choice of $\mathbf{V} = \mathbf{I}$, as in least-squares (LS) analysis, is misspecified, so (6) will not hold. The typical choice of GLS is $\mathbf{V} = \mathbf{S}$; then, $\mathbf{W} = \Gamma_N^{-1}$, and $T_{GLS} = n\hat{F}_{GLS}$ will meet (6). If $\mathbf{V} = \hat{\Sigma}$ is iteratively updated, F_{GLS} is the reweighted least-squares function F_{RLS}, yielding $T_{RLS} = n\hat{F}_{RLS}$. This also meets (6). In fact, Browne (1974) has shown that if $\mathbf{V}$ converges in probability to Σ (e.g. $\mathbf{V} = \mathbf{S}$ or $\mathbf{V} = \hat{\Sigma}$) then GLS and ML estimators are asymptotically equivalent.

Estimators and tests whose requirements fall between the normal and distribution-free theory are given by elliptical and heterogeneous kurtosis theory. In elliptical theory (Browne 1982, 1984), all marginal distributions of a multivariate distribution are symmetric and have the same relative kurtosis. This is more general than normal theory, yet estimators and test statistics can be obtained by simple adjustments to the statistics derived from normal theory methods. Let $\kappa = \sigma_{iiii}/3\sigma_{ii}^2 - 1$ be the common kurtosis parameter of a distribution from the elliptical class. Multivariate normal distributions are members of this class with $\kappa = 0$. The fourth-order multivariate moments σ_{ijkl} are related to κ by

$$\sigma_{ijkl} = (\kappa + 1)\left(\sigma_{ij}\sigma_{kl} + \sigma_{ik}\sigma_{jl} + \sigma_{il}\sigma_{jk}\right).$$

As a result of this simplification, the F_{QD} discrepancy function for an elliptical distribution simplifies to

$$F_E = \frac{1}{2}(\kappa + 1)^{-1}\mathrm{tr}\left\{[\mathbf{S} - \Sigma(\theta)]\mathbf{V}^{-1}\right\}^2 - \delta\left\{tr[\mathbf{S} - \Sigma(\theta)]\mathbf{V}^{-1}\right\}^2,$$

where as before $\mathbf{V}$ is any consistent estimator of Σ and

$$\delta = \kappa/[4(\kappa + 1)^2 + 2p\kappa(\kappa + 1)]$$

(Bentler 1983a). The selection of $\mathbf{V}$ as a consistent estimator of Σ and a kurtosis estimator such as

$$(\hat{\kappa} + 1) = \Sigma_1^N\left[(\underline{x} - \bar{\underline{x}})'\mathbf{S}^{-1}(\underline{x} - \bar{\underline{x}})\right]^2 / Np(p+2)$$

leads, under the model and assumptions, to an asymptotically efficient estimator of θ with $T_E = n\hat{F}_E$ meeting (6). If $\mathbf{V} = \hat{\Sigma}$ is iteratively updated, and the model is invariant with respect to a constant scaling factor, at the minimum of F_E the second term drops out yielding $T_E = T_{ERLS}$ (see Browne 1984, Shapiro & Browne 1987).

Heterogeneous kurtosis (HK) theory (Kano et al 1990) defines a still more general class of multivariate distributions that allows marginal distributions to have heterogeneous kurtosis parameters. The elliptical distribution is a special case of this class of distributions. Let $\kappa_i^2 = \sigma_{iiii}/3\sigma_{ii}^2$ represent a measure of excess kurtosis of the i-th variable, and the fourth-order moments have the structure

$$\sigma_{ijk\ell} = \left(a_{ij}a_{k\ell}\right)\sigma_{ij}\sigma_{k\ell} + \left(a_{ik}a_{j\ell}\right)\sigma_{ik}\sigma_{j\ell} + \left(a_{i\ell}a_{jk}\right)\sigma_{i\ell}\sigma_{jk},$$

where $a_{ij=(\kappa_i+\kappa_j)/2}$. If the covariance structure $\Sigma(\theta)$ is fully scale invariant and the modeling and distributional assumptions are met, the F_{QD} discrepancy function can be expressed as $F_{HK} = .5tr\{[S - \Sigma(\theta)]\hat{C}^{-1}\}^2$, where $\hat{C} = \hat{A} * \hat{\Sigma}$, and * denotes the elementwise (Hadamard) product of the two matrices of the same order. In practice, $\hat{A} = (a_{ij}) = (\hat{\kappa}_i + \hat{\kappa}_j)/2$ using the usual moment estimators for each variable $\hat{\kappa}_i^2 = s_{iiii}/3s_{ii}^2$, with $\hat{C} = \hat{A} * S$. [For another estimator, see Bentler et al (1991).] The HK estimator is asymptotically efficient, and the associated test statistic $T_{HK} = n\hat{F}_{HK}$, at the minimum meets (6). An attractive feature of the Kano et al theory is that fourth-order moments of the measured variables do not need to be computed as they do in ADF theory, because these moments are just a function of the variances and covariances and the univariate kurtoses. As a result, the HK method can be used on models with many measured variables. While ADF cannot be implemented with more than about 30–40 variables due to the large size of its weight matrix, this is not a limitation of the Kano et al HK method. Koning et al (1993) studied a generalization of F_{HK} in which the matrix C is unrestricted but, unfortunately, it must be related to an estimated ADF weight matrix.

Based on the general distribution (8), Satorra & Bentler (1986, 1988, 1994) developed two modifications of any standard goodness-of-fit statistic test T (T_{ML}, T_{HK}, etc.) so that its distributional behavior should more closely approximate χ^2. The mean of the asymptotic distribution of T is given by $tr(U\Gamma)$, where U is defined in (9). Letting $c = (df)^{-1} tr(\hat{U}\hat{\Gamma})$, where $\hat{U}$ is a consistent estimator of U based on $\hat{\theta}$ and $\hat{\Gamma}$ is an estimator based on the ADF matrix (14), the Satorra-Bentler scaled test statistic is

$$\bar{T} = c^{-1}T. \tag{15}$$

The scaling constant c effectively corrects the statistic T so that the mean of the sampling distribution of $\bar{T}$ will be closer to the expected mean under the model (see also Kano 1992). The scaled statistic that has been implemented in EQS since 1989 is based on the use of T_{ML} in (15). Chou & Bentler (1995), Chou et al (1991), and Curran et al (1994) found the scaled statistic to work well in simulation studies. In the study by Hu et al (1992), the Satorra-Bentler scaled statistic performed best overall under a wide variety of conditions of varied distributions and sample sizes, outperforming the ADF method at all but the largest sample sizes, where it performed equally well. Even though current evidence shows that the scaled statistic (15) performs better than others currently available in modeling programs, in principle some of the alternative statistics, such as those based on (8) and (10) might perform better because their sampling distributions are well specified. However, Bentler (1994) found (8) to break down under conditions where the scaled statistic remained well behaved, and essentially nothing is known about how (10) compares to (15).

Satorra & Bentler also reported the development of a test statistic that adjusts not only the mean, but also the variance, of the statistic to more closely approximate a χ^2 distribution. The adjusted test statistic $\overline{\overline{T}}$ is obtained by computing the integer d nearest to d', defined by $d' = [tr(U\Gamma)]^2 \div tr[(U\Gamma)^2]$, and computing the statistic

$$\overline{\overline{T}} = \frac{d}{tr(U\Gamma)} T. \tag{16}$$

The effect is to scale with a degrees of freedom adjustment, since (16) is χ^2 distributed with d df. If facilities permit χ^2 to be computed for noninteger df, one can calculate $\overline{\overline{T}} = \{d'/[tr(U\Gamma)]\} T$ and evaluate it with fractional df. Satorra & Bentler (1994) showed with an illustrative example that their statistic (16) can work well, but we are not aware of any systematic study of this statistic.

Because many of the potentially valuable statistics are not available in standard computer programs, in the Appendix we show how a standard matrix language available in SAS or SPSS can be used, along with extant programs such as LISREL and EQS, to yield some of the potentially useful tests. We now illustrate the similarities and differences with a short example.

AN EXAMPLE: TEACHER STRESS

In a study examining stress among school teachers, Bell et al (1990) used an 11 item measure of somatic complaints (e.g. dizziness, shortness of breath, headaches, etc). The questions were answered on a 5 point response scale for frequency of occurrence (1 = *rarely or never* to 5 = *very often*). The Pearson correlation matrix for these 11 items, as well as their standard deviations and measures of relative skewness ($g_{1(i)}$) and relative kurtosis ($g_{2(i)}$) are given in Table 1 for 362 primary school teachers out of the total teacher sample of 956 from primary, technical, and secondary schools. The data are quite obviously non-normal, with excessive kurtosis and skewness being evident for all items. Although structural models can be fitted to data of this kind using polychoric correlations, in applying such models one assumes that the underlying latent distribution for responses to each item is normal. For the sorts of data being considered in this example, the validity of that assumption may well be questioned.

The 11 items were fitted to a single factor model by LISREL using HK estimation. Details on how this is done are in the Appendix: In essence we minimize the F_{QD} discrepancy function (i.e. WLS in LISREL nomenclature) but supply our own computed weight matrix $\mathbf{W}$; $\mathbf{W}$ makes use of Browne's (1974) normal theory relation $\mathbf{W} = \Gamma_N^{-1}$, where $\Gamma_N = 2\mathbf{K}_p'(\mathbf{V} \otimes \mathbf{V})\mathbf{K}_p$, but where the general matrix $\mathbf{V}$ is in this instance given by $\hat{\mathbf{C}} = \hat{\mathbf{A}} * \Sigma$ from HK theory.

The HK parameter estimates and standard errors are displayed in Table 2. For comparative purposes, the results of using both ML and ADF (i.e. WLS) estimation are also provided in Table 2, along with the Satorra-Bentler scaled test of fit (Equation 15) and robust standard errors (Equation 12) for maximum likelihood. (Details of how these robust procedures can be computed for LISREL output are also given in the Appendix.)

The model test statistics for both ML ($T_{ML} = 79.89$, p. $< .001$) and ADF ($T_{ADF} = 66.82$, p. $= 0.015$) are considerably higher than either the HK ($T_{HK} = 36.14$, p. $= 0.794$) or the scaled ML statistics ($\bar{T}_{ML} = 45.89$, p. $= 0.394$). If we assume that the null hypothesis of a single factor model holds exactly, then the test statistics for both the HK estimator and the robust scaled ML estimator are quite acceptable. The corresponding probabilities for ML and ADF estimation

Table 1   Correlation matrix of 11 somatic complaints items and measures of item distribution ($N = 362$)

	1.	2.	3.	4.	5.	6.	7.	8.	9.	10.	11.
1.	1.000										
2.	0.503	1.000									
3.	0.375	0.388	1.000								
4.	0.542	0.498	0.459	1.000							
5.	0.444	0.471	0.451	0.472	1.000						
6.	0.419	0.411	0.382	0.364	0.369	1.000					
7.	0.291	0.302	0.272	0.262	0.274	0.380	1.000				
8.	0.468	0.509	0.295	0.455	0.402	0.450	0.245	1.000			
9.	0.274	0.224	0.230	0.270	0.285	0.232	0.173	0.256	1.000		
10.	0.351	0.294	0.200	0.308	0.284	0.340	0.256	0.402	0.280	1.000	
11.	0.396	0.399	0.399	0.445	0.382	0.409	0.342	0.394	0.290	.0.342	1.000
s.d.	0.648	0.809	1.210	0.809	0.837	1.005	0.917	0.877	1.045	0.671	1.224
$g_{1(i)}$	2.949	2.148	0.757	2.466	2.260	1.584	1.115	2.170	2.127	2.717	0.588
$g_{2(i)}$	9.229	4.547	-0.389	6.012	4.677	1.793	0.645	4.245	3.588	7.135	-0.641

Note: $g_{1(i)} = N^{1/2}\Sigma_1^N(x_{it} - \bar{x}_i)^3 / \left[\Sigma_1^N(x_{it} - \bar{x}_i)^2\right]^{3/2}$ and

$$g_{2i} = N\Sigma_1^N(x_{it} - \bar{x}_i)^4 / \left[\Sigma_1^N(x_{it} - \bar{x}_i)^2\right]^2 - 3$$

are both less than 0.02, thereby indicating that the null hypothesis would have been rejected if the latter two discrepancy functions had been employed in practice. Interestingly, the adjusted ML statistic ($\overline{\overline{T}}_{\text{ML}} = 51.07$, p. = 0.391), with fractional $df = 48.98$, has almost exactly the same probability of acceptance as the scaled $\overline{T}_{\text{ML}}$ statistic. The results here are consistent with those of Hu et al (1992) who found that the HK estimator tended to slightly underestimate the expected χ^2 statistic relative to the robust scaled ML statistic, but that the HK test statistic was more correct than either the ML or ADF statistics, which were inflated well above their expected values. If we inspect the parameter estimates and standard errors in Table 2, we see that the HK and ML values are more similar compared to the ADF estimates, although the difference is more pronounced for factor loadings than for unique variances. The

Table 2 Unstandardized parameter estimates and standard error values for the single factor model of somatic complaints under different estimation methods ($df = 44$)

	ML		ADF		HK		Robust ML
	$\hat{\theta}$	(S.E.)	$\hat{\theta}$	(S.E.)	$\hat{\theta}$	(S.E.)	(S.E.)
λ_1	0.453	(0.031)	0.289	(0.058)	0.403	(0.054)	(0.069)
λ_2	0.561	(0.039)	0.416	(0.056)	0.512	(0.058)	(0.064)
λ_3	0.702	(0.062)	0.632	(0.053)	0.751	(0.066)	(0.056)
λ_4	0.571	(0.039)	0.356	(0.060)	0.541	(0.060)	(0.067)
λ_5	0.542	(0.042)	0.425	(0.058)	0.531	(0.060)	(0.068)
λ_6	0.620	(0.051)	0.597	(0.064)	0.653	(0.063)	(0.068)
λ_7	0.411	(0.049)	0.373	(0.054)	0.459	(0.056)	(0.062)
λ_8	0.578	(0.043)	0.466	(0.061)	0.509	(0.063)	(0.071)
λ_9	0.418	(0.056)	0.388	(0.074)	0.414	(0.076)	(0.078)
λ_{10}	0.330	(0.035)	0.228	(0.048)	0.312	(0.054)	(0.054)
λ_{11}	0.762	(0.061)	0.661	(0.049)	0.795	(0.064)	(0.050)
ψ_1	0.215	(0.019)	0.167	(0.026)	0.209	(0.036)	(0.031)
ψ_2	0.340	(0.029)	0.281	(0.038)	0.325	(0.044)	(0.047)
ψ_3	0.971	(0.078)	0.839	(0.067)	0.855	(0.073)	(0.074)
ψ_4	0.329	(0.029)	0.194	(0.034)	0.295	(0.046)	(0.050)
ψ_5	0.407	(0.033)	0.302	(0.039)	0.382	(0.052)	(0.056)
ψ_6	0.626	(0.051)	0.439	(0.062)	0.551	(0.062)	(0.075)
ψ_7	0.672	(0.052)	0.571	(0.047)	0.611	(0.056)	(0.059)
ψ_8	0.434	(0.036)	0.325	(0.040)	0.384	(0.052)	(0.064)
ψ_9	0.918	(0.070)	0.734	(0.101)	0.879	(0.102)	(0.117)
ψ_{10}	0.341	(0.027)	0.198	(0.035)	0.302	(0.046)	(0.052)
ψ_{11}	0.916	(0.075)	0.829	(0.073)	0.861	(0.071)	(0.075)
χ^2 value	79.89		66.82		36.14		45.89

ML standard errors are lower than corresponding ADF and HK values, whereas the latter two are slightly lower on average than the robust ML standard errors.

It is also instructive to consider the effect of applying Browne's (1984) general quadratic test of fit (Equation 10) to the incorrectly specified ML discrepancy function. Under maximum likelihood, this statistic is 70.11 and is therefore an improvement on the inflated likelihood ratio statistic of 79.89. However, it is still not comparable to the robust scaled statistic. The HK estimator statistic under Browne's general quadratic test of fit is much higher at 68.23, compared with its corresponding T_{HK} value. Using the robust scaled ML statistic as a benchmark, these results suggest that Browne's general quadratic test of fit does not adequately correct for employing an inefficient estimation method in this example. When the complete sample of 956 teachers is analyzed (these results are not shown here), the ADF test statistic ($T_{ADF} = 101.27$) is now much closer to the scaled ML statistic ($\bar{T}_{ML} = 96.90$) and the HK statistic ($T_{HK} = 76.02$), compared to the ML statistic ($T_{ML} = 166.76$). Assuming from simulation studies such as those of Hu et al (1992) that the robust scaled statistic is the least biased test of fit of those available, the ADF estimator therefore appears to require a large number of cases to obtain relatively accurate tests of fit even in the present instance of a small-to-moderate number of variables.

DISCUSSION

It is remarkable that in spite of substantial technical innovation in the statistics of covariance structure analysis during the past 15 years, only a few of these developments have found their way into texts, commercial computer programs, or general knowledge among users. For example, one of the authors inquired about the robust covariance matrix through the SEMNET special interest internet user's group and found only scattered awareness about its existence. It seems that only the most dedicated methodologists will know about the technical inadequacies in the methods routinely available for application. This review aims at broadening the knowledge of proven and potentially useful statistics for this field, and, with the code accessible via the Appendix, permitting the applied researcher to incorporate some of the more promising into their own favorite computer program. Although we have concentrated on methods for a single group, the same principles hold for multiple population covariance structure models (e.g. Bentler et al 1987) and to mean and covariance structure models (e.g. Browne & Arminger 1995, Satorra 1992). Some parallel results have been reported in the econometric literature (Newey & McFadden 1994) and in the statistical literature on nonlinear regression (Yuan 1995). Clearly, these newer methods should prove useful toward the more accurate evaluation of psychological theories with nonexperimental data.

With a small number of variables to model, clearly there are several alternative test statistics that hold under potential misspecification. Currently, only the Satorra-Bentler scaled statistic (15) is known to behave well empirically under a wide variety of distributional misspecifications. Yet, there are other potentially useful statistics that have hardly been studied, e.g. the mixture test (8) and the quadratic form test based on (10). It is not clear why this should be so. Of course, simulation work is time consuming and few theoretical statisticians will undertake it, yet without such work we will never know the actual performance of statistics under less than textbook conditions. Certainly, future research should determine whether these ignored tests have any role to play in real data analysis. In such situations, there seems to be little excuse for not using the robust covariance matrix (12), at least until feasible and improved alternatives become available. The current practice of typically using the wrong formula (Equation 13) to evaluate parameter significance seems especially unfortunate because it tends to give misleadingly optimistic results.

The situation is more difficult for models based on say, 40 or more variables, where computer limitations make some estimators infeasible. Although not enough research has gone into establishing the types of nonnormal distributions that might be fruitfully modeled by the Kano et al (1990) HK approach, this method should be studied further in the future since it is one of the few that holds any promise of handling models based on a huge number of nonnormal variables. In such circumstances, methods that require computation of a distribution-free estimate of the true covariance matrix Γ of the sample covariances will become unavailable, and normal, elliptical, and HK theory (or transformations to such—see Mooijaart 1993) seem to be the only alternatives. Aside from asymptotic robustness theory, which if it could be applied wisely would suggest when use of normal theory methods would work (see, e.g. Hu et al 1992), HK theory would seem to be a promising alternative. In the Appendix we describe a way to implement this method. It could be implemented easily in other programs if software distributors followed Schoenberg & Arminger's (1990) LINCS program of permitting input of the matrix V in a normal theory method, since this method can be adapted to yield the HK method. The rationale for the HK method requires scale-invariant models (e.g. Krane & McDonald 1978), so equality restrictions could create a problem in practice (see also O'Brien & Reilly 1995). Extension of the theory to correlation structure models would permit a wider range of models to be used. The standard error estimates for the HK theory are easy to compute, though of course they are only strictly correct under an HK distributional assumption. Research will have to establish the robustness of the HK statistics to violation of its assumptions. Certainly, because of the need to estimate a very large Γ, the robust covariance matrix (12) will be difficult to compute. Perhaps computer-intensive resampling methods will have to be used instead (e.g. Bollen & Stine 1993, Ichikawa & Konishi 1995, Yung & Bentler 1995).

In addition to distributional misspecification and the number of variables and parameters in a model, sample size is a major factor influencing the quality of statistics in covariance structure models. Although projection of asymptotic theory onto small sample data analysis is an old problem (Boomsma 1983, Tanaka 1987), it remains a continuing one: More and more statistics rely on fourth-order moments of the data and these are unstable at the relatively low samples sizes that characterize most real data. Clearly, further research should be directed toward improving estimators of weight matrices that require such moments.

A FINAL NOTE

Since this review went to press, Yuan & Bentler (1995) developed some new test statistics for mean and covariance structure analysis. One of these can be computed as a simple Bartlett-type correction to the ADF test statistic. Specifically, considering a model fitted under arbitrary distributions using optimal ADF estimation, their corrected statistic can be computed as

$$T_{CADF} = T_{ADF} / (1 + T_{ADF} / n).$$

In a small simulation study with a covariance structure model, they replicated earlier results showing that the standard ADF test statistic is essentially unusable in small to intermediate sized samples. On the other hand, their corrected statistic yielded a dramatic improvement in performance. It behaved close to nominally at all sample sizes, though there was a tendency for the rejection rate under the null hypothesis to be somewhat too small. As sample size gets very large, as is obvious from the formula, $T_{CADF} \rightarrow T_{ADF}$, i.e. the Yuan-Bentler statistic becomes equivalent to the Browne-Chamberlain statistic in covariance structure analysis. This optimistic development clearly bears further study.

APPENDIX

This Appendix contains an overview of several procedures that have been written in the MATRIX command language of SPSS Release 4 (SPSS 1990) for carrying out a number of the above test statistics that are not available currently in structural modeling programs like LISREL or EQS. These procedures can be readily adapted to other matrix programming languages such as PROC IML (SAS Institute 1990) or GAUSS (Aptech Systems 1992) or incorporated into general matrix procedures for covariance structure analysis (see, e.g. Cudeck et al 1993). Files containing the MATRIX commands, as well as detailed instructions and test data, are available on the Internet via anonymous ftp at ftp.stat.ucla.edu in the directory \pub\code\statlib\csm or from either author. For those unfamiliar with using ftp, brief instructions are provided at the end of this Appendix. Further details concerning the use of the procedures are provided in files at the ftp site.

Heterogenous Kurtosis Estimation

Heterogenous kurtosis estimation can be obtained from standard covariance structure modeling programs if the program includes ADF estimation as an option. To implement the HK estimator, we make use of the equivalence between the normal theory GLS discrepancy function

$$F_{GLS} = \frac{1}{2} tr\left\{ [S - \Sigma(\theta)] V^{-1} \right\}^2 \tag{A1}$$

and the quadratic discrepancy function

$$F_{QD} = [\underset{\sim}{s} - \sigma(\theta)]' \hat{W} [\underset{\sim}{s} - \sigma(\theta)] \tag{A2}$$

where in the latter

$$\hat{W} = \left[2K_p'(V \otimes V)K_p \right]^{-1}$$
$$= \frac{1}{2} K_p^-\left(V^{-1} \otimes V^{-1} \right) K_p^{-\prime} \tag{A3}$$

and K_p^- is the Moore-Penrose inverse of K_p (see, e.g. Browne 1974, 1984). It is useful to remember that in this instance, $\hat{W} = \Gamma_N^{-1}$ because the discrepancy function is correctly specified. In any desired application of the HK discrepancy function to a particular covariance structure model employing SPSS MATRIX commands, we need to (a) calculate the estimates of $\hat{\kappa}_i = (s_{iiii} / 3s_{ii}^2)^{1/2}$ for the observed variables i = 1,...,p in the model, (b) calculate the product $\hat{C} = \hat{A} * \hat{\Sigma}$, where $\hat{A} = (\hat{a}_{ij}) = (\hat{\kappa}_i + \hat{\kappa}_j)/2$, (c) compute the required transition matrix K_p for the number of observed variables, and (d) compute (A3), where we substitute $\hat{C}$ for V and signify the resultant weight matrix as $\hat{W}_{HK}$. The LISREL or EQS user then minimizes the quadratic form discrepancy function

$$F\left[(S, \Sigma(\hat{\theta})) \Big| W = \Gamma_{HK}^{-1}, \Gamma_{HK} \right]$$

for heterogenous kurtosis estimation by taking the lower symmetric form of the resultant estimate of $\hat{W}_{HK}$, and inputting it as the external weight matrix file associated with WLS or AGLS estimation respectively. It should be noted that the weight matrix in both LISREL and EQS is inverted after it has been read in from an external file, so the SPSS MATRIX commands produce the noninverted form of (A3). Similar methods can be used to obtain estimates under elliptical distribution in LISREL or to compare the equivalence of estimation under the ML discrepancy function F_{ML} to that of the reweighted least-squares function F_{RLS}.

Scaled Test Statistics and Robust Standard Errors

The Satorra-Bentler scaled test statistic and robust standard errors are available already in EQS. To obtain these statistics for any covariance structure model that has been fitted by programs such as LISREL, we require (a) the ADF weight matrix, signified here as $\hat{\Gamma}$ and based on sample estimators for (14), (b) the appropriate consistent estimator of

$$\mathbf{W} = \hat{\Gamma}_N^{-1}, \hat{\Gamma}_E^{-1}, \text{ or } \hat{\Gamma}_{HK}^{-1}$$

using Equation (A3) for the particular estimation method being employed, (c) the matrix $\hat{\Delta}$ of partial first derivatives, and (d) the test statistic T and degrees of freedom (df) for the fitted model. The ADF weight matrix can be obtained from PRELIS, where it is called the asymptotic covariance matrix, or it can be computed directly using SPSS MATRIX commands. The matrix $\hat{\mathbf{W}}$ can be computed by a SPSS MATRIX procedure using (A3), where we substitute for $\mathbf{V}$ the appropriate sample matrix for the estimation method chosen in LISREL. Finally, a numerical approximation can be obtained in SPSS MATRIX for the matrix $\hat{\Delta}$ of partial derivatives using a forward finite-difference method (Kennedy & Gentle 1980, Section 10.2.6). Let h be a small constant, for instance 10^{-5}, and let c_i be a column vector of the same dimension as θ with a value of unity in its i-th element and zero values in all remaining elements. Then the $p^* \times 1$ vector of partial derivatives for the i-th value of θ is given by

$$\frac{\partial \sigma(\hat{\theta})}{\partial \theta_i'} = \frac{\sigma(\hat{\theta} + c_i h) - \sigma(\hat{\theta})}{h} = \sigma(\theta_i').$$

The $p^* \times q$ matrix $\hat{\Delta}$ can be derived from the concatenation of successive columns of $\sigma(\theta_i')$. The test statistic T can be found in the printout of the model.

Let us assume, for example, that we have estimated a model using maximum likelihood, and that we have calculated the three required matrices noted above (i.e. $\hat{\Gamma}, \mathbf{W} = \hat{\Gamma}_N^{-1}$, and $\hat{\Delta}$) and also obtained the values for T_{ML} and the df from the LISREL output. Then we can obtain (a) the Satorra-Bentler scaled test statistic $\overline{T}_{ML}$ by simple substitution to obtain $\mathbf{U}$ in Equation (9), and then solve Equation (15), and (b) robust standard errors by simple substitution into Equation (12), in which $\Gamma = \hat{\Gamma}$ and $\mathbf{W} = \hat{\Gamma}_N^{-1}$. The Satorra-Bentler adjusted test statistic (16) can be readily obtained in a similar manner. Note that SPSS MATRIX has a χ^2 cumulative distribution function routine that takes noninteger *df* values, so that it can compute the more precise form of (16).

Accessing the SPSS MATRIX Files by FTP

For persons who have not used anonymous ftp (file transfer protocol) procedures before, the following gives a few basic instructions. You will need access to the Internet and appropriate software for performing ftp. The hostname of the computer where the SPSS MATRIX files can be found is ftp.stat.ucla.edu. The account name that you must give to gain access is "anonymous" and the password is (usually) your email address. Once you have gained access, go to the subdirectory \pub\code\statlib\csm where the files are located (typically, this is done by typing "cd pub\code\statlib\csm"). All files are in ASCII format and can be transferred to your own computer by the appropriate commands for the particular ftp software implementation being used (typically, this is by typing "mget *.*"). Some ftp software implementations utilize graphical user interfaces, and so there is no way of covering all the possibilities of how to ftp the files, beyond the basic approach given here. It would be best to consult your local computer advisory service if you are uncertain about what to do.

Any Annual Review chapter, as well as any article cited in an Annual Review chapter, may be purchased from the Annual Reviews Preprints and Reprints service. 1-800-347-8007; 415-259-5017; email: arpr@class.org

---

Literature Cited

Amemiya Y, Anderson TW. 1990. Asymptotic chi-square tests for a large class of factor analysis models. *Ann. Stat.* 18:1453–63

Anderson TW. 1994. See Anderson et al 1994, pp. 1–20

Anderson TW, Amemiya Y. 1988. The asymptotic normal distribution of estimators in factor analysis under general conditions. *Ann. Stat.* 16:759–71

Anderson TW, Fang KT, Olkin I, eds. 1994. *Multivariate Analysis and Its Applications.* Hayward, CA: Inst. Math. Stat.

Aptech Systems. 1992. *GAUSS System, Version 3.* Kent, WA: Aptech Syst.

Arminger G. 1995. See Arminger et al 1995, pp. 77–183

Arminger G, Clogg CC, Sobel ME, eds. 1995. *Handbook of Statistical Modeling for the Social and Behavioral Sciences.* New York: Plenum

Arminger G, Schoenberg RJ. 1989. Pseudo maximum likelihood estimation and a test for misspecification in mean and covariance structure models. *Psychometrika* 53: 409–25

Bekker PA, Merckens A, Wansbeek TJ. 1994. *Identification, Equivalent Models, and Computer Algebra.* Boston: Academic

Bell RC, Wearing AJ, Conn M, Dudgeon P, McMurray N, Stanley GV. 1990. *Teacher Stress in Victoria.* Melbourne, Australia: Victorian Minist. Educ.

Bentler PM. 1980. Multivariate analysis with latent variables: causal modeling. *Annu. Rev. Psychol.* 31:419–56

Bentler PM. 1983a. Some contributions to efficient statistics for structural models: specification and estimation of moment structures. *Psychometrika* 48:493–517

Bentler PM. 1983b. Simultaneous equations as

moment structure models: with an introduction to latent variable models. *J. Econometr.* 22:13–42

Bentler PM. 1994. See Anderson et al 1994, pp. 123–36

Bentler PM. 1995. *EQS Structural Equations Program Manual.* Encino, CA: Multivariate Softw.

Bentler PM, Berkane M, Kano Y. 1991. Covariance structure analysis under a simple kurtosis model. In *Computing Science and Statistics,* ed. EM Keramidas, pp. 463–65. Fairfax Station, VA: Interface Found

Bentler PM, Dijkstra T. 1985. Efficient estimation via linearization in structural models. In *Multivariate Analysis VI,* ed. PR Krishnaiah, pp. 9–42. Amsterdam: North Holland

Bentler PM, Lee SY, Weng LJ. 1987. Multiple population covariance structure analysis under arbitrary distribution theory. *Comm. Stat. Theory* 16:1951–64

Bentler PM, Weeks DG. 1980. Linear structural equations with latent variables. *Psychometrika* 45:289–308

Bentler PM, Wu EJC. 1995a. *EQS for Macintosh User's Guide.* Encino, CA: Multivariate Softw.

Bentler PM, Wu EJC. 1995b. *EQS for Windows User's Guide.* Encino, CA: Multivariate Softw.

Bollen KA. 1989. *Structural Equations with Latent Variables.* New York: Wiley

Bollen KA, Long JS, eds. 1993. *Testing Structural Equation Models.* Newbury Park, CA: Sage

Bollen KA, Stine RA. 1993. See Bollen & Long 1993, pp. 111–35

Boomsma A. 1983. *On the robustness of LISREL (maximum likelihood estimation) against small sample size and nonnormality.* PhD thesis. Univ. Groningen

Borg I, Mohler PPh, eds. 1994. *Trends and Perspectives in Empirical Social Research.* Berlin: Walter de Gruyter

Breckler SJ. 1990. Applications of covariance structure modeling in psychology: Cause for concern? *Psychol. Bull.* 107: 260–73

Browne MW. 1974. Generalized least squares estimators in the analysis of covariance structures. *S. Afr. Stat. J.* 8:1–24

Browne MW. 1982. Covariance structures. In *Topics in Applied Multivariate Analysis,* ed. DM Hawkins, pp. 72–141. Cambridge: Cambridge Univ. Press

Browne MW. 1984. Asymptotically distribution-free methods for the analysis of covariance structures. *Br. J. Math. Stat. Psychol.* 37:62–83

Browne MW. 1987. Robustness of statistical inference in factor analysis and related models. *Biometrika* 74:375–84

Browne MW. 1990. Asymptotic robustness of normal theory methods for the analysis of latent curves. In *Statistical Analysis of Measurement Error Models and Applications,* ed. PJ Brown, WA Fuller, 112:211–25. Providence, RI: Am. Math. Soc.

Browne MW, Arminger G. 1995. See Arminger et al 1995, pp. 185–249

Browne MW, Cudeck R. 1993. See Bollen & Long 1993, pp. 136–62

Browne MW, Mels G, Coward M. 1994. Path analysis: RAMONA. In *SYSTAT for DOS: Advanced Applications, Version 6 Ed.,* pp. 163–224. Evanston, IL: Systat

Browne MW, Shapiro A. 1988. Robustness of normal theory methods in the analysis of linear latent variate models. *Br. J. Math. Stat. Psychol.* 41:193–208

Bullock HE, Harlow LL, Mulaik SA. 1994. Causation issues in structural equation modeling research. *Struct. Eq. Mod.* 1: 253–67

Byrne BM. 1994. *Structural Equation Modeling with EQS and EQS/Windows.* Thousand Oaks, CA: Sage

Chamberlain G. 1982. Multivariate regression models for panel data. *J. Econometr.* 18: 5–46

Chan W, Yung YF, Bentler PM. 1995. A note on using an unbiased weight matrix in the ADF test statistic. *Mult. Behav. Res.* In press

Chou CP, Bentler PM. 1995. See Hoyle 1995, pp. 36–55

Chou CP, Bentler PM, Satorra A. 1991. Scaled test statistics and robust standard errors for nonnormal data in covariance structure analysis: a Monte Carlo study. *Br. J. Math. Stat. Psychol.* 44:347–57

Cudeck RL, Henly SJ. 1991. Model size in covariance structures analysis and the 'problem' of sample size. *Psychol. Bull.* 109:512–19

Cudeck RL, Klebe KJ, Henly SJ. 1993. A simple Gauss-Newton procedure for covariance structure analysis with high-level computer languages. *Psychometrika* 58: 211–32

Curran PJ, West SG, Finch JF. 1994. The robustness of test statistics to non-normality and specification error in confirmatory factor analysis. In *Psychological Methods.* In press

de Leeuw J. 1988. Multivariate analysis with linearizable regressions. *Psychometrika* 53: 437–54

Dijkstra T. 1981. *Latent variables in linear stochastic models.* PhD thesis. Univ. Groningen

Dudgeon P. 1994. A reparameterization of the restricted factor analysis model for multitrait-multimethod matrices. *Br. J. Math. Stat. Psychol.* 47:283–308

Dunn G, Everitt B, Pickles A. 1993. *Modelling*

Covariances and Latent Variables Using EQS. London: Chapman & Hall

Faulbaum F, Bentler PM. 1994. See Borg & Mohler 1994, pp. 224–49

Finch JF, West SG, MacKinnon DP. 1995. The effects of sample size and non-normality on the estimation of direct and indirect effects in latent variable models. *Struct. Eq. Model.* In press

Gierl MJ, Mulvenon S. 1995. *Evaluating the application of fit indices to structural equation models in educational research: a review of the literature from 1990 through 1994.* Presented at 1995 Annu. Meet. Am. Educ. Res. Assoc., San Francisco

Haagen K, Bartholomew DJ, Deistler M, eds. 1993. *Statistical Modelling and Latent Variables.* Amsterdam: North Holland

Hoyle R, ed. 1995. *Structural Equation Modeling: Concepts, Issues, and Applications.* Thousand Oaks, CA: Sage

Hu LT, Bentler PM, Kano Y. 1992. Can test statistics in covariance structure analysis be trusted? *Psychol. Bull.* 112:351–62

Ichikawa M, Konishi S. 1995. Application of the bootstrap methods in factor analysis. *Psychometrika* 60:77–93

Jöreskog KG. 1969. A general approach to confirmatory maximum likelihood factor analysis. *Psychometrika* 34:183–202

Jöreskog KG. 1994. See Anderson et al 1994, pp. 297–310

Jöreskog KG, Sörbom D. 1993. *LISREL 8 User's Reference Guide.* Chicago: Sci. Softw. Int.

Jöreskog KG, Yang F. 1995. See Marcoulides & Schumaker 1995

Kano Y. 1992. Robust statistics for test-of-independence and related structural models. *Stat. Probab. Lett.* 15:21–26

Kano Y. 1993. See Haagen et al 1993, pp. 173–90

Kano Y, Bentler PM, Mooijaart A. 1993. Additional information and precision of estimators in multivariate structural models. In *Statistical Sciences and Data Analysis,* ed. K Matusita, ML Puri, T Hayakawa, pp. 187–96. Zeist: VSP (Int. Sci. Publ.)

Kano Y, Berkane M, Bentler PM. 1990. Covariance structure analysis with heterogeneous kurtosis parameters. *Biometrika* 77: 575–85

Kennedy WJ Jr, Gentle JE. 1980. *Statistical Computing.* New York: Dekker

Kenny DA, Judd CM. 1984. Estimating the nonlinear and interactive effects of latent variables. *Psychol. Bull.* 96:201–10

Koning R, Neudecker H, Wansbeek T. 1993. See Haagen et al 1993, pp. 191–202

Krane WR, McDonald RP. 1978. Scale invariance and the factor analysis of correlation matrices. *Br. J. Math. Stat. Psychol.* 31: 218–28

Lee S, Hershberger S. 1990. A simple rule for generating equivalent models in covariance structure modeling. *Mult. Behav. Res.* 25: 313–34

Lee SY. 1985. On testing functional constraints in structural equation models. *Biometrika* 72:125–31

Lee SY. 1990. Multilevel analysis of structural equation models. *Biometrika* 77:763–72

Lee SY, Bentler PM. 1980. Some asymptotic properties of constrained generalized least squares estimation in covariance structure models. *S. Afr. Stat. J.* 14:121–36

Lee SY, Poon WY, Bentler PM. 1992. Structural equation models with continuous and polytomous variables. *Psychometrika* 57: 89–105

Lee SY, Poon WY, Bentler PM. 1995. A two-stage estimation of structural equation models with continuous and polytomous variables. *Br. J. Math. Stat. Psychol.* In press

Lockhart RS. 1967. Asymptotic sampling variances for factor analytic models identified by specified zero parameters. *Psychometrika* 32:265–77

Loehlin JC. 1992. *Latent Variable Models: An Introduction to Factor, Path, and Structural Analysis.* Hillsdale, NJ: Erlbaum

MacCallum RC, Rosnowski M, Necowitz LB. 1992. Model modifications in covariance structure analysis: the problem of capitalization on chance. *Psychol. Bull.* 111:490–504

MacCallum RC, Wegener DT, Uchino BN, Fabrigar LR. 1993. The problem of equivalent models in applications of covariance structure analysis. *Psychol. Bull.* 114:185–99

Marcoulides GA, Schumacker RE, eds. 1995. *Advanced Structural Equation Modeling Techniques.* Hillsdale, NJ: Erlbaum. In press

McArdle JJ, McDonald RP. 1984. Some algebraic properties of the Reticular Action Model for moment structures. *Br. J. Math. Stat. Psychol.* 37:234–51

McDonald RP. 1989. An index of goodness-of-fit based on noncentrality. *J. Classif.* 6: 97–103

Micceri T. 1989. The unicorn, the normal curve, and other improbable creatures. *Psychol. Bull.* 105:156–66

Mooijaart A. 1985. Factor analysis for non-normal variables. *Psychometrika* 50: 323–42

Mooijaart A. 1993. See Haagen et al 1993, pp. 249–58

Mooijaart A, Bentler PM. 1986. Random polynomial factor analysis. In *Data Analysis and Informatics IV,* ed. E Diday, Y Escoufier, L Lebart, J Pages, Y Schektman, et al, pp. 241–50. Amsterdam: Elsevier

Mooijaart A, Bentler PM. 1991. Robustness of

normal theory statistics in structural equation models. *Stat. Neerland.* 45:159–71

Muthén B. 1984. A general structural equation model with dichotomous, ordered categorical, and continuous latent variable indicators. *Psychometrika* 49:115–32

Muthén B, Kaplan D. 1992. A comparison of some methodologies for the factor analysis of nonnormal Likert variables: a note on the size of the model. *Br. J. Math. Stat. Psychol.* 45:19–30

Muthén B, Satorra A. 1989. Multilevel aspects of varying parameters in structural models. In *Multilevel Analysis of Educational Data*, ed. RD Bock, pp. 87–99. San Diego: Academic

Newey WK, McFadden D. 1994. Large sample estimation and hypothesis testing. In *Handbook of Econometrics*, ed. RF Engle, D McFadden, 4:2112–245. Amsterdam: Elsevier Sci.

O'Brien RM, Reilly T. 1995. Equality in constraints and metric-setting measurement models. *Struct. Eq. Mod.* 2:1–12

Olkin I. 1994. See Anderson et al 1994, pp. 37–53

SAS Institute. 1990. *SAS/IML Software: Usage and References, Version 6.* Cary, NC: SAS Inst.

Satorra A. 1989. Alternative test criteria in covariance structure analysis: a unified approach. *Psychometrika* 54:131–51

Satorra A. 1992. Asymptotic robust inferences in the analysis of mean and covariance structures. In *Sociological Methodology 1992*, ed. PV Marsden, pp. 249–78. Oxford: Blackwell

Satorra A. 1993. See Haagen et al 1993, pp. 283–98

Satorra A, Bentler PM. 1986. Some robustness properties of goodness of fit statistics in covariance structure analysis. *Proc. Bus. Econ. Stat. Am. Stat. Assoc.*, pp. 549–54

Satorra A, Bentler PM. 1988. Scaling corrections for chi-square statistics in covariance structure analysis. *Proc. Am. Stat. Assoc.*, pp. 308–13

Satorra A, Bentler PM. 1990. Model conditions for asymptotic robustness in the analysis of linear relations. *Comput. Stat. Data Anal.* 10:235–49

Satorra A, Bentler PM. 1991. Goodness-of-fit test under IV estimation: asymptotic robustness of a NT test statistic. In *Applied Stochastic Models and Data Analysis*, ed. R Gutiérrez, MJ Valderrama, pp. 555–67. Singapore: World Sci.

Satorra A, Bentler PM. 1994. Corrections to test statistics and standard errors in covariance structure analysis. In *Latent Variables Analysis: Applications for Developmental Research*, ed. A von Eye, CC Clogg, pp. 399–419. Thousand Oaks, CA: Sage

Schoenberg R, Arminger G. 1990. *LINCS: A User's Guide.* Kent, WA: Aptech Syst.

Shapiro A. 1983. Asymptotic distribution theory in the analysis of covariance structures. *S. Afr. Stat. J.* 17:33–81

Shapiro A, Browne MW. 1987. Analysis of covariance structures under elliptical distributions. *J. Am. Stat. Assoc.* 82:1092–97

Sobel ME. 1995. See Arminger et al 1995, pp. 1–38

SPSS. 1990. *SPSS Reference Guide (Release 4).* Chicago: SPSS

Steiger J. 1994. See Borg & Mohler 1994, pp. 201–23

Steyer R. 1993. Principles of causal modeling: a summary of its mathematical foundations and practical steps. In *SoftStat '93: Advances in Statistical Software*, ed. F Faulbaum, pp. 107–14. Stuttgart: Fischer

Tanaka JS. 1987. "How big is big enough?": sample size and goodness of fit in structural equation models with latent variables. *Child Dev.* 58:134–46

Ullman JB. 1995. Structural equation modeling. In *Using Multivariate Statistics*, ed. BG Tabachnick, LS Fidell. New York: Harper & Row. In press

Weng LJ, Bentler PM. 1995. *Covariance Structure Analysis with Intraclass Dependent Observations.* Taipei: Natl. Taiwan Univ.

West SG, Finch JF, Curran PJ. 1995. See Hoyle 1995, pp. 56–75

Wiley DE. 1973. The identification problem for structural equation models with unmeasured variables. In *Structural Equation Models in the Social Sciences*, ed. AS Goldberger, OD Duncan, pp. 69–83. New York: Academic

Willett JB, Sayer AG. 1994. Using covariance structure analysis to detect correlates and predictors of individual change over time. *Psychol. Bull.* 116:363–81

Yuan KH. 1995. *Asymptotics for nonlinear regression models with applications.* PhD thesis. Univ. Calif., Los Angeles

Yuan KH, Bentler PM. 1995. Mean and covariance structure analysis: theoretical and practical improvements. *UCLA Stat. Ser. Rep. 180.* UCLA Cent. Stat. Los Angeles, Calif.

Yung YF, Bentler PM. 1994. Bootstrap-corrected ADF test statistics in covariance structure analysis. *Br. J. Math. Stat. Psychol.* 47:63–84

Yung YF, Bentler PM. 1995. See Marcoulides & Schumacker 1995

Annu. Rev. Psychol. 1996. 47:593–620

THE MOTIVATIONAL IMPACT OF TEMPORAL FOCUS: Thinking About the Future and the Past

Rachel Karniol

Department of Psychology, Tel Aviv University, Ramat Aviv, Israel

Michael Ross

Department of Psychology, University of Waterloo, Waterloo, Ontario, N2L 3G1 Canada

KEY WORDS: goals, autobiographical memory, prioritizing goals

ABSTRACT

In this chapter, we consider the degree to which individuals are pulled to behave by their conceptions of the future, pushed to act by their recollections of the past, or primarily driven by current exigencies. In examining conceptions of the future, we discuss how individuals bridge the present and the future, the origin of goals, their impact on behavior and cognition, and the motivational underpinnings for inferring other people's goals. We then outline four theoretical approaches to goal prioritization, the motivational impact of proximal vs distal goals, and the distinction between approaching positive vs avoiding negative outcomes. Turning to conceptions of the past, we discuss the motivational push of the past, the use of the past to select one's goals, the impact current goals have on recall and interpretations of the past, and individual differences in using the past. We conclude that temporal focus provides a meaningful framework for social cognitive approaches to motivation.

CONTENTS

0066-4308/96/0201-0593$08.00

INTRODUCTION

Most world languages mark time grammatically to differentiate future events from events in the past and the present (Binnick 1991). This linguistic attribute sensitizes individuals to the temporal status of events. Motivation is affected by *how* people think about past and future events. In some cultures, people view the future as so unpredictable that they fail to attempt to influence the course of their lives (Kluckhohn & Strodbeck 1961). In contrast, many individuals in Western cultures adopt long-term educational, financial, and health goals, engaging in activities that are nearly masochistic: attending graduate school, saving for retirement, and jogging. The past, represented in people's memories and in conceptions of history, also influences motivation. The traumatic recollections of Holocaust survivors influence their behavior in complex and disturbing ways (Chodoff 1986, Dor-Shav 1978). Individuals often react to the present as if they were reliving the past (e.g. Spiegel 1981). By the same token, many international conflicts have their roots in divergent interpretations of the past.

As these examples suggest, the past and the future are social cognitive constructions: They can be idiosyncratic or culturally held, more or less stable, and more or less realistic. Here, we consider the motivational relevance of such constructions and examine the degree to which individuals are pulled to behave by their conceptions of the future, pushed to act by their recollections of the past, or primarily driven by current exigencies.

Theorists have long recognized the importance of temporal focus to motivation. Lewin (1935, 1943) incorporated people's conceptions of the past, present and future into his concept of "life space," the subjective representation of one's current goals and social setting. Lewin defined goals as cognitive representations of states that people desire to attain. The past serves as the context in which people acquire knowledge about future possibilities.

More recently, sociologists Bell & Mau (1971) presented a model of social change that illustrates the impact of temporal focus on motivation. They suggested that people's images of the future influence their current decisions by determining their goals and the procedures they select for achieving them. Bell & Mau argued that views of possible futures differ on three major dimensions: positivity (i.e. Does the future hold good or bad outcomes?), controllability (i.e. Can one influence one's future outcomes?), and temporal distance (i.e. How far away is the envisaged future?). People derive their forecasts from their recollections of the past, conceptions of the present, attributions of social causality, and values. Values represent criteria for defining desirable and undesirable images of the future and provide the basis for evaluating alternative possible futures.

As we will show, many of the processes explicated by Bell & Mau are precisely the ones that personality and social psychologists have examined in their studies of motivation. We begin our analysis with how conceptions of the future—and goals in particular—affect motivational processes. We proceed to examine the motivational impact of the past, as well as the relations among people's views of the past, present, and future.

GOALS IN SOCIAL PSYCHOLOGICAL THEORY

The idea that people's expectations for the future can be used to understand their behavior extends back to Plato (Bolles 1974); however, Lewin's (1935, 1943) seminal discussion of goals has most affected current social psychological theory. According to Lewin, individuals are motivated to develop strategies and to invest effort in the pursuit of their goals. The future, as represented by goals, exerts a major influence on current behavior. Thus conceptualized, the goal concept has become critical to many social and personality theorists (e.g. Cantor & Fleeson 1991; Deci & Ryan 1985; Locke & Latham 1990; McIntosh & Martin 1992; Mischel & Shoda 1995; Pervin 1989a, 1992; Stein & Glenn 1991).

Bridging the Present and the Future

How do possible futures influence an individual's current motivational state? People can forge a connection between the future and the present in a number of ways. In general, people imagine various futures, consider the advantages and disadvantages of each, select their preferred end states, and then develop plans to achieve their desired goals while avoiding negative outcomes (e.g. Bandura 1989, 1990; Beach 1990; Locke & Latham 1990; Melges 1982; Mueller 1990).

Beach (1990) suggested that individuals' constructions of the future are guided by three types of images. The *value* image consists of prescriptive and proscriptive standards for adopting or rejecting both goals and associated actions. The *trajectory* image represents the goals that people pursue and the ideals they want to achieve. The *strategic* image consists of plans for attaining goals.

According to Beach, individuals assess the compatibility of plans with the relevant images by constructing scenarios of possible futures. Scenarios connect the present to the future and provide a basis for making decisions about how to pursue goals. Evaluations of possible plans are not based solely on expected utility; instead, Beach posits that individuals' actions are often dictated by the moral principles, social norms, and standards of appropriateness contained in the person's value image.

Markus and her colleagues suggested that individuals bring the future into the present by creating images of possible selves, representations of how they might act, look, or feel in the future (Cantor et al 1986, Markus & Nurius 1986, Markus & Ruvolo 1989). Guided by their experiences, self-knowledge, current moods, and expectations, people imagine selves they would like to achieve (positive selves) and to avoid (feared selves). Imagined end states motivate current behavior to the extent that people can link their present condition to these potential outcomes through a set of self-representations that lead to the end states (Markus et al 1990).

Yet individuals differ in their tendency to focus on the future. Norem & Illingworth (1993) reported that defensive pessimists are more inclined than optimists to construct possible futures. Such simulations apparently help defensive pessimists to channel their anxiety about failure into plans for effective behavior. Preferring to avoid contemplating negative possibilities, optimists are less disposed to think about possible futures. As well, individuals can be defensive pessimists in some contexts (e.g. academic tasks) and optimists in others (e.g. social settings), with attendant cognitive consequences (Cantor et al 1987, Norem & Cantor 1990, Norem & Illingworth 1993).

Thus, people may sometimes decline to think about the future and, as research on prediction indicates (e.g. Buehler et al 1994, Griffin et al 1990, Hoch 1984, Kahneman & Lovallo 1993), at any given time they may consider only a small subset of possible futures. This can occur because people may not contemplate futures that are incompatible with their values or preferences. People may also fail to consider that the future may not evolve as expected (Buehler et al 1994, Kahneman & Lovallo 1993, Kahneman & Tversky 1979).

The motivational bridge connecting the present to the future permits traffic to flow in both directions. Current knowledge and moods can affect people's constructions of the future, and their constructions of the future can influence their present cognitive and emotional states. Individuals who explicitly imagine possible futures provide higher estimates of the probability of the imagined events, and they are more likely to engage in behaviors associated with the imagined events than individuals who do not engage in such forecasts (e.g. Anderson 1983, Sherman et al 1981; see Johnson & Sherman 1990 and Koehler 1991 for reviews). Instructing individuals to develop more distal and more varied possible selves affects the objectives they subsequently set for themselves (Day et al 1994).

Origin of Goals

People may generate their own goals, develop them in concert with others (participatory goals), adopt goals proposed by others, or have goals thrust upon them. Social psychologists from the time of Lewin (1935) onward (e.g. Deci & Ryan 1985, Lepper & Gilovich 1981) have maintained that self or participatory goals are more motivating than goals imposed by others. For instance, externally imposed goals undermine people's interest in pursuing activities for their own sake (Deci & Ryan 1985, Lepper & Gilovich 1981). Organizational psychologists, however, reach a different conclusion when they examine the quality and intensity of people's performance under externally imposed goals (see Locke & Latham 1990 for a review). Such studies reveal no systematic differences in people's attainments as a function of whether goals are self-set, assigned, or participatory. The apparent discrepancy may have a number of explanations. Goals may not affect liking for the task in the same way they affect quality of task performance. Also, even when working toward assigned objectives, individuals are not fully constrained and may still be able to select their own strategies. Finally, in organizational settings, individuals fully expect to be assigned goals by others. Perhaps such assignment undermines motivation only when individuals believe they should be able to select their own goals (NL Stein, personal communication).

Evidence shows that personality also influences responses to externally imposed vs self-imposed goals (Harackiewicz & Elliot 1993, Racicot et al 1991). Harackiewicz & Elliot (1993) reported that externally imposed goals consistent with participants' achievement orientations enhanced intrinsic interest in an activity. An achievement goal (i.e. performance level would be compared with that of other participants) only increased the intrinsic interest of those high in achievement orientation.

Bargh (1990; Bargh & Barndollar 1996) proposed that recurring goals need not be generated by the individual. If an individual often pursues a goal in a specific situation, the goal may become linked to features of that situation. As a result of repeated association, environmental stimuli eventually elicit the goal automatically, without the person's conscious guidance. Once activated, this goal can evoke behaviors, even though individuals may not consciously select or intend those actions (Bargh & Gollwitzer 1994).

Impact of Goals on Behavior and Cognition

Goals affect people's behavioral choices, effort, and persistence at tasks (Locke & Latham 1990). The impact of goals on cognitive processing is equally pervasive; "Thinking begins with goals and cannot move without them" (Simon 1994, p. 19). Goals can monopolize people's attention as they plan ways to achieve their objectives and evaluate their progress. Goals can influence recollection, observation, and interpretation of information. Individuals may retrieve goal-relevant knowledge from memory, seek and attend to events in their environment that are relevant to their goals, and interpret behavior and events in light of their objectives (Ditto & Lopez 1992, Gollwitzer 1993, Kruglanski 1989, Kunda 1990, Lord et al 1979, Murray & Holmes 1993, Vorauer & Ross 1993, 1995).

Gollwitzer (1990, 1993; Bargh & Gollwitzer 1994) analyzed the impact of temporally distinct stages of goal pursuit on behavior and cognition. Intriguingly, progression through the stages of goal pursuit engenders transitions from impartial to biased evaluation of information. During the predecisional phase, people establish priorities by impartially processing information related to the feasibility and desirability of alternative goals. After choosing a goal, but before actively pursuing it, they develop plans. At this stage, they process information about issues of implementation in an unbiased fashion, but they disregard information about the desirability of the goal. Next, while actively pursuing the goal, people attend primarily to those aspects of the self and the environment that promote successful performance; they reject information that would trigger reevaluation of the goal or their adopted strategies. In the final evaluative phase, people compare their outcomes with their actual goals and initial desires. Such a comparison may lead to the cessation of goal pursuit, or it may trigger renewed attempts to attain blocked goals. In several studies, empirical support for the cognitive and behavioral impact of successive phases of goal pursuit has been found (Gollwitzer 1990, 1993; Gollwitzer et al 1990a,b).

Gollwitzer proposed that at each stage of goal pursuit, individuals focus primarily on information relevant to that specific phase. However, in their eagerness to attain their goals, people may exaggerate the goal relevance of ambiguous information (Vorauer & Ross 1993, 1995). For example, a man who is anxious to assess a woman's feelings about him may notice and read meaning into actions that do not actually reflect those feelings.

As well, Gollwitzer proposed that in the final, evaluative phase of goal pursuit, people willingly abandon unsuccessful strategies so that in the future they can attain their original goal or attractive alternatives. However, individuals may become committed to ineffective strategies (Staw 1976, Staw & Ross

1987), especially when they are personally responsible for negative consequences and need to justify their actions (Bobocel & Meyer 1994).

Individuals sometimes exhibit remarkable tenacity in goal pursuit. Based
on their analysis of the life histories of individuals in pre-Nazi and Nazi
Germany, Allport et al (1948) observed that many individuals spent years of
intense suffering before they gave up their original goals. Renewed planning
activities were only initiated after abandoning the original goals.

Gollwitzer's analysis is broadly applicable to many types of goals. Other
theorists have focused on more specific objectives; for instance, how individuals pursue knowledge-related goals. Kruglanski (1989) and Kunda (1990)
associated different cognitive sets with distinct types of knowledge-related
goals; for example, when the goal is to reach accurate conclusions rather than
to confirm a specific hypothesis, individuals analyze information more carefully. Baumeister & Newman (1994) distinguished the intuitive scientist's
goal of maximizing accuracy from the intuitive lawyer's goal of reaching
particular conclusions; they suggested that these different objectives affect
how people process information at each phase of goal pursuit. Webster &
Kruglanski (1994) recently reported an individual difference measure of the
need for closure, the tendency to prematurely terminate hypothesis testing and
information search.

Sternberg (1990) related distinct cognitive sets to personality styles of
"mental self governance." Individuals who adopt a *legislative* style enjoy
creative and constructive planning–based activities. Individuals with the *executive* style like to discover how to do things. Individuals with a *judicial* style
relish evaluating rules and procedures. Because these three styles seem to
reflect distinct phases of the goal execution process, it would be interesting to
examine whether the different personalities display the information search
patterns posited by Gollwitzer.

Dweck (1990) differentiated individuals both by the types of goals they
select and the information search patterns that characterize each objective.
Individuals facing the same task can conceptualize their objectives in different
ways. Individuals with performance goals strive to obtain favorable judgments
of their competence and to avoid unfavorable assessments. In contrast, individuals pursuing achievement goals seek to increase their actual competence
by, for example, learning new skills. Dweck and her colleagues have studied
the implications of both experimentally instigated (Elliott & Dweck 1988) and
naturally existing differences in children's goal preferences (Dweck & Leggett
1988).

Significant differences between those pursuing performance goals and
those pursuing learning goals have been found in patterns of attributions for
failure, display of affect, use of unproductive strategies, and likelihood of
persistence in the face of failure. Dweck and her associates (Dweck 1990,

Dweck & Leggett 1988) suggest that children pursuing performance goals process information in terms of its relevance for assessing their ability. Conversely, children with learning goals examine information for its relevance to their task mastery.

Inferring Other People's Goals

Individuals often attempt to assess other people's intentions and goals. Such attempts are directed at discovering whether others' goals are compatible with their own. Perceptions of goal compatibility encourage individuals to engage in mutually advantageous action. Perceptions of goal conflict may lead individuals to hinder, or at least not facilitate, one another's efforts (Kelley & Stahelski 1970, Kelley & Thibaut 1978). Aggressive as opposed to nonaggressive children tend to infer that others want to obstruct rather than aid their goal attainment, contrasting perceptions that predict attributions and actual behavior toward others (Crick & Dodge 1994).

In inferring goals and intentions, people sometimes appear to project their own motivations on other people. Demorest & Alexander (1992) found that the emotional scripts present in individuals' autobiographical memories resemble those scripts they used to interpret ambiguous affective stimuli such as TAT pictures. Markus et al (1985) suggested that projection occurs because people use self-schemas in the service of social perception. It is not clear, however, that the direction of inference is always from self to other. Karniol (1986, 1990) argued that memory is organized around prototypical knowledge structures. When based on the same prototypical representations, individuals' inferences about themselves will resemble their inferences about others, and such similarities will appear to reflect projection. Markus & Kitayama (1991a,b) suggested that the direction of inference differs according to culture: In cultures that encourage interdependent selves, people may derive self-perceptions from their social perceptions; in cultures that promote independent selves, people may base their social perceptions on self-perceptions. Recently, Singelis (1994) developed a scale to assess these two divergent orientations.

PRIORITIZING GOALS

People can pursue only a limited number of their potential goals. How do they choose which goals to pursue? Answers to this question focus on the impact of emotions, goal hierarchies, current concerns or life tasks, and self-control processes.

The Role of Emotions in Prioritizing Goals

Many theorists have analyzed emotions within the context of a goals framework (e.g. Bower 1992, Frijda 1986, Leventhal & Scherer 1987, Ortony et al

1985, Roseman et al 1994, Stein & Levine 1987, Stein et al 1993), noting that people experience positive emotions when they appraise events as furthering their goals and negative emotions when they appraise events as thwarting their goals. Emotions are particularly likely to be associated with events that unexpectedly advance or obstruct goal achievement (Mandler 1992, Stein & Levine 1987).

Theorists posit that the primary function of emotions is to mobilize attention to goal-relevant features of situations (Bower 1992, Frijda 1986, Simon 1994, Stein & Levine 1987). According to Frijda (1988, p. 354), "emotions exist for the sake of signaling states of the world that have to be responded to, or that no longer need response and action." Consistent with Frijda's analysis are findings that positive and negative emotions elicit different goals (Isen 1984, Schwarz 1990, Taylor 1991). Unlike positive affective states that reinforce the status quo, negative ones lead individuals to analyze the bases of their problems, explore possible mechanisms of change, and consider the potential outcomes of different actions.

In examining the impact of emotions on goals, theorists have seldom differentiated affect generated by current states from affect produced by *anticipated* states. Happiness, anger, and sadness are apparently generated by current states; fear and hope are generated by anticipated states (Roseman 1984, Stein & Jewett 1986, Stein & Levine 1987). Ortony et al (1985) distinguished the "well-being" emotions, which reflect the impact of events on current status, from the "prospect-based" emotions, which reflect the future implications of events. An important research question is whether emotions are temporally connected to goal choice, with prospect-based emotions affecting the selection of distal goals and well-being emotions influencing more proximal ones.

Using Goal Taxonomies to Prioritize Goals

The development of goal taxonomies is an ancient and still popular ritual. According to Plato, human actions are guided by a concern for virtue; St. Augustine postulated a conflict between the desire for good and a desire for pleasure (Bolles 1974). Modern thinkers have tended to posit more complex taxonomies. Maslow (1954) described a goal hierarchy with a pyramidal shape; individuals must satisfy lower needs before considering higher ones. In action identification theory, Vallacher & Wegner (1985, 1989) analyzed goals according to level of abstraction; they distinguished ultimate purposes (e.g. losing weight) from lower-level objectives (e.g. rejecting dessert).

More recently, Ford & Nichols (1987, 1991) and Schank and his colleagues (Schank & Abelson 1977, Schank & Wilensky 1978, Wilensky 1983) offered extensive taxonomies of goals. Ford & Nichols distinguished goals within the person (e.g. affective goals such as happiness and cognitive goals such as developing positive self-conceptions) from external goals (e.g. social relationship goals such as promoting the well-being of self or others and task goals such as acquiring wealth). Schank and his associates provided a classification that includes satisfaction goals (e.g. hunger, sex, sleep), enjoyment goals (e.g. entertainment), achievement goals (e.g. good job, skills), preservation goals (e.g. health, possessions), and finally, instrumental goals that arise in the pursuit of other objectives (e.g. get information, take a cab). It is evident that the taxonomies differ in focus and level of abstraction, and at this point it is unclear which will prove most useful.

Taxonomic theorists do not tend to discuss the factors that lead people to construct particular goal hierarchies or to alter their preferences. Stein & Levine (1990) argued that people change their goal preferences as a consequence of revising their values. Values are elastic yardsticks, changing with development and over time (Rokeach 1973). Although within any given culture goal taxonomies may be organized in a relatively stable hierarchy, goal hierarchies change with development and life transitions (Zirkel 1992).

Prioritizing Goals via Life Tasks and Current Concerns

Many researchers have proposed that people prioritize goals on the basis of their current concerns or important life tasks at a given point in time (Cantor et al 1986, Emmons 1986, Little 1989, Nikula et al 1993, Palys & Little 1983). Theorists assume that individuals selectively attend and make plans relevant to their life tasks (e.g. achieve high grades, find a spouse). Cantor and her colleagues (e.g. Cantor et al 1986) suggested that in pursuing particular life tasks, people are guided by distinct representations of themselves in the future. Life transitions (e.g. from college to work) lead people to alter their representations of both themselves in the future and the life tasks they need to pursue (Zirkel 1992).

A link between life tasks and emotions may also be relevant to goal prioritization. Emmons (1992) found that individuals who describe their goals in more general terms tend to be more depressed, perhaps because they feel further away from their goals. Zirkel & Cantor (1989) similarly reported that people who conceived of their life tasks in higher level terms (e.g. conceived independence as "not having parents to turn to" vs "having to balance my checkbook") experienced more stress and saw the tasks as more difficult, time-consuming, and challenging. Individuals reporting higher level goals also indicated being less satisfied with their lives than individuals who described lower level goals. The negative affective states associated with higher level goals may lead people to seek ways to alter their situation, to abandon such higher level goals in favor of more concrete or lower level objectives (Baumeister 1990, Vallacher & Wegner 1987).

Prioritizing Goals via Self-Control Processes

Individuals' goals range in time from those that are nearly immediate to those that are many months or years away (Jaques 1982). Goal choices generally reflect a "positive time preference" (Karniol & Miller 1983, Lowenstein 1988), the motivational pull of goals with immediate outcomes over the discounted value of distal goals. Even when individuals do decide to pursue distal outcomes, the value of such outcomes may spontaneously decrease during goal pursuit, making distal outcomes more similar in value to proximal outcomes that were of lower value originally (Karniol & Miller 1983). As the subjective values of proximal and distal outcomes converge and become more similar, the pursuit of long-term goals becomes more difficult.

When people do commit themselves to long-term objectives, how do they overcome the positive time preference? A self-control analysis explains the pursuit of distal goals in terms of psychological transformations that prevent or prolong the convergence of values of proximal and distal outcomes (e.g. Karniol & Miller 1983, Rachlin 1989). By using self-control processes to alter the subjective values of the outcomes, the situation, or both, individuals can maintain their priorities in the face of temptation and adversity. Individuals differ in their use of psychological transformations to render the subjective values of proximal and distal goals less similar and hence, in their commitment to distal goals (Kuhl & Beckmann 1985). Mischel's (1974, Rodriguez et al 1989, Mischel et al 1988) classic research on delay of gratification demonstrated how children distracted themselves and cognitively transformed incentives to overcome their preference for immediate rewards. Children's ability to engage in such cognitive transformations when faced with visible rewards correlated significantly with SAT scores at age 18 (Shoda et al 1990).

In order to choose between immediate and distal goals, individuals must not only determine how they feel about the distal goal now but they must forecast how they will evaluate it in the future. Kahneman (1994, Kahneman & Snell 1990) found that people's forecasts of their later food preferences on the basis of initial tastings were poor indicators of their actual subsequent preferences. Prior to possessing an object, people underestimated its eventual value to them (Kahneman et al 1991). If people are often unable to assess their future likes and dislikes accurately, over time they may become unhappy with decisions made on the basis of expected utility.

When individuals are aware that their immediate preferences and their long-term ones are inconsistent, they may be willing to adopt strategies such as precommitment that restrict the possible impact of their changing priorities over time (Schelling 1984, Thaler & Shefrin 1981). One instance of precommitment is a mandatory pension plan, which prevents people from being continually tempted to spend their savings.

People may also psychologically transform free choice situations into no-choice ones in order to sustain their priorities over time (Karniol & Miller 1981). Seeing themselves as compelled to go to work, for example, may relieve people of the daily temptation to stay at home. The same psychological transformation process may be operative in moral domains. Many people do not view murder, theft, or cheating as viable means of reaching their goals.

Summary

The processes implicated in the above four approaches to prioritizing goals may work in concert with one another. Individuals may acquire different hierarchies and taxonomies of goals that they use to think about themselves and others. Such hierarchies may influence the life tasks that individuals select in specific settings, and the relevance of events to their life tasks may determine the emotional reactions they experience (Singer & Salovey 1993). An individual's tendency to engage in self-control processes may then influence how he or she copes with emotions and adopts changing strategies to attain desired outcomes.

Alternative causal sequences are also likely, however. For example, although people may choose their life tasks on the basis of their goal hierarchies, they may also rank their goals on the basis of their current life tasks. Emotions, goal taxonomies, life tasks, and self-control processes surely all play a role in the establishment of goal priorities. Researchers and theorists have studied some of the relations among these constructs, but they have yet to establish how the constructs operate independently or in common to produce goal preferences.

THE MOTIVATIONAL IMPACT OF PROXIMAL VS DISTAL GOALS

People differ in the degree to which they spontaneously focus on proximal or distal goals (e.g. Cottle & Klineberg 1974, Nuttin 1985, Strathman et al 1994, Trommsdorff & Lamm 1975). Nonetheless, individuals may often be forced to focus on relatively immediate objectives (Klinger et al 1980). A number of theorists maintain that immediate goals exert a stronger motivational impact on behavior than distal goals. Bandura (1990) argued that proximal goals help people motivate themselves by enabling them to gauge their progress; the successful pursuit of distal goals often requires the support of proximal sub-goals (see also Kanfer & Ackerman 1989, Locke & Latham 1990).

Evidence on the motivating power of proximal goals vs distal ones is inconclusive. Kirschenbaum et al (1981) found that subjects who used monthly plans and goals for improving study habits benefited more than those who used four-day plans and goals. DM Wegner & RR Vallacher (unpublished manuscript) observed that individuals who engage in low-level action identification with regard to an ice water task removed their hands earlier and reported greater pain than those who engaged in high-level action identification. In contrast, Locke & Latham (1990) reviewed the literature on dieting and concluded that daily goals appear to be more effective for promoting weight loss than weekly objectives.

Further research is needed to compare the motivational effectiveness of immediate and long-term goals. The effectiveness of proximal or distal objectives may depend upon the nature of the activity (e.g. dieting vs pain tolerance). Vallacher & Wegner (1987) suggested that low-level act identifications are more motivating for difficult acts and that high-level identifications more effectively motivate easy acts. It is also possible that moderately distal goals are more effective than very proximal or very distal goals.

Definitive answers to the above questions may be difficult to obtain because individuals sometimes spontaneously generate proximal goals when assigned distal goals and distal goals when assigned proximal goals (Locke & Latham 1990). People desire both immediate and long-term goals, and they are capable of psychologically transforming one into the other.

Plans to reach one's goals can also vary in their temporal focus. In the *Republic*, Plato suggested that people should plan for the future by starting with their goals and working backward. Melges (1982) speculated that people actually do work backward in time from the future to the present, developing plans to obtain their goals. Researchers working within an artificial intelligence framework (e.g. Allen & Perrault 1980) similarly discuss planning by backwards chaining. In contrast, Markus proposed that people plan by moving forward in time: Individuals proceed from the present to the future by building a bridge of self-representations between their current states and their goals (Markus & Ruvolo 1989). Individuals may in fact employ both a forward and a backward planning strategy, depending on the specific goals involved. Alternatively, individuals may differ in terms of whether they construct immediate plans prior to distal ones, or vice versa. This is an important issue to examine empirically because people's efficiency at reaching their goals may vary as a consequence of the temporal pattern of their goal pursuit.

APPROACHING POSITIVE VS AVOIDING NEGATIVE OUTCOMES

Different motivational systems are associated with positive and negative outcomes (Gray 1987). A behavioral inhibition system promotes avoidance of negative outcomes and a behavioral approach system is oriented to positive outcomes. When individuals anticipate an aversive outcome, they may try to avoid it or to reduce its negativity. If they cannot avoid it, they may attempt either to delay or hasten its onset. Some people eat their spinach first, others leave it to the end. When individuals anticipate a positive state, they try either to improve their chances of reaching it or to hasten its arrival (e.g. joining a singles club to find a potential mate).

While some individuals aim primarily to avoid or eliminate negative states, others focus on achieving or maintaining positive states. For example, rejecting chocolates may be a sufficient goal for those desiring not to be obese, but it will be an insufficient one for those wanting to be slim. Chocolate avoiders and celery eaters need not be the same person.

This distinction between approach and avoidance tendencies is useful in explaining individual differences in behavior. Some parents [e.g. overprotective parents (Parker 1983)] concern themselves almost exclusively with helping their children avoid future negative outcomes, whereas others focus on positive outcomes their children may enjoy. Franzoi et al (1990) found that individuals low in private self-consciousness are more likely than those high in private self-consciousness to avoid potentially negative information about themselves. Schlenker & Weigold (1992) differentiated acquisitive (i.e. focused on opportunities for favorable social outcomes) from protective (i.e. intent on avoiding unfavorable social outcomes) styles of self-presentation—naturally occurring styles that can be induced situationally.

Approach and avoidance tendencies have been incorporated in several theoretical analyses of self-functioning. Carver & Scheier (1985) suggested that individuals can attempt either to attain desired end states by reducing discrepancies between their current self and their ideal or to avoid undesired end states by increasing discrepancies between their current self and those states (e.g. not being like cheating/alcoholic Uncle Henry). Recently, Carver & White (1994) developed a measure to assess these two motivational systems.

Oyserman & Markus (1990) similarly incorporated approach-avoidance tendencies into the possible selves framework, proposing that the pursuit of long-term goals is facilitated when individuals possess mental representations of both feared and desirable possible selves that can offset each other by specifying how the person must act to avoid the feared end state or to approach the desirable possible self. Preliminary evidence for this hypothesis comes from their study relating adolescents' possible selves to their likelihood of committing delinquent acts.

In recent elaborations of self-discrepancy theory, Higgins (1989, Higgins et al 1985, 1994) also emphasized the importance of approach-avoidance tendencies. He proposed two basic types of guiding end states, ideal-self guides that represent people's hopes, wishes, and aspirations and ought-self guides that include duties, obligations, and responsibilities. The ideal-self regulatory system focuses on the presence or absence of positive outcomes (e.g. performing well in school); the ought-self regulatory system focuses on the presence or absence of negative outcomes (e.g. being criticized for poor school perform- ance). The ideal-self regulatory system promotes approach tendencies (e.g. working hard to achieve a good grade); conversely, the ought-self regulatory system encourages avoidance tendencies (e.g. not reporting bad grades to parents in order to escape criticism).

Higgins and his associates have reported a number of studies that provide support for this conceptualization (Higgins et al 1994). In addition, they have shown that desired and undesired end states have different motivational effects (Higgins et al 1994; Roney et al 1995): Emphasizing the positive outcomes associated with success seems to encourage better performance than does emphasizing the negative outcomes associated with failure.

Approach and avoidance goals may require the deployment of different strategies for coping in contexts that require continued persistence. For in- stance, Lazarus et al (1980) discussed *sustainers* (i.e. cognitive activities such as imagining rewarding outcomes, which sustain motivation), *breathers* (i.e. activities such as watching TV, which allow one to disengage from the current task or plan), and *restorers* (i.e. activities such as vacations, which allow recuperation). The use of sustainers may be more beneficial when approach goals are involved, whereas breathers and restorers may be more beneficial when avoidance goals are involved.

THE PAST: FRIEND OR FOE?

As we discussed in the introduction, for Lewin (1943), the past is always contained in the psychological field existing at any given time but plays no direct motivational role. Bell & Mau accorded the past an important positive role in determining the possible futures individuals envisage. The past is not always so favorably viewed. The deleterious, motivational push of the past is emphasized in psychoanalytic theory (Kihlstrom 1995). Psychoanalysis "has always been concerned with how and why the past contaminates the present, with how and why the influence of the past can become excessive" (Lamm 1993, p. 178). The past, then, can be viewed as a foe. Can it also be a friend as Bell & Mau suggest? We argue that the relation of the past to the present and imagined future is a two-way street, with reciprocal motivational connections between people's goals and recollections. The past can come to mind unin- vited, color the present, and push individuals into action; people can use their memories to guide their selection of goals and plans; and people can use their memories to help them achieve their chosen goals. Finally, goals can affect how people retrieve, construct, and interpret their memories.

The Push of the Past

The push of the past is evident in studies that have examined the impact of memories of negative and sometime catastrophic, past events. Remembering distressful past episodes spontaneously or via experimental instructions (e.g. Salovey 1992, Wood et al 1990) can evoke negative emotions, such as sadness and anger. In everyday life, distressful episodes sometimes produce repetitive and intrusive memories (Loftus 1993, Pennebaker 1990, Rothbaum et al 1992, Silver et al 1983, Tait & Silver 1989). Nolen-Hoekesma & Morrow (1991) found that frequency of rumination about a severe California earthquake ten days after its occurrence was positively related to depression and to symptoms of posttraumatic stress disorder seven weeks later. Individuals who actively try to suppress such thoughts often find themselves dwelling on them at even greater length (Kelly & Kahn 1994, Wegner 1992).

When people recall past episodes, they can think about *how* or *why* the events occurred. Most of the research on the impact of remembering distressful events has focused on people's memories for how the episodes unfolded. Thinking about how events occurred leads to assimilation effects in assessments of current well-being; thinking about the causes of events tends to produce contrast effects in assessments of current well-being (Clark et al 1994, Strack et al 1985). Little is known about the impact of reminiscing about positive past experiences (e.g. one's first kiss, wedding day) on current well-being. The proliferation of home movies and videos suggests that there is a motivational benefit to reminiscing about positive past events.

People's conceptions of the past may motivate them to take dramatic actions to alter their worlds. In his analyses of several autobiographies, Freeman (1993) examined how major life decisions and changes were driven by evaluations of the past. In many cases, individuals break with the past, not because they envisage a possible self for which they strive, but because their negative conceptions of the past and the present provide an impetus for change. As evidenced by his cry of "No more war, no more bloodshed," Egyptian President Sadat's signing of a peace treaty with Israel seems to have been impelled by a need to break with the past rather than by a picture of the future. A similar pattern appears in many instances of emigration, separation, and disappearance (e.g. Sinha & Ataullah 1987).

On the other hand, interpretations of the past may lead to a reluctance to break with it. Individuals who view the past positively are reluctant to admit to themselves that the past carries no implications for the future; consequently, they hesitate to dramatically alter their behavior, strategies, or goals (Allport et al 1948).

Many therapeutic interventions are explicitly aimed at restricting the motivational push of the past by helping people change their interpretations of their pasts. Psychoanalysts often lead patients to adopt alternative explanations for events, explanations that may improve their current functioning (Spence 1982). The elicitation of childhood recollections is a prime example. Disputants in the current lively debate about whether adults' "recovered" memories of childhood abuse should be accepted at face value (Kihlstrom 1995; Loftus 1993; Masson 1984; Ross 1995; Stein et al 1995) do not doubt that people's recollections of the past, whether valid or not, affect current emotions, thoughts, and behavior.

Similarly, social psychologists who use attributional retraining (e.g. Wilson & Linville 1982) assume that patterns of causal explanations for past success and failure can have deleterious effects on current functioning. Attributional retraining procedures attempt to shift people's explanations of previous failures from stable, uncontrollable causes (e.g. I am not good at mathematics) to unstable, controllable causes (e.g. I don't work hard enough at mathematics) and thereby to alter their related emotions, goals, and subsequent behavior.

The Past Guides Selection of Goals and Plans

There is research evidence that memories can help people establish their goals and devise strategies to attain them (Buehler et al 1995, Neisser 1988, Singer & Salovey 1993, Stein & Levine 1987, Trabasso & Stein 1994). Similarly, in the model of planning advanced by Schank and his colleagues (Hammond 1989, Riesbeck & Schank 1989, Schank 1982), all planning represents a memory task that requires the retrieval of relevant cases of goal failure and goal success. Consistent with Zeigarnik's classic demonstration, Thorne & Klohnen (1993) suggested that individuals tend to remember "unfinished business" to which they have to attend. Stein & Levine (1987) proposed that negative memories remind people of their past errors and of circumstances they should avoid in the future. In contrast, positive memories remind people of their past accomplishments and provide cues for how to attain future success.

The Past in the Service of Goals

The recounting of past experiences forms the basis of a great deal of people's discourse throughout their lives (Edwards & Potter 1992, Fivush 1993). People report personal experiences for a variety of reasons, including to entertain and to inform their audiences (Ross & Buehler 1994). Autobiographical narrative helps people establish and convey their own and others' public identities. People selectively communicate their memories in an effort to manage their impressions and to register their opinions of other people in their social environment (Blumstein 1991, Ross & Buehler 1994).

Memories do not need to be communicated to serve current goals. Several investigators have theorized about the functions of uncommunicated reminiscences. One intriguing hypothesis is that memories promote self-regulation of ongoing affective states. Robinson & Swanson (1990) proposed that individuals sustain desirable moods by retrieving mood-congruent personal memories and alter undesirable moods by retrieving mood-incongruent memories. Evidence supporting this account of mood self-regulation is not strong. The authors of two recent reviews concluded that unhappy and depressed people take longer than happy people to recall pleasant memories and recall fewer of them (Brewin et al 1993, Dalgleish & Watts 1990). Mood does not seem to influence systematically the recall of unpleasant memories. Contrary to Robinson & Swanson's hypothesis, unhappy people's memories sustain rather than counteract their moods.

There are other ways in which individuals might use recall to govern their affect—for example, by engaging in cognitive processing that promotes emotional self-regulation. Mueller (1990) presented a model of daydreaming in which reminiscence is a spontaneous activity that both regulates people's emotions and guides their behavior. Mueller described *rationalization* as the modification of the interpretation of a past goal failure to reduce the associated negative emotional state; *roving* as the shifting of attention to a positive past or imagined future scenario to reduce a negative emotional state; *reversal* as the generation of imaginary scenarios in which a real or imagined goal failure is prevented; and *recovery* as the generation of possible future scenarios for achieving a failed personal goal.

Consistent with Mueller's analysis, people can use counterfactual thinking for both emotional self-regulation and planning (Boninger et al 1994, Kahneman & Miller 1986, Roese 1994). Roese (1994) induced individuals to think about how their outcomes could have been worse or better. Individuals who imagined how their outcomes could have been worse experienced positive affect. Individuals who considered how their outcomes could have been better did not report increased negative affect; instead, they reported an increased intention to perform success-enhancing behaviors. Although such research does not provide direct evidence that people *spontaneously* engage in counterfactual thinking to regulate their emotions or guide their behavior, it seems likely that unprompted counterfactual thinking plays an important role in these psychological processes. Lecci et al (1994) found that regrets, defined as unpursued goals that a person currently wishes had been undertaken, account for about 20% of the variance in reported life satisfaction. Similarly, McIntosh & Martin (1992) found that cognitions about unattained goals foster unhappiness in those individuals who see themselves as able to influence their own happiness.

An issue that has not been discussed is how far back individuals search their past to guide emotional self-regulation and planning. Some individuals may consult the immediate past while others may be biased toward using memories of the distant past. Grandparents are notorious for their use of ancient memories rather than more recent events to buttress their current claims. Focusing on distant rather than recent past events seems to have some important correlates. When Gilovich & Medvec (1994) asked individuals to list their regrets, recent regrets tended to involve actions, whereas distant regrets tended to involve failures to act. The time frame of memories also seems relevant to judgments of well-being; more distant memories produce a contrast in assessments of current well-being, and relatively recent memories lead to assimilation in assessments of current well-being (Clark et al 1994, Strack et al 1985).

Goals Affect Memory Retrieval

Occasionally individuals seem remarkably impervious to the effects of earlier, apparently relevant experiences. For example, some people hurdle from one romantic alliance to the next, showing little evidence that they have learned from previous relationships. One reason for this apparent neglect of the past is that people may fail to see the relevance of past events to current circumstances. Apparent differences between past and current events may preclude meaningful comparisons between them (Kahneman & Tversky 1979). Buehler et al (1994) found that people repeatedly underestimated how long it would take them to complete various tasks; people judged the causes of their previous tardiness to be relatively unique and unlikely to recur.

Motivational accounts of people's tendency to ignore the relevance of the past portray such attempts as furthering current goals and plans (e.g. Holmes & Boon 1990, Kunda 1990, Ross 1989, Ross & Buehler 1994, Santioso et al 1990). Individuals tend to discount the implications of episodes from the past that are inconsistent with their current goals or preferences and stress ramifications that validate their choices. Holmes & Boon (1990) noted that people make their decisions to marry on the basis of positive feelings and seem determined to explain away negative experiences. World leaders' tendency to minimize the relevance of negative past events to their present concerns has been documented in a variety of historical contexts (Neustadt & May 1986). Perhaps decision makers deny the relevance of previous experiences, especially past failures, to maintain their feelings of control over future outcomes. If people see themselves as bound to the past, they lose their sense of agency. By deemphasizing the relevance of past failures, people can maintain the belief that they are in command of their futures and that they have the power to produce success.

In many cases, current goals do not affect the retrieval of episodes but rather alter the interpretation placed on the retrieved episodes (Holmes & Murray 1995). For example, Murray & Holmes (1993) reported that individuals in love explain the past actions of their romantic partners in ways that minimize their imperfections. Happy couples make "relationship-enhancing" attributions that stress the importance of their partner's positive behaviors and decrease the impact of negative behaviors; distressed couples interpret the past behaviors of their partners in ways that are "distress maintaining," discounting the value of positive actions and emphasizing the importance of negative behaviors (Bradbury & Fincham 1990). Although the causal direction of the relation between attributions and marital satisfaction is ambiguous (Holmes & Boon 1990), it is clear that current goals can color the interpretations placed on the past. Individuals use the past in a selective manner to support their current position.

Individual Differences in Using the Past

Individuals differ in how and whether they use the past. For example, Type A individuals seem to reminisce less about the past than Type B individuals (Bryant et al 1991). Repressors are less able to recall emotional episodes that reflect negatively on the self (Davis 1987). Similarly, people with discrepancies between their current and ideal selves differ in their use of the past from those with discrepancies between their current self and the self they feel they ought to be (Higgins 1989). Strauman (1990) provided subjects with self-guide cues and asked them to recall childhood incidents related to the cues. Ought-self cues led to significantly shorter retrieval times of childhood memories than ideal-self cues. In addition, individuals accessed memories more quickly when the cues referred to dimensions on which they differed from their ought selves than from their ideal selves, which suggests that individuals with an ideal self-focus—who tend to be depressed (Scott & O'Hara 1993, Strauman 1992)—are like depressives in their reluctance to reminisce about the past (Bachar et al 1990).

Individual differences in learned helplessness (e.g. Abramson et al 1978) can be conceptualized as identifying individuals who use the past to predict the future vs those who discount the past. Individuals with a global attributional style tend to perceive the causes for uncontrollable events as extending across many events in their life; individuals with a specific attributional style tend to perceive the causes of uncontrollable events as limited to particular events and circumstances. In turn, those with a global attributional style use the past to guide their expectations about the future and those with a specific attributional style minimize the effect of the past, assuming that it is irrelevant in predicting future outcomes. Researchers studying attributional retraining as a remedy for learned helplessness (e.g. Dweck 1975) assume that discounting the past, at least in the case of failures, is beneficial. Their findings contrast markedly with research with the elderly where reminiscence training has been shown to be therapeutic (Bachar et al 1991, Kaminsky 1984). Conceivably, either age or the affective quality of the relevant memories is the critical variable in this context, but we know of no research that addresses this issue.

In discussing people's efforts to escape from the self, especially via suicide, Baumeister (1990) described the psychological state of "cognitive deconstruction," where deconstruction includes a narrowing of temporal focus to the present, rather than the past or the future. In a similar vein, Ball & Chandler (1989) observed that adolescents at risk for suicide are less able to relate the person they were in the past to the person they currently are. This research suggests that minimizing the importance of the past can sometimes be extremely destructive, especially when people's visions of the future are insufficiently well developed.

CONCLUSIONS

The cognitive revolution has often been blamed for demoting motivational processes from their rightful status in social and personality psychology. During the last decade, social-cognitive researchers and theorists have again turned to examine motivational processes, incorporating them within the information processing paradigm that swept social psychology. The motivational pull of the future was evident in studies of the impact of individuals' goals, expectancies, self-schemas, and possible selves on their processing of social-cognitive information and on their subsequent behavior. The excitement that these new developments generated is evidenced by the hundreds of articles that have been published recently dealing with just these issues.

At the same time that many researchers were analyzing the pull of conceptions of the future on behavior, others were investigating the study of memory in everyday contexts. Consistent with psychoanalytic claims, memories do color the present and the imagined future. In addition, however, the present and the imagined future color people's recollections of the past.

We have shown in this chapter that motivation reflects an interweaving of one's present into the fabric of one's past and the prospects of one's future. Individuals engage in an ongoing, internalized "re-interpretative temporal dialogue" (Rotenberg 1987, p. 74) that allows them to reshape their past and to mold their future. To quote from T. S. Eliot's poem *Burnt Norton* (1934), "time present and time past are both perhaps present in time future, and time future contained in time past." Forging cognition and motivation together in a more complex pattern than ever before, temporal focus provides a research agenda for the future.

ACKNOWLEDGMENTS

We thank Peter Gollwitzer, John Holmes, Ziva Kunda, Larry Pervin, Peter Salovey, Nancy Stein, and Daniel Wegner for their helpful comments on a previous version of this manuscript.

Literature Cited

Abramson LY, Seligman MEP, Teasdale J. 1978. Learned helplessness in humans: critique and reformulation. *J. Abnorm. Psychol.* 87:49–74

Allport GW, Bruner JS, Jandorf EM. 1948. Personality under social catastrophe: ninety life-histories of the Nazi revolution. In *Personality in Nature, Society and Culture*, ed. C Kluckhohn, H Murray, DM Schneider, pp. 436–55. New York: Knopf

Allen JF, Perrault CR.1980. Analyzing intention in utterances. *Artif. Intell.* 15:143–78

Anderson CA. 1983. Imagination and expectation: the effect of imagining behavioral scripts on personal intentions. *J. Pers. Soc. Psychol.* 45:293–305

Bachar E, Dasberg H, Shapira B, Lerer B. 1990. Reminiscing in depressed aging patients: effects of ECT and antidepressants. *Int. J. Geriatr. Psychiatr.* 5:251–56

Bachar E, Kindler S, Schefler G, Lerer B. 1991. Reminiscing as a technique in the group therapy of depression: a comparative study. *Br. J. Clin. Psychol.* 30:375–77

Ball L, Chandler M. 1989. Identity formation in suicidal and nonsuicidal youth: the role of self-continuity. *Dev. Psychopathol.* 1: 257–75

Bandura A. 1989. Self regulation of motivation and action through internal standards and goal systems. See Pervin 1989, pp. 19–85

Bandura A. 1990. Self-regulation of motivation through anticipatory and self-reactive mechanisms. *Nebr. Symp. Motiv.* 36: 69–164

Bargh JA. 1990. Auto-motives: preconscious determinants of social interaction. See Higgins & Sorrentino 1990, pp. 93–130

Bargh JA, Barndollar K. 1996. Automaticity in action: the unconscious as repository of chronic goals and motives. In *The Psychology of Action: Linking Motivation and Cognition to Behavior,* ed. PM Gollwitzer, JA Bargh, pp. 457–81. New York: Guilford.

Bargh JA, Gollwitzer PM. 1994. Environmental control of goal directed action: automatic and strategic contingencies between situations and behavior. *Nebr. Symp. Motiv.* 41:71–124

Baumeister RF. 1990. Suicide as escape from self. *Psychol. Rev.* 91:3–26

Baumeister RF, Newman LS. 1994. Self-regulation of cognitive inferences and decision processes. *Pers. Soc. Psychol. Bull.* 20: 3–19

Beach LR. 1990. *Image Theory: Decision Making in Personal and Organizational Contexts.* New York: Wiley

Bell W, Mau JA. 1971. Images of the future: theory and research strategies. In *The Sociology of the Future: Theory, Cases, and Annotated Bibliography,* ed. W Bell, JA Mau, pp. 6–44. New York: Russell Sage Found.

Binnick RI. 1991. *Time and the Verb: A Guide to Tense and Aspect.* New York: Oxford Univ. Press

Blumstein P. 1991. The production of selves in personal relationships. In *The Self-Society Dynamic: Cognition, Emotion, and Action,* ed. JA Howard, PL Callero, pp. 305–22. Cambridge: Cambridge Univ. Press

Bobocel DR, Meyer JP. 1994. Escalating commitment to a failing course of action: separating the roles of choice and justification. *J. Appl. Psychol.* 79:360–63

Bolles RC. 1974. Cognition and motivation: some historical trends. In *Cognitive Views of Human Motivation,* ed. B Weiner, pp. 1–20. New York: Academic

Boninger DS, Gleicher F, Strathman A. 1994. Counterfactual thinking: from what might have been to what may be. *J. Pers. Soc. Psychol.* 67:297–307

Bower GH. 1992. How might emotions affect learning. See Christianson 1992, pp. 3–31

Bradbury TN, Fincham FD. 1990. Attributions in marriage: review and critique. *Psychol. Bull.* 107:3–33

Brehm SS, Kassin SM, Gibbons FX, eds. 1981. *Developmental Social Psychology.* New York: Oxford Univ. Press

Brewin CR, Andrews B, Gotlib IH. 1993. Psychopathology and early experience: a reappraisal of retrospective reports. *Psychol. Bull.* 113:82–98

Bryant FB, Yarnold PR, Morgan L. 1991. Type A behavior and reminiscence in college undergraduates. *J. Res. Pers.* 25:418–33

Buehler R, Griffin D, Ross M. 1994. Exploring the "planning fallacy": why people underestimate their task completion times. *J. Pers. Soc. Psychol.* 67:366–81

Buehler R, Griffin D, Ross M. 1995. It's about time: optimistic predictions in love and work. In *Eur. Rev. Soc. Psychol.,* ed. W Stroebe, M Hewstone, 6:1–32. Chichester: Wiley

Cantor N, Fleeson W. 1991. Life tasks and

self-regulatory processes. *Adv. Motiv. Achiev.* 7:327–69

Cantor N, Markus HR, Niedenthal P, Nurius P. 1986. On motivation and the self concept. See Sorrentino & Higgins 1986, pp. 96–121

Cantor N, Norem JK, Niedenthal PM, Langston CA, Brower AM. 1987. Life tasks, self concept ideals and cognitive strategies in a life transition. *J. Pers. Soc. Psychol.* 53: 1178–191

Carver CS, Scheier MF. 1985. A control-systems approach to the self-regulation of action. See Kuhl & Beckmann 1985, pp. 237–65

Carver CS, White TL. 1994. Behavioral inhibition, behavioral activation, and affective responses to impending reward and punishment: the BIS/BAS scale. *J. Pers. Soc. Psychol.* 67:319–33

Chodoff P. 1986. Survivors of the Nazi Holocaust. In *Coping with Life Crises: An Integrated Approach*, ed. RH Moos, pp. 407–14. New York: Plenum

Christianson S-A, ed. 1992. *The Handbook of Emotion and Memory*. Hillsdale, NJ: Erlbaum

Clark LF, Collins JE II, Henry SM. 1994. Biasing effects of retrospective reports on current self-assessments. In *Autobiographical Memory and the Validity of Retrospective Reports*, ed. N Schwarz, S Sudman, pp. 291–304. New York: Springer-Verlag

Cottle TJ, Klineberg SL. 1974. *The Present of Things Future*. New York: Free Press

Crick NR, Dodge KA. 1994. A review and a reformulation of social and information-processing mechanisms in children's social adjustment. *Psychol. Bull.* 165:74–101

Dalgleish T, Watts FN. 1990. Bases of attention and memory disorders in anxiety and depression. *Clin. Psychol. Rev.* 10:589–694

Davis PJ. 1987. Repression and the accessibility of affective memories. *J. Pers. Soc. Psychol.* 53:585–93

Day JD, Borkowski JG, Punzo D, Howsepian B. 1994. Enhancing possible selves in Mexican-American students. *Motiv. Emot.* 18:79–103

Deci EL, Ryan RM. 1985. *Intrinsic Motivation and Self Determination in Human Behavior.* New York: Plenum

Demorest AP, Alexander IE. 1992. Affective scripts as organizers of personal experience. *J. Pers.* 60:645–63

Ditto PH, Lopez DF. 1992. Motivated skepticism: use of differential decision criteria for preferred and nonpreferred conclusions. *J. Pers. Soc. Psychol.* 63:568–84

Dor-Shav NK. 1978. On the long-range effects of concentration camp internment on Nazi victims: 25 years later. *J. Consult. Clin. Psychol.* 46:1–11

Dweck CS. 1975. The role of expectations and attributions in the alleviation of learned helplessness. *J. Pers. Soc. Psychol.* 31: 674–85

Dweck CS. 1990. Self-theories and goals: their role in motivation, personality, and development. *Nebr. Symp. Motiv.* 36:199–236

Dweck CS, Leggett EL. 1988. A social-cognitive approach to personality and motivation. *Psychol. Rev.* 95:256–73

Edwards D, Potter J. 1992. The chancellor's memory: rhetoric and truth in discursive remembering. *Appl. Cogn. Psychol.* 6: 187–215

Elliott ES, Dweck CS. 1988. Goals: an approach to motivation and achievement. *J. Pers. Soc. Psychol.* 54:5–12

Emmons RA. 1986. Personal strivings: an approach to personality and subjective well being. *J. Pers. Soc. Psychol.* 51:1058–68

Emmons RA. 1992. Abstract versus concrete goals: personal striving level, physical illness, and psychological well-being. *J. Pers. Soc. Psychol.* 62:292–300

Fivush R. 1993. Developmental perspectives on autobiographical recall. In *Child Victims, Child Witnesses*, ed. GS Goodman, BL Bottoms, pp. 1–24. New York: Guilford

Ford ME, Nichols CW. 1987. A taxonomy of human goals and some possible applications. In *Humans as Self Constructing Systems: Putting the Framework to Work*, ed. ME Ford, DH Ford, pp. 289–312. Hillsdale, NJ: Erlbaum

Ford ME, Nichols CW. 1991. Using goal assessments to identify emotional patterns and facilitate behavioral regulation and achievement. *Adv. Motiv. Achiev.* 7:51–84

Franzoi SL, Davis MH, Markwiese B. 1990. A motivational explanation for the existence of private self-consciousness differences. *J. Pers.* 58:641–59

Freeman M. 1993. *Rewriting the Self: History, Memory, and Narrative.* New York: Routledge

Frijda NH. 1986. *The Emotions.* Cambridge: Cambridge Univ. Press

Frijda NH. 1988. The laws of emotion. *Am. Psychol.* 43:349–58

Gilovich T, Medvec VH. 1994. The temporal pattern to the experience of regret. *J. Pers. Soc. Psychol.* 67:357–65

Gollwitzer PM. 1990. Actions phases and mind-sets. See Higgins & Sorrentino 1986, pp. 53–92

Gollwitzer PM. 1993. Goal achievement: the role of intentions. *Eur. Rev. Soc. Psychol.* 4:141–85

Gollwitzer PM, Heckhausen H, Ratajcsak H. 1990a. From weighing to willing: approaching a change decision through pre- or postdecisional mentation. *Org. Behav. Hum. Decis. Process.* 45:41–65

Gollwitzer PM, Heckhausen H, Steller B.

1990b. Deliberative and implemental mind sets: cognitive tuning toward congruous thoughts and information. *J. Pers. Soc. Psychol.* 59:1119–27

Gray JA. 1987. Perspectives on anxiety and impulsivity: a commentary. *J. Res. Pers.* 21:493–509

Griffin DW, Dunning D, Ross L. 1990. The role of construal processes in overconfident predictions about the self and others. *J. Pers. Soc. Psychol.* 59:1128–39

Hammond KJ. 1989. *Case-Based Planning: Viewing Planning as a Memory Task.* San Diego: Academic

Harackiewicz JM, Elliot AJ. 1993. Achievement goals and intrinsic motivation. *J. Pers. Soc. Psychol.* 65:904–15

Higgins ET. 1989. Self-discrepancy theory: What patterns of self beliefs cause people to suffer? *Adv. Exp. Soc. Psychol.* 22: 93–136

Higgins ET, Klein R, Strauman T. 1985. Self-concept discrepancy theory: a model for distinguishing among different aspects of depression and anxiety. *Soc. Cogn.* 3: 51–76

Higgins ET, Roney CJR, Crowe E, Hymes C. 1994. Ideal versus ought predilections for approach and avoidance: distinct self regulatory systems. *J. Pers. Soc. Psychol.* 66: 276–86

Higgins ET, Sorrentino RM, eds. 1990. *Handbook of Motivation and Cognition.* Vol. 2. New York: Guilford

Hoch SJ. 1984. Availability and interference in predictive judgment. *J. Exp. Psychol.: Learn. Mem. Cogn.* 10:649–62

Holmes JG, Boon SD. 1990. Developments in the field of close relationships: creating foundations for intervention strategies. *Pers. Soc. Psychol. Bull.* 16:23–41

Holmes JG, Murray SL. 1995. Memory for events in close relationships: applying Schank and Abelson's story skeleton model. In *Knowledge and Memory: The Real Story*, ed. RS Wyer Jr, 8:185–202. Hillsdale, NJ: Erlbaum

Isen AM. 1984. Toward understanding the role of affect in cognition. In *Handbook of Social Cognition*, ed. RS Wyer, TK Srull, 3: 179–236. Hillsdale, NJ: Erlbaum

Jaques E. 1982. *The Form of Time.* New York: Crane Russak

Johnson MK, Sherman SJ. 1990. Constructing and reconstructing the past and the future in the present. See Higgins & Sorrentino 1990, pp. 482–526

Kahneman D. 1994. New challenges to the rationality assumption. *J. Inst. Theor. Econ.* 150:18–36

Kahneman D, Knetsch J, Thaler R. 1991. The endowment effect, loss aversion, and status quo bias. *J. Econ. Perspect.* 5:193–206

Kahneman D, Lovallo D. 1993. Bold forecast-

ing and timid decisions: a cognitive perspective on risk taking. *Manage. Sci.* 39: 17–31

Kahneman D, Miller DT. 1986. Norm theory: comparing reality to its alternatives. *Psychol. Rev.* 93:136–53

Kahneman D, Snell J. 1990. Predicting utility. In *Insights in Decision Making: A Tribute to Hillel J. Einhorn*, ed. RM Hogarth, pp. 295–310. Chicago: Univ. Chicago Press

Kahneman D, Tversky A. 1979. Intuitive prediction: biases and corrective procedures. *TIMS Stud. Manage. Sci.* 12:313–27

Kaminsky M. 1984. *The Use of Reminiscence: New Ways of Working with Older Adults.* New York: Haworth

Kanfer R, Ackerman PL. 1989. Motivation and cognitive abilities: an integrative/aptitude-treatment interaction approach to skill acquisition. *J. Appl. Psychol.* 74:657–90

Karniol R. 1986. What will they think of next? Transformation rules used to predict other people's thoughts and feelings. *J. Pers. Soc. Psychol.* 51:932–44

Karniol R. 1990. Reading people's minds: a transformation rule model for predicting others' thoughts and feelings. *Adv. Exp. Soc. Psychol.* 23:211–47

Karniol R, Miller DT. 1981. The development of self-control in children. See Brehm et al 1981, pp. 32–50

Karniol R, Miller DT. 1983. Why not wait? A cognitive model of self-imposed delay termination. *J. Pers. Soc. Psychol.* 45: 935–42

Kelley HH, Stahelski AJ. 1970. The social interaction basis of cooperators' and competitors' beliefs about others. *J. Pers. Soc. Psychol.* 16:66–91

Kelley HH, Thibaut JW. 1978. *Interpersonal Relations: A Theory of Interdependence.* New York: Wiley

Kelly AE, Kahn JH. 1994. Effects of suppression of personal intrusive thoughts. *J. Pers. Soc. Psychol.* 66:998–1006

Kihlstrom J. 1995. Exhumed memory. *Truth in Memory*, ed. SJ Lynn, NP Spanos. New York: Guilford. In press

Kirschenbaum DS, Humphrey LL, Malett SD. 1981. Specificity of planning in adult self-control: an applied investigation. *J. Pers. Soc. Psychol.* 40:941–50

Klinger E, Barta SG, Maxeiner ME. 1980. Motivational correlates of thought content frequency and commitment. *J. Pers. Soc. Psychol.* 39:1222–37

Kluckhohn FK, Strodbeck FL. 1961. *Variations in Value Orientations.* Evanston, IL: Row, Peterson

Koehler EJ. 1991. Explanation, imagination, and confidence in judgment. *Psychol. Bull.* 110:499–519

Kruglanski A. 1989. *Lay Epistemics and Hu-*

man *Knowledge: Cognitive and Motivational Bases.* New York: Plenum

Kuhl J, Beckmann J. 1985. *Action Control: From Cognition to Behavior.* Berlin: Springer-Verlag

Kunda A. 1990. The case for motivated reasoning. *Psychol. Bull.* 108:480–98

Lamm LJ. 1993. *The Idea of the Past: History, Science, and Practice in American Psychoanalysis.* New York: New York Univ. Press

Lazarus RS, Kanner AD, Folkman I. 1980. Emotions: a cognitive phenomenological analysis. In *Emotion: Theory, Research, and Experience,* ed. R Plutchik, H Kellerman, 1:189–217. New York: Academic

Lecci L, Okun MA, Karoly P. 1994. Life regrets and current goals as predictors of psychological adjustment. *J. Pers. Soc. Psychol.* 66:731–41

Lepper M, Gilovich TJ. 1981. The psychological functions of reward: a social-developmental perspective. See Brehm et al, pp. 5–31

Leventhal H, Scherer K. 1987. The relationship of emotion to cognition: a functional approach to a semantic controversy. *Cogn. Emot.* 1:3–28

Lewin K. 1935. *A Dynamic Theory of Personality: Selected Papers of Kurt Lewin.* New York: McGraw-Hill

Lewin K. 1943. Defining the 'field at a given time'. *Psychol. Rev.* 50:292–310

Little BR. 1989. Personal projects analyses: trivial pursuits, magnificent obsessions, and the search for coherence. In *Personality Psychology,* ed. DM Buss, N Cantor, pp. 15–31. New York: Springer-Verlag

Locke EA, Latham GP. 1990. *A Theory of Goal Setting and Task Performance.* Englewood Cliffs, NJ: Prentice-Hall

Loftus E. 1993. The reality of repressed memories. *Am. Psychol.* 48:518–37

Lord CG, Ross L, Lepper MR. 1979. Biased assimilation and attitude polarization: the effects of prior theories on subsequently considered evidence. *J. Pers. Soc. Psychol.* 37:2098–109

Lowenstein GF. 1988. Frames of mind in intertemporal choice. *Manage. Sci.* 34: 200–14

Mandler G. 1992. Memory, arousal, and mood: a theoretical integration. See Christianson 1992, pp. 93–110

Markus H, Nurius P. 1986. Possible selves. *Am. Psychol.* 41:954–69

Markus H, Cross S, Wurf E. 1990. The role of the self-system in competence. See Sternberg & Kolligian 1990, pp. 205–25

Markus HR, Kitayama S. 1991a. Culture and the self: implications for cognition, emotion, and motivation. *Psychol. Rev.* 98: 224–53

Markus HR, Kitayama S. 1991b. Cultural vari-

ation in the self concept. In *The Self: Interdisciplinary Approaches,* ed. J Strauss, GR Goetahls, pp. 18–48. New York: Springer-Verlag

Markus H, Ruvolo A. 1989. Possible selves and personalized representations of goals. See Pervin 1989, pp. 211–41

Markus HR, Smith J, Moreland RL. 1985. Role of the self-concept in the perception of others. *J. Pers. Soc. Psychol.* 49:1494–1512

Masson JM. 1984. *The Assault on Truth: Freud's Suppression of the Seduction Theory.* New York: Farrar, Strauss, Giroux

Maslow AH. 1954. *Motivation and Personality.* New York: Harper

McIntosh WD, Martin LL. 1992. The cybernetics of happiness: the relation of goal attainment, rumination, and affect. *Rev. Pers. Soc. Psychol.* 14:222–46

Melges FT. 1982. *Time and the Inner Future: A Temporal Approach to Psychiatric Disorders.* New York: Wiley

Mischel W. 1974. Processes in delay of gratification. *Adv. Exp. Soc. Psychol.* 7: 249–92

Mischel W, Shoda Y. 1995. A cognitive-affective system theory of personality: reconceptualizing situations, dispositions, dynamics, and invariance in personality structure. *Psychol. Rev.* 102:246–68.

Mischel W, Shoda Y, Peake PK. 1988. The nature of adolescent competencies predicted by preschool delay of gratification. *J. Pers. Soc. Psychol.* 54:687–96

Mueller ET. 1990. *Daydreaming in Humans and Machines: A Computer Model of the Stream of Thought.* Norwood, NJ: Ablex

Murray SL, Holmes JG. 1993. Seeing virtue in faults: negativity and the transformation of narratives in close relationships. *J. Pers. Soc. Psychol.* 65:707–22

Neisser U. 1988. Time present and time past. In *Practical Aspects of Memory: Current Research and Issues,* ed. MM Gruneberg, PM Morris, RN Sykes, 2:545–60. New York: Wiley

Neustadt RE, May ER. 1986. *Thinking in Time.* New York: Free Press

Nikula K, Klinger E, Larson-Gutman MK. 1993. Current concerns and electrodermal reactivity: responses to words and thoughts. *J. Pers.* 61:63–84

Nolen-Hoeksema S, Morrow J. 1991. A prospective study of depression and postraumatic stress symptoms after a natural disaster: the 1989 Loma Prieta Earthquake. *J. Pers. Soc. Psychol.* 61:115–21

Norem JK, Cantor N. 1990. Cognitive strategies, coping, and perceptions of competence. See Sternberg & Kolligian 1990, pp. 190–204

Norem JK, Illingworth KS. 1993. Strategy-dependent effects of reflecting on self and tasks: some implications of optimism and defensive pessimism. *J. Pers. Soc. Psychol.* 61:822–35

Nuttin J. 1985. *Future Time Perspective and Motivation.* Leuven: Erlbaum, Leuven Univ. Press

Ortony A, Clore GL, Collins A. 1985. *The Cognitive Structure of Emotions.* Cambridge: Cambridge Univ. Press

Oyserman D, Markus HR. 1990. Possible selves and delinquency. *J. Pers. Soc. Psychol.* 59:112–25

Palys TS, Little BR. 1983. Perceived life satisfaction and the organization of personal project symptoms. *J. Pers. Soc. Psychol.* 44:1221–30

Parker G. 1983. *Parental Overprotection: A Risk Factor in Psychosocial Development.* New York: Grune, Stratton

Pennebaker JW. 1990. *Opening Up: The Healing Power of Confiding in Others.* New York: Morrow

Pervin LA. 1989a. Goal concepts in personality and social psychology: a historical perspective. See Pervin 1989, pp. 1–17

Pervin LA, ed. 1989b. *Goal Concepts in Personality and Social Psychology.* Hillsdale, NJ: Erlbaum

Pervin LA. 1992. Transversing the individual–environment landscape: a personal odyssey. In *Person-Environment Psychology: Models and Perspectives,* ed. WB Walsh, KH Craik, RH Price, pp. 71–87. Hillsdale, NJ: Erlbaum

Rachlin H. 1989. *Judgment, Decision, and Choice: A Cognitive/Behavioral Synthesis.* New York: Freeman

Racicot BM, Day DV, Lord RG. 1991. Type A behavior pattern and goal setting under different conditions of choice. *Motiv. Emot.* 15:67–79

Riesbeck CK, Schank RC. 1989. *Inside Case-Based Reasoning.* Hillsdale, NJ: Erlbaum

Robinson JA, Swanson KL. 1990. Autobiographical memory: the next phase. *Appl. Cogn. Psychol.* 4:321–35

Rodriguez ML, Mischel W, Shoda Y. 1989. Cognitive person variables in the delay of gratification of older children at risk. *J. Pers. Soc. Psychol.* 57:358–67

Roese NJ. 1994. The functional basis of counterfactual thinking. *J. Pers. Soc. Psychol.* 66:805–18

Rokeach M. 1973. *The Nature of Human Values.* New York: Free Press

Roney CJR, Higgins ET, Shah J. 1995. Goals and framing: How outcome focus influences motivation and emotion. *Pers. Soc. Psychol. Bull.* 21:1151–160

Roseman IJ. 1984. Cognitive determinants of emotion: a structural theory. *Rev. Pers. Soc. Psychol.* 5:11–36

Roseman IJ, Wies C, Swartz TS. 1994. Phenomenology, behaviors, and goals differentiate discrete emotions. *J. Pers. Soc. Psychol.* 67:206–21

Ross M. 1989. The relation of implicit theories to the construction of personal histories. *Psychol. Rev.* 96:341–57

Ross M. 1995. Validating memories. In *Memory for Everyday and Emotional Events,* ed. NL Stein, PA Ornstein, B Tversky, C Brainerd. Hillsdale, NJ: Erlbaum. In press

Ross M, Buehler R. 1994. Creative remembering. In *The Remembering Self,* ed. U Neisser, R Fivush, pp. 205–35. New York: Cambridge Univ. Press

Rotenberg M. 1987. *Rebiographing and Deviance: Psychotherapeutic Narrativism and the Midrash.* New York: Prager

Rothbaum BO, Foa EB, Roggs S, Murdock T. 1992. A prospective examination of posttraumatic stress disorder in rape victims. *J. Traum. Stress* 5:455–75

Salovey P. 1992. Mood-induced self-focused attention. *J. Pers. Soc. Psychol.* 62:699–707

Santioso R, Kunda Z, Fong GT. 1990. Motivated recruitment of autobiographical memories. *J. Pers. Soc. Psychol.* 59:229–41

Schank RC. 1982. *Dynamic Memory: A Theory of Learning in Computers and People.* London: Cambridge Univ. Press

Schank R, Abelson RF. 1977. *Scripts, Plans, Goals, and Understanding.* Hillsdale, NJ: Erlbaum

Schank R, Wilensky R. 1978. A goal-directed production system for story understanding. In *Pattern-Directed Inference Systems,* ed. DA Waterman, F Hayes-Roth, pp. 415–30. New York: Academic

Schelling T. 1984. Self-command in practice, in policy, and in a theory of rational choice. *Am. Econ. Rev.* 74:1–11

Schlenker BR, Weigold MF. 1992. Interpersonal processes involving impression regulation and management. *Annu. Rev. Psychol.* 43:133–68

Schwarz N. 1990. Feelings as information: informational and motivational functions of affective states. See Higgins & Sorrentino 1990, pp. 527–61

Scott L, O'Hara W. 1993. Self-discrepancies in clinically anxious and depressed university students. *J. Abnorm. Psychol.* 102:282–87

Sherman SJ, Skov RB, Hervitz EF, Stock CB. 1981. The effects of explaining hypothetical future events: from possibility to probability to actuality and beyond. *J. Exp. Soc. Psychol.* 17:142–58

Shoda Y, Mischel W, Peake P. 1990. Predicting adolescent cognitive and self-regulatory competencies from preschool delay of gratification: identifying diagnostic conditions. *Dev. Psychol.* 26:978–86

Silver RL, Boon C, Stones MH. 1983. Searching for meaning in misfortune: making sense of incest. *J. Soc. Issues* 39:81–102

Simon HA. 1994. The bottleneck of attention: connecting thought with motivation. *Nebr. Symp. Motiv.* 41:1–21

Singelis TM. 1994. The measurement of independent and interdependent self-construals. *Pers. Soc. Psychol. Bull.* 20:580–91

Singer JA, Salovey P. 1993. *The Remembered Self.* New York: Free Press

Sinha VNP, Ataullah MD. 1987. *Migration: An Interdisciplinary Approach.* Delhi: Seema

Sorrentino RM, Higgins ET, eds. 1986. *Handbook of Motivation and Cognition.* New York: Wiley

Spiegel D. 1981. Man as timekeeper. *Am. J. Psychoanal.* 41:5–14

Spence DP. 1982. *Narrative Truth and Historical Truth.* New York: Norton

Staw BM. 1976. Knee-deep in the big muddy: a study of escalating commitment to a chosen course of action. *Org. Behav. Hum. Perf.* 16:27–44

Staw BM, Ross J. 1987. Behavior in escalation situations: antecedents, prototypes, and situations. *Res. Org. Behav.* 9:39–78

Stein NL, Glenn LJ. 1991. Making sense out of emotion: the representation and use of goal-structured knowledge. In *Memories, Thoughts, and Emotions: Essays in Honor of George Mandler,* ed. W Kessen, A Ortony, F Craik, pp. 295–322. Hillsdale, NJ: Erlbaum

Stein NL, Jewett J. 1986. A conceptual analysis of the meaning of basic negative emotions: implications for a theory of development. In *Measurement of Emotion in Infants and Children,* ed. CE Izard, P Read, 2:238–67. New York: Cambridge Univ. Press

Stein NL, Levine L. 1987. Thinking about feelings: the development and use of emotional knowledge. In *Aptitude, Learning, and Instruction: Cognition, Conation, and Affect,* ed. RE Snow, M Farr, 3:165–97. Hillsdale, NJ: Erlbaum

Stein NL, Levine L. 1990. Making sense of emotional experience: the representation and use of goal-directed knowledge. In *Psychological and Biological Approaches to Emotion,* ed. NL Stein, B Leventhal, T Trabasso, pp. 45–73. Hillsdale, NJ: Erlbaum

Stein NL, Trabasso T, Liwag M. 1993. The representation and organization of emotional exprerience: unfolding the emotional episode. In *Handbook of Emotion,* ed. M Lewis, J Haviland, pp. 279–300. New York: Guilford

Stein NL, Wade E, Liwag MF. 1995. A theoretical approach to understanding and remembering emotional events. In *Memory for Everyday and Emotional Events,* ed.

NL Stein, PA Orenstein, B Tversky, C Brainerd. Hillsdale, NJ: Erlbaum. In press

Sternberg RJ. 1990. Prototypes of competence and incompetence. See Sternberg & Kolligian 1990, pp. 117–45

Sternberg RJ, Kolligian J Jr, eds. 1990 *Competence Considered.* New Haven: Yale Univ. Press

Strack F, Schwarz N, Gschneidinger E. 1985. Happiness and reminiscing: the role of time perspective, affect, and mode of thinking. *J. Pers. Soc. Psychol.* 49:1460–69

Strathman A, Gleicher F, Boninger DS, Edwards CS. 1994. The consideration of future consequences: weighing immediate and distant outcomes of behavior. *J. Pers. Soc. Psychol.* 66:742–52

Strauman TJ. 1990. Self-guides and emotionally significant childhood memories: a study of retrieval efficiency and incidental negative emotional content. *J. Pers. Soc. Psychol.* 59:869–80

Strauman TJ. 1992. Self-guides, autobiographical memory, and anxiety and dysphoria: toward a cognitive model of vulnerability to emotional distress. *J. Abnorm. Psychol.* 101:87–95

Tait R, Silver RC. 1989. Coming to terms with major negative life events. In *Unintended Thought,* ed. JS Uleman, JA Bargh, pp. 351–38. New York: Guilford

Taylor SE. 1991. Asymmetrical effects of positive and negative events: the mobilization-minimization hypothesis. *Psychol. Bull.* 110:67–85

Thaler R, Shefrin H. 1981. An economic theory of self control. *J. Pol. Econ.* 89: 392–410

Thorne A, Klohnen E. 1993. Interpersonal memories as maps for personality consistency. In *Studying Lives Through Time: Personality and Development,* ed. DC Funder, RD Parke, C Tomlinson-Keasey, K Widaman, pp. 223–54. Washington, DC: APA

Trabasso T, Stein NL. 1994. Using goal/plan knowledge to merge the past with the present and the future in narrating events online. In *The Development of Future-Oriented Processes,* ed. MM Haith, J Benson, R Roberts, BF Pennington, pp. 323–49. Chicago: Univ. Chicago Press

Trommsdorff G, Lamm H. 1975. An analysis of future orientation and some of its social determinants. In *The Study of Time II,* ed. JT Fraser, N Lawrence, pp. 343–61. Berlin: Springer-Verlag

Vallacher RR, Wegner DM. 1985. *A Theory of Action Identification.* Hillsdale, NJ: Erlbaum

Vallacher RR, Wegner DM. 1987. What do people think they are doing? Action identification and human behavior. *Psychol. Rev.* 94:3–15

Vallacher RR, Wegner DM. 1989. Levels of personal agency: individual variation in action identification. *J. Pers. Soc. Psychol.* 57:660–71

Vorauer J, Ross M. 1993. Making mountains out of molehills: a diagnosticity bias in social perception. *Pers. Soc. Psychol. Bull.* 19:620–32

Vorauer J, Ross M. 1995. The pursuit of knowledge within close relationships: an informational goals anlaysis. In *Knowlege Structures in Close Relationships: A Social Psychological Approach*, ed. G Fletcher, J Fitness. Hillsdale, NJ: Erlbaum. In press

Webster DM, Kruglanski AW. 1994. Individual differences in need for cognitive closure. *J. Pers. Soc. Psychol.* 67:1049–62

Wegner DM. 1992. You can't always think what you want: problems in the suppression of unwanted thoughts. *Adv. Exp. Soc. Psychol.* 25:193–225

Wilensky R. 1983. *Planning and Understanding*. Reading, MA: Addison-Wesley

Wilson TD, Linville PW. 1982. Improving the academic performance of college freshman: attribution therapy revisited. *J. Pers. Soc. Psychol.* 42:367–76

Wood JV, Saltzberg JA, Goldsamt LA. 1990. Does affect induce self-focused attention? *J. Pers. Soc. Psychol.* 58:899–908

Zirkel S. 1992. Developing independence in a life transition: investing the self in the concerns of the day. *J. Pers. Soc. Psychol.* 62:506–21

Zirkel S, Cantor N. 1989. Personal construals of life tasks: those who struggle for independence. *J. Pers. Soc. Psychol.* 58:172–85

AUTHOR INDEX

SUBJECT INDEX

CUMULATIVE INDEXES

CONTRIBUTING AUTHORS, VOLUMES 37–47

CHAPTER TITLES, VOLUMES 37–47

666   CHAPTER TITLES

PSYCHOLINGUISTICS

See COGNITIVE PROCESSES

PSYCHOLOGY AND CULTURE

PSYCHOLOGY IN OTHER COUNTRIES

PSYCHOPATHOLOGY

ANNUAL REVIEWS INC.
4139 El Camino Way • P.O. Box 10139
Palo Alto, CA 94303-0139 • USA

BB96

Step 1 *Ordered by:*

Name _____

Address _____

_____ Zip Code _____

Please Mention
Priority Code
BB96
when placing
orders by phone.

Call from USA or Canada
1.800.523.8635
FAX orders 24 hours a day
1.415.424.0910

Today's Date _____ Day Phone: (_____)

Fax (___) _____ e-mail _____

Step 4 *Payment Method*

☐ Check or money order enclosed. Make checks payable
to "Annual Reviews Inc."   *or charge*

☐ VISA   ☐ M/C   ☐ AMEX

Account Number _____

Expiration Date Mo __ / Yr __ / __

Signature _____

Print name exactly as it appears on credit card.

Qty	Annual Review of	Vol.	Place on Standing Order? Save 10% now with payment	Price	Total
			☐ Yes, save 10% ☐ No	$	
			☐ Yes, save 10% ☐ No	$	
			☐ Yes, save 10% ☐ No	$	
			☐ Yes, save 10% ☐ No	$	
			☐ Yes, save 10% ☐ No	$	

Step 2
*Enter
Order*

☐ **Student / Recent Graduate** (past three years) discount **30% off.** Not applicable to standing orders. Proof of status enclosed.

☐ **California customers.** Add applicable California sales tax for your location.

☐ **Canadian customers.** Add 7% Canadian GST. **(Reg. # 121449029 RT)**

Step 3

✔ **Handling Charges.** Add $3 per volume. Applies to all orders.

*Shipping
and
Handling*

☐ **Standard shipping,** US Mail 4th class bookrate (surface) No extra charge.   **N/C**

☐ **Optional UPS Ground service,** $3 extra per volume in 48 contiguous states only. UPS not available to PO boxes.

UPS Next Day Air ☐   UPS Second Day Air ☐   US Airmail ☐   Note option at left. We will calculate amount and add to your total.
Optional shipping to anywhere. Charged at actual cost and added to total. Prices vary by weight of volumes.

Total _____

Call Toll Free **1.800.523.8635**
from USA or Canada 8am-4pm, M-F, Pacific Time. From elsewhere call 1.415.493.4400 ext. 1

 Mail Orders, fill in form, send in attached envelope. · e-mail **service@annurev.org**

Orders may also be placed through booksellers or subscription agents or through our Authorized Stockists
From Europe, the UK, the Middle East, and Africa contact: Gazelle Book Service Ltd., Fax 44 (0) 1524-63232
From India, Pakistan, Bangladesh or Sri Lanka contact: SARAS Books, Fax 91-11-941111.

ANNUAL REVIEWS INC. on the Web **http://www.annurev.org**